ECONOMICS

AN INTRODUCTORY TEXT

Fifth Edition 2007

Mordechai E. Kreinin
Michigan State University

To my wife Marlene

Cover images courtesy of Getty Images, Inc.

Printed in the United States of America

10 9 8 7 6 5 4 3 2 1

ISBN 0-536-21938-9

2006160252

EC/TT

Please visit our web site at *www.pearsoncustom.com*

PEARSON CUSTOM PUBLISHING
75 Arlington Street, Suite 300, Boston, MA 02116
A Pearson Education Company

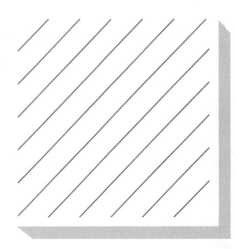

Contents

PART THREE

PART FIVE

BEYOND OUR SHORES 423

24 International Trade and Protectionism 428

25 Foreign Exchanges and the International Currency System 450

Preface

"Too wordy" is a common complaint by instructors and students alike about many principles of economics texts. One objective of this book is to remedy this problem. It presents economic principles as well as contemporary policies and controversies in a succinct, yet comprehensive manner.

A running glossary, designed to highlight, summarize, and define important concepts was continued in the 5th edition.

International economic relations was included in the last three editions. Part 5, entitled "Beyond Our Shores," contains three chapters dealing with international trade and protectionism (Chapter 24), international financial relations (Chapter 25), and economic development (Chapter 26). These chapters follow a short introduction to the field of international economics.

Apart from these changes, the entire book has been revised and brought up to 2006. Most examples and illustrations have also been updated. Likewise, analytical concepts have been sharpened, including such matters as the demise of the the Phillips curve, the development of rational expectations analysis, and new explanations on non-clearing labor markets.

As in the case of previous editions, the book is designed for a one-semester course in economics. Because its fundamental objective is to familiarize students with enough economic analysis to understand the financial press and follow contemporary economic issues, the book "squeezes" as much economic literacy and understanding as possible out of simple analytical tools. The theory necessary to meet this object is covered in a clear and simple fashion, yet accuracy is not sacrificed for the sake of brevity, nor is rigor compromised for the sake of simplicity.

Some topics must be deleted from the standard one-year introductory material to produce a one-semester text. A main criterion for inclusion in this book is the value of the topic for understanding current events. Thus, the necessary institutional material, such as a description of the private and government sectors is covered in one chapter (Chapter 3); and elements of the marginal analysis of microeconomics are included in an abbreviated form (Chapter 9) to the extent needed to highlight the difference between the market behavior of a perfectly competitive firm and that of a monopolist or oligopolist. Part 1 contains material (e.g., income distribution) normally classified under the micro part of a standard two-semester text. The topic of resource allocation is handled mainly with the tools of supply and demand, as are other problems of the market economy (Part 2). The usual lengthy treatment of long-run economic growth is reduced to a few pages. Parts 3 and 4 are devoted to macroeconomics and money, respectively, including the monetarist-fiscalist debate and supply-side economics. Short reviews of the contributions of great economists, such as Adam Smith and J. M. Keynes, are incorporated in appropriate sections.

This book can also be used as a text for the macroeconomic part of a two-term sequence by deleting Chapters 7–11 (as well as part of Chapter 5), and including the appendices to Chapters 17–18.

As in the first edition, display boxes are scattered throughout the book. They are designed to highlight certain controversies, to introduce contemporary ideas and issues from various sources, and to add a "light touch" to otherwise serious economic discourse.

I wish to thank Professor Kent Olson of Oklahoma State University for his helpful comments on an early draft of the manuscript. I also wish to express my gratitude to the users of previous editions who sent many helpful comments and suggestions, as well as words of encouragement about this revision.

MEK

PART ONE

ECONOMICS AND THE ECONOMY: AN OVERVIEW

OVERVIEW

WHAT ARE ECONOMIC PROBLEMS?

Economic problems: include **unemployment** and **inflation**.

We have often heard it said during election campaigns, "This election will be won or lost on 'bread and butter' issues." The reference is invariably to one or more economic problems that dominate the social landscape. Of course, the appearance of economic dilemmas is not confined to election time; rather, it is a continuous process. Only the nature of the issues—not their existence—changes. Thus, the main concern in the late 1950s and early 1960s was about a sluggish economy, curtailed production of goods and services, and high **unemployment** of workers and machines, with President Kennedy promising to "get the economy moving again." By the second half of the 1960s, especially in 1968–69, high **inflation**—rapidly **rising** prices of goods and services—replaced unemployment as the major issue. But the declining output and rising unemployment resumed in 1970, and re-appeared in 2002, only to decline in 2004–6.

In 1973, the large increases in food prices and the quadrupling of oil prices led the list of major economic troubles, and in 1974, public debate centered around the 12–13 percent inflation coupled with spreading unemployment. By 1975, unemployment superseded the abating inflation as "public enemy number one." But toward the end of the 1970s, the situation reversed itself and the fight against inflation became the number one priority. In 1981–82, spreading unemployment again occupied the center stage. During 1983–88, the economy experienced a robust noninflationary growth of output, with unemployment declining sharply. But large deficits in the government budget and in the country's external trade loomed as the important problems of the day. Most of the 1990s were low unemployment, low inflation, and declining budget deficits. But in 2001–02 unemployment re-emerged as a main concern, only to decline in 2003–6.

Because economic issues affect the well-being of all, they often evoke high emotions, and their importance can outweigh that of other problems in the minds of the voters. The effects on the populace of such questions as inflation and unemployment, environmental pollution, government spending and taxes, minimum-wage laws, interest rates, farm subsidies, rent control, and energy are all-pervasive.

Finally, there are economic issues with direct effects on certain geographical sections of the country. A shift in consumer preferences away from coal and to oil is of grave concern to the coal miners of West Virginia; and a switch by the buying public from American to foreign-built cars upsets the residents of Michigan, the U.S. auto capital.

Even noneconomic problems, such as abortion or law and order, may have an economic component, since they require the financing of certain social activities.

These cases constitute a sample of what we consider "economic problems." *One feature common to all of them is that, directly or indirectly, they revolve around production, pricing, and consumption of goods and services.*

Some problems relate to the *entire range of goods and services* produced and consumed; others are limited to *specific commodity categories.* It is to the understanding of such issues, their causes and effects, and to considerations of possible remedies by means of public policy (when cures are necessary), that the subject matter of economics is devoted.

Yet economics as a field of study does not tackle these and other issues one at a time, as they appear over space and time. Rather, it offers a coherent body of principles, a kit of tools that equip the student to analyze problems whenever and wherever they arise. This is fortunate. For the issues change over time in both nature and importance, yet the analytical tools remain the same.

Mastery of these principles will enable the student to deal with future issues, even those unforeseen at the time of his or her studies. And this is one of the exciting things about economic analysis. The financial press provides ample coverage of economic events, but these make little sense to those who have not mastered the analytical tools, often referred to as economic theory. Furthermore, mastery of these tools would make possible an understanding of diverse events and controversies.

SCARCITY—THE HEART OF ECONOMICS

Why are the issues of production, pricing, and consumption of goods and services considered *problems* for individuals as well as for society at large? In the Garden of Eden, all Adam and Eve wanted (before they wised up) was provided for them by nature. They could spend their time and energy at play and did not have to do anything to meet their needs. All they desired was available in unlimited quantities. It was free for the asking. *Nothing was* **scarce**. A commodity available in unlimited quantities is known as a **free good.** In a world dominated by free goods, nothing needs to be produced, and *no choices* need to be made by consumers. They can have as much as they wish of any good or service known to them. Consideration of production and consumption choices is irrelevant.

Scarcity: The study of economics revolves around how people satisfy their unlimited wants with limited resources. Consequently resources must be used efficiently. Resources, or factors of production, are: labor, capital, and land. These are scarce.

Free Good: Good available in unlimited quantities. It need not be produced.

But even casual observation will convince us that the situation in Eden has never been repeated. It certainly does not apply to the contemporary world. Today, one would be hard put to think of a single free good. Even clean air and fresh water are no longer free. Goods and services must be produced and distributed before they can be consumed.

People's wants are unlimited. Once their need for food is satisfied, they desire clothes, and beyond that, shelter. Once these **basic needs** are met, they turn their attention to fancier clothes, housing, and household equipment. From there they move on to an infinite array of luxury goods and services, such as overseas travel, cars, theater, racing boats, sailboats, or the like.

But the goods and services available to satisfy people's desires are very limited. There is today no Garden of Eden where wants are met through the abundance of nature. Rather, goods and services must be produced and distributed. And their production requires the coordinated effort of (1) workers (labor), (2) machines (capital), and (3) land and materials. These are known as **resources or inputs or factors of production.** They are not available in unlimited quantities. Resources *are scarce.* Hence, the goods and services they produce are also scarce. Very few people—and certainly not society at large—can satisfy all their wants and perceived needs. It is because of this scarcity that the economic system must ensure first that the goods desired most avidly by consumers are produced, and then that they are allocated among consumers in a way that yields maximum satisfaction.

CHOICES AND TRADEOFFS

Scarcity imposes on individuals as well as on society the need to make choices. A consumer may have to choose between a fur coat and a trip to Florida, or between a theater ticket and a meal at a nice restaurant. Life is full of such choices. They are invariably based on preferences of the person involved and are subject to the total amount of money he or she has to spend. This is the sense in which all goods and services compete for the consumer's dollar.

Tradeoff: what one must give up to obtain what he/she desires.

Opportunity cost: The cost of the next best good or service given up in order to obtain the desired good or service.

In making these choices, people—knowingly or unknowingly—engage in **tradeoffs.** A tradeoff refers to what they must give up to obtain what they desire. In the examples above, there is a tradeoff between a coat and a trip, between seeing a play and eating out.

This brings us to another, related concept, **opportunity cost.** The opportunity cost of obtaining a good or a service is the next-best good or service that must be given up in order to obtain the preferred one. The opportunity cost of attending college is not only the out-of-pocket cost of tuition, books, and related expenses. To that one must add the (frequently larger) sum that the college student *could have earned* over the four-year period by working at the best job for which he or she is suited. In general, the opportunity cost of doing something is the loss of opportunity of doing the next-best thing.

All these terms apply equally to society at large. Society must choose among an array of goods and services that can be produced with its limited resources. It tends to choose goods and services that make its members, collectively, best off—those that maximize its collective satisfaction. Society must choose the least costly method of producing these goods and services. Only then would the scarce resources be put to their best use; that is, produce the maximum quantities of the most desired goods and services.

Thus, as in the case of the individual, society faces tradeoffs. There is a tradeoff between producing war goods (guns) and civilian goods (butter). There is a tradeoff between making available university education and vocational training. For society as a whole, the opportunity cost of increasing defense production is the next most desirable civilian goods or services that could have been produced with the same resources and must be foregone.

As a student, your main available resource is your time. You want to allocate it in a way that would maximize your output (learning).

"You do the best you can with what you have," is the motto of this class.

ECONOMICS AND ECONOMISTS

Economics: economics is concerned with the efficient allocation of limited resources. The questions it deals with include: How to insure full employment of resources; and how to insure that resources are allocated in a way that the goods and services desired most avidly by society are produced in the most efficient way.

This brings us back to the subject matter of **economics**. Dealing with the organization of production and consumption in the economy, economics is concerned with the efficient management of limited resources for the purpose of obtaining maximum satisfaction of human material wants. The types of questions addressed by the discipline are these: (1) How do we ensure that the limited resources (both workers and machines) at the disposal of society are fully employed (or fully utilized) and do not lie wastefully idle? (2) By what process does the economy identify the goods and services that people want most avidly? (3) What mechanism ensures that it is precisely these goods, and not those further down on the priority list, that are produced, each in the desired quantity? (4) How do we ensure that these goods and services are produced in the most efficient way so as to make the most of scarce resources?

Partly because of the increasingly complex nature of the economy, the discipline of economics has come of age in the postwar period. The advice of economists is widely sought in the councils of governments and by business organizations. The president receives direct economic advice from the Council of Economic Advisers; congressional committees benefit from the analysis and views of their staff economists. The annual *Economic Report of the President* contains a comprehensive review of the economy and of pressing policy issues. And a Nobel Prize for economic science is awarded every year by the Swedish Riksbank.

Yet, in rendering advice, economists often disagree with each other. And judging from press reports, such disputes seem to be the order of the day. Not so. There is a wide array of issues on which economists are in agreement. But it is the debates that capture the headlines.

Economic advice is often rendered in the following form: "On the one hand if you do this, the following result would ensue; on the other hand, doing such and such would produce the following result."

President Truman is reported to have said, "Find me an economist with one hand."

There are at least two reasons that economists sometimes disagree. The first relates to differences in philosophy or values, as these affect the choice of economic objectives. Thus, "conservative" economists place great emphasis on price stability and the need to combat inflation, whereas "liberal" economists are more concerned about unemployment, ranking the objective of full employment ahead of price stability. Second, economists disagree on technical grounds: how best to attain an agreed-upon objective.

Despite such disagreements, or perhaps because of them, the demand for economic advice has mushroomed in recent years. Economics has become a subject of immense consequence to government, business, and private individuals. It is simply impossible to understand the world around us or even to vote intelligently without a rudimentary knowledge of economic principles.

As is the case in most disciplines, economics employs a variety of analytical tools. In particular, many an economic principle lends itself to visual expression by a two-dimensional diagram. Because of its simplicity and clarity, such graphical analysis is widely employed in economics, and it will be heavily emphasized in this book. A review of this analytical tool is offered next.

THE TWO-DIMENSIONAL DIAGRAM—A TOOL OF ECONOMIC ANALYSIS

The Four Quadrants

It is customary to divide the space into four parts, known as quadrants, by drawing two intersecting straight lines, as in Exhibit I–1. The horizontal line is called the *X* axis, and the vertical line the *Y* axis. Their point of intersection is the **origin** (O). *X* and *Y* units are measured from the origin; they can be either positive or negative. The four quadrants, identified in the exhibit by roman numerals, have the following characteristics:

Origin: The point of intersection of two axes.

Quadrant	X *Units*	Y *Units*
I	Positive	Positive
II	Negative	Positive
III	Negative	Negative
IV	Positive	Negative

Each point on the chart can be located by identifying its pair of *X* and *Y* magnitudes, in that order. This is illustrated on the chart by points *A*, *B*, *C*, *D*, and *E*. Since economics is concerned mainly with positive magnitudes, it makes most use of quadrant I, although quadrant IV is also used on occasion.

Any relation between *X* and *Y* can be expressed by a schedule of figures such as the following:

Exhibit I–1 The Four Quadrants: A space is divided into four quadrants by the intersecting X and Y axes. Once the axes are scaled, any point on the space can be located by identifying its pair of X and Y magnitudes.

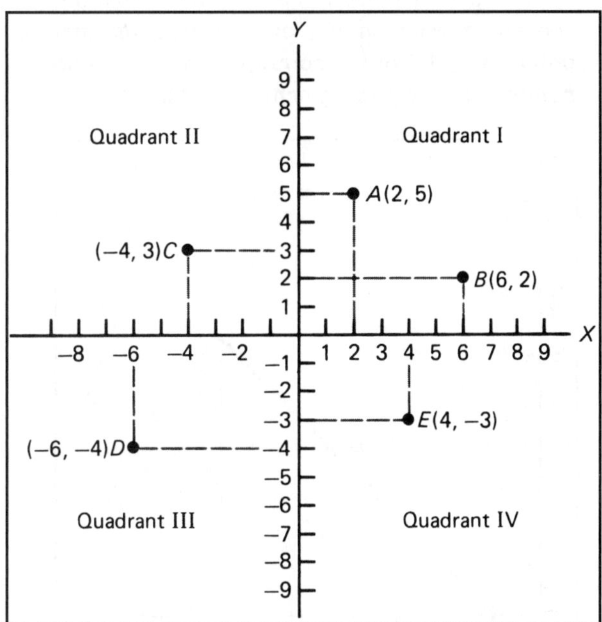

Point	X	Y
K	1	0
L	2	1
M	3	2
N	4	3

It can be read as follows: If X is 1, then Y is O; if X is 2, then Y is 1; if X is 3, then Y is 2; if X is 4, then Y is 3. The longer the schedule of figures, the more cumbersome it becomes, and the more difficult it is to discern and comprehend the nature of the relationship from the raw numbers.

Slope: the slope of a line represents the change in the vertical distance divided by the change in the horizontal distance. The steeper the line the greater its slope.

Plotting the numbers on the X,Y space of quadrant I gives a clear visual expression to the relation, as shown in Exhibit I–2. The result is a straight line. It is the simplest of all relations, because two points are sufficient to determine and plot the entire line. The **slope** of a straight line has a very definite and important meaning. From any point, such as N, drop a perpendicular to the X axis. The slope is the ratio of the vertical segment over the horizontal segment: a/b.[1] The steeper the line, the greater is its slope; the flatter the line, the smaller its slope. *The slope is constant over a*

[1]More precisely the slope is the vertical change divided by the horizontal change as we move to the right along the line.

Exhibit I–2 A Straight-Line Relation: Any relationship between two changing magnitudes can be represented on a two-dimensional diagram. A straight line is the simplest form of such a relation. It has a constant slope, and only two points are needed to establish the entire line. ***Note* that points *K, L, M,* and *N* correspond to the same points in the preceding schedule of figures.**

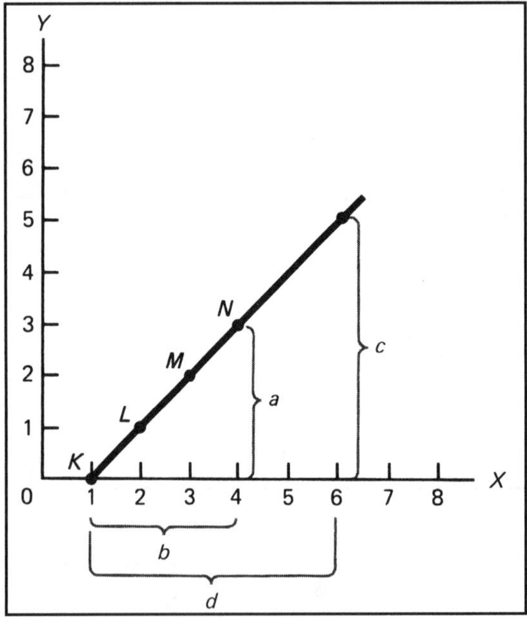

straight line (that is, $a/b = c/d$) but not over a curved line. And here lies another advantage of using straight-line relationships, even at the cost of oversimplification.

In what follows, we illustrate graphically two of the economic ideas discussed later in the book. Here, they are used mainly to illustrate the value of graphical presentation.

Supply schedule: In a graph with quantity measured on the horizontal and price on the vertical axis, the supply curve (a straight line sloping upward and to the right) shows that as the price of a good rises, more of it is offered for sale. This is a positively sloped curve.

Supply Schedule

As a matter of common sense, the quantity of a commodity *supplied* in the marketplace depends on its price: The higher the price, the greater the quantity supplied. This relation between supply and price of an individual commodity is well rooted in economic analysis and has been observed empirically countless times. A hypothetical supply schedule for wheat is given in Table I–1. It shows the number of millions of bushels farmers stand ready to supply at each of four alternative prices: If the price were $2 per bushel, suppliers would offer 100 million bushels; at a price of $4 per bushel, they would provide 200 million bushels; and so on.

Table I–1 Supply Schedule for Wheat

	Price per Bushel	Number of Bushels Supplied (in Millions)
(A)	$2	100
(B)	$4	200
(C)	$6	300
(D)	$8	400

These figures are plotted in Exhibit I-3, where prices are shown on the Y axis and quantities on the X axis. This is a positive relation: As price rises, so does the quantity supplied. A line sloping upward and to the right, such as the supply curve, is said to have a **positive slope** (or be positively sloping). The flatter the curve, the smaller is its slope; the steeper the curve, the higher its slope.

Demand schedule: As the price of a good rises consumers buy less of it. This is shown by a line sloping downward and to the right (negatively sloped curve).

Demand Schedule

As a matter of common sense, the quantity of a single commodity purchased depends on its price: The higher the price, the smaller the quantity bought. Again, this is a well-established relation, based on theoretical reasoning and empirical observation. A hypothetical demand schedule for wheat is given in Table I–2. It shows the number of millions of bushels consumers would be willing to buy at each of four alternative prices: At $8 per bushel, consumers would purchase 200 million bushels; at a price of $6 per bushel, they would buy 300 million bushels; and so on.

Exhibit I–3 Supply of Wheat: The supply schedule for a given product shows the relation between price and quantity supplied. It has a positive slope: The higher the price, the greater the quantity. ***Note* that points *A*, *B*, *C*, and *D* correspond to the same points in Table I–1.**

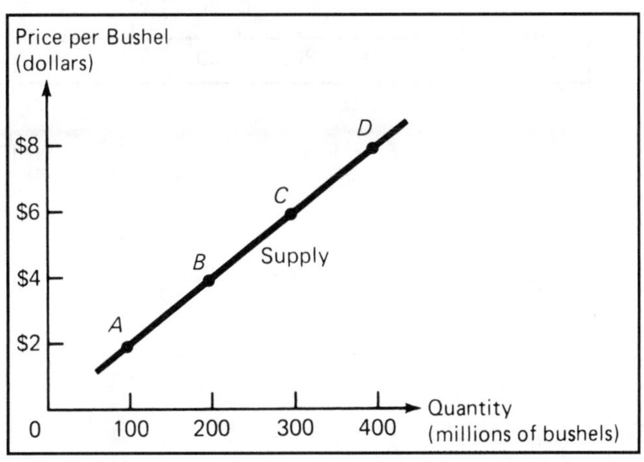

Table I–2 Demand Schedule for Wheat

	Price per Bushel	Number of Bushels Supplied (in Millions)
(A)	$8	200
(B)	$6	300
(C)	$4	400
(D)	$2	500

These points are plotted in Exhibit I–4, where prices are shown on the *Y* axis and quantity on the *X* axis. As in the case of supply, we have chosen the simple case of a straight line. Only two points are needed to draw the entire line. This simplification is not essential; a curved line is also easily presentable. Unlike supply, the demand curve demonstrates a *negative* relation between price and quantity: As price declines, the quantity that buyers wish to purchase rises. The curve, sloping downward and to the right, is said to have a **negative slope** (or be negatively sloping).

Exhibit I–4 Demand for Wheat: A demand schedule for a given product shows the relation between price and quantity demanded. It has a negative slope: The higher the price, the smaller the quantity. ***Note* that points *A, B, C,* and *D* correspond to the same points in Table I–2.**

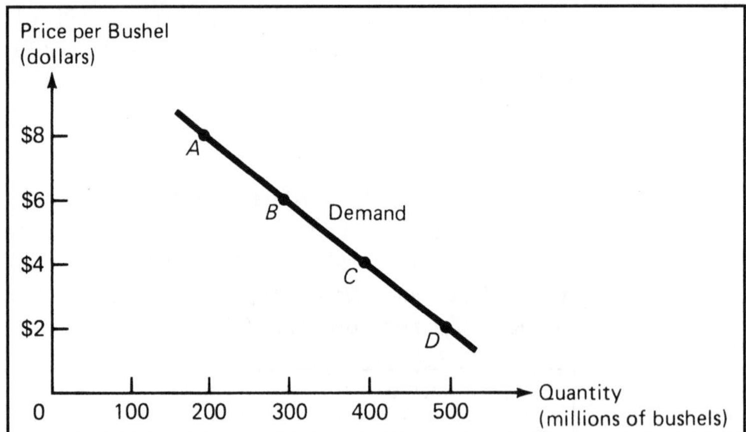

Economics—What Is It About?

ECONOMICS DEFINED

There is no shortage of definitions of what the discipline of economics is all about. In a simplified yet precise way, *economics may be described as the study of people's behavior in producing, exchanging, and consuming the goods and services they desire*. Producers and consumers are the main actors of economic analysis.

The main body of economic analysis is divided into two interrelated areas, each yielding a wide array of policy applications. The field of macroeconomics is concerned with the overall or aggregate performance of the entire economy; microeconomics is devoted to the units in the economy—the individual consumer, firm, and industry. Whereas macroeconomics is concerned with aggregate economic activity, microeconomics deals with the distribution of economic activity among sectors of the economy, and the relative performance of these sectors compared to one another.

Macroeconomics

In particular, macroeconomics highlights several main issues: fluctuations in the level of output and employment, the rate of inflation, and the long-term growth of the economy.

Unemployment rate: the number of workers who are involuntarily out of work expressed as a percentage of the labor force.

Employment and Unemployment In 2005 there were about 140 million civilian workers in the United States. The **unemployment rate** is the number of workers who are involuntarily out of work expressed as a percentage of the labor force. In 2000 the rate of unemployment was 4.5 percent of the labor force, while in early 2006 it was just under 5 percent. The larger the total production or output of goods and services, the greater the number of workers needed to produce it. Consequently, the level of output and the level of employment are positively related. Conversely, the level of output and the level of unemployment are negatively related: *The* *lower the output, the higher the unemployment.* In 2001 output declined and unemployment rose to 5.9 percent, while during 2003–06 output rose and unemployment declined below 5 percent.

In inquiring into the determinants of output, we are indirectly inquiring into what determines the level of employment or unemployment.

Much of macroeconomic analysis is indeed concerned with the determination of aggregate output, and thus indirectly with the determination of employment. Policy measures to expand or contract aggregate output are also included. The most widely used measure of aggregate output is the **gross domestic product,** or GDP.

Gross Domestic Product (GDP): The dollar value of all final goods and services produced in an economy in one year. It is also known as **Money GDP or Nominal GDP**. U.S. GDP in 2005 was $12.5 trillion, accounting for one-fifth of the world GDP.

GDP Gross domestic product is the dollar value of all *final* goods and services produced in one year. The price of each final good or service is multiplied by the quantity produced to obtain the total dollar value of its output. Then the output value of all final goods and services is added up. Because it expresses the value of output at prevailing prices and in money terms, GDP is also called **money GDP** and **nominal GDP**.

More concretely, suppose a simplified economy produces three goods and services: food, clothing, and a variety of services (dry cleaning, education, entertainment, medical care, and so on), all lumped together. How can one add up quantities of food, clothing, and services into one figure? The only way to aggregate diverse items to one figure is to price each of them on its respective market, multiply the price by the quantity produced to obtain the dollar value of each good and service produced, and add up these dollar values. The total dollar value of all final goods and services produced over one year is the economy's gross domestic product, or GDP.

Remember that what is added up is the value of *final* goods and services, abstracting in each case from raw materials and intermediate products that go into the production of the final good—for example, steel that enters the production of cars, lumber that is used in manufacturing desks, or yarn that enters the production of clothes. Such materials are already included in the value of the final product.

In 2005, the U.S. GDP was $12,480 billion; the United States accounts for about one-fifth of the world GDP.

Inflation: a *rising average* price level.

Inflation The next major concern of macroeconomics is **inflation** which is defined as a *rising price level.* Assume for simplicity that the economy consists of food, clothing, and services, and that each of these three items produced and consumed in the economy is equally important. In other words, the average or representative consumer divides his or her spending among the three items equally.

In the normal course of a year, some prices fall, some stay constant, and some (perhaps most) rise. From all these changes we can calculate a *weighted-average* price change, where the weight of each product is the proportion of consumer spending expended on it—its importance in the average consumer's shopping basket. In our "economy" of three equally important goods and services, this translates into an unweighted mean (or simple-average) price change. Thus, if the price of food declined by 5 percent, the price of clothing increased by 5 percent, and that of services increased by 15 percent, then the average price increase in the economy is:

$$\frac{(-5) + 5 + 15}{3} = \frac{15}{3} = 5 \text{ percent}$$

Thus, 5 percent would be the rate of inflation from one year to the next. It measures the annual increase in the cost of living.

But not all goods need be of equal importance in the representative consumer's budget. Indeed, we know that as the economy advances and incomes rise, a smaller and smaller portion of income is devoted to the bare necessities of life, such as food, and an increasing share to luxury goods, such as services. When goods possess unequal weights, the calculation of the average price increase is slightly more complicated.

Suppose the representative consumer spends a quarter of her budget on food, one-quarter on clothing, and one-half on services. (Note that the sum of these fractions must add up to 1.) Then the price change in services is of double importance (has a double weight) compared to that of each of the two goods. To obtain the average, we multiply each price change by the weight of its respective product:

$$(-5)(1/4) + (5)(1/4) + (15)(1/2) = 7\ 1/2$$

The annual inflation rate, measuring the increase in the cost of living from one year to the next, is then 7.5 percent. Both price and employment statistics are compiled by the Bureau of Labor Statistics at the U.S. Department of Labor.

The *average rate* of price increase is known as the **rate of inflation.** Inflation is a sustained process of *rising* prices, not *high* prices. Once prices have stabilized at a new level, however high, inflation is said to have stopped. Also, it is a rising average of **all** prices, rather than a price increase of a single commodity that constitutes inflation. A declining price level is known as **deflation**. But that has not happened continuously since the Great Depression of the 1930s. (It occurred in Japan during 1990–2005.) In 1979 and 1980, U.S. annual inflation was at 12–13 percent (double digit). But by 1998–2005, it declined to around 2 percent.

Deflation: A declining price level.

Macroeconomics is concerned with the change in the average price level, the causes and effects of inflation, and possible remedies for it. It is not concerned with the behavior of individual or sectoral prices.

Real GDP: GDP minus inflation.

Real GDP **Real gross domestic product** is gross domestic product adjusted for, or net of, inflation.

In most years the price level changes; mainly, it moves upward. In a year of unstable price levels, the rise in GDP is made up of two components: a rise in prices (inflation), and an increase in the *physical volume* or *quantity* of goods and services produced. Real GDP is money GDP net of inflation; it measures the physical volume or quantity of output. If money GDP rose by 10 percent during a given year while the average price level increased 4 percent, then real GDP—the physical volume of goods and services produced—increased by (10 – 4), or 6 percent. If in the same year the price level had risen by 13 percent, then real GDP actually declined by 3 percent.

It is the changes in *real* GDP that are positively related to changes in employment and negatively related to changes in unemployment.

Recession: A period of two or more successive quarters of decline in real GDP. It usually involves a rise in unemployment.

Stagflation: the simultaneous existence of unemployment and inflation.

A **recession** is defined as a period of two or more successive quarters of decline in real GDP.[1] It is usually associated with a rise in unemployment. In 1991–92, the U.S. economy experienced a recession, so unemployment rose to 7.5 percent. During 1993–2000 the economy recovered from the recession, and by April 1999 unemployment was down to 4.2 percent. The recession of 2001 raised unemployment to 5.9 percent. But the economy recovered during 2002–6. The coexistence of unemployment and inflation at the same time is known as **stagflation**.

Long-Run Economic Growth In any given year, the resources of the economy are fixed in quantity. But over the years, these resources—mainly workers and machines—grow. And with them grows the output of the economy, determining the extent to which increasing wants can be satisfied. In turn, the growth rate in output depends on the expansion in the country's resources, such as its labor force and capital stock (machines and structures), on improved quality of these resources (such as improved labor skills), on increased efficiency in the use of these resources, and on the degree of technological advance. The causes and effects of economic growth are a concern of macroeconomics.

Summary The field of macroeconomics is concerned with the aggregate performance of the economy. It is devoted to explaining the overall level of economic activity, as measured by the aggregate volume of real output or *real* GDP, and the level of employment (or unemployment) of productive factors associated with that output. Equally important, it attempts to explain the rate of inflation.

Although inflation is often viewed as the opposite of unemployment, the two concepts are not strictly symmetrical. The term *unemployment* refers to a large—not rising—number of people out of work, whereas *inflation* describes a situation of rising—not high—prices. Macroeconomic analysis is also concerned with stagflation, the dual occurrence of inflation and unemployment at the same time.

And finally, macroeconomics is concerned with the long-term growth of the economy.

Microeconomics

By contrast, the subfield of microeconomics is concerned with the activities of individual economic units—consumers, firms, and resource owners—the allocation and flow of goods and resources among these units, and the operation of the price system. It deals with the *industrial composition* of the output, or how resources are allocated among industries, and the price of one good *relative* to the price of another.

Scarcity The purpose of economic activity is to satisfy consumers' wants and society's needs. But although the appetite for goods and services is practically unlimited, the resources available for production—and, there-

[1]A quarter is a three-month period. The year is divided into four quarters: January through March, April through June, July through September, and October through December.

fore, the potential availability of output—are limited. By their very nature, resources are scarce. Even clean air and fresh water, which used to be considered "free goods" (available in unlimited quantities), are now recognized as scarce, since there is a limit to the industrial and auto pollution that the atmosphere can absorb and still remain habitable.

Allocation of resources: a fundamental problem in microeconomics is how can resources be deployed to their most valuable uses.

Scarcity imposes upon society a need to choose between competing wants, and the attendant problem of **allocation of resources** among the various pursuits. Society must first select the most desired combination of consumer and capital goods, and then the proper mix within each category. This is sometimes referred to as the problem of *choice*. Each good and service must then be produced at maximum efficiency. Available resources (workers, machines, land, and raw materials) need to be allocated among industries in a way that will produce the best match between the resource and the industry need.

These and other issues must be settled by any economic system. And they are no small problems. Reflect for a moment upon the amazing versatility and diversity of talents and occupations possessed by the millions who make up society and the equally baffling diversity of their wants. Yet somehow all those talents are put to use in a concerted fashion, to produce precisely the product mix that coincides with the desires of millions of consuming households. Somehow, the system hangs together. And the fact that we have come to take these results for granted is merely an indication of how smoothly the system functions.

How does it all fall into place? What "invisible hand" channels millions of people entering the labor force each year into their desired occupations and guide millions of producers to produce efficiently what the millions of consumers want? These questions are of major concern to microeconomics. Specifically, the following four questions are asked.

Three important questions in economics: 1) What goods and services shall be produced and in what quantities? 2) How shall each good be produced? 3) How shall income be distributed?

What Goods and Services Shall Be Produced, and in What Quantities? In the United States economy these two questions are determined by consumers in their decisions on how to spend their income. The consumer, through the decision on allocation of income between consumption and savings—that is, between present and future consumption—is also partly responsible for the allocation of output between consumer goods and capital goods, and therefore, for the rate of economic growth. This central role that consuming units play in the allocation decisions is confined to market economies. In the socialist states with centrally planned economies, such decisions are made by the state planning authority.

How Shall Each Good Be Produced? This is determined by firms taking account of available technology and the prices of the productive resources or inputs. For the production of each commodity there is usually a range of available technologies. Equally important, there are several or even numerous possible combinations of productive inputs that can be employed. Thus, food can be produced with little land and much labor or with little labor and much land. Similarly, the amount of capital equipment (machines) combined with labor and land can be varied. The producer would choose the combination that would minimize production costs. Thus, in a country such as India, where unskilled labor is abundantly available and therefore cheap, producers would tend to use as much labor and as little machinery as the appropriate technology permits. Precisely the reverse would be the case in the United States, where capital is relatively abundant and labor scarce and therefore expensive.

How Will the Income Be Distributed? Total income of households is generated by their participation in the production process. In a free-enterprise market economy, distribution of income among groups in society depends on the market-determined prices of productive factors. And that in turn reflects *the contribution of each factor to production:* that is, how important the particular factor is for the production of the product. This income gives households command over goods and services, and by spending money in the marketplace, they signal to firms which goods are to be produced and in what quantities. The market-determined distribution of income among households is modified by government redistributional measures, executed through taxes and subsidies.

There are in the world distributional systems that are not determined by market forces, and in which a person's earnings are not determined by his or her productive contribution. In the Israeli kibbutz, or collective, income is divided equally among members regardless of their contribution to output. In other words, the production and distribution system of the kibbutz is embodied in the slogan, "From each according to his ability and to each equally." An alternative system, which formed the ideological base of world communism, although it was never put into full practice, is, "From each according to his ability and to each according to his needs."

Summary In sum, the field of microeconomics is concerned with the sectoral composition of output and employment, with the price of one good relative to another, and with the distribution of income among productive factors or segments of society.

MACRO AND MICRO RELATIONS

Macroeconomics views the economy in its totality, concentrating on the size of the total "pie" (the total real value of goods and services produced), whereas microeconomics is devoted to the composition and the distribution of the "pie." One should never forget, however, that macroeconomics has micro foundations, for the pie is made up of its parts. Thus, the double-digit inflation of 1974 has been correctly viewed as a macro problem and treated as such. Yet to some extent, it could be traced to forces operating in specific sectors, such as agriculture or energy, requiring cures at the micro level.

On the other hand, there are many instances in which what is true of the part is not necessarily true of the whole. The often-quoted illustration is that of a stadium full of spectators: When one person rises while everybody else remains seated, the standing person can see better; but should everybody rise at the same time, no one would see better.

This so-called **fallacy of composition** suggests that not all generalizations from microeconomics are applicable to macroeconomics. One individual can effectively protect herself against future uncertainties of economic life by the act of saving (consuming less than her income); but should everyone in society try to increase her or his savings, a depression could result, in which case everybody's effort to save more would be frustrated. Hence it is important to be careful when generalizing from micro to macro and vice versa.

Graphic Illustration

In introducing microeconomics, it was emphasized that scarcity of resources forces upon society the need to make choices. The issue of choice is often illustrated graphically by a so-called opportunity-cost curve.

Constant Opportunity Costs Consider an economy that produces two commodities, food and textiles. Employing *all* its resources, at *maximum* efficiency, the alternative combinations of the two products that can be produced in a particular year are shown in Table 1–1. These alternatives can be plotted on a two-dimensional diagram as in Figure 1–1.

If all resources were devoted to food production, then 0*A* (300 million) units of food and no textiles would be manufactured. Conversely, if all resources were devoted to textiles and none to growing food, then 0*D* (600 million) units of textiles and zero food would be produced. Along the curve *AD* lie combinations of some food and some textiles that can be manufactured with a given amount of resources and at a given level of technology.

Production possibilities curve (PPC): represents all possible production mixes for the economy. The slope of the PPC, or Opportunity cost curve, represents the opportunity cost of one commodity in terms of another. **The marginal rate of transformation (MRT):** the ratio at which one good can be transformed into the other (i.e. slope of the PPC) in terms of resource conversion.

For example, at point *B*, *OM* of food and *ON* of textiles would be produced; at *C*, *OP* of food and *OR* of textiles will be made available. Points *A*, *B*, *C*, and *D* represent graphically the four alternatives shown in Table 1-1.

Points inside the line, such as *G*, indicate either some unemployment of workers and machines or less than maximum efficiency, for they represent smaller outputs of the two goods than it is possible to produce. They would be avoided if at all possible. Points outside the line, such as *F* or *H*, are unattainable, because they require more resources than the economy possesses. Consequently, an efficiently functioning economy would produce a combination of goods lying somewhere on line *AD*.

Line *AD* indicates two things: First, it is a measure of the productive potential of the economy in a given year, for it shows the limit to possible output. That explains the first of its names: **production-possibilities curve**.

Second, its slope measures the amount of one commodity that needs to be given up to obtain a certain quantity of the second good. Thus, starting

Table 1–1 Combinations of Maximum Outputs

Alternative Combinations	Food Output (In Millions of Bushels)	Textile Output (In Millions of Yards)
A	300	0
B	200	200
C	100	400
D	0	600

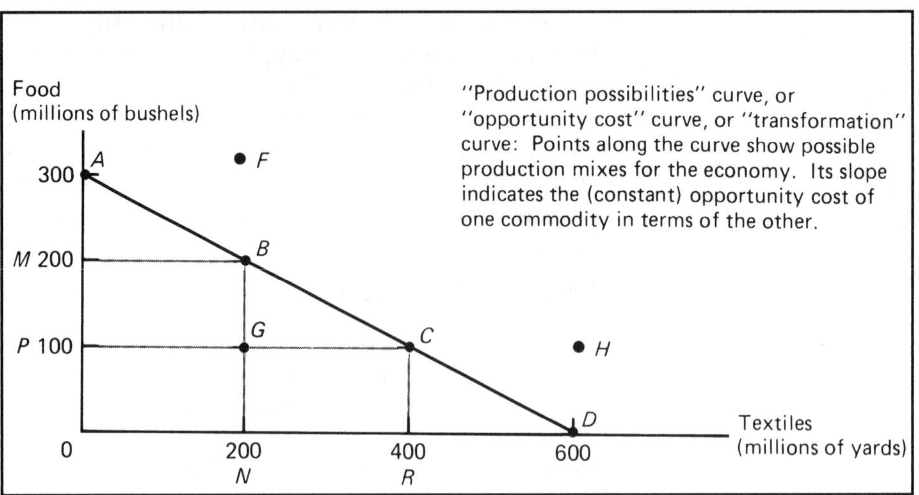

Figure 1–1 Transformation Curve

at Point *A*, *AM* of food must be given up to get *MB* of textiles; between *B* and *C*, *MP* (= *BG*) of food must be sacrificed for an additional *NR* (= *GC*) of textiles; and further, *PO* (= *CR*) of food is "exchangeable" for *RD* of textiles. Not that food is transformable into textiles in any mechanical sense; it certainly is not. But by the giving up *MP* of food, enough *resources are released* from the food industry and absorbed in the textile industry to produce *NR* of textiles. It is in that sense that one good is transformed into the other.

For that reason, line *AD* is known as the **transformation curve**; its slope indicates the ratio at which one good can be transformed into the other in the sense of resource transfer. The line is also called the **opportunity-cost curve**. For the economy as a whole, *the cost of producing one commodity* (textiles) *is the amount of other commodities* (food) *that must be given up to free the necessary resources*. In a war economy, this is often exemplified by the "guns-or-butter" problem: To obtain more guns and other military goods, society must give up butter and other civilian goods. It can't have both, because resources are limited. Note that this analysis applies only to movements along the transformation curve. From points inside the line, such as *G*, it is possible to increase the output of one commodity (or both) without giving up any of the other.

This cost of one product in terms of the next best good foregone is known as *opportunity cost*. The fact that *AD* is a straight line implies that the ratio between "food given up" and "textiles gained" is constant throughout: *AM/MB* = *BG/GC* = *CR/RD* = the *slope* of the transformation line, or *AO/OD*. This would hold true for any segment of the line. Thus, a straight transformation line illustrates a situation of *constant transformation* ratio of one product to the other, and is a reflection of certain cost conditions prevailing in the economy.

Note that the transformation curve has a negative slope: An *increase* in the output of textiles is associated with a *decrease* in the output of food.

Increasing Opportunity Cost But constant opportunity cost is not common in the economy. Usually the transformation curve is depicted as concave to the origin, as in Figure 1–2, implying an increasing transformation ratio of one product to the other. It is referred to as an *increasing-opportunity-cost curve.*

Increasing-opportunity cost curve: Successive increases in the production of one good requires increasingly greater reductions in the production of the other good. Concave to the origin, this curve is common to most economies, because resources are not equally suitable to produce both goods.

Starting from point *A*, where *OA* of food and no textiles are produced, we move gradually along the line towards point *F*, where *OF* of textiles and no food are produced.

At each step (from *A* to *B*, from *B* to *C*, and so on), we are adding equal quantities of textiles, as shown by the equal segments on the horizontal textiles axis. To acquire additional textiles we must give up food, and the cost in terms of food given up is shown by the segments along the vertical food axis. For example, moving from *C* to *D*, we add *RN* to textile output and give up *PM* of food.

It is clear that equal successive additions to textile output require *increasingly* sizable *reductions* in food production. The opportunity cost of textiles in terms of food is rising.

What production conditions give rise to such a situation? It would arise if the economy's resources were *not equally suitable* to produce the two goods. At point *A*, the food industry presumably employs some resources that are better suited for textile production (for example, weavers). Consequently, the first unit of textiles is obtained by shifting out of the food industry resources that are better suited for textile production. The cost in terms of food foregone (*AL* on the vertical axis) is necessarily very small. But as textile output rises, we begin to transfer out of the food industry resources that are more suitable for food production (for example, farmers). Consequently, the cost of successive units of textiles in terms of food output foregone (*LP, PM,* and further segments down the vertical axis) must rise. This is the rationale behind the increasing-opportunity-cost curve.

Figure 1–2 Increasing-Opportunity-Cost Curve

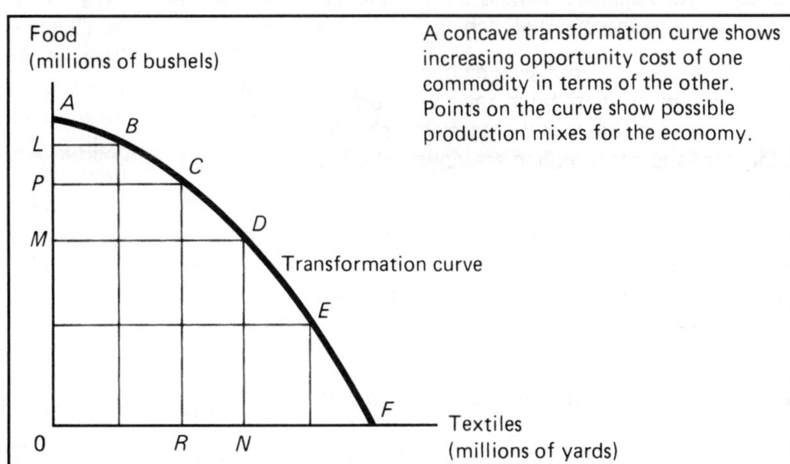

In contrast, the case of *constant cost* (straight-line transformation curve) occurs when resources are *identically suited* to produce both commodities. The *ratio of exchange* of one commodity for another remains constant throughout. Increasing opportunity cost is far more common in the economy than constant cost conditions.

What has been shown thus far is that a fully employed economy, functioning at top efficiency, would operate somewhere on the transformation line. Its precise location on that curve indicates how much of each commodity is produced. For example, at point *D*, *ON of* textiles and *OM* of food are manufactured, and *resources are distributed accordingly between the two industries.* Determining the precise location on the transformation curve requires knowledge of society's demand for the two goods, or its preference between the two goods.

Outward shift in PPC: shows long run growth in the economy.

Long-Run Growth Over time, the economy grows. Its resources expand with the increase in the capital stock (structures and machines) as well as in the labor force. The quality of its labor and capital improves with education, training, and new inventions. And efficiency of production may also increase. All these changes make it possible to expand output of both commodities. Graphically, this is shown by an outward shift in the transformation curve, as in Figure 1–3, indicating that more of both commodities can be produced after growth. But usually the outward shift is not symmetrical.

▶ STORY OF A BURMESE FISHERMAN—ECONOMIC GROWTH

An American fishery expert is sent to Burma to teach the Burmese how to improve their fishing.

He finds a Burmese fisherman who catches fish with his bare hands. In an eight-hour day (he is unionized), he catches eight fish and eats eight fish. His output, income, and consumption are equal, at eight fish per day.

Says the visiting American expert, "Why don't you fish only six hours, catching and eating only six fish per day, and devote the two hours so freed to the construction of a fishing net?"

Fisherman: Why do I need a net?
Expert: With a net, you can catch 50 fish a day.
Fisherman: Why do I need 50 fish? I only eat eight.
Expert: You'll eat eight and sell 42 fish.
Fisherman: What will I do with the money?
Expert: Buy yourself a fishing boat.
Fisherman: What do I need a boat for?
Expert: With a boat, you can catch 100 fish a day.
Fisherman: But I only eat eight fish!
Expert: You eat eight and sell 92.
Fisherman: And what shall I do with the money?
Expert: You buy yourself a fishing fleet; send them fishing, and you go fishing for pleasure, just like an American entrepreneur.
Fisherman: But that's what I am doing now.

Figure 1–3 Transformation Curves before and after Growth

Food
Economic growth over the years is represented by pushing the transformation curve outward. More of the two commodities can be obtained.
Transformation curve after growth
Transformation curve before growth
0
Textiles

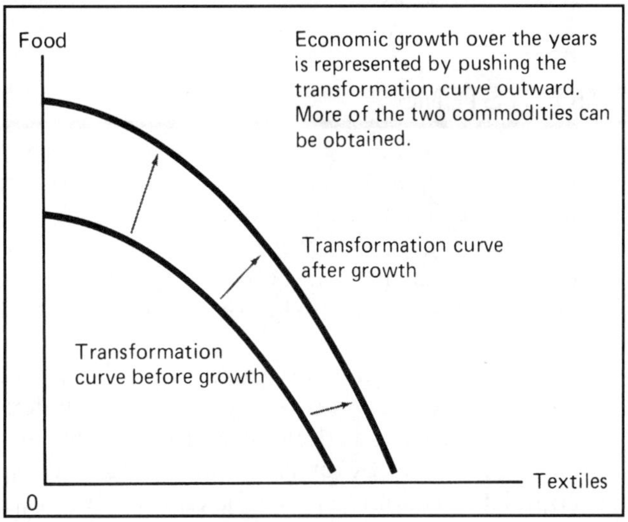

THE METHODOLOGY OF ECONOMICS

Variables: changing values or magnitudes. Economics studies the relationships between such changing values.

In the discussion of diverse economic issues in the introduction to Part I, economic analysis was described as a "kit of tools" that can be applied to a variety of problems. At this point, a word about methodology is in order.

For the most part, economic analysis searches for stable *relationships* between changing magnitudes, known as **variables**. Indeed, much of economics is concerned with *cause-and-effect relationships that are stable over time*. The influence of the price of a particular commodity on the quantity purchased is an example of such cause and effect from microeconomics; and the effect of aggregate income on aggregate savings in society at large is an example from macroeconomics.

Once a stable relationship is uncovered, it is presented in a variety of ways, and it also lends itself to statistical measurement. For example, *how strong* is the influence of price on the quantity of a commodity purchased? Then, the various stable relationships may interact with one another, thus forming a coherent body of analysis. This book concentrates on the analysis rather than measurement of the relationships' strength.

In many cases, more than one magnitude influences the phenomenon in which we are interested. For example, both the price of automobiles and the income of society determine the number of automobiles sold in a given year. Perhaps the price of gasoline is a third determining factor. Such cause-and-effect relations are complex, and require a mathematical expression.

In sum, economic analysis revolves around *relationships* between related magnitudes (variables) where each relationship is *stable* over time. The array of such relationships make up the body of economic analysis. When combined with facts and statistical information, it can yield predictions as well as prescriptions for public policy.

TYPES OF ECONOMIC SYSTEMS

Pure capitalism: means of production are privately owned and the coordination of economic activity is done through markets and prices. **Communism:** means of production are owned by the state, and a state planning authority coordinates economic activity.

In discussing the four questions of microeconomics, it was mentioned that there are different ways of organizing economic activity. Societies differ in their ideologies, and these differences give rise to alternative social systems. The distinction between types of economies is made on two grounds: (1) the ownership of means of production, and (2) the organization of economic activity.

At one extreme lies **pure capitalism,** where means of production (plants, machines, farms) are privately owned, and the coordination of economic activity is done through markets and prices. All economic decisions are made by private consuming and producing units, who have complete freedom to make the choices that would maximize their welfare as they perceive it. And markets, free of government control, are relied upon to coordinate the diverse decisions of millions of units. Because of these characteristics, the system is sometimes referred to as a market system or *free enterprise economy.*

At the other extreme is **communism,** a system where means of production are owned by the state ("public" ownership of resources), and the state planning authority coordinates economic activity; it makes the resource-allocation and income-distribution decisions. Because of *the latter feature,* this system is often referred to as a command economy. Decisions

▶ ONE-SIDED VIGNETTES

The inherent vice of capitalism is the unequal sharing of blessings. The inherent virtue of communism is the equal sharing of miseries.

—Winston Churchill

Bustling capitalist Kenya and socialist Tanzania are neighboring countries in East Africa.

They say in Tanzania, "Kenya is a country in which man eats man."

Reply the Kenyans, "Tanzania is a country in which man eats nothing."

The Russians joke about their living standards. Their favorite is the "Adam and Eve" joke. The scene is the classroom, and the teacher goes down the list of famous people, asking their nationality. All are Russians. Finally, the teacher comes to Adam and Eve. "Now class, what was the nationality of Adam and Eve?" "They were Russians," roars the class. "And how do we know they were Russians?" asks the teacher. "Because they had no clothes to wear, no roof over their heads, only an apple to eat between them, and they called it paradise." ("Who can they be but Russians!").

Source: The Wall Street Journal, April 17, 1979, p. 22.

are centralized and people's freedom of choice is highly restricted by government directives.

Perhaps the most cherished feature of capitalism is the degree of individual freedom it affords. Each person is free to pursue his or her own interests, and the market mechanism ensures that the interest of society is also served in the process. The point is strongly highlighted in the contemporary book, by the Nobel prizewinner Prof. Milton Friedman, entitled *Capitalism and Freedom*. When dealing in the marketplace, he states, every person has freedom of choice to accept or reject what is offered, or to select a preferred item or even brand out of a variety of alternatives. This is not the case in the political sphere, where decisions are made collectively. There, the minority must accept and live with the preferences of the majority. Hence, individual freedom is enhanced by increasing the scope of the market economy to encompass as many spheres of life as possible, and correspondingly reducing the scope of the political sphere. It is further alleged that political freedom is inextricably tied in with economic freedom; by maximizing the latter, we maximize the former.

But equally distinguished economists, such as another Nobel prizewinner, Prof. Paul Samuelson of M.I.T., question the value of such freedom for the poor people in our society, who are partly a product of unbridled capitalism. This point has particular relevance to citizens of underdeveloped countries; to them, freedom from hunger is often more important than freedom to make economic decisions. These scholars advocate government intervention to change the distribution of income that emanates from the purely capitalistic system, so as to eliminate poverty.

Democratic socialism: a combination of the most attractive features of both capitalism and communism. **Mixed economy:** a mixed system of private and public ownership of resources, governed somewhat by markets but modified by government intervention.

Democratic socialism can be viewed as an attempt to merge what socialists consider the most attractive features of both capitalism and communism. In the original conception of *pure socialism,* all means of production would be owned by the state, and all major economic decisions made by the planning authority rather than by markets. But in contrast to communism, the freedoms of consumer and occupational choice are retained by the individual, and the democratic process is fully preserved.

In recent decades, many socialist leaders in Western Europe have come to doubt the compatibility of economic freedoms and central controls. They have opted for a mixed system of private and public ownership of resources, reliance upon market forces that is tempered by some government planning, and freedom of choice of private economic units that is somewhat restricted by government intervention. Because of the mixed nature of resource ownership, this is often referred to as a **mixed economy.** In addition, the government modifies the distribution of income that is generated by the market and generally assumes responsibility for the least fortunate members of society. It may also provide certain basic services, such as free medical care, and education. Such an economy is known as a "welfare state."

In reality, there is no clear-cut dichotomy between capitalism and communism. Rather, there is a continuum, and countries vary in the degree of government ownership of means of production and the level of responsibility the government assumes for the social welfare of the citizenry. In practically all countries, the nature of the system is subject to constant change and evolution; it is far from being frozen. And in recent years, just as the communist states have shifted toward greater reliance on markets in carrying out the state's economic plan, so have certain Western economies moved to assign the government a greater role in the economy. Even China has moved to liberalize its economy.

On the continuum, the United States lies closer to pure capitalism than does any other country. It emphasizes private ownership of means of production, freedom of individual choice, and reliance on markets as the coordinating mechanism. Although the U.S. government budget is large, the government buys goods and services in the private sector rather than producing them in publicly owned enterprises. On the other side of the continuum are communist states like China, which feature state ownership of means of production and rely on central planning as a coordinating mechanism. In between lie the economies of Western Europe.

SUMMARY OF MAIN CONCEPTS

Macroeconomics is concerned with the *aggregate* performance of the economy. It highlights the problems of unemployment, inflation, and long-run growth.

Inflation is a process of rising price levels. It is computed as a weighted average of the yearly change in prices of individual products, where the weight of each product corresponds to its relative importance in the consumer basket.

Unemployment, the proportion of the work force that is involuntarily unemployed, varies inversely with real physical output. The higher the level of output, the lower the unemployment.

Gross domestic product or **GDP** is the most widely used measure of national output. It is the money value of all *final* goods and services produced during a year. Because it is measured in terms of money, it is also called ***money GDP*** or ***nominal GDP***.

Real GDP is GDP adjusted for inflation. It measures the quantity or volume of final goods and services produced.

Recession is a decline in real GDP for two or more successive quarters.

Stagflation is the simultaneous existence of unemployment and inflation.

Economic growth indicates the growth of available resources over time, and with them the rise in potential output of the economy. Demographic factors and labor-force participation determine changes in the size of the labor force. The rate of investment in the economy determines changes in the capital stock. Besides the quantity of resources, their quality and the efficiency of their use determine the rate of economic growth.

Microeconomics is concerned with the sectoral *distribution of output*, prices of commodities *relative* to one another, and the *distribution of income*. Its four leading questions are, What shall be produced? In what quantity shall each good and service be produced? How shall it be produced? and How shall income be distributed?

A graphic demonstration of these questions is offered by a curve known alternatively as the **transformation curve, opportunity-cost curve,** or **production-possibilities curve.**

In terms of methodology, much of economics inquires into **stable relationships between variables**: how one magnitude varies with another; for example, how the quantity of a commodity demanded by consumers varies with its price, or how the quantity of a commodity offered by suppliers varies with its price. The simplest way of presenting such relations is a two-dimensional graph.

The **two-dimensional diagram** is an analytical tool used widely in economics. Straight lines will be employed for reasons of simplicity: Only two points are necessary to determine the entire line, and the slope of a straight line is constant throughout the line.

Economies differ from each other on two grounds: ownership of resources or means of production, and organization of economic activity. In a capitalist, free-enterprise system, means of production are privately owned, and markets are relied upon to coordinate economic activity. Under communism, resources are publicly owned, and the state planning authority coordinates economic activity. In between these lies a spectrum of mixed economies and welfare states.

QUESTIONS AND PROBLEMS

1. What is the difference between microeconomics and macroeconomics? What type of question does each part of the discipline deal with?
2. Define the following concepts:

- ☐ Economics
- ☐ Inflation
- ☐ Unemployment
- ☐ Economic growth
- ☐ Stagflation
- ☐ GDP
- ☐ Real GDP
- ☐ Recession
- ☐ Resource allocation
- ☐ Constant opportunity cost
- ☐ Increasing opportunity cost
- ☐ Investment
- ☐ Capital stock
- ☐ Transformation curve

3. Draw a transformation curve of the *increasing-cost* variety between *guns* and *butter*. Show on it three points: (a) unattainable combination of the two goods; (b) a combination indicating unemployment or less than full efficiency; (c) an

attainable combination when the economy functions at full employment and at maximum efficiency. Indicate the nature of opportunity cost on your chart. Show on your chart the growth of the economy over time.

4. Repeat question 3 by drawing a *constant*-opportunity-cost curve between machines and consumer goods.
5. What can you say about the methodology of economics?
6. Explain the terms *a straight line, slope, positive and negative relation.*
7. Describe the main advantages and disadvantages of the market economy.
8. How does pure socialism compare economically with capitalism?
9. You often hear that a choice must be made in the economy between "guns and butter." In the government budget, this may translate into an increase in defense spending *or* an increase in spending for social services.
   a. Briefly explain the aforementioned statement in the light of the fact that resources are scarce.
   b. Had resources been unlimited, would the preceding statement make any sense?

The Nature of Economic Processes

Economics is concerned with production—the creation of a good or service—and consumption of goods and services. Consumption in turn depends on the availability of income to finance purchases. Consequently, it is necessary to examine how goods are produced and income generated in the economy.

THE NATURE OF PRODUCTION PROCESSES

A One-Stage Process

Although most production processes are highly complex, their principle can be illustrated by a simple example. Consider Ms. Smith, who decides to grow cucumbers and sell or market them at a road stand along the highway. What are the requirements for such an enterprise?

Smith must first have *land*, which she rents from a landowner, and for which she pays *rent*. Should she herself own the land, we could think of her as paying rent to herself (known as imputed rent), equaling the money value that the use of the land commands. Second, she hires *labor*, with the workers' compensation taking the form of *wages and salary*. Again, part of the labor might be supplied by the person herself or by her immediate family, in which case we think of her as paying wages to herself (imputed wage), equaling the money value that labor commands on the labor market. Third, she must borrow funds with which to purchase structures (such as a tool shed), machinery, and equipment, known as **capital goods**. For these borrowed funds she pays *interest*.

Capital goods are: structures, machinery, and equipment. **Primary factors of production** are: labor, land and natural resources, and capital. These factors receive compensation in the form of wages and salaries, rent, and interest, respectively.

All the economic agents she hires—labor, land and natural resources, and capital—are known as **primary factors of production,** or **primary inputs,** or alternatively, resources**.** And these factors command remunerations or compensations in the form of wages and salaries, rent, and

Table 2–1 Factors of Production (Inputs) and their Forms of Remuneration

Factor of Production	Form of Remuneration (or compensation)
Labor, skilled and unskilled	Wages and salaries
Land and other natural resources	Rent
Capital	Interest
Entrepreneurship	Profit

interest, respectively. Together, these make up the outlays incurred in the production process.

To be successful, she must sell the cucumbers at a price that exceeds her production outlays, and the difference between the sales revenue she obtains and total outlays is her profit.[1]

Profit: the return to entrepreneurial ability or entrepreneurship, the fourth factor of production. The entrepreneur assumes risk, and is responsible for **inventions** (new scientific ideas) and **innovation** (transformation of inventions into commercial use). Production takes place within **firms**. **Income** is compensation for the services provided by the four factors of production.

Profit is a return to a fourth factor of production, known as entrepreneurship or entrepreneurial ability. The entrepreneurial functions are of vital importance. They include the bringing together of the three factors into the framework of one productive unit, the coordination of their activity in a way designed to produce the product, the making of the necessary business decisions, the introduction of **inventions** (new scientific ideas) into commercial use **(innovation)**, and the all important assumption of **risk.** For our cucumber grower may lose as well as gain, and her profits in that case would be negative. The person who performs these functions is known as the **entrepreneur.** And the productive unit within which production takes place is known as the **firm.** All production in a modern economy is organized in firms. Although often calculated as a residual—the difference between earnings and outlays—profit is nothing but a form of remuneration for the contribution of a productive factor: entrepreneurship. Factor inputs and their forms of remunerations are summarized in Table 2–1.

Income is generated in the productive process as compensations for the services provided by the factors. It takes the form of wages and salaries, rent, interest, and profit. In other words, the remuneration received by owners of each of the factors, in return for the productive service they perform, constitute their income.

To ensure simplicity, the example of the cucumber grower was artificially contrived in one important respect: The entire productive process, from the initial preparation of the land to the final sale of the product to the consumer, was executed by one firm. The fact that there may be millions such identical enterprises producing cucumbers does not change matters. What was said above about the individual farmer can be duplicated millions of times for the entire cucumber industry. Each farmer is assumed to carry through the entire productive process. Another way of stating this is that cucumbers are produced in only one *stage of production.* The simplification involves assuming away multistage production.

[1]For the sake of simplicity, this chapter uses the accountant's rather than the economist's definition of profit. The distinction between the two concepts is made in a subsequent chapter.

Multi-stage production: a process where each firm performs only a part of the process and sells its output to another firm for further fabrication. **Raw materials** are materials in their natural state, such as coal or iron ore, **intermediate products:** are processed goods that are sold to other producers for further fabrication, such as steel; and **final products**: Output sold to consumers, such as autos.

Multistage Production

In a complex economy, practically all products are produced in multistage operations, where each firm performs only a part of the process and sells its output to another firm for further fabrication.

We distinguish among three types of products: Materials in their natural state, such as coal or iron ore, are called **raw materials.** Processed goods that are sold to other producers for further fabrication, such as steel, are known as **intermediate products.** Output sold to final consumers, such as autos, is called **final products.**

Thus, the production and sale of clothing may involve several stages: (1) the *raw-materials* stage, such as the growing of cotton or wool; (2) the fabrication of *intermediate* materials, such as yarn; (3) the design and production of clothing—the final product; (4) the sale of clothing—by manufacturers to wholesalers, by wholesalers to *retail* outlets, and by retail stores to the consumer—together known as the distribution stage.

Likewise, the production of a desk may involve four stages: (1) the *raw-materials* stage of growing the forest and cutting the trees, (2) one *intermediate* stage of producing lumber, (3) one *final-production* stage of designing and manufacturing the desks, and (4) *distribution*—the sale of the desks by manufacturer to wholesaler, by wholesaler to retail store, and by retailer to the final consumer.

These two examples can be described schematically as in Figure 2–1.

Since each stage of production involves separate firms, there are many *interbusiness transactions* as a product moves through the production process from the raw-materials stage to the intermediate stage to the

Figure 2–1 Hypothetical Stages of Production in Clothing and Desk Manufacturing: Product moves from the raw material stage to the intermediate and final product stages. Beyond that it goes through the distribution system before reaching the consumer.

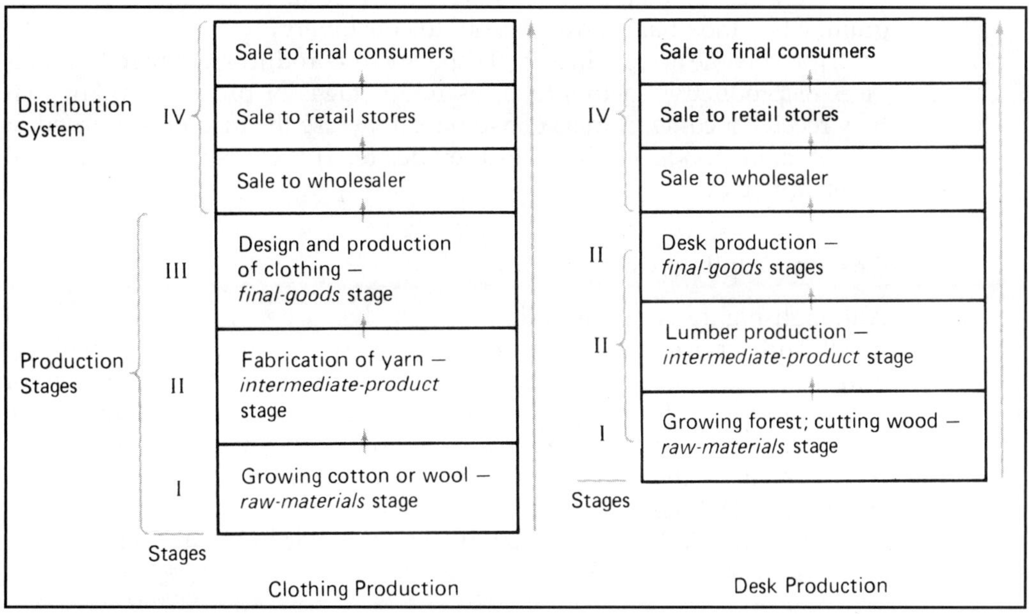

final-good stage. (Only final goods are included in the calculation of GDP.)

Even the examples above are oversimplified. The production of sophisticated items such as electronics or aircrafts involves many intermediate stages. Thousands of subcontracting firms, each manufacturing one part, may be involved. Each large auto manufacturer has hundreds of supplying firms each providing one part, such as glass, tires, steel, or aluminum.

At the first stage of production, each firm employs the four primary inputs to extract raw materials in the manner of the cucumber grower. At each subsequent stage, the firm employs primary inputs, such as labor and capital, and uses materials purchased from firms in an earlier stage. These materials are subjected to further fabrication and are sold "onward" to other firms, until the final stage of production is reached.

By the same token, it is analytically possible to move "backward" through the production process. Consider stage III in desk manufacturing (Figure 2–1). The final desk can be *decomposed* (broken down or separated) into materials purchased from stage II and the primary factors used. In turn, the intermediate materials of stage II can be decomposed into the raw materials purchased from stage I plus the primary inputs employed to fabricate it. And finally, the raw materials of stage I can be decomposed into the four primary inputs used to extract it: labor, capital, land and natural resources, and enterprise.

Each final product, however complex, can be decomposed into the four primary inputs embodied in it by working backward through the stages of production. In the final analysis, each good and service owes its existence to, or is produced by, the four primary factors of production.

These four factors receive remuneration, which is their income, for their productive contribution at all stages of production. With that income they exercise their rights as consumers and purchase the goods and services they desire. In Figure 2–1, this is shown at the upper end of each diagram, when the final product is sold to consumers.

Thus, people appear in a dual capacity: As producers, they sell the services of productive factors to firms in all stages of production. For that they receive income. And as consumers, they use the income so earned to purchase the goods and services they desire. This leads us to the general statement below.

General Application

Although highly simplified, this analysis has a general application. All goods and services produced in the economy are known collectively as **output.** And resources or factor inputs are required for the production of output. In return for their contributions, factors or their owners receive incomes in the four forms outlined previously. In turn, the income they receive enables the owners of productive factors to purchase (or "lay claims against") the output.

Output: All goods and services produced in the economy.

Schematically, the process can be illustrated as in Figure 2–2.

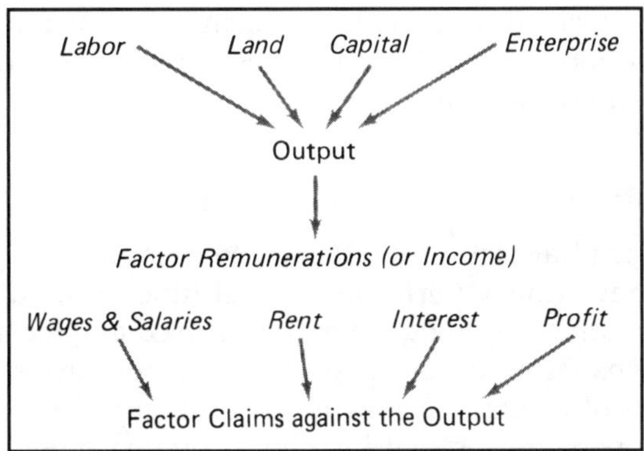

Figure 2–2 Primary Factors of Production (or Inputs)

THE CENTRAL IDEA OF SCARCITY

In the United States, as well as in other Western industrial countries, the final objective of economic activity is to satisfy the wants of society and its individual members, through the provision of the goods and services they desire. But these goods and services, referred to collectively as output, are not available free for the asking. They must be produced and distributed. And their production requires the concerted and coordinated effort of several primary productive resources: labor, land and natural resources, capital, and enterprise.

At any given time, society has a given amount of each of these resources; they are not available in unlimited quantity. We express this by saying that *resources are scarce.* Consequently, the output they can produce is also limited, or scarce, relative to the wants of society and its individual members. We simply cannot obtain and consume all the goods and services we may wish, because our desires far exceed what can be made available with limited resources.

The fact that resources are scarce, while society's desire to consume their product is unlimited, makes it necessary to use resources efficiently. By this we mean it is necessary to obtain maximum output out of a given amount of the scarce resources, or, alternatively stated, to obtain a given amount of output with a minimum amount of productive resources.

THE NATURE OF EXCHANGE

Transactions: the sale or purchase of goods and services. The costs involved in making transactions or finding the necessary information are called **transaction costs**.

Transactions

All production and other economic processes involve the sale or purchase of goods or services. Thus, in stage I of desk production (Figure 2–1), the producing firm buys the services of productive factors, then sells its product to firms in stage II, and so on up the line. Finally, the consumer who had received income in the form of factor remunerations purchases the final goods and services. Sales or purchases of goods and services are called **transactions**.

Money

Money: is a means of payment or medium of exchange.

In each transaction, a commodity or a productive service is exchanged for **money.** Money performs several functions, but first and foremost it is a **medium of exchange**; that is, it is used as a means of payment in all transactions. Thus, a person supplying labor, professional services, or the services of capital receives remuneration in the form of money. And when that person uses that income to purchase goods and services, he or she pays for them in money.

We all take the use of money so much for granted that we lose sight of what a magnificent social invention it actually is. Yet think how difficult life would be without the use of money.

What would an automobile worker do if he got paid in steering wheels, or a worker in a furniture factory if she had to accept payment in desks? The worker would have to barter the wheels or desks for other products and services desired, such as food, clothing, shelter, medical care, and entertainment. Every transaction would become highly laborious and even painful. For in each case, the factory worker would have to find a seller who would agree to accept the desks in payment. And the sellers in turn would wish to trade some of their surplus desks (whatever they receive beyond their needs) for other commodities. Or consider the possibility that your economics instructor, instead of being paid in money, were paid in goods and services supplied by parents of the students in this class.

Barter is the exchange of goods for other goods (as opposed to goods for money).

The alternative to the use of money is **barter**, the exchange of one good for another. A barter system is very cumbersome. Under such a system, people would spend most of their time and effort exchanging things instead of engaging in the production of goods and services to satisfy consumer wants. The existence of a universally accepted means of payment—money—is absolutely essential to the functioning of a complex economic system. And the wider the area money serves, the more useful it is. A monetary unit serving only a few people would still necessitate barter transactions between that and other similar groups. But if all these groups used the same monetary unit, the need for such barter would be avoided.

Uniform money makes it possible for a Pittsburgh steel mill to purchase Upper Midwest iron ore and West Virginia coal for its furnaces, and sell the steel it produces to Michigan auto makers; and then for Michigan to trade the surplus cars it produces for Florida oranges, Idaho potatoes, Iowa corn, and Washington-manufactured aircraft. Imagine the hardship if all these transactions had to be bartered; they would simply be impossible to execute.

Prices

Prices: The price of a good or service is the number of dollars paid for one unit.

Each transaction involves the exchange of a good or a service for money. In the United States, the monetary unit is the dollar. The **price** of a good or a service is the number of dollars paid for one unit.

Economic processes include many prices of final goods and services sold to consumers, the prices of intermediate inputs or raw materials sold by one firm to another, and the prices of productive services or primary inputs—labor, land, and capital—sold by their owners to firms.

Markets

Markets: any situation where buyers and sellers come together. The price that clears the market is the price at which the amount of the product sellers are willing to sell equals the amount buyers are willing to buy.

Every one of these prices is determined in a market in which buyers (or demanders) and sellers (or suppliers) interact. The buyers and sellers of a product are usually *different groups of people.* In each market, there are many buyers who register their preferences and the intensity of their desire for the product (on the demand side) by the number of dollars they are ready and willing to spend. As a general rule, buyers of a particular product stand ready to purchase increasing quantities as its price declines. Sellers of the same product are willing to supply increasing quantities as its price rises. The price of each good and service is established on its respective **market** at a level that *equates* the quantity sellers are ready to supply with the quantity that buyers are ready to purchase.

The word **market** is a general description of any situation in which buyers and sellers come together. It can be a highly organized national market, such as the New York Stock Exchange, on which corporate stocks are traded, where prices and quantities traded are posted continuously on a highly visible "Big Board," and where buyers and sellers are represented by stockbrokers. It can be a market for credit or foreign currencies, where buyers and sellers are represented by banks with a closely knit international communication network. Or it may be a labor exchange in which the services of workers are offered and purchased; a local farmers' market where sellers and buyers converge to exchange fruits and vegetables for money; a department store or shopping center; or any of a large variety of other markets.

Specialization

Specialization: Each person, region, or country specializes in the activity it can do best.

One feature of a complex economic society that is made possible by the existence of markets and a universally accepted means of payment is a high degree of **specialization.** It enables each individual, each firm, each region of the country, or indeed each country, to specialize in the activity it can do best. Receiving earnings in the form of money, each can buy whatever it needs in highly organized markets and pay for the purchases in money.

Each of us produces directly very little of what each consumes, and consumes virtually nothing of what each produces. It is taken for granted that we sell our productive services to firms and use our income to buy what we need. Without the existence of markets and of money, such specialization would be highly difficult, if not impossible. For specialization requires exchange, and exchange is made possible by the use of money.

In turn, it is partly the ability of each person or firm to specialize in the pursuit for which it is most suited that accounts for the high productivity of industrial societies. Workers can better perform the one task for which they are best suited than they can a variety of tasks. In addition, devoting one's time to a single task, one can improve skill while also avoiding the loss of time involved in switching from one task to another. Furthermore, specialization makes possible the use of machinery and equipment and the consequent development of advanced technology; for each piece of machinery is usually suitable for only one repetitive operation. Indirectly, therefore, the existence of organized markets and the use of money contribute to the high standard of living of industrial societies.

THE CIRCULAR-FLOW DIAGRAM

A simplified view of the economy can now be obtained through the use of a common device known as the circular-flow diagram. Assume that the economy consists only of business firms and individual households, that no government exists. Assume further that there are *no interbusiness transactions;* firms produce goods and services for sale to households. In terms of Figure 2–1, this means that all stages of production, from the raw materials to the final product, are carried out by one firm. Such a firm is called vertically integrated, because it includes under one organization all the vertical steps shown in Figure 2–1. It sells its final product to consuming households.

In turn, all productive services are supplied by households to firms. Households are viewed as the owners and suppliers of the factors of production: labor, land, capital, and enterprise. In return, households receive factor remunerations in the form of wages and salaries, rent, interest, and profit. These remunerations constitute household income, which is used to buy the goods and services produced by firms. The price of each good and productive factor is determined on its respective market. The situation is commonly summarized by the diagram shown in Figure 2–3.

Firms demand productive factors, and households supply such factors on the markets for productive services, shown at the bottom of the diagram. The price of each factor is determined by supply and demand in its market. In turn, *firms supply and households demand final goods and services on their respective markets,* depicted at the top of the diagram.

Firms function in the economy in a dual capacity: as buyers of productive inputs from households, and as sellers of goods and services to households. Households also function in a dual role: as sellers of productive inputs to firms, and as purchasers of final goods and services from firms.

Households earn income, in the form of factor remunerations, for the sale of their productive services; and they spend that income on the purchase of goods and services from firms. Firms earn income from the sale of their output to households; and in turn they spend it on the purchase of productive services from households. The circuit is complete.

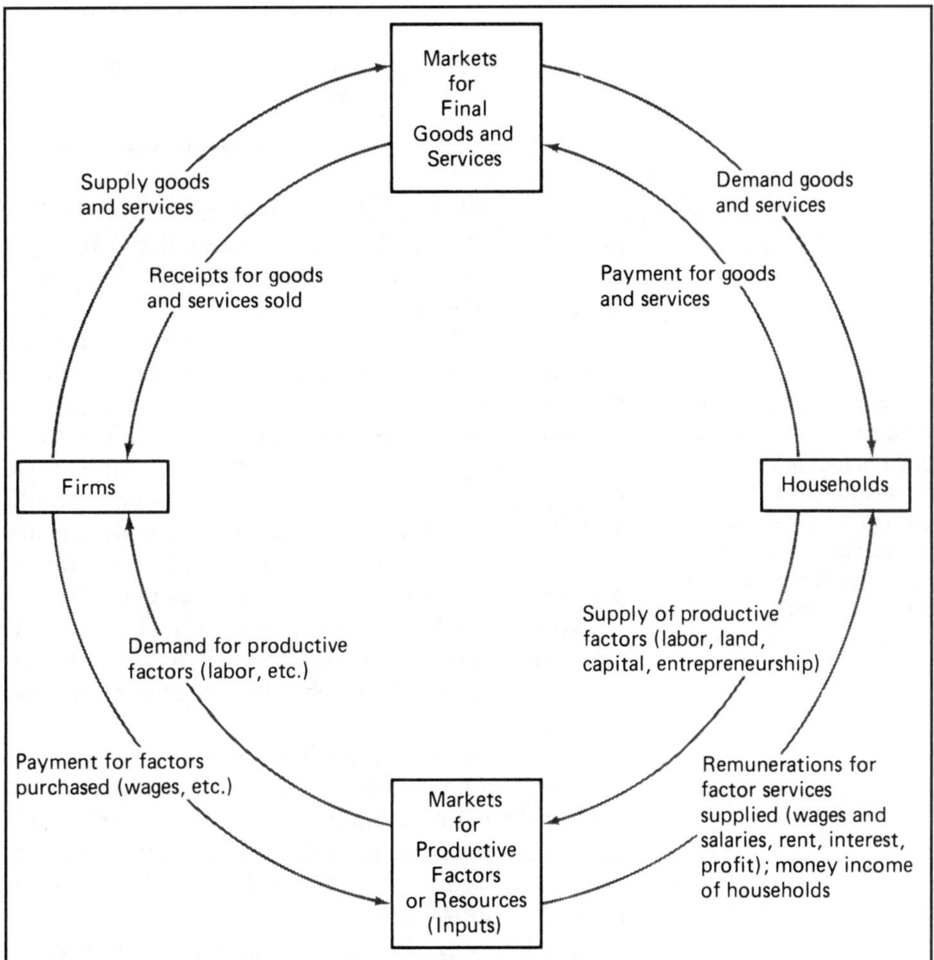

Figure 2–3 The Circular-Flow Diagram Productive services flow from households to firms. Payments flow in the opposite direction. Goods and services flow from firms to households. Payments flow in the opposite direction. All transactions take place on markets.

Circular-flow diagram: a diagram that shows the direction and flow of money and resource in the economy. Productive services flow from households to firms. Payments flow in the opposite direction. Goods and services flow from firms to households. Payments flow in the opposite direction.

EQUALITY OF OUTPUT AND INCOME

How much household income, in the form of factor remunerations, is generated in the process of producing goods and services? The answer is not immediately obvious, yet it is of utmost importance.

Consider the simple one-stage production case of our cucumber grower. She hires the services of three productive factors—labor, land, and capital—for which she pays, respectively, wages and salaries, rent, and interest. Assume that these outlays are as follows:

Wages and salaries	$500
Rent	$200
Interest	$100
Total outlays	$800

If she sells her crop of cucumbers for $1,000, then her *profit* is $200 ($1,000 – $800 = $200). But profit is also a return to a productive factor, enterprise. By adding up the return to all four factors, we obtain precisely the price of the product, $1,000.

Equality of output and income: The dollar value of all output produced equals the total income earned by all factors of production (including profit), generated in the production process.

This result suggests the following all-important proposition: **In any productive activity, the dollar value of any product or service produced equals the total income—in the form of wages and salaries, rent, interest, and profit—generated in the production process.**

This is easy to see in the case of a simple barter economy, where the fish Robinson Crusoe catches with his bare hands constitute his output and his income at one and the same time. It was also shown above for the simple case of one-stage production. But it is far from apparent in a complex money economy. Yet it holds true even there.

At this point we merely wish to rely on an intuitive extension of the simple case to the entire economy. **The dollar value of all final goods and services produced equals the income generated in the production process.**

This principle has an implication for the circular-flow diagram. Over any period of time, the dollar value of the goods and services produced and sold by firms, shown at the upper left-hand corner of Figure 2–3, equals the total remunerations to productive factors employed by firms, shown at the lower right-hand side. These remunerations make up the income of households.

If all household income is spent on goods and services (that is, in the absence of saving by the households) it would be exactly sufficient to purchase all the goods and services produced. The circuit would then be complete and self-perpetuating: In the process of production, firms generate an *income stream* that accrues to households. In turn, if households spent their entire income, they would purchase the entire output of goods and services produced.

A COMPREHENSIVE DEFINITION OF THE DISCIPLINE

It is now possible to offer a more complete definition of economics than the one introduced in Chapter 1: **Economics is concerned with the production, processing, and distribution of goods and services among consumers; the distribution of incomes among productive factors; the level of employment or unemployment of such factors; and the purchasing power of their money income (how much goods and services their money income will buy).**

SUMMARY

Many of the problems confronting society are economic in nature. And even noneconomic problems are apt to have an economic component, whenever the question of financing certain social activities arises.

Economics is defined as the study of people's behavior in producing, exchanging, and consuming the goods and services of their choice.

Production of goods and services, or of output, is carried on in firms. Within the framework of a firm, factors of production or inputs (or resources) are organized to produce output. In the process, factors receive remuneration, which is their income. The four primary inputs and their form of compensation are:

Primary Factors	Form of Remuneration
Labor	Wages and salaries
Land and natural resources	Rent
Capital	Interest
Entrepreneurship	Profit

(Note that profit is also a return to a productive factor.) The sum total of the returns to all factors of production equals the dollar value of the output produced. *Income and output are equal.*

A single-stage process is the simplest form of production. But practically all goods and services require several or many stages, starting from raw materials, moving on to intermediate products, and then to final commodities. These then reach the consumer through *wholesale* and *retail* distribution outlets (stores).

In all cases, the final product can be decomposed into the four primary inputs. The *equality of income and output values is preserved.*

Income, obtained as compensation for productive contributions in their capacity as inputs, enables households to purchase the output produced by firms.

In the circular-flow diagram, which offers a simplified description of the economy, both firms and households appear in a dual role. Firms buy factors from households and sell them output. Households purchase output from firms and sell them productive inputs.

It is in *markets* that the buying and selling of each good, service, or input is carried on. In each market, demanders and suppliers interact to determine the dollar price. And each transaction involves an exchange of a good, a service, or an input for money.

Money is a medium of exchange, or means of financing transactions. Without a universally accepted means of payment to finance transactions—money—no sophisticated economy can exist. Indirectly, the existence of money makes specialization possible, and it thereby contributes to mechanization of production, and to a high living standard.

Last but not least, note the central idea of *scarcity*. Because *resources* are limited, so is their output. In contrast, *society's wants are unlimited*. That feature makes it necessary to use resources *efficiently*, to obtain maximum output for a given amount of scarce resources.

QUESTIONS AND PROBLEMS

1. Give four examples of problems that are economic in nature.
2. Define *economics*.
3. Distinguish between one-stage and multistage production processes.
4. What are the four primary inputs and their forms of remuneration?
5. Explain these terms:

- ☐ Raw materials
- ☐ Intermediate products
- ☐ Final products
- ☐ Output
- ☐ Income
- ☐ Money
- ☐ Markets
- ☐ Transactions
- ☐ Specialization
- ☐ Price

6. Explain the following statement: "If resources were not scarce, it would not be necessary to use them efficiently." What is the meaning of *efficiency* in economics?
7. Show and explain the circular-flow diagram.
8. What do we mean by the equality of income and output?

The Economic Agents—An Overview

Chapter 2 presented a simplified analysis of the process of production and income generation in the economy in the form of a circular-flow diagram. Firms and households are two basic economic agents, producing and selling goods and services and receiving income. Combined, they are often referred to as the private, or nongovernment, sector. But there is also a *public sector,* in the form of three levels of government: federal, state, and local (municipalities). Indeed, the government is another economic agent, omitted from the previous discussion for the sake of simplicity.

Both firms and households pay *taxes* to the government. In turn, the government supplies public services to both. The goods the government needs for the provision of public services, such as tanks required for national defense, are largely produced by and purchased from private firms. All these "flows" are incorporated in the modified circular-flow diagram shown in Figure 3–1.

This chapter reviews briefly the three agents: firms, households, and government in their various capacities.

THE FIRM, INDUSTRY, AND SECTOR

General Nature of Firms

Firms: the organizational unit within which economic activity is conducted.
Plants: a physical establishment set up to carry out a specific production or distribution function.
Multinational firm: A firm that owns plants in several countries.

The **firm** is the organizational unit within which economic activity is conducted. A firm may operate one or more **plants,** the plant being a physical establishment, such as a factory, a mine, or a store, set up to perform a specific production or distribution function. Firms can also operate in more than one country. A firm that owns plants in several countries is known as a **multinational firm.**

There are millions of firms in the United States. They range in size from the corner drugstore or small shop, employing one or two people, to giant corporations, such as General Motors or General Electric, each

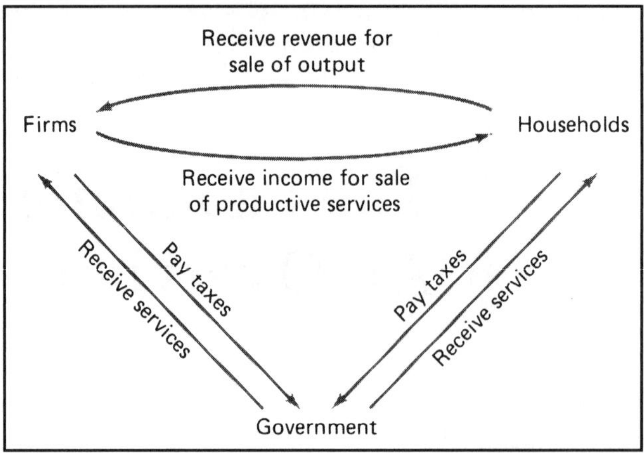

Modified Circular Flow Diagram includes the government sector.

Figure 3–1 A Modified Circular-Flow Diagram: Extension of the circular-flow diagram to incorporate tax payments by firms and households to the government and the provision of services by government to firms and households.

employing hundreds of thousands of workers, each operating many plants both here and abroad, and each with annual sales of tens of billions of dollars.

Not all firms are profitable; some suffer losses and are forced to go out of business. Hundreds of thousands of new firms are established every year, but a similar—although somewhat smaller—number fail and close their doors. At times, even huge firms, such as the Penn Central Railroad or Enron, fail. And on occasion, large firms are bailed out with government assistance, as in the case of the Lockheed and Chrysler corporations. Reasons for failure are many and varied. They include poor management, a change in consumer taste away from the products produced by the firm, changes in technology that undermine the competitive position of the firm, and the like.

There are numerous ways of classifying enterprises: by size of assets, by dollar value of sales, by industry or economic sector, or on the basis of legal forms by which firms are organized.

Legal Forms of Business Organizations

Sole proprietorship: A business owned by one person, who is subject to unlimited liability.

Partnership: a business owned and operated by two or more people. Also subject to unlimited liability.

In terms of its legal structure, a firm can be (1) a **sole proprietorship**, a business owned and operated by one person; (2) a **partnership**, owned and operated by two or more people; or (3) a **corporation**; which is a legal entity distinct and separate from the people who own it. Of the millions of firms, 75 percent are sole proprietorships, 7 percent are partnerships, and 18 percent are corporations.

Sole Proprietorship A sole proprietorship has the advantage of being easy to organize and set up. The owner, being her own boss, has substantial freedom in managing the business. But there are three disadvantages: The financial resources available to one person may not be sufficient to set up a large-scale enterprise. One proprietor needs to carry out all the management functions, leaving no scope for specialization. And the owner is subject to **unlimited liability**; she risks not only the assets of the firm but also her entire personal wealth. Should the business fail and be unable to pay all the creditors, creditors can lay claim against any or all of the owner's personal wealth.

Unlimited liability: The owner of an indebted business can lose not only the assets of the business, but personal assets as well, to creditors.

Partnership A partnership has the advantages of being relatively easy to organize; of affording some measure of specialization between the partners in discharging management responsibilities; and of permitting access to greater financial resources, as the partners pool their funds to set up the business. The disadvantages include possible disagreements and disputes between the partners; at the extreme, such disputes can lead to a dissolution of the partnership. Withdrawal or death of one partner may lead to the same outcome. Financial resources remain limited, although less so than in the case of a sole proprietorship. Finally, a partnership is also subject to *unlimited liabilities*. If the business fails, creditors can lay claim to the entire personal wealth of the owners, regardless of whether it is invested in the firm.

Corporation It is the financial and managerial limitations outlined above that have led to the creation of the corporation. Designated by law as an independent entity, separate and distinct from its owners, it can raise capital funds; produce, distribute, and sell goods and services; incur debt or extend credit; sue and be sued; and conduct all business affairs.

Corporation: A legal entity separate from the people who own it. It is able to raise capital funds; produce, distribute, and sell goods and services; incur debt; sue or be sued; and conduct business affairs. **Stocks or shares:** certificates used to raise initial capital through their sale. **Dividends:** part of a corporations profits which are distributed to the stockholders of the company. **Retained earnings:** the part of a company's profits that are withheld in anticipation of future investments. **Bond:** An IOU issued by a company to raise additional funds. Owners receive **interest**. Corporations have **Limited liability**: Their risk extends only to the number of shares they own.

Following the legal process of *incorporation*, the corporation raises its initial capital by selling **stocks** or **shares** to the public.[1] The buyers and owners of these shares own the corporation. But ownership changes when the shares change hands, as they are traded on one of the country's stock exchanges. The corporation is run by a board of directors elected by the stockholders. The board in turn hires the management, headed by a president, to manage the day-to-day affairs of the company.

In years when the corporation realizes profit on its transactions, the profits are usually divided three ways: Part is consigned to the government in payment of the corporate profit tax; part is withheld in anticipation of future investments (known as *undistributed* or **retained earnings**); and the remainder is distributed to the stockholders in the form of **dividends**.

Dividends are the form in which the owners of the corporation receive their profit. A corporation is not obligated to distribute dividends, and the board of directors may choose not to do so in unprofitable years. In general, the size of the dividends depends on how profitable the corporation is. In turn, the price of the company's stock, traded on the stock exchange, depends in no small measure on its current and expected profitability.

[1]The corporation must submit any sizable new issue of stock for review by the Securities and Exchange Commission (SEC), and prove that no misleading claims are involved.

Should the corporation wish to raise additional funds, it can also sell bonds. A **bond** is an IOU issued for a specific number of years, at the end of which the bond "matures," and the corporation redeems it from the owner; that is, it pays back the principal amount. While the bond is in force, its owner is a creditor, and the issuing corporation is the debtor. The bond carries a commitment by the corporation to pay the holder a *specific dollar amount* in **interest** each year. The proportion of interest to the value of the bond is the interest rate, expressed as a percentage. Unlike the case with dividends, the commitment to pay interest does not depend on the profitability of the company during the year. Unlike stockowners, bondholders do not own the corporation or any part of it; they only lent it money.

Finally, the corporation can raise funds by borrowing directly from banks and paying them interest.

In sum, **dividends are the form of profit distributed to the owners of the corporation. Interest is payment for loans advanced to the company**. It is a return on "debt" capital.

What are the advantages of a corporate form of business enterprise? First, it is able to raise large sums of money through the methods outlined above, and at the same time spread the risk of ownership over many owners. Additionally, since the corporation's stock is registered on one of the country's **stock exchanges**, individual owners can dispose of their stocks by selling them on an exchange. However, in most cases, an enterprise needs to be a "going concern" at the time of incorporation in order to entice people to purchase its stocks. Often, a firm starts out as a sole proprietorship or partnership and only after it reaches a certain size do its owners decide to incorporate through the public sale of stock ("go public").

Stock exchanges: The place where people buy or sell stocks.

Second, the owners of the corporation have **limited liability**. Their risk extends only to the number of shares they purchased. Creditors can sue the corporation as a legal entity, but not the owners as individuals. The owners' personal wealth cannot be claimed in case of corporate bankruptcy.

Third, the corporation has a life of its own, independent of that of its owners. Its continuity is not disrupted when ownership changes hands through the sale or other transfer of its stocks.

Finally, its size permits the corporation to hire specialized and efficient management. The separation of ownership from management gives the corporation a life of its own, separate and distinct from that of its stockholders.

Against these advantages there are some drawbacks. First, the very process of incorporation involves legal expenses as well as some red tape.

Second, once incorporated, the business becomes subject to double taxation: (1) A corporate profit tax ranging up to 32 percent is levied on the profits realized by the corporation, and (2) the amount distributed to shareowners as dividends is subject to personal income tax when shareholders file their individual tax returns. By contrast, income from an unincorporated enterprise is subject only to the personal income tax. In 2003 President Bush proposed the elimination of personal tax on dividends.

Third, the *separation of ownership from management* and control invites abuse. In annual meetings of stockholders, and in the election of the corporate board of directors, each share carries one vote. Ownership is often diffused among thousands or even millions of shareholders, many of whom have only a passing interest in the affairs of the corporation. They

▶ THE STOCK EXCHANGE

By far the most important stock exchange in the country is the New York Stock Exchange, on which most of the large corporations are registered and their stocks are traded. It is followed by the American Stock Exchange, also located in New York City, and the regional exchanges in other cities, such as the Midwest Exchange in Chicago and the Boston and Pacific Exchanges.

Trading in corporate stocks is done by brokers, such as Merrill Lynch or Paine Webber, who have a seat on the exchange. With offices all over the country, they execute "buy" or "sell" orders on behalf of their customers.

Each day the press reports the transactions in all company stocks registered on the major exchanges. The accompanying report describes transactions in General Electric stocks on February 2, 2006:

52 weeks				Yld	P-E	Sales		Net
High	Low	Stock	Div.	%	Ratio	100s	Close	Ch.
37.3	32.6	GenEl	1.0	3.0	21	304511	32.9	-0.2

Skip for a moment the two left-hand columns. Following the abbreviated name of the company, (GenEl), there is a column showing the current annual dividend per share ($1.0 in the case of GE), based on the latest quarterly declaration.

Next comes "Yield" (Yld) or the annual dividend as a percent of the current stock price (3.0%). The price-earning (P-E) ratio is the current stock price dividend by the latest twelve month dividends (21 for GE). "Sales 100s" refers to the number of shares traded during the day (30,451,100). Stock prices are then shown in dollar amounts: the price at the end ("close") of the day ($32.9). The change is the difference-plus, minus, or no change-between the day's closing price and the previous day's closing price (price declined by $0.2). The two left-hand columns show the high and low prices for the particular stock over the last 52 weeks ($37.5 and $32.6 respectively).

On February 2, 2006, a total of 1.9 billion shares of all corporations were traded on the New York Stock Exchange.

Each day the New York Stock Exchange publishes a composite average price of stocks traded, better known as the Dow Jones Index. It is a price index of the shares of the thirty largest industrial corporations and it stood at 10,852 on February 2, 2006. Comparable price indexes are available for the stocks of transportation and utility companies.

are interested mainly in corporate profitability. The control over the affairs of the corporation is entrusted to its managerial staff. And the management may have additional interests: It may also be interested in corporate size and the prestige and power that accompany bigness. The two sets of interests often diverge.

Moreover, management is accountable to shareholders only in a roundabout and limited fashion. Corporate officials can pay themselves high salaries, bonuses, fringe benefits, and other perquisites,[2] leaving a smaller portion of corporate earnings for dividends distribution.

In the year 2002, it was discovered that several huge corporations, such as Enron, vastly exaggerated their sales revenues and profits. The top corporate officers collected millions in salaries and bonuses before the corporations went bankrupt, leaving workers and pensioners penniless.

[2]Perquisites, or "perks," refer to nonfinancial remuneration, such as a chauffeur-driven car or a trip to a baseball game in the company jet. Fringe benefits include such things as health or life insurance.

Large accounting firms, such as Arthur Andersen, often acquiesced and covered up these misdeeds. Public confidence in corporate America was eroded as a result.

Should a group of stockholders wish to replace the management, they would have to amass enough votes at the annual meetings. Since few stockholders attend these meetings, the rebellious group would have to collect proxy votes (permission to cast a vote in the name of the absentee) to attain a majority. And because management would try to do likewise, a *proxy fight* may ensue, with an uncertain outcome. Corporations may also be subject to takeover bids by other companies, and such bids were very widespread in 1988. Conflicts of interest between owners and managers are absent in the case of a single proprietorship or a partnership.

Preferred Form With all these pros and cons, the critical factor that determines the desirability of incorporation is the amount of funds required by the business. In most manufacturing industries, firms must be of reasonably large size for efficient operations, and consequently, large capital investments are crucial. Such industries as autos, steel, metal products, computers, machinery, electrical equipment, household appliances, and aircraft production are dominated by the corporate form of business organization.

Although only 18 percent of U.S. business enterprises are incorporated, large corporations own by far the greatest share of manufacturing assets, and they account for 89 percent of sales. Each year, *Fortune*, the business magazine, publishes a list of the 500 largest manufacturing corporations in the United States. Known as the *Fortune* 500, the list includes such particulars as assets, employment, and annual sales of each firm. Similar lists of the largest foreign firms are also available, as are lists of the largest nonmanufacturing companies, such as those in banking and insurance.

▶ LEGAL FORMS OF BUSINESS ORGANIZATION

Type of Firm	Advantages	Disadvantages
Individual Proprietorship	Easy to organize Owner makes all decisions Earnings taxed only once, as personal income	Unlimited liability (owner risks personal wealth) Limited financial resources Unspecialized management
Partnership	Not difficult to organize Some specialization in management Earnings taxed only once	Unlimited liability for partners Possible disputes between partners Limited financial resources
Corporation	Limited liability for owners Ability to raise capital by issuing stocks and bonds Specialized management Life continues beyond that of owners	Income taxed twice: once as corporate profit and once as personal income of dividend recipients Possible disagreements between managers and owners

Most of the largest corporations, based either in the United States or abroad, are *multinational* firms. They own production plants in several or even many countries, and distribution facilities in many countries.

Corporate Growth

Mergers: Horizontal merger: Merger of two companies in the same industry. **Vertical merger:** merger of two companies at different stages of production, as when a firm acquires one or more of its suppliers. **Conglomerate merger:** merger of companies from totally different industries.

Many corporations tend to grow in size, either by internal expansion or by purchasing or merging with other independent firms. The latter type of expansion is said to be **horizontal** if it enables the company to expand its sales of a similar range of products—for example, when one steel company buys another, one auto company merges with another, or one supermarket chain purchases a controlling interest in another. The expansion is said to be **vertical** if a company acquires one or more of its suppliers—as when an auto company acquires a steel or aluminum producer, where steel and aluminum are materials used in auto production; when a steel company acquires an iron or coal mine; or when a furniture company buys a forest or lumber yard.

Finally, a company such as Textron, Litton, or IT&T that owns plants producing *unrelated* and diverse products and services (such as electronics, banking, insurance, and printing) is known as a **conglomerate.** A conglomerate merger occurs when firms in diverse and unrelated lines of production are merged.

Incentives on the part of corporations to expand are many and varied. The need to attain higher efficiency and "mass-production economics" is one. The desire to acquire power and prestige is another. And seeking security protection against losses in diversification of output into many goods and services—that is, to avoid "putting all the eggs in one basket"—is still another.

Society reaps certain benefits from large corporate size, inasmuch as bigness contributes to greater efficiency through mass production and specialization within firms. But this is a double-edged sword. Bigness also confers upon a firm market power, wherein it can partly escape the discipline of competition. Very large corporations are able to manipulate the consuming public to some degree, to the benefit of the company's own needs. Bigness undercuts the degree to which the firm caters to consumer wants. The pros and cons of size must be balanced against each other.

Industries

Sector: a broad industry classification that contains many industries.
Industry: a group of firms producing the same or similar products. The commodity producing sectors: (Agriculture, mining, construction and manufacturing) provide less than 1/4 of economic activity while services account for over 2/3 of economic activity.

Thus far, the discussion has concentrated on the individual firm. This subsection defines broader business groups in the economy, each consisting of more than one firm.

An **industry** is a group of firms producing the same or similar products. Thus, the automobile industry consists of all firms producing automobiles, the chemical, steel, footwear, and textile industries contain firms producing the products indicated by their respective industry titles. There are hundreds of industries in the American economy, classified in a standardized manner known as the Standard Industrial Classification (SIC). Information about them, such as their output, employment, and geographical locations, is compiled in quadrennial censuses and annual surveys.

Some industries, such as automobiles, electrical appliances, and aircraft, consist of very few firms. Others, such as textiles, comprise a multitude of firms. In cases where the "economics of mass production" is important, there is a tendency for firms to be very large and, therefore, for the number of firms in the industry to be very small.

Some industries, such as automobiles, supply their output to final consumers; others, such as steel, sell mainly to other industries. And still other industries, such as chemicals, sell part of their output to consumers and part to other manufacturers.

Sectors

A **sector** is a broad industry classification that contains many industries. Thus, the manufacturing sector includes all manufacturing industries; the agricultural sector contains the dairy, wheat, cotton, and other farm industries. Table 3–1 shows the eight main private sectors in the U.S. economy, plus the government sector. In particular, the table shows how the nation's firms (proprietorships, partnerships, and corporations), its work force, and its national income are divided among these sectors.

Less than 2 percent of all workers are employed in agriculture and only 1.5 percent of all income is generated there. The figures attest to the immense productivity of American agriculture: It requires only 1.7 percent of the nation's work force to feed the entire population, with significant quantities

Table 3–1 Major Sectors in the U.S. Economy

Sector	Number of Firms (2002)		Contribution to GDP (2003)		Full Time Workers Employed (2003)	
	Million	%	*Billion Dollars*	%	*Million*	%
Agriculture, forestry, and fisheries	N/A		114	1.0	1.3	1.1
Mining	*		130	1.2	0.5	0.4
Construction	0.7	10.3	501	4.6	6.7	5.5
Manufacturing	0.3	4.4	1,402	12.7	14.0	11.4
Wholesale and retail trade	1.6	23.5	1,416	12.9	18.9	15.4
Finance, insurance, and real estate	0.8	11.8	2,250	20.4	7.7	6.3
Transportation, communications, and public utilities	0.4	5.9	1,035	9.4	7.6	6.2
Services	**3.0	44.1	2,755	25.0	46.4	37.9
Government			1,400	12.7	20.0	16.3
Rest of world			N/A		–0.6	–0.5
Total	6.8	100.0	11,004	100.0	122.5	100.0
	Source: Statistical Abstract of the U.S. 2004, Table No. 728		Source: BEA, Gross Domestic Product by Industry Accounts, Feb. 2005		Source: BEA, National Income and Product Accounts Table 6.5D, Feb. 2005	

*data not reported because it did not meet publication standard

**does not include "Management Services" because data did not meet publication standards

Sources: Statistical Abstract of the United States, 2004, and *Survey of Current Business, 2005.*

of food left over for export. Highly mechanized techniques and sophisticated use of fertilizers have made the U.S. farm economy very efficient.

Less than one fifth of the labor force is employed by the manufacturing sector, and a similar proportion of national output is generated there. However, because it contains huge companies, the number of firms in that sector is relatively small.

Of the remaining sectors, the wholesale and retail trade and services (such as educational and cultural activities) are the most important, followed by finance and transportation. Government at all levels employs 16.9 percent of all workers.

Agriculture, mining, construction, and manufacturing can be described as the *commodity*-producing sectors of the economy. They account for less than one quarter of economic activity. The remaining industry classes, providing various *services*, account for over two thirds.

This division of the work force and output is characteristic of a highly advanced industrial economy. At the early stages of development of a society, most workers are employed in agriculture, in order to feed the population. With the introduction of fertilizers and of increasingly advanced tools of production, the agricultural economy becomes more productive. This makes possible the release of labor from the farm sector and enables manufacturing production to expand. At a subsequent stage, the same phenomenon occurs in manufacturing. As the scale of operations expands and production processes become increasingly mechanized, *output per worker*, called **labor productivity**, rises. Eventually it becomes possible to release workers to service activities, and these expand rapidly.

Labor productivity: output per worker. As productivity rises, output shifts from manufacturing to services, and consumption shifts in the same direction.

This process of economic development is accompanied by parallel changes in consumption patterns. At the society's early levels of development, incomes are low, and expenditures on bare necessities, such as food, occupy the greatest part of the consumer's budget. As productivity and output rise, so does consumer income. (Recall that output and income are equal.) It becomes possible to devote an increasingly higher share of that income to manufactured products. And at the final stage, with further boosts in income, consumers begin to devote increasing proportions of their income to services. What is considered a luxury when incomes are low becomes a necessity as incomes rise.

Such changes in consumption patterns are common in all or most countries. Thus, the changes in the production mix as the country develops correspond to the changes in the pattern of consumption. As a result, employment in the U.S. service industries rose from 60 percent of total employment in 1956 to 80 percent in 2005.

HOUSEHOLDS

As shown by the circular-flow diagram, households play a dual role in the economy. First, they supply productive services to firms, in exchange for which they receive income in the form of factor remunerations. Second, they spend their income on goods and services. We shall consider each role separately.

Table 3–2 Distribution of Personal Income, 2004

Personal-Income Class	% of All Households in Each Class
Under $10,000	9%
$10,000–24,999	20%
$25,000–49,999	27%
$50,000 and over	44%
Total	100%
Median Income $42,409	

Source: Bureau of the Census, *Money Income in the United States, 2005, Table A-1.*

Households as Income Receivers

Functional Distribution of Income Income is received by households in return for productive services. The functional distribution of income in the economy shows how aggregate personal income is distributed among the four productive factors—that is, according to the function performed by the income receivers.

In 2005, total personal income in the United States amounted to $10,238 billion, of which $7,114 billion was in the form of wages and salaries (and supplements). In other words, about 70% of all household income is return from the labor factor of production (wages and salaries). The remaining third is divided among interest, rent, and profit.

Size and Rank Distribution of Income An alternative form of reporting distribution is by classifying all households according to the size of income: for example, under $10,000; between $10,000 and $24,999; between $25,000 and $49,999 and $50,000 and above. Table 3–2 shows the percentage of all households falling within each income bracket. In 2004, 9 percent of all households earned less than $10,000 per year while 44 percent earned $50,000 or more.

Rank distribution of income: The ranking of households by the level of their income from the lowest to the highest, and dividing them to five groups of equal numbers (quintiles).

Another method that highlights the degree of equality or inequality of income in society is known as the **rank distribution of income**. All households are ranked by the level of their income from the lowest to the highest. The income of the household that falls exactly in the middle is called **median** income; half the households earn less than the median, and half earn more. The median is the midpoint income. In 2004, median income of households in the United States was $40,400—among the highest in the world. In contrast, the mean (or simple average) income is obtained by adding up all incomes in the economy and dividing by the number of households.

Return now to the original ranking of households from the lowest to the highest income earnings. Once such an array is made, households are grouped into five groups of *identical size*, known as **quintiles**.[3] Thus, the lowest fifth of the income distribution is the lowest quintile, followed by the next lowest quintile, and so on up the line to the highest quintile. The advantage

[3]A more detailed division, into ten groups, is also common. Each group contains one tenth of all families, and is known as a *decile*. Deciles are also ranked from lowest to highest.

of such a division is that each group contains an *identical number* of households (one fifth of all), and that they are ranked from lowest to highest.

As a next step, add up total income received by households in each group, and calculate that figure as a percentage of incomes received by *all* households in society. This is done in Table 3–3. The degree of inequality is reflected in the fact that the fifth of all households at the lowest end of the distribution earns under 4 percent of all income, whereas the uppermost fifth earns 50 percent. In a perfectly equal income distribution, each quintile would account for exactly 20 percent of all income; that is, the percentage of households in each group and the share of income they receive would be identical. Indeed, the degree of inequality can be assessed by measuring the extent to which the actual income distribution departs from a hypothetical perfectly equal distribution.

Between 1967 and 2004 there has been an increase in income inequality in the U.S.: The share of the top quintile in total income increased while that of the bottom quintile declined (shares of the middle quintiles also declined).

Reasons for Inequality What accounts for the inequality in income distribution? In a market economy, people's earnings are determined by their productive contribution, their contribution toward the production of goods and services. And that in turn depends on a variety of factors, including native ability; training, skill, and education; advancement opportunities in a particular job situation; property ownership, where the property yields income and may or may not have been inherited; and presence or absence of discriminatory practices against certain groups in particular labor markets. A market-based reward system inevitably generates unequal income distribution.

The Case For and Against Inequality In the minds of most people, the case against inequality is built around some concept of social justice: We can increase total satisfaction if money is taken from the rich and given to the poor. Additionally, income inequality leads to political inequality, since rich people exercise greater political clout.

Against these arguments is the idea that the extra financial rewards embedded in inequality enhance people's incentives to acquire skills, work hard, and advance. All that, in turn, contributes to an increase in output.

Table 3–3 Rank Distribution of Income in the United States, 2004

Quintile	% of All Households	% of Income Received by Households in Each Quintile
Lowest	20	3.4%
Second	20	8.7
Third	20	14.7
Fourth	20	23.2
Highest	20	50.0
	100	**100.0**

Source: Bureau of the Census, Money Income in the United States, 2005, Table C

▶ A SIMPLIFIED ILLUSTRATION

Following is a simplified example of how a table such as Table 3–3 is derived.

Assume an economy consisting of ten households. Ranking them in terms of their hypothetical income, from the lowest to the highest, we obtain the first two columns of the following table:

The incomes of the ten households add up to $300,000. Divide the ten households into five equal groups (quintiles) and add up the total income of each group, as shown in the third column. The fourth column computes the income of each quintile as a percent of total income of the community.

Household	Annual Income	Income of Each Quintile	% of Total Income Received by Each Quintile
1	6,000		
2	9,000	$ 15,000	$\frac{15}{300} \times 100 = 5\%$
3	12,000		
4	18,000	$ 30,000	$\frac{30}{300} \times 100 = 10\%$
5	23,000		
6	27,000	$ 50,000	$\frac{50}{300} \times 100 = 17\%$
7	30,000		
8	37,000	$ 67,000	$\frac{67}{300} \times 100 = 22\%$
9	48,000		
10	90,000	$138,000	$\frac{140}{300} \times 100 = 46\%$
	Total: $300,000		100%

The absence of such incentives impedes economic growth. Why work harder or improve skills if such changes go unrewarded? Additionally, it is thought that inequality contributes to investment and capital formation in the economy, because these activities are generally undertaken by the high-income groups.

Both arguments have merit. Ideally, one wants to strike a proper balance and achieve just the amount of inequality that provides maximum incentive to work and to advance. But finding that balance is a difficult if not impossible task, and we must be satisfied with a more modest objective. Although it is essential to maintain a strong incentive system and therefore retain a measure of inequality, it is also desirable to eliminate its most serious outcome: stark poverty. Not only is that a matter of social and political consensus; even in terms of output, underfed, underclothed, and under-sheltered people make poor workers. The government budget plays a useful role in redistributing income from the rich to the poor, thereby modifying the outcome of the market system. It does so by taxing the rich and subsidizing the poor.

Households as Spenders

Households receive income mainly in return for productive services they render, and partly in the form of transfers from the government. Part of that income goes to the government in the form of the **personal income**

Household income is compensation for work. After payment of the **personal income tax**, what is left is **disposable income,** which may be saved, or spent on: durable goods, nondurables, or services.

tax, and the remainder, known as **disposable income**, is in the hands of households to dispose of as they wish. It is divided into two components: consumption and savings, where savings is defined as the part of income not consumed.

Households save for a variety of reasons: protection against unforeseen financial contingencies, reserves for a rainy day, a nest egg for retirement, and financing of the children's college education, to name just a few. Savings are usually placed in a variety of financial instruments that earn interest or dividends. These include bank checking accounts, passbook savings accounts, bank certificates of deposit, (CDs),[4] corporate or government bonds, and corporate stocks. Some of these forms, such as CDs, involve a commitment of the funds for a specified time. With other forms, such as passbook savings accounts, the money can be withdrawn upon request.

Both the perceived need for savings and the ability to save determine how much a family saves. And that ability depends on income: The higher the income, the more the people are able to save. The positive relation between savings and income is indeed reflected in empirical data. People with very low incomes often *dissave*, or experience *negative savings;* they spend more than they earn. To finance the difference, they either borrow or use up previously accumulated savings.

In turn, consumption expenditures are divided among thousands of goods and services. In that sense, all goods and services compete for the consumer dollar. Total consumption expenditures rise with income. Any increment or addition to household income is divided between added consumption and added savings.

It is customary to classify products consumed into three categories, on the basis of their durability: (1) durable goods, which may last for years, such as automobiles, household appliances, and furniture; (2) nondurable goods, such as clothing, shoes, food, and gasoline; and (3) services, such as transportation, entertainment, and education.

Durable-goods purchases are *discretionary,* or postponable in nature. In a bad year, consumers can forego the purchase of a new car, but they can hardly postpone expenditures on food and clothing. For that reason, sales of durable goods tend to fluctuate much more with the ups and downs of the economy than do sales of nondurables.

THE PUBLIC SECTOR

Deficit: a deficit occurs when government expenditures exceed its tax revenue. A budget surplus occurs when tax revenue exceeds expenditures.

Government at the federal, state, and local levels provides many services ranging from national defense to education, park maintenance, and highway construction. To finance these services, the government levies a variety of taxes. The government budget shows expenditures or outlays on one side and tax revenues or receipts on the other. It is in **deficit** if expenditures exceed revenues and in surplus if revenues exceed expenditures.

[4]These are certificates sold by banks to depositors for a specific time period (such as 6 months or 2 years) and paying interest at a rate far above that of passbook savings accounts.

Public Expenditures

Public goods: are goods that are enjoyed collectively, such as a park: one person cannot exclude others from enjoying it, and one person's use of the good does not interfere with someone else's use or enjoyment of that good. The classic example of a public good is national defense.

Public and Private Goods What kind of goods and services are provided by government? With some exceptions, these are known as **public goods**, as distinguished from private goods that are provided by private firms.

A private good is one that, when used by one person, cannot be used by anyone else. If I purchase a suit, a car, or a theater ticket, no one else can buy the same suit, car, or theater ticket. Individual purchases of such goods can be guided by the private motive of maximizing satisfaction out of consumer expenditures.

Not so with respect to a park. The fact that I use a park on a Sunday afternoon does not prevent other people from using it. The same holds for police protection and national defense. These are known as *public goods*. A **public good** is one that can be enjoyed *collectively* by many people at the same time. It is indivisible, consumed by all citizens regardless of whether each has paid toward it.

For that reason, no one person would be willing to finance such goods as police protection, public parks, or national defense, whose benefits accrue to society at large. If left to the private sector, such activities would be either underfinanced or not financed at all. Yet they are absolutely essential for a stable environment conducive to the conduct of private business.

Externality: The benefit to society from an activity exceeds the sum of direct benefit to individuals. These activities would be underfinanced if left to the private sector.

In other, less extreme cases, the provision of government services is justified by what is known as **externalities**. Consider, for example, higher education. It benefits individual students directly, by enhancing their future income. And to that extent, they should pay for their own education. But above and beyond this benefit, there are gains to society at large. These include, among others, an educated citizenry, better-informed voters, an improved labor force, the attraction that a good state university may hold for newly hired executives, and reduced crime. Such benefits are "external" to the individual, but "internal" to the society of which he or she is a part. It is the same as the case with vaccination against infectious disease: When a person is vaccinated, everybody benefits, since the risk of contracting the disease from that person is reduced. To the extent that such externalities exist, a government subsidy of that activity is justified.

Although the lines of demarcation between private and public goods are sometimes blurred and often controversial (as in the case of postal services), the paragraphs above offer general guidelines for the type of services usually offered by the public sector. Political "liberals" define public goods as broadly as possible, allowing maximum scope for the government sector; political "conservatives" define them as narrowly as possible.

Finally, it should be noted that the public sector mainly finances these services. It does not produce them. The goods and services it needs are purchased from the private sector.

Growth of the Public Sector Growth in public spending has accelerated in the past forty years, and it now claims one fifth of the national output.

The reasons for that growth are many and varied. They include a rise in national security expenditures because of wars and international tensions;

the provision of more public services, owing to population growth and the increasing urbanization of society; and the assumption of greater government responsibilities for the poor and less fortunate members of society.

Level of Government Which level of government provides what services? National defense looms large in federal-government expenditures. A variety of services in the areas of education, health, energy, the environment, technology, commerce, and agriculture are also provided. And finally, a very sizable item is transfers in various forms. These are income-maintenance programs that assist the aged, the disabled, the poor, and the unemployed.

State-government expenditures are concentrated in the areas of higher education, highway construction and maintenance, health and hospital services, and public welfare. Much the greatest share of local government expenditures is absorbed in K-12 education. Other areas of local responsibility include police and fire protection, health and welfare, and highway maintenance.

This information is summarized in Table 3–4.

Taxes

Since the public sector generates little or no output of its own, its expenditures are financed by taxes. Taxes are compulsory levies. Each level of government tends to draw upon different types of taxes.

Personal income tax: is the most important source of revenue for the federal government. It is followed by **payroll taxes,** levied on employers and employees at an equal rate, and used to finance the **Social Security** payments to retirees.

Revenue Sources of Each Level of Government The most important source of federal revenue is the **personal income tax**, imposed on the income of individuals and proprietors. Next in importance are **payroll taxes,** such as the Social Security tax, which is levied equally on employees and employers, and at a higher rate on self-employed people. The revenue these taxes generate is channeled into a special **Social Security** fund used to finance payments to the retired and other transfers.

This is followed by the corporate profit tax, levied on the profit of corporations. The remainder of federal-government revenue is made up of excise (a tax imposed on a few specific products at the time of purchase) and other taxes.

States vary a great deal in the type of taxes they impose. The most common as well as most important source of state revenue is the **general**

Table 3–4 Important Expenditure Items of Each Level of Government

Federal Government	State Government	Local Government
National defense	Higher education	K-12 education
Social Security payments	Highways	Police and fire protection
Interest on the public debt	Public welfare	Public welfare
Education and manpower	Health and hospitals	Health and hospitals
Commerce and transportation		Highways
Natural resources, energy, and environment		

▶ THE SOCIAL SECURITY FUND

Payroll taxes, levied on both employees and employers, are channeled into a special fund, the Social Security Fund. Retired people draw their Social Security benefits out of that fund. The following illustration describes the operation:

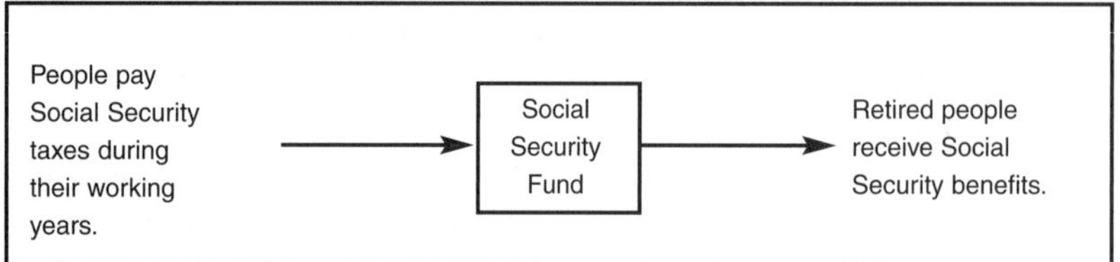

The benefits received by retirees are indexed to the cost of living: They increase automatically each year in proportion to the rise in the cost-of-living index, which measures the rate of inflation. Unemployment-insurance schemes, paid for by employers, are operated by state governments in a similar manner.

General sales tax: A uniform tax levied (as a percentage of price) on goods and services at the time of purchase. **Property tax:** A tax levied as a percentage of the assessed value of a person's property.

sales tax, a uniform tax levied (as a percentage of price) on goods and services at the time of purchase. Some states also levy a personal income tax and/or a corporate profit tax, and these (combined) come next in importance. They are followed by license and permit fees and related sources of revenue.

Finally, the **property tax**—levied as a percentage of the assessed value of a person's property, such as a home—is the mainstay of local revenue. In some localities, it is supplemented by sales, excise, and income taxes. License and permit fees are also common.

This discussion is summarized in Table 3–5.

An additional source of state and local revenues is contributions from the federal government. A large part of these contributions are grants ear-marked for specific programs, but unrestricted grants are also provided. Of the latter grants, the states retain one third, and two thirds are allocated to localities.

Following are some distinctions commonly made between the various types of taxes.

Direct and Indirect Taxes **Direct taxes** are taxes that are imposed on a factor of production and are paid by the entities upon which they are levied. The two outstanding examples are the personal income tax, imposed on the earnings of individual households and paid by them, and the corporate profit tax, levied on the profits of corporations.

Indirect taxes are taxes levied on commodities. They are then shifted either to the buyer or to the seller of the commodity, who in fact pays the tax. A general sales tax is an example, where a uniform levy (of, say, 4 percent of the price) is imposed on all goods and services sold. The store clerk

Table 3–5 Important Revenue Sources of Each Level of Government

Federal Government	State Government	Local Government
Personal income tax	Sales and excise taxes	Property tax
Payroll taxes	Personal income tax	Sales and excise taxes
Corporate profit tax	Corporate profit tax	Personal and corporate taxes
Excise and other taxes	License and permit fees	Fees

Direct taxes: taxes that are imposed on a factor of production, such as the personal income tax and the corporate profit tax.
Indirect taxes: taxes levied on commodities, and are then shifted to the buyer or seller.
Progressive tax: A tax-system where the *percentage* or proportion of *income* paid in taxes rises with income. **Proportional tax (or flat tax):** where the percentage of income paid in taxes remains constant as income rises.
Regressive tax: when the proportion of income paid in taxes declines as income rises.

adds that levy to the purchase price of any item bought. Although the tax is general, at times certain items that are considered essential, such as food and medicines, are excluded.

Another example of an indirect tax is the excise tax. It is similar to a sales tax, except that it is imposed only on a few commodities, such as alcohol and cigarettes.

Progressive, Proportional, and Regressive Tax A tax is **progressive** if the percentage or proportion of income paid in taxes rises with income. It is **proportional** if the percentage of income paid in taxes remains constant as income rises. And it is **regressive** if that proportion declines as income rises. Note that the distinction between the three cases lies not in the dollar amount paid in tax; that absolute amount may well rise in all three cases. Rather, it lies in the *proportion of income* paid in taxes, or the tax *rate*. It is the tax *rate* that rises, remains constant, or declines, respectively, in the three cases.

To illustrate the point, observe the hypothetical figures in Table 3–6. In the first column, a progressive tax is shown: The tax rate rises from 10 to 20 percent of income as income increases from $10,000 to $30,000. The dollar amount paid in tax rises steeply from $1,000 (10 percent of $10,000) to $6,000 (20 percent of $30,000). In the second column, the tax is proportional, with the rate remaining at 10 percent of income regardless of the income level. Yet the dollar amount paid in taxes rises from $1,000 (10 percent of $10,000) to $3,000 (10 percent of $30,000). In the third column, labeled "Regressive Tax I," the tax rate declines from 20 to 10 percent as income rises from $10,000 to $30,000. Yet the dollar *amount* paid in tax still *rises* with income, from $2,000 (20 percent of $10,000) to $3,000 (10 percent of $30,000). In the last column, labeled "Regressive Tax II," the degree of regressivity is increased, so as to generate a decline in the absolute dollar amount paid in tax with the rise in income.

Table 3–6 Hypothetical Illustration Distinguishing Between the Three Types of Taxes

Annual Income	Progressive Tax		Proportional Tax		Regressive Tax I		Regressive Tax II	
	Tax Rate	*Tax*	*Tax Rate*	*Tax*	*Tax Rate*	*Tax*	*Tax Rate*	*Tax*
$10,000	10%	$1,000	10%	$1,000	20%	$2,000	35%	$3,500
$30,000	20%	$6,000	10%	$3,000	10%	$3,000	10%	$3,000

Table 3–7 The Federal Tax Schedule for 2001 (Married Filing Jointly)

Taxable-income Bracket[1]	Marginal Tax Rate	Computation of Tax		
		Pay +	% on excess	of the amount over
A) 0–$ 45,200	15%	$0	15%	$0
B) $45,200–$109,250	28%	$6,780	28%	$45,200
C) $109,250–$166,450	31%	$24,714	31%	$109,250
D) $166,450–$297,300	36%	$39,446	36%	$166,450
E) $297,300 and over	39.6%	$86,552	39.6%	$297,300

Progressivity or Regressivity of Particular Taxes

Income Taxes Some states and municipalities impose a proportional income tax; but other local governments, and especially the federal government, levy a progressive income tax: As income rises, a higher **proportion** of **income** is paid in Federal income taxes. The mechanics by which this is done is of interest: successively higher income brackets are subject to successively higher **marginal tax rates**. This is the rate that applies to income above a certain cutoff point. Table 3–7 illustrates this principle by reference to the Federal tax for 2001 for a married couple filing jointly.

Marginal tax rates: A tax rate applied to income above a certain cutoff point. Successively higher income brackets are subject to successively higher marginal tax rates.

There are five tax brackets shown in the first column. The dollar amounts refer to family taxable income; namely, income minus the itemized deductions and personal exemptions. The first bracket is subject to a 15 percent tax, so that income of $45,200 (top of the bracket) the tax is ($45,200 × 15%) $6,780. People in the second bracket pay $6,780 plus 28 percent of any income over $45,200; namely over the threshold of that bracket. Thus on income of $109,250, the tax is $6,780 plus 28 percent of (109,250 – 45,200) = $64,050, which adds up to ($6,780 + $17,934) = $24,714.

People in the third bracket pay $24,714 plus 31 percent of income over $109,250, namely over the threshold of that bracket. For a family with $166,450 in taxable income, this amounts to $24,714 plus 31 percent of ($166,450 – $109,250) $57,200; or $24,714 + $14,732 = $39,446.

People in the fourth bracket pay $39,446 plus 36 percent of income over $166,450. For a family with taxable income of $297,300 this amounts to [39,446 + 36% ($297,300 – $166,450) =] $86,552. Finally, people with income over $297,300 pay $86,552 plus 39.6% of income over $297,300. For example with taxable income of $500,000 people would pay [$86,552 + 39.6% ($500,000 – 297,300)] = $166,726.

[1]The income brackets to which the tax rates apply are adjusted annually (upward) according to the rate of inflation.

To compute the average tax rate of the above families, perform the following calculations:

(A) Taxable Income	(B) Income Tax	(C) Income Tax as % of Income (B/C)
$45,200	$6,780	15%
$109,250	$24,714	23%
$166,450	$42,446	26%
$297,300	$89,547	30%
$500,000	$169,726	34%

col. C, which is col. B divided by col. A, shows the progressivity of the Federal income tax. Similarly, the Federal Corporation income tax is progressive, with marginal tax rates ranging from 15 to 32 percent.

Tax rates are being gradually reduced under the Bush II administration.

Sales Tax A general sales tax set at, say, 5 percent of the price of all purchases is regressive (despite the appearance of proportionality). It is the percentage of **income** paid in tax that determines its nature. Higher-income people are better able to save. And since savings are not subject to the tax, such people pay a lower percentage of their income in sales taxes.

Thus, a person earning $10,000 per year and spending all of it pays $500, or 5 percent of that income, in sales taxes. By comparison, a person earning $30,000 and spending $20,000 (while saving $10,000) pays $1,000 (5 percent of $20,000) in sales taxes, which works out to 3⅓ percent of income ($1,000 is 3⅓ percent of $30,000).

One reason for the popularity of the sales tax is that it is paid a little at a time, in "nickels and dimes." People do not feel the burden when the tax is not paid in one big lump. To remove some of the regressivity in the sales tax, certain necessities, such as food or medicine, are sometimes exempt from it.

The Role of Government In the Economy

Although the government does not directly produce goods and services, relying instead on purchases from the private sector, it performs certain critical functions. Two roles of the public sector were identified in this chapter. First, it supplies certain services that would not be provided at all by the private sector, or would be underfinanced from society's point of view, if left strictly to market forces. Second, through its tax and expenditures system, the government redistributes income in society. Social consensus, expressed through the political process, indicates the measure of social dissatisfaction with the income distribution that emerges from the market system. It shows the extent to which the degree of income inequality should be altered or modified. That alteration is then carried out through the progressive federal income tax system which taxes the rich more heavily than the poor and various expenditures that benefit the poor.

A third role of government is to stabilize the level of economic activity; that is (1) to lower unemployment or raise employment, and (2) to reduce the rate of inflation or promote price stability.

Although there is general agreement about the appropriateness of these functions of government, their scope is a matter of dispute. Political conservatives define each function as narrowly as possible, suggesting a very limited scope for government intervention in a market economy, and the leaving of practically all activities to the private sector. This is the view of the Reagan and Bush (first and second) Administrations. At the other extreme are political liberals, such as Senator Kennedy. They define these roles as broadly as possible, suggesting a wide scope for government intervention in the market economy. In between lies an entire spectrum of views, giving rise to many shades of opinions. Attitude toward degree of government intervention is one of the main dividing lines between conservative Republicans on the one hand and liberal Democrats on the other.

SUMMARY

This chapter is devoted to an institutional analysis of the firm, the household, and government. The firm is the basic unit within which economic activity is organized. It can be single- or multiplant. It can range in size from a corner drugstore to a huge multinational corporation. It can realize large profits, but it may also sustain losses.

In terms of its legal form, the firm can be a single proprietorship, a partnership, or a corporation, the last being an independent legal entity separate from its owners. Each form has advantages and disadvantages.

A firm is usually a "going concern" before its owner decides to incorporate. Usually that decision is predicated on the need for capital funds to expand the business. Incorporation is carried out by selling stocks or shares to the public. The shareowners become the owners of the corporation, and the return they receive is called dividends. A corporation is not obligated to distribute dividends, especially in unprofitable years; it is, however, obligated to meet interest payments on bonds that it has sold to the public.

Over time, many corporations tend to grow in size, and some become multinationals. We distinguish between horizontal, vertical, and conglomerate-type expansion. Respectively, these may be illustrated by a company's merging with a competitor, buying up a supplier, and buying up a firm engaged in a totally unrelated activity.

An industry is a group of firms producing similar products. They may produce final or intermediate products, or a raw material.

A sector is a broad classification that contains many industries. In the United States, the commodity-producing sectors—agriculture, mining, manufacturing, and construction—employ less than one third of the labor force. The service sectors employ the rest. This is typical of a highly advanced economy. Indeed, as an economy develops, both the supply mix and the demand mix for goods and services gradually evolve in the direction of proportionally larger service sectors.

Households interact with firms in a dual capacity: of income recipients, and of spenders on goods and services. As income recipients, their interest attaches to the functional distribution of income; that is, how income is distributed among factors. Equally interesting is the size distribution of income, which highlights the degree of inequality prevailing in the economy.

There are many reasons why a market economy, where factors are paid according to their productive contribution, would generate an unequal income distribution. Moreover, a certain degree of inequality is absolutely essential to the maintenance of work and investment incentives. And such incentives in turn are critical to a robust and growing economy.

Still, it is desirable, for both social and economic reasons, to equalize income to some extent, and in particular to eliminate stark poverty. This is done through both sides of the government budget: the progressive income tax on the revenue side, and spending that benefits the poor on the expenditures side.

As spenders, households divide their income into three parts: the personal income tax, savings, and consumption.

Savings is the part of disposable income (income after taxes) not consumed. People save for many reasons, and they place their savings in a variety of financial instruments. Their ability to save is determined by income; savings is positively related to income.

Consumption is also positively related to income. It is customary to classify the products consumed into durables, nondurables, and services.

Government, the third economic agent under review, exists on three levels: federal, state, and local. The government budget consists of revenues derived from taxes and levies, and expenditures on many programs. The difference between revenue and expenditures measures the surplus or deficit in the budget. Government expenditures consist largely of purchases from the private sector.

On the expenditures side, the government provides "public goods," and goods and services that offer "external" benefits. The three levels of government differ in the type of services they provide.

Main sources of tax revenue also vary from one level of government to another. Income, payroll, and corporate profit taxes are the mainstay of federal revenues; states draw most of their revenues from sales taxes, and localities from property taxes.

Common distinctions between various types of taxes include (1) direct versus indirect taxes, depending on whether the tax is levied on a factor or a commodity; and (2) progressive, proportional, and regressive taxes, depending on whether the tax *rate* (as a proportion of *income*) rises, remains constant, or declines as income increases. The personal income and corporate profit taxes are direct; the sales tax is indirect. The federal personal income tax is progressive; state income taxes are progressive or proportional; sales taxes are usually regressive.

Provision of public goods, income redistribution, and economic stabilization are the three roles of government in a market economy.

QUESTIONS AND PROBLEMS

1. Define or explain briefly each of the following concepts:

Firm
Plant
Shares in a corporation
Corporate bonds
Undistributed corporate profit
Dividends
Corporate stocks
Stock exchange
Interest
Limited liability
Industry
Sector
Stages of production
Disposable income
Personal savings
Durable goods
Personal services
Public goods
Externalities
Income redistribution
Sales tax
Excise tax
Property tax
Personal income tax
Multinational corporations
Corporate profit tax
Government budget:
   Revenue
   Expenditures
   Surplus
   Deficit
Progressive tax
Regressive tax
Marginal tax rate
Political conservative
Political liberal

2. What are the three legal forms of business organization? Explain the differences between them. What are the advantages and disadvantages of each?
3. Relate the following concepts to each other:

☐ Corporate stocks
☐ Dividends
☐ Corporate bonds
☐ Government bonds
☐ Interest

4. Use examples to explain the difference between the horizontal, vertical, and conglomerate-type expansion of firms.
5. Explain the difference between final goods, intermediate goods, and raw materials.
6. What are the main sectors of the U.S. economy? What happens to the employment and output distribution among sectors as an economy develops over time, and why?
7. Explain the difference between the functional and the size distribution of income.
8. Is a perfectly equal income distribution a desirable economic objective? Why, or why not?
9. How does the government sector contribute to greater income equality in the population?
10. What is the relation between savings and income; between consumption and income?
11. What types of goods or services are appropriately provided by the public sector?
12. What are the three levels of government? What type of taxes does each level rely upon to generate revenue? What types of services does each level provide?

13. Distinguish clearly (with illustrations) between direct and indirect taxes; between progressive, proportional, and regressive taxes. Why is the sales tax considered regressive?
14. What is the "marginal income tax," and how is it used in the calculation of the federal personal income tax? Is that tax regressive or progressive? Why?
15. What are the three roles of government in a market economy?
16. What conflicting considerations must be weighed in setting up a tax system?

PART TWO

PRICE DETERMINATION AND RESOURCE ALLOCATION

OVERVIEW

A modern economy is so complex that it is difficult to contemplate the mechanisms that make it function so smoothly. How is it that millions of producers of diverse goods and services know exactly the product mix desired by tens of millions of consuming families? And how do millions of potential workers (and college students) in various skills and professions know what type of training to seek, what occupations to prepare for, and what types of skills will be required by the economy? Moreover, the types of goods people want and the kinds of occupations the economy requires change continuously. "Change is the only constant." How does the economy accommodate itself to these changes?

All these questions come under the label of the "resource allocation problem." In a capitalistic economy, markets and prices constitute the mechanism that coordinates economic activity and provides answers to these questions.

As seen earlier, a market is any place where sellers and buyers come together. There is a market for each commodity, service, or productive service. And on that market, the price of the product or service and the quantity bought and sold are determined.

TYPES OF MARKETS

Economic analysis classifies markets into four categories, or **structures,** *according to the degree of competition* prevailing in them.

Pure or Perfect Competition

Perfect competition: A market structure in which the number of buyers and sellers in an industry is very large; products are standardized; and there are no barriers to entry. These conditions yield one uniform price.

Price taker: A firm that does not have influence over the price: it takes the market price for granted and adjust to it.

Perfect competition is said to prevail in a market for a given product or service if (1) the number of buyers and the number of sellers are very large, (2) the same product produced by different firms is uniform or standardized or *homogeneous,* and (3) entry into and exit from the market by firms is reasonably easy—that is, no important barriers to entry exist.

The first condition ensures that no one seller (or buyer) is large enough to affect the price or the condition of sale by its own actions. The quantity supplied by each firm is a "drop in the bucket" relative to the industry total, so that even if the individual firm withdraws totally, or conversely doubles its supply, the market price does not change. Such a firm is known as a **price taker**; it takes the market price as given and adjusts its actions to it. The single wheat farmer, one of hundreds of thousands, is a purely competitive firm. It cannot by its action affect the market price. The second condition ensures that the individual producer cannot *differentiate* its product (make it distinguishable) from that of its competitors (for example, by packaging it differently or by introducing a brand name), thereby enabling it to command a higher price. Milk is milk, whether produced by farmer A or by farmer B. And the third condition ensures that firms in the industry cannot block entry of other firms: New firms come in readily if profit opportunities exist, and old firms depart if they sustain losses.

Under perfect competition, one uniform price prevails in the market for each product, and no brand advertising is possible because no brands exist. No firm advertises its wheat, corn, or cotton. One may occasionally hear a commercial about milk, but not about a particular brand of milk. Agriculture, the stock market, and the markets for foreign currencies are examples of perfectly competitive markets.

Monopolistic Competition

Monopolistic competition: exists when there are a large number of buyers and sellers in an industry; firms sell a differentiated product; and there are no barriers to entry. Sellers have a limited control over price, but long run profit is zero.

Monopolistic competition is a variant of perfect competition, where conditions 1 and 3 are met but condition 2 is absent. The product of a particular firm is differentiated by packaging, brand name, or some other means, giving the seller some *limited* control over price, although it faces many competitors. This condition is characteristic of much of the retail trade. Thus, brand-name gasoline can command a somewhat higher price than a nonbrand name sold across the street, although the product itself is identical. Advertising and other modes of nonprice competition (such as gift coupons) abound, as sellers try to convince buyers of the supposed superiority of their products. Yet the outcome is somewhat similar to that of perfect competition, for the price difference between brands cannot be large.

Oligopoly

Oligopoly: is a market structure in which there are few firms. Firms do have some control over the market price, which means they are **price makers**. Firms are interdependent: the actions of one firm influences the actions of other firms. **Price-leadership** is said to exist when one firm raises or lowers its price and other firms in the industry follow.

Oligopoly is said to exist when a few large firms dominate the market for a given product. The automobile industry, consisting of a few firms, is a case in point. Each company has a sizable share of the market; by its very actions, it can affect price and the condition of sale. Such a firm is known as a **price maker**. It does not merely take the market price for granted; rather, the firm has a certain amount of market power. Since by its action the firm affects the position of its competitors, it can expect them to react. In turn, the anticipation of response places some limit on the firm's control over its price. Mutual interdependence of firms in the industry is the result.

Products may be standardized (such as raw materials) or differentiated (automobiles, durable goods). In the latter case, advertising is widely used. In part, such advertising is useful in dispensing information, but to some extent, it can be wasteful and even deceptive. Although entry of new firms is possible, the barriers to entry are formidable, for production usually requires large-scale operation, much capital, and advanced and often unavailable technology. Most U.S. durable-goods and capital-equipment industries are oligopolistic in structure. In some cases, such as steel, many firms exist; but the industry is dominated by a few large firms that account for a large share of total output. The oligopolistic nature of such a market is determined by the **price-leadership** role exercised by the large firms; all other firms tend to follow.

Monopoly

Monopoly: a one-firm industry, producing a unique product for which there are no substitutes. There are high barriers to entry.

A **monopoly** is a one-firm industry, producing a unique product for which *no good substitutes* are available. The monopolist is certainly a price maker and has much market power. Barriers to entry are formidable, ranging all the way from advanced technology and patent rights to access to critical materials, and even to legal limitations. Local public utilities (gas and electric companies) are examples of such monopolies.

Duopoly is a two-firm industry, such as the production of commercial jet aircraft.

Monopolistic competition, oligopoly, and monopoly are sometimes referred to as *imperfect competition*.

A variety of factors determine the market structure of any particular industry. If large-sized plants are required to produce efficiently and large sums of capital are necessary to form a company (perhaps reinforced by a need to employ advanced technology), an oligopolistic structure is likely to emerge. In the case of public utilities, the law usually mandates a monopoly firm. Gas and electric companies are characterized by huge fixed costs, such as electric lines or gas pipelines, which would be uneconomical to duplicate. Known as **natural monopolies**, they are accorded a monopoly status by law but are placed under government regulations. In most states, the regulatory agency is the public utilities commission. In the absence of the conditions such as those specified above, competitive markets are likely to emerge.

Natural monopolies: a natural monopoly is said to exist when it is cheaper for one firm to supply the entire market than for two or more firms (e.g., a public utility).

We turn next to demand and supply analysis and price determination in individual markets. The next five chapters analyze perfectly competitive markets. They develop the tools of demand and supply (Chapters 4 and 5) and explain price determination in competitive markets (Chapter 6). Elasticities of demand and supply are considered in Chapter 7, followed by applications of supply and demand, and examination of resource allocation in a competitive economy (Chapter 8). Chapter 9 analyzes a monopoly or oligopoly and compares its behavior to that of a perfectly competitive firm. It contains the necessary elements of the "marginal analysis." Chapters 10 and 11 describe a wide array of departures from competitive markets and assess their implications for the U.S. economy.

QUESTION

Describe the essential features of each of the four market structures. Offer two examples of each category.

Market Demand

It is often said that "Price is determined by demand and supply." Indeed, demand and supply, when properly used, constitute a powerful tool for understanding a wide range of economic phenomena. The next three chapters develop and employ these concepts in perfectly competitive markets.

Demand for a given product (or service) is a *schedule* that shows the various quantities of the product that consumers are able and willing to purchase at *various prices* over a *specified period of time.* In what follows, we construct the demand side of the market step by step, beginning with the individual consumer.

DEMAND SCHEDULE OF THE INDIVIDUAL CONSUMER

Each consuming unit, such as a family or an individual, has a given income to spend over a given period of time. That maximum limit is known as the *budget constraint.* The income must be allocated among many lines of expenditures, such as food, clothing, shelter, travel, durable goods, entertainment, and the like. Many of the goods and services the family purchases are immediate *substitutes* for each other, in the sense that they serve a similar purpose. Travel by air, rail, bus, and car is one example; dresses and pantsuits another. However, given the family's budget constraint, all goods and services compete for its expenditures, and in that sense they are all substitute products. If the family takes a trip to Florida, it may not be able to purchase a new washing machine. A choice must be made between the two items; they are substitute products even though they do not serve the same purpose. All *goods and services compete for the consumer's dollar.*

How will the family allocate its given amount of total expenditures among hundreds of goods and services it needs or desires? Casual observation suggests that its dollars will be spread over a large number of goods and services rather than being concentrated on very few items. Clearly, buying a little of each of many items contributes more to the family's satisfaction than spending all its income on very few goods and services, however useful these may be. Why? Because no matter how useful a specific product is, the fourth unit is not as useful as the third, the third is not as useful as the second, and the second is not as useful as the first. For example, a car may be deemed immensely useful and thus considered much more necessary than a freezer. Consequently, starting from scratch, the consumer would rank a car ahead of a freezer, and buy it first. She might even purchase a second car ahead of a freezer; even though the second car may yield less satisfaction than the first, it is still more useful than a freezer. But once the family owns two cars, the value of a third car would not be considered high at all; a freezer would be purchased ahead of a third car. The fact that a car is more useful than a freezer does not mean that the *third* car is more useful than the *first* freezer. And this applies throughout the entire range of the family's spending.

It is useful to think of a consuming family as having a maximum number of dollars to spend on hundreds or even thousands of desirable goods and services. The budget constraint prevents the consuming unit from buying all it wants. *Its financial resources are scarce relative to its wants.* The family must choose, and in those choices, all goods and services become substitutes for each other. The family allocates its income among all desirable lines of expenditures in a manner that would maximize its total satisfaction. The first unit of each of the highly useful products is ranked ahead of that of the less useful ones. But that does not mean that the entire income will be spent on goods and services deemed the most useful, so that less useful products will not be bought. Rather, after one or two units of the most useful products are purchased, extra units yield much less additional satisfaction, inducing the family to buy some items that it deems less useful. This principle governs the family's purchase of an individual good or service: The more units of it the family owns, the smaller the *added* satisfaction it obtains from an *extra* unit of the product. The rule underlies consumer demand for a single product. Let us see how it applies to the purchase of hats.

Consider a woman who owns no hats and decides to acquire one or more hats in succession. Starting from a "zero hat" position, she regards the first hat to be acquired as very important, for it would serve a variety of purposes: protection from the elements, beauty, and the like. The satisfaction that she would derive from that first hat is presumably very high. Once the first hat is purchased, she must decide whether to buy a second one. But the importance she attaches to the second hat is presumably less than that attached to the first one. Since the need for protection from the elements is already largely met, a second hat is useful only for beauty purposes. Judged in a rational manner, the *additional* or *incremental* satisfaction obtained from the second hat is less than that derived from the first hat. When she already owns two hats and considers buying a third one, the incremental satisfaction is even less. For the third hat may be needed only to match a certain dress. This reduction in incremental satisfaction

Table 4–1 Demand Schedule for Hats

Price of Hat	Number of Hats Purchased
(a) $20	1
(b) $15	2
(c) $10	3
(d) $ 5	4

from newly *added* (fourth, fifth, and so on) units of the product continues. Economists use the word **marginal** to denote *incremental* or *additional.* In the present context, we say that the marginal satisfaction from the added hat (but not total satisfaction from all hats combined) declines with the number of hats owned.

This discussion assumes for simplicity that the marginal or incremental satisfaction begins to decline after the first unit. This need not be so. It may remain constant with the second unit, and start declining with some subsequent unit. The important point is that *at some level, it begins to decline. This is the* **Law of Diminishing Marginal Satisfaction** or **Utility.**

Law of Diminishing Marginal Utility or Satisfaction: The more of something a person consumes the less *additional* utility she derives from consuming *additional* units.

This principle applies to practically all goods or services. Thus, the satisfaction obtained by the family from its first car exceeds the marginal satisfaction obtained from the second car. Although total satisfaction rises with the acquisition of the second car, marginal satisfaction declines (that is, total satisfaction rises at a declining rate).

The next logical step is to move from marginal satisfaction to price. The amount of money a consumer is willing to pay for a unit of the product (price) is related to the level of satisfaction she obtains from it. The woman in our example would be willing to pay a good deal for her first hat and somewhat less for the second hat.[1] She would acquire a third hat only if she could get it for a considerably lower price. This merely reflects the declining marginal value she attaches to a succession of additional hats. Hypothetically, the first hat may be worth $20 to her, the second $15, the third $10, and the fourth only $5. The fifth hat may be worth nothing; it merely takes up space in her closet. Table 4–1, showing this relation between the price of a hat and the quantity purchased, is the woman's **demand schedule** for hats.

Demand schedule: A relationship between prices of a product and the amount that a person is willing to buy at each price. This is an inverse relationship: The **Demand curve** slopes downward and to the right.

The lower the price, the more hats she would purchase. It is convenient to present this information on a two-dimensional graph, Figure 4–1. Following tradition, price is shown on the vertical axis and quantity on the horizontal axis. The resulting curve is known as a **demand curve.**

Note that the demand schedule, or demand curve, slopes downward and to the right. The relation it represents is a *negative* one: The lower the price, the greater the quantity purchased. For that reason, it is called a **negatively sloping curve.** Demand curves are negatively sloped because they

[1]As corroborative evidence, just reflect on how many families buy an expensive first car and content themselves with the purchase of a used second car.

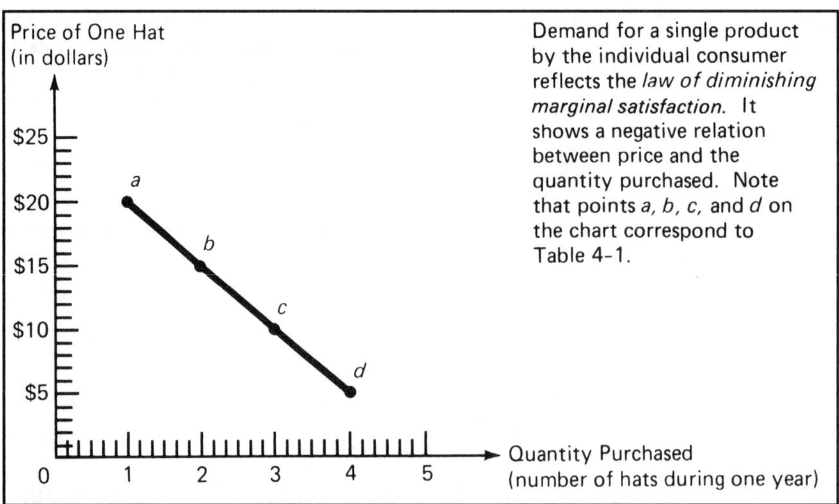

Figure 4–1 A Graphical Representation of the Woman's Demand Schedule for Hats

invariably represent an inverse relation between price and quantity. They may or may not be straight lines. But a straight-line demand curve has the advantage of geometrical simplicity: Only two points are sufficient to determine the entire line. For this reason, and for this reason only, we use straight-line demand curves throughout this chapter.

THE MARKET-DEMAND SCHEDULE

The woman described above is one of millions of consumers in the market for hats. Their demand schedules may or may not be similar to each other. The only required feature is that they be negatively sloped. The *market-demand schedule shows the amount purchased by all consumers at each price.* Thus, to move from the individual- to the market-demand curve, we *add up the quantities purchased by all individual consumers at each price.* Geometrically, the market-demand curve is the *horizontal summation of the individual consumers' curves.* Since it is not possible to show millions of consumers on one page, we derive the demand schedule for a hypothetical market in which there are only three consumers. Each consumer may be thought of as representing a million consumers; the principle is the same regardless of the number involved. The derivation is done first in tabular form and then in graphical form.

Consider a market for hats in which each of three buyers represents 1 million consumers. Their respective demand schedules are shown in Table 4–2. At a price of $10 per hat, the first consumer would purchase 3 hats, the second 4 hats, and the third, 7 hats. Altogether, 14 hats would be purchased per year. Since each consumer is assumed to represent 1 million consumers, a total of 14 million hats would be purchased. At a price of $20,

Table 4–2 Derivation of a Market-Demand Schedule for Hats (Per Year)

First Consumer		Second Consumer		Third Consumer		Market Demand	
Price	*Quantity*[a]	*Price*	*Quantity*[a]	*Price*	*Quantity*[a]		
$10	3	$10	4	$10	7	$10	14
$20	2	$20	3	$20	5	$20	10
$30	1	$30	2	$30	3	$30	6

[a] *In millions of units. Each consumer in the first three columns represents one million consumers.*

the quantities bought are, respectively, 2, 3, and 5, for a total of 10 hats per year. And at a price of $30, they are 1, 2, and 3, for a total of 6 per year. Again, all these figures should be multiplied by one million. Thus, to generate the market-demand schedule, we add up the quantities purchased by consumers at each price. The resulting schedule on the right-hand side of the table shows market demand for 3 million consumers.

In a similar fashion, the market-demand curve can be constructed diagrammatically. Figure 4–2 shows the demand curve of each of the three consumers, representing the price-quantity relationships shown in Table 4–2. At a price of $10 per hat, the first consumer would buy 3 hats, and that quantity is represented by segment *a* on the left-hand panel of the figure; the second consumer would purchase 4 hats (segment *b*), and the third consumer would buy 7 hats (segment *c*). Total market purchase at that price is 14 hats, represented on the right-hand panel by segment $(a + b + c)$; it is obtained by a horizontal summation of the three individual segments. At the price of $20 per hat, the three people would buy respectively 2 (segment *d*), 3 (segment *e*), and 5 (segment *f*) hats, for a total of 10 (segment $d + e + f$) on the right-hand panel. Finally, at the price of $30 per hat, the purchases would be 1 (segment *g*), 2 (segment *h*), and 3 (segment *i*) for a total of 6 hats (segment $g + h + i$).

Market demand is the horizontal summation of the individuals demand curves: As the price of a product declines, the quantity purchased rises.

Figure 4–2 Graphical Derivation of the Market-Demand Curve for Hats: The market-demand curve is obtained by horizontal summation of the quantities purchased by individual consumers at each price. Each consumer in the first three panels represents one million consumers.

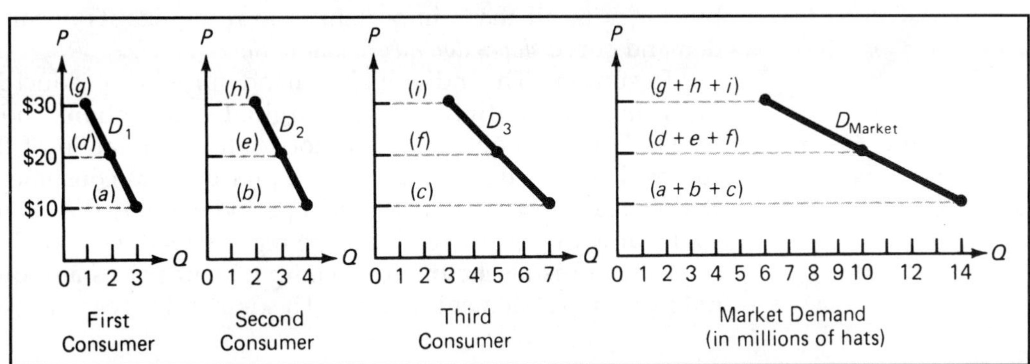

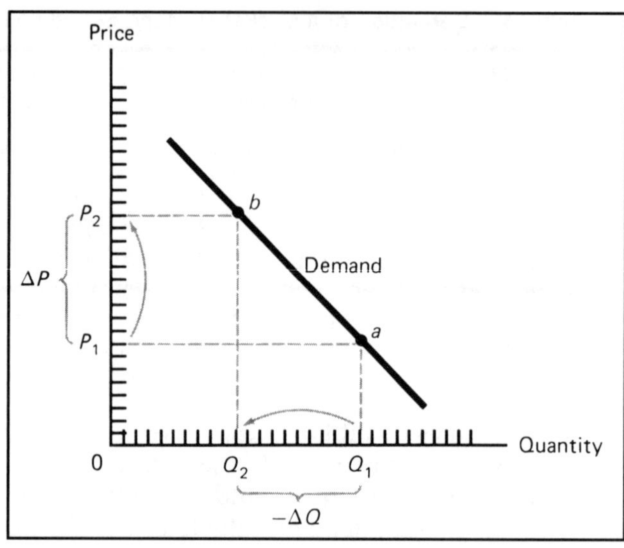

Figure 4–3 Market-Demand Schedule for Oil: The market demand schedule for a product such as oil, shows a negative relation between price and quantity purchased.

Connecting the resulting price-quantity combinations on the right-hand panel of Figure 4–2, we obtain the market-demand curve for hats. Its negative slope represents the **law of demand: As the price of a product declines, the quantity purchased rises**. This law corresponds well to a legion of empirical observations in contemporary periods and throughout history.

In more general terms, a market-demand curve for product *X*—such as oil—is seen in Figure 4–3, connecting two price-quantity combinations: P_1Q_1 (point *a*) and P_2Q_2 (point *b*). As price rises from OP_1 to OP_2, quantity purchased declines from OQ_1 to OQ_2,. For the sake of brevity, we frequently dispense with the reference to the point of origin and simply state that as price rises from P_1 to P_2, the quantity purchased declines from Q_1 to Q_2. The change in price (P_2 minus P_1) and in quantity (Q_2 minus Q_1) is shown on the chart as ΔP and ΔQ, where the Greek letter delta (Δ) denotes change. It matters a great deal whether the demand curve is flat or steep. But for now, all that's important is to recognize its negative slope: The demand curve *slopes downward and to the right.*

To sum up: The individual demand curve for product *X* is rooted in the **principle of diminishing marginal satisfaction**, and the market-demand curve is obtained as a horizontal summation of the individual curves. It shows the quantity of the product that consumers would purchase at each price over a specified period; namely the quantity demanded. Its downward or negative slope represents the law of demand.

Demand is a schedule or a composite of prices and quantities. It is not a point. A statement such as, "The demand for cars in 1988 was 10 million units," makes no sense, for the number of cars consumers would wish to purchase depends on price. Demand relates various prices to their corresponding quantities demanded.

MOVEMENT ALONG THE MARKET-DEMAND CURVE VS. SHIFT IN THE ENTIRE CURVE

Shifts in Demand vs. Movement along the demand curve: Movements along the demand curve shows the effect of changes in the price of the product itself while shifts in the entire demand schedule reflect the effect of other factors. These are changes in income, change in the price of substitute or complementary products; anticipation of future price change; or a change in the number of consumers.

A pitfall of which the reader should be wary is the distinction between movements along the demand curve and shifts in it. This often tricky distinction must be fully mastered before the analytical tools of supply and demand can be put to good use.

In the two-dimensional graph of Figure 4–3, the quantity of the product bought is shown to depend on the product's own price. And *movements along the demand curve* describe this relationship: The higher the product's own price, the smaller the quantity purchased; the lower the price, the greater the quantity purchased. Indeed, the product's price has an important influence on the quantity purchased (and it provides the link to the supply side of the market). But it is not the only influence. There are several other factors that affect the quantity of a product bought. Since only price can be plotted on a two-dimensional diagram, the effect of these factors is shown by *shifting the entire curve.* Six important factors will be considered in turn, in each case assuming that only the change in question occurs, while all other influences on price remain unchanged.

Income

Consider a market-demand curve for automobiles. It relates car prices to the number of cars purchased. Suppose that a significant increase occurs in the income of the community. People can afford more cars, and presumably will purchase more. But this increase in car sales is *not due to a reduction in auto prices. Rather, at each and every price, more cars would be purchased than before.* Table 4–3 illustrates these changes. The number of cars consumers would be willing and able to purchase annually at $4,000 per car rises from 3½ to 4½ million; at a price of $6,000 per car, it rises from 2½

Table 4–3 Two Demand Schedules for Automobiles

Before the Rise in Income (D_1)		After the Rise in Income (D_2)	
Price per Car (In Thousands of Dollars)	*Millions of Cars Purchased per Year*	*Price per Car (In Thousands of Dollars)*	*Millions of Cars Purchased per Year*
4	3 1/2	4	4 1/2
6	2 1/2	6	4
8	1 1/2	8	3 1/2

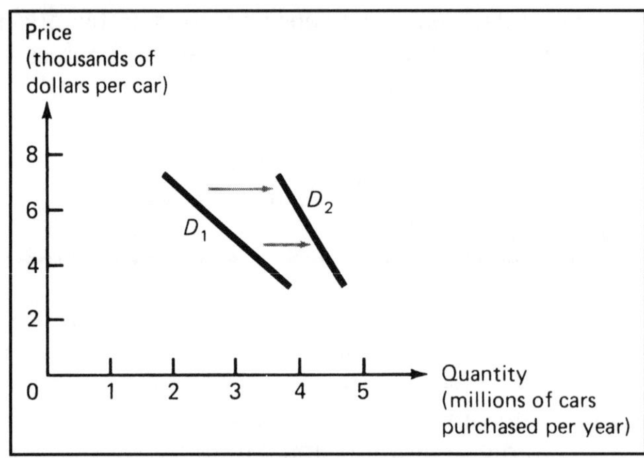

Figure 4–4 Market for Automobiles: A rise in income increases demand for D_1 to D_2. At each price a larger number of automobiles is purchased.

to 4 million; and at $8,000 per car, the rise is from 1½ to 3½ million, all as a result of the increase in the community's income.

These figures are given a diagrammatic representation in Figure 4–4. Line D_1 represents the original demand schedule. As a result of the rise in income, the quantity purchased at each price rises; in terms of the diagram, this is shown by a shift to the right of the quantity segment at every given price, as the direction of the arrows indicates. As a result, the *entire demand curve shifts to the right,* from D_1 to D_2. The term **increase in demand** is reserved to such a shift in the entire curve. It is not—repeat, *not*—used to indicate a movement downward *along* a given demand curve. Such a movement merely describes an increase in *quantity* purchased because of a reduction in the commodity's own price.

Conversely, a reduction in the community's income *lowers* the number of cars per year consumers are willing and able to buy at each price. Diagrammatically, this *shifts the entire demand curve leftward.* And such a shift is labeled a *decrease* or *reduction in demand.* It is to be sharply distinguished from a reduction in the number of cars purchased because of a rise in automobile prices. The latter event involves moving upward along a given demand curve, and it is not described by the term *decrease in demand.* Rather, it is properly described by stating that the quantity purchased declined as the price rose. In sum, a change in income changes demand in the same direction: **A rise in income increases demand (shifts the demand curve to the right), and a decline in income lowers demand (shifts the demand curve to the left).**

Change in the Price of Substitute Products

Consider the market demand for beef, where beef and lamb are regarded by consumers as close substitutes in consumption. If the price of lamb

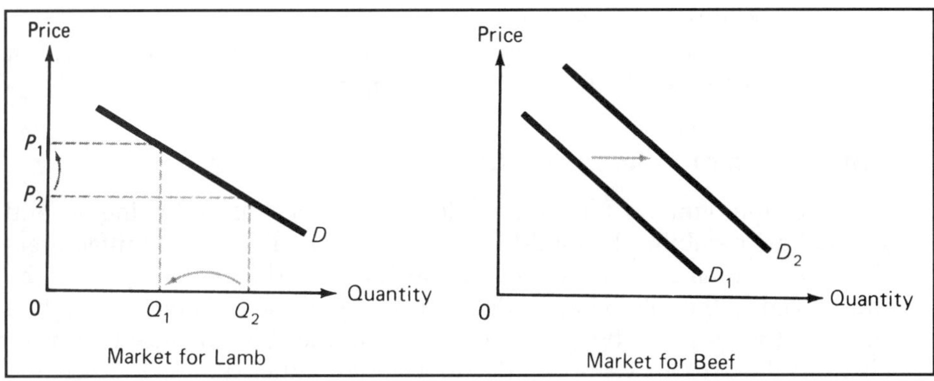

Figure 4–5 Markets for Beet and for Lamb (substitute products in consumption): An increase in the price of lamb raises the demand for beef, as people switch from lamb to beef.

should drop, some consumers would switch from beef to lamb. Consequently, at *each and every price of beef, less beef would be consumed.* The demand for beef would decline; that is, the demand curve would shift leftward. Conversely, a rise in the price of lamb would induce consumers to shift from lamb to beef. The demand for beef would rise, with the demand curve shifting to the right. This is shown diagrammatically in Figure 4–5, which describes two separate but interrelated markets: that for beef (the product of our primary interest), and that for lamb (a close substitute for beef). If the price of lamb rises, for whatever reason, demand for beef increases. Note that the change in demand occurs in the beef market. In the lamb market, we merely move along the demand curve.

In sum, a change in price of a substitute product (lamb) changes the demand for the product itself (beef) in the *same* direction.

Change in the Price of a Complementary Product

Consider the demand for men's ties. A tie is *complementary* to a man's suit, in the sense that they are generally worn together. Assume that, for whatever reason, there has been a sharp increase in the price of men's suits. Then fewer suits would be purchased, moving up along the demand curve for suits. But consumers would also require fewer matching ties; at every price of ties, fewer would be purchased. The demand curve for ties shifts leftward, denoting a decrease in demand. Conversely, a decrease in the price of suits will raise the quantity purchased, and consequently would raise the demand for ties; the demand curve would shift rightward.

In sum, a change in price of a complementary product (suits) changes the demand for the product itself (ties) in the *opposite* direction.

This discussion was limited to the effect of a price change of substitute and complementary products. In fact, a variation in the price of any product influences demand for the commodity in question, because it changes the amount of money left in the hands of the consumer to spend on it. Under the budget constraint, all goods compete for the consumer's dollar.

Thus, a substantial boost in the price of gasoline may leave the family with less money to spend on other goods and change its demand for them. But these effects are usually weaker than those considered here.

Anticipation of Future Price Change

Consider the demand for automobiles *in a given year,* following several years of price stability. It is suddenly announced by the auto manufacturers that a substantial price boost is being considered and will most probably be introduced in the following model year. Many of the consumers who had planned to buy a car the next year may be induced to advance their purchase to the present year, in order to save the anticipated price increase. Since demand is always defined over a given time period, such as one year, this would raise this year's demand for cars, shifting the demand curve to the right. At each price, more cars would be purchased in the present year.

A Change in the Number of Consumers

The market demand for a product is constructed as the horizontal summation of the demand curve of the individual consumers. Consequently, an increase in the number of consumers increases demand for the product, and the demand curve shifts to the right. A decrease in the number of consumers would have the opposite effect. For example, a large-scale sale of wheat to Russia would increase substantially the number of consumers of American wheat, and shift the demand curve for U.S. grains to the right.

Change in Taste

A shift in consumer preferences away from a given product means that at every price, less of the product will be purchased. The demand curve shifts to the left, showing a decrease in demand. Conversely, a shift in preferences *toward* a product raises demand for it and is represented by a rightward shift in the demand curve.

As an illustration, suppose that there has been a shift in women's preference from skirts to pants. In the two markets, demand for skirts shifts to the left and demand for pants to the right. A recent newspaper headline depicted a shift in preferences of the movie-going public to cable TV and video cassettes (popcorn sales also decline as a result). The student should draw this demand shift in the two markets.

SUMMARY

A demand schedule exists in the market for each product, service, and productive factor. It relates the price of the product or service to the quantity demanded.

Based on the law of diminishing marginal satisfaction (or utility), the demand by a single consumer for a given product or service is negatively sloped: The lower the price, the greater the quantity purchased. The market-demand curve is obtained by a horizontal summation of the quantities demanded by all people at each price. It has a negative slope; it slopes downward and to the right.

It is of the utmost importance to distinguish between (1) movements along the curve and (2) shifts in the entire curve. The first refers to change in the *quantity* purchased caused by a change in price of the commodity itself. The second, labeled a *change in demand,* refers to variations in the quantity purchased at each and every price. The entire demand schedule shifts upward or downward. We identified such factors that may cause either an increase or a decrease in demand: changes in income, changes in the price of substitute products, changes in the price of complementary products, anticipation of future price changes, changes in the number of consumers, and changes in taste. These should be committed to memory.

QUESTIONS AND PROBLEMS

1. *a.* Arrange the following figures into a demand schedule of the usual form: \$4.50, 4,000 units; \$2.50, 8,000 units; \$5, 3,000 units; \$4, 5,000 units; \$3, 7,000 units; \$3.50, 6,000 units. Draw the demand curve.
   b. Construct a new demand schedule assuming that demand doubled (double the quantity at each price).
   c. If before the demand changed, the price being charged was \$4, how many units of the good would be bought? How many after the demand changed?
   d. If the price being charged before the change in demand occurred was \$4 and it then increased to \$4.50, what change in the amount bought would occur?
   e. If the price being charged after the change in demand occurred was \$4 and it then increased to \$4.50, what change in the amount bought would take place?
2. You are given the following demand schedule for Canadian wheat:

Price (Dollars per Bushel)	Quantity Purchased (Millions of Bushels)
\$2	40
\$3	30
\$4	20
\$5	10

   a. Draw a demand curve representing this schedule.

b. Suppose that a drought in China caused the Chinese government to purchase Canadian wheat. As a result, the quantity purchased at each price doubled. Show that effect on your demand schedule and on the diagram.

3. Automobiles and gasoline are complementary goods. Suppose the oil producers quadrupled the price of gasoline. Show the effect of that action on the market demand curve for (a) gasoline; (b) automobiles.

4. Coal and oil are competing sources of energy. Sketch a market-demand curve for each of these two products. Now, suppose that the price of oil doubled. Show the effect of that change on each of the two market-demand curves.

Supply in a Perfectly Competitive Industry

Supply schedule: A relationship between prices of a good and the quantities sellers are willing to sell at each price. This is a positive relationship; the Supply curve slopes upward and to the right.

Facing consumers, on the other side of the market, is a group made up of different people: the sellers, or suppliers. Their market position is represented by a **supply schedule** or a supply curve. It is a schedule that shows the *amounts of the product suppliers are willing to sell at various prices.* Alternatively stated, it shows *the prices needed to induce suppliers to sell various quantities.*

TWO EXPERIMENTS

The following experiments are useful in generating a supply schedule. Assume that this class consists of 500 students. Your instructor is about to participate in a racquet ball tournament and is in need of cheerleaders. If the instructor offers an A grade for each student who comes to cheer, there would undoubtedly be 500 volunteers. For a promise of a B, 350 students would volunteer; for a C, 200 students; and for a D, only 50. This information can be tabulated (Table 5–1) and also plotted on a chart (Figure 5–1). Clearly, *the higher the price* (in terms of a grade), *the greater the number of cheerleaders supplied.* This is a *positive relation* between price and quantity: The supply curve slopes upward and to the right.

Table 5–1 Supply Schedule of Cheerleaders

Price (Grade)	Number of Volunteers
A	500
B	350
C	200
D	50

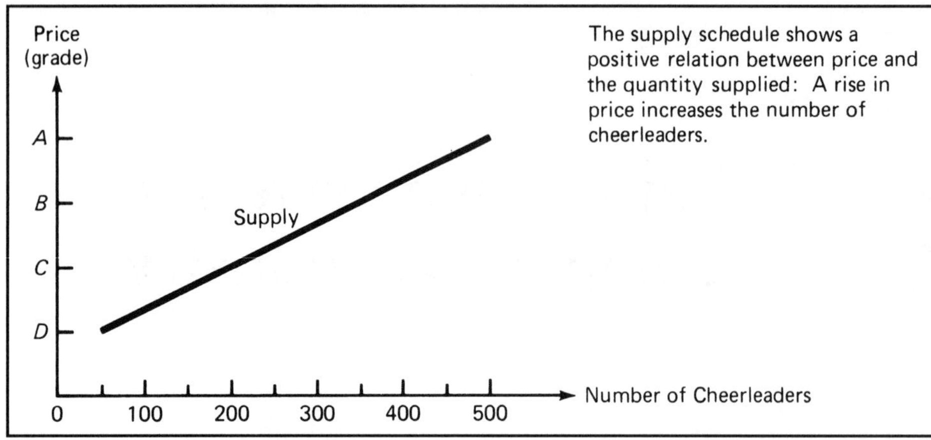

Figure 5–1 Supply Schedule of Cheerleaders: Clearly, *the higher the price* (in terms of a grade), *the greater the number of cheerleaders supplied.* This is *a positive relation* between price and quantity: the supply curve sloped upward and to the right.

As another experiment, assume that your instructor is in possession of a fruit basket containing 100 apples. She likes apples, and would rather consume them herself. But the students in the class also want apples, and wish to induce her to offer apples to the class. To overcome her reluctance to part with her cherished apples, they offer her money.

Should they offer 10¢ per apple she would sell nothing, for at such a low price she would rather keep her beloved fruit. At a price of 20¢, still no apples would be supplied. A price of 30¢ per apple would be sufficient incentive for her to sell 20 apples; for 40¢ she would be induced to sell 40 apples; for 50¢ per apple she would offer her students 60 apples; for 60¢ per apple, 80 apples; for 70¢ per apple she would be induced to part with her entire stock and sell 100 apples. The higher the price, the greater the incentive to part with her apples, and the more apples she would be induced to supply. This information is tabulated in Table 5–2 and Figure 5–2.

Both the table and the chart indicate a positive relation between price and quantity supplied: The higher the price the greater the number of apples supplied. The supply curve slopes upward and to the right.

Table 5–2 Supply Schedule for Apples

Price (per Apple)	Quantity (Number of Apples Supplied)
20¢	0
30¢	20
40¢	40
50¢	60
60¢	80
70¢	100

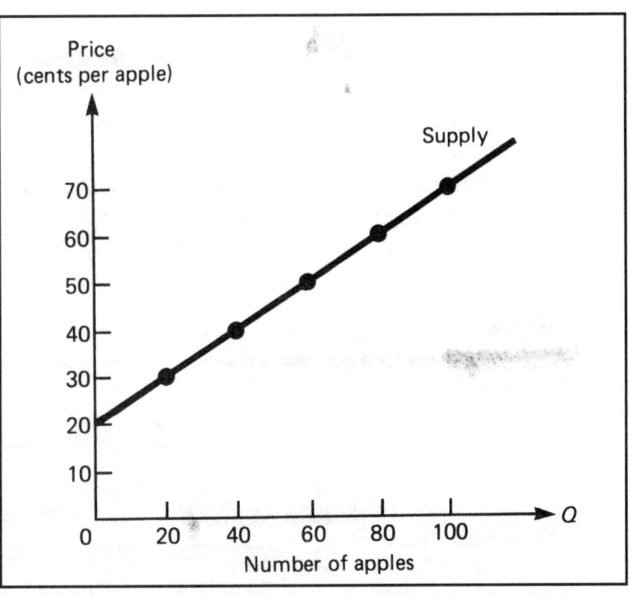

Figure 5–2 Supply Schedule for Apples: The higher the price the greater the quantity of apples supplied. This is a positive relation between price and the quantity supplied.

This positive relationship between the price of a particular good or service and the quantity supplied, known as the **law of supply,** applies to all products. Supply is a schedule and not a point. We next develop such a schedule in a production situation, for *a perfectly competitive* industry. In doing so, we distinguish between the short and the long run.

A customer approaches an apple vendor:
Customer: How much are your apples?
Vendor: 50¢ a piece!
Customer: Why is it that across the street they cost only 30¢ each?
Vendor: Why don't you buy apples there?
Customer: They are out of them!
Vendor: When I am out of apples, I shall also sell them for 30¢!

THE SHORT RUN AND THE LONG RUN

Consider a manufacturing firm. It has a given number of *buildings* (or structures) housing its *machinery* and *equipment.* Together, they are called the firm's capital stock. These machines are combined with labor

Short-run: a period of time over which the firm's capital stock (structures and machinery) is fixed.

to produce the final product out of some raw materials that the firm buys elsewhere. *The* **short run** *is defined as a period over which the firm's capital stock is fixed*. The period is not defined in terms of months, years, or any other specific length of time. Rather, it is a period too short for construction of an additional building or installation of new machinery. Nor is the period long enough for existing machines to be depreciated and put out of use. The only way a firm can expand output in the short run is by more intensive utilization of its existing capital stock. For example, this can be accomplished by putting on a second or a third shift, or by working during weekends and holidays. In other words, *production can expand in the short run only by combining a greater quantity of the labor input with a fixed quantity of machinery and equipment.* Production can contract only by reducing the amount of labor applied to a fixed amount of machinery. Likewise, *no new firms can enter the industry* and start production in the short run, nor can old firms leave the industry. It is defined as a period during which the number of firms in the industry and their capital stock are fixed.

Long-run: A period of time in which all inputs, including machines and structures, can be changed.

In contrast, the **long run** is a period long enough to allow firms to **expand or to contract** the quantity of their machinery and structures. And old firms can leave the industry and new firms can enter in the long run. Clearly, the long run allows a greater expansion or contraction of output than does the short run, because the change in production can come about by changing the capital stock and the number of firms, as well as the number of workers.

We now derive a hypothetical long-run supply schedule by using a simplified example of an oil-drilling firm. The industry is assumed to be perfectly competitive, consisting of 2,000 firms.

LONG-RUN SUPPLY CURVE OF THE SINGLE PRODUCER

Consider a drilling company (one of 2,000 such firms) that owns small oil fields in three regions of the country: Texas, Michigan, and offshore in the Mexican Gulf. The fields vary greatly in the degree of ease with which oil can be extracted, and therefore in the cost of extraction. In Texas, oil is very close to the surface, requiring very shallow drilling to extract it, and the cost per barrel is very low. In Michigan, the oil is less accessible, requiring deeper wells, and the cost of production per barrel is higher. And oil is most difficult and even hazardous to extract offshore in the Mexican Gulf, where the producer must also guard against environmental hazards of oil spills. Thus, offshore oil is most expensive to produce.

What implication does this gradation in production costs have for the firm's supply schedule? At a price of $10 per barrel, only the most efficient, least-cost field is profitable—that is, the firm produces only in its East Texas field—and that field yields 2,000 barrels per day. The other fields, where one must drill deeper for oil, are not profitable at this price.

Table 5–3 Hypothetical Long-Run Supply Schedule of a Single, Competitive Oil Producer

Price	Output in Barrels per Day			Supply
Dollars per Barrel	*Texas Field*	*Michigan Field*	*Offshore Field*	*Total Barrels per Day*
(a) $10	2,000	0	0	2,000
(b) $25	2,000	1,000	0	3,000
(c) $40	2,000	1,000	500	3,500

Should the price rise to $25 per barrel, the less-efficient Michigan field would come into production, producing 1,000 barrels per day; the total output from the two fields would then be 3,000 barrels per day. It would take $40 per barrel to bring into production the offshore field in the Mexican Gulf. Output there is assumed to be 500 barrels per day, so the three-field total would be 3,500 barrels per day.

These figures are summarized in Table 5–3, showing the supply schedule of the individual oil producer. The left-hand and right-hand columns constitute its supply schedule. They show the quantities supplied at various prices. As the price rises, so does the quantity supplied. These figures can be presented diagrammatically on the price-quantity graph in Figure 5–3, showing the supply curve of the single producer. The curve may or may not be a straight line. But it must slope upward and to the right,

Long-run supply curve and the single producer: A rise in the price of a good allows the firm to develop less productive resources and thereby increase the supply of the good.

Figure 5–3 Long-Run Supply Schedule of the Single Oil Producer: A rise in price induces the oil producing firm to work less-productive oil fields and thereby increase the amount of oil. The supply schedule of the single producer is positively sloped.

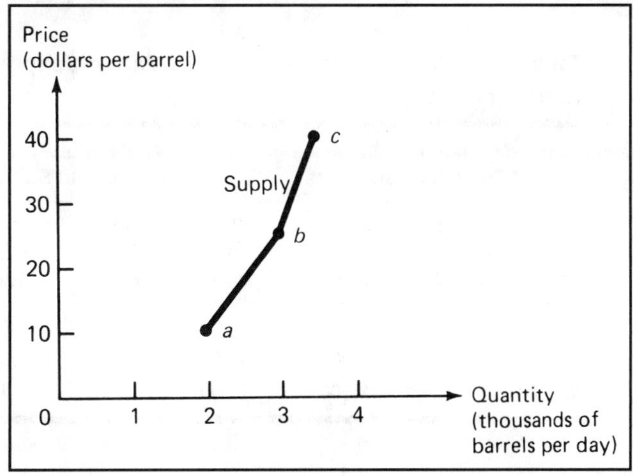

showing that the higher (lower) the price, the greater (smaller) the quantity supplied. The supply curve of the firm is positively sloped.

THE LONG-RUN MARKET-SUPPLY SCHEDULE IN A COMPETITIVE INDUSTRY

Long-run market supply schedule in a competitive industry: It is the horizontal summation of the quantities supplied by individual firms at each price.

The firm described above is one of many oil drillers, whose supply schedules may or may not be similar to each other. The only required feature is that they be positively sloped. *The market-supply schedule shows the quantities supplied by all producers at each price.* Thus, to move from the single-firm to the market-supply schedule, we add up the quantities supplied by the individual producers at each price. Geometrically, the market-supply curve is the horizontal summation of the individual suppliers' curves. Since it is not possible to show thousands of producers on one page, we assume that the supply schedule above is representative of 1,000 identical firms. Each of a second thousand identical firms owns fields in Michigan and offshore in the Mexican Gulf.

At a price of $10 per barrel, only the first set of producers would supply oil (from the Texas fields), because only they own fields in that most productive part of the country. And they would supply 2 million barrels per day (2,000 barrels by each of 1,000 producers). At a price of $25 per barrel, the first set of producers would supply a total of 3 million barrels from the fields in Texas and Michigan, and the second thousand producers would bring their Michigan fields into production, supplying 1 million barrels per day. Such entry into the industry is possible only in the long run. Total market supply at that price is 4 million barrels per day. At $40 per barrel, it is profitable to exploit the (least-productive) offshore field. Thus, the first thousand producers now supply out of fields located in all three states a total of 3.5 million barrels per day, and the second thousand supply 1.5 million barrels per day, for a total of 5 million.

This information is summarized in Table 5–4, where the resulting market-supply schedule is shown in the right-hand column. Note that

Table 5–4 Derivation of a Long-Run Market-Supply Schedule for Crude Oil (in Barrels per Day)

Each of First Thousand Suppliers			Each of Second Thousand Suppliers			Market Supply	
Price per Barrel	*No. of Producing Fields*	*Quantity Supplied*	*Price per Barrel*	*No. of Producing Fields*	*Quantity Supplied*	*Price*	*Quantity Supplied*
(a) $10	1	2,000	(d) $10	0	0	(A) $10	2 million
(b) $25	2	3,000	(e) $25	1	1,000	(B) $25	4 million
(c) $40	3	3,500	(f) $40	2	1,500	(C) $40	5 million

the opening of new fields and the entry of new firms into the oil-production industry take time. They are possible only in the long-run as defined above.

Figure 5–4 shows the derivation of the long-run market-supply curve diagrammatically. The two left-hand panels show each of the 2,000 suppliers, on price-quality graphs. The lowercase letters correspond to the respective points in Table 5–4. At the price of $25 per barrel, each of the first thousand producers supplies 3,000 barrels per day, shown as segment 1 on the left-hand panel, and each of the second thousand suppliers supplies 1,000 barrels per day (segment 2). Daily market supply at that price is the sum total of the 2,000 supplies, or 4 million barrels, shown as segment 1 + 2 multiplied by 1,000, on the right-hand panel of the figure. At a price of $40 per barrel, the supplies offered daily by each firm in the two sets of suppliers are 3,500 barrels (segment 3 on the left-hand panel) and 1,500 barrels (segment 4) respectively, for a total of 5 million barrels (segment 3 + 4 multiplied by 1,000 on the right-hand panel). The three price-quantity points in the market (right-hand) panel are shown in capital letters, corresponding to the points in the right-hand column of Table 5–4. By connecting them, one obtains the long-run market-supply curve. This curve may or may not be a straight-line, but a straight-line example offers the advantage of simplicity.

The crucial property of the long-run supply curve is that it has a positive slope. As price rises, the quantity supplied increases, because (1) each producer or producing firm expands capacity by opening new fields as

Figure 5–4 Derivation of Long-Run Market-Supply Schedule from Supply Schedules of 2,000 Individual Suppliers: The industry supply schedule is obtained by horizontal summation of the quantities supplied by individual firms at each price.

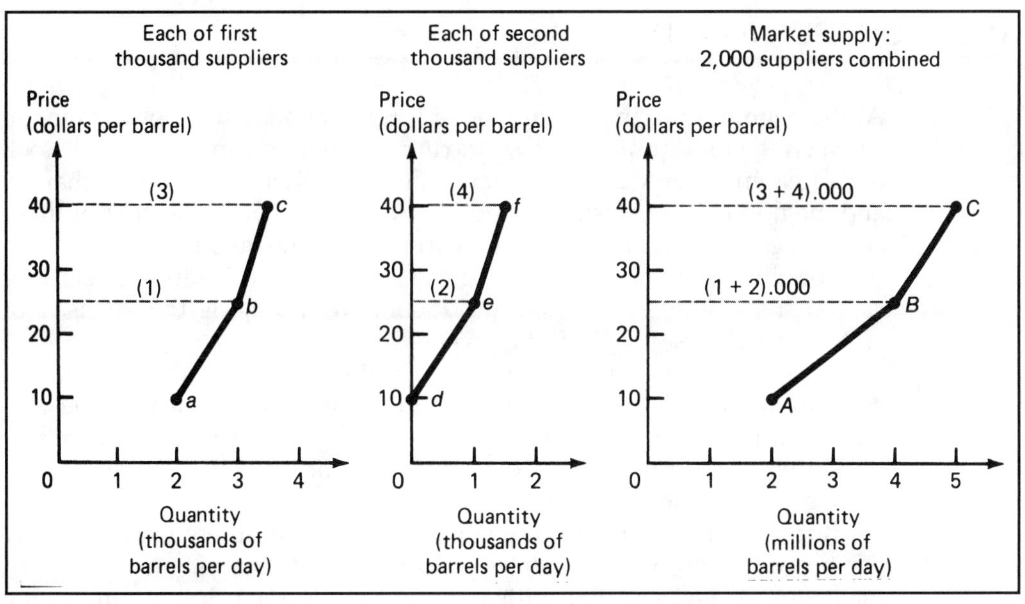

less-productive fields can be brought into production; and (2) new producers, which by reason of their lesser efficiency could not supply at the lower price, can now start supplying.

This pattern applies to the production of many commodities. In the long run, individual firms can expand their supplies in response to a rise in price by dipping into less-efficient and more-costly resources. In our example, the gradations in efficiency were determined by the depth at which crude oil could be found. In agricultural production, it may be determined by the difference in productivity of land, where only the most productive land would be used at a relatively low price of the farm product, and each individual farmer would expand into less-productive land as the price of the product rises. In other words, it requires higher prices of the final product (corn, wheat, or whatever) to justify the cultivation of less-productive land. As the price rises, farmers would supply more by cultivating new and less-productive land.

With respect to the entry of new firms into production, it is generally possible to rank potential producers in each industry (such as textiles) by the degree of their productive efficiency. Any number of productive inputs can determine this ranking—the natural resource the firms own, such as oil fields; the quality of labor they traditionally employ; the quality of machinery they use; and last but not least, the quality of their management. At any given price, there will be firms with highly profitable operations, others making just about enough profit to stay in business (known as *normal profit*) and still others that cannot function profitably and would enter the industry only if the price rose sufficiently to justify operations. Firms in the second category are known as the *marginal* firms; those in the third group are called *submarginal* firms. It is in this fashion that industry size expands as price increases.

LONG-RUN AND SHORT-RUN SUPPLY

At the beginning of this discussion, a fundamental distinction was made between the long run and the short run: In the long run, the capital stock (also known as productive capacity) of the individual firm can change; and the number of firms in the industry can also change. Neither of these changes can occur in the short run; variations in the quantity supplied can be brought about only by changing the intensity of utilization of existing capital stock or, in agricultural production, by changing the intensity of cultivation of a plot of land of a given size.

How would the firm respond to a rise in price in the short run? In some industries output cannot be changed at all without varying the capital stock. The short-run supply curve would then appear as a straight *vertical* line. It represents a fixed quantity supplied in the short run irrespective of price.

But in many industries, the situation could be different. A firm may begin production with an *optimal* utilization of its machinery and equipment, employing, say, two shifts per day. Should the price per unit of the product rise, the firm might be induced to utilize its machines more intensely, by putting on an extra half shift. This may leave too few hours for maintenance and repair of the capital stock. Thus, the extra half shift would not be as productive as the first two shifts, thereby increasing the cost of production per unit of the added output. But this drawback is offset by a higher price fetched for the product. Indeed, it required a rise in price to induce the firm to put on the extra half shift. In these circumstances, the quantity supplied would rise as price increases even in the short run, but not by as much as in the long run, when capacity itself can be changed.

This difference has an important implication for the relative shape of the short-run and long-run supply curves. Suppose that in the market for product X (Figure 5–5), there is a rise in price from OP_1 to OP_2. In the short run, only *existing* firms can respond, each expanding output but only through more intensive utilization of its fixed capital stock. Consequently, the quantity supplied rises from $0Q_1$ to $0Q_2$. But in the long run, the output expansion in response to the same rise in price (ΔP) can be much more substantial: Existing firms can install new *capacity* (machines and equipment), and altogether new firms can enter the industry. Output expansion in the long run can be much greater; to wit, from $0Q_1$ to $0Q_3$. Although both supply curves are positively sloped, a given price change will elicit a far greater quantity response in the long run than in the short run.

Law of supply: As the price of the product rises, the quantity supplied increases; the market supply curve has a positive slope. The long-run supply schedule is flatter than that of the short run, representing greater supply response to price changes.

To recapitulate, the market-supply curve has a *positive slope,* representing the **law of supply. As the price of the product rises, the quantity supplied increases.** This law corresponds well to empirical observations. The supply schedule may or may not be a straight line, but it is convenient to employ straight-line supply curves.

Figure 5–5 Comparison between the Short-Run and the Long-Run Market-Supply Schedules for a Given Product: In the long run, the size of firms as well as their number can change; in the short run both are fixed. Production can vary only by changing the intensity of use of a fixed capital stock of a given number of firms. Therefore, a given price increase causes a greater increase in the quantity supplied in the long run than in the short run. *This is the general case.*

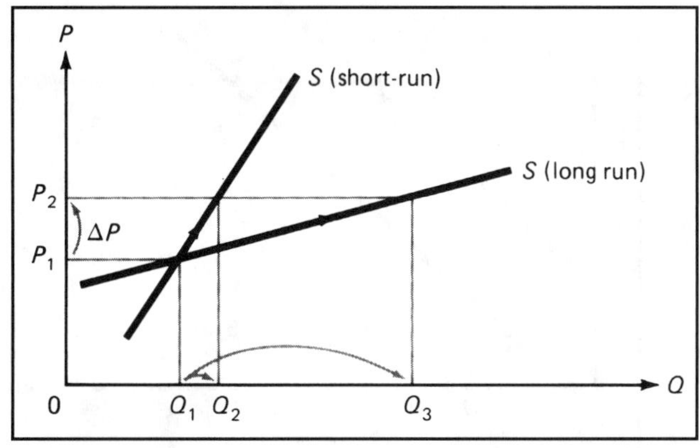

MOVEMENTS ALONG THE MARKET-SUPPLY CURVE VS. SHIFTS IN THE ENTIRE CURVE

Shifts in the supply schedule vs. movements along the supply curve: Movements along the supply curve are due to the change in the product's own price while shifts in the entire supply curve are caused by other factors (i.e. changes in technology; changes in factor prices; and changes in the prices of other goods.) The latter means that the quantity supplied at each and every price changes.

As in the case of demand, it is of the utmost importance to make the often tricky distinction between movement along the supply curve and shifts in it. The supply curve relates the product's own price to the quantity supplied. Movements along it show changes in quantities occurring because of changes in price, where the price and quantity move in the same direction. *These are NOT labeled changes in supply!* Rather, they are described as a variation in the *quantity* supplied. But the product's own price is only one factor affecting the quantity supplied; there are other important factors influencing that quantity. These bring about *changes in the quantity supplied at each and every price; they cause a shift in the entire supply curve.* The term *change in supply* is reserved for such shifts. These factors will now be considered in turn.

Improvement In Technology

Suppose that a new and improved technology is developed and introduced. This may be a new lubricating oil for machines or some other maintenance procedure, or it may be a new oil rig for deep drilling that makes it easier and cheaper to drill. Because production costs decline, it would now require a lower price than before to induce each supplier to supply a given quantity (or for new suppliers to enter the industry). This is shown in Figure 5–6 by a shift in supply from S_1 to S_2, each given quan-

Figure 5–6 Market-Supply Schedules before (S_1) and after (S_2) the Introduction of New Technology: An increase in supply means that at each price a greater quantity is supplied. The supply schedule shifts to the right.

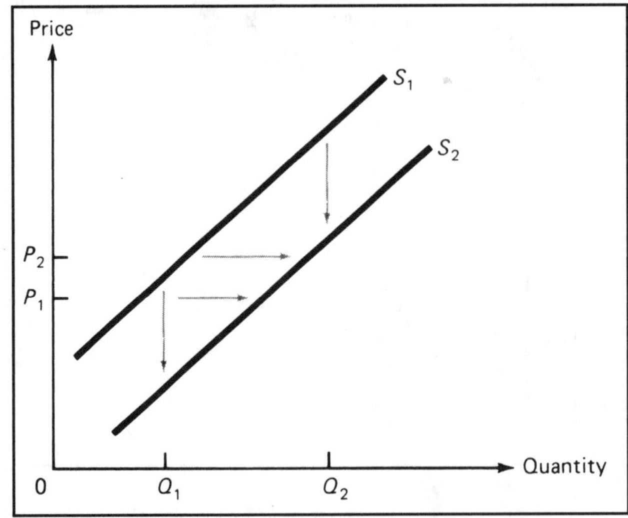

tity is now offered at a lower price than before. It is highlighted by the two downward-pointing arrows, each pinned at a quantity level, Q_1 and Q_2. An alternative way of looking at the same change is horizontally instead of vertically: *At any given price, a greater quantity is now supplied than before.* This is highlighted in the figure by the two arrows pointing to the right, each pinned at a price, P_1 and P_2. Clearly, the **supply curve has moved to the right.**

Shifts in supply: A shift to the right of the supply curve indicates an increase in supply, whereas a shift to the left indicates a decrease in supply.

Either the horizontal or the vertical shift describes correctly what has happened to supply. But it is more customary to emphasize the horizontal shift, showing that **a greater quantity is offered at each price.** This is known as an **increase in supply.**[1] It should be sharply distinguished from a movement *along* the supply curve, where a greater (lesser) quantity is supplied because of a higher (lower) price. The term *change in supply* (increase or decrease) is reserved strictly for a shift (rightward or leftward) in the entire supply curve. Movements along the curve are described as *changes in quantity supplied.*

Change in Factor (or Input) Prices

Suppose that wage rates decline because an increased availability of cheaper migrant workers in the United States, or suppose that the price of equipment declined substantially. Then production becomes profitable at lower prices. By reasoning analogous to that employed above, the reduction in production costs lowers the price required by producers to supply a given quantity. At any given price, a greater quantity is supplied. The supply curve shifts *to the right* indicating an *increase in supply.*

Conversely, a sharp hike in wage rates **reduces supply, shifting the curve to the left.** A similar reduction in supply could occur for other reasons: Freezing weather in Florida would reduce the supply of oranges; a drought in the Middle West would reduce the supply of wheat; a rise in the price of wheat would reduce the supply of bread. In all these cases, a smaller quantity would be supplied at each and every price or, alternatively, each given quantity would be supplied only at a higher price than before.

Changes in the Prices of Other Goods

Suppose a manufacturer could use his production equipment to produce tennis balls or racquet balls. The two types of balls are different and serve different games. But they are substitutes in production, in the sense that output of one can be expanded at the expense of the other by switching production equipment to it. The product of our primary interest is racquet balls. A rise in the price of tennis balls would induce producers to switch facilities from racquet-ball to tennis-ball production. At any given price of

[1]The diagrammatic presentation is deceptive, for it appears as though the curve shifts downward, yet this shift actually describes an increase in supply: More is supplied at each price. The student should avoid being deceived by the chart's appearance.

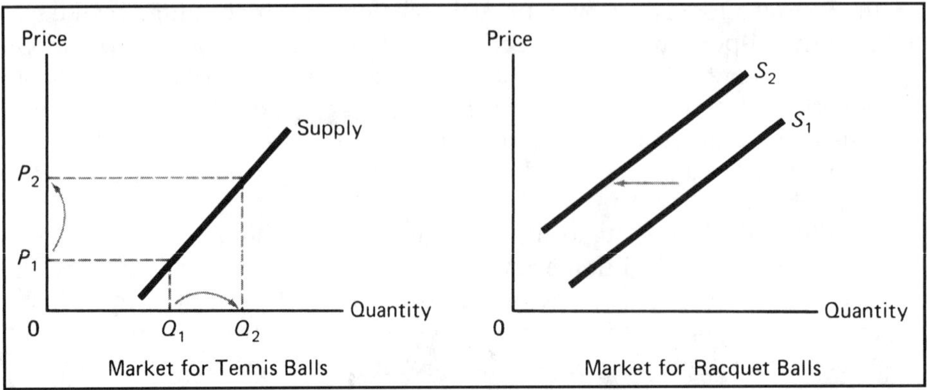

Figure 5–7 Market for Tennis Balls and Racquet Balls (substitutes in production): A rise in the price of tennis balls induces producers to switch productive factors from racquet balls to tennis balls, thereby reducing the supply of racquet balls.

racquet balls, fewer of them would be supplied. The supply of racquet balls would decrease, and the supply curve would shift to the left.

These changes are shown in Figure 5–7 for the two commodities that are substitutes in production. As the price of tennis balls rises from $0P_1$ to $0P_2$, output rises from $0Q_1$ to $0Q_2$ and the supply of racquet balls declines from S_1 to S_2. Note that *no* change in *supply* took place in the tennis-ball market, only a change in the quantity offered as we move along a given supply curve. A reduction in supply occurred in the market for racquet balls. Conversely, a decline in the price of tennis balls would increase the supply of racquet balls.

The analysis above illustrates a relation between two goods that are *substitutes* in production: The production of one can be expanded at the expense of the other. In contrast, products can be *complementary* in production, in the sense that they are produced jointly. For example, beef and liver are produced jointly and in fixed proportions. Suppose that liver is the commodity of our primary interest, and there has been a rise in the price of beef. Moving up along the supply curve of beef, more beef would be produced. But as a direct consequence, there would be an increase in the supply of liver: At any given price of liver, a greater quantity of it would be supplied.

In sum, when two goods are substitutes in production, a rise (decline) in the price of one reduces (increases) the supply of the other; when two goods are complements in production (produced jointly), a rise (decline) in the price of one increases (decreases) the supply of the other.

SUMMARY

A supply schedule exists in the market for each good, service, or productive service. It relates the price of a good to the quantity supplied. *The price,* shown on the vertical axis, *provides a link to the demand side of the market.* The market-supply schedule is positively sloped (slopes upward and to the right), reflecting a positive relation between price and the quantity supplied. It is obtained by a horizontal summation of the quantities supplied by the constituent firms at each price.

The long-run supply schedule of a *single perfectly competitive firm* reflects expansion or contraction of output by varying the use of **all** its productive factors as the price of the product changes. The numbers of firms can also change in the long run. The short-run supply schedule of the firm reflects a more limited response to a change in the price of its product: a change in quantity produced, obtained from a more or less intensive utilization of its fixed capital stock. The number of firms is constant in the short run.

Although both the long- and short-run schedules are positively sloped, the long-run curve is flatter, showing a greater response of quantity to price change.

It is critical to distinguish between (1) movements along the supply curve and (2) shifts in the entire curve. The first, labeled a change in the *quantity supplied,* shows how the quantity changes in response to a change in the product price. The term *change in supply* is reserved for the second type: At each and every price, more or less is supplied, and the entire supply schedule shifts upward (increases) or downward (decreases). We identified three factors that may cause an increase or a decrease in supply: changes in technology, changes in input prices, and changes in the prices of related goods. These should be committed to memory.

QUESTIONS AND PROBLEMS

1. You are given the following supply schedule for coffee by Brazilian producers:

Price per Bushel	Quantity supplied (Millions of Bushels)
$2	10
4	20
6	30
8	40

   a. Draw a supply curve for coffee.

   b. Suppose a weather freeze in Brazil *halved* the quantity supplied at each price. Show the new supply curve on your chart.

   c. Return now to the original situation (under *a*). Suppose new planting and harvesting machines make it possible to supply each quantity at half the price originally charged. Tabulate and draw the new supply curve. Relate it to the original supply curve.

2. Sketch two hypothetical market-supply curves: (a) for wheat; (b) for corn. Use figures of your choice. Suppose farmers can use their land to plant *either* wheat *or* corn. Show on your two charts the effect of a sudden doubling of the price of wheat.

Price Determination in Competitive Markets

EQUILIBRIUM PRICE AND QUANTITY IN A SINGLE MARKET

For any given demand and supply curves, the intersection of the two determines the price that would prevail on the market and the quantity changing hands. At that price, the quantity supplied equals the quantity demanded; it is the price that "clears the market."

Consider the market for shoes, illustrated in Table 6–1. To each price shown in the first column, there corresponds a quantity demanded (second column) and a quantity supplied (third column). The figures represent the laws of demand and of supply respectively, with price being the link between the two sides of the market.

At a price of $10 per pair of shoes, 100 million pairs are demanded and only 20 million pairs are supplied, generating **excess demand** (quantity demanded minus quantity supplied) of 80 million pairs (fourth column). This leads consumers to offer a higher price, or to "bid up" the price, as each tries (in competition with other consumers) to secure the supplies desired. The price of $10 is not sustainable; it will be bid up to, say, $20 a pair. As the price rises gradually, consumers' purchases decline, reaching 80 million pairs at the new price, while the quantity supplied by producers rises to 40 million. Excess demand declines to 40 million. But the incentive of consumers to offer a higher price remains, until the price reaches $30 per pair. At that point, the quantities supplied and demanded are equal. No excess demand exists; $30 per pair is a price that **clears the market,** the price that equates the quantities supplied and demanded.

Approaching Table 6–1 from the other end, consider the price of $50 per pair. The quantity demanded is 20 million pairs, while 100 million are supplied. An **excess supply** of 80 million pairs appears at this price; it is shown in the fifth column of Table 6–1. In an attempt to get rid of the excess supply, sellers would quote a lower price, or bid down the price, to,

Table 6–1 Market Demand for and Supply of Shoes

Price (Dollars per Pair)	Quantity Demanded[a]	Quantity Supplied[a]	Excess Demand	Excess Supply
(a) $10	100	20	80	
(b) $20	80	40	40	
(c) $30	60	60	0	0
(d) $40	40	80		40
(e) $50	20	100		80

[a] *In millions of pairs per year.*

say, $40 a pair. As the price declines, buyers expand their consumption while sellers curtail the quantity supplied. Consequently, excess supply declines to 40 million pairs. But as long as excess supply exists, the incentive of suppliers—competing with each other—to bid down the price in order to unload these quantities remains. When the price reaches $30 a pair, the excess supply disappears, and with it the incentive to cut the price further.

Equilibrium price is $30 a pair. It is the price that **clears the market.** Sixty million pairs of shoes are sold and purchased at that price; at equilibrium, the quantity supplied equals the quantity demanded. In other words, the market price performs the **rationing function;** it allocates available supplies among purchasers. Finally, note that total revenue (TR) of all shoe sellers, which equals total expenditures on shoes by all buyers, equals the price per pair ($30) times the quantity sold or purchased (60 million pairs), for a total of $1.8 billion per year.

An identical analysis is presented in Figure 6–1, displaying the demand and supply schedules of Table 6–1. In their joint appearance, the

Figure 6–1 Market for Shoes

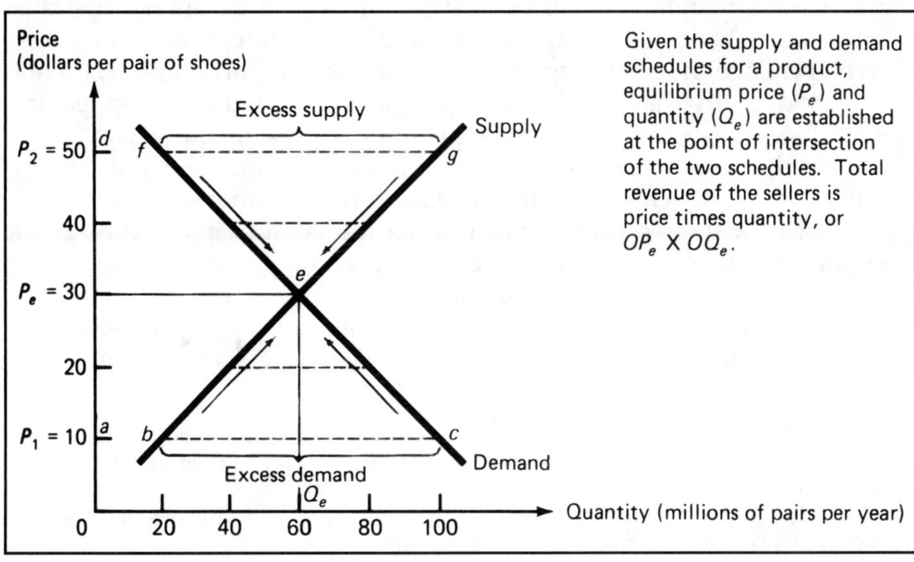

Given the supply and demand schedules for a product, equilibrium price (P_e) and quantity (Q_e) are established at the point of intersection of the two schedules. Total revenue of the sellers is price times quantity, or $OP_e \times OQ_e$.

two schedules are similar to an open pair of scissors.[1] Suppose the price were \$10 per pair, or $0P_1$. Then the quantity demanded is 100, or segment *ac* (as shown on the demand curve), while the quantity supplied is 20, or segment *ab* (as shown on the supply curve). Since the quantity demanded exceeds the quantity supplied, there is *excess demand* of 80 million pairs, shown as segment *bc*. It leads consumers to bid up the price as each tries (in competition with the other consumers) to secure the supplies desired. Price P_1 is not sustainable; it will be bid up. As the price rises gradually, two things happen: Consumers purchase less, moving upward along the negatively sloped demand curve; and producers supply more, moving upward along the positively sloped supply curve. These movements are indicated by the upward-pointing arrows; the quantities demand and supplied converge. The excess demand gradually narrows as the price moves up. It is eliminated when the price reaches $0P_e$ (\$30 per pair). Only at that price will the bidding-up process stop.

Conversely, if the price were \$50 a pair, or $0P_2$, then the quantity supplied (as shown on the supply curve) is 100, represented by segment *dg*, and the quantity demanded (as shown on the demand curve) is 20, represented by segment *df*. Since the quantity supplied exceeds the quantity demanded, the excess supply is 80, or segment *fg*. But this cannot last. For it leads each producer to bid down the price (in competition with other producers) in order to sell the desired quantities. As the price declines gradually, two things happen: Producers supply less, as they move down along a positively sloped supply curve, and consumers purchase more, as they move down along a negatively sloped demand curve. These movements are indicated by the downward-pointing arrows; the quantities supplied and demanded converge, and the excess supply narrows. The process will go on until price $0P_e$, or \$30 per pair, is reached. At that price, there is no longer an incentive to bid down the price.

Equilibrium price: is the price that equates the quantity supplied with the quantity demanded; it is also known as the market-clearing price.

Equilibrium quantity is the quantity that exchanges hands at the equilibrium price.

Price P_e is called the **equilibrium price** for the given pair of supply and demand curves. Any other price would bring about market forces that would push the price back to P_e. At price P_e, there are no frustrated buyers or sellers; both groups are satisfied. Therefore, there is no incentive to change the price. Corresponding to the equilibrium price, there is a given quantity changing hands—quantity demanded and supplied. It is 60 million pairs, represented by segment $0Q_e$ on the quantity axis. This is the **equilibrium quantity.** The market price performs the highly important rationing function: It rations available supply among demanders.

Consider the rectangle formed under the point of intersection of the supply and demand curves, referred to as the equilibrium point (point *e* in Figure 6–1).[2] Its area equals the equilibrium price times quantity: $0P_e \times 0Q_e$. But price times quantity sold yields total revenue of the sellers, or total expenditures on shoes by consumers. Thus, *the rectangular area under*

[1]For that reason, they are sometimes referred to as the "Marshallian scissors," named after the great English economist Alfred Marshall, who first used supply and demand together as an analytical tool.

[2]More precisely, the rectangle formed by joining point *e* and the two axes. In future references, it is called the area under the equilibrium point.

the point of intersection of supply and demand represents total revenue (TR) of all sellers or total expenditures by all buyers. In our case, it is 60 million pairs of shoes times \$30 per pair, or \$1.8 billion.

SHIFTS IN SUPPLY AND/OR DEMAND

Starting from an equilibrium situation of a given pair of supply and demand schedules, any shift in one of the curves or in both will change the equilibrium price, quantity, and total revenue (price times quantity). The effect of some such shifts is demonstrated next.

Figure 6–2 shows the effect of an increase in demand, from D_1 to D_2, holding supply constant. The equilibrium point (intersection of supply and demand) moves from e_1 to e_2 as we move up along the constant supply curve. Price rises from $0P_1$ to $0P_2$, with the increase shown as ΔP (the Greek letter delta, written Δ, is used to denote change). Quantity exchanged increases from $0Q_1$ to $0Q_2$, with the increase shown as ΔQ. Total revenue of the sellers (which equals total expenditures by the buyers) rises from $0P_1 \times 0Q_1$ to $0P_2 \times 0Q_2$, or from the rectangular area under equilibrium point e_1 to that under e_2.

Conversely, a decrease in demand from D_2 to D_1, holding supply constant, moves the equilibrium point downward along the supply curve from e_2 to e_1. Price declines from $0P_2$ to $0P_1$; quantity bought or sold declines from $0Q_2$ to $0Q_1$; and total revenue declines from $0P_2 \times 0Q_2$ to $0P_1 \times 0Q_1$.

Shift in demand: When the demand curve shifts up (down), holding supply constant the equilibrium price and quantity all goes up (down). TR rises (declines).

Figure 6–2 Effects of an Upward Shift In Demand (from D_1 to D_2) Holding Supply Constant: Price, quantity, and total revenue all rise. Price rises from P_1 to P_2. Quantity rises from Q_1 to Q_2. Total revenue rises from ($0P_1 \times 0Q_1$) to ($0P_2 \times 0Q_2$).

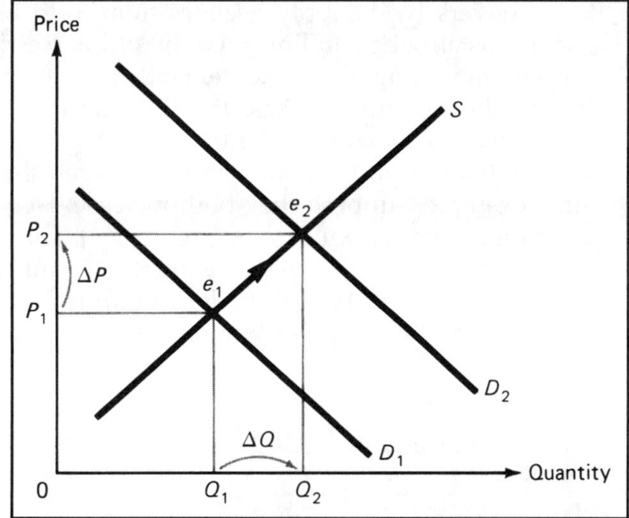

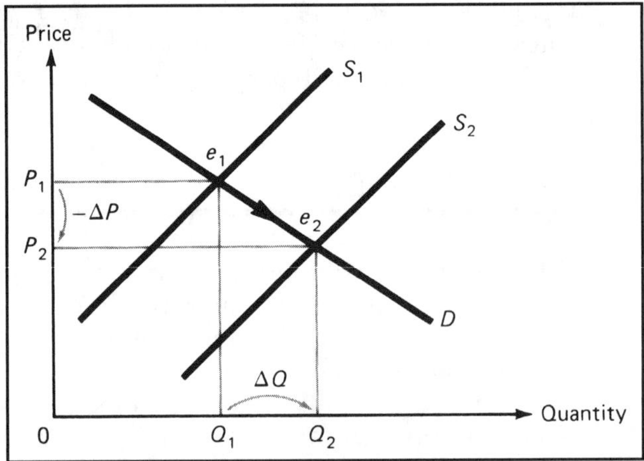

Shifts in supply: When the supply curve shifts up (down), holding demand constant, the equilibrium price declines (rises) while the quantity increases (declines). The direction of change in TR is indeterminate.

Figure 6–3 Effects of an Upward Shift in Supply (from S_1 to S_2,), Holding Demand Constant: Price declines, quantity rises; the direction of change in total revenue is indeterminate. Price declines from P_1 to P_2. Quantity rises from Q_1 to Q_2. Total revenue changes from $(0P_1 \times 0Q_1)$ to $(0P_2 \times 0Q_2)$.

Figure 6–3 shows the effect of an increase in supply, from S_1 to S_2, holding the demand curve constant. The equilibrium point (point of intersection between supply and demand) moves down along the demand curve from e_1 to e_2. Price declines from $0P_1$ to $0P_2$ while quantity exchanged *rises* from $0Q_1$ to $0Q_2$. What then happens to total revenue, which is the product of price and quantity (TR = $P \times Q$)? The answer depends on which of the two changes is proportionally larger—the decline in price, or the increase in quantity purchased. Without additional information, we can only say that TR can move in either direction (up or down) or else remain unchanged. In other words, the change in TR is classified as indeterminate, pending later discussion of demand elasticity.

Conversely, if supply declines from S_2 to S_1 with the demand curve held constant, the equilibrium point of intersection between demand and supply moves up along the demand curve from e_2 to e_1. Price rises from $0P_2$ to $0P_1$; quantity purchased declines from $0Q_2$ to $0Q_1$; and TR can move either way or remain constant.[3]

Both the supply and demand curves can shift at the same time. In the first example, suppose they both increase: Demand rises from D_1 to D_2, and supply rises from S_1 to S_2 (Figure 6–4). The equilibrium point of intersection shifts from e_1 to e_2. Clearly, the quantity exchanged increases; it rises as a result of the shift in demand from D_1 to D_2, holding supply constant at S_1 (that is, equilibrium moves from e_1 to the imaginary intermedi-

[3]*Note:* The direction of change in TR is clear-cut when demand shifts along a constant supply curve. It is indeterminate when supply shifts along a constant demand curve.

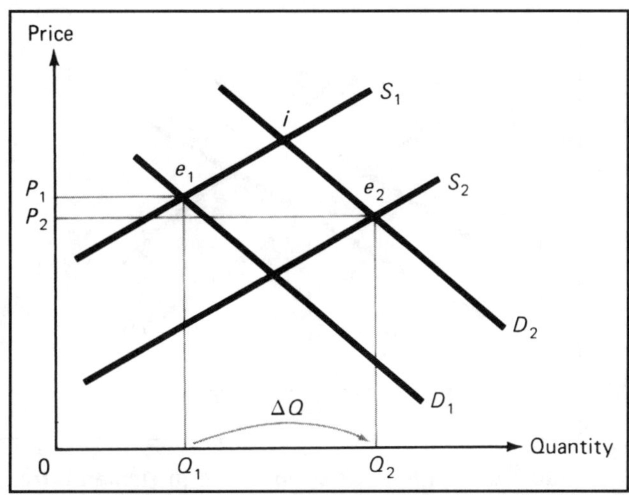

Figure 6–4 Effect of an Increase in both Supply (from S_1 to S_2) and Demand (from D_1 to D_2): Quantity rises from Q_1 to Q_2; direction of change in price and total revenue is indeterminate.

Shifts in supply and demand: If both supply and demand rise, the equilibrium quantity increases but the direction of change in price and TR is indeterminate.

ate point i); and then it rises when supply shifts from S_1 to S_2, holding demand constant at D_2 (equilibrium moves from i to e_2). Since both demand and supply changes affect the quantity in the same direction, the total effect is clearcut—quantity rises from $0Q_1$ to $0Q_2$. Not so with respect to price. Here, the rise in demand from D_1 to D_2, holding supply constant at S_1 (equilibrium moves from e_1 to i), raises the price. But the rise in supply from S_1 to S_2, holding demand constant (equilibrium moves from i to e_2), lowers the price. The net effect on price cannot be predicted without knowing the magnitude of the shift in the two curves. Thus, in Figure 6–4, price happens to decline from $0P_1$ to $0P_2$. But if we allowed for only a very small reduction in supply and/or a much larger increase in demand, price would have increased. Therefore, the direction of change in price is indeterminate. And because TR is the product of price and quantity, the direction of change in TR is also determinate.

Conversely, a decrease in both demand and supply shifts the equilibrium point from e_2 to e_1. Quantity definitely decreases. But the direction of change in price and TR depends on the relative magnitude of the shift in the two curves, and is therefore indeterminate.

A rise in D but decrease in S: If demand increases but supply decreases price rises but the change in quantity and total revenue is indeterminate.

Finally, if demand increases and supply decreases, the price rises, but the direction of change in quantity and TR is indeterminate (Figure 6–5). Conversely, if demand decreases and supply increases, price declines, but the direction of change in quantity and TR is indeterminate. The student is invited to illustrate these changes on a diagram.

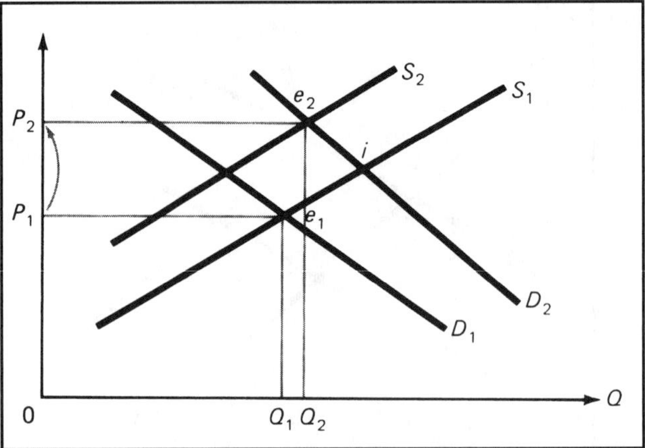

Figure 6–5 Effect of an Increase in Demand (from D_1 to D_2) and a Decrease In Supply (from S_1 to S_2): Price rises from P_1 to P_2; direction of change in quantity and *TR* is indeterminate.

SUMMARY

Each good and service (including productive services or inputs) is traded on a market. The product's own price forms the link between the demand and supply sides of the market. For a given set of *D* and *S* schedules, their intersection determines equilibrium quantity, price, and TR. This helps fill some of the gaps left open in the circular-flow diagram (Part I). On each commodity market, there is a supply schedule by the firms selling that commodity and a demand schedule by the households purchasing it. Conversely, in the market for a productive service, the supply schedule is by households and the demand schedule is by firms. The equilibrium price clears the market and performs the rationing function. Any shift in the demand and/or supply curves changes the equilibrium price, quantity, and total revenue.

QUESTIONS AND PROBLEMS

1. You are given the demand and supply schedules for wheat found at the top of the next page.
   a. Draw a demand and supply curve based on this information.
   b. What is the equilibrium market price, and what quantity would exchange hands at that price? Why?
   c. What is the total revenue of the producers? Is it equal to the total expenditures on wheat by the buyers?
   d. Suppose now that the quantity demanded at each price doubles. Show in the table as well as the diagram the effect of that change on the market price, quantity, and total revenue.

PriceQuantity (per Bushel)	Quantity Demanded[a]	Supplied[a]
$1	500	100
$2	400	200
$3	300	300
S4	200	400
$5	100	500

[a]*In millions of bushels per year.*

e. Returning to the situation under *c*, show the effect on market price, quantity, and TR of doubling the quantity *supplied* at each price.

2. Add the following supply schedule of Canadian wheat to question 2 at the end of Chapter 4:

Price (per Bushel)	Quantity Supplied (Millions of Bushels)
$2	20
$3	30
$4	40
$5	50

Draw the supply and demand schedules on the price-quantity space. Determine and explain the equilibrium price, quantity, and TR. Show and explain the changes in all three under the conditions specified in question 2b, Chapter 4.

3. Add the following demand schedule for Brazilian coffee to question 1 at the end of Chapter 5:

Price (per Bushel)	Quantity Demanded (Millions of Bushels)
$2	40
$4	30
$6	20
$8	10

Draw and determine *from your chart* the equilibrium price, quantity, and TR. Show *diagrammatically* the changes in all three under conditions specified in questions 1b and 1c, Chapter 5.

Degree of Response to Price Change: Supply and Demand Elasticities

In Chapter 4, the demand curve was shown to be negatively sloped: As price declines (rises), the quantity purchased rises (declines). We did not address the question, "By *how much* does the *quantity demanded* change as a result of a given change in price?" Yet the **degree of response** to price change is important to every seller. Before deciding on any variation in price, the seller wishes to know the *magnitude* of its effect on the quantity purchased. Another illustration comes from the area of energy conservation. We know that a given rise in price would reduce the quantity of energy (such as gasoline) consumed; but *by how much*? A measure of this degree of response, or the sensitivity of quantity purchased to price change, is known as the price **elasticity of demand**. It will be recalled that when examining the effects of a shift in the supply curve (holding demand constant), the direction of change in total revenue was indeterminate. It too depends on the demand elasticity.

Elasticity: The term used as a measure of the degree of response to price change. It applies to demand as well as to supply.

A similar question exists with respect to supply. A variation in price alters the quantity supplied in the same direction. But by how much does the quantity supplied change in response to a given change in price? In the case of energy production, we know that a rise in the price of oil, coal, or natural gas would stimulate greater output of the respective commodity; but how much greater? A measure of the degree of response is known as the price elasticity of supply.

Elastic demand: A flat (steep) demand curve tends to show high (low) response by consumers to a price change. We refer to it as a relatively elastic (inelastic) demand curve.

These two concepts, their measurement and applications, are examined in this chapter. Remember throughout the discussion that sellers and buyers are two different and distinct groups of people. In the product markets consumers are the demanders while firms are the suppliers.

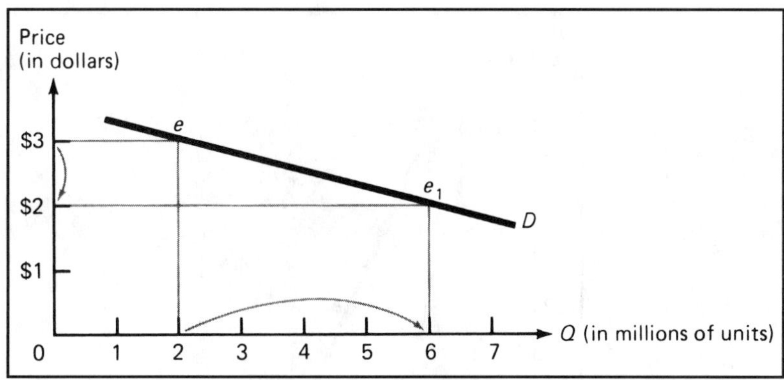

Figure 7–1 Relatively Elastic Demand: A reduction in price from $3 to $2 per unit increases the quantity purchased from 2 to 6 million units. The **percentage** increase in quantity is greater than the **percentage** decrease in price. TR rises from $6 to $12.

PRICE ELASTICITY OF DEMAND

Schematic Illustration

Empirical observations suggest that the degree of consumers' responsiveness to price change varies from one commodity or service to another. Furthermore, consumer responsiveness may vary substantially between different price ranges for the same commodity.

In the case of some products, a given reduction (boost) in price generates a very large increase (decrease) in the quantity purchased. Schematically, this is illustrated by a very flat demand curve, such as that in Figure 7–1. A price reduction from $3 to $2 per unit generates a large increase in quantity purchased, all the way from 2 to 6 million units. We call this a *highly responsive* or a **relatively elastic** demand. A moment's reflection would lead to the conclusion that the extreme case of *most* responsive demand is illustrated by a flat or horizontal demand curve.

By contrast, the demand schedule for another commodity may display very little response to price change; that is, a given reduction (boost) in price generates a very small increase (decrease) in the quantity purchased. Schematically, this is shown in Figure 7–2. A price reduction from $3 to $2 per unit generates a small increase in the quantity purchased—from 2 to only 2¼ million units. This is called a **relatively inelastic** demand. You can see that the most extreme case is a vertical demand curve where a price change elicits no change in the quantity purchased.

Elasticity coefficient: A quantitative measure of response of buyers to a price change. It is a ratio between two *percentages*: Percentage change in quantity divided by percentage change in price. It varies along a linear demand curve, with the mid-point equaling 1.

The Elasticity Coefficient

In seeking a precise measure of the response of buyers to price change, economists developed the concept of demand elasticity (η_D). It measures

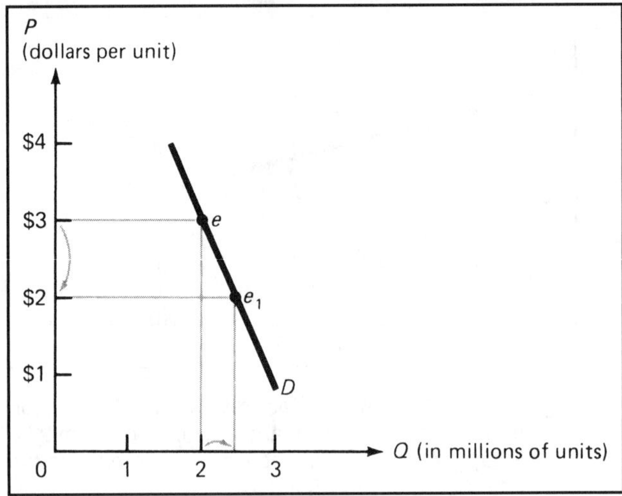

Figure 7–2 Relatively Inelastic Demand: A reduction in price from \$3 to \$2 per unit increases the quantity purchased form 2 to 2¼ million units. The **percentage** increase in quantity is smaller than the **percentage** decrease in price. TR declines from \$6 to 4½.

the relation between the change in price and the accompanying change in quantity where both changes are expressed in **proportionate or percentage terms**. In particular, elasticity is defined as a ratio of two percentages:

$$\text{Elasticity coefficient } (\eta_D) = \frac{\text{Percentage change in the quantity demanded}}{\text{Percentage change in price}}$$

Alternatively, in symbols using the Greek delta (Δ) to denote change:

$$\eta_D = \frac{\%\Delta Q}{\%\Delta P} = \frac{\Delta Q/Q}{\Delta P/P} = \frac{\Delta Q}{\Delta P} \times \frac{P}{Q}$$

Elasticity is a number; it is a ratio between two percentages. To illustrate its meaning, suppose you are told that the elasticity of demand for oil is –.25, or –1/4. Then a 20 percent increase in oil price reduces the quantity of oil consumed by one quarter of that, or by 5 percent. Conversely, a 5 percent increase in the quantity consumed is caused by a price cut of 20 percent. An elasticity of demand of –2 means that a 10 percent rise in the product's price reduces the quantity purchased by 20 percent, and a 15 percent reduction in the product's price increases the quantity purchased by 30 percent. Because price and quantity move in opposite directions, demand elasticity is negative. But economists often ignore the negative sign for reasons of convenience.

Measurement

To show the meaning of the definition above, we select the demand schedule in Table 7–1.

Demand Elasticity: Demand is relatively elastic, of unitary elasticity, or relatively inelastic if the coefficient is greater than, equal to, or smaller than 1.

Table 7–1 Calculation of Demand Elasticity Along a Straight-Line Demand Curve

	Price	Quantity Purchased	Calculated Demand Elasticity	Total Revenue (Price × Quantity)
	$6	1		6
(a)			–3.67	
	$5	2		10
(b)			–1.80	
	$4	3		12
(c)			–1.00	
	$3	4		12
(d)			–0.55	
	$2	5		10
(e)			–0.27	
	$1	6		6

Range (a) Along the range labeled (a) in the table, price declines from $6 to $5. The change in price, ΔP, is –$1. To convert that change into a percentage change *($\Delta P/P$)*, a base (P) is needed. Either the prechange price ($6) or the postchange price ($5) can serve as a base. To avoid bias and ambiguity, we use the **midpoint** between them, or $5 1/2 = $11/2. The percentage change in price (the denominator in the elasticity formula) is then:

$$\frac{-\Delta P}{P} = \frac{-1}{11/2} = -2/11$$

Over the same range, quantity increased from 1 to 2 units—that is, by 1: $\Delta Q = 1$. To convert that change into a percentage change, a base (Q) must be used. Again, we employ the midpoint between the pre- and postchange (between 1 and 2) as a base: $Q = 1\ 1/2 = 3/2$. The percentage change in quantity (the numerator of the elasticity formula) is:

$$\frac{\Delta Q}{Q} = \frac{1}{3/2} = \frac{2}{3}$$

Combining the two results, we obtain the demand elasticity over range (a):

$$\eta_D = \frac{\Delta Q/Q}{\Delta P/P} = \frac{2/3}{-2/11} = -11/3 = -3\,2/3 \cong /3.67/$$

(The last number is expressed in "absolute value," so as to disregard the negative sign.)

The Appendix to this chapter presents the elasticity calculations for ranges (b) – (e), the results of which are entered in the third column of Table 7–1. The student should review these calculations at this time. The following discussion often ignores the negative sign.

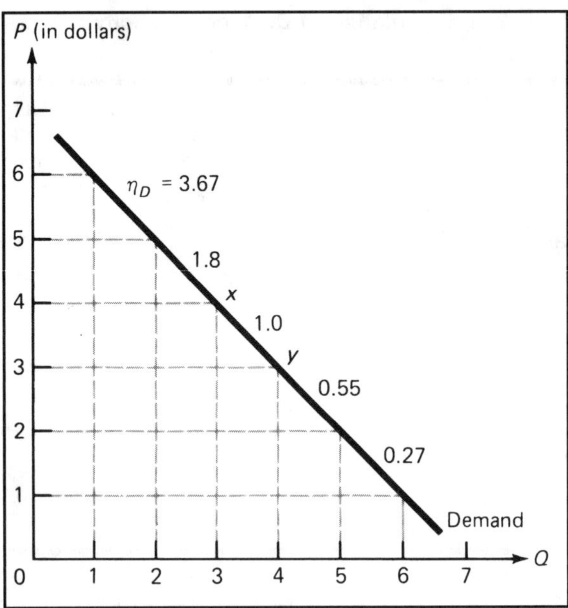

Figure 7–3 Elasticity Along a Hypothetical Demand Curve: Demand elasticity varies along a straight-line demand curve: It is unitary in the middle range (assuming that the curve stretches between the two axes), higher than 1 above it, and lower than 1 below it.

Figure 7–3 presents the hypothetical demand curve of Table 7–1 along with the elasticity results, expressed in *absolute values*, inserted in the respective ranges. Clearly, the *elasticity varies along a straight-line demand curve*. This is so because it is defined as *a ratio of two percentages* and not a ratio of two values ($\Delta Q/\Delta P$). Only the letter ratio is constant over a straight line.

One advantage of defining the elasticity concept as a ratio of two percentages is that the result is independent of the unit of measurement. To see this, assume for a moment that the price values in Table 7–1 were expressed in terms of cents rather than dollars, so that the numbers in the first column were 600, 500, 400, 300, 200, and 100. Consider range (b):

$\Delta P = -100$; P (midpoint between 500 and 400) = 450
Percentage change in price = $\Delta P/P = -\ 100/450 = 2/9$
$\Delta Q = 1$; Q (midpoint between 2 and 3) = 2 1/2 = 5/2

$$\text{Percentage change in quantity} = \frac{\Delta Q}{Q} = \frac{1}{5/2} = 2/5$$

$$\eta_D = \frac{\Delta Q/Q}{\Delta P/P} = \frac{2/5}{-2/9} = -9/5 = -1.8 = /1.8/$$

The elasticity result is not affected by the change in the unit of measurement. If, on the other hand, elasticity were defined as the ratio of two quantities, $\Delta Q/\Delta P$ (equivalent to the slope of the demand curve), then the calculations in terms of dollars (as in Table 7–1) would yield

$\Delta Q/\Delta P = 1/{-1} = -1$. But by the use of cents instead of dollars to express prices, the results would be different:

$$\Delta Q/\Delta P = 1/{-100} = /0.01/$$

The use of **percentages frees the concept of elasticity from dependence on the unit of measurement and makes it comparable across demand for different commodities** with differing units of measurement. We can thus compare the elasticity of demand for houses (expressed in thousands of dollars per unit) with the elasticity of demand for gasoline (expressed in cents per gallon) with the elasticity of demand for wheat (expressed in dollars per bushel), and so on.

Returning to Figure 7–1, we observe that for a straight-line demand curve, elasticity exceeds 1 (in absolute value) at the upper range, is below 1 at the lower range, and equals 1 in the middle. With a little imagination, this result can be extended further. Had the demand curve been extended at both ends to intersect the two axes, then elasticity would equal /1/ at the midpoint of the demand curve, be greater than /1/ at the upper half, and be smaller than /1/ at the lower half.

Demand elasticity and TR: A reduction in price will increase, leave unchanged, or decrease TR if demand elasticity is greater than, equal to, or lower than one.

Demand Elasticity and Total Revenue

To explore the significance of these three ranges, we fill in the total-revenue (fourth) column of Table 7–1, by multiplying price and quantity in each row. Consider range (c), over which the elasticity is unity, and recall that the elasticity is a ratio of two percentage changes. The number one means that the numerator and denominator are equal; in other words, the percentage change in price equals the percentage change in quantity. Since price and quantity move in opposite directions, this is equivalent to saying that the increase in quantity (from 3 to 4 units in Table 7–1) is exactly sufficient to offset the fact that each unit now sells for less ($3 instead of $4 per unit). This leaves their product, $P \times Q$ (total revenue) unchanged at $12. The rectangular areas under the demand curve at prices $4 and $3 are the same, as can be verified by observing the two areas, under points x and y, in Figure 7–3. This then is the **significance of unitary elasticity: Total revenue is constant as price changes over that range.**

In the upper part of the demand curve, **elasticity exceeds 1**. In terms of the ratio: Percentage change in quantity/Percentage change in price, this means that the numerator is greater than the denominator. As price declines and quantity rises, the increase in quantity is *more than sufficient* to offset the fact that each unit sells for less. **Total revenue increases with a reduction in price.** This can be verified by inspecting the areas under the demand curve of Figure 7–3: As price declines from 5 to 4, the area rises from 10 to 12.

In the lower half of the demand curve, **the elasticity is less than 1**. In terms of the ratio, the denominator is greater than the numerator. **As price declines and quantity rises,** the increase in quantity is *not sufficient* to compensate for the fact that each unit now sells for less. **Total revenue declines.** This the reader can verify by inspecting the area under the

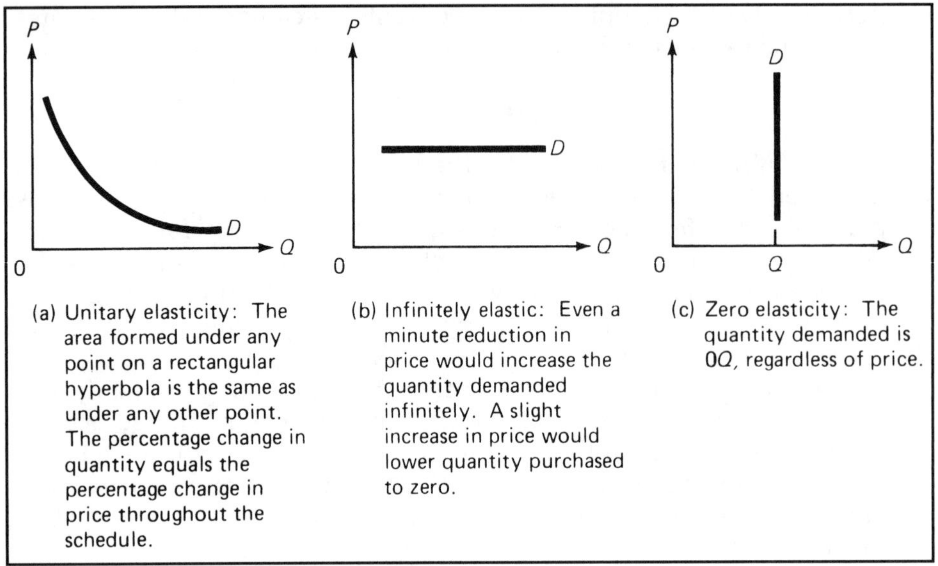
P
D
Q
0
P
D
Q
0
P
D
Q
0
Q
(a) Unitary elasticity: The area formed under any point on a rectangular hyperbola is the same as under any other point. The percentage change in quantity equals the percentage change in price throughout the schedule.
(b) Infinitely elastic: Even a minute reduction in price would increase the quantity demanded infinitely. A slight increase in price would lower quantity purchased to zero.
(c) Zero elasticity: The quantity demanded is 0Q, regardless of price.

Figure 7–4 Three Demand Curves

demand curve of Figure 7–3: As price *declines* from $2 to $1, total revenue *declines* from $10 to $6.

When the demand elasticity is greater than 1, total revenue changes in an opposite direction to price; it rises as price declines and declines as price rises. When the demand elasticity is smaller than 1, total revenue changes in the same direction as price; it declines when price declines and rises when price rises. When the demand elasticity is 1, total revenue is invariant to the change in price; it remains constant when price changes in either direction. Total revenue reaches its maximum where the demand elasticity is 1. We call the three cases, respectively, *relatively elastic demand, relatively inelastic demand,* and *demand of unitary elasticity.* This fills the gap of indeterminacy expressed in Chapter 4, when it was not possible to know what happens to total revenue as the equilibrium point moves up or down the demand curve. Total revenue rises if the movement *down* the demand curve occurs over the elastic range. It declines if the *downward* movement is over the inelastic range. The reverse holds for a movement up the demand curve. The student is invited to go back to Chapter 4 and relate the change in TR to the demand elasticity in the cases where the ΔTR was classified as indeterminate.

A demand curve along which the demand elasticity is unity at all points is a rectangular hyperbola (Figure 7–4a), under which the area (total revenue) is the same at all points. Demand is said to be infinitely elastic when the demand curve is horizontal, because in that case, the percentage change in price (denominator) is zero (Figure 7–4b). On the other hand, a vertical demand curve, where quantity is unchanged, portrays zero elasticity (Figure 7–4c).[1] Finally, recall that elasticity varies along a straight-line

---

[1]Infinity and zero are difficult concepts. To avoid confusion, the student may wish to draw several alternative demand curves, *gradually approaching* a horizontal line in the first place and a vertical line in the second, and then examine their elasticity properties.

demand curve. Therefore, when economists draw two straight-line demand curves and characterize the flatter one as more elastic, such a statement must be construed as a loose description of the situation.

What Determines Demand Elasticity

Substitutes: Availability of good substitutes for a product is one factor that determine its demand elasticity: The better the substitutes, the higher the demand elasticity. Other factors that determine elasticity include the size of the good relative to the consumer's budget, and how dispensable it is. Elasticity is higher in the long run than in the short run.

Three characteristics of the product determine the elasticity of demand for it. First is the availability of good **substitutes** for the commodity. The more readily available they are, the more likely is the average consumer to switch to the substitute products as the price of the commodity in question rises, and the more elastic is the demand for that commodity. As its price rises, the quantity taken declines substantially, since consumers switch to substitute products. Demand for Coca-Cola, for which substitute beverages are available, is likely to be more elastic than demand for gasoline, for which there is no substitute (the quantity consumed can decline only through reduced driving). Second, the more **dispensable** the product (easy to do without), the more elastic is the demand likely to be. Third, the smaller the item in question is in the consumer's budget, the less elastic the demand for it is likely to be. A case in point is salt. Even the doubling of its price is unlikely to induce consumers to lower the quantity of salt they purchase.

For all products, demand is likely to be more elastic in the long run than in the short run. Consider the demand for gasoline. In the short run, consumers can respond to a rise in price only by curtailing their driving. In the long run, they can drive less *and* in addition replace their vehicles by smaller or more gasoline-efficient cars. Then response in the long run to a given price increase is likely to be greater than in the short run.

Because the size of the elasticity is important in many policy issues economists have spent much effort in estimating it for many products. Examples of demand elasticities in the United States are: gasoline –0.5; beef –1; and automobiles –2. Observe for example the case of airline traffic. For many years, the nation's airlines believed that the demand elasticity for their service was low. Consequently, they resisted any reduction in fares. When fares were reduced in the 1980s, the airlines found that the elasticity was rather high, and they started flying full planes.

ELASTICITY OF SUPPLY

Parallel to the concept of demand elasticity is the elasticity of supply, which measures the response of suppliers to price change. It is defined as:

$$\eta_s = \frac{\text{Percentage change in the quantity supplied}}{\text{Percentage change in price}}$$

$$= \frac{\%\Delta Q_s}{\%\Delta P} = \frac{\Delta Q_s/Q_s}{\Delta P/P} = \frac{\Delta Q_s}{\Delta P} \bullet \frac{P}{Q_s}$$

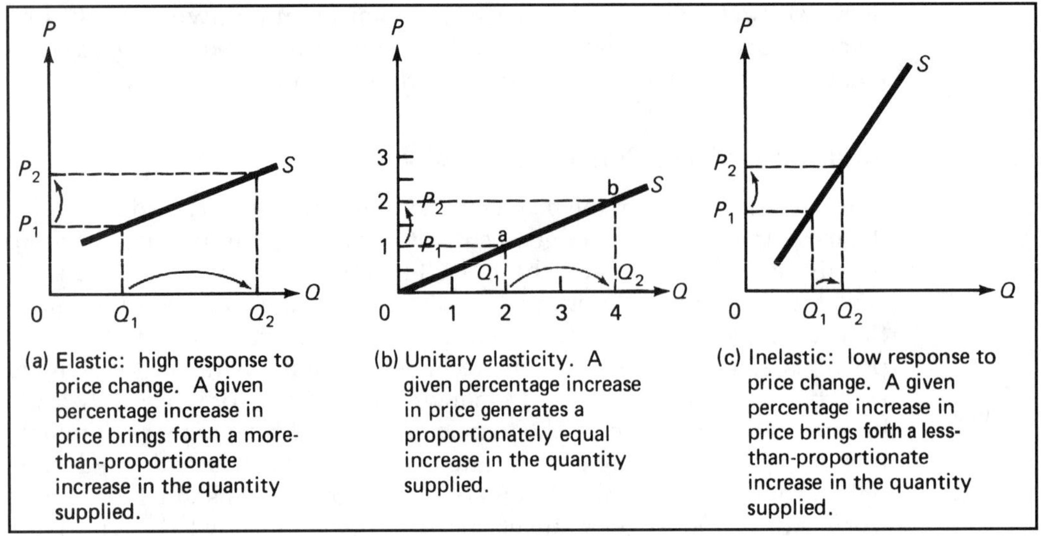
P
P2
P1
S
Q
0
Q1
Q2
(a) Elastic: high response to price change. A given percentage increase in price brings forth a more-than-proportionate increase in the quantity supplied.
P
3
2
1
P2
P1
a
b
S
Q1
Q2
Q
0
1
2
3
4
(b) Unitary elasticity. A given percentage increase in price generates a proportionately equal increase in the quantity supplied.
P
S
P2
P1
Q
0
Q1 Q2
(c) Inelastic: low response to price change. A given percentage increase in price brings forth a less-than-proportionate increase in the quantity supplied.

Figure 7–5 Supply Curves on Various Elasticities

Because the price and the quantity supplied move in the same direction, the supply elasticity is positive. Since there is no need to repeat the computations of the preceding section, Figure 7–5 merely illustrates various supply curves. The reader can compare the three quantity responses to an identical price change, from P_1 to P_2. Vertical and horizontal supply curves portray zero and infinite supply elasticities respectively.

A straight-line supply curve that extends to the origin is of unitary elasticity. To illustrate this, we measure the supply elasticity between points *a* and *b* in Figure 7–5(b).

$$\Delta Q = 4 - 2 = 2;\ Q_{\text{base}} = 3;\ \%\Delta Q = \frac{\Delta Q}{Q} = \frac{2}{3}$$

$$\Delta P = 1;\ P_{\text{base}} = 1\text{-}1/2 = 3/2;\ \%\Delta P = \frac{1}{3/2} = 2/3$$

$$\eta_s = \frac{\%\Delta Q}{\%\Delta P} = \frac{2/3}{2/3} = 1$$

Supply elasticity is measured in the same fashion as demand elasticity except that it relates to the quantity supplied. Because price and quantity move in the same direction along a supply curve, supply elasticity is positive. Supply elasticity equals 1 along a supply ray from the origin.

Energy production can be used to illustrate the importance of supply elasticity. There is no doubt but that a rise in the price of oil and natural gas would stimulate output. The question is, By how much? How vigorous will be the supply response to a price increase? It was seen in Chapter 5 that the **supply elasticity** *is greater in the long run* (when the capital stock and the number of firms can be changed) *than in the short run* (when only the intensity of utilization of the fixed capital can be changed). Estimates of the elasticities in both the short and the long run are necessary for policy formulation.

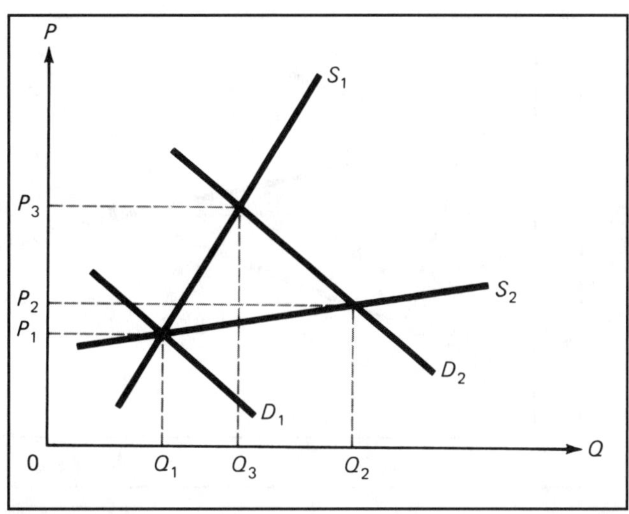

Figure 7–6 Comparative Effect of a Rise in Demand from D_1 to D_2 on Price, under Elastic (S_2) and Inelastic (S_1) Supply: Price rises more and quantity less under the inelastic supply; a substantial price boost is required to induce producers to expand output significantly.

APPLICATION: ELASTICITIES AND PRICE STABILITY

Price stability: Highly elastic (inelastic) demand, and supply generate a stable (unstable) market price, because a small (large) price change is required to accommodate a given change in quantity supplied or demanded.

The greater the elasticities of supply and demand in the market for a given commodity, the more stable the price of the product. The general notion behind this proposition is simple: With high elasticities, it takes a small price change to induce changes in the quantities supplied or demanded, when such changes are called for in the marketplace. Consequently, prices do not vary much.

Specifically, Figure 7–6 compares the effect of a rise in demand (from D_1 to D_2) on market price under elastic and inelastic supply conditions. When supply is elastic (S_2), it takes a relatively small increase in price (from P_1 to P_2) to bring forth the greater quantity desired by consumers (quantity rises from Q_1 to Q_2). By contrast, when supply is inelastic (S_1), it requires a much greater increase in price (from P_1 to P_3) to satisfy the expanded demand, with equilibrium quantity rising only from Q_1 to Q_3. A parallel result would obtain for a decrease in demand from D_2 to D_1. In short, the more elastic the supply, the more stable the price.

Figure 7–7 considers the case of an increase in supply (from S_1 to S_2) under two alternative demand conditions. When demand is elastic (D_2), it takes a relatively small decline in price (from P_1 to P_2) to induce consumers to purchase the increased quantity offered, with equilibrium quantity rising from Q_1 to Q_2. In contrast, when demand is inelastic (D_1), the price reduction required to absorb the expanded supply is much larger, all the way from P_1 to P_3. And the equilibrium quantity rises only from Q_1 to Q_3. A parallel result obtains for a decrease in supply from S_2 to S_1. The more elastic the demand, the more stable the price.

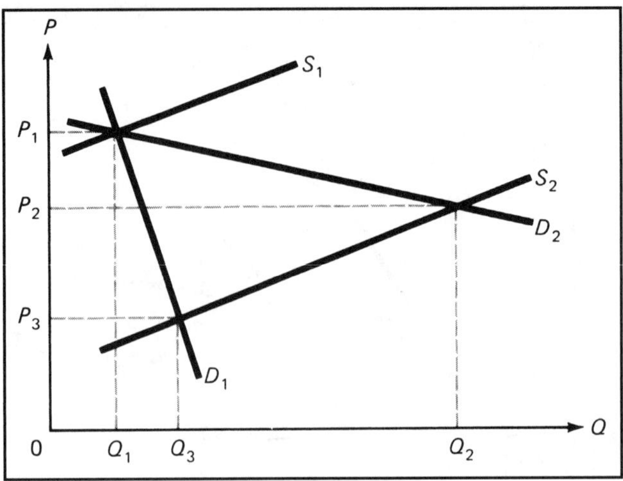

Figure 7–7 Comparative Effect of a Rise in Supply on Price under Elastic (D_2) and Inelastic (D_1) Demand: Price declines more and quantity rises less under the inelastic demand: A large price reduction is required to induce buyers to expand purchases significantly.

This discussion is summarized in Figure 7–8. Panel *a* describes a market for a commodity characterized by relatively inelastic supply and demand. The reader is invited to shift either of the two curves and examine the effect on price: Price will show sizable fluctuations. By contrast, panel *b* describes a market for a commodity where supply and demand are relatively elastic. Shifting either of the curves would generate very modest price changes: The price is reasonably stable.

Intuitively, you can see the desirability of having elastic supply and demand conditions. For the functioning of the price system depends on the response of economic agents (demanders and suppliers) to price change. The greater the response, the more smoothly the system functions. Agriculture is a sector of the economy characterized by inelastic supply and

Figure 7–8 Elastic and Inelastic Schedules: Prices are more stable in markets characterized by elastic supply and demand than in markets governed by inelastic supply and demand. It requires a smaller change in price in the first case than in the second to induce the requisite change in quantity (either demanded or supplied).

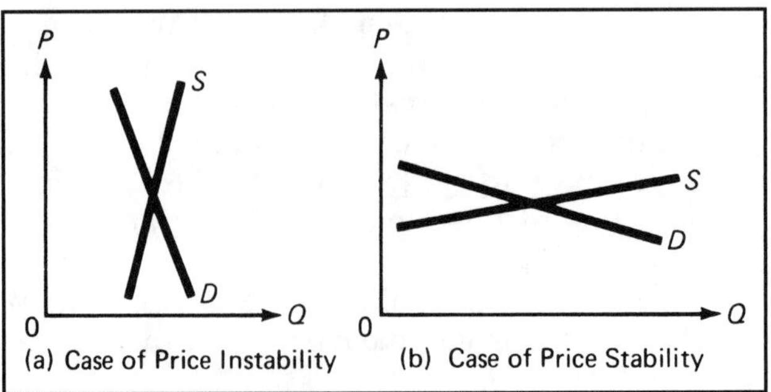

demand, and with them, unstable prices. Complaints are often heard about violent price fluctuations of farm products. Hence, farm organizations demand the introduction of price-stabilization schemes by the government.

A second application of the elasticities concept is presented in the appendix at the end of this chapter.

SUMMARY

Elasticities of demand and supply measure the degree of response of consumers and producers, respectively, to price change.

Demand elasticity is defined as a ratio of the *percentage* change in the quantity of the product demanded to the *percentage* change in its price. Because price and quantity move in opposite directions, demand elasticity is negative. The elasticity varies along a straight-line demand schedule: it is higher than /1/ (or relatively elastic) over the top half; below /1/ (or relatively inelastic) over the bottom half; and /1/ (unitary elasticity) in the middle. A demand curve shaped as a rectangular hyperbola has unitary elasticity throughout. Elasticity is zero or infinite in the case of vertical or horizontal demand curves, respectively.

Factors that determine the size of the demand elasticity include (1) the availability of good substitutes for the product in question, (2) how dispensable the product is, and (3) the importance of the product in the consumer budget.

In turn, demand elasticity determines the behavior of total revenue ($P \times Q$) as price changes. When demand is relatively elastic (inelastic), a decline in price elicits a greater (smaller) than proportionate rise in the quantity purchased, so that total revenue rises (declines). Under unitary elasticity, price and quantity change in the same proportion (but in opposite directions) so that total revenue is invariant with respect to price.

The elasticity of *supply* is the percentage change in the quantity supplied divided by the percentage change in price. Because price and quantity supplied move in the same direction, this elasticity is positive. It is larger in the long run than in the short run. The flatter the supply curve—the greater the elasticity. A unitary supply elasticity is represented by a straight line from the origin. Zero and infinite supply elasticities are represented, respectively, by vertical and horizontal supply curves.

In turn, the size of the elasticities is important for a variety of business decisions and policy issues. It was shown to be a determining factor in the degree of price stability.

QUESTIONS AND PROBLEMS

1. Given the following demand schedule, complete the total-revenue and elasticity columns. Compute the demand elasticity over each portion, and determine in which portion the demand is elastic, if at all; in what portion unitary elasticity exists, if at all; in what portion the demand is inelastic, if at all.

Price per Unit	Quantity of Units	Total Revenue	Elasticity of Demand
$.90	400		
.80	500		
.70	600		
.60	700		
.50	800		
.40	900		
.30	1,000		
.20	1,100		
.10	1,200		

Draw the demand curve, and insert in your chart the elasticities you computed in the relevant ranges.

2. What is meant by the statement, "The elasticity of demand for gasoline is –0.2 in the short run and –0.7 in the long run"? Why should the figures differ with the length of the run?
3. Recall the distinction between short-run and long-run supply made in Chapter 5. Would you expect supply elasticity to vary with the length of the run? If so, in which direction? Why?
4. Draw two panels of demand and supply curves as in Figure 7–8. Increase the demand (holding supply constant) by the same (horizontal) amount on both panels. What happens to the price in each case?

   Now increase the supply (holding demand constant) by the same (horizontal) amount on both panels. What happens to the price in each case?

   What conclusion can you draw from that experiment?

APPENDIX TO CHAPTER 7

Calculations of Demand Elasticities for Table 7–1

Range (b)

$\Delta P = -1$; P (midpoint between 5 and 4) = 4 1/2 = 9/2

Percentage change in price = $\dfrac{\Delta P}{P} = \dfrac{-1}{9/2} = -2/9$

$\Delta Q = 1$; Q (midpoint between 2 and 3) = 2 1/2 = 5/2

Percentage change in quantity = $\dfrac{\Delta Q}{Q} = \dfrac{1}{5/2} = 2/5$

$$\eta_D = \frac{\Delta Q/Q}{-\Delta P/P} = \frac{2/5}{-2/9} = -9/5 = -1\,4/5 = -1.8 = /1.8/$$

Range (c)

$\Delta P = -1$; P (midpoint between 4 and 3) = 3 1/2 = 7/2

Percentage change in price = $\dfrac{\Delta P}{P} = \dfrac{-1}{7/2} = -2/7$

$\Delta Q = 1$; Q (midpoint between 3 and 4) $= 3\,^1/_2 = 7/2$

$$\text{Percentage change in quantity} = \frac{\Delta Q}{Q} = \frac{1}{7/2} = -2/7$$

$$\eta_D = \frac{\Delta Q/Q}{-\Delta P/P} = \frac{2/7}{-2/7} = -1 = /1/$$

Range (d)

$\Delta P = -1$; P (midpoint between 3 and 2) $= 2\,^1/_2 = 5/2$

$$\text{Percentage change in price} = \frac{\Delta P}{P} = \frac{-1}{5/2} = -2/5$$

$\Delta Q = 1$; Q (midpoint between 4 and 5) $= 4\,1/2 = 9/2$

$$\eta_D = \frac{\Delta Q/Q}{-\Delta P/P} = -\frac{2/9}{2/5} = -5/9 \cong /0.55/$$

Range (e)

$\Delta P = -1$; P (midpoint between 2 and 1) $= 1\,^1/_2 = 3/2$

$$\text{Percentage change in price} = \frac{\Delta P}{P} = \frac{-1}{3/2} = -2/3$$

$\Delta Q = 1$; Q (midpoint between 5 and 6) $= 5\,1/2 = 11/2$

$$\text{Percentage change in quantity} = \frac{\Delta Q}{Q} = \frac{1}{11/2} = 2/11$$

$$\eta_D = \frac{2/11}{-2/3} = -3/11 \cong /0.27/$$

Application of the Elasticities Concept

The Incidence of Sales Taxes

A sales tax is a tax levied on the product at the time of sale. But since only people and not products can pay taxes, the tax is shifted either to the consumer or to the producer. As far as can be observed, it is added onto the price of the product, so the buyer pays the tax. In other words, the tax appears to be passed on in its entirety to the consumer. But this impression is often more apparent than real. Consider a 10 percent sales tax on men's suits. It would increase the price of suits, and consequently fewer suits would be bought. But that reduction would force producers to absorb part of the tax, by lowering the price they receive. In other words, the market mechanism causes a split in the burden of the sales tax between consumers and producers. And the word *incidence* is used to measure that split: How much is passed forward to the consumers and how much is passed backward to the producers?

A sales tax can be imposed as a certain percentage of price (for example, 5 percent of the price) or as a fixed dollar amount per unit (for example, $100 per unit) regardless of price. These are known respectively as an *ad valorem* and a *specific* tax.

In Figure 7–9, a sales tax in a fixed dollar amount is imposes on product X (a specific tax). It is measured by the segment t on the vertical axis. Prior to the tax, suppliers were willing to supply quantity $0Q_1$ for price $0P_1$. Now the government adds a tax, in the amount t, so that quantity $0Q_1$ would be supplied only for $0P_2$ ($0P_1$ plus the tax, t). Likewise, quantity $0Q_2$ was first supplied for price $0P_3$. After the tax, it would be supplied only for $0P_4$ ($0P_3$ plus the tax, t). The upshot is that supply curve S shifts to

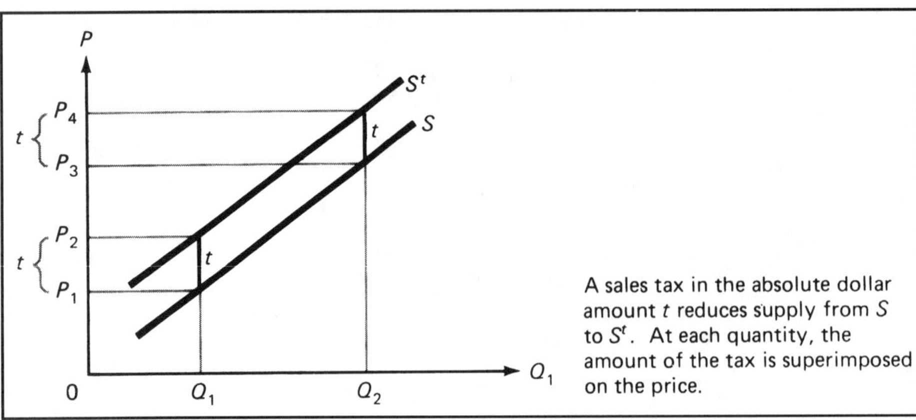

Figure 7–9 Marked for Product *X*

S^t, where the vertical distance between the two is equal to the tax, t. S and S^t parallel each other, where S^t is the tax-ridden supply schedule. That change can be reinterpreted as a leftward shift in supply: At any given price, less will be supplied than before the tax. In sum, a *sales tax decreases supply.*

In the (more realistic) ad valorem case (a tax levied as a percentage of price), the supply schedule shifts in the same direction, but the two curves are not parallel. Rather, the vertical distance between them widens as we move to the right, because a fixed *percentage* is applied to a larger base as the base price rises. And that translates into a greater absolute dollar amount.

This is shown in Figure 7–10, where a 33⅓ percent sales tax is represented by a decrease in supply from S to S^t. Thus, quantity Q_1 was offered by producers at price P_1 before the imposition of the tax. After the government levies the tax, suppliers offer that quantity only at price P_1^t, with the government collecting $P_1\, P_1^t$. In a similar vein,

Figure 7–10 Effect of an Ad Valorem Sales Tax: At each quantity, the fixed *percentage* tax is superimposed on the price. The vertical distance between S and S^t widens, because the higher the base price, the greater the absolute dollar amount of the tax.

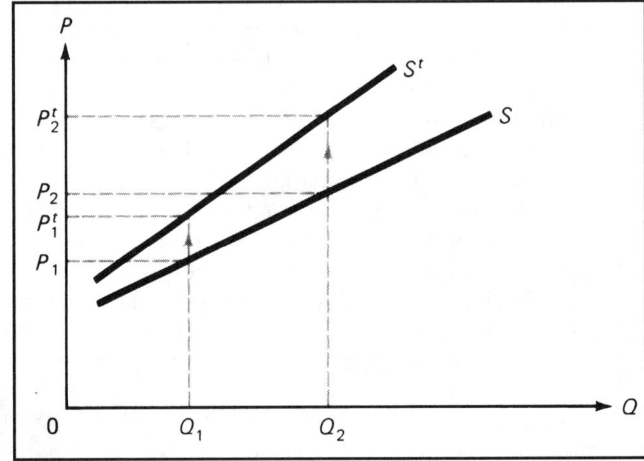

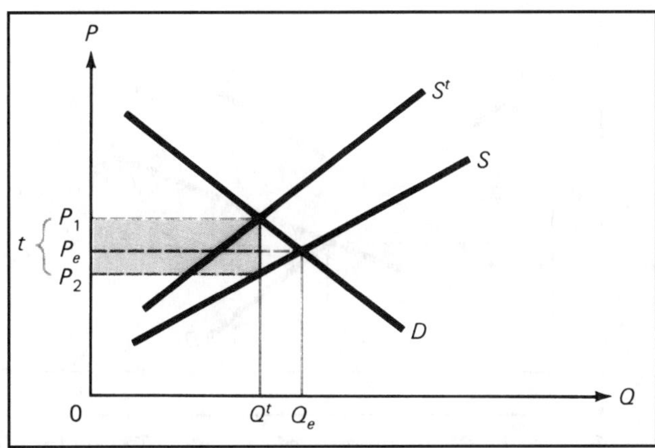

Figure 7–11 Incidence of an Ad Valorem Sales Tax: Supply declines from S to S^t. Price rises from P_e to P_1, of which the government receives t and producers receive P_2. Quantity declines from Q^e to Q^t. Consumers pay P_eP_1 of the tax; producers absorb P_eP_2 per unit.

quantity Q_2 will be offered at an after-tax price of P_2^t, with the price being pushed up in the direction of the arrow by the amount of the tax. The tax equals the vertical distance between the two supply curves at quantity Q_2. In this fashion, the entire supply curve is moved from S to S^t.

Sales tax burden: A sales tax is split between the buyer and the seller according to the relative elasticities of demand and supply.

Figure 7–11 combines this shift in supply with a demand curve. Prior to the tax, the price paid by consumers equaled that received by the sellers, P_e. Quantity sold and bought was Q_e. After imposition of the tax, the two prices are no longer the same, the difference between them being collected by the government. The new equilibrium is determined by shifting the supply curve to S^t. The quantity traded declines to Q^t. That is the quantity that consumers are willing to purchase at price P_1 (determined by D) and that sellers are willing to sell at P_2 (determined by S). The difference between the two prices ($P_1 - P_2 = t$) is the tax per unit, and the tax (t) times the number of units sold ($0Q^t$) is the total tax revenue to the government. It is shown by the shaded rectangle. The incidence of the tax is observed by comparing the pretax price (P_e) with the post-tax prices paid by consumers and received by producers: P_eP_1 of the tax (per unit) is passed on to consumers, and P_eP_2 of the tax (per unit) is passed on to producers (the price they receive declines by that amount). In Figure 7–11, the burden is about evenly divided between the two groups.

It is the distribution of the tax burden between producers and consumers that is determined by the relative elasticities of demand and supply. Given the demand schedule, the more elastic the supply curve, the less of the burden is borne by producers and the more of it borne by consumers. Highly elastic supply means that a considerable expansion of output is induced by a small rise in price. But it also implies that a considerable contraction of output is induced by a small reduction in price. Producers are unwilling to "take a beating" on the price they receive; they would rather withdraw from the market. This outcome is shown in Figure 7–12. The consumers bear P_1P_e of the tax (per unit), and the producers bear only P_2P_e. In the extreme case where the supply curve is infinitely elastic, the entire burden is borne by consumers and none by producers.

Conversely, given the supply curve, the more elastic the demand, the more of the burden is borne by the producers. For highly elastic demand means that a large reduction in the quantity purchased is triggered by even a small rise in price. Consumers are unwilling to "take a beating" on the price. They would either consume less or switch to substitute products. This outcome is shown in Figure 7–13. Consumers pay only P_eP_1 of the tax (per unit), and producers pay P_eP_2. On the other hand, under highly inelastic

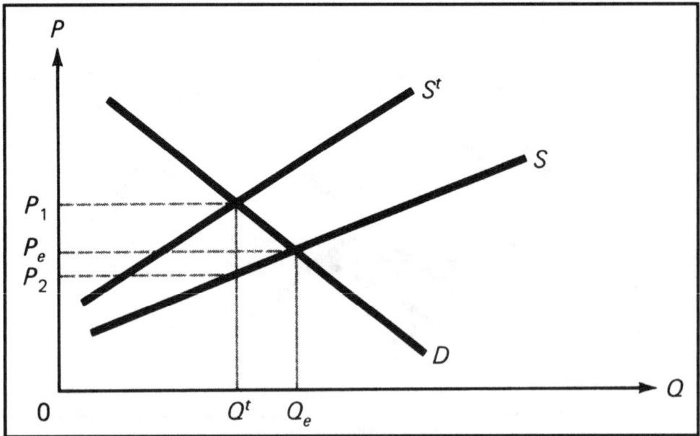

Figure 7–12 Incidence of a Sales Tax with Highly Elastic Supply: Given the demand curve, the more elastic the supply the greater the proportion of the tax paid by consumers: Producers would rather withdraw from the market than absorb a large price cut. In this chart, consumers pay P_eP_1 of the tax; producers absorb only P_eP_2.

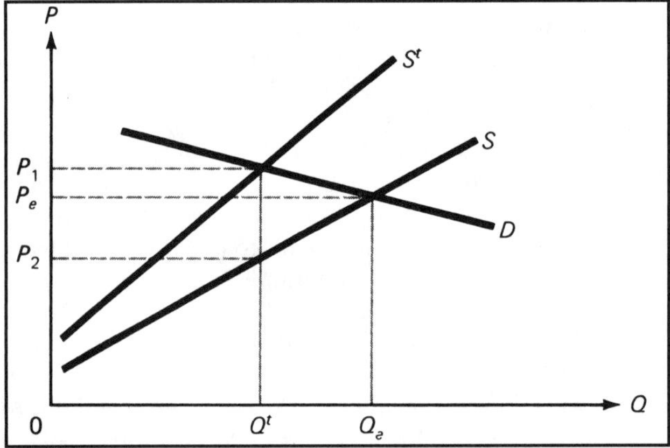

Figure 7–13 Incidence of a Sales Tax with Highly Elastic Demand: Given the supply schedule, the more elastic the demand, the smaller the proportion of the tax paid by consumers: They would rather withdraw from the market than pay a much higher price. In this chart producers absorb P_eP_2 of the tax; consumers pay on P_eP_1 per unit.

demand, the consumers pay most of the tax. This can be verified by drawing a chart with an identical supply curve to that in Figure 7–13, but with a very inelastic demand.

Clearly, it is the elasticities of supply and demand, *relative to each other*, that determine the incidence of a sales tax.

PROBLEM

Using supply and demand curves in the markets for (a) small cars and (b) large cars, show the effect of a tax levied on large cars on price and quantity on both markets. Why can such a tax be used as an energy-conservation measure?

Applications of Supply and Demand: Resource Allocation in a Competitive Market Economy

Supply and demand are powerful tools for understanding real-world phenomena. Several examples are presented below. In tackling each problem, one must first determine which curve or curves shift, and why. Examples start with short-run changes and then extend to long-run adjustments. They are designed to lead into a discussion of resource allocation. Purely competitive markets are assumed throughout.

SHORT-RUN ADJUSTMENTS

Effect of a Change in Income on the Market for Beef

A rise in income increases demand, as shown in Figure 4-4 with respect to automobiles. The same analysis applies to beef. As a result, the price of beef, its quantity sold, and total revenue rise. A reduction in income would have an opposite effect. A good the demand for which rises as income rises is referred to as **normal good**.

Normal good: A good, the demand for which rises when income rises.

Substitute: Two goods that are related in such a way that when the price of one good rises the demand for the other good increases.

Complement: Two goods that are related in such a way that when the price of one rises the demand for the other good declines.

Effect of a Weather Freeze in Florida on the Price of Apples in Europe

The uninitiated observer may think that there is no connection between Florida weather and European apple prices, but in fact there is a rather close relation. And that relation demonstrates the fact that national and, indeed, international markets are interrelated.

A one-year, nonrecurring freeze in Florida reduces the supply of Florida oranges. With a constant-demand curve, the worldwide price of oranges rises, since Florida is a major supplier of citrus fruits. Because oranges and apples are substitute goods in consumption, some consumers would switch from oranges to apples, as well as to other deciduous fruits. As the demand for apples rises, their price rises as well.

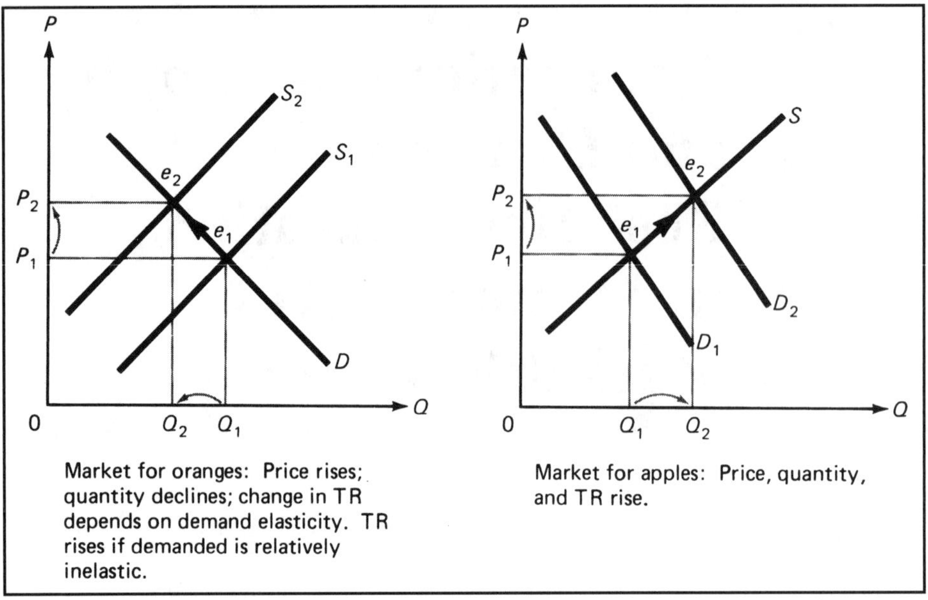

Figure 8–1 Effect on the Orange and Apple Market of a Florida Freeze: As supplies of oranges decline from S_1 to S_2 their price rises, inducing consumers to switch from oranges to apples. Demand for apples rises from D_1 to D_2.

All this is shown in Figure 8–1. In the orange market (shown in the left-hand panel), supply declines from S_1 to S_2. As a result, the price of oranges rises from $0P_1$ to $0P_2$; quantity sold declines from $0Q_1$ to $0Q_2$; and total revenue of the sellers changes from the area under equilibrium point e_1, to that under e_2: It rises if demand is relatively inelastic and declines if demand is relatively elastic. The rise in the price of oranges increases demand for apples (right-hand panel) from D_1 to D_2. Their price rises from $0P_1$ to $0P_2$; quantity rises from $0Q_1$ to $0Q_2$; and total revenue of the apple growers increases from the area under equilibrium point c_1 to that under e_2.

Effect of a Florida Freeze on the Market for Orange Juice and Orange Juice Cans

The rise in the price of oranges would have effects on other markets as well. Consider the market for orange juice. Since fresh oranges are the raw materials from which orange juice is made, a rise in their price reduces the supply of orange juice. In Figure 8–2, the market for oranges is shown in the left-hand panel, with effects similar to those in Figure 8–1. The center panel shows the market for orange juice, where the rise in the cost of oranges reduces supply from S_1 to S_2. Note, however that the decline in supply of orange juice is less than the decline in supply of oranges, because fresh oranges are only one factor input entering orange-juice production, the others being labor, machinery, and other materials, such as sugar. As a result, price rises, quantity declines, and TR of the growers

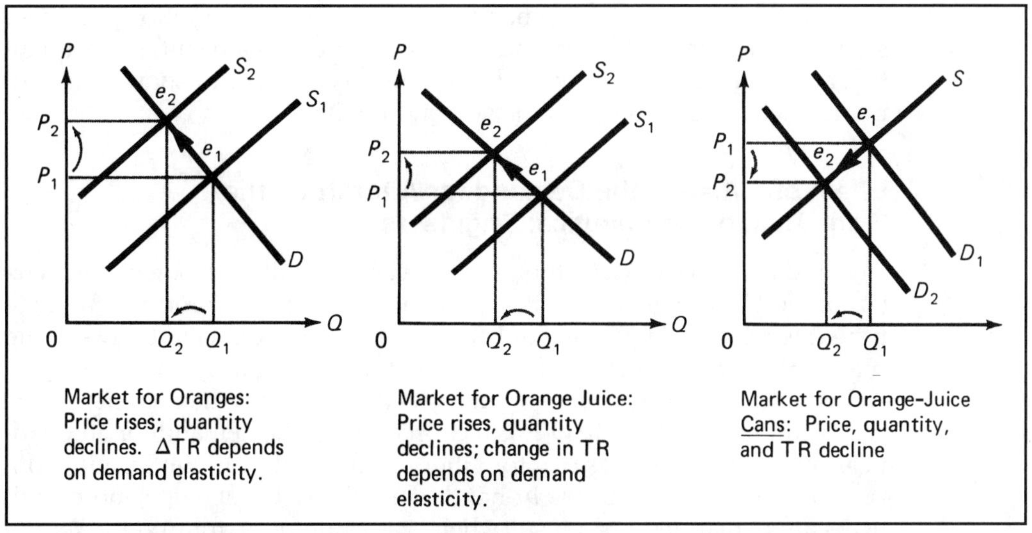

Figure 8–2 Effect of a Florida Freeze on the Markets for Orange Juice and Orange-Juice Cans: As supplies of oranges decline from S_1 to S_2, their price rises from P_1 to P_2. Because oranges are an input in orange-juice production, the price increases: lowers the supply of orange juice from S_1 to S_2, raises the price of orange juice from P_1 to P_2, and lowers their quantity from Q_1 to Q_2. Because cans are an input into orange-juice production, the demand for cans declines from D_1 to D_2 as the quantity of orange juice drops from Q_1 to Q_2.

changes from the area under equilibrium point e_1 to that under e_2: It rises if demand is relatively inelastic and declines if demand is relatively elastic.

Orange juice is marketed in frozen form in specialized cans and in other containers. Since less orange juice is produced, there is less need for cans, and the demand for them declines from D_1 to D_2 (right-hand panel of Figure 8–2). Moving down along a constant, positively sloped supply curve, price, quantity, and TR of the suppliers all decline. All inputs into orange-juice production, be they labor or materials, are affected in a similar manner. The demand for factor inputs is a **derived demand,** because it depends on (or is derived from) the demand for the product in the production of which the factor is used.

Derived demand: The demand for labor and capital to produce a product depends on the demand for the product.

There may be ripples in other markets caused by the Florida freeze. For example, because of the rise in the price of orange juice, there may be an increase in demand for pineapple juice—a substitute product in consumption. That would raise the price, quantity, and TR of pineapple growers. In turn, there would be a rise in demand for all factor inputs in the pineapple industry, and their price and quantity would rise. In other words, repercussions of any one change are felt in many markets.

Effect of a Large Rise in Tailors' Wage Rate on the Prices of Suits and Ties

A large boost in tailors' wage rates increases production costs in the suit industry. Supply of suits declines, their price rises, and quantity sold declines.

Suits and ties are complementary products in consumption. As fewer suits are purchased, the demand for ties declines. As a result, price, quantity, and total revenue decline. The student is advised to show diagrammatically the adjustments in the suit and tie markets.

Effect of a Rise in the Demand for Aircraft on the Wage Rate of Aeronautical Engineers

Demand for productive factors, such as various skills of labor, depends on (among other things) the demand for the product they produce. To illustrate this relation, suppose that because of a rise in demand by the flying public, the airlines increased their demand for aircraft from D_1 to D_2, as shown in the left-hand panel of Figure 8–3. This raises the quantity of aircraft produced from Q_1 to Q_2. As a consequence, the demand for aeronautical engineers (as well as that for other inputs used in aircraft production) rises from D_1 to D_2, on the right-hand panel. At each wage rate, more engineers are demanded. As a result, their wage rate rises from W_1 to W_2, and the number employed rises from Q_1 to Q_2.

It is seen in this example that the demand for an input (engineers) depends on the demand for its output. The same applies to any input; hence, it is called *derived* demand. Additionally, the demand for input such as labor (on a competitive market) depends on the price of inputs for which labor may be a *substitute.* For example, a rise in the price of energy increases demand for labor, because firms are led to substitute labor for energy. Some substitution of labor for energy did in fact occur in U.S. manufacturing industries in the 1970s, when, because of the sharp rise in the price of energy relative to that of other inputs, certain functions—formerly performed

Figure 8–3 A Rise in Demand for Aircraft Increases Demand for Aeronautical Engineers: As demand for aircraft rises from D_1 to D_2, the quantity manufactured increases from Q_1 to Q_2. That requires more engineers (and other inputs). Consequently, demand for engineers rises from D_1 to D_2.

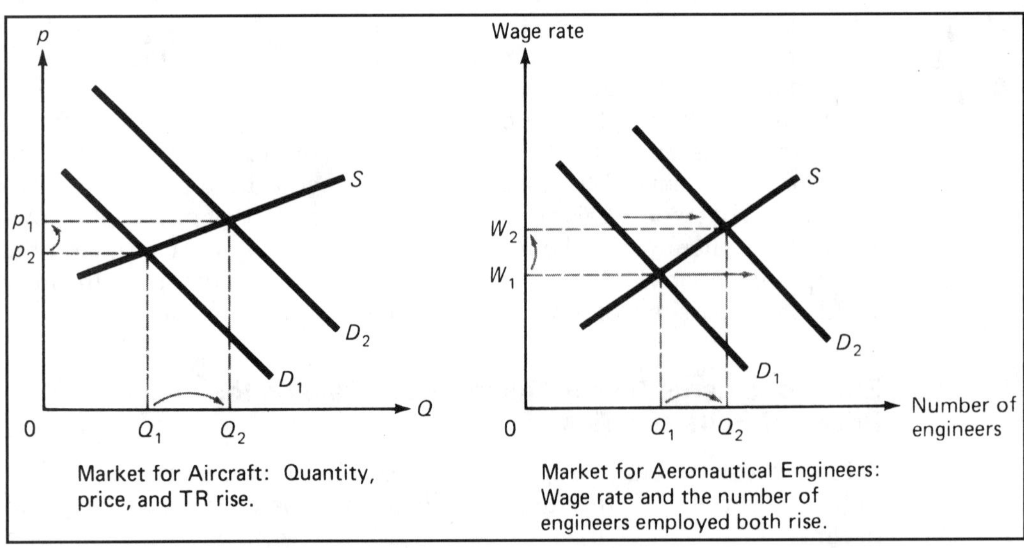

▶ PRICES OF PRODUCTIVE FACTORS

Prices of productive factors are determined on their respective markets through the demand and supply mechanism. Some people may consider it callous to treat labor as a commodity traded on a market. But it should be remembered that the subject is the *services* of labor, not the workers themselves. And indeed, there is a market for the services of each type of labor skill (such as assistant professors of economics): where the equilibrium price of labor (wage rate), and quantity are determined by supply and demand. However, in many industries wage rates are not determined by competitive markets, as assumed here. Rather, they are negotiated between unions and management in collective-bargaining agreements.

Suppose that a certain skill of labor is required to manufacture a product called a widget. The demand for labor by the widget manufacturers depends upon two factors: (1) How productive or efficient is labor in producing widgets? In part, that depends on how much machinery each worker has to work with. (2) How much are widgets worth in the marketplace? If no one wishes to purchase widgets, there would be no demand for widget-producing workers, no matter how efficient they are.

mechanically—came to be performed manually. Thus, the demand for labor rises (falls) with the rise (decline) in the price of inputs for which labor is used as a substitute.

Productive inputs—labor services in various skills, natural resources, capital, and entrepreneurial ability—are owned by people. Therefore, the corresponding factor remunerations—wages and salaries, rent, interest, and profit—that are determined on their respective markets accrue to people. They become the income of households, and indirectly they determine the distribution of income in society.

Effect of Antipollution Requirements on the Automobile Industry

In an attempt to reduce auto-exhaust pollution, Congress legislated the maximum amounts of pollution that may legally be emitted from cars. That restriction requires the installation of special antipollution equipment on automobiles, which in turn raises production costs. As a result, the supply of automobiles declines, their price rises, and the quantity sold declines.

Antipollution Requirements in Petrochemicals

Maximum allowable water and air pollution have been legislated for many industries. The petrochemical industry is an example of a high polluter that would be affected by such a law. If, for example, the law lowers supply and raises the price of synthetic rubber, it may cause rubber users, such as tire companies, to switch from synthetic to natural rubber, at least in part. This raises demand for natural rubber, increasing the price, quantity, and total revenue, as illustrated in Figure 8–1, where the markets for synthetic and natural rubber would appear on the left- and right-hand panels, respectively.

This example has a more general application. *A rise in the price of any commodity,* for whatever reason, *encourages the development of substitute products.* In the energy field, a rise in the price of oil would lead producers to expand output of petroleum, and at the same time would encourage output of substitute energy sources, such as coal, shale oil, nuclear energy, and perhaps solar energy. These new sources are expensive to develop. But as the price of conventional energy sources rises, it would become profitable to develop them. This possible substitution is a long-run constraint on the price action of the international OPEC oil cartel. Even though in the short run there is no good substitute for oil, in the long run there are several.

Multiple Factors Affecting the U.S. Automobile Industry

Suppose the following events occurred in mid-1999: (1) As a result of renegotiations of the labor contract between the United Auto Workers Union and the automobile companies, wage rates and/or workers' fringe benefits were reduced considerably. (2) Because of an across-the-board cut in the federal personal income tax and other reasons, there was a significant increase in income in the United States. (3) For various reasons, including an increase in the value of Japanese yen, there was a significant increase in the dollar price of Japanese cars. Let us trace the effect on the U.S. auto industry.

We begin with the original equilibrium P and Q in Figure 8–4. Event 1 increases the supply of American-made automobiles from S to S'. Event 2 increases demand for all cars, imports as well as U.S. makes. Demand for American cars rises from D to D'. Event 3 increases the demand for

Figure 8–4 The U.S. Car Market: Decline in UAW wage rates raises supply from S to S'. Rise in income raises demand from D to D'. The price increase of Japanese cars (substitutes) raises demand from D' to D''. As a result, equilibrium shifts from e to e': Quantity increases from Q to Q', but effect on price and TR is indeterminate.

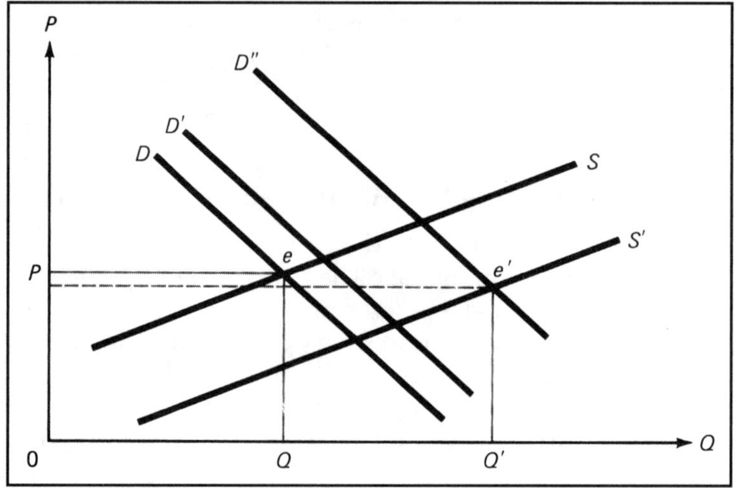

U.S.-made cars, from D' to D''. In the final equilibrium, e', the quantity sold, rises, but the effect on price is indeterminate.

Exchange rate: The price of one currency in terms of another. It is determined by demand for, and supply of, the foreign currency.

Foreign-Exchange Rates

A unique and important price is the foreign-exchange rate. It is the price of one national currency in terms of another. Thus, the U.S. dollar ($1) may be worth one European euro ($1=1€) or 100 Japanese yen ($1=¥100). These are two dollar-exchange rates. Each exchange rate has an inverse. If the dollar is worth 100 yen then one yen is worth 1 cent. Each exchange rate is determined by the supply of and demand for the currency in question, and it fluctuates with shifts in one of the curves or both.

Consider the market for euros in New York, where the dollar-euro exchange rate is determined. It is depicted diagrammatically in Figure 8-5. On the vertical (price) axis, we show the exchange rate defined as the dollar price of one euro. That price rises from $0.80 to $1.00 to $1.20. On the quantity axis, we show millions of euros purchased or sold.

Unlike the case with the demand for goods and services, Americans demand euros not for any utility or satisfaction value embodied in the euros themselves. Rather, they demand euros in order to purchase European goods and services and in order to invest in Europe. In turn, the supply of euros represents American exports to Europe and European investments in the United States. Despite these unique features, there is good reason to expect the supply and demand schedules to display normal slopes, as shown in Figure 8-5. The intersection of the two curves determines the market exchange rate ($1=1€) and the quantity of euros purchased and sold ($0Q_E$). But the demand and supply curves are subject to numerous influences that continuously move them up or down. And with those shifts come daily changes in the market exchange rate.

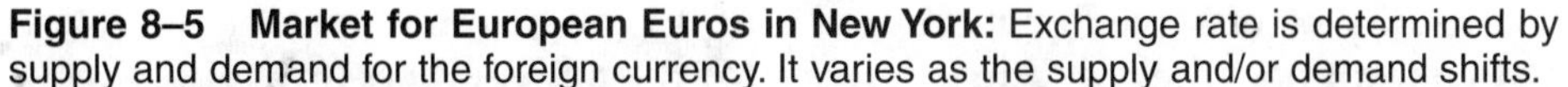

Figure 8–5 Market for European Euros in New York: Exchange rate is determined by supply and demand for the foreign currency. It varies as the supply and/or demand shifts.

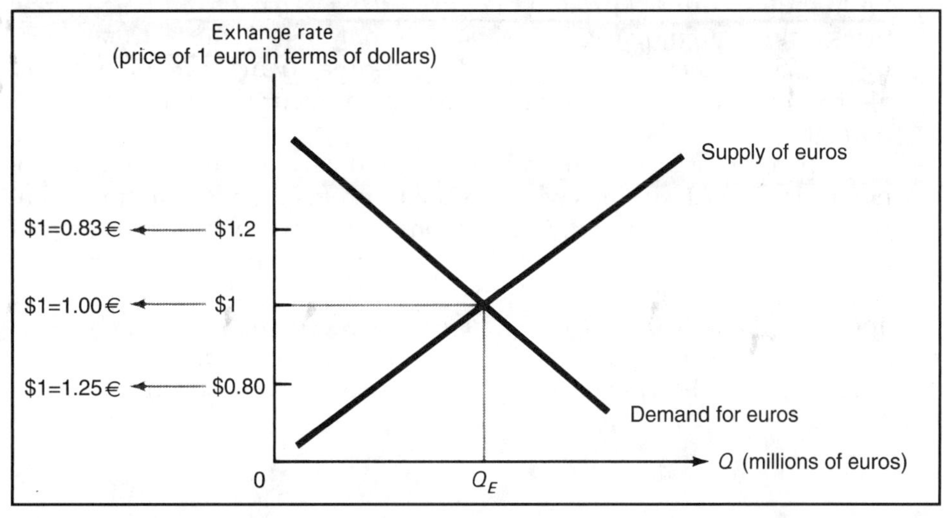

SHORT-RUN AND LONG-RUN CHANGES

Short Run (SR): A period of time in which only one input can vary. **Long Run (LR)** is a period of time in which all inputs can vary.

In the previous illustrations, no distinction was made between short-run and long-run adjustments in supply. It will be recalled that in the short run, the capital stock of firms (or productive capacity) is fixed, and only the intensity of utilization can vary. In the long run, firms can alter their capital stock, and the number of firms can change as well.

What gives rise to long-run variations in the capital stock? In a competitive-market economy, the motivating force is **profit**. But that answer requires elaboration. Profit, the return to entrepreneurship, is the difference between the firm's total revenue from selling its products and its total cost, which includes payments for labor, capital, and natural resources, as well as for materials purchased from other firms. In sum: *Profits = Total revenue – Total cost.*

Normal profit: Profit sufficient to induce the firm to stay in business without changing its size. *Economic profit* is profit above the level of normal profit. Its existence induces firms to expand, and new firms to enter the industry. Economic loss, or profit below normal profit, induces firms to contract and/or leave the industry.

We now make a conceptual distinction between two components of profit. **Normal profit** is the amount of profit exactly sufficient to induce the firm to stay in business and maintain its capacity at a constant size. A firm making exactly normal profit would not expand or contract its capacity, nor would it go out of business. Any profit in excess of, or less than, that level is called **above- or below-normal profit.** Thus:

$$\text{Profit} = \text{Normal profit} \begin{array}{l} + \text{ Above-normal profit, or economic profit} \\ - \text{ Below-normal profit, or economic loss} \end{array}$$

This distinction modifies the use of the term *profit*, introduced in Chapter 1. Economists include normal profit as a part of production costs. Thus, the $200 profit realized by our cucumber grower may contain $50 in normal profit and $150 in above-normal profit or **economic** profit. The division of profit into two categories may appear artificial, because the amount of normal profit varies between firms and industries and cannot readily be observed or measured. But it is an extremely useful analytical concept nonetheless: **The existence (or the appearance) of above-normal profit induces firms to expand their productive capacity and attracts new firms into the industry. Conversely, profit below the normal level induces firms to contract their productive capacity or leave the industry altogether.** Changes in either direction do not occur if profits are at their normal level.

Expansion of a perfectly competitive industry occurs as long as economic profit exists; it stops when economic profits drop to zero (the incentive to expand disappears). Contraction of an industry occurs as long as economic profits are negative or below zero (economic losses exist); it stops when economic profit returns to zero (the incentive to contract disappears). *In a perfectly competitive industry, economic profit is zero in long-run equilibrium.* Free entry into and exit from the industry brings about this outcome. The following examples make use of this distinction.

Effect on the U.S. Market for Wheat of a Large Sale of Wheat to Russia

Suppose that, starting from an equilibrium condition in the U.S. wheat market, Russia experiences a drought and purchases huge quantities of American wheat to feed its population. (This actually happened several times.) The effect on the U.S. wheat market is to increase the number of consumers and to shift the demand for wheat upward.

In Figure 8–6, this is depicted by a shift in demand from D_1 to D_2. Moving up along the constant short-run supply curve, (S_{SR}), price rises from $0P_1$ to $0P_2$; quantity sold increases from $0Q_1$ to $0Q_2$; and total revenue of the wheat farmers increases from the rectangular area under e_1 to that under e_2. The latter increase shows clearly why U.S. farmers are so very interested in promoting and expanding foreign sales.

If the Russian wheat sale is a one-time affair—that is, if it occurs only in one given year and "disappears" thereafter—then in subsequent years, the market equilibrium would return to point e_1. But should the Russian crop failures become more permanent, U.S. farmers would be induced by the above-normal profit at price P_2 to expand both their acreage under cultivation (presumably using some of their less-productive land) and their stock of machinery. Also, new farmers would come into the business. The long-run supply curve becomes appropriate, and it is shown by a broken supply line in Figure 8–6. The expansion of the industry will continue until (above-normal) profits disappear and there is no longer an incentive for new farmers to enter. In the long run, equilibrium will settle at e_3, with price being $0P_3$, quantity $0Q_3$, and TR of the American farmers at the area under e_3 ($0P_3 \times 0Q_3$). The price change is smaller and quantity change larger in the long run than in the short run. As price recedes from $0P_2$ to $0P_3$, profit in the industry declines. In the long run, equilibrium economic profit is zero.

Figure 8–6 Effect of a Russian Wheat Purchase on the U.S. Wheat Market

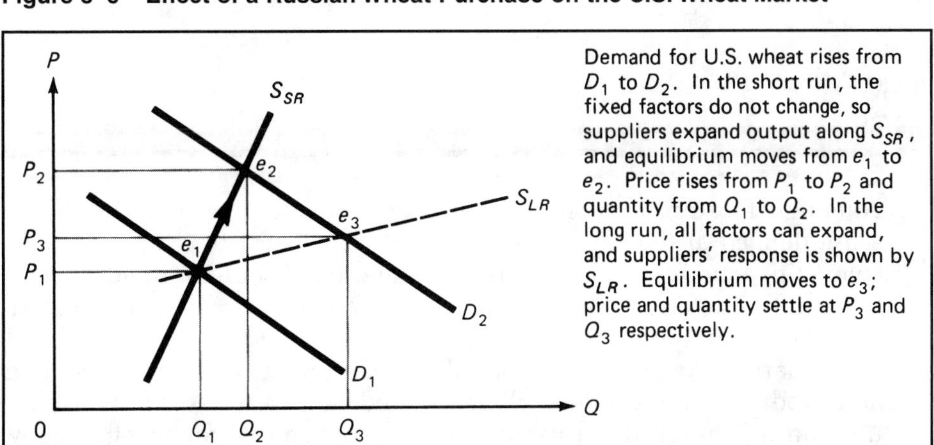

Demand for U.S. wheat rises from D_1 to D_2. In the short run, the fixed factors do not change, so suppliers expand output along S_{SR}, and equilibrium moves from e_1 to e_2. Price rises from P_1 to P_2 and quantity from Q_1 to Q_2. In the long run, all factors can expand, and suppliers' response is shown by S_{LR}. Equilibrium moves to e_3; price and quantity settle at P_3 and Q_3 respectively.

Effect of a Rise in Income on the Air-Travel Market

The following discussion assumes the airline industry to be purely competitive.

The Short Run The market for air travel is very sensitive to the income of the community. A rise in income induces an increase in demand for air travel, partly because of an increase in travel generally, and partly because some people can afford to switch to air travel from cheaper modes of transport, such as buses.

Figure 8–6 can be used to show the demand for and supply of travel (instead of wheat) in the price-quantity space. In the short run, the quantity supplied can expand only by more intensive utilization of a fixed number of aircraft. Once aircraft fly at near full capacity, this can be done by scheduling more frequent flights for each aircraft. This requires an increase in the number of employees per aircraft, because additional crews and servicing personnel (such as mechanics), flight attendants, ticket agents, and other personnel are needed to service the same number of aircraft.

Starting from an original equilibrium position e_1 in Figure 8–6, a rise in income increases demand from D_1 to D_2, the price of airline tickets rises from $0P_1$ to $0P_2$, quantity of tickets sold rises from $0Q_1$ to $0Q_2$, and total revenue of the airline industry is boosted from the rectangular area under equilibrium point e_1 to that under equilibrium point e_2. At P_2, profits rise above the "normal" level, constituting an inducement for the industry to expand in the long run.

The Long Run If these changes persist, enlargement of capacity would take place in the long run. Existing airlines would order additional aircraft, spare parts, and support equipment. At the same time, new airline companies might appear. The more elastic long-run supply schedule (S_{LR}) becomes relevant, yielding a new long-run equilibrium at point e_3. The price retracts to $0P_3$, and quantity rises to $0Q_3$. The (above-normal) profit disappears. In the long run, the price increases resulting from a given rise in demand are smaller than in the short run, and the quantity exchanged is greater.

HOW COMPETITIVE MARKETS ALLOCATE RESOURCES

Although the U.S. economy is not purely competitive in the technical sense defined at the beginning of Part II, it is instructive to employ the competitive model to see how markets allocate resources. In addition to the insight it offers, the model provides a yardstick by which economists often assess the outcome of noncompetitive markets.

A market economy contains millions of economic agents—consumers and producers, buyers and sellers of goods and services. Producers are unaware of the product mix desired by consumers (for instance, how many automobiles, fur coats, trips to Florida, and the like consumers will demand). Buyers of labor services have no direct knowledge of the occupation mix that the current generation of university students is training for, nor are aspiring students fully aware of the occupation mix required by the economy. There is no central planning authority that determines the allocation of resources—of people and machines—among various industries, or that coordinates production plans among industries, making sure that precisely enough intermediate products are produced to meet the requirement of final goods demanded by consumers. Likewise, there is no authority that determines the number of people that must train for each of many occupations.

Resource allocation Competitive markets allocate resources through the free interaction between buyers and sellers.

And yet the economy "hangs together." Somehow the pieces fall into place. For the most part, consumers buy what they demand without the producers' direct knowledge of the composition of demand. And 139 million people find jobs for which they are reasonably qualified. How does all this happen? It is the market mechanism that provides the "invisible hand" guiding resources to where they are needed.

To see how the mechanism functions, assume for a moment a position of long-run equilibrium in all markets of a competitive economy. Starting from such an equilibrium, assume that a change occurs in consumers' tastes from clothing to shoes, both industries assumed to be purely competitive. This is shown in Figure 8–7 by an increase in the demand for shoes and decrease in the demand for clothing, from D_1 to D_2 on panels *b* and *a* respectively. Moving along the *short-run* supply curves in the two markets, the points of equilibrium shift to P_2 and Q_2. These are short-run adjustments in supply in the two markets, attained through less intensive and more intensive utilization of a fixed capital stock in the clothing and shoe industries respectively.

At price P_2, some clothing producers make below-normal profit, and some shoe manufacturers make above-normal profit. In the long run, both industries would be induced to change their capacity. The clothing industry moves down along its long-run supply schedule (S_{LR}), contracting in two ways: The least-efficient firms, which can no longer realize normal profit, close down, and existing firms discard or do not replace their least-efficient equipment. Supply contracts further, to Q_3, and the final price is P_3—a new long-run equilibrium is reached. The shoe industry moves up along its long-run supply curve (S_{LR}), and expands its activity in two ways: New equipment is added by existing firms, and new firms enter the industry. Output rises to Q_3, and the new long-run equilibrium price is P_3. In the new long-run equilibrium, above-normal profit is zero in both industries.

This is the process by which consumers signal to firms a desire to change the product mix of their consumption. It involves a two-stage adjustment. In the short run, the magnitude of price change is large, and the quantity adjustment is small. It is constrained by the fixed capacity. But the large price change generates above-normal profit in some firms of the shoe industry and below-normal profit in some firms of the clothing industry. And it is these variations in profit that guide the movements of resources in the long run. Firms are motivated to exit the clothing industry by inadequate profit, whereas new firms (and capital) are attracted by

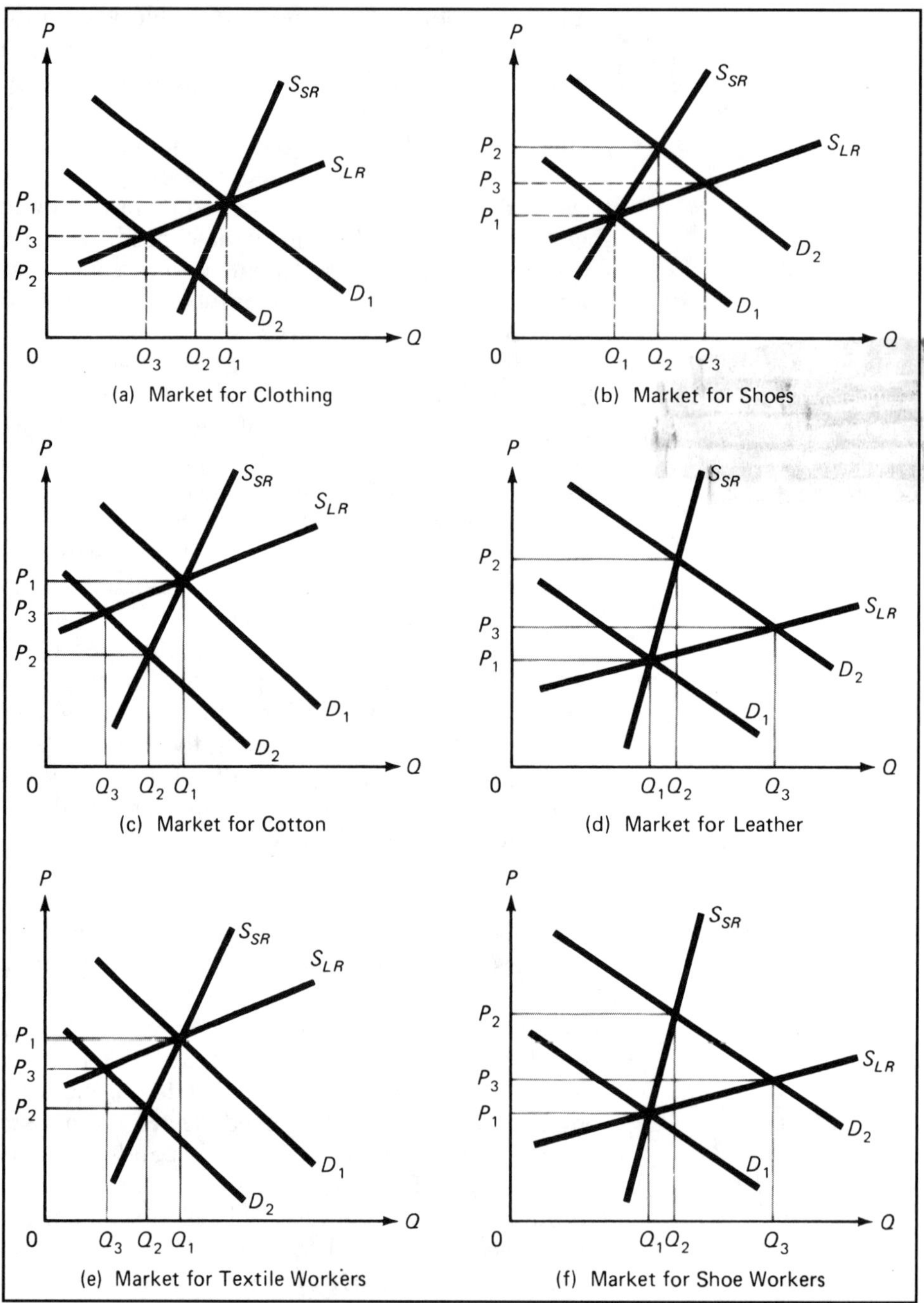

Figure 8–7 Selected Market Adjustments to a Shift in Consumer Demand from Clothing to Shoes: As demand for shoes rises and demand for clothing decreases from D_1 to D_2, the two top panels show the short-run and the long-run market adjustments, along S_{SR} and S_{LR} respectively. The two lower sets of panels show short-run and long-run market adjustments of two inputs into the shoe and clothing industries.

Prices as signals: Prices act as signals to producers and consumers and influence their respective behaviors. An economy where prices do not convey accurate information about relative scarcity of goods will achieve poor resource allocation.

the large profit to the shoe industry. This is why supply is more elastic in the long run than in the short run.

It would be a mistake to suggest that the process affects only these two markets. Industries that supply materials to the two industries in question (for example, cotton for clothing, leather for shoes) are affected, as are the factors of production employed in the two of them and in the supplying industries. Various complementary and substitute products are also affected. In other words, **ripple effects of the change are felt throughout the economy.** The effect is strongest in the areas most closely related to the expanding and contracting industries, and declines as we move away from them. It can be likened to a stone dropped into a tranquil body of water; it produces waves in concentric circles, and these decline in intensity as one moves further away from the point of impact. For example, all industries connected with the clothing sector will contract. Demand declines for woolens, synthetics, chemicals and other materials used in synthetics production, chemical engineers, cotton pickers, sales clerks in clothing stores, and so on. In the long run, the decline of profit to below-normal levels induces an exit of resources from these industries, until normal profit is restored to zero.

Only a few selected repercussions are shown in Figure 8–7. Panels *c* and *d* show the decline in demand for cotton (and other materials used in clothing production) and an increase in demand for leather from D_1 to D_2. Both short-run and long-run adjustments are pursued, with the final points of equilibrium resting at P_3 and Q_3. Similar adjustments are shown in panels *e* and *f* for the two types of labor inputs in the two industries.

This interrelation among sectors cannot be overstressed. For example, if residential construction rises in a given year from 1 1/2 to 2 million homes, then demand rises for lumber, nails, construction workers, refrigerators and other household appliances, and perhaps autos. In turn, the expansion of appliance production increases demand for steel and other metals, appliance and steel workers, electrical engineers, and so on. And the increase in automobile production provides employment in hundreds of firms supplying the automobile companies with glass, ball bearings, and other specialized products. Conversely, the contraction of the space program in the United States affected adversely thousands of firms supplying the major companies under government contracts.

Although the illustration above employed changes in demand as the forces motivating economic adjustment, in effect the cause can be changes in supply. Thus, a technological breakthrough in computer production would reduce cost and increase profit, thereby attracting new resources to the industry. Conversely, the near exhaustion of easily accessible sources of petroleum and natural gas would motivate some users to switch to alternate energy sources, such as coal and nuclear energy. Resources would follow the demand in the fashion described above. An increase in price of conventional forms of energy may also induce producers to develop more exotic forms, such as solar and wind energy, as these become profitable.

In all cases, the principle guiding the allocation of resources is the same. It is the "invisible hand" of the marketplace. In each market, supply and demand are moved by the **forces of competition** to determine equilibrium price and quantity. When these are disturbed, redistribution of resources occurs (again, moved by competitive forces) until a new equilibrium is established. In effect, the economy is in a continuous state of motion from one equilibrium to another. And even before the new equilibrium is reached, new changes take place, creating further disturbances. Such is the "magic of the market." Its attractiveness has been underscored in recent years as most socialist states abandoned certain aspects of their planned economy in favor of market-determined allocation of resources. Central planning has failed as a regulatory mechanism under which an economy can thrive.

Allocative efficiency is reached when maximum output is obtained from a given amount of resources.

Two main advantages make the competitive market system an attractive mechanism for allocating resources: efficiency and freedom. In a perfectly competitive industry, the individual firm has no control over price. Competitive forces ensure that a uniform market price will prevail, settling at the point that equates supply and demand, because entry into (and exit from) the industry is easy. The individual firm is a price taker, and has no pricing policy of its own. It merely adapts itself to the market price. Perfect competition ensures **maximum efficiency** *in production, because* **inefficient firms would be priced out of the market.** It also ensures **efficient resource allocation,** in the sense of *bringing the* **production mix** *of the economy into* **conformity with consumers' preferences.** Free entry and exit ensure that in the long run **only normal profits** are realized in a competitive industry. Economic profits or losses disappear in the long run.

Efficiency of production and resource allocation are the great advantages of a competitive economy. And these are accomplished with **maximum freedom for the individual** consumer and producer to act as they please. With a minimum of guidance by and intervention from government, people are free to organize and disband enterprises, to work where they please, and to buy and sell whatever they choose. Their sole guide is economic self-interest, and their sole constraints are market-determined incomes, prices, and profits. So important is this efficiency outcome that economists use it as a yardstick by which to assess the outcome of alternative, noncompetitive market structures. Our understanding of this mechanism dates back to the great economist, Adam Smith.

ADAM SMITH: THE FATHER OF POLITICAL ECONOMY (GLASGOW, SCOTLAND, 1723–1790)

A graduate of Oxford University, Adam Smith occupied the chair of Moral Philosophy at the University of Glasgow beginning in 1751. Already famous for his important work in philosophy, he published in 1776 the monumental *Wealth of Nations,* destined to become an economics classic.

This masterpiece provides a panoramic view of the market economy. Consumption, wrote Smith, is the sole end and purpose of all production. But how is it that the production process, carried out by millions of diverse individuals, each motivated strictly by self-interest, is somehow directed to satisfy precisely the wants of consumers and the needs of society, by providing the kinds and quantities of goods they desire? The answer offered by Smith to this momentous question remains largely true today: The market is the regulatory mechanism, the **invisible hand,** that channels people's energy to satisfying consumer wants.

Invisible hand: self-interest guides the actions of buyers and sellers leading to efficient allocation of resources. This notion was developed by Adam Smith in *The Wealth of Nations* published in 1776.

How do the laws of competitive markets perform this function? Self-interest drives each person to do whatever society is willing to pay for. This is how production comes about. And competition from other people providing the same good or service works as a disciplinary force against anybody's charging excessive prices and obtaining exorbitant earnings. If a man raises his price, competitors will undersell him, forcing him out of the market should he refuse to lower his price to the level charged by other sellers. Competition among sellers protects the buyers from being charged excessively high prices.

And how does the market ensure the availability of the right quantity of each good? Suppose consumers suddenly decide to reduce the number of shirts and increase the number of shoes they wish to purchase. Then the price of shirts would be bid down because of slumping sales, and the price of shoes would be bid up, as sales rise in the face of constant supply. As a consequence of these price changes, profits would decline in the shirt industry and rise in the shoe industry, so that resources would be released from shirt production and attracted to shoe production. Thus, shirt output declines while shoe output rises, in conformity with the new desires. The market mechanism, and not any governmental planning authority, has regulated the reallocation of society's resources to fit demand. Self-interest and competition are seen as the central elements in the process. And just as the market mechanism regulates the price and quantities of the goods produced, it also regulates the income of those who participate in their production. It is the laws of the market that give society its cohesiveness.

Specialization: When each person (or country) produces what he can do best—output is maximized.

Within the productive process itself Smith singled out one important feature that contributes to the tremendous increase in industrial productivity: **specialization** *of labor*. His famous example tells how ten workers, each charged with one tiny task in the production of a pin, can make

▶ ECONOMICS—A DISMAL SCIENCE?

Given Smith's optimistic view of the economy, why was economics ever called "the dismal science"? The answer dates back to the English economist Thomas Malthus. In his *Essay on* the *Principles of Population* (1798), he tried to explain the poverty and misery observable among the lower classes of every nation. His explanation was rooted in a nation's inability to produce enough food. Population, he maintained, grows at a constant geometric rate (2, 4, 8, 16, 32 . . .), whereas food output increases at a constant arithmetic rate (1, 2, 3, 4, 5 . . .). In time, the population inevitably runs out of food.

More specifically, according to Malthus, food is produced with land and labor. Land is fixed in quantity. The amount of labor, in contrast, grows as rapidly as food supplies permit. *The larger the amount of labor, the less each additional amount adds to total food output.* People continue to have children as long as they can feed them. Labor continues to grow, and the amount of food per person continues to fall, until there is just enough food to keep people alive. At times, if population grows too fast, there may be famine, disease, and war. Any time the food supply is more than what is needed for the survival of the existing population, the surplus leads to more children and eventually more labor. The added labor soon drives food per person back down to bare subsistence.

Although certain underdeveloped countries are still caught in the Malthusian trap, the industrial countries clearly escaped it. What Malthus did not foresee was the tremendous rise in farm productivity through mechanization, advanced technology, and the use of fertilizers. Today in America, less than 2 percent of the population feed the entire nation, with ample amounts of food left over for export.

upward of 48,000 pins a day, whereas the same ten, each doing the entire operation separately and independently, would each make fewer than 20 pins a day. Of course, the degree of specialization is determined by the *size of the market.* Should the market be too small to absorb tens of thousands of pins, specialization, however beneficial, would not come about.

Self-interest is also the mechanism that propels society toward greater wealth, for it drives people to save and accumulate. When these savings are transformed into investment in plants and machinery, they increase the volume of output.

Laissez-faire or "Let it alone": The idea that the government should not be involved in the economy. It is only through the free-interaction of buyers and sellers that the invisible hand can function properly.

It is easy to see that Smith's theory leads to the doctrine of **laissez-faire**. Each economic unit is completely free to pursue its own self-interest, and the market mechanism ensures that these individual decisions will also serve the interest of society at large. Smith was against government interference with the market mechanism and vehemently opposed to monopoly power. All impediments to competition should be removed, he said, and market forces must be free to determine the level of prices, wages, profits, and production.

Although much has changed since Smith's day—and so has the relevance of some of his conclusions—his panoramic view of the market remains a lasting contribution. In subsequent generations, great economists have perfected the analytical tools of economics and sharpened the analysis of the market mechanism. It was Alfred Marshall (U.K., 1890)[1]

[1]In each reference, the year refers to the appearance of the person's principal work in economics.

who introduced the widely used supply and demand curves, which, like the blades of a scissors, intersect to determine the market price. David Ricardo (U.K., 1817) and John Bates Clark (U.S., 1899) were concerned with the market-determined distribution of income among groups in society. And the French economist Leon Walras (1875) introduced the idea of general equilibrium—that is, many mutually determined market prices at one and the same time. In the 1930s, Edward Chamberlin (U.S.) and Joan Robinson (U.K.) introduced into the analysis of markets theories of noncompetitive behavior, such as monopolistic competition.

SUMMARY

Supply and demand analysis was used to consider various situations that can develop in the marketplace. In each case, the situation was translated into a shift in either demand or supply, and the effect on price, quantity, and total revenue was examined. In three of the cases, the discussion was extended to encompass long-run effects on resource allocation among industries. The examples led to a discussion of resource allocation in a competitive market economy, where industries shrink and expand in response to variations in prices and profits. The contribution of Adam Smith to our understanding of the market mechanism was highlighted.

QUESTIONS AND PROBLEMS

1. Show diagrammatically and explain the effects of a frost in Brazil on the markets for coffee and for tea. In each case, determine the changes in price, quantity, and total revenue. *(Hint:* See Figure 8–1.)
2. Suppose that, as a result of an advertising campaign by the Florida orange growers' association, there has been a large-scale shift in consumer demand away from soft drinks and toward frozen orange juice. Using supply and demand curves, trace the short-run and long-run effects of this change on the markets for orange juice; oranges; fertilizers used in orange growing; soft drinks; soft-drink bottles; and labor in the soft-drinks industry.
3. Suppose that a new oil rig is invented that lowers considerably the cost of offshore oil drilling. *(Hint:* Supply of crude petroleum rises.) Using supply and demand diagrams, show the short-run and long-run effects of that on the markets for crude petroleum; gasoline; workers in oil production; coal; and coal miners.
4. In the 1950s, there was a change in the form of energy preferred by consumers for heating purposes: away from coal and toward oil (oil is a cleaner fuel than coal). Show diagrammatically and explain the effect of this change on the markets for coal and for oil (a) in the short run; (b) in the long run. Indicate the changes in market prices, quantities, and TR.

   This shift in taste was the cause of problems of industrial adjustment in the 1970s, when crude petroleum became scarce. U.S. energy legislation encouraged industrial conversion back to coal. Elaborate verbally on this reconversion process.
5. Assume that aluminum and steel are substitute metals in automobile production, with aluminum being the lighter metal. As one of several energy-conservation

measures, the U.S. Congress legislated that the fleet of cars of each manufacturer must average at least 25 miles to the gallon. Among other things, that led producers to substitute lighter for heavier metals. Show diagrammatically and explain the effect of this substitution on the markets for aluminum and steel (prices, quantities, and TR).

6. Suppose that in year *X* there has been a drought in Argentina (beef-producing country) *and* a rise in income in the beef-consuming countries. Show the combined effect of these events on the worldwide markets for beef and for fish (fish and beef are substitutes in consumption).
7. Show diagrammatically and explain the short-run and long-run adjustments occasioned by a shift in consumer preferences from dresses to pant-suits. Sketch the reallocation of resources in the economy that might ensue.
8. Do the same to explain the effects of a shift in consumer preferences from visiting movie theaters to watching videocassette movies on television.
9. The U.S. government is considering large-scale aid to palm-oil producers in Southeast Asia, to help them expand the area under cultivation. Why should American soybean producers demonstrate and protest against such action? In your answer, show the markets for palm oil and soybeans, and remember that both products are a source of energy in the diet.

APPENDIX TO CHAPTER 8

Karl Marx: The Philosopher of Communism

Karl Marx and The Communist Manifesto: The view of Marx was that the free enterprise system will destroy itself due to the "exploitation" of the laborers (proletariat) by the capitalists.

An alternative view of the market system is presented in the writings of **Karl Marx** (1818–1883). He maintained that the system contains the seeds of its own destruction. A short and simplified summary of his ideas is in order.

In 1848, Marx and his collaborator, Friedrich Engels, published a pamphlet entitled ***The Communist Manifesto***. In it they called for the violent overthrow of the capitalist system and its replacement by communism: "The proletarians have nothing to lose but their chains. They have the world to win." The revolution, they argued, was not only desirable but inevitable, for the capitalist system contains an inherent contradiction: On the one hand, the complexities and interdependencies of industrial production cry out for social planning, and on the other, capitalists insist on full individual freedom. Planless production, they said, will destroy itself.

Although the world views Marx primarily as a revolutionary, his lasting contribution was that of a great scholar. It is embodied in the four volumes of ***Das Capital*** that were published during 1867–1910; three of the volumes were edited and appeared after his death.

Das Capital: Published in 1867–1910 by Karl Marx, put forth the **Labor theory of value:** The price of a good is determined by the value of labor required to produce it.

In a purely competitive world of perfect capitalism, wrote Marx, each commodity sells for a price that equals its value. And that value is the amount of labor *embodied in it*. Such labor need not be direct; part of it may be embodied in a machine used to produce the commodity. But all commodities can be reduced to their labor content and will be priced accordingly. The capitalist, who owns the means of production, buys labor services in the marketplace. And like any other commodity, labor services are priced at their labor content—at *the amount necessary for the laborer to perpetuate himself or to keep himself alive.* This is the laborer's *subsistence wage.*

Surplus value: A term coined by Marx, synonymous with profit; it is generated only by workers.

How are profits generated in such a system? By the worker's contracting to work longer than is necessary to maintain himself. If five hours of labor constitute what is socially necessary to keep the worker alive, he would be paid accordingly. But since, in a competitive labor market, he normally contracts to work eight hours a day (otherwise he would not get the job), the difference accrues to the capitalist in the form of profit, or what Marx called **surplus value**. This unpaid work is the difference (three hours, in our example) between a full day's work and labor's worth on the market, which equals his subsistence wage. Since the product that the capitalist sells embodies a full day of labor, the difference is his profit.

Competition forces capitalists to expand their operations and hire more workers. To do so, they must bid up wages, and surplus value tends to fall. The capitalists react to this decline by introducing labor-saving machinery and laying off part of their work force. And these unemployed workers form the *Industrial Reserve Army,* which serves to keep wages at their subsistence level. But substituting machines for labor is unprofitable. For there is no surplus value in machines; the capitalist buys a machine from another capitalist for the full labor value embodied in it. Only workers generate surplus value. And as they decline proportionately relative to machines, profits also decline. When the process reaches the point where production becomes unprofitable, bankruptcies occur, and a capitalist crisis is at hand.

What then? As man and machines become idle, workers are forced to accept subvalue wages, and the strongest capitalists can purchase machines at less than their true value. Surplus value reappears, and the expansion starts all over again. But it can only lead to its own collapse. The process repeats itself, with expansions following crises. However, in each crisis, the large capitalists swallow the little ones, and firms get progressively bigger. These industrial magnates are capable of exploiting the workers, leading to mass misery, oppression, and degradation. This would eventually lead to a revolt of the working class, and the inevitable breakdown of the capitalist system. All means of production would then be transferred to society's ownership. Marx did not spell out the structure of the system that would replace capitalism. It remained for his successor, Lenin, to do that during the first quarter of the twentieth century.

Even on the contemporary American scene, socialist ideas have taken at least some hold. Expounded by the Union for Radical Political Economics (still outside mainstream economics), they are based on Marxian views. The following quotation from a recent article shows that despite the different economic scene, radical economics in the United States is deeply rooted in the Marxian philosophy:

> Individual employers earn profits only on the basis of "value added" within their own enterprises, profiting from the margin between the value their workers produce and the wages their workers earn. Machines can't add value because the individual producers must pay some other capitalist, the one who made the machine, the full worth of that machine. The only purchase on which the producers may earn some extra money is the purchase of the workers' labor time. The fewer workers the employers hire, therefore, the narrower the base for profit accumulation. As they replace workers by machines, the rate of profit may fall. . . . Continuous prosperity eventually threatens profits through the market mechanism. Individual capitalists invest feverishly during a boom. Sooner or later they begin to exhaust the reserve supplies of workers. The labor market tightens. This over-investment has two shattering consequences for corporations. Wages begin to rise rapidly, cutting into profits. And workers take advantage of their scarcity by resisting the "werewolf hunger" more militantly and more effectively; workers' productivity slows, directly undercutting capitalist control of the production process.[2]

---

[2]From David M. Gordon, "Recession Is Capitalism as Usual," *The New York Times Magazine,* April 27, 1975.

How did Marx's forecast of the collapse of capitalism fare in reality? In Russia, capitalism disappeared after the revolution of 1917, as it did subsequently in Eastern Europe and China. But in the West, capitalism thrived, affording a high standard of living and economic freedom at the same time.

Much of Marx's theory cannot be accepted as an accurate description of reality. Prices based on supply and demand, rather than values based on labor content, regulate the market economy. Profits are regarded as a return to a productive factor (Part I) rather than treated as "surplus value." Labor has risen far above the subsistence level; the American labor movement functions and thrives within the capitalistic system, and does not wish to change it. Economics has developed alternative explanations for business fluctuations (Part III), and has devised means for coping with them within the context of a free-enterprise system. Rather than self-destroy, capitalism has continued to evolve and adjust to meet the demands for social justice and equality of opportunity. And in recent years European socialist states and China adopted capitalist economies, thereby acknowledging the superiority of markets over a central plan as a mechanism for regulating the allocation of resources.

A Monopolist or Oligopolist Compared to a Competitive Firm

Resource allocation in a perfectly competitive economy was analyzed in Chapter 8 by the use of market demand and supply curves. Although the role of the individual firm was discussed, the focus was on markets. Competitive markets were shown to yield efficient production and resource allocation in the economy. This favorable outcome must now be compared with that of alternative market structures: monopoly and oligopoly.

A monopoly is a single-firm industry. By definition, the industry and the firm are one and the same. Consequently, to unravel the essential features of monopolistic practices and how they differ from perfect competition, we must delve into the behavior of a single firm. This chapter does so to the extent necessary to highlight the different outcomes of alternative market structures. The reader is invited to review the introduction to Part 2, where the four market structures are described.

OBJECTIVE OF THE FIRM

Economic profit: Total Revenue – Total Cost, where cost includes the opportunity cost of resources used in production. These costs are not included in calculating accounting profit.

It is the objective of a firm, be it perfectly or imperfectly competitive, to **maximize profit**. There are two sides to the profit equation: revenue and costs. The firm realizes revenue or **receipts** from the **sale** of its **product.** These receipts are called **total revenue (TR).** They are equal to the number of units of the product sold times the price of each unit. Thus, a farmer who sells 10,000 bushels of wheat in a given year at $10 per bushel realizes total revenue of $100,000. TR = Quantity of sale × Price per unit.

To produce the product, the firm incurs production costs. These consist of the outlay for materials purchased from other firms and payments to the primary inputs employed: wages and salary to labor; rent to land

and natural resources; interest to capital; *and normal profit. In* other words, the profit required to keep the firm in business, operating on a constant scale, is a part of production costs.

Variable costs: Costs that vary with the level of output produced. **Fixed costs:** Costs that do not vary with the level of output (i.e. plant facilities and heavy equipment and capital). **Total cost:** Variable costs plus fixed costs.

In the short run, one or more factors are fixed in quantity and others are variable. The cost of the fixed factor(s) is known as **fixed cost**; the cost of the variable factor(s) is called **variable cost**. Combined, they make up **total cost (TC).**

Total cost of the farmer mentioned above is the sum total of costs involved in growing and selling 10,000 bushels of wheat. It might be $90,000. The difference between total revenue and total cost is economic profit ($10,000 in our example). The total-cost schedule is the cost of producing various amounts of output.

Profit = TR – TC. The firm's objective is to make this difference positive—that is, to avoid losses, or ensure that TR exceeds TC—and to *maximize* its value. It is the pursuit of this objective that will be shown to yield a different outcome in case of the perfectly competitive firm, the monopolist, or oligopolist.

THE MARGINAL WAY OF THINKING

Marginal analysis: Economic decisions are made by comparing marginal (incremental) benefits and marginal cost.

It is convenient to think of the firm as making **marginal decisions.** The term *marginal* is used to describe *additional* or *incremental* values. It was encountered in Chapter 4 in the context of utility derived by the consumer: "Marginal satisfaction" is the incremental satisfaction obtained from consuming an additional unit of the product. And it applies equally to *positive* or *negative* increments (an added or a subtracted unit).

Knowingly or not, we all make marginal decisions in our daily lives. A student enrolled in four courses and considering taking a fifth asks herself, "What are the extra (marginal) costs, in time and money, of taking the fifth course, and how do they compare to the extra (marginal) benefits from the course, in terms of knowledge gained or graduation requirements?" Only if the marginal benefits exceed the marginal cost would she sign up for the fifth course. Similar considerations may apply to a decision by a person who subscribes to two publications of whether or not to subscribe to an additional magazine. A comparison between the marginal costs and the marginal benefits is inherent in such a decision. Another example would be a student working in a book store and being offered an extra hour's work per week. In deciding whether she should increase her workweek, she weighs the benefit of the extra pay against the marginal cost of study and leisure she would have to give up.

Our daily life is full of *marginal decisions*, or *decisions at the margin*. And these determinations operate as well in reverse. Should the student drop one of her five courses? Should the reader cancel the subscription to one of the three magazines? The student makes the decision by comparing the marginal *saving* in time and money with the marginal *loss* of benefits in terms of knowledge, information, or progress toward a degree. Only if the marginal savings exceed the marginal loss would she proceed with the cut.

In a similar way, the firm makes marginal decisions. Starting from a certain scale of operations, the farmer in our previous example may ask, "Should I hire one additional (marginal) farmhand, so as to grow an extra (marginal) 100 bushels of wheat?" Such a decision involves incremental costs of paying for the new worker; but it also yields additional revenue from selling the extra wheat. The farmer would proceed only if the added revenue exceeded the added cost. Alternatively, she may ask the question in reverse: "Should I lay off one of my farmhands, and allow the crop to drop by 100 bushels?" In doing so, she would save the wages of one worker, but would also lose the proceeds from the sale of 100 bushels. Only if the marginal savings exceed the marginal loss (from reduced sales) would she proceed with the cut.

Bearing these concepts in mind, we proceed with the analysis of the firm. The next three sections demonstrate a critically important difference between a single perfectly competitive firm and a monopolist/oligopolist: the way each views the demand schedule for its product, and the implications that this difference has for their revenue. This is followed by a section on production costs, the other side of the profit equation. Revenue and costs are then brought together, to determine the profit-maximizing output of the two types of firms.

THE COMPETITIVE FIRM'S DEMAND CURVE

Price taker: the market sets the price and the firm must sell at that particular price; no more and no less.

A competitive industry is defined as one consisting of a great multitude of firms. The individual firm is exceedingly small relative to the entire industry. It supplies an infinitesimally small portion of the industry's total output—"a drop in the bucket." A single wheat farmer, one out of a million such farmers, is a case in point. She faces a price for her product that is determined by the intersection of *market* demand and supply. Nothing she does can influence this price, for her share in the industry output is much too small. She can double her output without causing the price to decline. Or she can halve her output, and the price would not rise. It requires a concerted action of thousands like her to affect the market price.

Put differently, the single competitive firm takes the market price for granted. It can sell as much as it wants to at the going market price. It need not lower its price one iota below the one established on the market to attract customers and increase sales. On the other hand, should it raise its price one iota above that prevailing on the market, it would lose all its customers and sell nothing.

These conditions are illustrated in the following hypothetical figures:

Hypothetical Demand Conditions for the Output of a Single Farmer

Price	Quantity Demanded (Bushels)
$10	1
$10	2
$10	3
.	.
.	.
.	.

This relationship is graphed in Figure 9–1a, yielding a horizontal or an infinitely elastic demand cure. With the market price established at $10 per bushel, the farmer need not lower her price to $9.99 in order to expand sales, and she cannot sell a single bushel at $10.01. But she can sell as much as she pleases at $10 per bushel without affecting that price.

What constrains the firm's output is its positively sloping supply curve, which in turn is rooted in its cost conditions (Chapter 5). Its intersection with the demand cure determines output.

Figure 9–1 shows the individual firm on panel (a) and the competitive industry of which it is a part on panel (b). Price and quantity for the industry are established by a positively sloped supply schedule and a negatively sloped demand schedule in the right-hand panel. The $10-per-bushel price determines the horizontal (infinitely elastic) demand as seen by the single firm, in the left-hand panel.

Figure 9–1 The Market for Wheat and the Single Wheat Farmer Demand: The latter is horizontal at the going market price.

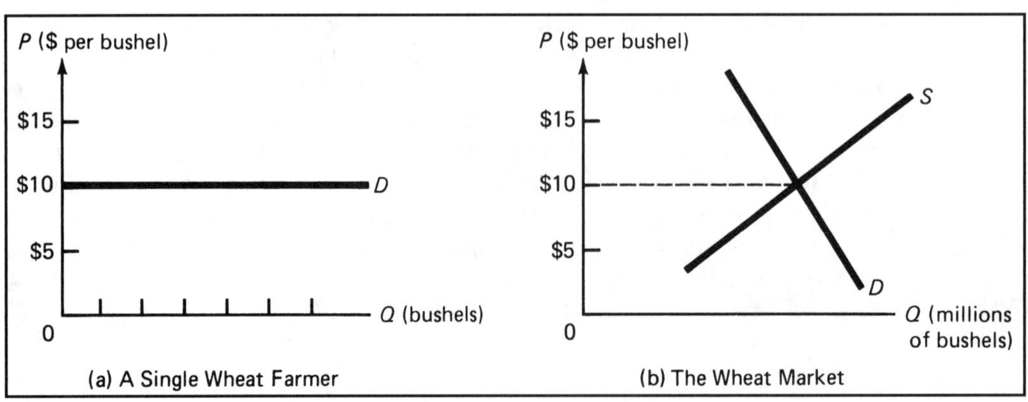

Table 9–1 Total Revenue and Marginal Revenue of the Competitive Firm

Output	Price	TR (Output × Price)	MR (ΔTR)
1	$10	$10	
			(20 – 10 =) 10
2	10	20	
			(30 – 20 =) 10
3	10	30	
			(40 – 30 =) 10
4	10	40	
			(50 – 40 =) 10
5	10	50	
			(60 – 50 =) 10
6	10	60	
			(70 – 60 =) 10
7	10	70	

DEMAND AND MARGINAL REVENUE OF A SINGLE COMPETITIVE FIRM

We now return to the demand for the output of a single wheat farmer, as shown in Figure 9–la. Total revenue (or receipts from sales) of the firm is its output times the constant price. At output of one bushel, TR is $10 (1 × $10); at output of two bushels, TR is $20 (2 × $10); and so on. At each level of output, TR is obtained by multiplying that output by the constant price. It is shown in the third column of Table 9–1.

Marginal revenue: The additional revenue obtained from selling one more unit of output. MR=ΔTR/ΔQ. For the perfectly competitive firm MR=Price; its demand and MR curves are identical.

We next define an important concept: **Marginal revenue (MR) is the addition or increment to total revenue from selling an additional unit of output.** Calculated as ΔTR/ΔOutput, it is computed in the fourth column of Table 9–1 as the change in TR between rows; that is, the rise in TR as output increases by one unit. Because the price is constant throughout, it constitutes the addition to total revenue from selling an extra unit of the product. At each level of output, price equals MR, as can be verified by comparing the second and fourth columns of Table 9–1. This leads to an important conclusion: **For the competitive firm, price equals marginal revenue.** The demand curve shown in Figure 9–1a is also the marginal-revenue curve for the single firm.

DEMAND AND MARGINAL REVENUE OF A MONOPOLIST OR OLIGOPOLIST

In contrast to a competitive firm, a monopolist or oligopolist cannot sell as much as it pleases at the going market price. General Motors must lower its prices if it wishes to sell additional cars. Indeed, by its very action, GM

Table 9–2 Hypothetical Demand and MR of a Super-Computer Manufacturer

Price	Quantity Sold	TR ($Millions)	MR ($Millions)
(In Millions of Dollars per Computer)	*(Number of Computers)*	*(Price × Quantity)*	*(ΔTR)*[a]
10	1	(10 × 1 =) 10	
			(18 – 10 =) 8
9	2	(9 × 2 =) 18	
			(24 – 18 =) 6
8	3	(8 × 3 =) 24	
			(28 – 24 =) 4
7	4	(7 × 4 =) 28	
			(30 – 28 =) 2
6	5	(6 × 5 =) 30	
			(30 – 30 =) 0
5	6	(5 × 6 =) 30	
			(28 – 30 =) –2
4	7	(4 × 7 =) 28	

[a] *Note: If the quantity increments were greater than 1, the calculation of MR would require a division of change in TR by the change in quantity: MR = ΔTR/ΔQ. MR figures are placed between rows.*

Price maker: A firm that has the ability to affect the market price. It's marginal revenue lies below the demand curve, because in lowering its price to promote sales, it must lower not only the price of the marginal unit but of all units that previously sold for more.

affects auto prices: Halving its output would certainly increase prices, and doubling its output would depress them. Unlike the case with a perfectly competitive firm, the single oligopolist's demand curve has a negative slope. In the case of a pure monopolist, the market-demand curve is identical with that of the firm. Both are negatively sloped. The firm's demand curve is not infinitely elastic. This is an essential difference between a perfectly competitive firm and a monopolist/oligopolist. It has an important implication for the MR curve.

A monopolist or oligopolist must lower the price to increase sales. However, in doing so, **he lowers not only the price of the last unit sold, the marginal unit: he must also reduce the price of all the units that previously sold for more.** Consequently, the marginal revenue is lower than the price.

To see this, consider the demand schedule faced by a manufacturer of large computers, assumed to be an oligopolist, shown in Table 9–2. Hypothetical prices and quantities sold are shown in the first two columns. The third column presents total revenue for each quantity (row); it is price times quantity. The fourth column shows marginal revenue (MR). The MR is the *change in total revenue obtained from selling one additional unit of the product (output);* MR = ΔTR. Note that the MR figures are inserted *between the rows* to which they apply.

In each row, **MR is lower than price.** In order to increase sales from one to two computers, the manufacturer lowers the price from $10 to $9.[1] But in doing so, it must lower the price not only of the second unit; the

[1]All price figures in this paragraph refer to millions.

first unit's price (previously $10) is also reduced to $9. The firm earns $9 from selling the second computer. But the MR from the second unit is $9 minus the $1 "loss" incurred from the price cut on the first unit, or $8. In order to sell the third unit, the company must lower the price from $9 to $8. But in doing so, it reduces the price of the first two units as well. Although it earns $8 from selling the third computer, its MR is $8 minus $2 ("lost" on the first two units), or $6. In order to increase sales from three to four, it must lower the price from $8 to $7. But in doing so, it needs to shave $1 off the price of each of the first three units. The MR is $7 (the new price) minus $3 (the "loss" on the first three units), or $4. A further increase in sales from four to five requires a price reduction from $7 to $6—on the fifth (marginal) unit as well as on the previous four. The firm earns $6 on the fifth unit. But its MR is $6 minus (the "loss" of) $4, or $2. Verify for yourself how MR is calculated in the last two rows.

Figure 9–2 shows the demand and MR curves using the figures in Table 9–2. Demand indicates the relation between quantity and price (second and first columns), and MR is built on the relation between quantity and MR (second and fourth columns). At each quantity sold, marginal revenue is lower than price. **The MR curve lies under the demand curve.**

Figure 9–2 Demand and MR of a Single Computer Manufacturer (Table 9–2): ***Note*** that because demand is negatively sloped (not horizontal), marginal revenue lies under the demand schedule. Mechanically, the MR curve can be obtained from the demand schedule as follows: Extend the demand curve so that it reaches both the price and the quantity axes. Bisect the resulting *0Q* distance, and connect the midpoint with the beginning of the demand curve on the price axis. The resulting line is MR.

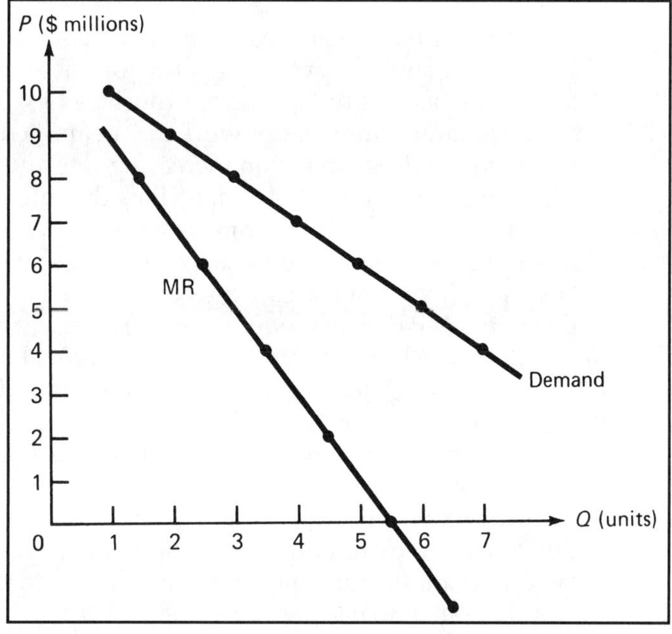

This is a critical difference between a purely competitive firm and a monopolist or oligopolist. The perfect competitor need not lower its price to expand its sales. The demand curve for its product is horizontal, and it *coincides with the MR curve.* At each quantity, MR = Price, for TR rises by the price of the marginal unit sold. Not so in the monopoly/oligopoly firm. Because it must lower the price to sell more, the MR is less than price at each quantity. The MR curve *lies under the demand curve.*

THE FIRM'S SHORT-RUN COST

Revenue is one side of the profit equation. The other side is production costs, which consists of purchases of materials and payments by the firm for the services of primary factors: wages and salaries for labor, rent for land and natural resources, interest for capital, and normal profit. In other words, the part of profit that induces the firm to stay in business and maintain its scale of operations is considered part of production costs. Finally, the short run is defined as a period in which the plant's capacity is unaltered; only its degree of utilization (The number of workers employed with a fixed amount of capital or of land) changes.

The Law of Diminishing Returns

Law of diminishing marginal returns: When units of the variable factor are added to the fixed factor, then beyond a certain point the marginal product declines.

What characterizes the short run is the fact that at least one factor of production is fixed in quantity (known as the *fixed* factor), whereas another one can vary (known as the variable factor). Under such conditions, production is subject to the **law of diminishing returns**. The law states: *As successive units of a variable factor* (such as labor) *are combined with a given amount of a fixed factor* (such as land), *then beyond some point, the marginal product declines.*

For your understanding of the principle, Table 9–3 presents hypothetical data for a wheat-producing farm, one acre in size. Total product refers to the number of units produced (bushels of wheat) by the farm. As successively larger numbers of workers are applied to one acre of land, total product (TP) rises, first at an increasing rate and then at a decreasing rate. **The marginal product (MP) describes the rate of increase in TP. It is the increase in TP resulting from a one-unit increase in the variable factor, labor.** It is seen that with no labor, nothing can be produced. Then, as the labor employed increases up to two workers, the MP rises. But beyond that point, MP declines; equivalently TP rises at a decreasing rate. At some point (six workers, in our example), workers begin to get in each other's way, and the TP declines in absolute amount; MP becomes negative. Our concern is the region of declining but not negative MP (where TP rises at a decreasing rate): that is, between two and five workers employed on a fixed amount of land.

Production costs of various amounts of output reflect the law of diminishing returns and depend upon the prices of the fixed and variable factors. Without our going into details, it can be understood intuitively that *the cost of production is inversely related to productivity: As productivity*

Table 9–3 Hypothetical Production Conditions in a Wheat Farm

Fixed Factor (Land)	Variable Factor (Labor)	Total Product (Bushels of Wheat Produced	Marginal Product (Bushels of Wheat)
1 acre	0	0	
			(3 – 0 =) 3
1 acre	1	3	
			(10 – 3 =) 7
1 acre	2	10	
			(16 – 10 =) 6
1 acre	3	16	
			(20 – 16 =) 4
1 acre	4	20	
			(21 – 20 =) 1
1 acre	5	21	
			(19 – 21 =) –2
1 acre	6	19	

rises, costs decline; as productivity declines, costs rise.[2] Production costs in the short run (when one factor is fixed in quantity) reflect the law of diminishing returns: **As output expands, total costs of producing the output first rise at a declining rate and beyond a certain point begin rising at an increasing rate.**

Production Costs

To simplify the presentation, Table 9–4 shows hypothetical short-run cost conditions of a firm when total product (the firm's output) *rises by single units.* Note that the first column shows output rising in increments of one unit of the product,[3] whereas in Table 9–3 it was labor input rising in increments of one unit of the factor (worker). As output rises, production costs increase, first at a decreasing rate (reflecting the rising MP of labor), and then, beginning with three units of output, at an increasing rate (reflecting declining MP of labor).

Marginal cost: The additional cost incurred from producing an additional unit of output.

We next define a highly important concept: **Marginal cost (MC) is the addition to total cost incurred from producing one extra unit of the product.** It is the rate of increase in total cost as output expands by increments of one unit, and is calculated in the third column of Table 9–4 (and graphed in Figure 9–3) as the increments to total cost from one row to the next. Note that the MC is shown *between* the relevant rows. Marginal cost declines up to the third bushel of output and rises beyond that point. To

[2]Suppose that a worker producing "widgets" earns $10 per hour. If he produces 10 widgets per hour then the cost per widget is $1. If his productivity doubles so that he makes 20 widgets per hour (wage remaining the same), then the cost per widget declines to (10/20) 50¢.

[3]Note the switch from a farm to a computer manufacturer.

Table 9–4 Hypothetical Short-Run Cost Conditions of a Computer Manufacturer

Total Product	Total Production Costs (Millions of Dollars)	Marginal Cost[a] (Millions of Dollars)
0	10	
		(18 – 10 =) 8
1	18	
		(24 – 18 =) 6
2	24	
		(28 – 24 =) 4
3	28	
		(34 – 28 =) 6
4	34	
		(42 – 34 =) 8
5	42	
		(52 – 42 =) 10
6	52	
		(64 –52 =) 12
7	64	
		(78 – 64 =) 14
8	78	
		(94 – 78 =) 16
9	94	

[a] *Had TP expanded at increments larger than 1, marginal cost would be $\Delta TC/\Delta$ Output.*

Short-run supply curve is the rising segment of the firm's MC curve.

simplify the presentation, our example shows MC rising at a constant rate of two units. Our interest lies in the rising segment of the MC curve.

Both the MC and the MR are strategic concepts. The relation between them guides the firm's decision whether to expand or contract output, or to remain at a constant level of production. In the short run, the farm

Figure 9–3 The Marginal-Cost Schedule of a Computer Manufacturer: MC first declines and then rises as output expands.

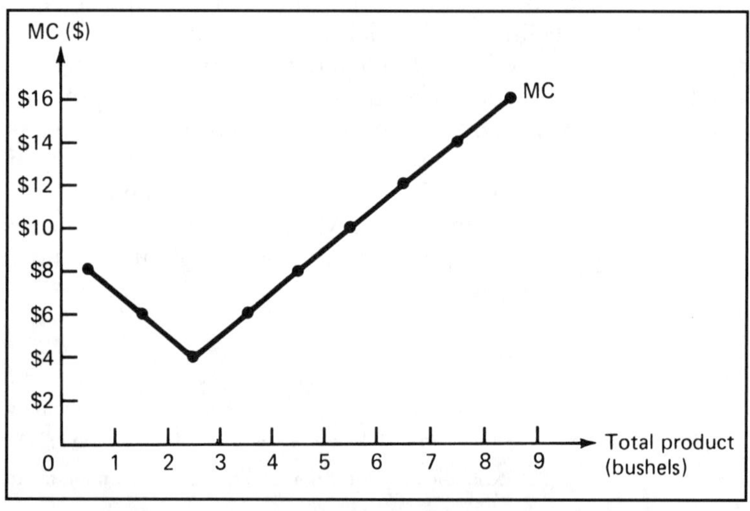

makes marginal decisions: to add (subtract) a few units to (from) its output. It evaluates these options by comparing how much an added unit of the product adds to its total cost (MC) and to its total revenue (MR). Conversely, in considering a small contraction of output, it compares by how much the contraction would curtail its total cost (MC) and its total revenue (MR). The concepts of MC and MR apply in both directions, to an expansion as well as a contraction of output.

THE PROFIT-MAXIMIZING OUTPUT OF THE COMPETITIVE FIRM

At the beginning of the chapter, we identified the objective of the firm as profit maximization. It wishes to set output at a level where the excess of TR over TC would be the greatest. To do so, the firm equates marginal revenue with marginal cost. Why does equality of MR and MC imply maximum profits?

Consider first the competitive firm, where the demand and MR schedules are identical and horizontal, and the relevant segment of MC slopes upward and to the right. This is shown in Figure 9–4. What is the profit-maximizing output?

Starting at output level *0A*, where MR ($10) exceeds MC ($5), the firm must decide whether to expand output, contract it, or stay put. Recall that marginal revenue is the addition to TR from one unit of extra output. Therefore, increasing output by one unit would add $10 (MR) to its total revenue. Marginal cost is the increment to total cost incurred by adding one unit to output. Expanding production by one unit would add $5 (MC) to total cost. Therefore, a one-unit increase in output would raise profit by

Figure 9–4 Marginal Cost and Marginal Revenue of the Perfectly Competitive Firm: Profit maximizing (equilibrium) output is set at a point where MC = MR. At output *0A*, MR > MC and the firm would increase profit by expanding. At output *0B*, MC > MR and the firm would increase profit by contracting. *0E* is equilibrium output: Movement in either direction reduces profit.

For a perfectly competitive firm, price = MR (the demand and MR schedules coincide), and so *MC also equals price.*

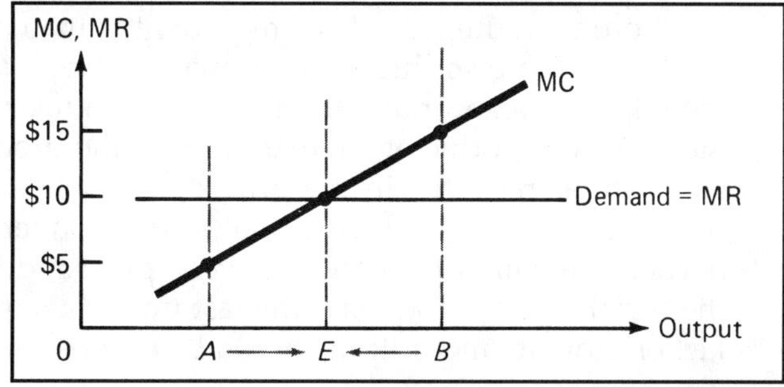

$10 – $5, or $5. The firm would expand production. In a more general way, the firm weighs the contribution of an added unit of output to its total revenue (MR) and to its total cost (MC): **As long as MR exceeds MC** (output to the left of point *E*), **the firm would expand output.** For the extra unit of output adds more to total revenue than to total cost, thereby increasing profit.

Profit maximizing output: occurs where MR=MC in imperfect competition; or where P=MC in perfect competition (where price equals MR).

Conversely, at output level *0B*, the firm again considers its options. It discovers that by contracting output by one unit, it can reduce its total cost by $15 (MC). Correspondingly, its total revenue would then decline by $10 (MR). Because total cost declines by a greater amount than total revenue, profits rise. It would pay the firm to contract output. In a more general way, the firm weighs the cost savings from the contracted unit of output (MC) against the loss in revenue (MR). **As long as MC exceeds MR** (output is to the right of point *E*), **it would pay the firm to contract production.** By doing so, it increases profit. The two arrows along the horizontal axis of Figure 9–4 describe the movement of output indicated above.

At point *E*, MC = MR. Any movement from *E* in either direction reduces profit. *0E* is *equilibrium output for the firm*, in the sense that profit is maximized. Should the firm expand production beyond *0E*, it would add to total cost more than total revenue, for to the right of *E*, MC exceeds MR. Should the firm contract output, it would lose more in total revenue than cost, for to the left of *E*, MR exceeds MC. ***0E is the equilibrium output of the single firm.***

What price would the competitive firm charge? That can be read off the demand curve facing it. Because it is horizontal and coincides with MR, the price is $10 per unit. **Equilibrium for the competitive firm is where MC = MR = Price.**

EVALUATION OF COMPETITIVE MARKETS

An advantage of a competitive system: is efficiency in resource allocation.

Advantages

Three important advantages of perfectly competitive markets follow from the foregoing analysis.

First, under perfect competition, **price equals marginal cost.** Price reflects the value society places on the commodity. Marginal cost reflects its cost to society, in terms of opportunity cost of the resources required to produce the particular commodity. Setting P = MC equalizes, at the margin, the satisfaction derived from the last unit of the product (marginal satisfaction) with the "sacrifice" required to obtain it.

Had price been higher than marginal cost ($P >$ MC), then resources would have been underallocated to the industry, from society's point of view. For by producing an extra unit of the product, we add more to satisfaction (as reflected in the price people are willing to pay) then to the resource cost of producing that unit. Conversely, if production goes beyond the point of equality between price and MC, so that $P <$ MC, then the social cost of producing the last unit of the product exceeds the satisfaction from it, and output should be reduced.

Equality of price and MC in all markets, which would obtain under perfect competition, ensures maximum satisfaction from the limited resources at the disposal of society. In a perfectly competitive economy, resource allocation conforms best to consumer wishes.

Long run: in a competitive industry, firms make zero economic profit in the long run.

Second, free entry into and exit of firms from the industry ensures that in the long run, firms would realize no economic profit. Existence of above-normal profit attracts new firms, a process that increases industry supply and depresses the market price. The process would go on until economic profits decline to zero and the incentive for the industry to expand disappears. Conversely, existence of economic loss induces firms to leave the industry. That reduces supply and raises the price until economic losses disappear, and with them the incentive for the industry to contract.

A third important result can be seen intuitively. Competitive pressure induces all firms to produce at the point of maximum efficiency, at the lowest production costs per unit of the output. It also forces them to introduce and use the latest technology. In a competitive environment, only the fittest survive.

Drawbacks

What are the shortcomings of a competitive system? First, a system in which factors' remuneration is commensurate with their productive contribution may generate an income distribution that is considered unacceptable to society. Government policy to equalize the income distribution was discussed in Chapter 3.

Second, no allowance is made for positive or negative externalities. Government action is required to adjust for these: Subsidize activities with positive externalities, and tax those with negative externalities (see Chapter 11).

Disadvantages of the perfectly competitive system: Possible excessive income inequality; inability to deal with externalities without government intervention; limited ability to incorporate technologies that require large-size firms.

Third, in certain industries, reasonably large firms are required to develop and exploit the best technology. And such size may not be compatible with perfect competition, where a great multitude of firms must exist in each industry. Finally, product standardization, implied by perfect competition, restricts consumer choice and may therefore lower satisfaction.

On balance, however, the advantages of competitive markets far outweigh the drawbacks, especially if public policy deals adequately with the first two problems.

PROFIT-MAXIMIZING OUTPUT AND PRICE OF A MONOPOLIST OR OLIGOPOLIST

Consider next a monopolist or oligopolist. Because of its negatively sloping demand curve, its MR is also negatively sloped. This is shown in Figure 9–5.

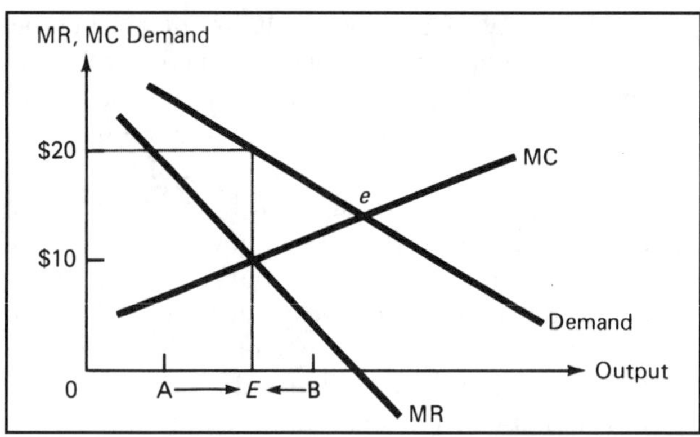

Figure 9–5 Equilibrium Output and Price of a Noncompetitive Firm: Profit maximizing (equilibrium) output is set at a point where MC = MR = $10. At output *0A* MR > MC and the firm would increase profit by expanding. At output *0B* MC > MR and the firm would increase profit by contracting. *0E* is equilibrium output: Movement in either direction reduces profit.

However because the demand schedule lies above the MR schedule, price ($20) exceeds MC ($10). Equality of price and MC, similar to the perfectly competitive outcome, would occur only at *e*. The oligopolist restricts output to *0E* and charges a *higher price than the perfectly competitive firm.*

But identical reasoning applies to the determination of its equilibrium output. It would be *0E*, the point where MR = MC ($10). From that output level, any expansion adds more to total cost than to total revenue, for to the right of *E*, MC exceeds MR. Any contraction of output subtracts more from total revenue than from total cost, for to the left of *E*, MR exceeds MC. From any point along the output axis, the firm would move to *E*. But once output *E* is reached, there is no incentive to expand or to contract production. *0E* is equilibrium output. The solution to problem 4 at the end of this chapter demonstrates that profit reaches its maximum at the level of output where MC = MR. The accompanying table demonstrates the same point.

Monopoly or oligopoly (few sellers). Charge a higher price and produce less than a perfectly competitive firm. As a consequence resources are underallocated to monopolistic or oligopolistic industries.

But here the analogy to the competitive firm ends. As we see in Figure 9–5, **given output *0E*, the price charged is determined by the demand schedule.** And that schedule lies above the MR curve. The price charged for output *0E* would be $20 per unit. The equality between MC and price is broken. **Price exceeds marginal cost.**

To equate price and marginal cost, the firm would have to produce at point *e*. And this leads to an important conclusion. **Profit maximization requires a monopolist or oligopolist to produce less and charge a higher price than the perfectly competitive firm does.** On these two counts, an imperfectly competitive industry is less efficient from society's point of view than is a perfectly competitive one. Resources are **under-allocated** to the monopolistic or oligopolistic industries. Monopolies and oligopolies produce less (and charge more) than what is warranted by the criterion of efficient allocation, as evidenced by the behavior of perfectly competitive firms.

The following hypothetical table is constructed to demonstrate the fact that profit (TR – TC) is at the maximum at the level of output at which MC = MR.

Demand and Cost Schedule of an Aircraft Producer

Price ($ Millions)	No. of Airplanes Purchased	TR ($ Millions) ($P \times Q$)	TC ($ Millions)	Profit ($ Millions) (TR – TC)	MR (ΔTR)[a]	MC (ΔTC)[b]
(1)	(2)	(3)	(4)	(5)	(6)	(7)
20	1	20	24	–4		
					(38 – 20 =) 18	(30 – 24 =) 6
19	2	38	30	8		
					(54 – 38 =) 16	(34 – 30 =) 4
18	3	54	34	20		
					(68 – 54 =) 14	(40 – 34 =) 6
17	4	68	40	28		
					(80 – 68 =) 12	(48 – 40 =) 8
16	5	80	48	32		
					(90 – 80 =) 10	(58 – 48 =) 10
15	6	90	58	32		
					(98 – 90 =) 8	(70 – 58 =)12
14	7	98	70	28		
					(104 – 98 =) 6	(84 – 70 =) 14
13	8	104	84	20		
					(108 – 104 =) 4	(100 – 84 =) 16
12	9	108	100	8		

Note: Columns 1 and 2 constitute the demand schedule, and are given. Column 4 is also given. The remaining columns are computed as shown in the table. Maximum profit is $32 million, occurring at 5 and 6 units of output. Between these two levels, MC = MR = 10.

[a]First differences in the TR column.

[b]First differences in the TC column.

Another difference applies to the long run. Because entry is free, a competitive firm cannot realize above-normal profit in the long run. That would merely attract new firms into the industry. Not so a monopolistic or oligopolistic firm. Entry into such an industry is difficult and sometimes impossible. Consequently**, the firm can realize above-normal profit even in the long run.**

SUMMARY

In order to compare the performance of a perfectly competitive industry with that of a monopolistic or oligopolistic one, it is necessary to delve into the behavior of a single firm. The prime objective of the firm is to maximize profit: the difference between total revenue (price per unit times output sold) and total cost. But realization of that goal results in different outcomes in the two types of firms.

A perfectly competitive firm is one of a multitude of similar firms. Its output is tiny relative to the industry's total output. The market price is established at the intersection of the "normal" sloping demand and supply schedules of the entire industry. But the single firm can sell all it wishes at that price. It can sell nothing at a price above this, and it need not lower its price below the market level to expand sales. This translates into a horizontal demand curve faced by the *single* firm.

Marginal revenue is the addition to total revenue accruing from an added unit of output. It applies equally to a loss in revenue from a one-unit contraction in output. Because the perfectly competitive firm expands or contracts its sales at a constant price, price is also MR. The demand and MR schedules are the same, and they are both horizontal.

Since the monopolist is a single-firm industry, its demand curve coincides with that of the industry. Both are negatively sloping. Similarly, an oligopolistic firm faces a negatively sloped demand schedule for its product. It must lower its price to expand sales. Conversely, a reduction in its output would trigger an increase in market price.

Because of this feature, MR is less than price. To expand sales by one (marginal) unit, the oligopolist/monopolist needs to reduce the price not only of the marginal unit, but also of the units that previously sold for more. MR is the new price minus the price reduction on those earlier units. The MR curve lies under the demand curve.

Costs are the other side of the profit equation. Total cost (TC) is the cost incurred by the firm in producing varying amounts of output. Marginal cost (MC) is the increase or decrease in TC incurred by adding to or subtracting from output one unit of the product, which in turn is governed (in the short run) by the law of diminishing returns. Our interest lies in the rising segment of the MC curve.

Equilibrium output of the firm is that level at which MC = MR. An increase in output from that level adds more to cost than to revenue, and a decrease in output depletes revenue by more than it lowers cost. That level is the profit-maximizing output.

Operating at that level, the perfectly competitive firm would charge a price that is equal to MC, because its demand and marginal-revenue schedules are identical. In contrast, a monopolist or an oligopolist would charge a price in excess of MC, because its MR schedule lies under its demand schedule; at each level of output, price exceeds MR. It would produce less and charge more than a perfectly competitive firm with the same cost structure. Here lies the central conclusion of this chapter: Resources are underallocated to the monopolistic/oligopolistic sectors of the economy. Such firms interfere with efficient resource allocation. This analysis provides the rationale for public policy toward monopolies and large oligopolies, to be addressed in the next chapter.

QUESTIONS AND PROBLEMS

1. Define:
   - ☐ Pure or perfect competition
   - ☐ Monopoly
   - ☐ Oligopoly
   - ☐ Monopolistic competition

Consult introduction to Part 2.

2. A supermarket is considering the possibility of staying open one extra hour per day. Describe the marginal considerations that enter this decision.
3. You are given the *market* supply and demand schedules for Canadian wheat (a perfectly competitive industry):

Price	Quantity Supplied (in Millions of Bushels)	Quantity Demanded (in Millions of Bushels)
$2	20	40
$3	30	30
$4	40	20
$5	50	10

   Draw the market supply and demand curves, and determine equilibrium price and quantity. Next, draw the demand and MR curves of a *single* wheat farmer. How would the price and quantity supplied by the single farmer be determined?

4. You are given the following demand schedule and total-cost figures for a large oligopoly firm producing jet aircraft:

Price (in Millions of Dollars)	Quantity Demanded (in Units)	TR ($P \times Q$)	Total Cost[a]	Profit (TR − TC)	MR (ΔTR)	MC (ΔTC)
9	2		20			
8	3		22			
7	4		26			
6	5		32			
5	6		40			

[a] *Total cost of producing the various levels of output.*

   Complete the columns for TR, profit, MR, and MC. At which output is profit at the maximum level? What is the relation between MR and MC at the profit-maximizing output? Is this an accident? Why, or why not? Explain fully.

   Now draw the demand, MR, and MC curves of the firm. Identify on your chart the (profit-maximizing) equilibrium output. Explain why you selected that point. What price would the firm charge at that output? Show this on your chart. What conclusion can you draw from this result concerning the market outcome of an oligopolistic industry relative to that of a perfectly competitive one?

5. Sketch demand, MR, and MC curves for General Motors—a large (oligopolistic) automobile manufacturer. Identify on your chart the equilibrium output and price. Explain why this is the equilibrium position.

   In 1982, the United Auto Workers granted GM wage concessions. As a result, wages and benefits of the workers (their "compensations") declined, reducing GM's (labor) production costs. Show that event on your diagram: At each level of output, MC is less than before. What effect would the reduction in labor compensation have on equilibrium output and price?

10 Departures from Competitive Markets—Market Power

Chapter 8 described an economy in which perfectly competitive markets allocate resources. But this idyllic description is more of an exception than the rule. Most sectors of the American economy do not conform to it, and some sectors do not even approximate it. Several deviations from a purely competitive economy are examined in this and the next chapter, the most glaring one being oligopolistic or monopolistic markets, and we shall make use of the results obtained in Chapter 9. At this point, the student is advised to review the classification of markets in the introduction to Part 2.

IMPERFECTLY COMPETITIVE MARKETS

Market power: A firm's ability to influence the price it charges.

Market Power

Competitive product and resource markets—many sellers and buyers of each product, and free entry—do not prevail in many industries. The landscape is often dominated by giant corporations and huge labor unions. In part, the emergence of large firms has resulted from the fact that exploitation of modern technology requires much capital, large markets, vast and complex organizations, and reliable access to raw materials. But in large measure, this development has come about because competition is irksome, and the individual producer tries to avoid it by forming combinations with competitors or by dominating the market. The massive size of large American corporations (often multinationals), such as General Dynamics, General Electric, General Motors, and all the other "generals,"[1] is far in excess of what is thought necessary to exploit "economies of

[1]Each year *Fortune* magazine publishes lists of the 500 largest corporations in the United States and of the 500 largest foreign corporations.

scale"[2] and reach maximum productive efficiency. And finally, at least in part, it represents the desire to attain visibility, power, and prestige.

Large corporations and labor unions (such as the United Auto Workers) have a great deal of market power with the consequent diminution of competition. They can fail to respond to slumping sales with a reduction in prices and wages, so that *prices and wages have become somewhat rigid or inflexible in a downward direction.* All this weakens the price system as a mechanism for allocating resources—that is, for providing precisely what society wants. It also weakens the protection afforded to the consumer in being able to choose among many competing sellers. Huge corporations are not subject to the same market restraints that limit the power of the competitive firm and force it to conform to society's desires.

In contrast to the perfectly competitive firm, a monopolist—and to a lesser extent, an oligopolist—has a measure of control over its price. With entry restricted, it is not pushed by market forces to the point of earning no more than normal profit, because it exercises a degree of control over these forces. Yet this control is not unlimited; even a monopolist faces some restraint on price behavior. Much economic analysis has been devoted to describing the pricing behavior of monopolists and oligopolists.

Pricing Behavior of Oligopolistic Firms

Oligopolistic behavior Oligopolies produce less and charge more than perfectly competitive firms, thereby creating allocative inefficiency. Entry into the industry is restricted.

A monopolist or an oligopolist is usually led to *restrict output* in order to *raise price* above the competitive market-equilibrium level. Because barriers to entry are high, this price does not attract new firms into the industry as in the competitive case. This rather common outcome has several undesirable implications: (1) The consumer must pay a price higher than the competitive price for the product. (2) Allocative inefficiency results, since fewer resources are employed in the oligopolistic industry than are warranted by consumer preferences. Consumer sovereignty in guiding resources from one industry to another is abridged. (3) Competitive pressure on firms to improve production efficiency and to introduce technological innovations is insufficient. (4) Market power forms the foundation of "cost—push" inflation, to be addressed in the parts of this book dealing with macroeconomics.

Monopolistically competitive markets depart somewhat from pure competition, in the direction of less efficiency. But because barriers to entry are minor and competitive forces are strong, the difference is not as great as in the case of oligopoly or monopoly.

Advertising

Advertising abounds in both monopolistically competitive and oligopolistic industries. But the social verdict concerning advertising is far from clear. On the one hand, advertising contains important information about

---

[2]When production costs per unit of output decline as the size of the operations expands, "economies of scale" are said to exist. (See Figure 10–1.)

products, services, processes, and the like. This is doubly important when new products are introduced into the market. Advertising can even be somewhat educational. On the other hand, it can be misleading, misinforming, and deceptive, or a sheer waste of resources. Most advertising contain both negative and positive elements. Billboards mar the landscape; but they also inform drivers of available accommodations, food, and fuel. The role of public policy is to minimize the deception and abuse while retaining the positive elements of advertising.

Mitigating Considerations

Economies of scale: As a firm increases its production, long run average cost declines. Scale economies, countervailing power, "workable" competition, and imports, mitigate the harmful effect of large oligopolies on the economy.

The verdict against oligopolies is somewhat tempered by certain advantages derived from **economies of scale**. If the development and utilization of the best technology require large firms, perfect competition may be ruled out. More generally, some industries require large-scale production just to attain maximum efficiency. "Economies of scale," where production costs per unit of output decline as the size of operations expands, may be obtained from greater specialization of labor and machines in production processes; from the development and introduction of new technology; from better utilization of management; from securing financing on the capital markets (it is easier for General Electric to raise funds than for a corner drugstore); from product distribution, advertising, and promotion; and from other aspects of the firm's activity. In multiplant firms, the specialization argument applies mainly at the plant level, while the other arguments apply to the firm as a whole. Firms in many manufacturing industries function under such scale economies

Where scale economies exist, it is customary to depict the cost per unit of the product—known as average cost—in a manner shown on Figure 10–1. The size of the firm, measured by the level or quantity of its output,

Figure 10–1 Relation of Size of Firm (as Measured by its level of output) to Cost per Unit of the Product: As output expands to point *OB*, cost per unit of output declines. This is the "economies of scale" range. In the next range, costs per unit of output are constant, describing "constant returns to scale." This is followed by the "diseconomies of scale" range, where costs per unit of output increase as output rises.

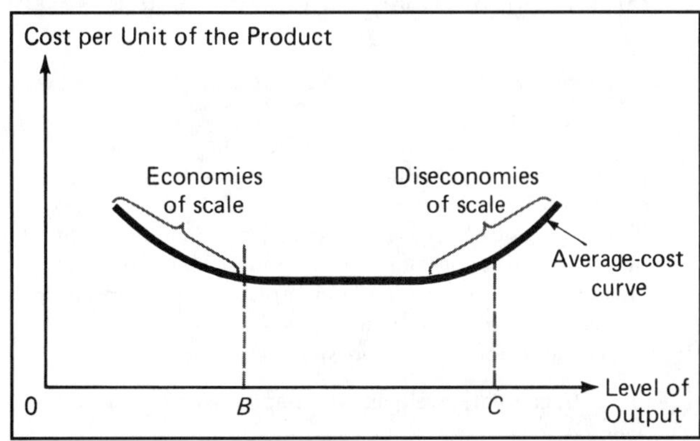

is shown on the horizontal axis, and the average cost is shown on the vertical axis. As the firm expands in size (namely, it increases the use of *all* factors), the average cost first declines, then remains flat at a certain minimum level, and over the subsequent range, it rises. Over the first stage of expansion, the firm benefits from scale economies, as outlined above. Maximum efficiency or minimum average cost is reached at some level of output, where the curve flattens out. Then, over a certain range of output, the same minimum average cost prevails. That is the range of maximum efficiency. For beyond a certain point, "diseconomies of scale" set in. The firm gets too big and complex to manage, and for a variety of reasons, the average cost turns up.

Optimum size of firms varies among industries. It is reached at a relatively small size in the textile and perhaps the shoe industries. But in steel, autos, aircraft, electrical appliances, and computers, output must reach a rather high level before economies of scale are fully exploited and minimum average cost is reached. And where there are great advantages to size, the number of firms in the market and the level of competition among them are necessarily limited. In the case of jet aircraft, world output can support only two or three firms operating at maximum efficiency.

However, in many industries, corporate size far exceeds the level that can be justified by these mitigating considerations.[3] In Figure 10–1, a firm producing *0B* of output already enjoys all the available economies of scale. Yet many corporations are of size *0C* or beyond where the damage in the form of production and allocative inefficiency is not offset by benefits from economies of scale.

Consumer Protection

Competition among sellers protects the consumer against market power exercised by large firms. Is the consumer left unprotected when such competition is weak? Not completely, argue some economists, for three possible reasons. In some industries, "countervailing powers" are said to exist.[4] Consider the oligopolistic electrical-appliance market. It is dominated by a few huge firms, such as General Electric and Westinghouse. But these firms do not face directly the "helpless" consumer. Rather, they sell to equally huge distribution companies, such as Sears. It is through such channels that the product reaches the consumer. And these companies are large enough to bargain effectively with the big manufacturers, so they

---

[3]Minnesota Mining & Manufacturing Company (87,000 employees; $6 billion in sales) is an example of a company that ferociously attacked bigness, by dividing itself into 37 divisions and nine subsidiaries. Most of its plants are of average size. See "Manageable Size: Some Firms Fight Ills of Bigness by Keeping Employee Units Small," *Wall Street Journal*, February 5, 1982, p. 1. The same problem applies often to individual plants. For example, in September 1981, Ford closed its huge Flat Rock (Michigan) engine plant that had been opened only ten years before. It was viewed as too big and too inflexible for conversion to making new types and different sizes of engine blocks for six- and four-cylinder cars.

[4]A concept developed and popularized by J. K. Galbraith in his book, *The New Industrial State*.

constitute a countervailing power. In turn, when they retail the product to the consumer, these outlets face ample competition.

Second, some economists believe that even in oligopolistic industries, there is a sufficient number of firms to provide at least "workable" competition. Stiff competition for market shares in an oligopolistic industry is a case in point. Even though the results do not square with those of perfect competition, strong competitive forces still exist to guarantee at least some measure of protection for the consumer. Clearly, the larger the number of firms, the better the outcome.

Third, benefits from competition in oligopolistic industries is obtained by opening our borders to foreign imports (as is attested to by the automobile industry) and inducing foreign countries to open their doors to our exports. For the world as a whole is the biggest attainable market. In the automobile industry, for example, instead of competition being limited to the big three domestic firms (GM, Ford, and Chrysler) it is extended also to several large Japanese and European producers. This is one analytical foundation to the policy of gradual and reciprocal reduction of import tariffs that has taken place among the countries of North America, Western Europe, and Japan over the past fifty years. Even a small country can enjoy the benefits of scale and competition if foreign trade is free to flow without obstruction. This is also one reason why 25 European countries[5] have formed the so-called European Union (EU), or Common Market. A main feature of the EU is the abolition of all trade restrictions among its members, thereby forming one huge market where many firms compete in each industry.

Summary

In the view of most economists, the benefits outlined above are only mitigating circumstances to an otherwise overconcentrated market power in the hands of giant corporations. Because of several barriers to entry, oligopolistic firms can **make above-normal profit** even in the long run. And since competition is restricted, **they cannot be forced** by competition to operate at a point of **maximum production efficiency.** Also, the consumer would be **charged a higher price** than under pure competition, and **resources would be underallocated** to the oligopolistic sector.

INTERNATIONAL CARTELS

International cartels: An organization of producers located in different countries that agree to set prices and restrict output.

Action to raise prices and limit competition is not restricted to national oligopolies. An **international cartel** is an organization of producers located in different countries and designed to set prices, allocate markets among themselves in an arbitrary fashion, or in other ways interfere with the workings of the market mechanism. An example is the International

[5]France, Germany, the United Kingdom, Italy, Belgium, Holland, Luxemburg, Denmark, Ireland, Greece, Spain, Portugal, Sweden, Austria, and Finland. Ten additional countries were added in 2005.

Air Transport Association (IATA). It is an organization of most of the international airlines, many of which are owned by their respective governments. They meet every year to set fares, and generally their decisions are backed up by the governments that have control over landing rights. (In the same manner, international ocean freight rates are determined by cartels of shipping conferences.) While air fares in the United States are set competitively, fares within Europe are set by a cartel and are therefore much higher than in the United States.

Another example of an international cartel is the Organization of Petroleum Exporting Countries (OPEC), which is controlled by the governments of the oil-producing countries rather than private companies. OPEC succeeded in quadrupling the price of crude petroleum within less than a year (1974), and then in doubling it again in 1979. Such price increases could occur in a commodity for which no close substitutes exist in the short run. But during the 1980s, oil prices declined sharply because of the emergence of new suppliers, and by reason of conservation activities that reduced demand. In 2005–06 oil prices rose to the $70's a barrel range, due to increased demand reinforced by OPEC market power. In general, the ability of a cartel to raise prices is limited by the availability of substitute products to which consumers can turn.

PUBLIC POLICY

It is generally recognized that many firms are much bigger than they need to be to enjoy the benefits of size. Thus, many economists insist that very large firms could be broken up and still remain highly efficient. Conversely, it would cause much harm to competition, and bring very few scale benefits, if the two largest chemical companies merged into one, or if executives of the large manufacturers of electrical appliances met periodically to agree upon common pricing and marketing policies rather than competing with each other.

U.S. public policy has attempted to strike a balance between the conflicting considerations outlined earlier. While recognizing the benefits of large size, it tries to deal with the most flagrant abuses that follow from large-scale enterprises. That policy is two-pronged: public regulation of the so-called natural monopolies, and antitrust legislation designed to enforce competition in other cases.

Natural monopoly: When fixed costs are high (e.g. utilities) one firm may be able to supply the entire market cheaper and more efficiently than a number of firms.

A **natural monopoly** is said to exist when fixed costs, such as power lines, are so high that it would not pay to duplicate them. Public utilities such as electric and gas companies are a case in point. They are granted monopoly positions by law but are made subject to regulation by state public-utilities commissions. These commissions may at times restrain firms under their jurisdiction from raising prices. One possible objective may be to force the utility to establish a price at point *e* ($15) in Figure 9-5, thus making it conform most closely to the competitive outcome.

▶ EXAMPLES OF MAJOR ANTITRUST SUITS

The term antitrust describes laws and programs designed to curb monopoly power and prevent business combinations and other practices that lead to the accumulation of market power. In the biggest suit in antitrust history, AT&T was charged with restricting competition in telephone equipment. In 1982, seven years after the suit was filed, an out-of-court settlement was reached between the company and the U.S. Justice Department. AT&T divested itself of the 22 local subsidiaries that account for two thirds of its $136 billion in assets. It kept its intercity and interstate phone operations, its equipment-producing arm (Western Electric), and its research facilities (Bell Laboratories). Following the divestiture, the local companies are now able to purchase equipment from sources other than Western Electric. On the other hand, AT&T is free to enter and compete in the lucrative data-processing and communications fields. AT&T continues to be supervised by the Federal Communications Commission, and the local companies (operating monopolies) are supervised by their respective state public-service commissions.

The longest-running antitrust case, the government suit against IBM, was filed in 1969 and dropped in 1982.

In September 1981, a judge dismissed a suit lodged by the government in 1972 against three cereal companies—Kellogg, General Mills, and Quaker Oats—charging that they had conspired to fix prices. In the same month, the Federal Trade Commission (FTC) dropped its long-standing antitrust suit against the nation's eight largest oil companies. In 1982, an FTC judge dismissed charges that General Foods used unfair practices and tried to monopolize the coffee market with its Maxwell House brand. And in 1984, the FTC approved a $13 billion acquisition of Gulf Oil by Standard Oil of California.

On the other hand, Mobil Oil Company was twice prevented from purchasing another oil company—first Conoco and then Marathon. In the end Conoco was purchased by the chemical company DuPont in 1981, and U.S. Steel acquired a controlling interest in Marathon.

In 1998, the Justice Department sued Microsoft, the software giant, for monopolistic and exclusionary practices. The case (in the U.S.) was settled in 2001, but as of early 2006 it was still pending in Europe. And in 1999, five vitamin-producing companies were fined over a billion dollars for price fixing.

Antitrust: Legislation which prohibits anti-competitive behavior such as price-fixing agreements by companies in the same industry.

In the case of oligopolistic firms, the **antitrust** legislation prohibits (subject to fines and even imprisonment) a variety of business practices that restrict competition and otherwise abuse market power.[6] In particular, price-fixing agreements by companies in the same industry are illegal, as are mergers between two firms in the same industry if both have substantial market shares. U.S. law also limits participation of American firms in international cartels. But the court battles to enforce laws have often been very protracted, and the courts have not been consistent in enforcing the legislation (see display box). During the Reagan years antitrust enforcement has been lax. Thus, between 1982 and 1986 the government challenged only 0.7 percent of the deals in which the parties were required to file for antitrust approval, compared to 2.5 percent during the Carter administration. Indeed, several major mergers took place in 1988. This trend continued unabated in the late 1990s, and beyond.

[6]These are laws designed to curb monopoly power.

Labor union practices include negotiating wage rates above market-equilibrium level; artificially raising demand for workers (featherbedding), or restricting their supply.

Corporate size is not the only source of allocative inefficiency. In many industries, an important input market—that of labor—is concentrated in the hands of labor unions. Wage determination is governed by negotiations between large corporations and large unions. Labor unions may negotiate wage rates above equilibrium market level, or engage in other practices that interfere with efficient resource allocation.

Consider the market for primary and secondary schoolteachers, shown in Figure 10–2. Equilibrium wage rate is at W_E. But teachers throughout the country form labor unions (affiliated with the National Educational Association) to bargain collectively with their respective school boards. They succeed in raising their salaries to OW, above the equilibrium rate. Certainly that is to the benefit of those teachers who are employed in the system. But at that salary there is excess supply of teachers in the amount of *bc*. In other words, newly trained teachers ready to join the labor force cannot find jobs. Although voters may be willing to pay somewhat higher taxes toward the defrayal of higher teacher salaries, they fail to raise taxes sufficiently over the years to cover the entire increase in cost. School budgets do not expand enough to accommodate the higher salaries. As a result, class size must rise in some areas. But mainly, teachers outside the system cannot find employment.

Two other modes of behavior of labor unions might be mentioned. A union may negotiate an increase in demand for its members, shifting the entire demand curve for labor upward and to the right. Thus, pilots' unions may negotiate the mandatory employment of a three- instead of a two-member crew in the cockpit of a certain type of aircraft, or perhaps fewer hours of flying time per month (Figure 10–3). On U.S. railroads,

Figure 10–2 The Market for Schoolteachers: A teacher's union may negotiate wage rate *W*, above the market-clearing rate, W_E. At that rate, the number of teachers available for work is *ac*, the number in demand is *ab*, resulting in excess supply of teachers *bc*.

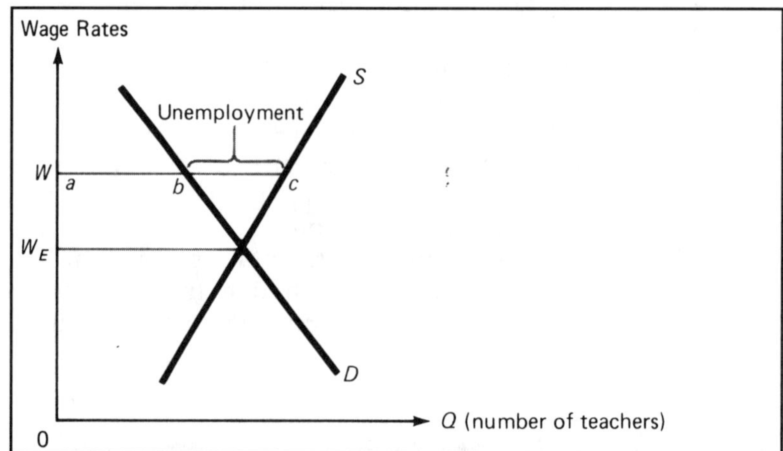

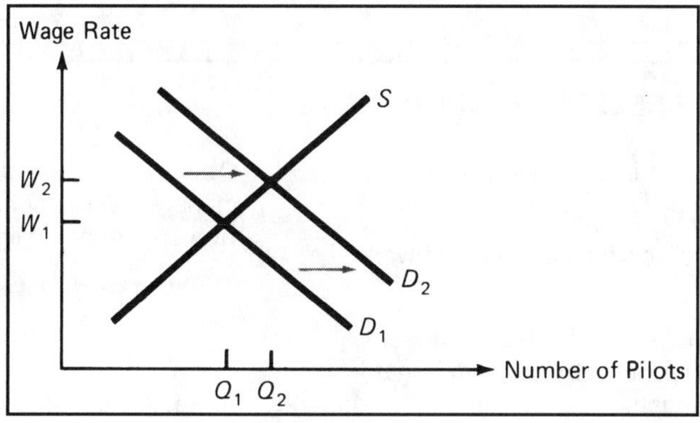

Figure 10–3 Airline Pilots Union Increases Demand for Labor from D_1 and D_2: Wage rates and the number of jobs rise.

employee unions insist on artificially raising the size of the crew serving each train. Known as *featherbedding*, this increases employment of union members while at the same time raising wage rates above the market equilibrium.

As a second alternative, a union may artificially limit the supply of workers in the particular skill it encompasses by restricting membership. This is true in certain building trades as well as some craft unions (such as electricians and plumbers). The effect of such barriers to entry is to shift the supply curve downward (to the left) and raise wage rates of union members above equilibrium level, while potential entrants into the labor force are kept out of these occupations (Figure 10–4).

Figure 10–4 Craft Union Reduces the Supply by Restricting Membership: Supply declines from S_1 to S_2. The number of workers employed declines from Q_1 to Q_2; the wage rate rises from W_1 to W_2.

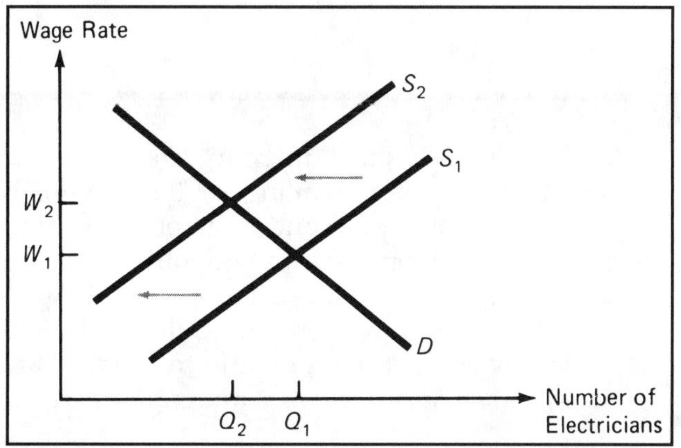

GLOSSARY OF SELECTED LABOR TERMS

Following are terms used in conjunction with labor legislation or collective bargaining:

1. **Labor union:** A collective organization of workers.
2. **Industrial union:** A union that represents employees of a single industry or a firm, regardless of their occupation.
3. **Craft union:** A union that represents workers of a single occupation, regardless of the industry they work in.
4. **Collective bargaining:** A process whereby a union bargains with management as a representative of its members. It usually leads to a labor contract, covering compensations and working conditions.
5. **Closed shop:** An arrangement under which only union workers may be hired by the firm.
6. **Union shop:** An arrangement that permits nonunion workers to be hired, but on condition that they join the union within a specified period of time.
7. **Open shop:** An arrangement under which management may hire nonunion workers, and workers are not obligated to join the union.
8. **"Right to Work" laws:** Laws that make compulsory union membership (and hence a union shop) illegal.
9. **Strike:** A work stoppage by all unionized workers, that lasts until management agrees to certain union demands, or until a compromise is reached.
10. **Lockout:** The closing down of a plant by management, to force striking workers to come to terms. It is the management counterpart of a strike.
11. **Injunction** (or a restraining order): A court order directing that some act not be carried out. For example, employers can obtain such a court order prohibiting a strike.
12. **National Labor Relations Board (NLRB):** A government board that protects labor from unfair labor practices, supervises union elections, and otherwise deals with employee relations.

In many Western countries, industrial unions have become very powerful, able to bargain for ever-higher wage rates and improved working conditions. Their market power matches that of many large corporations. But in the United States union membership has declined in recent years, and now amounts to only 15 percent of the labor force.

SUMMARY

Markets are classified in four categories, according to the degree of monopoly power prevailing in them: pure competition, monopolistic competition, oligopoly, and monopoly. In contrast to the purely competitive firm, an oligopolist or monopolist has a measure of control over price. Such firms can maintain prices above competitive equilibrium level by restricting supply. Not only does the consumer pay more, but the firm is not led by competitive pressure to produce at a point of maximum efficiency; and resources are underallocated to oligopolistic industries.

Despite some mitigating factors such as the benefits from economies of scale, most economists believe that large oligopolies interfere with production and allocative efficiency.

Large labor unions also exercise market power.

QUESTIONS AND PROBLEMS

1. *a.* Why is the market outcome in the case of oligopoly different from the outcome in the case of monopolistic competition?

   b. Define the two market structures mentioned in question 1a, and state how each of them differs from perfect competition.

2. Suppose the governments of Italy, Germany, France, and the U.K. decided to form a common market, so as to enjoy the benefits of competition and large-scale production at one and the same time.

   a. Can a market-sharing agreement among Fiat, Volkswagen, Renault, and British Ford—restricting each company to its national market—frustrate the intent of the governments involved with respect to the auto industry? How?

   b. Would anticartel legislation be necessary and helpful? What might the law say?

3. Bauxite, the mineral from which aluminum is made, is produced in several countries. There are two other ores that are almost equally well suited for aluminum production.

   a. Can the bauxite producers form a cartel and quadruple bauxite price the way the OPEC countries did with oil? Why, or why not?

   b. Suppose now that the substitute ores did not exist. Could a bauxite cartel be formed?

   c. Show diagrammatically the effect of a large increase in bauxite price on the prices of (i) aluminum, (ii) aircraft, (iii) airline fares.

4. Had shale oil been easy and cheap to extract, would the OPEC cartel have been successful? Why, or why not?

Departures from Competitive Markets—Government Intervention

GOVERNMENT PRICE CONTROLS

Price ceiling: A government regulation that sets an upper limit to price (as in rent control); this usually results in excess demand or shortage.

Price floor: A government regulation that sets a minimum price (as in agriculture); this usually results in excess supply and surplus.

Often the government interferes with efficient resource allocation by imposing a **price ceiling** or a **floor,** thus not permitting price to reach equilibrium. An inevitable result is a shortage or a surplus of the commodity or service in question.

Price Ceiling

Figure 11–1 displays the market for gasoline. Equilibrium price OP_E is the price that clears the market and performs the rationing function. But the government may impose an upper limit on the price at $0P_C$, as it did in the 1970s, and not permit it to rise to $0P_E$. The reasons for such price control may be many and varied. Most often, the government considers the product in question to be an essential consumption good and believes that the free market would price it out of the reach of vast segments of society. Thus, the U.S. government imposed price controls on meat, bread, and other products during World War II. Under the controlled price, the quantity demanded (*ac* in Figure 11–1) exceeds the quantity supplied (*ab*), and excess demand, or shortage (*bc*), emerges. It is *only* under price control that a *shortage* can develop.[1] In these conditions, price no longer performs the rationing function. Other forms of rationing may then be introduced. For example, customers may have to line up for the commodity, as they did in the case of gasoline in two summers of the 1970s, with the sellers selling until they ran out of supplies, leaving some customers frustrated ("first come, first served" as long as the supply lasts). Alternatively, each seller

[1] A phenomenon that frequently accompanies price control is the "black market." It emerges when owners of the commodity agree to sell part or all of their holdings at a price that exceeds the control price. If caught, the seller or the buyer may be subject to government penalty.

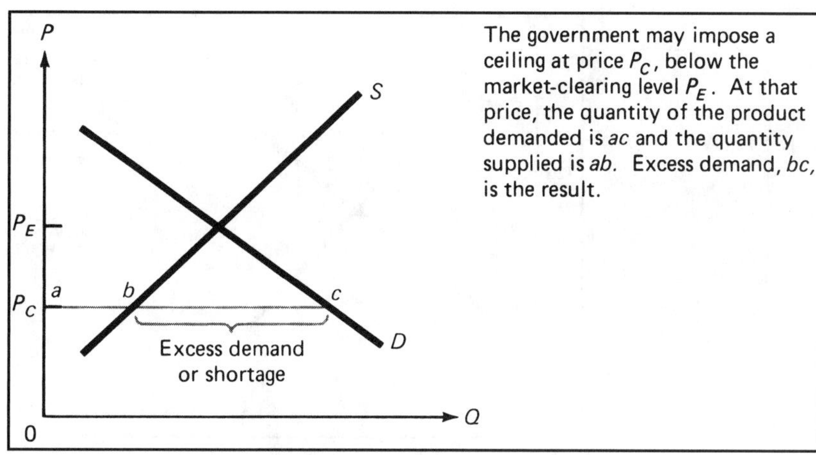
P
S
P_E
P_C
a
b
c
D
Excess demand
or shortage
0
Q
The government may impose a ceiling at price P_C, below the market-clearing level P_E. At that price, the quantity of the product demanded is *ac* and the quantity supplied is *ab*. Excess demand, *bc*, is the result.

Figure 11–1 Results of Price Control on Gasoline

may ration the commodity informally by offering to sell only a limited amount to each customer. Customers may then be induced to run from one seller to the next until their demand is fully satisfied. Closing all gasoline stations on Sundays is another form of informal rationing.

Alternatively, the government may introduce official rationing by printing and distributing coupons, each entitling its holder to a given quantity of the rationed commodity. An optional feature of a coupon rationing system develops if the coupons may be sold on the free market. Thus, consumers who require less than the allocated amount would sell the unneeded coupons to those who require more. If coupon rationing is used, a new bureaucracy is needed to administer it. And the bureaucrats are usually given special decision-making power over who deserves extra rations, and other important matters. The wielding of such power may become arbitrary and even capricious. In all cases, rationing is inefficient, and in many cases, it is also inequitable. For example, in the case of gasoline rationing, does an accountant who works at home deserve the same rations as a traveling salesman or a physician?

The appearance of shortages following the imposition of price controls need not be immediate. Consider the case of rent control imposed by a city council on apartments in the city. No change will be apparent immediately. But in time, some apartment owners will lose their incentive to maintain and keep up their property, and no new apartment buildings will be constructed. So the quality of rental housing will deteriorate and the quantity supplied will decline (moving from a free-market equilibrium point down along a positively sloped supply curve). At the same time, consumers will have an incentive to increase the quantity demanded by substituting apartment living for individual homes. The quantity demanded will increase, as consumers move down from a free-market equilibrium point along a negatively sloping demand curve. In time, shortages will appear. Thus, rent control imposed in a college town may not affect adversely the student population residing there at the time. But subsequent

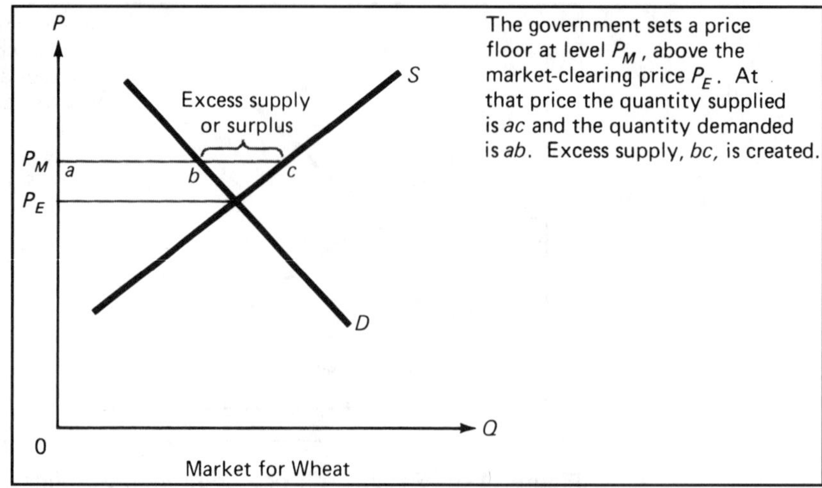
P
S
Excess supply
or surplus
P_M
a
b
c
P_E
D
Q
0
Market for Wheat
The government sets a price floor at level P_M, above the market-clearing price P_E. At that price the quantity supplied is *ac* and the quantity demanded is *ab*. Excess supply, *bc*, is created.

Figure 11–2 Imposition of a Minimum Price for Wheat by the Government: The only way a surplus can develop is by the introduction of a floor below which the price is not allowed to fall.

generations of students will find quality apartments unavailable, or in short supply.

Price Floor

In certain markets, the government may set a price floor below which the price is not allowed to fall. For example, Congress has set minimum wages by legislation—currently at $5.15 per hour. Because the law is set at the low end of the U.S. wage scale, it affects mainly (but not exclusively) the unskilled segments of the labor force.

Figure 11–2 may be applied to the unskilled labor market, with wage rate (price of unskilled labor) on the vertical axis (substitute *W* for *P*) and the number of unskilled workers demanded by firms and supplied by individuals on the horizontal (quantity) axis. The market-equilibrium wage rate is determined at $0W_E$, by the interplay of supply and demand. But the government sets the minimum wage at $0W_M$, above $0W_E$. The effect is to give those who happen to be employed a wage rate above market equilibrium. But at that wage rate, the number of unskilled workers demanded, *ab*, falls short of the number supplied, *ac*, that **excess supply** or **unemployment** develops in the amount *of bc*. Some firms cannot afford to hire all the dishwashers or peanut pickers they may need at the $0W_M$ wage rate. They will substitute machines for labor, or in some other way avoid employing as many workers as they would at wage rate W_E.[2] The result is that every time Congress raises the legal minimum wage, it also contributes to unemployment in the least-privileged segments of society. However, the analysis does not show *how much* unemployment results.

[2]With the passage of time, the general price levels rises, so that previously set minimums lose their effectiveness, and the minimum wage is therefore raised periodically.

This analysis is not in itself a justification for abolishing the minimum-wage legislation. Society may have other objectives in mind, such as redistributing income (from profit to wage earners) and may be willing to pay the cost of the legislation in terms of unemployment. What the analysis does is point out the cost of the legislation to society. It forces certain dislocations on employers, who may be induced to substitute machines for workers, and at times even go out of business because of too high a wage burden. But mainly it increases unemployment among the unskilled. For that reason, consideration is being given to establishing a subminimum wage for teenagers.

In most cases, the objective of the legislation is to redistribute income in society. In some popular discussion, it is at times justified as a means of raising living standards by paying higher wage rates. But higher living standards cannot be legislated. They depend solely on the productivity of economic agents in producing goods and services. An increase in wage rates that is not backed up by a rise in labor productivity would have two undesirable effects: In part, it would cause an increase in prices as employers pass on to consumers the increase in their labor costs; and in part, it would cause unemployment. Although there may also be some reduction in profit for firms that are forced to pay the higher wage rates, causing income redistribution from profit receivers to wage earners, most of the increase would dissipate in price increases and unemployment. There would be no increase in the average standard of living of the population as a whole.

GOVERNMENT REGULATIONS

There are certain industries in the United States, such as trucking and broadcasting, that are (or were) regulated by government agencies. With the support of the industry itself, the regulatory agency sets prices above

▶ GOVERNMENT CREATED-CREATED INEFFICIENCY

Congress has banned the export of Alaskan oil. As a result, supertankers carry 600,000 barrels of oil per day from Valdez, Alaska, down to the Panama Canal. The oil is then transshipped in smaller vessels through the canal, whereupon it is transferred back to supertankers bound for the U.S. Gulf Coast. The entire journey is in U.S. flagships, and costs $5.50 per barrel of oil.

Had there been no export ban, the same oil could have been shipped to Japan at 60¢ a barrel, and the difference made up by Mexican oil shipped to the Gulf Coast at 50¢ a barrel, or by Middle Eastern oil, shipped at $2–$3 per barrel.[3]

Opposition to the export of Alaskan oil comes from U.S. shipowners and maritime unions. Because under the law all interstate shipping must be done in American-made bottoms and by U.S. crews, the banning of export is an indirect subsidy of the shipping industry by U.S. oil producers, refiners, and consumers.

[3]Estimates are taken from a *Wall Street Journal* editorial, August 19, 1981.

those that would prevail on competitive markets. Thus, even though the industry itself may be highly competitive, government regulations confer upon it an oligopolistic status. In doing so, it inhibits competition, raises prices above the equilibrium level, and causes production and allocative inefficiencies.

As a consequence, many economists have long advocated **deregulation** (abandonment of regulation) of such industries. The U.S. airlines were deregulated in 1978, resulting in a widespread reduction in fares and increased capacity utilization of the airlines. Current proposals include deregulation of the trucking industry, and its relaxation in the case of railroads.

GOVERNMENT INVOLVEMENT IN THE MARKET SYSTEM TO ADJUST FOR EXTERNALITIES

Not all government interferences inflict damage on allocative efficiency. In sharp contrast to the cases considered above, government subsidies or taxes in cases of external benefits or external costs (respectively), improve the functioning of markets and promote allocative efficiency.

What Are Externalities?

External benefit (positive externality): Benefits to society from a good or service that exceed the sum of the benefits to individual consumers. Such goods are under-supplied by the private sector.

External benefits It will be recalled that the market-demand curve for a product is obtained by adding up the demand schedules of individual consumers. Thus, on the demand side, the price system tabulates only *individual* wants as translated into market demand (that is backed up by dollars). But there are goods and services—such as health and education—that are important to society as a whole. Their social importance exceeds the sum of their importance to the individuals benefiting from them directly. This excess of social benefits over the sum of individual benefits is known as **external benefits,** for it is external to the individuals that make up society. If left to the market mechanism, the economic system would produce too little of such goods and services, for production would then reflect only the sum of individuals' demand and ignore the external benefits to society.

Public good: Goods possessing two features: one person's use of the good does not prevent someone else from using it; and it is not possible for one person to exclude another person (e.g. who does not pay) from using it. Examples are national defense or a public park.

In Figure 11–3, *D* shows the sum of the demands by individual students for college education. *D'* (>*D*) reflects the tabulation of individual demands *plus* the external benefits accruing to society-at-large from college education. These cases call for government subsidy of the industries involved. Government aid to health or education is justified on these grounds.

An extreme case of such externality is known as **public** or *social* **goods**. These are goods that are consumed collectively. The distinguishing features of such a good are: (1) Its use by one person does not preclude use by others; and (2) it is not possible to exclude anyone who does not pay for the good from consuming it or enjoying its benefits National defense is a case in point. If the matter were left to market forces, no defense would

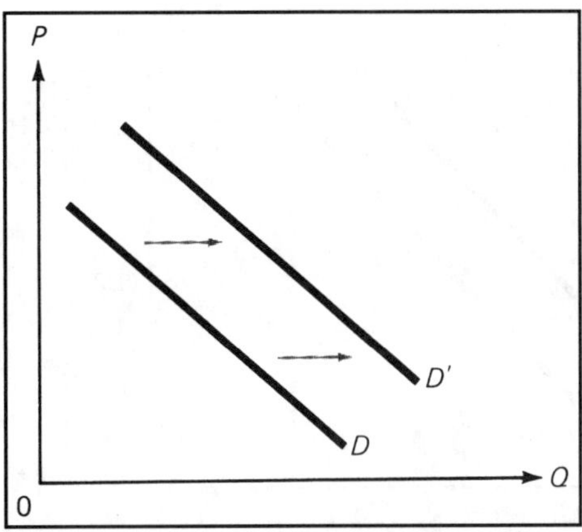

Figure 11–3 Market Demand for College Education, with (*D'*) and without (*D*) External Benefits

be provided, for no individual would be willing to pay for it. Public goods must be wholly financed by the state.

External costs (negative externality): Costs to society of producing a good exceed the sum of the marginal costs of individual firms (e.g. pollution). Such goods would be oversupplied by the private sector.

External costs Turning to the supply side of the market, supply decisions of firms are based only on the production costs the firms themselves must bear. The market supply curve is derived by adding up the supply schedules of the firms making up the industry. But there are costs to society—such as air and water pollution—that exceed the sum of the costs to individual firms. These are known as **external costs.** Using only the unchecked market mechanism, society would produce too much of the goods subject to such external costs, for the firm's production costs would appear too low; they do not incorporate the total cost to society (including the cost of environmental pollution) of producing the product.

In Figure 11–4, *S* shows the horizontal summation of the supply curve by the individual steel-producing firms, reflecting their private costs. When external costs (costs to society but not to the private firms) are also included, market supply of steel declines from *S* to *S'*.

In this case, the government may tax the firms involved and use the proceeds for cleaning up the environment, or it may promulgate regulations that force the firms to clean up after themselves. In sum, the need to adjust for such *externalities* is one reason for modifying the outcome of the price system.

In what follows, we illustrate this discussion with reference to adjustment for one external cost: pollution.

Controlling Environmental Pollution

One of the proper functions of government in a market economy is to deal with externalities. Environmental pollution is a cost external to the firm but internal to society as a whole. It is not incorporated in the firm's cost and supply curve and therefore is not reflected in the industry supply

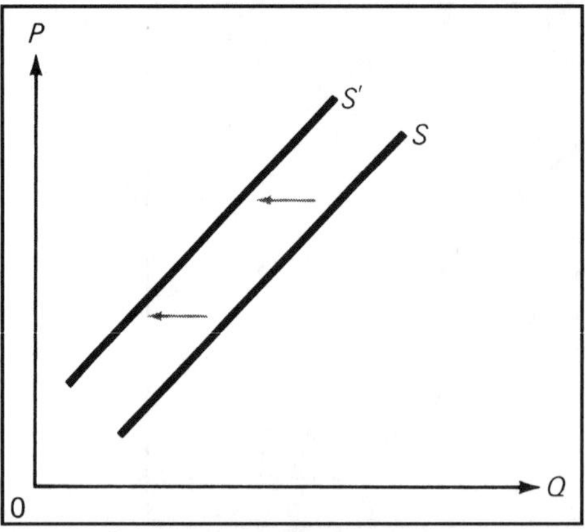

Figure 11–4 Market Supply of Steel with (S') and without (S) External Costs

Internalize an externality: incorporate the social cost into the firm's cost. A tax approach to controlling pollution is more efficient than government decree. A market for pollution rights, charging people a "market price" for the "right to pollute," is another method.

schedule. Had it been so included, the supply curve of a polluting industry would have been lower (shifted to the left) than it actually is. The government role is to see to it that such external costs are **internalized** by the industry, so that the supply curve is indeed shifted to the left, and the resulting market price is high enough to enable the industry to clean up after itself, to leave behind clean water and air. Additionally, the resulting equilibrium quantity would be lower than if only private cost were taken into account. Such a supply curve would reflect both the private and the social costs of producing the product, and would therefore be lower than the curve based solely on private costs. But without some form of government regulations, firms restrict themselves to private-cost calculations and have no incentive to defray the social costs. The agency in charge of promulgating the enforcing environmental clean-up regulations in the United States is the Environmental Protection Agency, or the EPA.

There are several alternative methods of reducing pollution, and they are not all equally efficient. Consider a case in which ten firms operate ten plants along a river, and all emit pollutants into the water. Suppose that the EPA wishes to clean up the river to a point of eliminating, say, 50 percent of the pollution. It can *decree* that each plant must meet that standard of cleanliness, forcing each firm to install pollution-control equipment that will remove half the pollutants resulting from its production processes. That is, although the EPA is interested only in reducing by one half the *aggregate* pollution in the river, the "decree method" accomplishes this by forcing each *individual* plant to meet that standard. But plants vary a great deal in the cost of reaching that standard. Some can attain it at minimal cost; for others, it is very costly. So the aforementioned method of pollution control is inefficient, since it makes no distinction among plants on the basis of the cost of compliance. Yet this is the method commonly employed.

Suppose that, as an alternative, the EPA imposed a tax on polluters. Firms would be free to pollute as much as they wished but would be subjected to the tax if they did. Then each individual firm would calculate the relative cost of paying the tax versus eliminating or lowering pollution. Only where the installation of antipollution equipment is cheaper than the

God said to Moses: "I have good news and bad news."
MOSES: Give me the good news first.

GOD: I shall bring upon the Egyptians the ten plagues, and they will let your people go.

MOSES: And what is the bad news?

GOD: You, Moses, will have to write an environmental-impact statement.

tax would it be installed. The tax could be set at a level that would reduce overall emission by 50 percent. But that reduction would come only from the firms that found it cheaper than the tax. Some plants would continue to emit as before, and others would eliminate pollution altogether. Only the overall outcome matters, and it would be achieved at a smaller cost than through the "decree method."

There is another sense in which the tax method may result in a more efficient outcome: if there are economies of scale in pollution control. In that case, instead of having each firm install pollution-control equipment, it would be cheaper to impose a tax and use the proceeds to construct a water-treatment plant downstream that would service the ten firms combined. The large-scale plant would then be built by a state or local government unit; but only the tax approach lends itself to such a solution.

This discussion has general application in economics. Whenever public policy wishes to nudge the economy in a certain direction, the indirect method of taxes and/or subsidies is often superior to the direct method of government decrees. And that for two reasons: First, because taxes and subsidies interfere less with economic freedom; offering a financial inducement is less restrictive than issuing a direct order. And second, the indirect approach may be more efficient or less costly because it permits a distinction among firms on the basis of costs of compliance.

Consider, for example, alternative policies to reduce congestion in downtown areas. The city government can prohibit private cars from entering a prescribed area. Such outright prohibition interferes with individual freedom and also necessitates the setting up of a (sometimes costly) bureaucracy to issue licenses exempting certain people—such as doctors or salesmen—from the regulation. This can be arbitrary and inefficient. Instead, the city government can impose a stiff parking tax in the downtown area. This would induce most commuters to switch to public transportation. But those willing to pay the tax—and that includes doctors and salesmen—can park to their heart's content. The objective is achieved in the most efficient way and with minimum interference with economic freedom.

As another example, consider the major airports in the country. They are overloaded during certain peak hours of the day, resulting in long delays for aircrafts taxiing for take-offs or waiting to land. The efficient remedy to this negative externality is to levy a tax on the airlines for the use of the airports during the highly congested hours. The airlines

▶ OTHER USES OF TAXES AND SUBSIDIES

Taxes and/or subsidies to induce people to behave in a certain way can be used in other areas. In the 1980 presidential campaign, Independent candidate Anderson proposed a gasoline tax to promote energy conservation. To counter criticism that such a tax would weigh too heavily on the poor, he proposed to couple it with a direct income subsidy. Many people thought this would merely shift money from one pocket to another and accomplish nothing. The following highly simplified example illustrates the validity of his proposal.

Consider an "average" family that consumes 1,000 gallons of gasoline per year. At an assumed price of $1 per gallon, it spends $1,000 on gasoline. Suppose now that the government levies a $1-per-gallon tax, and assume (unrealistically) that the price rises by the full amount, to $2 per gallon. The tax costs our representative family $1,000. It receives from the government a check (income subsidy) in that amount.

Should the family spend its entire $1,000 subsidy on gasoline, it would purchase 1,000 gallons as before, but now at a cost of $2,000. No conservation would occur.

But the family is unlikely to behave in that fashion, because gasoline has doubled in price relative to all other goods and service. Rather, it would spend only part of the subsidy on gasoline, to cushion the effect of the price increase, and devote the rest to other goods and services. If, for example, half the subsidy is spent on gasoline, the family would purchase 750 gallons for $1,500. Conservation of 250 gallons would result.

would pass all or part of the tax to the flying public by raising fares for flights during these hours. As a result, travelers who do not need to fly during these hours would shift to other hours, and the congestion would be alleviated.

Returning to the pollution case, a third method of reducing pollution is known as "a market for pollution rights." Suppose the EPA wanted to restrict the amount of pollutant X in the atmosphere to a level considered safe. The agency would then issue and auction off permits to pollute, with the total permits issued adding up to the amount the agency considers safe. In Figure 11–5, this quantity is depicted as $0Q_s$, and the supply of permits is of zero elasticity at that level. Polluters will bid for the permits, with the intersection of demand and supply determining their price, OP_E. A rise in demand would merely increase the price, leaving quantity unchanged. This method also yields revenue, which the government can use to install a large-scale plant for pollution control.

Clean air and water are scarce commodities that need to be rationed. And a market for pollution rights is an efficient way of rationing them. In 1982, the EPA took a step in that direction. The government assumes that an area including several plants is covered by an imaginary "bubble." It permits companies to expand their industrial operations as long as total emissions within the bubble do not increase. And within this overall limitation, companies are allowed to trade with each other "rights to pollute."

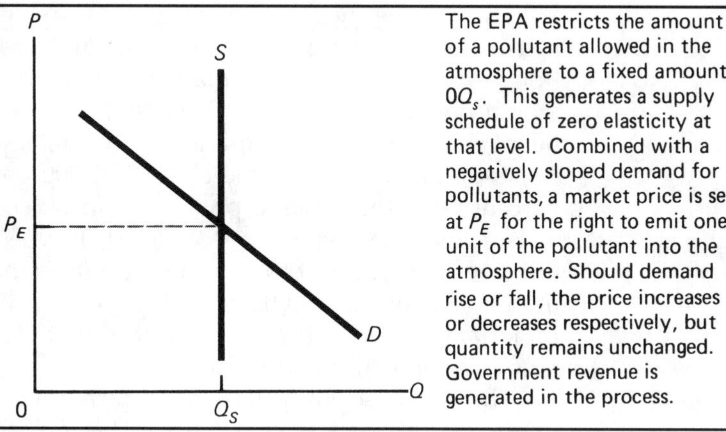

P
S
P_E
D
0
Q_S
Q
The EPA restricts the amount of a pollutant allowed in the atmosphere to a fixed amount $0Q_s$. This generates a supply schedule of zero elasticity at that level. Combined with a negatively sloped demand for pollutants, a market price is set at P_E for the right to emit one unit of the pollutant into the atmosphere. Should demand rise or fall, the price increases or decreases respectively, but quantity remains unchanged. Government revenue is generated in the process.

Figure 11–5 Market for Pollution Rights

GOVERNMENT INTERVENTION TO REDISTRIBUTE INCOME

Prices of factor inputs, established on their respective markets, determine the earnings of workers possessing various skills and of the owner of other factors of production. Indirectly, they determine the way income ends up being distributed among various segments of society. Clearly, people whose productive contribution is great—because they possess native ability, training, and education, or own capital and natural resources—command greater income than others. Given the great variations in people's native ability or acquired endowment, there is no reason to expect the income distribution that emerges from the market system to be equal, or even to approximate equality. It would be anything but equal.

Yet there is a deep and even emotional interest in this outcome. Some observers argue for a reasonably equal income distribution; others maintain that the market outcome should be preserved, however unequal it may be. There are potent arguments on both sides of the issue. The case against undue inequality is that it involves too much poverty at the lower end of the distribution. Not only is such poverty socially unacceptable, but it impairs the economic productivity of people below the poverty line. People who are ill-fed, poorly clothed, and poorly sheltered cannot perform well on their jobs. On the other hand, people at the top end of the distribution spectrum possess too much political power. Also, excessive inequality tends to foster unequal opportunities for future development and advancement, including educational and economic opportunities for the next generations. In other words, the inequality tends to be preserved and perpetuated in coming generations.

The case for inequality is threefold. First, it provides strong monetary incentives for people to invest, work, and produce. With equal distribution, such an incentive is inadequate; why work hard if your income would not be much affected? Indeed, it is known that in societies where people reach a very high marginal tax rate at just above average incomes (for example, if any income above $25,000 per year were taxed at an 85 percent rate), the drive to produce is low. Second, it is the upper middle class—whose existence is occasioned by unequal income distribution—that generates most of the savings and investment in society, thereby promoting economic growth. It is members of that class that are willing to undertake risky ventures. Third, it is that class that creates markets for new and sophisticated products.

There is no scientific base for determining the optimal income distribution. We can only say that it can be too even for adequate economic growth or too uneven to be socially acceptable. In the United States and other Western countries, the government alters the market outcome in the direction of greater equality. Disproportionately high taxes are levied on the rich through the progressive income tax system (Part I) and a variety of subsidies are offered to the poor. They include welfare benefits, unemployment benefits, retraining programs, health-care programs, and the like. It is through such a tax-subsidy combination that the federal budget redistributes income in society. There are even proposals to eliminate poverty altogether by giving each family below an arbitrarily defined poverty line a direct grant that would raise it up to a "socially desired" income level. Such a scheme has been enacted under the label "earned-income credit." While the middle and upper classes pay taxes to the government, the poor would receive a subsidy from the government. The thorny issue is how to provide such automatic income subsidies and still preserve work incentives of the poor.

GOVERNMENT INTERVENTION TO STABILIZE THE ECONOMY

It was suggested above that the functioning of today's markets is far from perfect. Market imperfections include insufficient competition, leading to inflexible prices and wages. If prices do not move swiftly in response to supply and demand conditions, at least two things may happen. It may require a considerable *time lag* before the economy responds to changes in private demand and social needs. And second, the market mechanism does not guarantee full employment and price stability. This last point is the centerpiece of the contributions made by another giant of economics, J. M. Keynes. Falling under the heading of macroeconomics, it will be addressed in Parts 3 and 4 of this book.

SUMMARY

Apart from market power exercised by large firms, there are other ways in which private groups and government agencies distort or impede the operations of markets. The reason may be the pursuit of some social goal (minimum wage); political power of the group benefiting from the action; or economic power of a group exercising private power (labor unions). Only a sample of such activities was selected for inclusion in this chapter. Economic analysis enables us to explore the effect, damage, and benefit in each case.

On the other hand, public action may be undertaken to help improve the operation of markets by correcting for externalities, as in the case of environmental pollution. Alternative means for controlling air and water pollution were discussed, with emphasis on the relative cost of achieving a desired goal. Government actions to modify the distribution of income and to stabilize economic activity were also considered.

QUESTIONS AND PROBLEMS

1. Show diagrammatically and explain the long-run effect of government control over the price of natural gas.
2. Hawaii is a major sugar-growing state, with three main individual growers responsible for most of the state's sugar output. In 1977, the U.S. Congress debated a proposal:

   a. To increase the support price for sugar.

   b. To limit the sum paid to any individual grower in sugar price support to $50,000.

   How do you suppose the Hawaiian congressional delegation voted on each of the proposals, and why?
3. Europeans are reported to be increasingly concerned about the "butter mountains" and the "wine lakes" that have been accumulated as a result of their agricultural policy of price support. Using supply and demand diagrams, explain the meaning of this statement.
4. Using a supply and demand diagram for the market for steel, show the effect on equilibrium quantity and price of the introduction by the federal government of antipollution standards for the industry. *(Hint:* Costs rise, so supply declines.)

   Can you tell what would happen to the total revenue of the industry? What would that depend on, and how?
5. *a.* Using a supply and demand diagram for the unskilled labor market, analyze the effect of an increase in the minimum wage from $3.35 to $ 5.35 per hour on that market.

   b. What do you suppose the effect might be on the wage rate in the market for semi-skilled workers?

   c. On January 16, 1979, *The Wall Street Journal* reported that the "boost in minimum wage tipped the scales [in several companies] in favor of taking labor-saving steps." Self-service gas stations and replacement of restaurant cashiers by special cash registers that can be used by waitresses are given as examples. Explain the connection between parts *a* and *c* of this question.

6. "Unemployed people receiving high unemployment compensation are less likely to actively seek and accept new employment than those not receiving jobless benefits." Do you agree? Explain why.
7. On October 11, 1988, (p. A22) *The Wall Street Journal* ran a story entitled "Why Berkeley Is Turning Into a Commuter School." A strict rent control introduced in Berkeley in 1980 has now induced thousands of students to find living accommodations in Oakland and other Bay-area communities, so that they need to commute to the famous university. Explain the relation between the rent control and the commuting phenomenon.

PART THREE

OUTPUT, EMPLOYMENT, AND FISCAL POLICY

OVERVIEW

Macroeconomics: the study of the economy as a whole.

Part 2 of this volume sketched out the mechanism by which scarce resources are allocated among sectors and industries in a market economy to produce the product mix desired by consumers, and the mechanism by which the given aggregate income—corresponding to the total output—is distributed. The *composition* of output, the *distribution* of income, and the determination of *individual prices* held the center of the stage. To highlight the problems of scarcity and choice, the analysis assumed implicitly that resources are fully employed. Nothing was said about what determines the **aggregate level of output** to be so distributed among sectors and industries, the corresponding **aggregate level of income** to be divided among groups in the economy, or the **average price level** prevailing in the economy as a whole, as distinguished from the price of one good relative to that of another. These are topics of macroeconomics.

In particular, macroeconomics highlights three main issues: the long-run growth potential of the economy, the short-run (annual) *aggregate* level of economic activity, and the rate at which the price level changes. Rather than being concerned with the output and sale of a specific product, it deals with total output of all goods and services put together.

LONG-RUN GROWTH

The economy is endowed with a given amount of productive resources: labor, capital, land and natural resources, and entrepreneurial ability. It also has a given level of technology based upon previous technological inventions. Employing that technology, and combining all its available resources in the most efficient way, the economy can produce a given aggregate volume of (real) goods and services to the benefit and enjoyment of the populace. This volume is a measure of the *productive capacity* or the **potential output** of the economy.

Potential output: The total amount of goods and services which *can* be produced if all available resources were employed in their most efficient way. Potential output rises over time with the increase in resources and improvement in technology.

Over the years or decades, the country's resources—its labor force as well as its capital stock (machines and structures)—expand. The efficiency in the use of these resources and the level of technology also improve. Consequently, the economy's potential output rises. This is called long-run growth. Exhibit 3–1 is a schematic illustration of the main sources of economic growth: increased quantity and improved quality of labor and capital. Economic growth can be depicted by "pushing outward" the transformation curve shown in Figure 1–3 in Chapter 1. It determines the extent to which increasing wants can be satisfied.

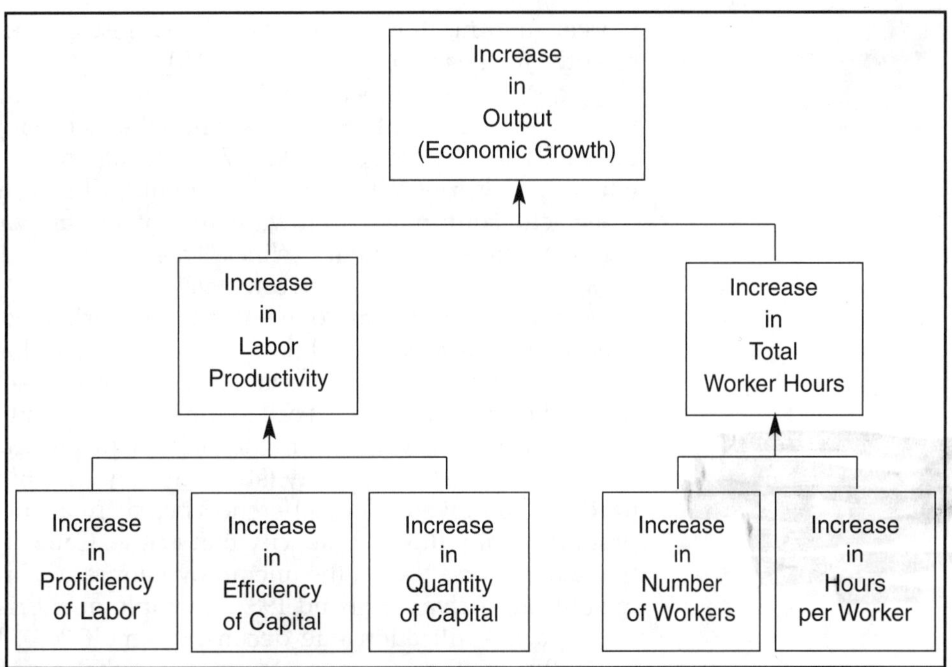

Exhibit 3–1 Sources of Economic Growth

Source: "U.S. Economic Performance in a Global Perspective," New York Stock Exchange, New York, February 1981, p. 16.

SHORT-RUN FLUCTUATIONS IN ECONOMIC ACTIVITY

In Exhibit 3–2, the bold line shows the growth potential in real GDP (net of inflation) over the 1976–2004 period. It is the growth in the economy's output at full capacity and at top efficiency. The smooth upward movement of the line reflects long-run growth resulting from increased resources and improved productivity. But in fact, the economy does not grow in a smooth fashion. It moves forward in fits and starts. And its actual growth is shown by movement in actual GDP, subject to these fluctuations, represented by the lighter line in Exhibit 3–2.

A central question of macroeconomics is: Will the economy operate at its *full capacity,* employing all its resources, and producing the maximum possible goods and services? Or will some of its resources, both labor and capital, be unemployed, and aggregate output fall short of its full potential? If so, what forces cause such unemployment, and how can the situation be remedied?

GDP gap: The difference between potential output and actual output. When the gap is large, unemployment increases.

This issue is highlighted by the relation between the potential and actual GDP, both expressed in real terms (adjusted to exclude inflation). The vertical distance between the light and bolder lines in the figure represent the shortfall between potential and actual output at any given year. Known as the **GDP gap**, it indicates the extent to which the economy failed to utilize its entire productive capacity—the extent to which some workers and machines were idle. The largest gap occurred in 1982. Most recently, the negative gap closed in 2003.

Indeed, it can be seen in 3–2(b) that the rate of unemployment rises in years when actual output declines and falls increasingly short of potential output. This happened in 1974–75, and again in 1980–82. Conversely, when the divergence between the two output measures declines—that is when actual output moves toward and catches up with potential output—the rate of unemployment declines. This occurred between 1976 and 1979, between 1983 and 1988, between 1992 and 2000, and in 2003–05.

Capacity utilization: the percent of available plants, equipment, industrial structures and machines that are employed.

Although the unemployment rate of workers is an important social concern, we also wish to know the level of employment of plants and equipment, that is, of industrial structures and machines. The degree to which they are employed is called the rate of **capacity utilization,** and the measure is usually confined to the manufacturing sector. It shows the percentage of industrial capacity (structures and machines) that is being utilized or employed. The difference between it and 100 percent is the proportion of industrial capacity that is idle. Capacity utilization tends to fluctuate inversely with the unemployment rate. Thus, in years of declining output, such as 1974 and 1982, unemployment rises (Exhibit 3–2), and the capacity-utilization rate declines (Exhibit 3–3). During 1976–79 and 1983–88 output increased, and with it rose the rate of capacity utilization. In turn, unemployment was on the decline. Note that even in years of rising output, capacity utilization does not reach 100 percent. It hovers below the 90 percent mark. In the 1990s a mild recession occurred early in the decade, with rising unemployment, followed by economic expansion into 1999–2000 when unemployment declined to around 4 percent. Again, following the 2001 recession, capacity utilization rose in 2003–05.

Growth in output is not necessarily commensurate with the rise in economic welfare. People concerned with the quality of life have criticized the economists' preoccupation with growth, and the use of aggregate output as the barometer of economic well-being. What if output rose 5 percent in a given year, but so did the level of air and water pollution and the degree of congestion in urban areas? Was society made better off by such an advance? Should we not adjust the measures of total output downward to allow for the social costs (externalities) incurred in its production? These questions have not yet received satisfactory answers.

Finally, inflation rose during the expansion of 2003–06.

INFLATION

Price level: A weighted average of all the prices in the economy. **Inflation** occurs when the price level rises continuously and **deflation** occurs when it falls continuously.

The next interest of macroeconomics is prices and inflation. As in the case of output, it is not concerned with the price of an individual commodity and its determination, nor with the price of one product relative to another. Rather, it focuses on the **price level**, a weighted average of all prices prevailing in the economy. A continuous increase in the price level is called **inflation**; that is, inflation is a *rising* price *level,* not *high prices.*

Exhibit 3–4 shows one measure of the U.S. inflation rate over the past twenty years. It is evident that the mid-1970s were years of high inflation, with its rate reaching into the "double-digit" range—exceeding 10 percent

Exhibit 3–2 Actual and Potential Aggregate (Real) Output in the U.S. Economy, and the Rate of Unemployment

(a) The GDP gap

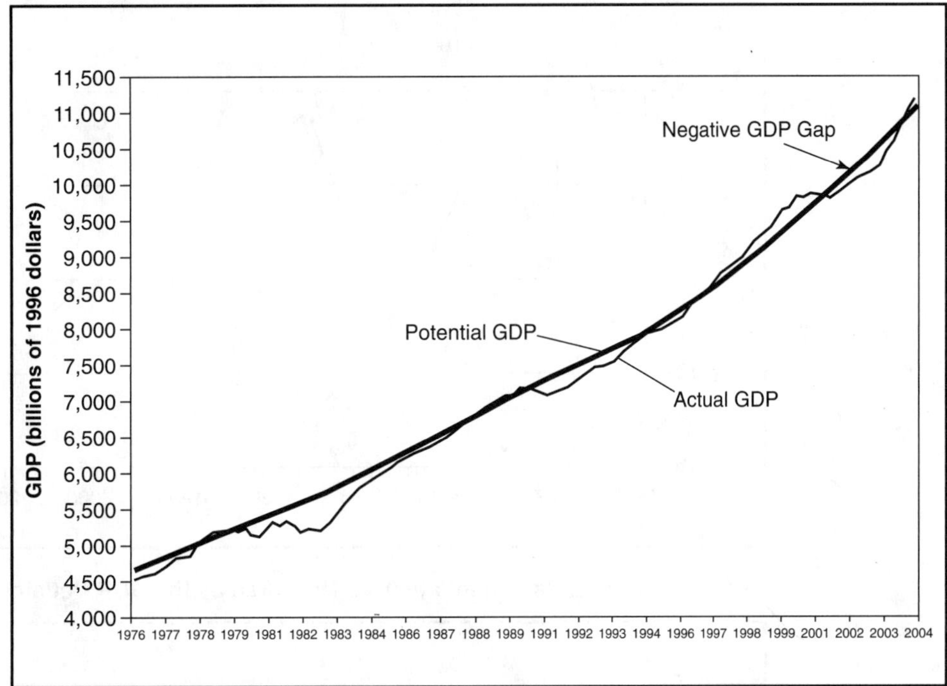

(b) Unemployment rate

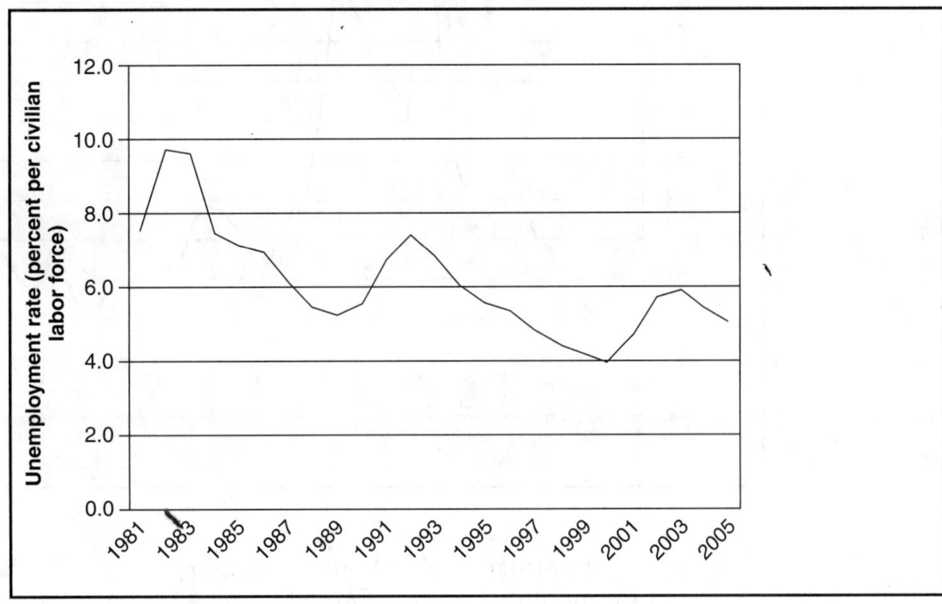

per year. In contrast, inflation declined sharply between 1982 and 1987, and between 1992 and 1998. It rose again beginning in 2003, and became a major concern in mid-2006.

Exhibit 3–3: Capacity Utilization in Manufacturing

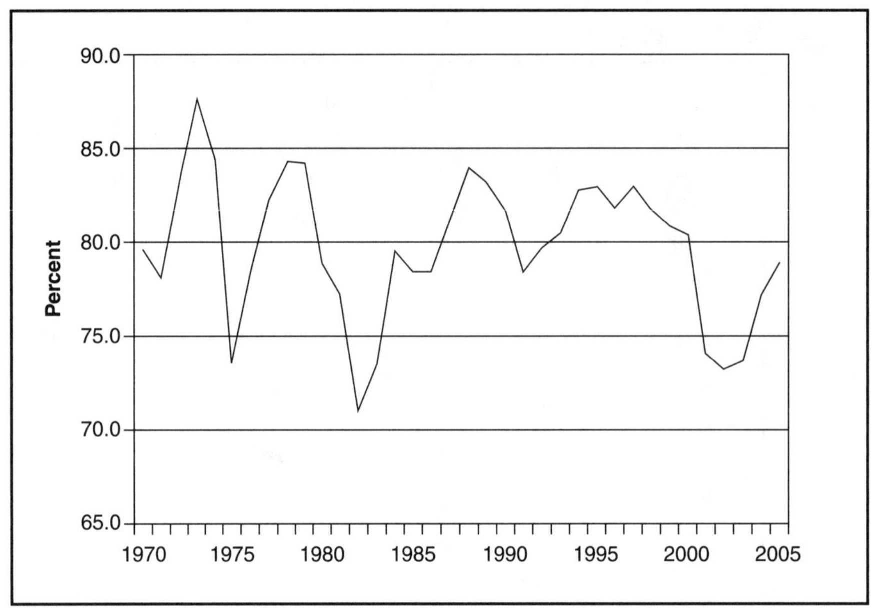

Exhibit 3–4: U.S. Rate of Inflation, as Measured by the GDP Deflator

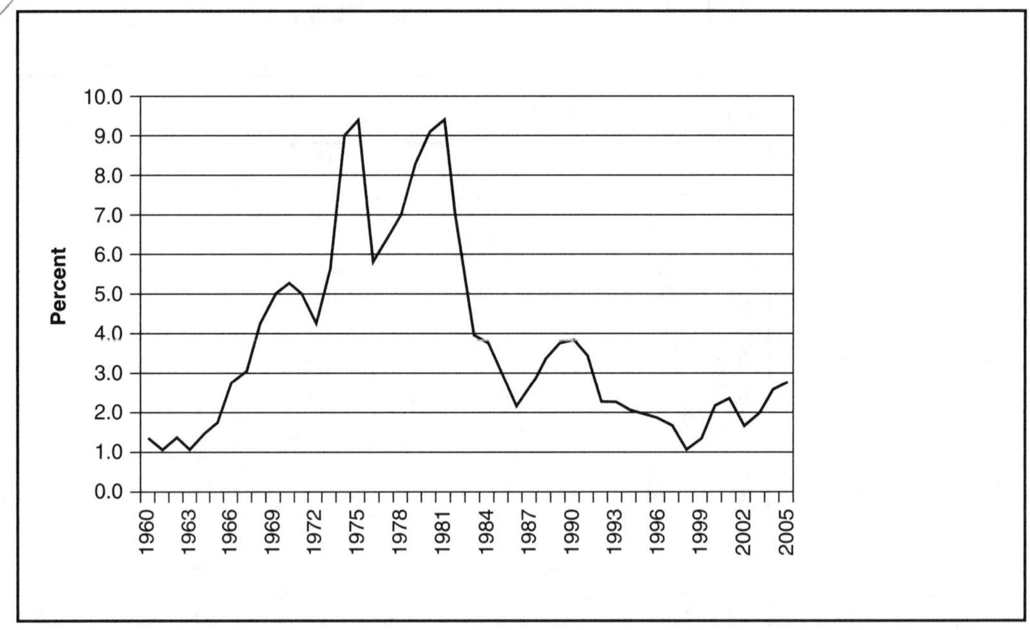

Information about output, employment, and inflation is published in the monthly *Survey of Current Business* (U.S. Department of Commerce); in the annual *Economic Report of the President* (Council of Economic Advisers); and in the monthly *Federal Reserve Bulletin* (Federal Reserve Board).

Before exploring the factors that determine aggregate output, we shall discuss how output and inflation are measured.

The National Income and Product Accounts

Macroeconomics deals with the aggregate level of economic activity. The most direct indication of that level is total output of goods and services produced in the economy over a given period, usually one year. Aggregate output also determines the level of employment, because the greater the output, the larger the number of workers and machines required to produce it. Finally, aggregate output can be compared to potential output, thereby indicating the degree of excess capacity in the economy.

Our first task is to examine how aggregate output is measured. This is done in the officially published National Income and Product Tables, compiled by the U.S. Department of Commerce and published in the *Survey of Current Business*. The accounts deal with the activity of the entire economy, measuring output of all firms combined. We start the exposition by examining a simple and hypothetical one-product case. Measuring output and income for that product can then be generalized over the entire economy.

OUTPUT AND INCOME—INTRODUCTION

The title of the official tabulations—National Income and Product Tables—brings to mind a concept alluded to in Part 1: The value of output equals the income generated in the productive process, where income includes wages and salaries, rent, interest, and profit. Since income and output are two sides of the official accounts, it is useful to demonstrate this equality in a one-product case.

In Part 1, this principle was shown in reference to a simple example of a person who grows cucumbers and markets them at a roadside stand. For that purpose, the person hires labor, rents land, and borrows capital. From the proceeds of the sale are paid wages and salaries, rent, and interest.

Anything left over constitutes profit. Clearly, the return of *all* factors (including profit) equals the value of the product (price times quantity).

This example is oversimplified in that the entire productive process, from the initial preparation of the land to the final sale of the product to the consumer, is executed by one firm. In a complex economy, virtually all products are produced in multistage operations, where each firm performs only a part of the process and sells its output to another firm for further fabrication. Yet in all cases, the principle of equality between product and income remains intact.

We demonstrate this point by reference to the production of a desk, involving four stages: (1) the raw-materials stage of growing the forest and cutting the trees, (2) one intermediate stage of producing lumber, (3) one final-production stage of designing and manufacturing the desks, and (4) the sale of the desks through retail outlets, which are assumed to purchase the product directly from the manufacturer.

Stage 1 A representative firm at the raw-materials stage is similar to the cucumber grower in Chapter 2. The entrepreneur must rent natural resources, hire labor, and borrow capital. Adding the payments she makes for these inputs in the form of rent, \$50, wages and salaries, \$30, and interest, \$10, we obtain his total outlays. Profit of \$10 places the final value of the raw wood at \$100. This is the price she obtains from the lumber-producing firm, to which the wood is sold.

Stage 2 The lumberyard operator pays \$100 for the raw materials purchased from the wood producer. In turn, the operator employs various factor inputs to convert the raw wood into cut lumber, then sells it to the desk manufacturer. The operator's factor payments are assumed to total \$50, in the following forms: wages and salaries, \$35; rent, \$3; interest, \$2; and profit, \$10. In other words, the operator paid \$100 for raw materials; paid out \$40 in wages and salaries, rent, and interest; and sold the finished lumber for \$150, making \$10 profit. The difference between what was paid for raw materials and what was obtained for the final product is known as the **value added** by the firm. In this case, the value added in the second stage of production is \$50.

Value-added: The difference between what the firm receives for the final product and what it pays to buy intermediate input.

Stage 3 The desk manufacturer buys the semifinished product, lumber, for \$150 and adds \$150 in productive services while manufacturing the desk. The value added in the third stage consists of the following factor remunerations: wages and salaries, \$80; rent, \$5; interest, \$35; and profit, \$30. In other words, the producer pays \$150 for materials, spends \$120 on primary factor inputs, and sells the desk for \$300. The profit, calculated as a residual, is \$30, the value added at this stage is \$150, and the total value of the desk is now \$300.

Stage 4 The retail furniture-store operator purchases the desk from the manufacturer for \$300. To this the retailer adds wages and salaries for the labor involved in crating, carting, and selling the desk, \$60; interest, \$10; rent, \$10; and profit, \$20; the total value added at the retail stage is \$100. The desk is sold to the consumer for \$400.

Summary

There are three ways of arriving at the final price of the desk, and they lead to an identical dollar value:

1. The price for which it was sold to the consumer—that is, $400.
2. Total value added in all stages of fabrication: $100 + $50 + $150 + $100 = $400. Note that we are adding only value *added* at each stage, not the prices for which the item is sold by each stage of production. The latter procedure would yield a far greater number ($100 + $150 + $300 + $400 = $950) but would involve much double counting.
3. Total remunerations to all productive factors in all stages of production, as is shown in Table 12–1. The final column shows that factor remunerations in all stages add up to wages and salaries, $205; interest, $57; rent, $68; and profit, $70, for a total of $400.

Thus, all three methods yield the same value. It will be noted in line 6 of Table 12–1 that counting the total receipts of each of the four firms at each stage results in a far greater number ($950). This is because such an approach involves double counting at all but the first stage (line 7). Thus, the value of the lumber at the end of the second stage is $150, made up of $100 in raw wood and $50 in value added by the lumber yard. If we added the $100 of the raw wood to the $150 value of the finished lumber, *which already incorporates the value of the raw material,* we would be counting the value of the raw wood twice. Similarly, the value of the desk in the third stage is $300, made up of $150 in purchased lumber and $150 in value added by the desk manufacturer. If we added the $150 in lumber to the $300 value of the desk, which already incorporates the value of the lumber, we would be counting the lumber twice. Similar double counting could occur in the fourth stage. In other words, the dollar value of all *transactions* involved in the productive process far exceeds the total value added at all stages, and the final value of the product. In measuring the national output, we include only the value of the final goods (such as the desk) and exclude that of intermediate products (such as the lumber), so as to avoid double counting.

Table 12–1 Factor Remunerations at Each Stage

	First Stage	Second Stage	Third Stage	Fourth Stage	All Stages Combined
1. Wages and salaries	$ 30	$ 35	$ 80	$ 60	$205
2. Interest	10	2	35	10	57
3. Rent	50	3	5	10	68
4. Profit	10	10	30	20	70
5. Total; equals *value added* at each stage	$100	$ 50	$150	$100	$400
6. Total value	$100	$150	$300	$400	$950
7. Double counting under total value	0	$100	$150	$300	$550

Output Equals Income

The three methods of measuring the value of a product, all yielding identical results, apply to all goods and services produced throughout the economy. The overwhelming majority of goods go through multistage processes, requiring the evaluator to calculate the value added as well as the (equal) income generated at every stage, inclusive of profit. Adding up the results for all stages until the final product is sold to the consumer, we always come up with the important triple equality: **The dollar value of the final product equals the sum of the value added at all stages of processing, equals the income generated in the production process in all forms of factor remunerations:**

Value of final output: The sum of the value-added at each stage of production equal output, which equals the sum of incomes generated in the production process.

$$\textbf{Value of Final Output} = \Sigma \textbf{ Values added} = \Sigma \textbf{ Incomes generated}$$

where the Greek letter Σ (capital *sigma*) denotes "the sum of." Income and product are two sides of the same coin. We are now in a position to generalize from the one-product case to the national economy.

GROSS DOMESTIC PRODUCT (GDP)

Definition

Aggregate output consists of thousands of diverse goods, produced in response to consumer demand and social needs. They must all be added up to obtain a comprehensive measure of the economy's performance But how does one add up apples, wheat, clothes, desks, education, houses, theater tickets, vacation trips, dry-cleaning services, and all other products into one single measure? It is done by pricing each good and service on its respective market; multiplying the price by the *quantity* (or *volume*) of the product delivered, to obtain a dollar value (price times quantity) of each good and service; and adding up these dollar values over all goods and services produced. **Gross domestic product**, or **GDP**, is the total market value of all final goods and services produced during *one year.* Because it is measured in terms of money, it is also called money GDP, or *nominal* GDP.

Gross Domestic Product (GDP): Total market value of all *final* goods and services produced in a year. Also called nominal or money GDP. It is an "output based" concept; and, it includes only market-bound activities.

A Simple Illustration A simplified example will serve to illustrate the principle. Suppose that four final goods were produced in a given year: bread (to represent food), pants (to represent clothing), desks (to represent furniture), and theater tickets (to represent services). They were sold in 1997 in the quantities and at the prices shown in Table 12–2.

To obtain the GDP, we price each product at its market value, multiply the price by the quantity produced to obtain the dollar value of output, and sum all the products. It is the *dollar value* of each product that serves as a common denominator and enables us to add up output of diverse goods and services. The GDP is the sum of all final products in their respective quantities times the market price. Using capital sigma (Σ) to indicate sum, P to indicate price, and Q to indicate quantity, it is customary to write:

Table 12–2 Hypothetical Output and Prices of Four Commodities in 1997

Item	Quantity Produced in 1997	Market Price in 1997	Dollar Value (Price × Quantity)
Bread	10 billion loaves	$1 per loaf	$10 billion
Pants	1 billion pairs	$25 per pair	$25 billion
Desks	60 million	$250 per desk	$15 billion
Theater tickets	1 billion	$10 per ticket	$10 billion
Gross domestic product			**$60 billion**

$$\text{GDP} = \sum_{\text{All final products}} QP$$

Special Features

Three features of the GDP measure are worth noting. First, it includes only *market-bound* activities. Thus, expenditures on food served in restaurants are included, but the cooking services of a person preparing meals at home are not. Services of cleaning establishments are included, but washing and drying one's clothes at home are not. In other words, productive activities that never reach the marketplace are excluded from GDP, because no one knows their magnitude and they would be impossible to measure. However, there are two exceptions to this rule: (1) Food produced *and* consumed on the farm is estimated and included in GDP, and (2) an imputed rental value of owner-occupied homes is also included in GDP. In order to avoid a distinction between people who rent their homes or apartments (whose rent is a part of market activities) and those who own their own homes (where no rent exchanges hands), the government estimates the rent that would have been paid by the latter group had they been renting their premises. That estimate is included in GDP. The size of the two aforementioned items justifies the departure from the exclusive preoccupation with market activities

Second, only *final* goods are included in GDP. If the market value of a car is $9,000, then that price already includes the steel, rubber, and other materials used in automobile production as raw materials or intermediate goods. To count them separately and add them along with the value of the car would mean double counting. This was shown previously, where the value of the lumber was already part of the price of the desk. Consequently, materials that enter into the production of final goods are not counted separately. Their value has already been included in that of the final product. In practice, this means that GDP *excludes interbusiness transactions*, such as General Motors' buying steel from U.S. Steel. The only exception to this rule is *plant, equipment, and machinery used by businesses* and purchased from other businesses. For the purpose of computing the GDP, such machinery is classified as a final product.

Third, the GDP is an *output-based* concept. Purely financial transactions, such as sales of stocks and bonds, as well as secondhand sales are excluded from GDP, because they are not part of current output. A notable type of

Table 12–3 U.S. Gross Domestic Product

Year	GDP ($ Billion)
1989	5,484
1990	5,803
1991	5,996
1992	6,338
1993	6,657
1994	7,072
1995	7,398
1996	7,817
1997	8,304
1998	8,747
1999	9,268
2000	9,817
2001	10,128
2002	10,487
2003	11,004
2004	11,734
*2005 (preliminary)	12,479

Source: Bureau of Economic Analysis, National Income and Product Accounts Trade, Table 1.1.5

Transfer Payments: Payments from the government to people not in return for productive services (e.g. retirement benefit). They are excluded from GDP because they do not emanate from current year's output.

financial transaction so excluded is known as **transfer payments**. These are payments made by the government *not* in return for productive services. They include Social Security payments paid to retired people, unemployment compensation paid to the unemployed, and welfare payments to the poor. All these are excluded from GDP because they do not reflect current output.

U.S. GDP

GDP per capita: The GDP divided by the population.

Table 12–3 shows the U.S. GDP estimates for 17 recent years. U.S. GDP is one fifth of the world's total. The West European countries combined have a GDP somewhat higher than that of the United States, and Japan's GDP is over one third its U.S. counterpart. Dividing the GDP by the number of people in the country yields an estimate of **GDP per capita,** which is often used as an indicator of the average standard of living. With a population of about 300 million, the U.S. per capita GDP of over $41,000 is among the highest in the world.

NOMINAL AND REAL GDP

Volume and Prices

Returning to Table 12–3, observe that the GDP rises over the years. For example, from 1996 to 1997 it increased by $445 billion, or by 5 percent. But that 5 percent increase is made up of two components: (1) an expansion of the physical quantities of the goods and services produced, known as the *volume of output*; and (2) an increase in prices of these goods and services. A distinction needs to be made between the two components, because only the first part reflects an increase in the community's satisfaction from the goods and services at its disposal. The common measure of

GDP, where all goods and services are priced at current market prices, is called *nominal* or *money GDP.* The changes in this aggregate occurring every year reflect both prices and volume changes. It is this measure that is shown in Table 12–3. An alternative concept, under which prices are held constant, shows only changes in the quantities produced. Called **real GDP**, it is a superior indicator of the productive performance of the economy over time. It is obtained by dividing nominal GDP by the average price level, in a manner explained in the next three sections.

Real GDP: GDP adjusted for inflation.

A Price Index

How is money GDP adjusted to net out the change in prices? Casual observation suggests that prices change nearly every year (mostly moving up), and that the annual changes differ from one product to another. Clearly, the aggregate price movement from one year to the next is a *weighted average* of the individual price changes, where the weight of each product reflects its importance in the economy.[1] These average price changes are related to a

---

[1]Suppose total output is made up of the four products shown in Table 12–2, and their prices changed as follows from one year to the next: The bread price decreased by 5 percent (–5%); the price of pants remained unchanged (0%); the price of desks rose by 5 percent (+5%); and that of theater tickets increased by 10 percent (+10%). If all four goods were equally important, then the combined rise in their prices is the unweighted or simple average of the four changes:

$$\frac{(-5) + 0 + 5 + 10}{4} = \frac{10}{4} = 2.5 \text{ percent}$$

But not all goods need be of equal importance. Indeed, we know that as the economy advances and incomes rise, a smaller and smaller portion of income is devoted to the bare necessities of life, such as food, and an increasing share to luxury goods, such as services. When goods possess unequal weights, the calculation of the average price increase is slightly more complicated. Suppose that ⅕ of the economy's output is made up of bread, ⅕ of pants, ⅕ of desks, and 2/5 of theater tickets. (Note that the sum of these fractions must add up to 1.) Then, the price change in tickets is of double importance (has a double weight) compared to that of each *of* the three goods. In a sense, we can divide total spending into five components, with each of the three goods receiving a weight of 1, and tickets a weight of 2. The average rate of price increase is then (–5)(⅕) + (0)(⅕) + (5)(⅕) + (10)(⅖) = 4 percent.

In the actual computations, statisticians do not make year-to-year comparisons. Instead, they select a base year (currently 2000) and compare it to the average price level in subsequent years. From such a series, stretching over a long time, one can readily make a comparison between two years by simple division. Both price and employment statistics are compiled by the Bureau of Labor Statistics at the U.S. Department of Labor.

Following is a hypothetical illustration

Item	Quantity Produced in 1997	1997 Prices	Q_{97} x P_{97}	1996 Prices	Q_{97} x Q_{96}
Bread	10 billion	$1	$10 billion	$0.75	$7.5 billion
Pants	1 billion	$25	$25 billion	$15.0	$15.0 billion
Desks	60 million	$250	$15 billion	$200.0	$12.0 billion
Theater tickets	1 billion	$10	$10 billion	$5.0	$5.0 billion
		1997 nominal GNP = $60 billion		1997 real GNP = $39.5 billion	

It can be seen that 1997 real GDP is equivalent to 1997 output of goods and services, where each item is priced at base-year (1996) prices. For that reason, it is also called GDP in 1996 dollars.

base year, which now happens to be 2000. The price level in 2000 is set at 100, and relative to that base year the average prices in 2001 were 102.4; in 2002, 104.1; in 2003, 106.0; and in 2004, 108.3. This amounts to saying that between 2000 and 2006 the average price level rose by 8.3 percent.

Price index: A series of average prices, which show the movement over time of prices from some base year.

The series of average prices just given is called a **price index**. To recapitulate, the price index shows the movement of a (weighted) average price level relative to a base period. The base period itself is changed periodically.

Types of Price Indexes

Several price indexes are used in the economy, differing from each other in their commodity coverage and other matters. The most important ones follow.

Consumer Price Index (CPI): A weighted average of the prices of goods and services included in a basket the average consumer consumes, priced at retail.

The Consumer Price Index (CPI) The **Consumer Price Index** contains a representative basket of the goods and services purchased by consumers in the base year, each assigned a weight according to its relative importance in that basket. Items not purchased by consumers, such as machinery, are excluded. Each commodity is priced at retail, the price paid by the consumer to the retail store. Because it directly affects the position of consumers, it is the most widely watched index and is reported every month.

Producer Price Index (PPI): A price index that covers all commodities traded at wholesale, priced at wholesale.

The Producer Price Index (PPI) The **Producer Price Index** covers all commodities traded at wholesale—that is, sold by factories or wholesale stores to retail stores. Items not traded at the producer or wholesale level, such as haircuts and other consumer services, are excluded. On the other hand, capital equipment is included. Consequently, the commodity composition differs from that of the CPI. Also, unlike the CPI, the PPI prices individual items at their factory or wholesale price, the price charged by the factory to the retail store. Because these prices will be reflected at the retail level two to three months later, movements in the PPI tend to foreshadow movements in the CPI.

GDP deflator: A price index of all goods and services included in GDP, used to convert nominal to real GDP.

The GDP Deflator The **gross domestic product deflator** is the most comprehensive index in its coverage; it includes all goods and services that enter the gross national product, both machinery and consumer services as well as all else. Each product is priced at the level of its final delivery. This is the index used to convert nominal GDP to real GDP. Each of these three indexes is available in the aggregate, as well as for the major commodity categories included in it.

Real GDP: equals Nominal GDP divided by GDP deflator.

Real and Nominal GDP **Real GDP** is obtained by dividing the nominal GDP by the GDP price deflator. It is also referred to as GDP *at constant* (2000) *prices*. The computation is illustrated in Table 12–4. Column 4 (real GDP) is obtained by dividing, or *deflating*, each year's nominal GDP (column 2) by the GDP deflator (column 3) of that same year. What the calcu-

Table 12–4 Real and Nominal GDP

(1) Year	(2) Nominal GDP ($ Billion)	(3) GDP Deflator (2000 =100)	(4) Real GDP, or GDP in 2000 Dollars (Billion) (Col. 2 / Col. 3) x 100	(5) Annual Percentage[a] Change in Real GDP
1979	2,563	49.6	5,173	3.2
1980	2,790	54.1	5,162	–0.2
1981	3,128	59.1	5,292	2.5
1982	3,255	62.7	5,189	–1.9
1983	3,537	65.2	5,424	4.5
1984	3,936	67.7	5,814	7.2
1985	4,220	69.7	6,054	4.1
1986	4,463	71.3	6,264	3.5
1987	4,740	73.2	6,475	3.4
1988	5,104	75.7	6,743	4.1
1989	5,484	78.6	6,981	3.5
1990	5,804	81.6	7,113	1.9
1991	5,996	84.5	7,101	–0.2
1992	6,338	86.4	7,337	3.3
1993	6,657	88.4	7,533	2.7
1994	7,072	90.3	7,836	4.0
1995	7,398	92.1	8,032	2.5
1996	7,817	93.9	8,329	3.7
1997	8,304	95.4	8,704	4.5
1998	8,747	96.5	9,067	4.2
1999	9,268	97.9	9,470	4.5
2000	9,717	100.0	9,817	3.7
2001	10,128	102.4	9,891	0.8
2002	10,487	104.1	10,075	1.9
2003	11,004	106.0	10,381	3.0
2004	11,734	108.3	10,842	4.4
*2005 (preliminary)	12,479	111.2	11,222	3.5

Source: Bureau of Economic Analysis, The National Income and Products Accounts, 2006

[a]Divide the figures for the year by the one for the previous year, multiply by 100, and then subtract 100.

lation in fact amounts to is this: The output of each good and service for a given year (say, 2003) is priced at base-year (2000) prices, and the result is added up over all products.[2] Column 3 shows the change in the price level since 2000. A continuous increase in the average price level is called *inflation,* while a decline in the price level is called *deflation.* Column 4 shows real GDP—that is, the physical output of goods and services. It is equal to nominal GDP with the effect of price increase netted out. Therefore, it is column 4 that shows the change in the quantity, or volume, of goods and

[2]As an illustration of this principle, we perform the computation with respect to the items shown in Table 12–2.

services produced by the economy and available to satisfy consumer wants and social needs. Column 5 shows the year-to-year percentage change in real GDP. Following three years of expansion in 1976–79, a dip in the real output appeared in 1981/82. There followed seven years of expansion (1983–90), with 1984 showing the sharpest rise in output. Note that with a robust expansion in real GDP, there tends to be an increase in employment (or a decrease in unemployment) and in capacity utilization, as more workers and machines are needed to produce the increased output. For example, unemployment declined from 9.5 percent in 1982 to 5.2 percent in mid-1989.

A slight recession appeared in 1991, followed by 10 years of expansion, and a recession again in 2001. The economy recovered during 2002–05.

A convenient place where all these and related statistics can be found is the annual *Economic Report of the President.*

Macro vs. Micro Once Again At this point, you may already detect major differences between micro- and macroeconomics. Whereas Chapter 4 was concerned with the determination of *individual* prices and their movements relative to each other (which guide the allocation of resources), here our interest is in the behavior of the *average* price *level.* Whereas Chapter 4 focused on the output of individual products, here our interest is in aggregate output of all goods and services combined

Another hint of things to come is this: An increase in demand for, and in expenditures on a certain product (such as gasoline) would raise the price of that product. But it would not necessarily raise the general price level; it may be offset by a decline in other prices.

Limitations of Real GDP

Although real GDP is the broadest and most widely used measure of economic activity, it is well to remember that it is far from a perfect indicator of social well-being. First, it excludes most nonmarket activities. Second, in measuring output, it cannot incorporate all improvements in product quality. For example, we price 2005 cars in 2000 dollars to obtain real auto output. However, the change between the two years is not exclusively an advance in automobile prices. Part of it is due to improved quality of the product itself. But since there is no way of sorting out that improvement, its cost is reflected in the price increase, overstating the rate of price rise.

And finally, the GDP measure overstates social output, because it does not include all the social costs of producing the output. If a rise in GDP is accompanied by increased air and water pollution, noise, congestion, and other social costs, then those should be subtracted from GDP if it is to be used as an indicator of the national well-being. Since this is not done, the GDP measure is deficient in this respect as well.

Quarterly Statistics

Although all the figures shown here refer to full calendar years, the U.S. Department of Commerce (which publishes the national income accounts) also provides quarterly figures.[3] *A period of two or more consecutive quarters in which real GDP is declining is called a* **recession**. Such a decline in real output is usually accompanied by increased unemployment of workers and machines, because it takes fewer workers to produce the reduced output. Thus, growing unemployment is one of the least desirable features of a recession. A sharp decline in real GDP occurred in 1982. By September 1982 the unemployment rate climbed to 10.1 percent—the highest in forty years.

Recession: A period of two or more consecutive quarters of decline in real GDP. Occurred in 2001.

The conversion of nominal to real figures is not restricted to total GDP. It is done also for various components of GDP, by constructing a price index appropriate for each component and dividing or deflating the nominal figure by that index. However, the discussion in the remainder of this chapter centers mainly on nominal magnitudes.

EXPENDITURE COMPONENTS OF GDP

Components of GDP: Consumption (C); Investment (I); Government Expenditures (G); and Net Exports (Exports-Imports) of goods and services.

Aggregate output can be divided in a variety of ways. It can be split up into its industrial composition (autos, appliances, dry cleaning, and so on) in as little or as great detail as desired. It can be decomposed into the regions of the country or even the states in which it is produced. Certainly, for the commodities-producing sectors of the economy—manufacturing, agriculture, and mining—these classifications are available. But for the analytical purposes of subsequent chapters, two different classifications are useful: expenditures and income. We first take up the classification by type of expenditure.

It is both logical and useful to ask which groups in the economy purchased the aggregate output. In turn, this classification shows the types of products (for example, consumer or investment goods) that were produced. We distinguish among four such groups: consumers, investors, government, and foreigners. Table 12–5 shows the four major categories of expenditures in 2004 and 2005 in nominal prices.

Consumption

Over two thirds of GDP consists of consumer goods, shown in the table as personal consumption expenditures. In subsequent chapters, consumption will be denoted by the letter C. It can be seen that services, such

[3]Each year is divided into four three-month periods, each known as a quarter: January through March, April through June, July through September, and October through December.

Table 12–5 Gross Domestic Product by Types of Expenditures, 2004–2005 ($ Billion)

		2005*		2004
Gross domestic product		12,480		11,734
Personal consumption expenditures (C):		8,746		8,214
Durable goods	1,026		988	
Nondurable goods	2,564		2,368	
Services	5,156		4,858	
Gross private domestic investment(I_g):		2,100		1,928
Business structures	335		298	
Producer's durable equipment	994		900	
Residential construction	756		674	
Change in business inventories	15		55	
Government purchases of goods and services (G):		2,360		2,216
Federal	875		828	
State and Local	1,485		1,388	
Net exports of goods and services (X_n):		–726		–624
Exports	1,299		1,174	
Imports	–2,025		-1,798	

*Source: Economic Report of the President, 2006, Table B-1 (*Preliminary)*

as education, travel, theater tickets, and dry cleaning, constitute over half of all consumption. This is followed by nondurable goods such as food and clothing, and the smallest (yet still substantial) portion of consumer spending is on durable goods such as autos and appliances. Expenditures on durable goods (goods that last, through repeated use, longer than one year) are more dispensable than those on nondurables. They are postponable from year to year. Thus, food is a necessity, but the purchase of a car can be considered a discretionary expenditure.

Investment

Gross private domestic investment (labeled I_g) amounted to $2,100 billion in 2005. It is made up of three components: (1) business investments in structures, plant and equipment (including computer software); (2) residential construction, which is classified as investment in the GDP accounts; and (3) changes in business inventories.

Inventories are the stocks of merchandize that dealers and other businesses keep on hand. Despite its small size, the *change in inventories* will turn out to be of extreme analytical importance, and its inclusion under investments should be committed to memory. An example will illustrate how this item comes about. If car dealers receive more auto units from the factories than they sell during a one-year period, the difference is added to their inventories, and we obtain a positive accumulation of inventories, as in 1997. Conversely, if, over a year's period, they sell to customers more cars than they receive from the factories, the difference reflects a *depletion* of inventories, and the item has a negative sign, as in 2001.

Economists define investment to include *only physical investments.* The purchase of stocks and bonds, referred to as investment in common parlance, is not investment by economists' definition, and in fact such transactions are excluded from GDP altogether.

Government

Government purchases of goods and services (labeled G) is the third main component of GDP, and it is subdivided into federal expenditures and state and local spending. Most of the government budget is spent on goods and services produced by and purchased from private enterprises. The size of federal spending ($875 billion) may appear small by comparison to what one sees in the media about the government budget. This is so because substantial portions of the budget are not included in GDP. In particular, government transfer payments (such as Social Security payments) and government interest payments to people and organizations that own government bonds are not part of GDP, and are excluded from G.

Foreigners

The final expenditure item is net purchases by foreigners of U.S. produced goods and services. It is what foreigners buy (U.S. exports) minus what Americans buy from abroad (U.S. imports). Exports are about one tenth of GDP in the United States but are approximately one half of GDP in the small European countries. In other words, despite its growing importance, foreign trade is less important here than in other, smaller countries. Because of the large size and diversity of the American economy, domestic output can satisfy much of our private and public needs. For that reason, the United States is sometimes referred to as a "relatively closed economy."

It is the difference between exports and imports of goods and services ($X - M$) that makes up net exports (labeled X_n). In 2005 the excess of imports over exports was $726 billion. Because imports exceeded exports, net exports has a negative sign.

Summary

Gross domestic product is the sum of personal consumption expenditures, gross private domestic investment, government purchases of goods and services, and net exports. This can be summarized by the equation:

$$\text{GDP} = C + I_g + G + X_n$$

Consumers, investors, government, and foreigners purchase the entire output. Hence, these four lines of expenditures make up the entire GDP.

NATIONAL INCOME

Depreciation or **Capital Consumption Allowance (CCA):** Wear and tear of equipment.

Let us return to the investment component of GDP. At first glance, one might think that the entire amount of investment constitutes an addition to the country's capital stock of plant and equipment. Not so. In the process of producing the $12 trillion of goods and services, much capital equipment wore out, or depreciated. The official name for this *depreciation,* or wear and tear, is **capital consumption allowance (or CCA)**. Consequently, a substantial portion of I_g (CCA = $1,574 billion in 2005), was required to replace the depreciated capital equipment. Only investment over and above that amount constituted a net addition to the country's capital stock. It is by this amount that the country's capital stock grew during the year, making it possible to increase aggregate output in subsequent years. Known as net investment, it is labeled I_n. In sum:

$$I_g = I_n + \text{Capital consumption allowance (or depreciation)}$$

Since the entire I_g is part of GDP, the GDP includes capital equipment that wore out in the production process. In this sense, the GDP overstates the amount of goods and services produced during the year. A measure of aggregate output net of the depreciated equipment is national income (NI). It is GDP minus capital consumption allowance. For 2005, NI = [$12,480 – $1,574 =] $10,906 billion. In 2004, NI was [$11,734 – $1,435 =] $10,353 billion. The only difference between GDP and NI is that the first concept includes I_g and the second includes I_n. Thus:

$$\text{GDP} = C + I_g + G + X_n$$
$$\text{NI} = C + I_n + G + X_n$$

where $I_n = I_g - \text{CCA}$.

Although conceptually NI is a superior measure of the economy's output, in practice the GDP is the more widely used measure. The reason is that the statistical estimate of CCA is unreliable.

THE INCOME SIDE OF THE ACCOUNTS—COMPOSTION OF NATIONAL INCOME

It will be recalled from the first section in this chapter that product and income are two sides of the same coin; they are necessarily equal. If $12.5 trillion worth of goods and services (GDP) was produced in 2005, then

Table 12–6 National Income by Type of Income, 2005 ($ Billion)

1. Compensation of Employees	7,125	
Wages and Salaries (W&S)		5,724
Supplements to W&S		1,402
2. Rental Income	74	
3. Net Interest (excludes government interest payments)	498	
4. Corporate Profits	1,352	
Profit Tax Liability		378
Corporate profits after tax		974
Dividends		514
Undistributed Profit		460
5. Proprietors' income	939	
6. Taxes on Production & Imports	903	
National income	**10,906**	

Source: Bureau of Economic Analysis, March 2006

Note: These are preliminary numbers; hence they don't exactly add up.

National Income: The part of GDP which can be assigned to factors of production; it includes compensation of employees, rent, interest, corporate profits, and proprietor's income

that much income was generated in the productive process and can be allocated among productive factors. However, part of that output, the CCA, was devoted merely to a replacement of plant and equipment that depreciated in the process of producing the GDP. Strictly speaking, it is NI that can be regarded as aggregate output. Conceptually, therefore, this amount equals aggregate income available for distribution among productive factors. **Indeed, while GDP focuses on the four channels of expenditures, the focus of NI is on the sources of income side of the accounts.**

Table 12–6 shows how national income is allocated among productive factors, with figures referring to 2005. The greatest part of aggregate income accrues to the labor factor: Wages and salaries were $5,724 billion, and supplemental labor income—such as employers' contribution to Social Security[4]—amounted to $1,402 billion. Note that what the government's Social Security fund receives during the year is part of output and is included in GDP and NI; the disbursements out of that fund are not included as part of this year's income, for they are made up of contributions to the fund derived from previous years' output and income.

The next two items are rental income on property and interest payments on capital. Interest paid by the government is excluded on the ground that much of the government debt (the government bonds on

[4]Employee contributions to Social Security are included in wages and salaries.

which this interest is paid) was incurred during wars to finance destructive rather than constructive activities.

There follows corporate profits ($1,352 billion), of which $378 billion is paid in taxes to the government. The remainder—corporate profits after taxes—is split two ways; much of it is paid by corporations as dividends to people who own shares (or stocks), and the remainder (undistributed profit or *retained earnings*) is retained by corporations for future investment and expansion purposes. The next item is proprietors' income. It includes the income of independent professional people (such as doctors, lawyers, or dentists), store owners, and other businesses. Their income is a composite; it contains elements of all four factor payments—compensation for their own labor (wages), rent on the property they own, interest on their own capital, and profit on their entrepreneurial activities. Since it is not possible to decompose this figure into the four functional components it is lumped together under proprietors' income.

Indirect Business Taxes (IBT): Taxes that are levied on goods and not on factors of production (i.e. sales, excise taxes).
Direct taxes: Taxes, which are levied directly on factors of production.

Finally, item 6 is made up of **indirect business taxes,** such as sales and excise taxes, which cannot be allocated to productive factors. **Direct taxes** are taxes levied directly on factors of production. We can identify the component of income from which they are collected by the government. The corporate profit tax is a part of profit, and the personal income tax is levied on wages and salaries of individuals. Both can be attributed to a particular component of income. In contrast, indirect taxes are taxes levied on products and collected at the time of sale. But only people or corporations, not products, can pay taxes. Indirect taxes tend to be split between buyers and sellers. There is not *a priori* way of knowing who paid them, and therefore whose income they are a part of. Indirect business taxes cannot be allocated or assigned to a factor of production.

Summary—The Two Sides of the Accounts

It is now possible to provide a schematic summary of the expenditure and income sides of the National Income and Product Accounts:

Output or Expenditure	Income
Gross domestic product	GDP – CCA= National Income:
Personal consumption expenditure (C)	
Gross private domestic investment (I_g)	Compensation of employees
Government expenditure on goods and services (G)	W&S
	Supplements
Net exports (X_n)	Rental income
$GDP = C + I_g + G + X_n$	Net interest (nongovernment)
GDP – CCA = NI	Corporate profit:
$NI = C + I_n + G + X_n$	Corporate profit tax
	Dividends } Corporate profit after tax
	Undistributed profit } Corporate profit after tax
	Proprietors' income

Conceptually, this amounts to writing

Consumption	+		Wages and Salaries	+
Investment	+		Rent	+
Government expenditure	+		Interest	+
Net expenditure by foreigners		= GDP =	Profit	+
			Nonincome charges (CCA and IBT)	

PERSONAL INCOME AND DISPOSABLE INCOME

Personal income (PI): Income received by individuals regardless of whether or not generated by same year output.

Disposable income is PI minus personal income taxes.

All product and income concepts discussed thus far are rooted in the economy's output during the year to which they relate. But there are two widely used income concepts that are not output based. The first of those is *personal income.* **Personal income** is *income accruing to (or received by) individuals over a given year, regardless of whether or not it is generated out of that year's output.* To move from national income to personal income, (1) add incomes received by individuals but not out of the current year's output, namely, government transfer and interest payments, and (2) subtract income generated by the current year's output but not accruing to individuals, namely, undistributed corporate profits, corporate profit tax, and Social Security contributions. In 2005 personal income amounted to \$10,904 billion, as shown in Table 12–7.

Subtracting personal taxes from personal income (PI), we obtain the second concept: personal disposable income (DI) (\$8,664 billion for 2004; \$9,031 billion for 2005). It is income at the disposal of people, to spend or to save as they wish. It can be either spent on consumption (C) (\$8,513 billion for 2004 and 9,073 billion for 2005) or saved (S) (\$152 billion in 2004; –\$42 billion in 2005). Personal savings is disposable income (DI) minus

Table 12–7 From National Income to Disposable Income, 2005 ($ Billion)

National Income			10,904
Plus:	Government transfers and interest payments	2,983	
Less:	Undistributed corporation profit (adjusted) Corporate profit tax Indirect business tax Social security contribution	3,649	
Equals:	Personal income		10,238
Less:	Personal tax	1,202	
Equals:	Disposable income		9,031
Less:	Personal outlays (mainly consumption)	9,073	
Equals:	Personal savings		–42
Personal saving as a percent of disposable income			–0.5%

Source: Economic Report of the President, 2006, Table B-27, 30

consumption C.[5] The personal savings rate (1.8 percent in 2004 and –0.5 percent in 2005), is personal savings as a percent of disposable income.[6]

▶ COMPILING THE GDP STATISTICS

Statistics on gross domestic product are compiled in the Bureau of Economic Analysis (BEA) of the U.S. Commerce Department. They are usually revised six times before becoming final. The immensity of the job is illustrated by the diversity of sources from which data must be obtained:

> For example, data on consumer spending come from the Census Bureau's monthly survey of retail stores and a tally of car sales put out by the Motor Vehicle Manufacturers Association; export estimates come from customs declarations; information about government purchases is taken from the Monthly Treasury Statement; farm income is estimated by the Agriculture Department.

These and other sources are used to compile the output side of the account, and another set of sources is used to obtain the income side. Because the two sides often don't match, a "statistical discrepancy" arises.

Life at BEA is rather hectic:

> There's an estimator for each of the four letters in the GDP equation, and each of these four chief estimators commands a team of assistants who specialize in separate subcategories. As the raw data come in, these statisticians have to process them, so the information matches the definitions required for the national accounts. After all, most of the sources used are really designed to serve the administrative needs of the organizations supplying the data.

[5]In effect, the figure subtracted from DI to obtain personal savings is not consumption but personal outlays. The latter figure includes personal consumption expenditures (C, as in Table 12–5) and a comparatively small item, interest paid by consumers to business.

[6]In Japan the savings rate approaches 20 percent. In the U.S., personal savings in 2005 was negative 0.5.

SUMMARY

The National Income and Product Accounts, available on an annual or a quarterly basis, describe the productive performance of the economy over a given period, be it a year or a quarter. They contain both an output or expenditure side and an income side, and the two are equal. Gross domestic product is the total dollar value of all final goods and services produced in the economy and traded on markets. Real GDP is GDP at constant prices; it is equal to nominal GDP deflated by the appropriate price index (the GDP deflator). National income is GDP minus capital consumption allowance (CCA). It is the part of GDP assignable to productive factors.

On the expenditures side, GDP is made up of consumption, gross investments, government purchases, and net exports, (C, I_g, G, and X_n), and NI consists of C, I_n, G, and X_n. On the income side, GDP is made up of capital consumption allowance and indirect business taxes (CCA and IBT), and the following five income components: compensation of employees, rent, interest, corporate profits, and proprietors' income. The two sides of the accounts are equal.

Personal income (PI) is income earned by individuals, regardless of whether it is generated out of the current year's output. It equals NI minus three items not accruing to individuals, plus one item received by individuals but not resulting from this year's output. Subtracting personal taxes out of PI, we obtain disposable income (DI), which in turn consists of consumption (C) and personal savings (S).

A period of two consecutive quarters or longer in which real GDP is declining is called a recession. Such a reduction of output is usually accompanied by a rise in unemployment. A period of continuously rising price levels is called inflation.

QUESTIONS AND PROBLEMS

1. Given the following data, compute gross domestic product, net domestic product, national income, personal income, disposable personal income, and personal savings (in billions of dollars):

Personal consumption expenditures	280
Indirect business taxes	40
Undistributed corporate profit	20
Transfer payments	20
Government expenditures on goods and services	90
Personal income taxes	40
Gross private investments	60
Depreciation (CCA)	30
Social Security taxes	10
Corporate taxes	20
Net export of goods and services	0

2. Define all the income and product concepts in question 1.
3. Explain the difference between nominal and real GDP.
4. Explain the following statement: "Aggregate output can be obtained (a) by adding up the market value of all *final* goods and services; (b) by adding up the *value added* of all firms in the economy; (c) by adding up all incomes generated in the economy.

   Can you explain all the national income and product concepts with reference to the preceding statement?

Unemployment and Inflation—Fundamental Concepts

Goals of macroeconomic policy: maintain full employment and price stability.

Microeconomics is concerned with the allocation of resources in the economy; attainment of efficient allocation is its prime policy objective. In order to focus attention on the allocation problem, it was implicitly assumed in Part 2 that all resources—workers and machines—were fully employed. For if they were less than fully employed, then concern with their efficient utilization is less overriding. In shifting from microeconomics to macroeconomics, we drop the full-employment assumption and switch the focus of analysis to the aggregate level of output and employment, and to the average price level. **The twin policy objective is the maintenance of full employment and price stability, or full employment without inflation.**

EMPLOYMENT AND UNEMPLOYMENT

Frictional and Structural Unemployment

The U.S. labor force is estimated at over 139 million workers. Clearly, many families have more than one wage earner. And with the entrance of many women into the labor force in recent years, the number of multiple-wage-earner families is on the rise.

Frictional unemployment: Workers who are unemployed because of changes in the composition of output which require shifts of resources between industries.

However, no one expects the entire labor force to be employed at any given time. There are two reasons: First, in a dynamic economy, there are continuous changes in the composition of output, requiring shifts of resources between industries. The implication of such shifts is that a certain number of workers always find themselves between jobs. They are unemployed for a short period of time while switching jobs or changing locations. In addition, there are workers who are laid off temporarily because of seasonal factors. Model changeover in automobile production and construction standstill in bad weather are examples that come to mind. These factors give rise to what is known as **frictional unemployment.**

Structural unemployment: Unemployment that exists because of changes in skill requirement as the economy becomes increasingly sophisticated.

A second reason for expecting some unemployment is structural changes in the economy. What is known as **structural unemployment** arises primarily because some people do not possess the skills required by an advanced economy. As the economy becomes increasingly sophisticated, there are always those who are "left behind." To an extent, they are unemployable rather than simply unemployed, in view of the minimum skill and literacy requirements of most jobs in a highly industrial economy.

But this reason is not as clear-cut as it may seem. Some unskilled workers might have been absorbed into the labor force at lower wage rates than are permitted by the legislated minimum wage of $5.15 per hour. Regardless of how sophisticated the economy is, there are menial jobs that would have been done manually had wage rates been low enough. At higher skill levels, large labor unions and corporations sometimes negotiate wage rates above the equilibrium market-clearing levels, causing excess supply of labor or unemployment, or engage in other practices that restrict entrance into certain occupations. Finally, government welfare and unemployment benefits often reduce the incentive of workers to seek employment: Why look for a new job if these benefits pay nearly as much as a person's wages while the person is unemployed? In a sense, such programs contain an element of subsidy for idleness.

All these factors combined are known as distortions in the labor markets. They suggest that part of the unemployment is *voluntary rather than involuntary,* and part of it depends on union and corporate market power and government wage policy.

Natural rate of unemployment: Unemployment that exists because of labor market distortions such as minimum wage laws and labor unions. Alternatively, it is the level of unemployment that would keep inflation from accelerating.

Unemployment that is due to such labor-market distortions is known as the **natural rate of unemployment.** Its size is extremely difficult to estimate, and it varies over time with changes in union and government policies. In part, it is a voluntary response to incentives to remain unemployed.

What Is Full Employment?

Full employment: When about 96% of the labor force is employed.

Although no one knows the exact magnitude of the phenomena just described, it is usually assumed that 4–5 percent of the labor force would be so unemployed. Consequently, full employment is defined as a situation in which 96 percent of the labor force is employed.

Similar considerations apply to the capital stock—industrial structures and machines. At any given time, some machines are obsolete, others are idle because consumer demand has shifted away from the product they produce, and still others may be kept idle deliberately for reasons of attaining maximum efficiency or for other causes. The level of capacity utilization consistent with full employment is somewhat below 90 percent. Thus, potential output is the real GDP that would be produced with 96 percent of the labor force and, say, 88 percent of the capital stock. For obvious social reasons, there is more concern with full employment of labor than of capital.

This definition of full employment sheds light on one peculiarity of Exhibit 3–2. It is seen that sometimes actual output rises above potential output, as was the case in the late 1960s. How can that be? The answer is rooted in the definition of full-employment output. There are periods in which aggregate expenditures (through all four channels) are so unusually high that they induce firms to hire some of the frictionally and structurally unemployed, so as to expand output to a point of satisfying these expenditures. On the capital side, firms strain their capacity beyond the point of maximum efficiency, perhaps even using machines that might otherwise be discarded. Capacity utilization is above the optimum of 88 percent. It is in that fashion that actual output rises above its potential counterpart.

Output and unemployment: Output and unemployment are inversely related. As output rises unemployment declines, because more workers are needed for production. Unemployment rises in a recession.

Unemployment and Output

It is the level of actual output, or real GDP, that determines the extent of employment or unemployment in the economy. The greater the employment of labor and capital required to produce it, the smaller the unemployment. Conversely, as output declines, unemployment rises. **Unemployment varies inversely with aggregate output.**

A recession is defined as a period of two or more consecutive quarters in which real GDP declines. Thus, Table 12-4 (last column) shows that 1982 was a recession year. Indeed, unemployment rose in that year, reaching 9.5 percent of the labor force. Recessions vary in depth and duration. However, none of the postwar recessions even approached the severity of the Great Depression of the 1930s, when a quarter of the labor force was unemployed.

There is no clear-cut demarcation between the definitions of a recession and a depression in terms of curtailment of output and employment. In popular parlance, one often hears the statement, "A recession is when my neighbor is unemployed; a depression is when I am unemployed." We can only say that a depression is an extremely severe, deep, and prolonged recession. A recession can be mild and short, but it always involves an *absolute* reduction in real output. Sometimes we wish to describe a situation in which real output keeps climbing but its growth rate declines (say, from 3 to 1 percent a year). This situation is referred to as a **growth recession**.

Growth recession: Real GDP rises but at a decreasing rate.

Cost of a Recession

Cost of a recession: The goods and services that could have been made available but were not due to the recession.

The economic cost of a recession is the **amount of goods and services that could have been produced and made available, but were not.** Known as the **GDP gap,** it is **the difference between potential and actual GDP, both measured in real terms.** If, in 1986, real GDP (actual output) was $3.7 trillion and potential GDP was $3.73 trillion, then the GDP gap was $300 billion. It is a measure of the goods and services that society had to forego because of the unemployment. To that economic cost, one must add other social costs of unemployment, such as increased crime, friction between children and parents resulting from idleness, and the like. These are high costs; hence the prime objective of avoiding recessions and maintaining full employment. If a recession occurs, the objective is to pull out of it as fast as possible.

Okun's Law: Beyond a growth rate of 3% every additional 3% increase in output lowers unemployment by 1% per year. While in the *short run* output depends on *aggregate expenditures*, in the *long run* output depends on the availability of capital and labor.

Okun's Law

How do we translate the measure of foregone output to unemployment? By observing a remarkable regularity, economist Arthur Okun suggests the following rule: Given the normal improvement in productivity and the annual increases in the labor force, the economy (real GDP) must grow at about 3 percent per year to keep unemployment at a constant level. Beyond the 3 percent growth rate, every additional 3 percent growth lowers unemployment by 1 percent per year. For example, if unemployment was initially at 7 percent of the labor force and the growth rate in real GDP was 3 percent, then a rise in the growth rate to 6 percent (that is, by 3 percentage points) would lower unemployment to 6 percent. This one-percentage-point reduction in unemployment would continue each year (that is, to 5 percent the following year) in which the growth rate was maintained at 6 percent. This has become known as *Okun's Law*. A reduction in unemployment is contingent upon an increase in output.

Output and Aggregate Expenditures

If the cost of foregone output and the level of unemployment depend on the level of real output, what determines real output? Furthermore, what can be done to increase it, if its level is inadequate to produce full employment? As a preview of coming attractions, it may be suggested that in the short run, in an advanced industrial economy such as the United States, **output depends on aggregate expenditures.** The volume of output that people wish to purchase determines the quantity that firms are able to sell and therefore the quantity that they will produce. As Table 12–5 shows, there are **four channels of expenditure: consumption, investments, government, and net exports. Together they make up aggregate expenditures. When the sum total of these expenditures is insufficient to generate output at the full-employment level, unemployment results.**

By contrast, in the long run output depended on the availability of capital and labor.

INFLATION

Definition

Inflation: Continuously rising average price level. It implies a reduction in the purchasing power of money.

Inflation is a **continuously rising average price level.** Because prices are expressed in terms of money, inflation implies a **decrease, or depreciation, in the value of money in terms of goods and services.** Whereas the term *unemployment* refers to a large, not necessarily rising, number of people out of work, *inflation* describes a situation of rising, not merely high, prices. Once the rise in prices has ceased, at however high a level, inflation is said to have stopped. Also, a rise of prices in one sector of the economy does not constitute inflation if it is offset by price declines in other sectors. Rather, the weighted average of all prices must be rising. Such a weighted average, calculated relative to a base year, is known as a *price index.* Three such indexes were discussed in Chapter 12.

Deflation: A period of declining average prices.

A condition of **declining** average price level is called **deflation.** But the U.S. has not experienced deflation since the Great Depression of the 1930s. (Japan was subject to deflation in the 1990s.)

The Economic Cost of Inflation

In contrast to that of unemployment, the economic cost of inflation is not immediately obvious, nor is it easy to measure, despite most people's strong aversion to inflation. That aversion is rooted in the widespread belief that price increases undermine the real value of earnings and therefore the standard of living, as when salary increments fail to keep up with inflation. But that notion of a simple and direct linkage from inflation to the family's living standard is largely a myth. Real income is made up of the relation between the rate of increase in money earnings and the rate of inflation. A 14 percent rise in money income accompanied by 13 percent inflation yields a 1 percent increase in real income. A stationary real income can result from zero inflation and zero rise in money earnings, or from any percentage increase in earnings matched by an equal rate of inflation. **Real income in the economy is determined only by the output of goods and services, which in turn depends on the productivity of factors** (such as labor). If productivity fails to grow, so that real output is stationary, society (collectively) decides on the rate of increase in money income, and a matching rate of inflation will follow. Inflation is a symptom; it does not in itself directly undermine real income. However, it does affect real income *indirectly,* to the extent that it undermines productivity and lowers real output in the economy.

Real income is nominal income minus inflation, and is determined by the output of goods and services.

What then are the costs of inflation?

Costs of inflation: These costs include: Redistribution Costs as wealth is transferred from creditors to debtors; loss to people living on fixed incomes; and possible loss to small savers as inflation may outpace interest earnings.

Redistribution Costs Its most pervasive cost is *redistribution of income* among various groups in society—redistribution that can be capricious and arbitrary and is certainly unintentional. **Debtors gain and creditors lose** as debts are repaid in dollars that are worth less in real terms—in terms of their purchasing power. If Linda lent Jack $100 to be repaid a year later, then Linda is the creditor and Jack is the debtor. When it comes time to repay the loan (when the loan **matures**), Linda receives back her $100, but it is worth less in terms of purchasing power. Because of the inflation that prevailed during the year, the same $100 now buys fewer goods and services than when the loan was extended. The value of money has declined during the year. It is beneficial to be a debtor (owe money) in years of high inflation.

People who live on fixed money income, as do millions of retirees, **lose in terms of real income** as the purchasing power of money declines. A retired couple receiving $750 per month from various sources, including Social Security, finds that because of inflation, that amount buys fewer and fewer goods and services. In the United States, Social Security payments **are indexed to the cost of living—they rise in proportion to the increase in the CPI**—affording retirees some protection against the ravages of inflation.

Small savers may lose **if the interest rate paid on passbook savings accounts falls short of the rate of inflation.** For at 10 percent annual inflation, a 6 percent interest rate means a 4 percent **negative interest** earned when viewed in terms of real purchasing power. For example, if Linda deposited $1,000 for one year at a local bank in a 6 percent savings account, she would receive back $1,060 when the *loan matures* at the end of the year: her $1,000 principal plus $60 in interest. But because of the 10 percent inflation, her principal lost $100 in real value during the year and is in fact worth only $900. By year-end, at maturity, she receives back $900 plus $60 interest, for a total of $960 (in real terms), or $40 less than the money she deposited. She has lost 4 percent (40/1,000) of the real value of her deposit, or earned a *negative* interest of 4 percent. Wealthy people, who have access to sophisticated financial instruments, may escape this problem, as they can select instruments that pay higher interest.

In a more general way, **people lose who maintain their wealth** (their accumulated lifetime savings) **in money or in financial instruments yielding low interest.** In the 1970s, even corporate stocks did not prove to be a good hedge (protection) against inflation. Those who maintain their wealth in real assets, such as real estate, may gain if the value of these assets rises faster than the rate of inflation. Businessmen who maintain stocks of inventories may gain if the money value of their inventories rises faster than inflation.

The effects of inflation can be compounded because its rate is unlikely to be at a standstill. If left unchecked, inflation tends to feed upon itself, as people begin to build it into their economic calculations and wage demands. The rate of inflation tends to rise, making the redistributional effects worse.

Variability of inflation causes uncertainty and may lower output.

Effects on Aggregate Output But high inflation may also have a negative effect on people's saving behavior, thereby curtailing the real growth rate in the economy. Why save if the real value of the accumulated savings is eroded away by inflation? Since savings is a major source of funds for investment purposes, the rate of investment in the economy declines, thus undermining future productivity and real output.

Not only that, but the *variability* of inflation (the degree to which it changes from year to year and quarter to quarter) increases with its average level. Double-digit inflation tends to be highly variable over time, and it is very difficult if not impossible to predict. People do not know how much inflation to anticipate in coming months and years. And consequently, economic agents have no firm basis on which to build costs, prices, wage contracts, and other economic calculations. Individuals and firms are reluctant to enter into long-term contracts, because they do not know what the real value of these contracts will be in the future. And that factor lowers investment and subsequently real output. People spend much time and energy on transactions designed to avoid the impact of inflation rather than on productive activity. All these factors, rooted in unanticipated inflation, interfere with efficiency of production and reduce the output of goods and services. They are the indirect effects of inflation in reducing real output and the standard of living, alluded to previously.

Finally, policy measures to curb or reduce inflation often cause unemployment and lost output, further exacerbating its cost to society.

Hyperinflation: A very high rate of inflation, where money cannot be used as store of value or medium of exchange.

If left unchecked, inflation may accelerate to a gallop, such as that experienced in some Latin American countries. **Hyperinflation**, averaging, say, at over 100 percent per year (triple-digit), hampers the orderly functioning of a monetary economy. Money with unstable value is not a very useful means of payment. And since a highly specialized economy depends on the use of money, the erosion of the real value of money through inflation interferes greatly with efficiency, and causes a curtailment in aggregate output. Imagine the waste of resources if storekeepers have to change all their posted prices every week.

The fact that inflation affects practically everybody in society explains the public aversion to it. But tolerance of inflation varies considerably among countries. And that is reflected in the historical record. In 1979, U.S. inflation was in the 10 to 13 percent range; in Germany and Japan, it was less than half that; in the Latin American countries, it averaged over 50 percent annually.

Causes of Inflation

Intuitively, inflation is the opposite of unemployment. **It occurs because aggregate expenditure on goods and services exceeds the aggregate output that the economy can produce at full employment, or the potential output of the economy.** When individuals, firms, and the government combined try to squeeze more goods and services out of the economy than can possibly be supplied, prices rise; there is too much demand relative to supply of goods and services in the aggregate. In common parlance, when there is "too much money chasing few goods," the value of money declines and inflation occurs.

Another cause of **inflation is rooted in cost conditions.** When the price of a productive factor such as energy (oil, coal, natural gas, or other forms) rises precipitously, it has an all-pervasive effect of increasing production costs throughout the economy. For energy is required for the production of almost all goods and services. Producers tend to raise the prices of their products to compensate for the increase in production costs. And when these price boosts work their way through the economy, inflation results. A sharp rise in the cost of labor, capital, or raw materials would have the same effects, resulting in inflation.

Natural rate of unemployment (revisited): the level of unemployment which keeps inflation from accelerating.

Because inflation results when the economy is strained to capacity, it is generally believed that some unemployment of people and machines is necessary to avoid it. The **natural rate of unemployment,** mentioned in the previous section, is defined as **the level of unemployment necessary to keep inflation from accelerating.**

Stagflation: Simultaneous existence of high unemployment and inflation.

Stagflation

The **existence of high unemployment and inflation at the same time is known as stagflation.** It is clearly the worst of all worlds, inflicting upon society both types of economic costs. In the mid-1970s, most industrial countries, including the United States, went through periods of stagflation.

Deflation is a process of declining price level. For reasons to be discussed later in the book, it can also be very costly to the economy.

THE BUSINESS CYCLE

Fluctuations in Real GDP

Secular trend of real GDP: A long run trend showing continuous economic expansion, as labor and capital increase and their productivity improves. **Business cycle:** fluctuations in the level of economic activity around this long-term trend; it has 4 phases: **expansion,** *peak,* **recession,** *trough.*

Consider the behavior of actual output in Figure 13–1. It exhibits two features. First, there is a fundamental long-run trend, showing continuous expansion of the economy. Known as the **secular trend of real GDP,** it reflects the increase in the quantity of labor and capital, and the improvement in their productivity that occurs continuously. Second, this expansion is not smooth, but is subject to ups and downs. And the fluctuations are not of equal duration; some are long and others are short.

Superimposed upon the secular or long-run growth trend are the variations in the level of economic activity. These fluctuations are known as the **business cycle,** which consists of four phases, as noted on the accompanying chart: **expansion** (or upswing) in real GDP; a **peak** occurring before the economy turns downward; a **recession** or contraction (or downswing) as real GDP declines; and a **trough,** reached before the economy turns upward. A complete cycle usually lasts from three to nine years.[1]

Real GDP and Employment

Unemployment is a lagging indicator; changes in it lag behind variations in real GDP.

As seen in Figure 13–1, it is fluctuations in real GDP that determine the position of the economy over the cycle. Associated with the GDP movements are variations in employment or unemployment. **Unemployment** *increases during the recession phase and declines during the recovery phase.* However, as a matter of empirical regularity, **variations in unemployment lag behind the variations in real output.**

At the beginning of a downswing when output declines, firms do not reduce their labor force by a proportionate amount. Some companies may consider the decline in orders and shipments as temporary and do not wish to dispense with their trained workers and other personnel. They tend to "hoard" labor in anticipation of a reversal in the situation. Other firms resist laying off workers and executives simply because it is an unpalatable thing to do. But such hoarding of labor is possible only as long as corporate profits remain high. When the profit squeeze comes,

[1]Seasonal fluctuations, such as a pre-Christmas spurt in economic activity, are superimposed upon the business cycle. They are disregarded here.

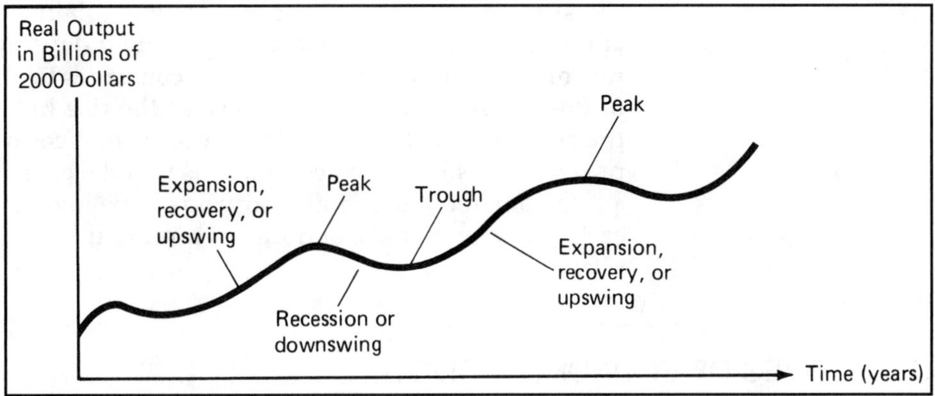

Figure 13–1 Cyclical Fluctuation (around a long-run trend) in the Movement of Real GDP: This schematic view shows the four phases of the business cycle: peak, recession, trough, and recovery.

firms are forced to adjust their labor force to the reduced level of output. The upshot of this practice is that only after a quarter or two into the recession will there be an observable increase in unemployment. *The rise in unemployment lags behind the decline in real GDP.*

Output per worker: a measure of labor productivity, rises during the initial recovery phase, and declines during the initial contraction phase. Inflation tends to rise during expansion, but only after the initial recovery stage.

This lag has an important implication for labor production costs. At the onset of a recession, output declines but employment remains stationary. Consequently, **output per worker** (output divided by the number of workers), which is a measure of **labor productivity, declines**. This means that **production costs per unit of output increase at the beginning of a recession,** and are adjusted downward only as the recession progresses and firms contract their labor force.

A reverse phenomenon occurs at the beginning of an upswing. Firms start expanding their output—first by making better use of their existing labor force; after that by hiring the most qualified workers out of the unemployed labor pool; and only when unemployment is down considerably by hiring the less qualified. *The decline in unemployment lags behind the expansion of output.* At the onset of the recovery phase, output expands but employment (and unemployment) remains stationary. Consequently, **output per worker increases, and conversely, production costs per unit of output decline.** Cost begin to rise only as the expansion progresses and firms increase their labor force.

In sum, employment fluctuations tend to lag behind variations in real GDP. And as a result, production costs tend to rise at the onset of a recession and decline at the onset of the recovery phase.

Inflation over the Cycle

Although subject to certain long-run trends, the rate of inflation tends to fluctuate over the cycle. As an increase in aggregate expenditures pushes the economy **toward the peak phase, resources tend to become fully employed and inflation heats up.** This trend **continues into the early stage of a downswing, primarily because of the increase in unit labor**

costs of production, as previously explained. **As the trough is approached, and slack and unemployment develop in the economy, the rate of inflation tends to subside. It continues to abate in the early stage of the recovery, primarily because of the rise in labor productivity and the associated reduction in labor production costs.** Only as the recovery proceeds does inflation accelerate, as was the case in mid-2006.

In sum, the rate of inflation tends to be highest around the peak and early recession phases, and lowest around the trough and early recovery phases.

OBJECTIVES OF ECONOMIC POLICY

Council of Economic Advisers (CEA): designed to advise the president on ways to achieve full employment and price stability.

In 1946, Congress passed a landmark piece of legislation known as the Employment Act. It assigned the federal government responsibility for attaining and maintaining full employment and created a special agency, the **Council of Economic Advisers (CEA),** to advise the president on policies designed to attain that objective. The *Economic Report of the President,* submitted each year to Congress, summarizes the state of the economy and contains a wealth of information and statistics about all phases of economic activity.

In subsequent years, the role of combating inflation was added to government economic policy. Thus, the twin objectives became full employment and price stability. And these two issues occupy the center stage of macroeconomics.

CAUSES OF INFLATION AND UNEMPLOYMENT—A PREVIEW OF COMING ATTRACTIONS

Parts 3 and 4 of this book provide a step-by-step analysis of the causes and cures of unemployment and inflation. An overview of this material is offered in this section.

It is useful to diagnose the twin problems in a framework similar to the traditional supply and demand analysis employed in Part 2. Whereas that analytical apparatus relates to the market for a single product, the variant used here applies to the aggregate economy. In the usual two-dimensional graph, the **vertical axis** represents a weighted average of all prices in the economy, or the **price level,** instead of the price of an individual commodity. The **horizontal axis** measures the quantity of all goods and services produced in the economy, or **real GDP,** instead of the quantity of one product.

Aggregate Demand

Figure 13–2 presents the demand schedule in such a two-dimensional diagram. Because it relates to the demand for all goods and services in the economy, it is known as **aggregate demand.** The **aggregate demand curve**

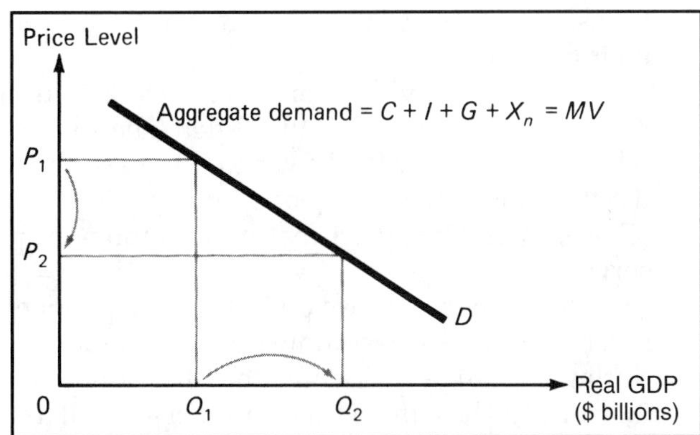

Figure 13–2 The *Aggregate-Demand* Schedule: This shows the relation between aggregate real output demanded and the price level. Aggregate demand consists of the four components of the expenditures side of GDP: consumption, investment, government purchases, and net exports. On the output-price-level space, it has a negative slope. Adding up to total output, it also equals money supply (M) times the velocity of circulation of money (V).

Aggregate demand: demand for all goods and services in the economy, consisting of consumption, investment, government spending and net exports. The **aggregate demand curve:** shows the quantity demanded declining as the price level rises.

describes the relation between the quantity of all final goods and services demanded and the average *price level* of these goods and services. Its negative slope shows that as the average price level declines, the quantity of all goods and services demanded increases. Because it deals with all goods and services combined, interproduct substitution is ruled out as an explanation for this relation. Rather, the nature of the slope can be explained as follows: Assume that the price level of all goods and services declines from P_1 to P_2, as indicated by the arrow along the vertical axis in Figure 13–2. That makes people feel wealthier, because the real value of their financial assets (such as savings accounts) rises. As a consequence, they spend more on all goods and services, as indicated by the arrow along the horizontal axis, and the quantity purchased rises from Q_1 to Q_2.

Expenditure Approach In line with the expenditures side of the national income accounts, there are four main components of aggregate demand. Consumer expenditures on nondurables, durable goods, and services (labeled C) constitute about two-thirds of the total in the United States. Next comes private domestic investment (labeled I), which include business expenditures on plant and equipment, residential construction, and changes in inventories. The third component is federal, state, and local government expenditures on goods and services (labeled G). Finally, net exports of goods and services (exports minus imports) is a relatively small item, labeled X_n. Thus, aggregate demand = $C + I + G + X_n$.

Monetary Approach There is another way of viewing aggregate demand. The four types, or channels, of expenditures just described are financed by money. They represent monetary transactions and are measured in dollar terms. Their dollar value must equal the amount of dollars expended on their purchase

Thus, an individual product, such as a desk, may sell for $400, and that sum is received by the seller. The other side of the transaction is what was spent by the buyer to purchase the desk—also $400. Similarly if $10 trillion of final goods and services was produced during 2000 (GDP), then it required that much money to purchase these goods and services.

Although the precise definition of the money stock (or money supply) must await Part 4, we know how much money circulates in the economy during a given year. Assume that the money stock in 2000, labeled *M*, was $1 trillion. Then this is the number of dollars available to all economic agents (consumers, investors, and the government alike) to purchase the final goods and services.

But how can $1 trillion purchase $10 trillions worth of goods and services? By having each dollar "work hard." The average dollar "turns around" more than once during a year, to finance more than just one dollar's worth of a (final-good) purchase. A given $100 bill may be used by Linda to buy a dress at a shop; the dress shop may then use it to pay a carpenter to build some shelves; the carpenter, upon receiving the money, spends it at the supermarket for food; and the supermarket chain may then use it in constructing a new store—all within the span of one year.

Velocity of money (v): the number of times the average dollar changes hands in a given year to finance purchases in *final* goods and services. [Velocity times money supply] is also a measure of aggregate demand.

The **number of times per year the average dollar turns around to finance purchases in final goods and services is called velocity** and is turned around 10 times and financed $10 worth of purchases. We say that velocity, *V*, equals 10. And $1 trillion × 10 = $10 trillion.

A general proposition emerges from this discussion. Since GDP equals aggregate expenditures on final goods and services, and because all expenditures are financed by money, GDP must also equal the money supply multiplied by the velocity. Thus, *aggregate demand* = *MV*. This definition does not distinguish between the channels of expenditures; rather, it lumps them all together. It is also indicated in Figure 13–2.

Both these definitions of aggregate demand are correct, and each is useful in its own way in gaining insights into the economy. Part 3 of this book highlights the expenditures approach, and Part 4 highlights the *MV* or monetary approach.

Aggregate supply: The supply of all goods and services in the economy. The **aggregate supply curve:** shows a positive relationship between the price level and the supply of goods and services in the economy. It has 3 phases: flat, mildly positive slope, and sharply positive slope.

Aggregate Supply

Shown on the same kind of two-dimensional graph, **aggregate supply** *describes the relation between the supply (by firms) of all goods and services and the price level of these goods and services.* The dashed vertical lines in Figure 13–3 divide the space into three regions; the solid vertical line marks the one level of output that generates full employment. At low levels of output, indicated as region I, the economy is functioning at far below full capacity. There is considerable unemployment in the labor force, and unused (or "excess") capacity in manufacturing plants. Starting, say, from output level *a* (which may represent $4.0 trillion in real GDP), the supply of output can expand without an increase in prices, for a simple logical

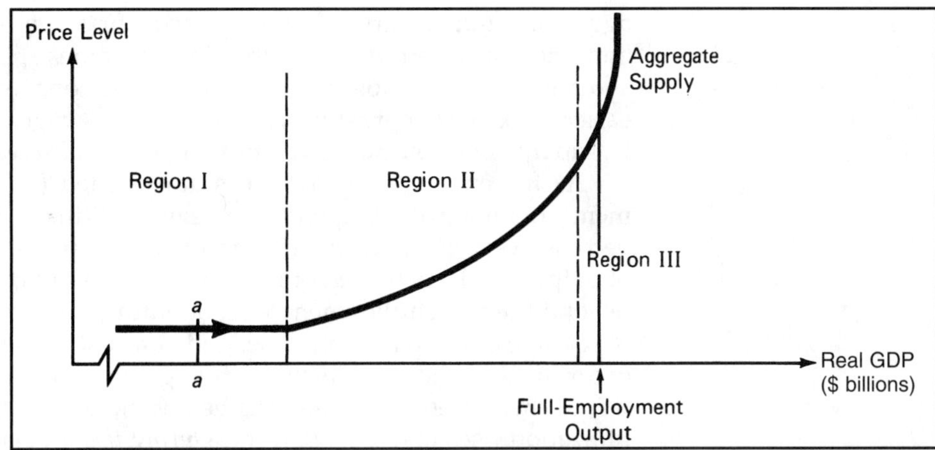

Figure 13–3 Aggregate Supply: This shows the relationship between aggregate real output supplied and the price level. It has three regions: (I) At low levels of economic activity, when considerable slack exists, output can be expanded at a constant price level, and the schedule is horizontal. (II) As the degree of slack in the economy declines, further expansion of real output requires an increase in the price level; aggregate supply acquires a positive slope, which becomes increasingly steeper as output rises. (III) In the neighborhood of full employment aggregate supply is very steep. Sharp increases in the price level are associated with further output expansion. Somewhat beyond the full employment level, aggregate supply becomes vertical; no further increase in output is possible (only prices rise).

reason: With so much slack in the economy, firms can expand production by hiring workers and machines at a constant price. They need not offer higher wages to attract workers from competing firms, because of much unemployment among workers of all skills and occupations. They can hire workers from the pool of the unemployed.

Moving in the direction of the arrow, as output rises to region II, unemployment of workers and machines declines. In this region, expansion of aggregate output can come about only if accompanied by an increase in the general price level. This is so for several reasons: First, bottlenecks begin to appear in certain industries, even when average output for the economy as a whole is well below full capacity.[2] Some specific plants and perhaps industries already function at near full capacity, and certain labor skills are in short supply. Also, certain labor unions experience high employment among their members and may become more militant in wage demands. Specific firms with market power approach full-capacity operations, and consequently begin to push up prices. A general increase in aggregate output in this region requires firms to bid workers away from other firms by offering higher wages, and these are passed on to consumers in the form of higher prices. Certain raw materials may also be in short supply, commanding higher prices. Consequently, the

[2] *Bottlenecks* describe a situation in which no unused capacity exists in firms in one stage of a multistage production process of a certain product. For example, inadequate supply of one part, such as glass, may hold up the entire output of autos.

aggregate-supply curve slopes upward—first gently, but as output rises and unemployment declines, the slope becomes steeper. Bottlenecks and shortages become more widespread, and unions as well as firms find it easier to exercise market power and push up wages and prices. **In region II, expansion of output is accompanied by an increase in the price level.**

As full-employment output is approached (at 5 percent unemployment), denoting the beginning of region III, the aggregate-supply curve becomes very steep. In the neighborhood of full employment, expansion of output can be achieved only at the cost of a rapid rise in the price level. Beyond the full-employment level of output, further economic expansion is possible only on a small scale, and at a cost of high inflation. This may occur at times of excessively high aggregate demand (such as during a war), when unemployment falls below the 5 percent mark and capacity utilization rises above 88 percent. *During the last two decades, the economy functioned mainly in region II,* and consequently, future graphs highlight that region.

Unemployment and Inflation

Figure 13–4 combines the aggregate-demand (*AD*) and aggregate-supply (*AS*) schedules in the same two-dimensional space. Their intersection at point *e* yields the equilibrium real GDP, Q_E on the horizontal axis, and the equilibrium price level, P_E on the vertical axis. The cause of unemployment is immediately apparent. It would be an unlikely coincidence for the *AD* and *AS* curves to intersect at a point corresponding to full-employment output. Inadequate aggregate demand is the root cause of unemployment. **The distance along the horizontal axis between equilibrium output (Q_E) and the unique full-employment output is the**

Figure 13–4 Aggregate Demand and Supply: The intersection of the two schedules at point *e* determines the equilibrium price level P_E, and equilibrium real output Q_E. A rise in aggregate demand from *AD* to *AD'*, within region II of the aggregate supply schedule, shifts the equilibrium to *e'*. Real output rises to Q'_E, but the price level also increases to P'_E.

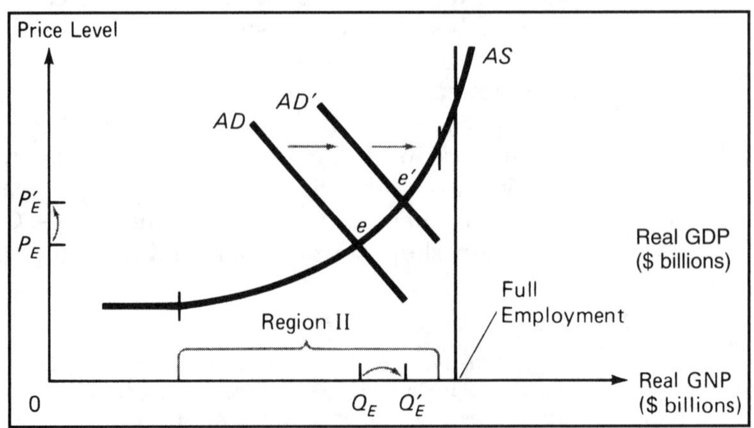

GDP gap: the difference between equilibrium real GDP and full employment (or potential) real GDP.

GDP gap at a given year. Its size determines the level of unemployment in the economy.

An upward shift in aggregate demand from *AD* to *AD′* moves the equilibrium position from *e* to *e′*. Output expands to Q'_E, toward the full-employment level (moving rightward along the horizontal axis), but prices also rise to P'_E (moving upward along the vertical axis). While it lasts, this process of rising prices is inflation. As *AD* moves gradually further to the right, the rise in the price level becomes more precipitous meaning a higher rate of inflation.[3] Because this inflation is caused by **successive increases in aggregate demand,** it is known as **demand inflation.** Demand inflation becomes high only in the neighborhood of full employment. This explains why inflation tends to heat up during the peak of a business cycle and subside during the trough.

Demand inflation: inflation that occurs due to excessive aggregate demand relative to ability of the economy to produce goods and services.

Such shifts in aggregate demand, in either direction, can occur in the private sector, as consumers (*C*), investors (*I*) or foreigners (X_n) change the level of their spending. Chapters 14–17 analyze in detail the determinants of these expenditure components and the causes of their shifts. Here it is important to note that the expansion of output can be attained only *at the cost of a rising price level* (that is, inflation). Conversely, a reduction in the rate of inflation comes about if and when aggregate demand moves downward (*AD* shifts to the left); it can be attained only *at the cost of shrinking real output and hence unemployment.* This underscores the **tradeoff between inflation and unemployment:** Inflation subsides only at the cost of rising unemployment, and unemployment declines only at the cost of rising prices.

Unemployment-Inflation trade-off. Bringing unemployment down, close to zero, would cause inflation.

Shifts in aggregate demand can also be brought about by government measures, known as demand-management policies. These are the policies traditionally employed by the government to stabilize the economy. But because they operate within region II of the aggregate-supply curve, they are also subject to the tradeoff between inflation and unemployment. The main reason for not reaching and maintaining full employment is its cost in terms of inflation. Conversely, the main reason for not attaining price stability is its cost in terms of unemployment.

Demand-Management Policies

Two types of policy are available to the government to influence aggregate demand: fiscal policy, which relies on changes in government expenditures (*G*) and/or taxes (*T*), and monetary policy, which relies on changes in the money supply.

Fiscal Policy Suppose the government wishes to increase output and employment, even at the cost of rising prices. It can, first of all, increase government expenditures, holding taxes constant. Government expendi-

[3]On a more technical level, the chart can be reinterpreted by showing inflation, or the rate of price *change,* rather than the price *level,* on the vertical axis. Thus, a rightward shift in *AD* stimulates inflation. A leftward shift in *AD lowers* the *rate of inflation;* it does not actually reduce prices.

▶ A GENERALIST AND A SPECIALIST

During the first 30 years after WW II the macroeconomic profession specialized in *demand* management policies.

What is the difference between a specialist and a generalist? A specialist is a person who knows a lot about very few subjects. A generalist is a person who knows a little about many subjects.

As times goes on the specialist knows more and more about fewer and fewer subjects until he knows everything about nothing; and the generalist knows less and less about an increasing number of subjects until he knows nothing about everything.

tures (*G*) is one of the four channels of expenditures, but its level is at the discretion of policy makers. A rise in *G* has the same effect as an increase in private expenditures; it pushes the *AD* schedule to the right. In the process, this measure moves the federal budget toward a deficit and increases the share of the government in the economy.

Second, the government can lower taxes. Although such a step has no direct effect on the economy, it leaves more purchasing power in the hands of the private sector. If the cut occurs in the personal income tax, consumers have more money to spend; consumption rises, and the *AD* schedule is shifted to the right. If the cut occurs in profit taxes, business firms have more money to invest, investment rise, and the *AD* schedule moves rightward. In both cases, the economy expands. As in the case of increasing *G*, the lowering of taxes pushes the federal budget toward a deficit. The government can, of course, increase expenditures and lower taxes at the same time.

A move toward a budgetary deficit—by raising expenditures and/or lowering taxes—stimulates economic activity, but at the cost of rising prices. Conversely, should the government wish to combat inflation, it would lower its expenditures, thereby directly curtailing aggregate demand, and/or raise taxes, thereby leaving less purchasing power in the hands of the private sector and causing consumers or investors to curtail their demand. These measures move the federal budget toward a *surplus.* They shift the *AD* curve to the left, curtailing inflation, but at the cost of reduced output and higher unemployment. Fiscal policy will be discussed in detail in Chapters 18 and 19.

Demand-management policies: Fiscal and monetary policies designed to promote full employment and price stability. **Fiscal policies:** changes in government taxes and expenditures. **Monetary policies:** changes in money supply and interest rates by the Central Bank.

Monetary Policy Monetary policy in the United States is in the hands of a legally independent agency, the Federal Reserve System, dubbed the Fed. Among its other responsibilities, the Fed regulates the quantity of money (*M*) in the economy. Many consumption and investment expenditures depend on borrowed funds, the cost of which is the rate of interest. These include purchases of homes, cars, durable goods, or plant and equipment. If the Fed wishes to expand economic activity (real GDP), it can make funds more readily available and reduce their cost, the rate of interest. This stimulates consumption and investment spending and pushes the *AD* curve to the right. Output rises, but so do prices. In terms of the monetary approach to aggregate demand, a rise in *M* shifts *AD* to the right. Conversely, should the Fed wish to dampen the rate of inflation, it would make funds scarcer and more costly, and thereby reduce private expenditures that depend on borrowed funds. A reduction in *M* shifts the *AD* curve to the left. Inflation abates, but real output declines and unemployment rises. Money and monetary policy are the subject of Part 4.

The Unemployment-Inflation Tradeoff

Both fiscal and monetary policy operate by influencing aggregate demand and consequently are subject to the tradeoff between inflation and unemployment. Only in periods when the economy operates in region I of the *AS* curve is that tradeoff averted. Accordingly, the twin policy objectives of maintaining full employment and price stability are not usually attainable jointly. Price stability can be achieved, but at the expense of high unemployment; indeed, this is the reason that inflation has not been wrung out of the economy. Conversely, full employment can be achieved, but at the cost of a rapid rise in prices; and this is the reason that unemployment has not been eliminated.

The tradeoff between inflation and unemployment induces periodic policy switches. Thus, in 1976, immediately after his election, President Carter declared unemployment to be "public enemy number one," and geared the government policy apparatus to promoting an increase in output (and therefore in employment) and an attendant reduction in unemployment. Unemployment declined from 9 percent of the labor force in 1975 (cyclical trough) to 5.6 percent in 1979 (cyclical peak). But the price paid for this economic expansion was an increase in the annual rate of inflation to 13.5 percent (CPI) by the fall of 1979. As a result, the president declared inflation public enemy number one, and the government policy apparatus switched gears to fight inflation, with the full expectation that unemployment would rise in the process. In 1982–83 unemployment stood at 9.5 percent and inflation declined to the 3 to 4 percent range. The subsequent expansion of 1983–88 lowered unemployment to under 5.5 percent, but in the second half of 1988 inflation again rose to 5 percent. In mid-2006 unemployment stood at 4.7 percent, and economic policy was directed at restraining inflation. Many "policy-induced" fluctuations result from such changes in objectives.

Attempts to alleviate the tradeoff problem by imposing price and wage controls while at the same time stimulating the economy have generally backfired. While in force, the controls tend to distort relative prices, and with them the pattern of economic activity; they promote inefficiency. Although prices and wages are held in check during the control period, a delayed reaction occurs when the controls are lifted; prices tend to rise sharply, compensating for the months of control. Even expectations of controls, prior to their imposition, tend to fuel inflation, as businessmen attempt to increase prices while that is still permissible.

Leftward Shift in Aggregate Supply—Stagflation

In the mid-1970s, both unemployment and inflation were on the increase in the United States and elsewhere. The simultaneous existence of inflation and unemployment is known as **stagflation.** How can it come about?

In the previous analysis, the *AD* schedule was shown to shift up or down, *holding the aggregate-supply schedule constant.* Suppose we reverse the process. Holding aggregate demand constant, we shift the *aggregate-supply schedule to the left:* In Figure 13–5, the *AS* curve is moved from AS_1 to AS_2. This is called a reduction in supply, because at *any given price level, a smaller quantity of goods and services is supplied,* as indicated by the two leftward-pointing arrows. With *AD* remaining unchanged, the equilibrium point of intersection moves from e_1 to e_2. Real GDP declines from Q_1 to Q_2, *and* the price level rises from P_1 to P_2.

Any economywide increase in production costs causes such a shift in aggregate supply. Thus, the worldwide boom of 1972–73 generated a large increase in the prices of raw materials, which enter production processes as inputs. This happened to coincide with drought conditions in certain areas of the world, raising food prices sharply. And following on the heels of that rise came the quadrupling of oil prices. Oil prices doubled again in 1979–80. Since energy enters into the production of everything in the economy, production costs rose; producers offered any given quantity of goods and services only at higher prices. That has the same effect as offering a

Figure 13–5 Leftward Shift in Aggregate Supply: A decline in aggregate supply can be interpreted as (a) each level of real output is supplied only at higher prices (upward pointing arrow); or (b) at each price level less real output is supplied (leftward pointing arrow). In both cases, the schedule shifts from AS_1 to AS_2. Holding *AD* constant, this *increases* the price level from P_1 to P_2, and *lowers* real output from Q_1 to Q_2. This combination, while it is happening, is called *stagflation.*

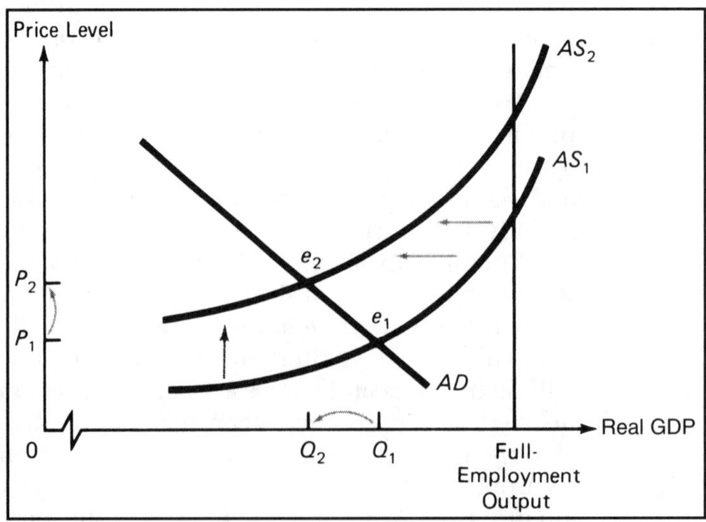

reduced quantity at each price. The upward-pointing arrow in Figure 13–5 indicates that each given volume of output will be supplied only at higher prices. As a result, aggregate supply shifts from AS_1 to AS_2. But this is equivalent to saying that at each given price, less is supplied, as shown by the leftward-pointing arrows. Thus, the all-pervasive rise in energy prices has the effect of moving aggregate supply to the left. Precipitous shifts of the *AS* curve to the left are often called **supply shocks.**

Supply shocks: events that cause the aggregate supply curve to shift to the left. They include sharp rise in energy prices, widespread draught or decline in labor productivity. These factors caused **stagflation** in the 1970s.

Environmental and safety regulations promulgated by the federal government require massive new investment expenditures (for example, to install scrubbers on the chimneys of steel mills) and have the same effect on aggregate supply, as does the strengthening of workplace health and safety standards. They all increase production costs and consequently shift *AS* to the left. And so is the effect of lagging labor productivity, coupled with a rapid rise in wage rates, implying a rise in labor production costs.

Another important cause for such a shift is **inflationary expectations.** When inflation heats up and becomes highly variable over time, both corporations and labor unions begin to build future price increases into their negotiated wage rates and price calculations. Anticipated inflation is built almost automatically into wage demands, and an added margin is sometimes included for unanticipated inflation. Because such wage increases are over and above the increase in labor productivity, they invariably raise production costs, prompting a leftward shift in *AS*. **In an inflationary environment, expectations of future inflation play an important role in further aggravating the inflationary process.**

With the help of Figure 13–5, it is easy to see the grave effects of the leftward shift in *AS*. Prices rise from P_1 to P_2, and continue to rise as long as *AS* keeps shifting to the left in response to rising production costs. While the process continues, this is inflation. Because it is caused by a shift in aggregate supply, which in turn is a result of rising production costs, it is known as supply or **cost inflation.**

Cost inflation: inflation caused by rise in production costs. It shifts the AS curve to the left, causing also contraction of output.

Next, observe what happens to output. Whereas demand inflation is accompanied by an expansion in real GDP, cost inflation is accompanied by a *contraction in real GDP* from Q_1 to Q_2, causing a rise in unemployment. If continued for two quarters or longer, this becomes a recession. And this combination of inflation and unemployment is *stagflation.* Thus, the classic cause of stagflation is a reduction in aggregate supply.[4] Its occurrence in the 1970s can be traced to the continuous increase in worldwide energy prices, the gradual tightening of environmental standards, inflationary expectations, the rise in labor production costs, and similar reasons. *Fears* of stagflation appeared in mid-2006.

---

[4]Besides the "classic" cause outlined in the text, stagflation can also arise temporarily when *AD* rises. In Figure 13–4 aggregate demand is shown to rise from *AD* to *AD′*, keeping *AS* constant. Equilibrium moves from *e* to *e′*. But the observed response of firms to a rise in demand for their products is first to expand output at constant prices. They overshoot the mark in terms of increased output. Only after a time lag, when the new conditions are perceived as permanent, do firms raise their prices. During this second phase, prices rise and output contracts (recedes from the overexpansion). While it lasts, this second phase is stagflation.

Finally, the leftward shift in AS worsens the tradeoff between inflation and unemployment. To highlight this point, we simplify Figure 13–5 by introducing a straight-line aggregate supply and concentrating on region II. This is done in Figure 13–6, where aggregate supply is shown to decline from AS_1 to AS_2 and equilibrium shifts from e_1 to e_2. To attain full employment at AS_1, AD must be shifted upward, so that it intersects AS_1 at point R. But on AS_2, such intersection can occur only at point S; attainment of full employment now requires more inflation than before. Conversely, to lower prices to a desired price level, P, aggregate demand must be shifted downward. On AS_1, the intersection would occur at point M. But on AS_2, AD must be lowered all the way to point N, involving a much greater loss of output and therefore more unemployment. The cost of controlling inflation in terms of unemployment rises.

Supply Management

Clearly, the leftward shift in aggregate supply that kept occurring in the 1970s was a major cause of the troublesome economic scene during that decade. Practically all the industrial countries were plagued by this phenomenon, although to varying degrees. The challenge of economic policy is to devise measures that would shift aggregate supply to the *right*. Such policies are known as **supply management.** Their great appeal is clearly

Supply management: government policies that attempt to shift AS to the right, thereby raising output and lowering inflation at the same time. **Reverse supply shock** can also come about by rapid increases in productivity without regard to government policies (e.g. the 1990s).

Figure 13–6 The Inflation—Unemployment Tradeoff: With AS_1, attainment of full employment requires a rise in AD so that equilibrium would shift from e_1 to R. With AS_2, attainment of full employment requires a much greater increase in AD, so that equilibrium would shift all the way from e_2 *to S.* The required increase in the price level is clearly greater in the second case than in the first. Conversely, attainment of price stability requires greater unemployment with AS_2 than with AS_1. Conclusion: A decline in aggregate supply from AS_1 to AS_2 worsens the trade-off between real output and changes in the price level.

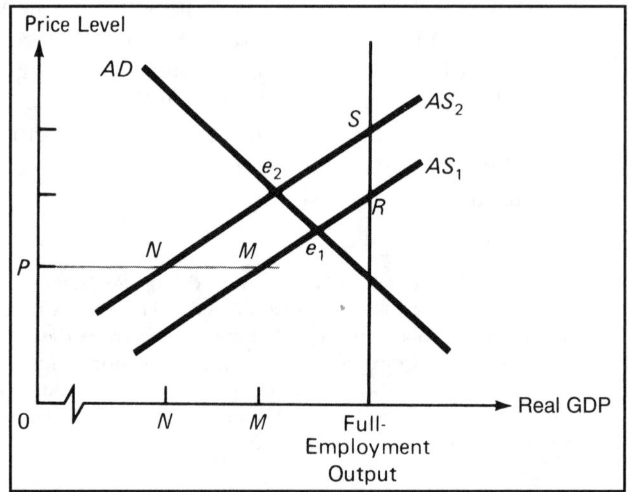

evident in Figure 13–5. By increasing aggregate supply, the equilibrium point moves from e_2 to e_1 and further down the *AD* curve. Not only does output expand toward the full-employment level, but inflation declines as well. Instead of the economy's being trapped by the inflation unemployment tradeoff, supply management can lick both problems at the same time: Inflation subsides and unemployment declines. Indeed, that was achieved with the decline in oil prices in 1981–82, caused by a glut on the international petroleum market (a reverse supply shock). In the late 1990s the economy again experienced a reverse supply shock; this time because of a precipitous rise in productivity occasioned by the "information revolution." That resulted in rapid non-inflationary growth.

But such policy measures are difficult to devise. What might such measures be? A reduction in business payroll (Social Security) taxes would lower production costs, and thereby shift the *AS* schedule to the right. Reduction in sales and excise taxes would have a similar effect. Beyond that, fiscal and monetary policies can be targeted in such a way as to stimulate investment (and therefore subsequent output) and increase productivity. Reduction in certain business taxes and an increase in the investment tax credit, or accelerated depreciation of plant and equipment, come to mind as possible steps. Finally, removal of redundant government regulations that increase production (and reporting) costs and infusing greater competition into the economy may also stimulate aggregate supply. Any measure that lowers production costs across the board would have the effect of increasing aggregate supply.

Supply-Side Economics

These were the considerations underlying the Reagan administration's preoccupation with the so called supply-side economics. Can the government devise an array of policy measures that would shift the *AS* curve to the right and produce the miraculous combination of an increase in output *and* a reduction in inflation?

Supply-side economics is not new. In the underdeveloped world (Asia, Africa, and Latin America), an increase in aggregate supply is the overwhelming policy objective. It is the only way to increase output and raise living standards. This was also the main policy target of the Western market-economy countries in previous centuries. In the writings of Adam Smith, for example, supply held the center stage. Attainment of maximum production and allocative efficiency was viewed as the crowning achievement of a competitive market economy.

All this changed dramatically with the Great Depression of the 1930s and the advent of Keynesian economics.[5] In the ensuing forty years, economists perfected, and policy makers employed, the tools of demand management. It was taken for granted that supply would be forthcoming. Indeed, in much of the 1930s, the economy was functioning in region I of the aggregate-supply schedule (often labeled the *Keynesian region*), so that aggregate output could be expanded without inducing inflation. (The

---

[5]Keynes's seminal book, *The General Theory of Employment, Interest and Money,* was published in 1936.

remainder of Part 3 of this book is devoted mainly to demand-management measures.) But the constellation of circumstances contributing to the supply shocks of the 1970s brought about another change of emphasis—a change that appeals to conservative philosophical predilections. President Reagan promulgated the new emphasis on supply-side economics, namely, policies designed to shift the *AS* curve to the right.

However, in contrast to demand management, there are only a few obvious supply-side measures that can be put into effect. Although all economists applaud the effects of increasing aggregate supply, (moving from AS_2 to AS_1 in Figure 13–5), many are skeptical about the effectiveness of most measures in accomplishing this.

Marginal tax rate: the tax rate on each additional dollar of income beyond a cut-off point. It *may* affect incentives to work and save.

One such measure, widely acclaimed by the Reagan administration, is a reduction in **marginal tax rates**. Indeed, in 1981 the administration introduced, and Congress passed, a 23 percent across-the-board cut in personal income taxes that was put into effect in three steps during 1981–83. Similar policies were subsequently introduced in other countries. At first, its supply-side effect was seen as inducing people to work harder by lowering their marginal tax rates. Such an outcome may occur in Sweden, where these rates are exceedingly high and are viewed as lowering work incentives. But in the United States, where income tax rates are not that high, this measure served mainly to increase aggregate demand, with only a slight effect on aggregate supply. As a second approximation, the measure is advocated as a way of stimulating savings, which would then flow into investment, thereby raising productivity and output. Yet an increase in the saving rate failed to materialize, as much of the resulting increase in disposable income was channeled into added consumption. Economists are still debating the effectiveness of an income-tax cut as a supply-side measure.

On the other hand, the investment tax credit, and the added flexibility in administering it, are generally considered an effective supply-side measure. And the same applies to the removal of government regulations that serve little or no social purpose.

HISTORICAL RECORD

To paint the historical record in broad strokes, the 1930s saw the Great Depression in the United States and the world at large. U.S. actual output was far below its potential, and unemployment reached a quarter of the labor force. Memories of the hard times of that period still dominate the thinking of many people of advanced age. By contrast, during the Second World War and its immediate aftermath, the economy functioned at full employment (in region III of the *AS* curve), and inflationary pressures were in evidence.

Moving to the last five decades, most of the 1950s (after the end of the Korean war) saw a period of low level of economic activity accompanied by price stability. Then in 1964, President Kennedy proposed, and Congress enacted, a cut in personal and business taxes designed to stimulate the economy. The *AD* curve shifted to the right, and the economy moved toward full employment without a significant increase in prices. But in

1967 came the escalation of the Vietnam War. President Johnson refused to increase taxes to match the $30 billion rise in defense spending, even though the economy was already approaching full employment. The large deficit so created, superimposed upon a fully employed economy, could not help but generate the inflation of 1968–69.

There followed attempts to deal with the inflation by demand-management policies. But in the first half of the 1970s, a constellation of circumstances combined to shift aggregate supply to the left. They included a worldwide drought and a rise in raw-material prices, followed later by successive huge hikes in energy prices. Environmental clean-up regulations were also tightened at that time. The stagflation set in. President Nixon attempted to stimulate the economy by demand management and to deal with the inflation by price-wage controls. But when the controls were lifted, a catch-up increase in prices fueled the inflation. In 1974–75, the world economy, including that of the United States, settled into a deep and prolonged recession accompanied by double-digit inflation (namely stagflation). The quadrupling of oil prices by the OPEC cartel was a significant cause of that stagflation. Under President Ford, fiscal and monetary policies were used to dampen aggregated demand. The rate of inflation declined to the 4 to 5 percent range, but unemployment rose to 9 percent. Upon assuming office, President Carter reversed the priorities and moved to stimulate the economy. Unemployment declined gradually to 5.6 percent in 1979, but inflation rose to 13.5 percent. (Incidentally, Europe did not experience a similar reduction in unemployment; its postrecession growth has been rather sluggish.) Another reversal of policy reappeared for 1979–80, emphasizing the battle against inflation. By 1982–83 unemployment reached 9.5 percent and inflation declined to 3 to 4 percent. Supply-side economics gained adherents with the advent of the Reagan administration in 1981.

During 1983–90 a combination of expansionary fiscal and (initially) monetary policies brought about a long period of economic recovery, with unemployment declining to 5.3 percent. But in 1988–89 inflation began to rise.

Following a short recession in 1990–91, the economy embarked upon a prolonged non-inflationary expansion, caused partly by rapid technological advance; by October 1998 unemployment declined to 4.4 percent. This expansion lasted until year 2000, and was interrupted in 2001 by a recession, with growth resuming in 2002–06.

SUMMARY

Macroeconomics is concerned with the level of output and employment and with the rate of rise in the average price level. Its policy objective is the maintenance of full employment without inflation.

Because of the existence of frictional and structural unemployment, and because not all the capital stock is suitable for efficient operations, full employment is defined as employment of 95 percent of the labor force and 88 percent of the existing capital stock. The level of employment or unemployment is tied to the level of real GDP. Consequently, a recession is accompanied by rising unemployment. A rise in output, which in turn requires a rise in aggregate expenditures, is called for in order to reduce unemployment. A growth rate of about 3 percent in real GDP is required to keep unemployment at a constant level. Each 1 percent growth rate above that level reduces unemployment by one-third of 1 percent per year.

The economic cost of a recession can be measured as the loss of output, or the GDP gap: It is the difference between potential and actual real GDP. A recession is caused by insufficient or inadequate aggregate expenditures. Output can be increased by expanding aggregate expenditures.

Inflation is a process of rising average price level. Its main costs are (1) redistribution of income among segments of society, and (2) loss of efficiency and aggregate output. Rapid inflation can also erode the functioning of a monetary economy and cause a great loss of output. The classic cause of inflation is excessive aggregate expenditures relative to the capacity of the economy to produce at full employment. This is known as *demand inflation.* Equally important is *cost inflation,* caused by a widespread increase in production costs.

The problems of inflation and unemployment can be analyzed within the framework of aggregate demand (*AD*) and supply (*AS*). Both schedules are drawn in a two-dimensional space, showing the price level on the vertical axis and real GDP on the horizontal axis. The *AD* curve slopes downward and to the right. The *AS* curve spans three distinct regions: It is horizontally flat in region I, where unemployment of workers and machines is high; it slopes upward and to the right in region II; and its positive slope becomes very steep in region III, which begins in the neighborhood of full employment. The intersection of the two schedules determines the equilibrium price level and real GDP.

Demand-management policies, both fiscal and monetary, can be used to push the *AD* curve to the right and thereby reduce unemployment. They are the traditional tools of economic policy. But because the economy functions mainly in region II of the *AS* schedule, increased output can be achieved only at the cost of rising prices. Conversely, a policy-induced reduction in aggregate demand would lower the rate of inflation, but at the cost of higher unemployment. Herein lies the tradeoff problem between inflation and unemployment. The twin objectives of macroeconomic policy cannot be attained by demand-management policies. Supply management can be used to attain these joint objectives, but such measures are still in their infancy. Supply-side economics is an attempt to develop or resurrect such measures.

A second cause of inflation is a shift to the left of aggregate supply, which is traceable to a general rise in production costs, such as a rise in energy prices. It is called *cost* or *supply inflation.*

Stagflation is the simultaneous occurrence of inflation and unemployment. Its main cause is a leftward shift in aggregate supply. Aside from inflicting upon society the cost of both inflation and unemployment, it makes the tradeoff between them worse.

Over the long run, the economy undergoes secular expansion as its labor and capital expand and efficiency improves. The business cycle is superimposed upon this long-run or secular trend. It has four phases: trough, recovery, peak, and recession. As a matter of empirical regularity, variations in employment (or unemployment) tend to lag behind fluctuations in real output. Consequently, production costs rise at the onset of a recession and decline at the onset of the recovery phase.

The Great Depression of the 1930s was followed by wartime inflation. In the post-war period, the relatively stagnant economy of the 1950s gave way to the prolonged expansion of the 1960s, culminating in a period of inflation at the end of the decade. A deep recession occurred in the mid-1970s, from which the U.S. economy recovered in the second half of the decade. But that recovery was accompanied by high inflation. Consequently, by the end of the decade, policies were employed to curtail aggregate demand and dampen the inflation. But unemployment rose as well. A turnaround of economic policies took place in the 1980s, leading to a prolonged expansion in 1983–889. After a short recession in 1991, the economy embarked on non-inflationary growth until 2000. Following a short slowdown in 2001, growth resumed in 2002–05.

QUESTIONS AND PROBLEMS

1. What are the economic costs of recession and inflation, and why is it important to attain full employment and price stability?
2. Define the following terms:

- ☐ Full employment
- ☐ Recession
- ☐ Inflation
- ☐ Stagflation
- ☐ Okun's law
- ☐ The business cycle and its four phases
- ☐ The Great Depression
- ☐ Supply shocks

3. Explain the time relation between fluctuations in real output and employment. What implications does this relation have for the labor cost of production and therefore for inflation?
4. Sketch the aggregate demand and supply schedules on a two-dimensional diagram.
   a. Explain clearly the nature of each curve and the reason it slopes the way it does.
   b. What does aggregate demand consist of under each of the two approaches?
   c. Use the diagram to identify the equilibrium output and price level.
   d. Identify the meaning of and reason for unemployment on your diagram.
   e. What might cause an upward shift in *AD*? How is demand inflation brought about?
   f. What might cause a downward shift in *AS*? How is supply or cost inflation brought about?
   g. Explain the cause of stagflation.
   h. Explain the nature of the tradeoff between inflation and unemployment. How is the tradeoff affected by stagflation?
   i. What is supply-side economics?

Classical Macroeconomics and the Keynesian Challenge

Until 1936, economics was concerned largely with microeconomic problems. The body of analysis developed in the 150 years preceding 1936 is referred to as *classical economics.* Devoting its attention mainly to the problems of resource allocation and the sectoral composition of output, classical economics had little to say about the great questions of unemployment and inflation. Indeed, its macroeconomic analysis rested on assumptions—not totally unrealistic for the past century—leading to a belief that the market economy is *stable,* in that it generates an automatic tendency to full employment.

CLASSICAL MACROECONOMIC ASSUMPTIONS

A World of Competitive Markets

Each of the many markets on which goods and services or productive factors are traded was believed to be purely competitive, in the technical sense of the word. A competitive market is defined as one composed of so many buyers and sellers that no one of them can influence the price or other conditions of sale. The individual seller (or buyer) is minuscule relative to all transactions on that particular market. Buyers and sellers take the market price for granted and adjust their behavior to it; they cannot by their own actions influence that price. The wheat market is a good example of such competitive conditions. At the time of the classical economists, this condition may also have been characteristic of many manufacturing industries.

An important feature of a competitive market is that prices are free to move unimpeded either up or down; they are flexible in *both* directions. And in each market, the price settles at a level that *clears the market;* that is, the one that equates the quantities supplied and demanded. This is the equilibrium price, determined by the supply and demand schedules.

Competitive conditions were assumed by the classical economists to prevail not only in the markets for goods and services but also in (1) the markets for productive factors, particularly labor; and (2) the market for savings and investment.

First we shall consider the labor market, depicted in Figure 14–1. The supply of labor by households is shown as a rising function of the real wage (that is, the wage rate deflated or divided by the cost of living), and the demand for labor by firms is a declining function of the real wage. The lower the real wage, the fewer workers are supplied and the more workers are demanded. The intersection of supply and demand determines the equilibrium real wage rate ($0P_E$) and the level of employment ($0Q_E$). Should the *entire* demand curve and/or supply curve shift, a new equilibrium point will be formed. But at any such point, the **real wage rate** is at a level that clears the labor market—that is, equalizes the number of workers willing to work with the number of workers firms wish to hire. By definition, there is no involuntary unemployment. The only possible unemployment is frictional in nature, occurring when workers change jobs or during other temporary adjustments in the economy.

Real wage rate: money wage rate minus the rate of inflation.

Only interference with the functioning of this market can cause more than frictional unemployment—for example, the introduction of a minimum-wage law setting the legal minimum at a level above the equilibrium real wage, as $0P_M$, and producing excess supply of labor in the amount *ab*. Likewise, if a powerful labor union negotiates a wage rate above the equilibrium level, excess supply of labor would result: At real wage $0P_M$, more workers would offer their labor services than firms found it profitable to employ, and involuntary unemployment, represented by segment *ab*, would result. But such impediments to market equilibrium—

Figure 14–1 The Labor Market: In competitive labor markets, equilibrium real wage and quantity of labor employed are established by the intersection of supply and demand for labor. Unless the wage rate is held artificially above the market clearing level ($P_m > P_E$), no involuntary unemployment can occur.

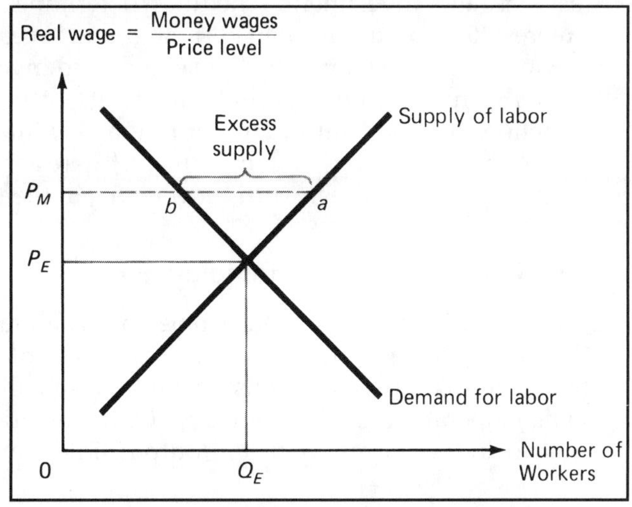

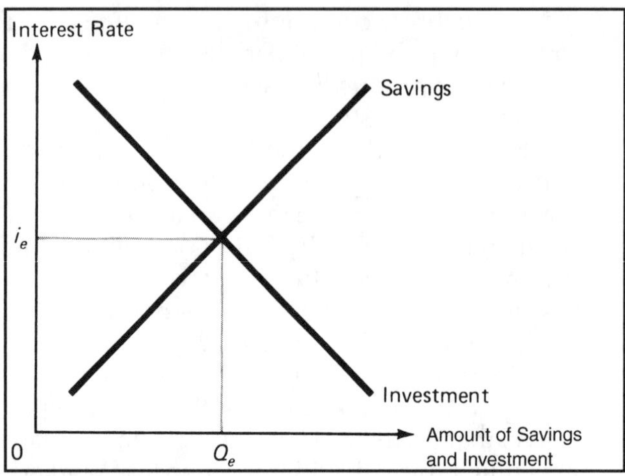

Figure 14–2 The Market for Savings and Investment: Savings and investment were assumed by the classical economists to be (positive and negative) functions of the rate of interest. The intersection of the two schedules determines equilibrium interest and equilibrium quantity of *S* and *I*. The rate of interest always equalizes desired savings and investment.

often referred to as *market imperfections* or *distortions*—were assumed not to exist in the classical world.

Second, we consider the market for savings and investment, which classical economists said was determined by the rate of interest. If people saved at all, the single alleged motivation was a desire to earn interest. The higher the rate of interest, the greater the amount saved. Put differently, savings is a *positive* function of the interest rate. In turn, the rate of interest represents the cost of investment capital. The lower the interest rate, the greater the amount firms would be willing to borrow and invest. Investment is a *negative* function of the interest rate.

These relationships are shown in Figure 14–2. The intersection of the savings and investment schedules determines the equilibrium rate of interest ($0i_e$) and the amount of savings and investment ($0Q_e$). Even though savings are done mainly by households and investment by firms, they are brought into equality by the market rate of interest. Should one of the functions (or both) shift in its entirety, a new interest rate would be found that equalizes savings and investment. There are no limits or impediments to the upward or downward movements in the market rate of interest.

The Impossibility of Unemployment

In a world such as this, there can be no involuntary unemployment. Why? In an advanced industrial society, unemployment (of people and machines) is caused by firms' inability to sell all the output they produce when operating at full capacity. Only insufficient aggregate demand would induce firms to curtail output, idle some machines, and lay off workers. But that could never happen in a classical world, because the classicals had two mechanisms of defense against such an occurrence.

It will be recalled that the value of goods and services produced equals the income generated in the productive process. On the simplest level of abstraction, the classicals assumed that the only reason people work is to be able to purchase goods and services. Why else should people part with their much cherished leisure time? Under this supposition, they would be expected to spend their entire income and save nothing. But then the entire output would be sold to consumers. People would work as much as they want to (that is, no involuntary unemployment) and then purchase the entire output they produce. This situation was described by the French economist J. B. Say in what has become known as **Say's Law: Supply creates its own demand.**

Say's Law: Classical economists maintained that supply creates its own demand. For two reasons anything that is produced will be sold to consumers or investors: savings and investment are equalized by the rate of interest; prices and wages are completely flexible. Unemployment cannot exist.

To illustrate the point, we employ the circular-flow diagram that was presented and discussed in Chapter 2. Figure 14–3 *presents only the financial-flows component of the original diagram.* The top flow shows payments by households to firms for the goods and services produced and sold by firms. The bottom flow shows payments by firms to households for productive services sold by households; these constitute household income. In the absence of household savings, the two flows are of identical magnitudes, because the values of output and income are equal. The circuit of output and income streams is self-perpetuating. If all income is spent, then it is precisely sufficient to purchase the entire output, regardless of how much is produced. There is no unsold output.

On a more sophisticated level, classical economists admitted the possibility of household savings. In other words, consumers may wish to withhold or withdraw part of their income from the income stream in the form of savings. Would not such savings give rise to unsold output? A resounding NO! was the answer of classical economists. Any withdrawal of funds into savings would be exactly matched by an *equal injection* by

Figure 14–3 The Circular-Flow Diagram in the Absence of Savings and Investment: Income received by households equals the value of goods and services produced by firms. If the entire income is spent, then all goods and services are sold. It is impossible for firms to be left with unsold output.

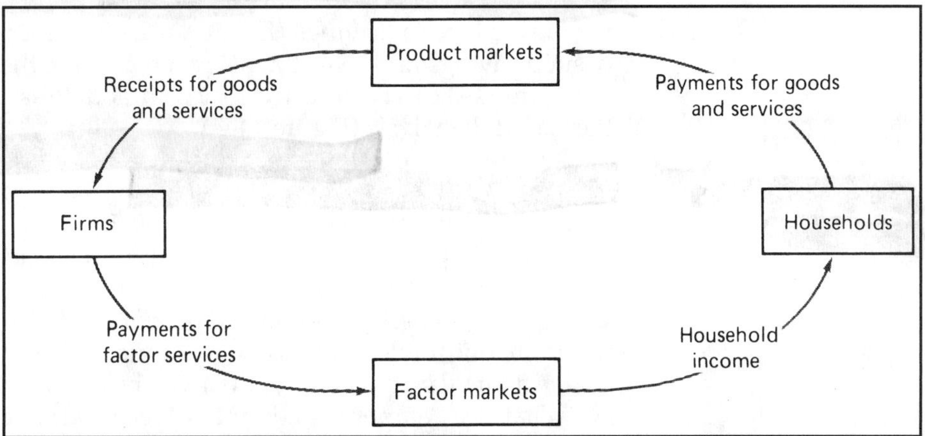

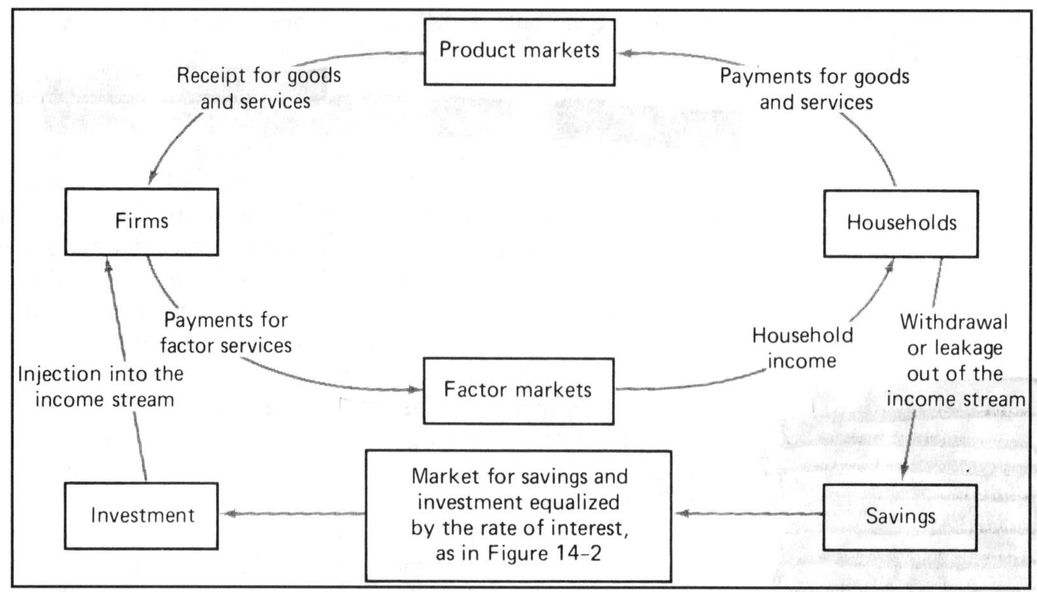

Figure 14–4 The Circular-Flow Diagram with Savings and Investment in the Classical Analysis: Income equals output, but the entire income is not necessarily spent on goods and services. Some of it is withdrawn (from the income stream) by households into savings. But in the classical analysis, that withdrawal is matched by an *equal* injection of investment by firms. Equality of savings and investment is assured by interest rate fluctuations. Consequently, there can still be no unsold output.

firms in the form of *investment.* Aggregate spending would continue to match total output; the entire output would be sold either to consumers or to investors. Savings merely make possible an equal amount of investment. Saving is always desirable, for it makes possible capital accumulation and economic growth.

Interest rate: Equates savings and investment in the classical model.

And what is the mechanism that guarantees the equality between desired savings and desired investment? It is none other than the rate of interest (Figure 14–2). The **interest rate** is the *price* of savings and investment funds; both flows of funds respond to interest variations. A rise in savings (supply of funds) merely depresses the rate of interest, and that in turn brings forth new investment (demand for funds) commensurate with the higher level of savings (Figure 14–2). Interest is the great equalizer of desired savings and investment. Schematically, the circular-flow diagram of Figure 14–3 can be adjusted to accommodate savings and investment in the classical analysis (Figure 14–4).

Savings: income minus consumption.

To recapitulate, household **income that is not spent on the purchase of goods and services is called savings. Savings** constitute a leak or a *withdrawal from the circular income stream.* But they would always be channeled into *investment* and *injected* back into the income stream by firms. What is not sold to consumers will be sold to investors. Consequently, there can be no problem of unsold output or of insufficient demand to buy the entire output. Regardless of how much is produced, all output will be sold. And if all output is sold, there can be no involuntary unemployment.

What if a temporary aberration occurred, and desired savings happened to exceed desired investment for a while? Would that not result in unsold output and unemployment? Never fear, maintained the classical economists. There is a second line of defense as strong as the first one: the competitive labor market, with perfectly flexible real wage rates. If some people are laid off, real wage rates will decline until demand and supply of labor are brought back into equality (Figure 14–1).

More specifically, observe that the vertical axis of Figure 14–1 is the real wage. It is a ratio of the money wage rate to the price level. Any unsold output caused by an excess of savings over investment lowers the price level of goods and services (the denominator). With money wage rates (the numerator) unchanged, real wages rise. As a result, the quantity of labor demanded falls and the quantity supplied rises, yielding excess supply (or surplus) of labor. Because money wage rates are assumed to be fully flexible in both directions, they fall as excess supply of labor appears, and consequently, real wages drop as well. That decline continues until the excess supply of labor is eliminated, and no involuntary unemployment remains. In sum, with flexible money wage rates, real wage rates adjust and serve to equate the supply of and demand for labor.

In sum, the idea was that the competitive private economy is **inherently stable. Flexible prices, including flexible wages and interest rates, ensure this desirable outcome.** So ingrained were these views that the classical economists tended to dismiss even protracted periods of unemployment as frictional adjustments of the economy to changes in its product mix. True, there were early writers, such as Thomas Malthus (1766–1834), who suggested that savings might cause a "general glut" on the market. But such notions were scoffed at by contemporaries. Not only were such ideas premature, but also they did not add up to a cogent theory to replace the classical analysis. When the Great Depression of the 1930s hit, it was little understood throughout much of the decade. Policy makers stumbled blindly from one remedy to the next, without diagnosing the malaise. It was left to **John Maynard Keynes**, in *The General Theory of Employment, Interest and Money* (1936) (often referred to simply as the *General Theory*), to provide a diagnosis and advocate a cure. This was the origin of modern macroeconomics.

THE KEYNESIAN CHALLENGE

Keynes, the son of a noted British economist, was born in Cambridge, England, in 1883. He was a genius; everything he touched turned into a great success. He amassed a fortune of over $2 million by speculating in the international currency and commodity markets; he wrote books on diverse subjects; he mastered the fields of mathematics and philosophy in addition to economics; he was a highly successful civil servant and carried out many a government mission; he was a patron of the arts; and for 33 years, he was the editor of the *Economic Journal*, the most distinguished economics publication in the United Kingdom.

John Maynard Keynes: The economist who introduced the theory that insufficient aggregate demand (AD) causes unemployment. Because savings are not a function of the rate of interest, interest does not equate savings and investment. Prices and wages are not flexible.

It was this giant of a man, already famous for his previous books in economics (written in the classical tradition), who in the mid-1930s came to grips with the central question of the day—the Great Depression. He offered a new theoretical structure to explain it and suggested fiscal policy (changes in government expenditures and taxes) to deal with it.

The Unlinking of Savings and Investment

In the first place, Keynes unlinked savings from investment. In a modern economy, savings and investment are done by two totally separate groups of people, motivated by totally different sets of factors. People save to guard against future contingencies, and therefore the amount of desired savings in society does not depend on the rate of interest. Indeed, it may have absolutely nothing to do with the rate of interest. Rather, savings vary positively with income: The higher the income, the more people are able and willing to save. As for investment, the desired amount depends to some extent on the rate of interest. But it is also influenced by expected profit opportunities, which in turn depend on a variety of dynamic factors affecting the economy. Since savings are not dependent on the rate of interest, interest cannot be the regulator mechanism equalizing desired savings and desired investment. The amount that people want to save can easily exceed what investors wish to invest, resulting in a net withdrawal of funds from the spending stream, and leaving part of total output unsold. In consequence, orders from factories would decline, causing a reduction in production and employment. The classical first line of defense against unemployment is demolished, offering a plausible explanation of depressions. This analysis is shown schematically in Figure 14–5, using the circular-flow diagram.

Price-rigidity: Prices do not adjust quickly, especially in a downward direction, because firms are not price takers (competition in most markets is imperfect). **Wage-rigidity:** In times of unemployment, wages do not adjust downward to clear the labor market because of labor unions and minimum wage laws. Hence, unemployment can persist.

Price-Wage Rigidities

What about the second line of defense? Would not real wages decline in a period of unemployment to a point that would clear the labor market? That, maintained Keynes, might have been true when commodity and factor markets were purely competitive, but it is not characteristic of vast segments of the economy today. Many manufacturing industries are dominated by a very few firms and large unions. Such corporations have at least partial control over the prices they charge. Known as price makers, they do not merely adjust to market prices; by their very action, they affect these prices. They possess varying degrees of market power. As a result of such industrial concentration, prices become rigid in a downward direction. The same applies to wage rates. Powerful unions, minimum-wage legislation, geographical labor immobility, immobility between industries (resulting in part from highly specialized skills), and other factors introduce rigidities into the labor markets. Wage rates are not flexible; they are rigid in a downward direction.

It will be recalled how the classical analysis treated the case of unsold output: The downward flexibility of money wage rates was relied upon to lower real wages to a point that clears the labor market. But with money wage rates rigid, such a reduction is not possible. Excess supply of labor,

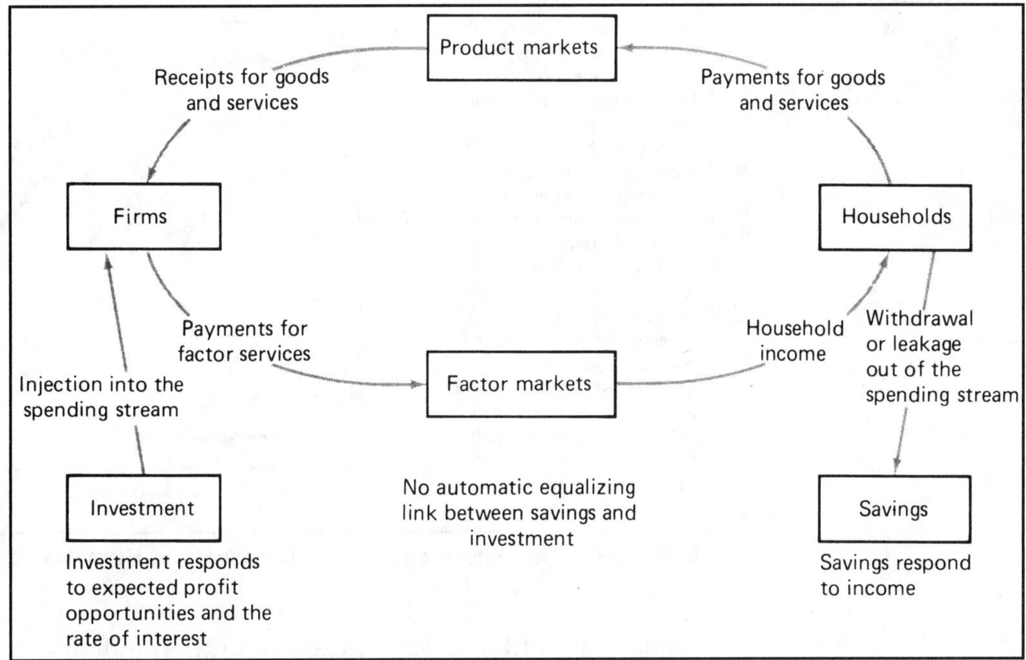

Figure 14–5 The Circular-Flow Diagram with Savings and Investment in the Keynesian Analysis: Keynes broke the link between savings and investment by making savings a function of income rather than the rate of interest. Because equality of *S* and *I* is no longer assured, savings may exceed investment, so that not all income is spent. Unsold goods would be the result.

or involuntary unemployment, can exist. And since there is no automatic mechanism that would restore full employment, unemployment can be protracted. Figure 14–6 highlights the difference between Keynes and the classical economists in terms of the region of the *AS* curve on which the economy is said to operate.

So much for the explanation of unemployment. Since desired investment can fall short of desired savings in the economy, aggregate demand can be inadequate to purchase the entire product at full employment. **Inadequate aggregate demand is the root cause of depressions.** Had prices and wages been flexible downward as well as upward, this would have presented no problem. But the rigidities in the factor (and product) markets prevent real wages from dropping to a point that would clear the market.

Result: Output can easily decline below the level that would generate full employment. The private economy is not stable at the full-employment level. Public policy is required to stabilize it.

The remedy proposed by Keynes was deliberate government spending (or a reduction in taxes) to pick up the slack in private spending. Like Adam Smith, *Keynes believed in the vitality of capitalism and the market system.* But in contrast to Smith, he arrived at the conclusion *that the government has an important role to play in market economy:* helping to maintain a high level of aggregate demand. In the United States, such government spending commenced in the 1930s under the "New Deal." But not until World War II did it reach sufficient magnitude to pull the

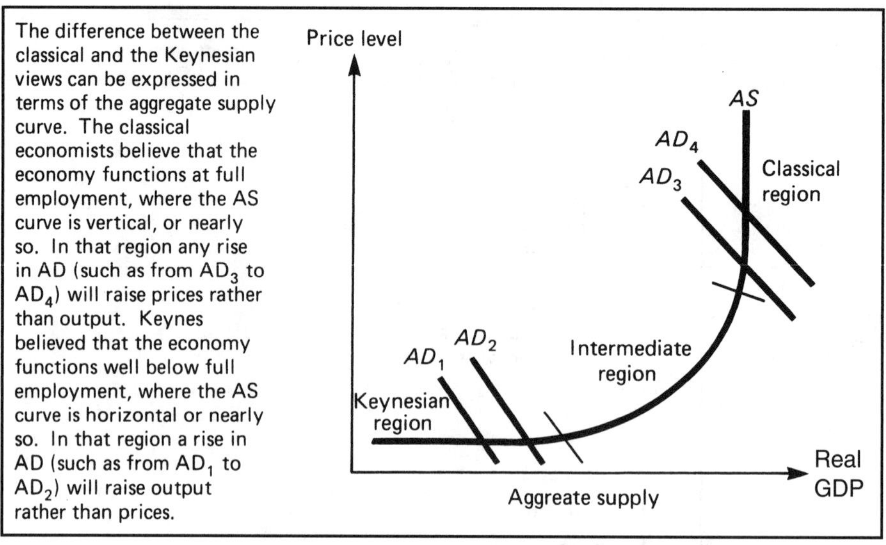

The difference between the classical and the Keynesian views can be expressed in terms of the aggregate supply curve. The classical economists believe that the economy functions at full employment, where the AS curve is vertical, or nearly so. In that region any rise in AD (such as from AD_3 to AD_4) will raise prices rather than output. Keynes believed that the economy functions well below full employment, where the AS curve is horizontal or nearly so. In that region a rise in AD (such as from AD_1 to AD_2) will raise output rather than prices.
Price level
AS
AD_4
AD_3
Classical region
AD_2
AD_1
Intermediate region
Keynesian region
Real GDP
Aggreate supply

Figure 14–6 The Difference Between Classical and Keynesian Macroeconomics

economy out of the deep depression. Indeed, military spending during the war became so vast as to *outpace the capacity of the economy to produce.* And that turned the entire problem on its head, for it caused inflation. At that point, Keynes applied the same analytical apparatus to the new problem and *suggested means to stimulate private savings so as to curtail demand and dampen the inflation.*

Keynes's analytical insights were later advanced and refined by many great economists. Abba Lerner, Alvin Hansen, Lawrence Klein, James Tobin, and Paul Samuelson were some of the great interpreters of Keynes. Their contributions made macroeconomics into a very elegant and refined body of analysis. Yet its policy implications are today the subject of a new and heated controversy between the "Keynesians" and the "monetarists," led by Prof. Milton Friedman formerly of the University of Chicago. We shall return to that controversy later in the book. But first we explore in detail the Keynesian analysis. For Keynes did more than just challenge the classical precepts. He offered an alternative analytical framework to explain the ups and downs in economic activity.

We have noted that a major contribution of Keynes was the unlinking of savings and investment, which in the classical analysis were both tied to the rate of interest. *What did he substitute for these relationships?* The answer to this question provides a convenient starting point, as it outlines the tools of the Keynesian analysis. It will occupy us in the next chapter. Subsequent chapters will employ these tools to explore the causes of unemployment and inflation.

SUMMARY

Classical macroeconomics rested on two fundamental assumptions: (1) Pure competition exists in all commodity and factor markets, yielding prices and wages that are flexible both upward and downward. All markets are cleared by price movements. This applies also to the labor market, which is cleared by variations in the real wage rates (money wage rates deflated by the cost of living). (2) Both savings and investment are functions of the rate of interest, so that savings and investment are always equalized by movements in the interest rate.

Under these conditions, aggregate demand will always be adequate to purchase the entire output, so that there is no possibility of unsold output and consequently no possibility of involuntary unemployment. The equality of savings and investment guarantees that the entire income generated in the production process will be spent in the form of either consumption or investment. Since income equals the value of output, this means that the entire output, whatever its level, will be sold. This is the first "line of defense" against involuntary unemployment. If by chance there appeared some unsold output, the second "line of defense" would come into play in the form of flexible prices and real wages. Prices would decline until the output was sold, and/or the real wage would decline until everybody who wished to be employed found employment. Involuntary unemployment cannot exist.

Keynes challenged both these postulates. Savings, he maintained, is governed by income and not by the rate of interest. Therefore, intended savings and investment are not equalized by variations in the interest rate. Savings can exceed investment, leading to a net withdrawal out of the income stream. Consequently, it is not true that the entire output, regardless of its level, will be sold, as implied by Say's Law, *Supply creates its own demand.* Unsold output, leading to involuntary unemployment, can result from insufficient aggregate demand. Nor will the "second line of defense" help, because of wage-price rigidity in a downward direction.

Not only did Keynes criticize the classical analysis; he offered an alternative analytical framework, which will be reviewed in the next three chapters.

QUESTIONS AND PROBLEMS

1. How did the classical economists describe the markets for:
   a. Onions?
   b. Automobiles?
   c. Labor?
   d. Savings and investment?
2. Why does the equality of (intended) savings and investment lead to Say's Law, that "supply creates its own demand"?
3. How did the classical analysis preclude the possibility of involuntary unemployment?
4. What was the nature of the Keynes challenge to classical macroeconomics? Why is involuntary unemployment possible under the Keynesian precepts?

The Keynesian Tools of Analysis

This chapter and the next present the Keynesian tools of analysis. They are the building blocks upon which the subsequent analysis rests.

SIMPLIFYING ASSUMPTION

Two important simplifications must first be introduced. The analysis begins by dealing strictly with a *private, noncorporate economy* in which there is *no government*—an assumption that will be eliminated later. In these circumstances, there are no taxes and no corporate savings (all saving is done by individuals), and therefore there is no difference between disposable income, personal income, and national income. They can all be lumped under the term *income* and labeled Y. Since consumption (C) and savings (S) add up to disposable income, they also add up to Y, so that $\boldsymbol{C + S = Y}$. Savings is the part of income that is not consumed. **By knowing consumption and income, we also know savings.** Likewise, knowledge of savings and income implies knowledge of consumption.

The second assumption is that all prices, including the rate of interest, are constant. This enables us to focus attention on real magnitudes without having to distinguish between money and real income or consumption. Any change in nominal (money) income represents an equal change in real income. This assumption implies that the economy operates in the horizontal range of the aggregate-supply curve (see Figure 14–6).

Note: While real NI is analytically "pure" in concept, real GDP is used to represent aggregate output, because NI cannot be measured accurately (CCA is not accurate).

THE CONSUMPTION FUNCTION

Introduction

Consumption function: the positive relationship between consumption and income: Consumption is a positive function of income.

To replace the relation between savings and the rate of interest, postulated by classical economics, Keynes introduced a causal relation between consumption and income and therefore between savings and income. Instead of depending on the rate of interest, savings (which equals $Y - C$) and consumption depend on income. The relation between consumption and income is called the **consumption function**, or the **consumption schedule**. It is a *positive relation*: **The higher the income, the higher the consumption.** Keynes viewed the consumption function as a **highly stable relationship**.

Indeed, the positive relation between C and Y has been verified time and time again in empirical investigations. During 1950–2005, U.S. consumption fluctuated between 89 and 96 percent of disposable income. This narrow range of fluctuations attests to the stability of the relation between the two variables. Figure 15–1 shows the long-run relation between consumption and disposable income. Nearly all the points, each representing one year, are in a straight line.

A Hypothetical Illustration

For analytical purposes, our interest lies in the dollar amounts that households **plan or intend** to consume out of possible levels of disposable income that might prevail at some point. Thus, the analytical consumption function postulates a **relation between intended consumption and expected income.** Just as the individual family would expect to spend more out of higher levels of income, so would all households in the economy combined. A positive relation between planned consumption and income for the economy as a whole is shown in Table 15–1, where hypothetical figures are employed. The first two columns show hypothetical income and consumption figures. For each possible level of income, there is a corresponding level of planned consumption expenditures. At income of $1,400 billion, planned consumption is $1,300 billion, and at income of $2,400 billion, planned consumption is $2,100 billion. Known as the consumption schedule, these figures illustrate a positive relation between consumption and income: **As income grows, so does consumption.**

Income and consumption are *changing magnitudes, or variables*. We say that the relationship between *these two variables is stable and positive.*

Geometrical Exposition

The relation between planned consumption and income can be displayed on a two-dimensional diagram by plotting income (Y) on the horizontal axis and consumption (C) on the vertical axis. This is done in Figure 15–2. To every level of income, shown on the horizontal axis, there corresponds a level of consumption, measured on the vertical axis, that can be read off

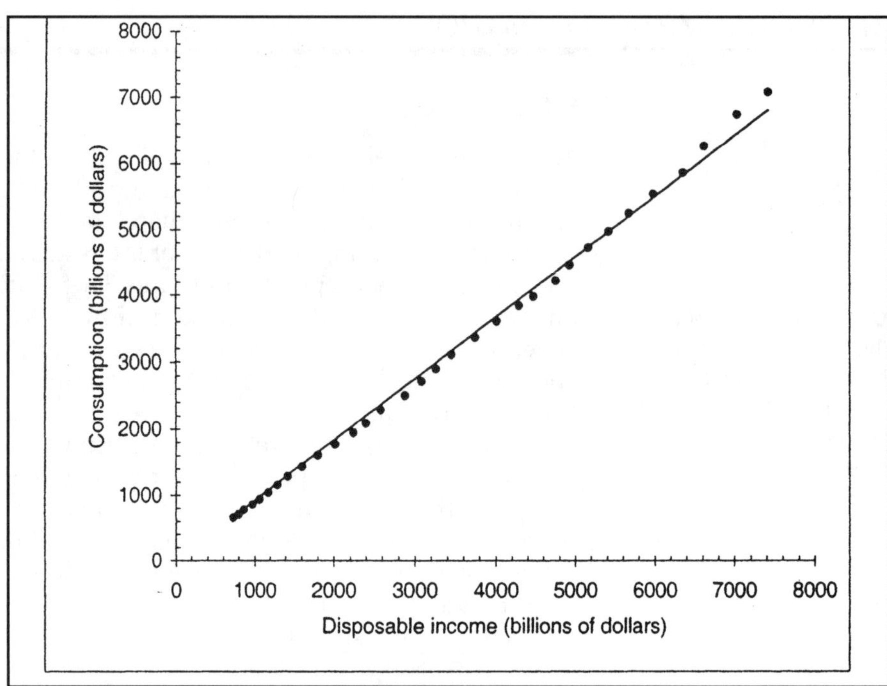

Figure 15–1 The Historical Relationship between Consumption and Disposable Income in the United States, 1970–2001: Each point along the "consumption" line shows disposable income (horizontal axis) and personal-consumption expenditures in the year indicated. Note the identical scales of the two axes.

Source: Economic Report of the President 2002, Table B-30 and *Survery of Current Business*, March 2002, Table B.2.

the consumption function. Thus, at income *0L*, consumption is *LB;* at income *0M*, consumption is *MC;* and at income *0Q*, consumption is *QE*. The same holds true for every other level of income. The reader should experiment by selecting alternative levels of income and reading off the corresponding levels of consumption. Clearly, the relation between the two is positive; the higher the income, the higher the consumption. For simplicity, the figures in Table 15–1 were selected so as to generate a straight-line consumption function. A curved function, concave to the horizontal axis, is also possible.

Average and Marginal Propensity to Consume

Average Propensity to Consume (APC): the proportion of aggregate income devoted to consumption, or C/Y.

Two concepts are defined in connection with the consumption schedule. The first is the **average propensity to consume (APC),** which is the part of income spent on consumption at each level of income. Computed as a ratio of consumption to income at each income level **(APC = C/Y),** it is

Table 15–1 A Hypothetical Consumption Schedule for the Economy ($ Billion)

	(1)	(2)	(3)	(4)	(5)	(6)
	Possible Levels of GDP (Y)	*Intended C*	*APC (= C/Y)*	ΔY	ΔC	*MPC* $= \Delta C/\Delta Y$
(A)	400	500	1.25			
				500	400	0.8
(B)	900	900	1.00			
				500	400	0.8
(C)	1,400	1,300	0.93			
				500	400	0.8
(D)	1,900	1,700	0.89			
				500	400	0.8
(E)	2,400	2,100	0.87			
				500	400	0.8
(F)	2,900	2,500	0.86			

shown in the third column of Table 15–1. Clearly, its size varies from one point on the consumption function to another. In the straight-line consumption function, portrayed in the table, the APC declines as income rises.

A little reflection will show you that this outcome is logical: As income rises, so does consumption; but the *proportion* of income spent on consumption declines and, correspondingly, the proportion saved rises. Families making $10,000 a year may consume their entire income and save nothing; those in the $25,000 bracket may consume $23,000 and save $2,000; and people earning $50,000 a year may spend $40,000 and save $10,000.

Marginal Propensity to Consume (MPC): The additional amount of income devoted to additional consumption. MPC=ΔC/ΔY. MPC equals the slope of the consumption function.

More important than the APC is the second concept to be defined, the **marginal propensity to consume (MPC). It is the proportion of change in income (in either direction) that is translated into a change in consumption**. Using the Greek letter delta, Δ, to denote change, **MPC =** $\Delta C/\Delta Y$. In Table 15–1, the change in income between any two rows (that is, between *C* and *B*, or *B* and *A*) is always 500 (1,900 – 1,400 = 1,400 – 900 = 900 – 400 = 500). It is shown in column 4. The corresponding change in consumption between any two rows is 400 (1,700 – 1,300 = 1,300 – 900 = 900 – 500 = 400), shown in column 5. The ratio between the two changes, $\Delta C/\Delta Y$, (column 5 divided by column 4) is the MPC. *It is 400/500 = 4/5, or 0.8, over the entire schedule.* Clearly, **the MPC is constant throughout a straight-line consumption schedule**. Herein lies a valuable property of a straight-line consumption function. Note that ΔY and ΔC are positioned *between* rows in Table 15–1.

To see how the MPC can be measured on a diagram, select points *C* and *D* in Figure 15–2, and drop perpendiculars to the horizontal axis at their respective income levels, 1,400 and 1,900. The horizontal distance between them represents the change in income, or ΔY (1,900–1,400). Next, connect point *C* with (imaginary) point *R* by drawing a horizontal line. *CR* also equals ΔY. Consumption at the two points is read off the

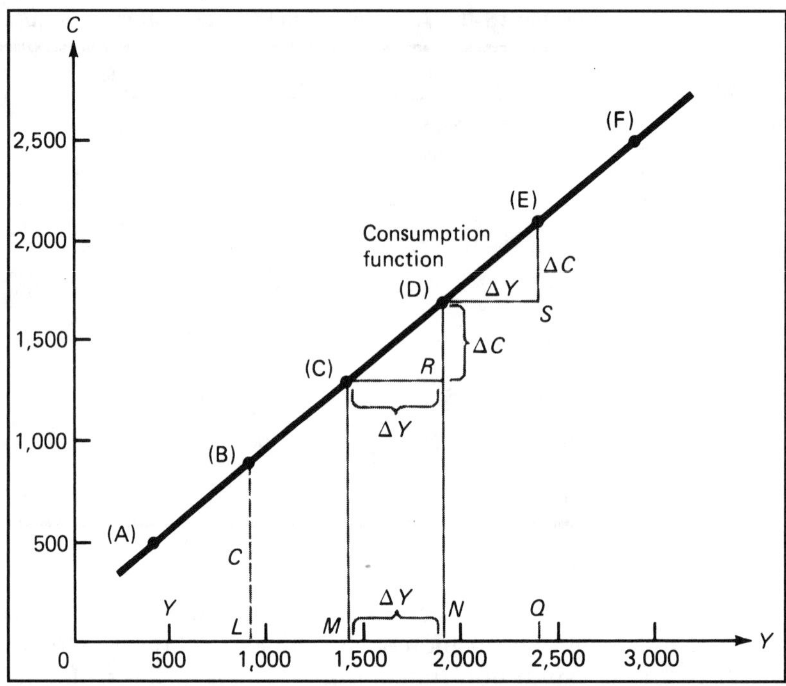

Figure 15–2 Hypothetical Linear Consumption Function (Figures based on Table 15–1): To each possible level of aggregate income (Y) corresponds a level of desired aggregate consumption. The relationship is positive: The higher the income, the higher the consumption. Consumption is a function of income. ***Note*** that the **scales** used on the two **axes** are identical.

vertical axis. It is 1,300 at point C and 1,700 at point D. The change in consumption, ΔC (400), is represented by the vertical distance DR in Figure 15–2. *The MPC, $\Delta C/\Delta Y$, equals the slope of the consumption function between points C and D.* The exercise is repeated between points D and E, where $\Delta C = ES$, and $\Delta Y = DS$, so that MPC $= \Delta C/\Delta Y = ES/DS =$ the slope of DE. The reader should repeat the exercise between points C and B and between B and A. Because the slope of a straight line is identical throughout, the MPC *is unchanged along a straight-line consumption function; it equals the slope of the function.*[1]

THE SAVINGS FUNCTION

Numerical Illustration

Savings, by definition, is the part of income not spent on consumption. Therefore, given the consumption schedule of Table 15–1 (first two columns), **the amount of savings at each level of income can be calculated**

[1]In a nonlinear consumption function (concave to the horizontal axis), the MPC declines as income rises.

Savings: Savings, the part of income not consumed, S = Y – C, is also a positive function of income.

by subtraction, *S* = *Y* – *C*. In Table 15–2, the first two columns are reproduced from the first two columns of Table 15–1. Column 3 is calculated by subtracting column 2 (*C*) from column 1 (*Y*) in each row. Columns 1 and 3 show the amount of planned savings out of each level of income; they constitute the **savings schedule**. It can be seen that at a very low level of income, consumption exceeds income, so that saving is negative. People spend their previously accumulated savings, or they borrow, in order to maintain a minimum standard of consumption. As income rises, savings increase, first to zero and subsequently to gradually increasing positive levels. The hypothetical figures in the table reflect reality and common sense: **As income rises, so does consumption, but by lesser amounts, so that savings are allowed to rise as well.** Between every two positions (rows) in the table, income rises by 500, consumption rises by 400, and savings increase by 100. It is logical that the higher the income, the easier it is to save (abstain from consumption), and therefore the greater the savings.

Geometric Representation of the Savings Function

In much the same way that the consumption function was plotted on an income-consumption space, the savings function—portrayed in columns 1 and 3 of Table 15–2—can be plotted on an income-savings space. This is done in Figure 15–3, where income is shown on the horizontal axis (drawn on an identical scale to that of the consumption function), and savings are shown on the vertical axis. The points *A, B, C, D, E,* and *F* correspond to the rows of Table 15–2. The relation between income and savings can now be read off the savings function: To each level of income, shown on the horizontal axis, there corresponds a unique level of intended savings, shown on the vertical axis. Thus, at income *0T*, savings are *TS*. The reader should experiment with other levels of income.

Clearly, **the relation between income and savings is positive:** The greater the income, the greater the savings. The savings function has a

Table 15–2 A Hypothetical Savings Function for the Economy ($ Billion)

	(1)	(2)	(3)	(4)	(5)	(6)	(7)
	Possible Levels of Y	***Intended C***	***Intended S (Y – C)***	***APS(S/Y)***	**ΔY**	**ΔC**	***MPS (ΔS/ΔY)***
(A)	400	500	–100	–0.25			
					500	100	0.2
(B)	900	900	0	0.00			
					500	100	0.2
(C)	1,400	1,300	100	0.07			
					500	100	0.2
(D)	1,900	1,700	200	0.11			
					500	100	0.2
(E)	2,400	2,100	300	0.13			
					500	100	0.2
(F)	2,900	2,500	400	0.14			

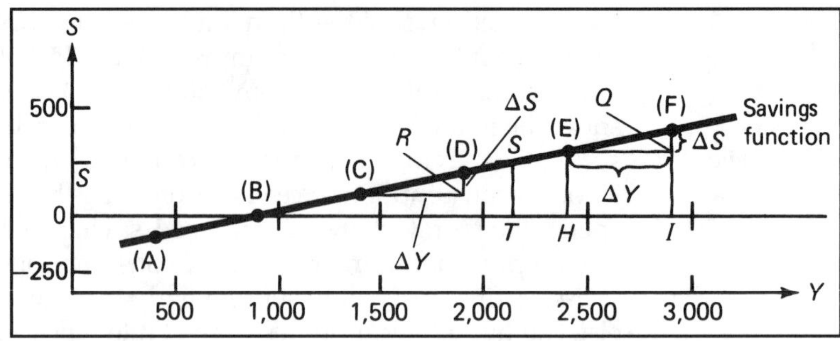

Figure 15–3 A Linear Savings Function: At very low levels of income, aggregate savings is negative. As income grows so does savings; the relation between them is positive. Savings is a function of income.

positive slope. As in the case of consumption (and because Table 15–2 is derived from Table 15–1), the hypothetical savings schedule displayed here is a straight line. This has the advantage of simplicity; only two points are necessary to construct the entire function.

Average Propensity to Save (APS): the proportion of income that is saved (S/Y). **Marginal Propensity to Save (MPS):** The addition to savings from an *increase in income* MPS = ΔS/ΔY. MPC + MPS = 1

Average and Marginal Propensity to Save

The two concepts defined in connection with the consumption function have corresponding counterparts relating to the savings function. The **average propensity to save (APS) is the proportion of income that is saved: APS =** ***S/Y.*** It is shown in column 4 of Table 15–2. In each row representing a given income level, it is obtained by dividing column 3 by column 1. **The APS rises with income: As income increases, the proportion of it that is saved rises.**

More important is the **marginal propensity to save MPS. It is the proportion of a change in income that is devoted to a change in savings (MPS = Δ*S*/Δ*Y*, where he Δ denotes change).** In Table 15–2, the changes in income and savings (in absolute amounts) between any two rows are shown in columns 5 and 6 respectively (positioned between rows). The MPS is computed in column 7 as a ratio of column 6 to column 5 at each level of income. It is *constant throughout the function,* at a value of 0.2 (= $^{100}/_{500}$).

Geometrically, the MPS is derived in Figure 15–3. If income rises from *0H* to *0I*—so that Δ*Y* = *HI* = *EQ*—then savings increase from *HE* to *IF,* so that Δ*S* = *IF* – *HE* = *QF.* The MPS = Δ*S* /Δ*Y* = *QF/QE* = the slope *of EF.* Similarly, the MPS between points C and D is Δ*S* /Δ*Y* = *RD/RC* = the slope of *CD.* Since the slope of a straight line is constant, **the MPS remains unchanged (invariant to the level of income), and it equals the slope of the savings function.**[2] It is important to note that the *concept MPS, like its MPC counterpart, applies equally to a reduction in income.* It shows the pro-

[2]Corresponding to a nonlinear consumption function, there is a nonlinear savings function. It is convex to the horizontal axis. The MPS is not constant along it; rather, it rises with income.

Table 15–3 Average and Marginal Propensities to Consume and to Save

	(1)	(2)	(3)	(4)	(5)	(6)
	APC	*APS*	$\sum$ *APC* *APS*	*MPC*	*MPS*	$\sum$ *MPC* *APS*
(A)	1.25	–0.25	1.00			
				0.8	0.2	1.00
(B)	1.00	0.00	1.00			
				0.8	0.2	1.00
(C)	0.93	0.07	1.00			
				0.8	0.2	1.00
(D)	0.89	0.11	1.00			
				0.8	0.2	1.00
(E)	0.87	0.13	1.00			
				0.8	0.2	1.00
(F)	0.86	0.14	1.00			

portion of a decrease in income that is translated into a decrease in savings, and it is calculated in the same fashion.

PROPENSITIES TO CONSUME AND TO SAVE

Table 15–3 "collects" four columns from Tables 15–1 and 15–2: the APC and APS, and the MPC and MPS. The third and sixth columns sum up, respectively, APC + APS and MPC and MPS. The Greek letter Σ (sigma) represents summation. Because $Y = C + S$, by definition the proportion of income not consumed is saved. Consequently, the sum of the APC and APS is 1: **APC + APS = 1**, as shown in the third column. Likewise, any increase (decrease) in income must be added to (subtracted from) either consumption or savings. Consequently, the sum of the MPC and MPS is 1: **MPC + MPS = 1**.

MOVEMENT ALONG FUNCTIONS VS. SHIFTS IN THEM

It is important to distinguish between movements along the function and a shift in the entire function. A movement up the consumption function means that because income rises, so does consumption. Similarly for the savings function. But suppose consumption changes for reasons other than a change in income. For example, in the immediate postwar period, consumption zoomed upward because of pent-up demand from the war period (when consumer goods were not available), and because consumers had accumulated large amounts of liquid assets, such as U.S. government bonds, which could be cashed in to finance long-awaited purchases. In circumstances such as this, *at every income level, consumption is higher than before.* **The entire consumption function shifts upward, and correspondingly, the savings function shifts downward.** The two functions necessarily move in opposite directions.

There are several factors that may cause an upward shift in the entire consumption function and a corresponding decrease in the savings function. A large accumulation of liquid assets in the hands of consumers and/or the existence of pent-up demand were already mentioned. High inflationary expectations may induce people to lower their rate of savings—to save less out of each given level of income—because inflation erodes the real value of savings. Such a change occurred in the 1970s, and it has its counterpart in an upward move of the consumption function.

Other possible reasons include reduced desire for thrift on the part of consumers, inducing them to save less out of any given level of income; a low level of consumer debt in the economy, making it easy to borrow to finance purchases; and a low stock of automobiles and consumer durables in the hands of consumers relative to the long-run trend, making consumers eager to replenish their stocks of such goods.

Despite these factors, **the consumption and savings functions are reasonably stable.** Most changes in consumption and savings occur because of movement along their respective functions rather than shifts in the entire functions. The last section of this chapter contains a geometric presentation of the relation between the consumption and savings functions, corresponding to the relation shown numerically in Tables 15–1 and 15–2.

THE INVESTMENT FUNCTION

If income replaces the rate of interest as the main determinant of savings, what determines net investment (I_n)? Net investment, it will be remembered, includes construction, plant and equipment, and change in inventories. Although residential construction directly serves the final consumer, the products of plant and equipment, reach the final consumer only after the investment project is completed and put into production.

Keynes maintained that a host of factors determine net investment. They include, first, expected sales and profit opportunities in future years, when plants designed today would come into production. Firms determine the need for such plants by their forecasts of the future market for the final product and the profit it might yield. Such estimates are derived from forecasts of future trends in the economy at large and are subject to considerable error. Also, they tend to vary greatly from one year to the next, as profits fluctuate considerably from year to year. A second factor is inventions of new products and production processes. These need to be put to use, and their exploitation often requires new production facilities. The invention of the personal computer is a case in point, as is the introduction of robots in automobile production. Both cases required new plants and machinery. Again, such innovations are difficult to predict and are highly variable from year to year. Also determining net investment are discoveries of new areas bearing raw materials, such as new oil fields, which require exploitation. For example, massive investments in drilling rigs, pipes, and other machinery were needed to exploit the oil and natural-gas discoveries in Alaska and the North Sea. These discoveries also vary greatly over time. Fourth is a possible rise in the rate of population growth, foreshadowing an increase in consumer demand. In turn, that increase must be satisfied out of new production facilities.

Then there are government policies that allow tax credit to investors, exempting part of reinvested profit from the corporate profit tax. These raise after-tax profitability and therefore encourage investment. When the government changes the tax law, a change in the level of investment is likely to ensue. And finally, the rate of interest determines the cost of borrowing capital for investment purposes and the cost of mortgage funds to finance residential construction. Although part of total investment is financed *internally*, out of business reserve funds, much of it must be financed *externally*, by business borrowing on financial markets. *A rise in the rate of interest increases the cost of such loans and discourages investment. A decline in interest rates lowers the cost of borrowing and encourages investment.* Keynes accepted the classical determinant of investment (the rate of interest), but only as one of several important factors.

Because the fruits of investment are borne only in future years, *expectations and uncertainty* play a role in determining its amount. This factor, plus the great variability of profit and the fact that inventions and discoveries tend to come in waves and are certainly subject to fits and starts, make **aggregate investment fluctuate considerably from one year to the next. Investment is viewed as a dynamic force that drives the economy.**

Conspicuously *absent* from the determinants of net investment outlined above is *current income.* Expected *future* income influences investment through its effect on expected sales and profit opportunities; but the effect of current income is considered small. As a first approximation, current income is assumed not to affect current investment. This is represented in Table 15–4, which shows a hypothetical investment schedule, postulating a relation between current income and investment: Regardless of the level of income, investment is $200 billion. Figure 15–4 offers a diagrammatic representation of the investment function. Since the simplified analysis assumes interest and prices unchanged, the relation between net investment and current income—the **investment function—is expressed as a straight horizontal line.**

Investment function: Relationship between net investment and Income. Investment does not depend on current income; hence the function is horizontal. But the reverse is not true: income or output depends profoundly on investment.

Table 15–4 Investment Schedule ($ Billion)

	Income (Y)	Net Investments (I_n)
(A)	400	200
(B)	1,400	200
(C)	2,400	200
(D)	2900	200

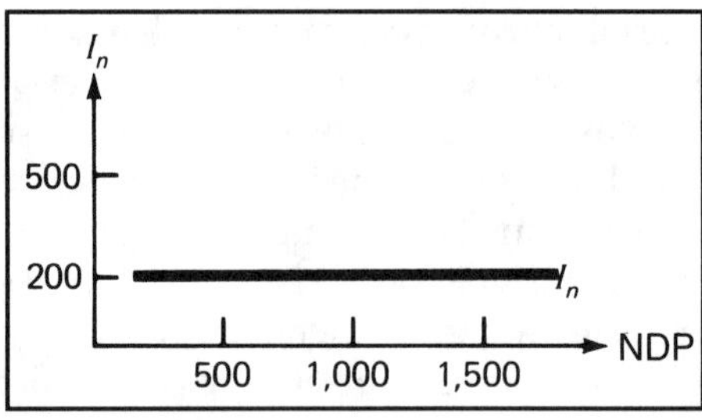

Figure 15–4 The Investment Function: Investment is a function of expected profit opportunities and other events. As a first approximation it does *not* depend on *current* income. This is depicted as a horizontal I schedule: Regardless of income, the level of investment is the same ($200 billion). Note however that investment does affect income.

It should be absolutely clear what such a horizontal line means: *Current income does not affect net investment, but the reverse is not true.* Investment does affect current income. In fact, because the factors that determine investment (outlined previously) are volatile, **the investment function**, in its entirety, **is subject to considerable fluctuations in both directions. The horizontal line shifts upward or downward as the factors that determine the level of investment change.** Such shifts are thought to occur much more frequently, and to be of far greater magnitude, than similar shifts in the consumption function. In the ensuing analysis, *the consumption* and *savings functions are assumed constant* while the *investment function fluctuates* in the manner just described.

Since *saving* and *investment* are done by two different groups of people, and because they are motivated by totally different sets of influences, *there is clearly no presumption that they will be equal.* Intended savings is determined by income, and the relation between the two variables is stable. Intended investment is determined by a wide array of forces and subject to wide gyrations. Savings and investment cannot be presented as two intersecting functions of one variable, such as the rate of interest in the classical analysis, for they are governed by two totally different sets of forces. There is no mechanism that would guarantee their equality at any level of output. *Say's Law does not hold.* In the next chapter, the investment and consumption (savings) functions will be integrated into one analytical framework.

The Consumption and Savings Functions Geometrically Related

Savings is defined as the part of income not spent on consumption. From the consumption schedule of Table 15–1 we derived the savings schedule of Table 15–2: At each level of income, the difference between consumption and income represents savings. The two schedules are not independent of each other; rather, given one of them, the other is uniquely determined. *Can the savings function be derived from the consumption function* (and vice versa) *diagrammatically?* Yes, with the aid of an imaginary **45° line** that bisects the right (90°) angle in the income-consumption space. Such a line is shown in Figure 15–5. Its important geometrical property is that every point on it (such as point *E*) is equidistant from the horizontal and vertical axes: *GE* (= *0F*) = *EF*, and *0M* = *MN*. In terms of the income-consumption space, this means that if income is *0F*, it is also *FE*; or if income is *0M*, it is also *MN*. The same property holds for every point on the 45° line. It enables us to represent income *vertically* by transposing its horizontal measure along the *Y* axis to a vertical distance up to the 45° line.

Figure 15–6 demonstrates the geometric derivation of the savings function from the consumption function. The upper panel shows the consumption function of Figure 15–2, but with the 45° line superimposed upon it. The lower panel shows the income-savings space. Income (*Y*) is drawn on the horizontal axis, with a *scale identical to that of the upper panel.* In other words, the income (horizontal) axes of the two panels are identical in all respects. The vertical axis of the upper panel measures consumption; that of the lower panel savings. However, their scales are identical, and are also equal to the income scale. Our task is to derive the savings function (relation between planned saving and income) from the consumption function (relation between planned consumption and income).

Observe income level *0N* (1,900) on the upper panel. Because of the property of the 45° line, it equals the vertical *NR*. Therefore, *NR* is income (*Y*). At income *NR* (= *0N*), consumption is *ND*; it is read off the consumption function. Since, by definition, savings is the part of income not consumed, $S = Y - C$; geometrically, $S = NR - ND = DR$. At income *0N*, savings is *DR*. This is now shown explicitly on the lower panel, by transposing the vertical segment *DR* to *ND* at the income level *0N*. We obtain one point on the savings schedule. Next, at income *0M* (1,400) on the upper panel, income is also *MQ* (= *0M*) by the property of the 45° line. Consumption at

Figure 15–5 The 45° Line: A line bisecting the right angle (90°) of the origin has a unique property: Perpendiculars dropped to the two axes from any point on the line are of equal length. For example *FE* = *GE*.

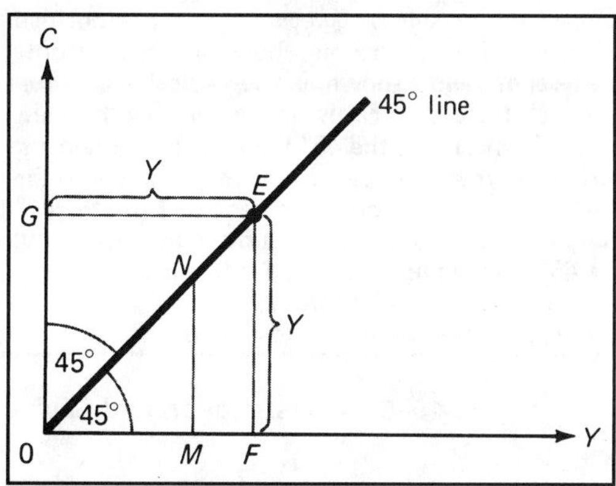

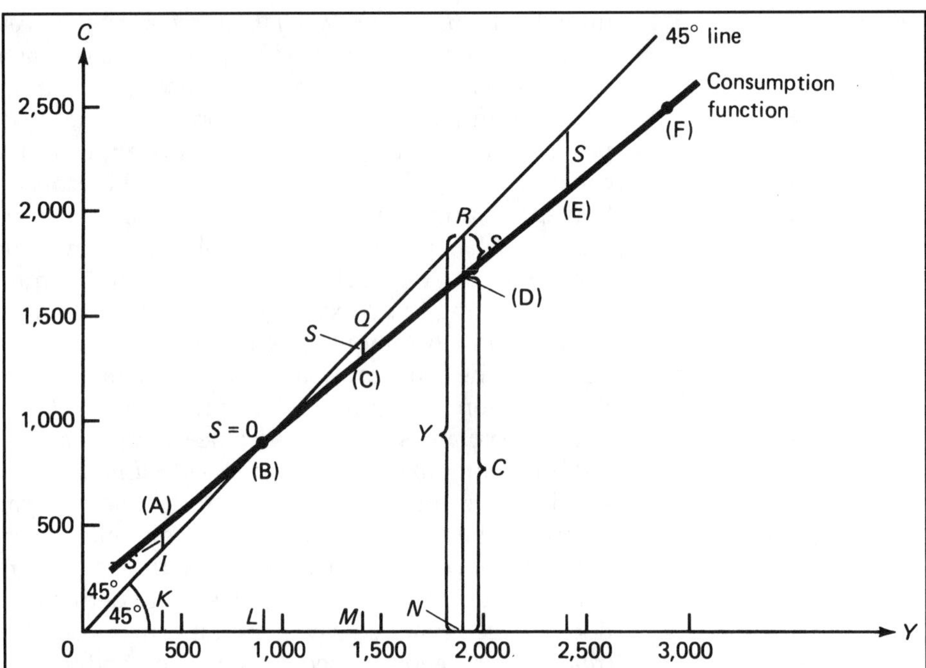

The consumption function shows aggregate consumption as a positive function of aggregate income. To alternative levels of income, shown on the horizontal axis, correspond various levels of consumption, shown on the vertical axis.
For example, hypothetical income $0N$ generates consumption $0D$. A 45° line is also drawn. Because of its unique property, vertical distances from it to the horizontal axis also measure income. Since $S = Y - C$, the vertical distance from any point on the 45° line to the C function (such as RD) measures savings. $S = 0$ where the consumption function intersects the 45° line. The entire savings schedule can be generated by using the vertical distance between the C function and the 45° line.

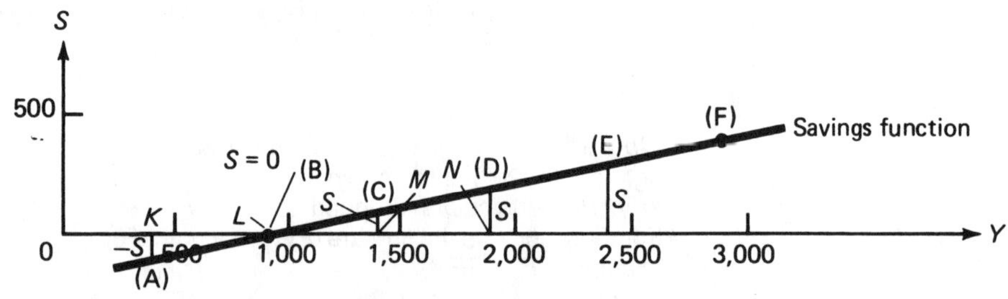

The savings function shows aggregate savings as a positive function of aggregate income. To each level of income, shown on the horizontal axis, corresponds a unique level of saving, shown on the vertical axis. Note that the income scales of the two panels (placed precisely one under the other) are identical.
From the C function and the 45° line, one can obtain a savings function (as described on the upper panel) and map it down to the lower panel. Conversely, given the savings function on the lower panel and the 45° line on the upper panel, the C function can be obtained by subtracting (vertically) various levels of savings from the 45° line. *On both panels, $S = 0$ at income level L.* The correspondence between the two panels is important.
Note that all *four axes* are drawn to an *identical scale.*

Figure 15–6 Consumption and Savings Functions

the level of income is *MC*, read off the consumption function. Savings, being $Y - C$, is then *CQ*. It is transposed to the lower panel as *MC* (= *CQ*) at income level *0M*.

At income level *0L*, *the consumption function crosses or intersects the 45° line:* Income is *LB* (= *0L*) by the property of the 45° line, and consumption is *LB*, as read off the consumption function. Since income equals consumption ($Y = C$), savings is zero ($S = 0$). *At the income level where the consumption function intersects the 45° line,* $C = Y$ *and* $S = 0$. Thus, at the corresponding income level (*0L*) on the lower panel, savings is shown to be zero; *the savings function crosses the horizontal (Y) axis.* The last two phrases in italics can be read as one full sentence. It represents an important link between the two panels, and it must be observed in constructing one from the other.

Finally, at income level *0K* (= *KI* by the property of the 45° line), consumption is *KA*, read off the assumption function. Consumption exceeds income by *AI*, showing negative savings of that magnitude. It is transposed to the lower panel as *KA*, a negative segment, at income level *0K*.

Connecting all the points so derived on the lower panel yields the savings function. It shows the amount of planned savings out of alternative levels of income. The relation is positive: The higher the income, the greater the amount saved. **This is the Keynesian substitute for the classical savings function. Instead of being a positive function of the rate of interest, savings is made a positive function of income.**

To summarize, the geometric derivation employs a pair of panels, showing the consumption function on the upper panel and the corresponding savings function on the lower panel. All four axes are measured to the same scale. The horizontal (*Y*) axes of the two panels are identical. From the upper panel showing the consumption function, we can also read savings: At any level of income, savings is the vertical distance between the corresponding points on the consumption function and the 45° line. These vertical distances are transposed to the lower panel, to form the savings function. Significantly, $S = 0$ when the consumption function intersects the 45° line. *The process can easily be reversed.* Given the savings function on the lower panel and the (imaginary) 45° line on the upper panel, the consumption function can be derived: At any level of income, consumption is obtained by subtracting vertically the segment measuring savings from the corresponding point on the 45° line. Straight-line functions have the advantage of simplicity: Only two points are needed to derive the entire function, and the marginal propensities are constant through the functions.

These geometric derivations are important because they will be built upon later in the analysis. Students are urged to construct a few of them themselves. They should note that *the 45° line appears only on the upper (consumption) panel, and not on the lower one*. Also, care should be taken to employ the *same scale* on all four axes. Because of its analytical convenience, this pair of panels goes together like a pair of gloves.

Finally, an upward (downward) shift in the entire consumption function is accompanied by a corresponding downward (upward) shift in the entire savings function. This is illustrated schematically in Figure 15–7.

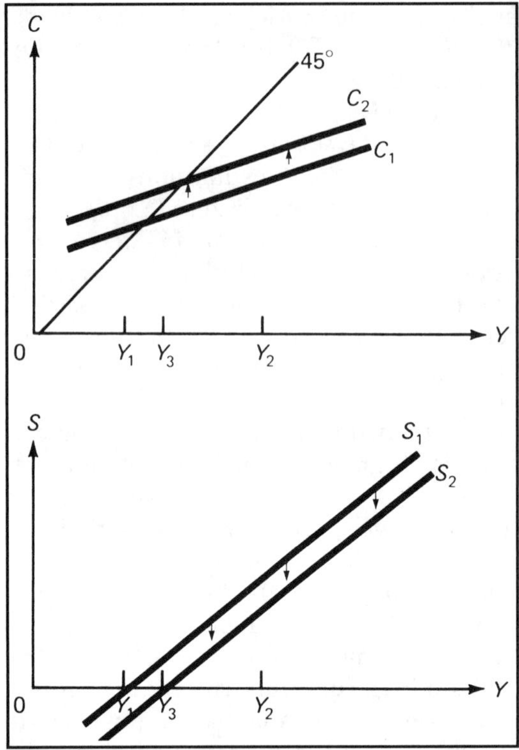

Figure 15–7 Upward Shift in the Consumption Function and Corresponding Downward Shift in the Savings Function: The point of zero savings always occurs where the C function crosses the 45° line.

SUMMARY

For a simplified economy, in which there is no government and no corporate sectors and where prices are assumed constant, the Keynesian analysis identifies two important relationships: (1) the consumption function and its related savings functions, and (2) the investment function.

Income is the main determinant of consumption and of saving. Consumption is positively related to income; it rises with income, but not in the same magnitude. The average propensity to consume (APC) is defined as the portion of income that is consumed (C/Y), and the marginal propensity to consume (MPC) is the portion of an increment (decrement) in income that is translated into an increase (reduction) in consumption ($\Delta C/\Delta Y$). The MPC is constant along a linear consumption function; it is equal to the slope of the function. Savings, the part of income not consumed, is also positively related to income. The average propensity to save (APS) is the portion of income that is saved (S/Y), and the marginal propensity to save (MPS) is the portion of an increment (decrement) of income that is translated into an increase (decrease) in savings ($\Delta S/\Delta Y$). The MPS is constant along a linear savings function; it is equal to the slope of the functions.

Because $Y = C + S$, it follows that (1) APC + APS = 1, and (2) MPC + MPS = 1.

Diagrammatic expression can be given to the consumption and savings functions, by showing them, respectively, on a consumption-income and on a savings-income space. Because the two are interrelated, it is possible to display them on a pair of panels and derive one from the other, as is done in the last section of the chapter. In the case of a linear function, the MPC and MPS equal the slopes of the consumption and savings functions respectively; they are constant throughout the function.

Factors other than income can affect consumption and therefore savings. They include among others a change in liquid-asset holdings, pent-up demand, and a change in attitudes toward thrift. In the 1990's the rise in stock prices is said to have shifted the consumption function upward as it increased people's wealth. They find diagrammatic expression by a shift of the entire consumption function up or down, and correspondingly a shift of the savings function down or up. At every level of income, more or less is consumed (less or more is saved). Despite their occasional variation, the two functions are generally stable.

This relation between savings and income is the substitute for the classical relation between savings and the rate of interest.

There are many determinants of investment. They include expected profit opportunities, inventions of products and production processes, population growth, discoveries, government tax policies, and the rate of interest. Interest rate, viewed by the classicals as the main determinant of investment, is only one of several. Investment is not dependent on current income to any major extent. Consequently, in a simplified economy, the investment function is shown as a straight horizontal line in the investment-income space. Current income does not affect investment, but the reverse is not true. Because the factors that determine investment are highly volatile, large shifts in the entire investment function in both directions occur frequently. The investment function (which replaces the classical function in the investment–interest-rate space) is much less stable than the consumption (or savings) function. There is no mechanism that equalizes savings and investment *at any level of output*, and therefore full employment is not assured, as in the classical analysis. Indeed, fluctuations in investment will be shown to affect output, employment, and income.

QUESTIONS AND PROBLEMS

1. With what constructs did the Keynesian analysis replace the classical savings and investment functions?

2. Define the following concepts:

☐ Average and marginal propensity to consume

☐ Average and marginal propensity to save

What do the two marginal propensities add up to? Why? What are the MPC and MPS equal to in the case of a linear consumption function?

3. What determines savings in the Keynesian analysis? What are the main determinants of investment in the Keynesian analysis? How does the investment function look?
4. Following are hypothetical income and consumption figures for a simplified U.S. economy, in which there is no government.

Possible Levels of GDP or Y	Intended Consumption
2,850	2,400
2,350	2,000
1,850	1,600
1,350	1,200
850	800
350	400

   a. Calculate the savings schedule.

   b. Compute the APC and APS. Add them up at each level of income. What do they add up to?

   c. Compute the MPC and MPS at each level of income. Must they add up to a specific number? Why, or why not? Are they constant throughout? Must they be?

   d. Draw separately the consumption and savings functions.

5. Sketch an investment schedule. Explain verbally the meaning of such a schedule.
6. Must intended savings and investment be equal at all levels of output (income) in the Keynesian analysis? Why, or why not?
7. Use the figures in question 4 above to draw the consumption function. Insert a 45° line. From it, derive diagrammatically and draw the savings function (on the lower panel).
8. Sketch a linear savings function. From it derive diagrammatically the corresponding consumption function on the upper panel with the help of a 45° line. Make sure that $S = 0$ and that the consumption function crosses the 45° line at the same level of income.
9. Suppose there were an increase in thriftiness in the community. Sketch the effect of the event on the pair of panels that you drew in question 2. Explain verbally the graphical expression given to that event.
10. Suppose stocks rose sharply as they did in the 1990's. What does that imply for people's wealth? What do you suppose happened to the consumption and savings functions?

Income Determination

FUNDAMENTAL PROPOSITION

With the help of the tools developed in Chapter 15, it is now possible to address this question: Given the consumption and investment schedules, what is the level of income or output (GDP) at which the economy would settle, or toward which the economy would gravitate? This level is known as the *equilibrium* level of income or output—a level that, once achieved, would be maintained. And because the level of employment is positively and uniquely related to output, the answer to this question also determines the level of employment or unemployment. This chapter is devoted to clarifying and demonstrating the following important proposition: **The equilibrium level of output (GDP) is one in which aggregate expenditures[1] for goods and services by consumers and investors ($C + I_n$) equals aggregate supply (GDP); this is equivalent to saying that it is the level at which planned savings equals planned investment.**

To demonstrate the meaning of this proposition, we employ the consumption, savings, and investment schedules of the preceding chapter They are reproduced in Table 16–1. Column 2 shows alternative volumes of real output that firms are willing to produce and supply, provided that they can be sold (aggregate supply, or GDP). Associated with each level of output is an equal amount of income received by households, also shown in column 2. Column 1 indicates the hypothetical number of workers (employment) needed to produce each level of output. Columns 3 and 5 show, respectively, the amount of goods and services (output or GDP) consumers and investors would be willing to purchase at each level of income. Whereas consumer demand (C) varies positively with

[1]Aggregate demand is the term used in the price-level-output space, as in Chapters 13 and 21. Aggregate expenditures are used in the C + I-output space, as seen in Chapters 16–18.

income, investment demand (I_n) is invariant with respect to income and is assumed to be $200 billion at all levels of GDP. Column 4, savings, is obtained by subtracting consumption (C) from income (Y) at each level of income (= output). Adding up consumer and investment spending yields aggregate expenditures ($C + I_n$) at each level of income, displayed in column 6.

EQUILIBRIUM INCOME

In this section, we employ a variant of the circular-flow diagram to analyze each row of Table 16–1. The top flow in each diagram represents the income stream from firms to households, which equals the output of firms. Both income and output are presented by that arrow. The bottom flow indicates how much of the income received by households is spent on consumption. The remainder is withdrawn out of the income stream into savings. On the other hand, firms are shown to inject funds into the income stream in the form of investment. There is no automatic mechanism that equates intended savings and investment at any level of output or income.

Row F

Employing 140 million workers, firms produce $2,900 billion of goods and services over the year (column 1), and generate an equal amount of income for households. Out of that income, households spend $2,500 billion on the purchase of consumption goods from firms, and save (leak out of the income stream) $400 billion, according to the consumption and savings functions. In turn, firms invest (inject into the income stream) $200 billion during the same year. Since, in our simple economy, we assume no government and no interfirm transactions, this information can be sketched in the form of a circular-flow diagram. The top flow in Figure 16–1 shows income of households, equaling total output or aggregate sup-

Table 16–1 Hypothetical GDP, Consumption, and Investment ($ Billion per Year)

	Employment (Millions of Workers)	Aggregate Supply GDP (= Y)	Intended C	Intended S	Intended I_n	Aggregate Expenditures $C + I_n$	Change in Output	Relation Between Planned S & I_n
	(1)	(2)	(3)	(4)	(5)	(6) (cols. 3 + 5)	(7)	(8)
(A)	40	400	500	–100	200	700	Increase	$I_n > S$ by 300
(B)	60	900	900	0	200	1,100	Increase	$I_n > S$ by 200
(C)	80	1,400	1,300	100	200	1,500	Increase	$I_n > S$ by 100
(D)	100	1,900	1,700	200	200	1,900	Equilibrium	$I_n = S$
(E)	120	2,400	2,100	300	200	2,300	Decrease	$I_n < S$ by 100
(F)	140	2,900	2,500	400	200	2,700	Decrease	$I_n < S$ by 200

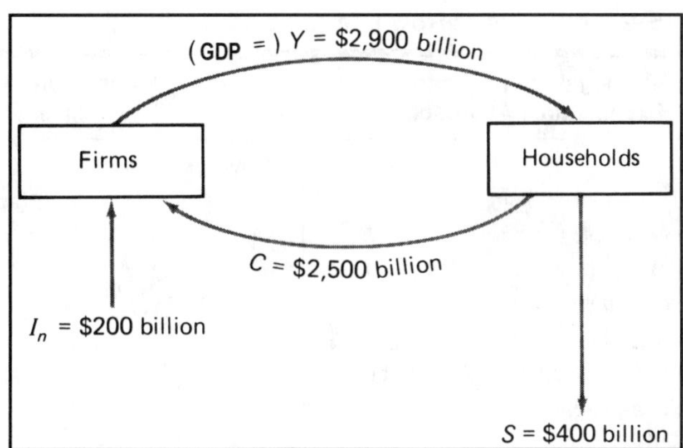

Figure 16–1 Circular-Flow Diagram Describing Row F of Table 16–1: This variant of the circular-flow diagram shows the income flow from firms to households (in return for production services rendered) on the top, and the consumption expenditures flow (in return for purchases of goods and services) from households to firms on the bottom. Savings by households are shown as a withdrawal or leakage from the income stream; investment by firms constitutes an injection into the income stream.

ply of $2,900 billion. The bottom flow shows how much of that income is returned to firms in the form of purchases of goods and services by households (C = $2,500 billion); the difference ($400 billion) is leaked out of the income stream in the form of household savings. In turn, an injection of $200 billion into the income stream is made by firms in the form of net investment. In total, firms produce $2,900 billion worth of goods and services; that is their aggregate supply. They sell only $2,700 billion—$2,500 billion to consumers and $200 billion to investors—and that represents intended aggregate expenditures at that level of income or output (column 6). **Aggregate supply exceeds aggregate expenditures** by $200 billion, and **this difference represents unsold output.** This is shown on the left-hand side of Table 16–2.

Such a situation is not sustainable. Firms would not go on producing output that could not be sold. Rather, they would be induced to curtail output, lay off workers, and consequently reduce employment. This outcome is indicated in column 7 of Table 16–1 (row F).

How is this relation between aggregate supply and expenditures reflected in the relation between savings and investment? *Savers and investors are two different groups of people, and they make their plans independently of each other.* At the beginning of the year, households plan to save $400 billion during the coming year out of expected income of $2,900 billion, and firms plan to invest $200 billion. **Planned savings exceed planned investment by $200 billion—precisely the amount by which aggregate supply exceeds aggregate expenditures, or the amount of unsold output.** This unsold output is **added to inventories.** For example, car and appliance dealers may be stuck with unsold autos and appliances because of inadequate demand. It will be recalled from Chapter 12 that

Table 16–2 Analysis of Row F in Table 16–1

Aggregate Supply and Expenditures Approach		Planned and Realized Savings and Investment Approach		
		Savings		Investment
			Planned	
Aggregate supply (GDP)	$2,900 billion			
Aggregate expenditures		$400	>	$200 billion
C = $2,500 billion				
I_n = $ 200 billion	$2,700 billion		Realized	
Excess of aggregate supply over expenditures	$ 200 billion		Planned investments	$200 billion
			Unplanned (Δ in inventories)	+ $200 billion
		$400 =	Total investments =	$400 billion

changes in inventories are part and parcel of investment (one of its three components, although the smallest one). Thus, planned investment plus unplanned investment (changes in inventories; in this case, undesired) adds up to savings of $400 billion.

This discussion underscores an **important distinction between planned and realized savings and investment.**[2] At the *beginning* of the period under discussion (in this case, a year), looking forward, savers and investors make their plans for the upcoming year. Because they are two different groups, *the plans need not match*; they are in fact unlikely to be of equal magnitudes. As shown in column 8 of Table 16–1, in row F, planned savings exceeds planned investment ($S > I_n$). During the period, the difference between the two figures results in a change in inventories—in this case, a buildup of unsold output (for example, in car dealers' showrooms). But a change in inventories is counted as investment. Consequently, at the *end* of the period, looking backwards, *realized* savings and investment are necessarily equal. This is shown on the right-hand side of Table 16–2 with respect to the figures of row F.

Inventories: Stocks of merchandise in retailer's warehouses, car dealerships, etc.

What is it that brings the unequal savings and investment plans into equality in a "realized" sense? It is *the change in* **inventories**—the unplanned, unintended, or undesired accumulation of stocks in dealers' showrooms or warehouses. That leads dealers to cut down their orders from the factories, so the factories curtail output and lay off workers. Here lies the analytical importance of the changes in inventories alluded to in Chapter 12. This item may be considered a **"valve," a regulatory mechanism in the savings-investment process.** Because *changes in inventories* constitute a guide to future orders from factories by dealers and stores, they *are watched carefully by financial observers* who wish to plot the future course of the economy.

It can be seen that the results obtained from the aggregate supply and expenditures analysis and those derived from the savings-investment analysis (both in Table 16–2) are identical. When aggregate supply exceeds

[2]Other terms used for the word *planned* are *intended* and *desired.*

aggregate expenditures planned savings exceeds planned investment and by the same amount. The outcome is clear: Output of $2,900 billion is not sustainable because it cannot be sold. It is not equilibrium output or income. Rather, it would *decline*—say, to $2,400 billion, shown in row E. The level of employment declines to 120 million workers.

The student is invited to draw a circular-flow diagram representing row E of Table 16–1, and then construct a table similar to Table 16–2 analyzing the figures in terms of the aggregate supply and expenditure approach as well as the planned savings and investment approach. The approaches show excess of aggregate supply over aggregate expenditures and excess of planned savings over planned investment of $100 billion. This unsold output results in an accumulation of inventories of $100 billion. It is the unintended accumulation of inventories that brings about equality between realized savings and investment. But such an accumulation affects the behavior of businesspersons, such as dealers. They curtail orders from the factories, which reduce output and lay off workers (column 7). GDP of 2,400 is not sustainable. It is not equilibrium output. Rather, GDP declines—say, to $1,900 billion—and employment declines to 100 million workers, as shown in row D of Table 16–1.

Row B

We now approach the analysis from the other end, starting with row B. Employing 60 million workers, firms produce $900 billion of goods and services during the year. Aggregate supply, or GDP, is $900 billion (column 2); that is also the income received by households. In turn, households spend $900 billion per year on goods and services (*C*) and save nothing. Firms invest $200 billion, for a total aggregate expenditures of (*C* of $900 + I_n of $200) $1,100 billion, shown in column 6. These flows are displayed in the circular-flow diagram of Figure 16–2. Aggregate supply falls short of aggregate expenditures by $200 billion, leading firms to expand output to meet the extra demand (column 7) and hire additional workers. Output and employment rise.

But precisely how is this excess aggregate expenditure satisfied until factory output is increased? The answer can be seen in the savings-investment approach. At the beginning of the year, looking ahead, households

Figure 16–2 Circular-Flow Diagram Depicting Row B of Table 16–1

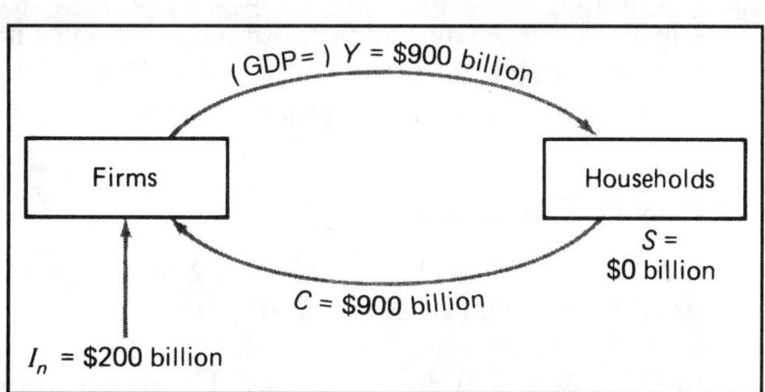

Table 16–3 Analysis of Row E In Table 16–1

Aggregate Supply and Expenditures Approach		Planned and Realized Savings and Investment Approach		
Aggregate supply		Savings		Investment
(GDP)	$ 900 billion		Planned	
Aggregate expenditures				
C = $900 billion		0	<	$200 billion
I_n = $200 billion	$1,100 billion			
			Realized	
			Planned investments	$200 billion
Excess aggregate			Unplanned (Δ in inventories)	–$200 billion
expenditures over				
supply	$ 200 billion	0 =	Total investments =	0

plan to save zero out of their income, and firms plan to invest $200 billion. The excess of planned investment over planned savings (column 7) of $200 billion equals the excess of aggregate expenditures over aggregate supply. It is met by *unanticipated depletion of inventories*. In other words, the excess aggregate expenditure is met out of dealers' stocks. In the national income accounts, a negative change in inventories is counted as negative investment. Therefore, in a *realized* sense (looking back at the end of the year), savings and investment are equal at zero. Table 16–3 summarizes the two approaches for row B.

When aggregate expenditures exceeds aggregate supply, planned investment exceeds planned savings, and by the same amount. The excess aggregate expenditures is supplied out of inventories. And the unintended depletion of inventories brings realized investment into equality with realized savings. But the unintended (undesired) **depletion of inventories causes dealers to step up their orders from the factories.** As a consequence, output expands—say, to $1,400 billion—while employment rises to 80 million workers, as shown in row C.

The student is invited to draw a circular-flow diagram depicting row C of Table 16–1, and then construct a table similar to Table 16–3 analyzing the figures in terms of the aggregate supply and expenditure approach as well as the planned savings and investment approach. The approaches show excess of aggregate expenditure over aggregate supply, and excess of planned investment over planned savings of $100 billion. The excess is supplied out of inventories. But a depletion of inventories induces dealers to step up orders from the factories. Output expands (column 7), say to $1,900 billion, and employment rises to 100 million workers.

Row D: Equilibrium

Employing 100 million workers, aggregate supply by firms over the year, or GDP, is $1,900 billion, and it equals the income received by households. Out of that income, households spend $1,700 billion on purchases from firms (column 3) and save $200 billion (column 4). In turn, firms invest

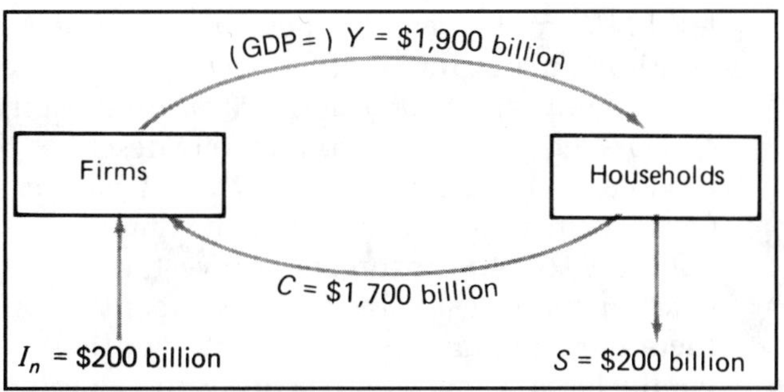

Figure 16–3 Circular-Flow Diagram Depicting Row D of Table 16–1

$200 billion (column 5). This is displayed in the circular-flow diagram of Figure 16–3.

Aggregate supply of $1,900 billion equals aggregate expenditures, which consists of $1,700 billion in consumption expenditures and $200 billion in investments. There is no unsold output; nor is there any unmet demand.

At the beginning of the year, looking ahead, households plan to save $200 billion, and firms plan to invest $200 billion. The two sets of independent plans are equal, and no change in inventories is needed to bring savings and investment into equality in a realized sense. **But this equality of planned savings and investment occurs only at one unique level of GDP—to wit, $1,900 billion. It, is the same level of output at which aggregate supply and aggregate expenditures are also equal.** The occurrence of these two equalities at the same level of output or income is **not a coincidence.** Rather, it is deeply embedded in the analysis. The two approaches are shown in Table 16–4.

At GDP of $1,900 billion, precisely the entire output is sold, no more and no less. Because no change in inventories takes place, there is no inducement for dealers either to step up or to reduce their orders from producing plants. And consequently, there is no incentive to change the

Table 16–4 Analysis of Row D in Table 16–1

Aggregate Supply and Expenditures Approach		Planned and Realized Savings and Investments Approach				
Aggregate supply	$1,900 billion	Savings				Investment
				Planned		
Aggregate expenditures						
C = $1,700 billion		$200 billion		=		$200 billion
I_n = $ 200 billion	$1,900 billion					
				Realized		
Excess of aggregate expenditures over supply	0	$200 billion	=	Planned investments No change in inventories	=	$200 billion

Equilibrium output: The level of output toward which the economy will gravitate given the consumption and investment schedules. It is the level at which aggregate supply (GDP) equals aggregate expenditures (C + I), or equivalently, where *planned*

level of output or employment. *That level of output can be maintained; it is* **equilibrium output** *(or income) and employment.*

It is important *not to associate the word* equilibrium *with a desirable state of affairs.* Equilibrium output merely describes the level toward which the economy will gravitate *given the consumption and investment schedules.* Once attained, that level can be maintained, for it is the level at which all output is sold to consumers or investors; aggregate supply equals aggregate expenditures. It is one out of many possible levels of output. **And there is no guarantee—indeed, it is unlikely—that equilibrium output would be at a level representing full employment.** Underemployment (that is, less than full-employment) equilibrium is clearly undesirable.

Planned Savings and Investment

That realized savings and investment are always equal was shown in the previous analysis. The equality also emerges from the national income accounts. For an economy without government and foreign trade, we have:

$Y = C + I$ Expenditures side of GDP
$Y = C + S$ Income side of GDP

and since $Y = Y$ and $C = C$, I must equal S.

Planned savings: Amount that people plan to save given the level of income.

Planned investment: Amount that businesses plan to invest. Equilibrium is reached when planned savings equals planned investment.

However, **planned savings** and investment are equal at *only one level of output, at equilibrium GDP.* Figure 16–3 may appear similar to the classical analysis shown in Figure 14–4, Chapter 14, where savings and investment were equal; but there is an important difference between the two cases. The classical economists viewed the equality of planned savings and investment as automatic, brought about by variations in the rate of interest, *at any and all levels of income.* Inequality between the two is of no great social concern; it merely changes the rate of interest until equality is restored. Income changes have nothing to do with savings and investment. By contrast, in the Keynesian analysis, this is the crux of income determination, and it is a matter of great social importance. For it is variations in income and employment that change intended savings and bring about or restore equality between planned savings and investment. And it is this equality between their planned magnitudes that determines the equilibrium level of income. The equilibrium will be different for a different consumption and investment schedule. But it is very unlikely that the planned savings and investment equality will occur precisely at the level of output that represents full employment. *Equilibrium income is the sustainable level* of GDP. There is nothing desirable or undesirable about it. And if it falls at a level representing unemployment, it is undesirable.

GEOMETRIC REPRESENTATION

Aggregate Supply and Expenditures Approach

It will be recalled that GDP, or income (Y), is measured along the horizontal axis in the consumption-income space. That axis represents aggregate

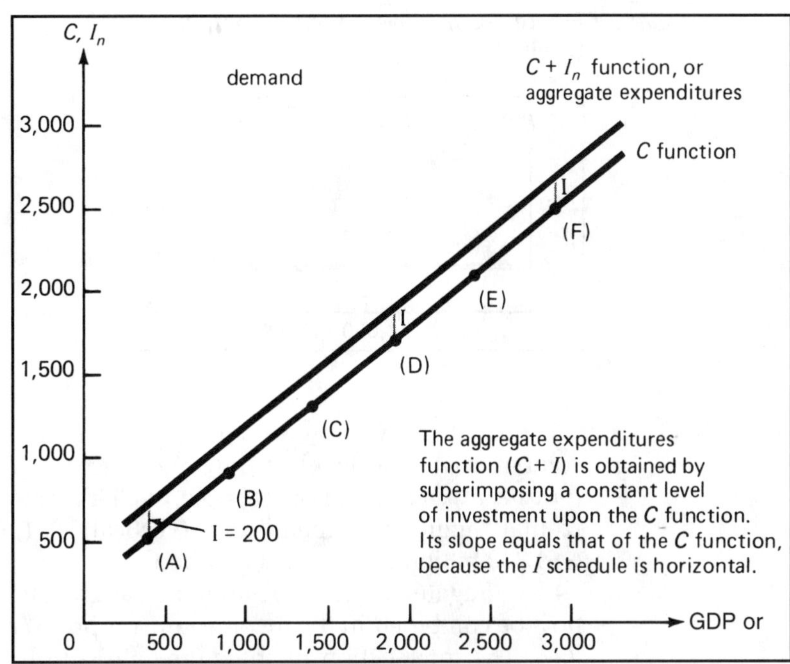

Figure 16–4 Consumption and Aggregate-Expenditures (consumption plus investments) Functions ($ billion)

supply, incorporating the levels of GDP shown in column 2 of Table 16–1. But the (imaginary) 45° line has the property of equidistance between the horizontal and vertical axes. As shown in Figure 15–5, each output level can be measured vertically up to the corresponding point on the 45° line. Consequently, the horizontal measure of aggregate supply (GDP) can be transposed vertically to the 45° line, *making the 45° line an equally valid, vertical measure of aggregate supply* (Column 2 of Table 16–1).

In turn, aggregate expenditures has two components: consumption (C) and net investment (I_n). Consumption is a positive function of income. And the consumption schedule, relating column 3 to column 2 in Table 16–1, can be drawn in the consumption-income space. It is shown in Figure 16–4 as a linear consumption function, with points A, B, C, D, E, and F, corresponding to Table 16–1, indicated along the line. In turn, net investment is invariant with respect to income; at any level of output or income, I_n is $200 billion. This is shown in Figure 16–5 as a linear horizontal investment function. Aggregate expenditures show how much would be spent on consumption and investment combined at each level of output or income. It is the sum total of C and I_n. The income-consumption space becomes income—consumption and investment space as shown in Figure 16–4. On the C functions of that diagram, one can read vertically how much consumers intend to spend at each level of income. To that is added (vertically) the $200 billion that would be spent on investment at each level of income, to obtain aggregate expenditures. In other words, the $C + I_n$ function is obtained by *superimposing vertically* the I_n function of Figure 16–5 upon the C function of Figure 16–4. Parallel to the consumption

Figure 16–5 Investment Function ($ billion)

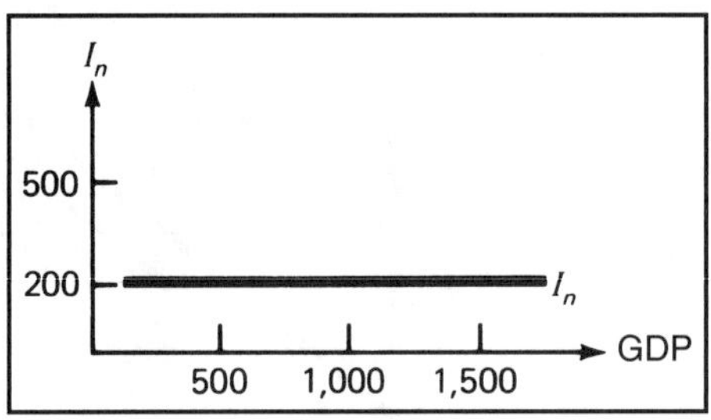

function, it shows how much is spent on consumption and investment combined at each level of output or income. Thus *it represents aggregate (private) expenditures.* For example, at GDP or income of $1,400 billion (horizontal), aggregate expenditures (vertical) is $1,500 billion, consisting of C = $1,300 billion and I_n = $200 billion.

Aggregate supply (45° line) and aggregate expenditures ($C + I_n$) can now be combined in the income-consumption/investment space of Figure 16–6. The intersection of the aggregate supply and expenditures curves occurs at annual output of $1,900 billion, and this is equilibrium income, labeled Y_E in Figure 16–6.

At annual output levels exceeding (to the right of) Y_E ($1,900 billion), aggregate supply exceeds aggregate expenditures, leading to a contraction of output. For example, at annual GDP = $2,900 billion, aggregate supply is $2,900 billion, measured vertically to the 45° line. Aggregate expenditure ($C + I$) is $2,700 billion, measured vertically to the $C + I_n$ function. The excess of aggregate supply over aggregate expenditures ($2 billion) represents unsold output. It induces firms to contract production, and with it output and employment. The region where aggregate supply exceeds aggregate expenditures is shown by the shaded area to the right of Y_E ($1,900 billion), and the resulting contraction of output is indicated by a leftward-pointing arrow at the bottom of the chart.

Conversely, at annual output or income below (to the left of) Y_E ($1,900 billion), aggregate expenditure aggregate exceeds supply, leading to a depletion of inventories, and inducing firms to expand output to meet demand. For example, at GDP = $900 billion, aggregate supply is $900 billion, measured vertically to the 45° line. Aggregate expenditures ($C + I_n$) is $1,100 billion, measured vertically to the $C + I_n$ function. The excess of aggregate expenditures over aggregate supply ($200 billion) represents depletion of inventories. It induces firms to increase production, and with it income and employment. The region where aggregate expenditures exceeds aggregate supply is shown by the shaded area to the left of Y_E ($1,900 billion in GDP), and the resulting expansion of output is indicated by a rightward-pointing arrow at the bottom of the chart.

Only at GDP of $1,900 billion is aggregate expenditures equal to aggregate supply. The entire output, no more and no less, is sold to consumers and investors. There is no inducement for firms to curtail or

Figure 16–6 Aggregate Expenditures and Aggregate Supply ($ billion): Equilibrium output or income is at Y_E. Equilibrium income or output occurs at the level where aggregate expenditures ($C + I_n$) equal aggregate supply, or where the aggregate-expenditures function intersects the 45° line.

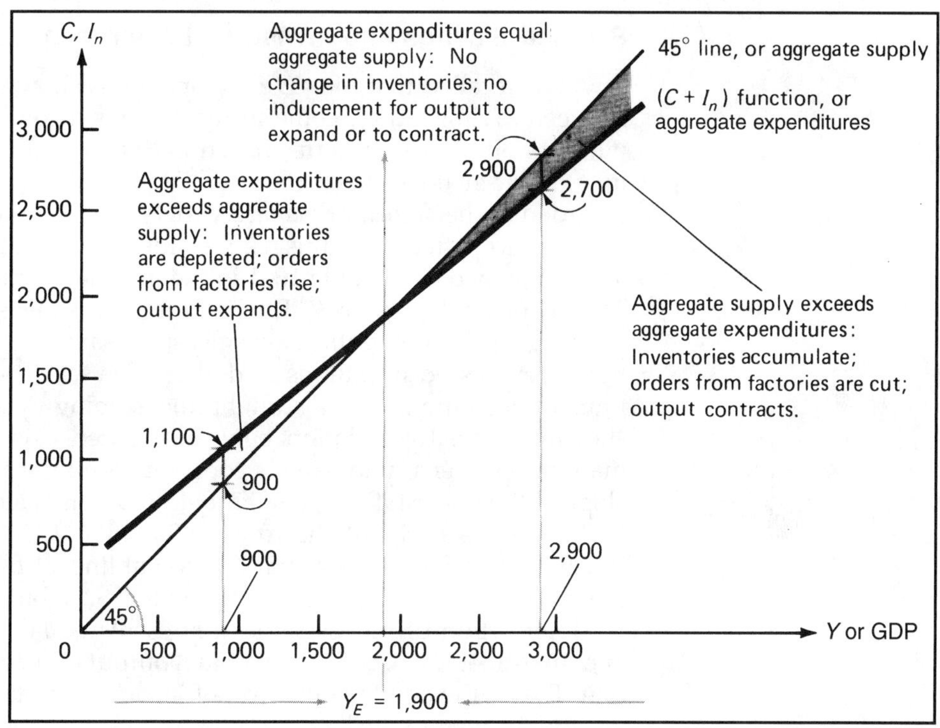

expand production. That output or income level would be maintained; it is equilibrium GDP, denoted by Y_E on the chart.

But there is nothing desirable or undesirable about equilibrium output. It is merely a sustainable level, with no inducement for change. A level of output representing full employment, or full-employment income Y_{FE}, can lie anywhere along the horizontal axis. It is one of an infinite number of possible output levels. Only by sheer coincidence, and an unlikely one at that, would Y_{FE} coincide with Y_E. *The difference between Y_{FE} and Y_E is the GDP gap.* For example, if full-employment equilibrium were $2,100 billion (that is, if Y_{FE} exceeded Y_E), then the GDP gap would be [$2,100 billion – $1,900 billion] $200 billion. The gap occurs because of insufficient aggregate expenditures by consumers and inventors to generate output at the full-employment level. Moving the economy to full employment implies adding $200 billion to its annual output of goods and services. Alternatively, had full employment equilibrium been $1,800 billion (if Y_E exceeded Y_{FE}), then the GDP gap would be [$1,900 billion–$1,800 billion] $100 billion. But this gap is of the opposite variety to the first one. Since full-employment output is less than equilibrium output, the situation describes an "excessive" aggregate expenditures: Consumers and investors demand more goods and services than the economy can supply when operating at full capacity. The average price level will rise. What is required is the dampening of aggregate expenditures to a point where Y_E coincides with Y_{FE}.

Planned Savings and Investment Approach

It will be recalled that the savings function is shown as a positive relation between savings and income in the savings-income space (Figure 15–3), whereas the investment function is a horizontal line in the investment-income space (Figure 15–4). Each of the two schedules is regarded as the *desired* or *planned* variety, and they will both be displayed in one space. Effectively, this means plotting columns 2 (Y), 4 (planned S), and 5 (planned I_n) of Table 16–1 in the income-savings/investment space. This is done in Figure 16–7. The horizontal axis measures output (GDP) or income (Y), and the vertical axis measures savings or investment, with all figures expressed in billions of dollars. The savings schedule relates column 4 to column 2. It is a straight line, sloping upward and to the right, showing a positive relation between desired savings and income. The marginal propensity to save is constant along the function; it equals the slope of the line: MPS = 1/5 = 0.2. Selected points along the line—A, B, C, D, E, and F—represent the rows of Table 16–1. In turn, the investment function is drawn as a straight horizontal line, at I_n = \$200. Regardless of the level of income, planned investment is \$200 billion.

Intersection of the two lines represents equality of planned savings and investment; it occurs at an annual output or income level of \$1,900 billion. That is the equilibrium level of income, denoted by Y_E.

At incomes exceeding Y_E, planned savings exceed planned investment. For example, at income of \$2,900, planned savings is \$400, mea-

Figure 16–7 Savings and Investment Function (\$ billion): Equilibrium output or income is at Y_E—the point at which planned $S = I_n$.

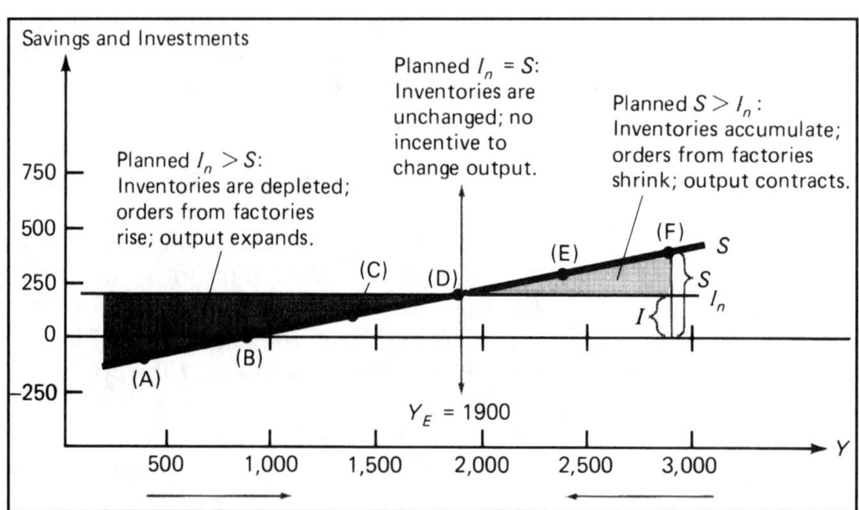

sured vertically on the savings schedule at point F, and planned investment is \$200, measured vertically on the I_n function at that income level. Since $S > I_n$, unplanned accumulation of inventories occurs, leading to curtailment of orders from the factories and reduction in output and income. A similar result is obtained at income of \$2,400 billion, point E on the savings schedule, and at all income levels in excess of \$1,900 billion. This is shown in a shaded area, denoted Planned $S > I_n$, and the resulting contraction of output is shown by a leftward-pointing arrow at the bottom of the chart.

At output or income levels below \$1,900 billion, planned investment exceeds planned savings. For example, at income level \$1,400 billion, planned savings is \$100 billion, measured vertically on the savings schedule at point C, and planned investment is \$200 billion. Since planned $I_n > S$, inventories are depleted. Dealers step up orders from the factories, and output, income, and employment expand. This applies to the entire income range to the left of Y_E and is shown by the shaded area where planned $I_n > S$. The resulting expansion of output is indicated by the rightward-pointing arrow at the bottom of the chart.

Although realized investment *always* equals realized savings, planned investment and savings are equal only at one level of output, and that level represents equilibrium GDP. Only at Y_E (\$1,900 billion), where planned $I_n = S$, is there no incentive to change the level of annual output. It is equilibrium output. From any other level of output or income, the economy will gravitate toward Y_E. *Only at that level of income, precisely the amount of planned savings is generated to match the amount of planned investment,* and there is no incentive to change output.

There is nothing particularly desirable about equilibrium output Y_E. **Full-employment output (Y_{FE}) can be anywhere along the horizontal, Y, axis. It would be a sheer coincidence—an extremely unlikely one—for full-employment output to coincide with equilibrium output; for Y_{FE} = Y_E.** If full-employment output were \$2,000 billion while equilibrium output (Y_E) were \$1,900 billion, then there would be a GDP *gap* of \$2,000–\$1,900, or \$100 billion. The gap occurs because of insufficient aggregate expenditures by consumers and investors to generate output at a full-employment level. In other words, Y_{FE} exceeds equilibrium output. Moving the economy to full employment implies adding \$100 billion to its annual output of goods and services. A gap of an opposite variety would exist had full-employment output been \$1,750 billion (where Y_E exceeds Y_{FE}). Here, equilibrium output represents *excessive* aggregate expenditures; consumers and investors demand more goods and services than the economy can provide at full employment.[3] The average price level would rise. This situation calls for the dampening of aggregate expenditures.

[3]In all cases of "excessive aggregate expenditures" and inflation, the economy no longer operates in region I of aggregate supply (Chapter 13). Rather, it is in region II or III.

SUMMARY

This chapter established an important proposition in macroeconomics. Equilibrium output or income is that level at which aggregate supply equals aggregate expenditures, or equivalently, at which planned savings equals planned investment. It is a unique level of GDP for any given set of consumption and investment schedules. Given the consumption and investment functions, that is the output level toward which the economy gravitates, and it is the only level that, once reached, will be maintained. The discussion highlights the role of *changes in inventories* as a regulatory mechanism. Indeed, businessmen are known to curtail (increase) orders from the factories when their *inventory/sales ratios* exceed (fall below) a desired level.

When aggregate supply exceeds aggregate expenditures, planned savings exceeds planned investment, and by the same amount. The result is unsold output and an accompanying accumulation of inventories. It is the inventory accumulation that brings savings and investment in a realized sense to equality—a sense in which they are always equal. As inventories pile up, dealers curtail orders from the factories, and output, income and employment decline toward the equilibrium level.

Conversely, when aggregate expenditures exceed aggregate supply, planned investment exceeds planned savings, and by the same amount. The result is unintended depletion of inventories. And it is this depletion that brings savings and investment in a realized sense into equality. As inventories get depleted, dealers step up orders from the factories, and output, income and employment rise toward the equilibrium level.

Only at equilibrium output is there no inducement to change the level of production. For a given set of consumption and investment functions, there is only one unique equilibrium output. Since employment is uniquely and positively related to output, equilibrium output also implies an accompanying level of employment.

For each set of consumption and investment schedules, there is one unique equilibrium output. However, there is nothing particularly desirable about the equilibrium output; it merely denotes a sustainable level. Rather, the desired level is full-employment output, and it can be anywhere along the horizontal axis. It is one out of an infinite number of possibilities and is therefore unlikely to coincide with the one unique equilibrium output. **The difference between full-employment output (Y_{FE}) and equilibrium output (Y_E) is the GDP gap. It represents inadequate aggregate expenditures if Y_{FE} exceeds Y_E, and excessive aggregate expenditures if Y_E exceeds Y_{FE}.**

Having established equilibrium output (or income) for a given set of consumption and investment schedules, in the next chapter we deal with moving from one equilibrium point to another as one of the schedules changes.

QUESTIONS AND PROBLEMS

1. a. Reproduce columns 2–4 of Table 16–1 in the text. What are the MPS and MPC at each level of GDP?

b. Let net investment (I_n) be $300 billion at all levels of GDP. Add an investment schedule.

c. Determine and explain equilibrium GDP, using (i) the aggregate expenditures and supply approach, and (ii) the planned savings and investment approach.

d. How can savings and investment diverge in a planned sense but be always equal in a realized sense?

e. Draw the information in your table on a savings-investment diagram (as in Figure 16–4).

f. Suppose that full-employment output were $2,600 billion per year (indicate it on your chart). What is the GDP gap? Does the gap represent inadequate or excessive aggregate expenditures?

g. Alternatively, suppose that full-employment output were $2,300 billion (indicate it on your chart). What is the GDP gap? Does the gap represent excessive or inadequate aggregate expenditures?

h. What would full-employment output have to be for a GDP gap to be absent?

2. You are given the following information (in billions of dollars) for the U.S. economy, which is assumed to have no government or foreign trade.

Possible Level of GDP (Y)	Consumption Schedule	Savings Schedule	Investment Schedule
3,850	3,400		250
3,350	3,000		250
2,850	2,600		250
2,350	2,200		250

a. Using these figures, answer questions 1a to 1e.

b. What would the size and nature of the GDP gap be, had full-employment output been:

(i) $2,700 billion per year?

(ii) $2,950 billion per year?

APPENDIX TO CHAPTER 16

The Two Approaches Combined

Because they yield identical results, the two approaches can be used separately. Still, it is useful to combine them in one diagram. As in the appendix to Chapter 15, this is done in two panels having an identical horizontal axis to represent income. The top panel shows the aggregate supply and expenditures approach in the consumption and investment-income space; the bottom panel displays the planned savings and investment approach in the savings and investment-income space. The drawing is done in two steps: First, draw the consumption function and the 45° line (aggregate supply) on the upper panel, and the corresponding savings schedule on the lower panel. Make sure that *the consumption function intersects the 45° line at the level of output (income) where savings is zero.* Second, draw the investment function on the bottom panel; and superimpose net investment upon the consumption function on the upper panel, obtaining

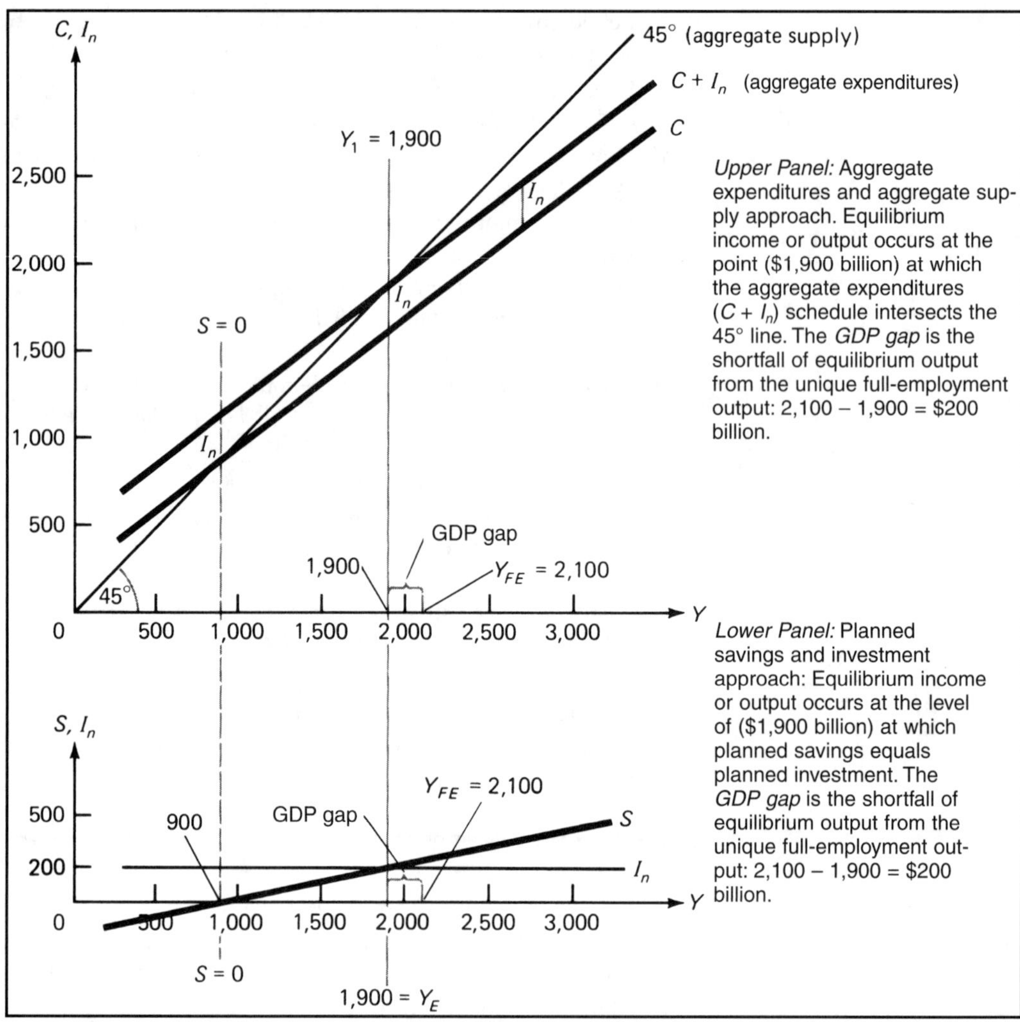

Figure A16–1 Diagrammatic Exposition of the Two Approaches to Income Determination: Note the correspondence between the upper and lower panels: Savings is zero on the panel at the same output level where the *C* function intersects the 45° line on the upper panel; and $S = I_n$ on the lower panel at the same output level where the $(C + I_n)$ function intersects the 45° line on upper panel.

the $C + I_n$ function or aggregate expenditures parallel to the consumption function. Make sure that *the* $C + I_n$ *function intersects the 45° line* (that is, aggregate expenditures equals aggregate supply) *at the level of output or income where planned savings equals planned investment.* The second (italicized) sentence in each of the steps above asserts a link between the upper and lower panels.

Figure A16–1 displays the two approaches combined. Note that the two indicated "links" between the upper and lower panels occur respectively at Y = $900 billion ($S = 0$) and at Y = $1,900 billion ($S = I_n$, and aggregate supply equals aggregate expenditures). Equilibrium income or output (Y_E) is at $1,900 billion per year on both panels. On the top panel, the vertical distance between the consumption function and the 45° line represents savings; the vertical distance between the consumption function and the $(C + I_n)$ function represents investment. Savings equals investment at the level of output where the two vertical distances are equal, namely where the $(C + I_n)$ function crosses the 45° line. This corresponds, on the bottom panel, to the level of output at which planned $S = I_n$.

The GDP gap is the difference between equilibrium output and full-employment output. On the diagram, Y_{FE} is shown at GDP of $2,100 billion implying a GDP gap of [$2,100–$1,900] $200 billion. It reflects *inadequate* aggregate expenditures. Alternatively, had Y_{FE} been less than Y_E, the difference between them, and also the GDP gap, would have represented *excessive* aggregate expenditures. These two related panels should become second nature to all students.

SUMMARY

The two approaches to income determination can find diagrammatic expression on a pair of two-dimensional panels. The top panel displays the aggregate supply and expenditures approach on a consumption and investments-income space. Aggregate supply is the 45° line, and aggregate expenditures is the $C + I_n$ function, parallel to the consumption function. Their intersection determines equilibrium output (Y_E). The lower panel displays the planned savings and investment approach on a saving and investment-income space. Income is shown on the horizontal axis in both panels, drawn to an identical scale. The intersection of the savings and investment schedules determines equilibrium output (Y_E). On both panels, Y_E occurs at the same level of output or income. Another link between the panels is the $S = 0$ (on the lower panel) at the output level where the consumption function intersects the 45° line (on the upper panel).

PROBLEMS

Refer to questions 1 and 2 at the end of Chapter 16. In each case, draw the information contained in the table on a pair of related panels—the top one representing the aggregate-expenditures and aggregate-supply approach, and the bottom one the savings-investment approach.

Movement from One Equilibrium GDP to Another—The Multiplier

CHANGES IN INVESTMENT

Given the consumption and investment functions, there is one unique level of GDP toward which the economy will gravitate and at which it will settle. That is the equilibrium output or income. But especially the investment function is not stable over time. Rather, it is volatile and subject to frequent gyrations. As it shifts up or down, so does the equilibrium level of GDP. In fact, the economy is subject to almost continuous disturbances that change its equilibrium output. As soon as one equilibrium is reached, or even before, one of the two functions may shift, moving the economy to a new equilibrium.

In what follows, we examine how shifts in the investment schedule move the economy from one equilibrium GDP to another, by inquiring into the effect of one change in the investment schedule. Specifically, we consider the effect of a rise in investment, which takes place when the economy functions at less than full employment of workers and machines, in region I of the aggregate-supply curve. Possible reasons for such a rise in investment are spelled out in Chapter 15.

Two types of variations in investment have to be considered. The first is a one-time change where investment rises over one period only—such as one quarter or one year—and then returns to its original level. This is sometimes called "pump-priming." Its effect would be to raise GDP, but only temporarily. Eventually, GDP would settle back to the old equilibrium level. The second, more interesting, case is a permanent increase in investment—when year in and year out, investment is at the new instead of the old level. Such a change would increase GDP to an entirely new equilibrium level, at which it would settle permanently.

A ONE-TIME RISE IN INVESTMENT: THE IDEA OF THE MULTIPLIER

A one-time increase in investment would boost GDP temporarily; subsequently, GDP would decline gradually to its original level. The total accumulated increments in income, until it reverts to its old level, are much greater than the rise in investment; in fact, the amount is a multiple of that increase. The reason for that phenomenon is not difficult to see. A rise in investment of $100 means that various factors of production are hired, say, to construct a new plant. For such an investment requires labor, capital, natural resources, and entrepreneurship, as well as materials supplied by other enterprises. The $100 ends up as new income in the hands of the owners of these factors of production, in the form of wages and salaries, profit, interest, and rent. In other words, a $100 temporary (one-period) boost in investment ends up as a one-time injection into the income stream in the form of factor incomes. But most of an addition to income in society is spent (on durable and nondurable goods as well as on services), and part of it is saved. **The division of the incremental income between spending and saving depends on the marginal propensities to consume and to save.** If the MPC = 0.8 and the MPS = 0.2, then $80 of the added income would be spent and $20 saved. If the original investment of $100 is called the "primary round" of spending, then the expenditure of $80 by its recipients is the "second round" of spending. At that round, $20 is leaked out of the income stream in the form of savings.

But the $80 injected back into the income stream ends up as added factor income in the hands of those who contributed to the production of consumer goods purchased by the second-round spenders. They in turn would spend 0.8 of that amount, according to the MPC, and save 0.2 of it, according to the MPS. Thus, the "third round" of spending is $64, with $16 leaked out of the spending stream in the form of added savings. Recipients of the $64—those who sold goods and services to the "third-round" spenders—would spend 0.8 of it, or $51.20, and save $12.80. That is the "fourth round" of spending. In turn, recipients of the $51.20 spent by the "fourth-rounders" would spend $40.96 (51.20 × 0.8) and save $10.24 (51.20 × 0.2); and recipients of this "fifth round" of spending would spend 0.8 of the $40.96 and save 0.2 of it. This process continues, as each group of income recipients from the preceding round of spending spends part of its newly found income and saves the rest, in accordance with the marginal propensities to consume and to save prevailing in society. At each round, part of the incremental income is saved, but most of it is reinjected into the income stream in the form of new spending. The reader is urged to continue the process through five more rounds.

At each round of spending, new income or output is created somewhere in the economy. Starting from the original one-time injection of $100 in new investment, we may add up the new incomes:

	ΔY =	100 +	80 +	64 +	51.20 +	40.96 +	32.77 +	26.27 + . . .	= 500
Spending round:		I	II	III	IV	V	VI	VII	

Continuing the process through many more rounds, all the newly created incomes add up to \$500. Of this, \$100 was the original income, and the remaining \$400 (added up from the second round onward) is new consumption. In turn, the new savings can also be added up over all rounds of spending; they add up to \$100:

$$\Delta C = 80 + 64 + 51.20 + 40.96 + 32.77 + \ldots = 400$$
$$\Delta S = 20 + 16 + 12.80 + 10.24 + 8.19 + \ldots = 100$$

Spending round: II III IV V VI

A primary injection into the income stream results in successive rounds of spending, each round being smaller than its predecessor. The process is like the effect of a stone dropped into a tranquil body of water. It makes concentric waves of ever-decreasing height as we move further away from the point of impact. The reason for this reduction in magnitude of successive rounds of spending is that part of the income in each round is leaked out of the spending stream in the form of savings.

All the increments to income, over all rounds of spending, add up to a multiple of the original primary injection. For a given primary injection (ΔI), **the smaller the amount withdrawn from the spending stream at each round in the form of savings—that is, the smaller the MPS—the greater will be the total rise in income.** Clearly, **this process** of spending → income → spending → income **takes time to work its way through the economy.** Most of the increase in income occasioned by a given ΔI usually occurs over a subsequent two-year period.

The effect of a one-time increase in investment on income over subsequent quarters is sketched in Figure 17–1, using figures from the previous

Figure 17–1 Effect on Output of a One-time Rise in Investments of \$100: Output first rises by the amount of the investment, and then it declines gradually to the original level. There is **no permanent effect on output**, but the increments to output while the adjustment is taking place add up to $\Delta I \times 1/MPS$.

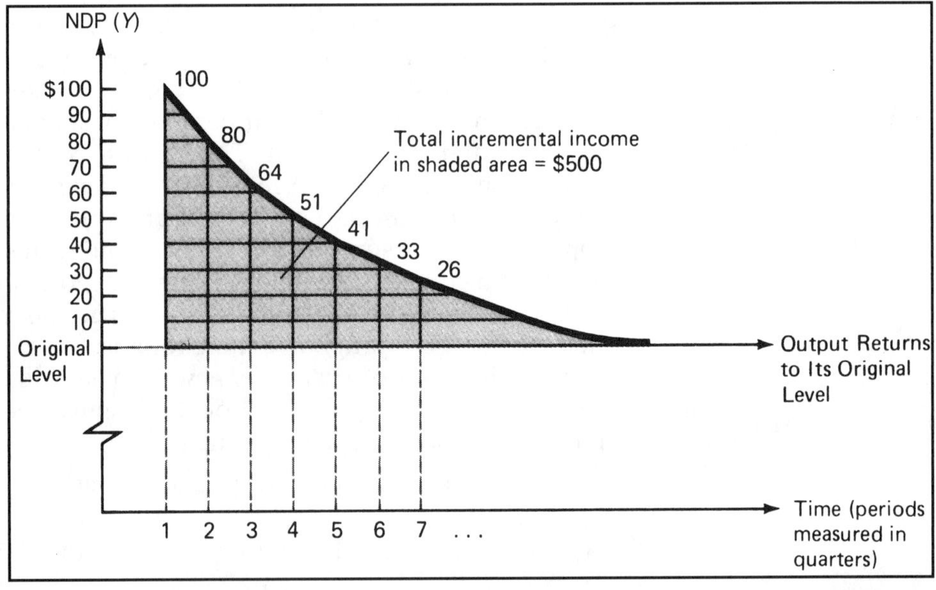

illustration. During the quarter in which the investment project is carried out, income shoots up by $100—the sum invested. The investment project *ceases at that point,* but ever-decreasing increments to income continue over subsequent quarters, through the successive rounds of income and spending described earlier. The addition to income in each quarter is marked on the chart and is shown to be declining, as in the previous calculations. *Eventually, income returns to its original level.* But this is a gradual process, during which the community collects a total incremental income of $500. Because a *one-time change in investments has no effect on the long-run level of income,* its interest lies mainly in the light it sheds on the spending-income process.

A PERMANENT RISE IN INVESTMENT: THE MAGIC OF THE MULTIPLIER

We now tackle the more interesting case in which investment rises to an altogether new level—that is, a permanent increase in investment. Again the initial equilibrium output is well below the full-employment level, so that unused capacity is assumed in the economy.

Suppose General Motors increases its investment by $100 million per quarter (three-month period) to build a series of new plants. Such investment may be financed either from *internal* funds, accumulated within the company out of previous profits, or by raising *external* funds on the capital markets, through borrowing from banks, issuing (selling) bonds, or even issuing new common stock. Either way, that money is spent by the company on hiring new workers to man the construction sites, buying materials from other suppliers, and purchasing new machinery and equipment from independent suppliers or companies. The funds so expended find their way to another set of people in the form of factor remunerations: wages and salaries for workers, profit to supplying entrepreneurs, and so on. In the first quarter, when the new investment is first undertaken, output and income in the economy go up by $100 million.

What would the second set of people do with their newly added factor income? They would spend part of it and save the rest. **The proportions of the added income allocated to additional spending and savings depend on the marginal propensities to consume and to save.** Suppose, as before, MPC = 0.8 and MPS = 0.2, and assume further that there is a *time lag of one quarter* between the receipt of newly added income and the expenditure of part of it on new goods and services. In that case, the recipients of the new $100 million would spend in the second quarter (a subsequent three-month period) $80 million and save $20 million. In other words, the primary investment injection of $100 million in quarter I results, during quarter II, in a second round of spending of $80 million. **But unlike the one-time case outlined before, GM's investments (the primary injections) also continue in the second quarter** at a rate of $100 million per quarter, also adding to income. Together, output and income rise in the second quarter by $180 million ($\Delta Y = \Delta I + \Delta C$), while savings rise by $20 million.

In the third quarter, the (new) investment process continues at a rate of \$100 million. But in addition, 0.8 of the \$180 million new income added in the second quarter is spent on new consumption. Consumption rises by 180×0.8, or \$144 million, and savings increase by 180×0.2, or \$36 million. The rise in income is now \$244 million. ($\Delta Y = \Delta I + \Delta C$). These figures represent new levels of income, consumption, and savings attained in the third quarter following the initiation of the new investment.

In the fourth quarter, the investment process continues with another \$100 million. Consumption rises by 0.8 times the increase in income in the preceding quarter, or by \$195 million (244×0.8), and savings rise by \$49 million (244×0.2). The rise in income relative to the original level now stands at $100 + 195$, or \$295 million. And the process continues in the manner described in Table 17–1.

Each row in the table depicts one quarter and shows the change in investment, consumption, income, and savings respectively (in successive columns), *relative to the original situation prevailing before the permanent change in investments was initiated.* The changes in consumption and savings lag one quarter behind the change in income that induces them. Also note that at each round, ΔY is *the sum of* ΔI and ΔC, based on the expenditures side of the national income accounts, $Y = C + I$, in a private, closed economy. Income is seen to rise gradually and attain a level of 500 above the preinvestment situation; consumption and savings rise gradually to levels

Table 17–1 The Multiplier Process: $\Delta I = 100$; MPC = 0.8; MPS = 0.2

Quarter	ΔI	$\Delta C(\Delta Y_{-1} \times \text{MPC})$	$\Delta Y(\Delta I + \Delta C)$[a]	$\Delta S(\Delta Y_{-1} \times \text{MPS})$
1	100		100	
		100 × 0.8		100 × 0.2
2	100	80	180	20
		180 × 0.8		180 × 0.2
3	100	144	244	36
		244 × 0.8		244 × 0.2
4	100	195	295	49
		295 × 0.8		294 × 0.2
5	100	236	336	59
		336 × 0.8		336 × 0.2
6	100	269	369	67
		369 × 0.8		368 × 0.2
7	100	295		74
⋮	⋮	⋮	⋮	⋮
Final	100	400	500	100

[a]*Note: In a private, closed economy,* $Y = C + I$, *so that* $\Delta Y = \Delta C + \Delta I$. *See Chapter 12.*

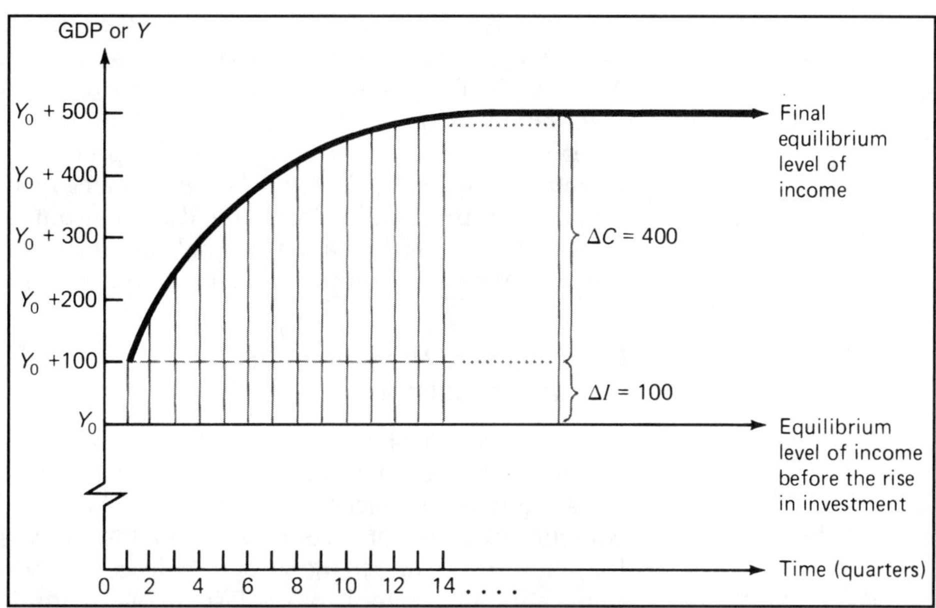

Figure 17–2 Schematic Illustration of the Effect on Output of a Permanent Rise in Investment: Output rises gradually to a new equilibrium level, which is higher than the original level by $\Delta I \times 1/MPS$.

of 400 and 100 respectively above those prevailing prior to the new investment. In the final equilibrium position, savings rise by the same amount as investment, thereby preserving the savings-investment equality.

Figure 17–2 shows schematically the rise in income (Y) over time. The original (pre-ΔI) level of income is shown as Y_0. In the period when the new investment is undertaken, income rises by the amount of the new investment expenditures ($\Delta Y = \Delta I = 100$). In each successive quarter, part of the previously added income is reinjected into the income stream. But (unlike the "pump-priming" case) all the while, the original investment continues. **Income converges gradually on a new, higher plateau. Eventually, income or output settles at a permanent equilibrium level, which is higher by 500 than the original level.** The change in income is **permanent,** and it is five times greater than the primary change in investment **that brought** it about. The ratio between the two magnitudes is called the **multiplier,** usually labeled **k.**

Multiplier (k): the ratio between the permanent change in income and the change in investment that brought it about. k = ΔY/ΔI.

$$\text{Definition of the multiplier: } k = \Delta Y / \Delta I$$

Several insights can be gleaned from this example. A *permanent* rise in investment raises income by a multiple of the ΔI, and *income settles at a new, permanent, higher equilibrium level.* The reason for this "multiplier effect" on income is the successive rounds of increased consumer spending that follow from the increases in income. At each successive round, a part of the previous-period increase in income is leaked out of the spending stream into savings. And the magnitude of that part depends on the MPS = (1 – MPC). The greater the MPS, the larger the withdrawal into savings at each round, and the smaller the rise in income for a given primary increase in investment. In other words, the size of the multiplier is inversely related to the MPS. The eventual rise in savings equals the rise in investment ($\Delta I = \Delta S = 100$). It takes some time for the successive rounds of spending to work themselves out and for the new equilibrium income to be established.

It is important to recognize that **the process works in the opposite direction** as well. A primary *reduction* in investment generates successive rounds of *cuts* in income and spending. Output and income eventually settle at a *lower* level than the original equilibrium, and the decline in output or income is a multiple of the primary reduction in investment.

Diagrammatic Presentation: Savings-Investment Approach

It is convenient to show the effect of a permanent rise in investment in the savings and investment-income space. (The appendix to Chapter 17 presents the two approaches.) The diagram shows only the *initial* and *final* equilibrium levels of income, and not the process of spending rounds leading from the first to the second. It describes the aggregate economy by duplicating the example of the last chapter, with figures given in billions of dollars. Figure 16-4 is reproduced in Figure 17–3, but it is drawn to a somewhat larger scale. The initial investment, I_1, is \$200 billion, yielding equilibrium income or GDP of \$1.9 trillion, which in turn generates savings of \$200 billion; at equilibrium output, intended savings equals intended investment. As in the case of problem 1 at the end of Chapter 16, annual investment rises to \$300 billion; that is, the entire investment function is shifted upward to I_2, with ΔI being \$100 billion. A new equilibrium income or output is established at GDP = \$2.4 trillion, although it takes

Figure 17–3 Effect on Income of a \$100 Billion Rise in Investments (figures in billions of dollars): As investments rise from I_1 to I_2 (by 100), equilibrium output or income rise from Y_1 to Y_2 or by 500. The rise in income generates a rise in savings of $\Delta Y \times MPS = 500 \times 1/5 = 100$, which equals the original increase in investment. Thus desired $S = I$ at both Y_1 and Y_2 (the properties of equilibrium income are preserved). The multiplier k is defined as $\Delta Y/\Delta I$. Because

$$\Delta I = \Delta S,\ k = \Delta Y/\Delta S \text{ or } \frac{1}{\Delta S/\Delta Y} = \frac{1}{MPS} = \text{ the slope of the savings function.}$$

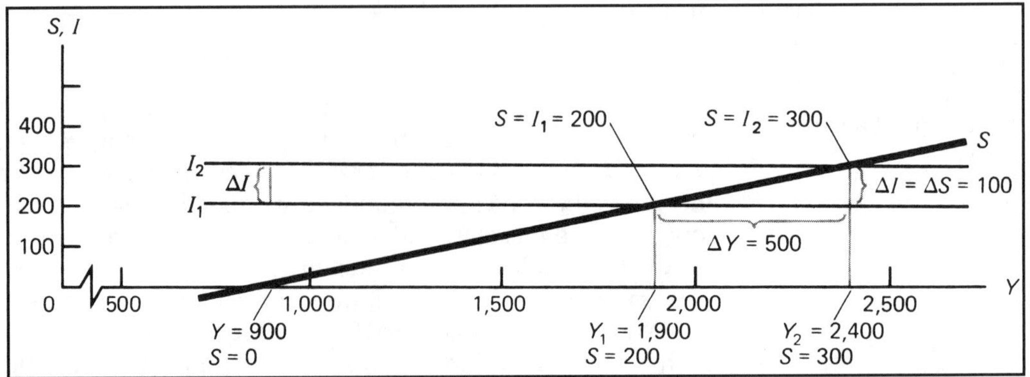

time for the economy to move from Y_1 to Y_2. And at the new, higher level of income, \$300 billion of savings is generated (moving up along the savings function) to match the new level of investment. Again, at equilibrium, intended investment equals intended savings. In sum, given the slope of the savings function) a (permanent) \$100 billion increase in investment raises income by \$500 billion, which in turn induces an increase in savings by \$100 billion. This is the nature of a movement from one equilibrium output to the next. Although Figure 17–3 shows only the initial and final equilibrium, the analysis of the preceding section demonstrates unmistakably that this process takes time, as successive rounds of spending work their way through the economy.

Centering attention on the two points of equilibrium, we see that a \$100 billion rise in investments increased income by \$500 billion. The size of the multiplier in this case is 5:

$$k = \Delta Y/\Delta I = 500/100 = 5$$

THE MULTIPLIER FORMULA

Multiplier formula: k = 1 / MPS = 1 / (1 – MPC)

We saw intuitively earlier that the size of the multiplier is inversely related to the MPS, or to the proportion of income leaked out of the spending stream in the form of savings at each round of spending. We are now in a position to develop a more precise formula for measuring the multiplier.

In Figure 17–3, $\Delta I = \Delta S = 100$, and $\Delta Y = 500$. Consider the slope of the savings function between points Y_1 and Y_2. It equals the MPS.

$$\text{Slope} = \Delta S/\Delta Y = \Delta I/\Delta Y = \text{MPS}$$

By definition, the multiplier k is the inverse of $\Delta I/\Delta Y$, and it is therefore the inverse of $\Delta S/\Delta Y$, or of the MPS:

$$k = \Delta Y/\Delta I = 1/\text{MPS} = 1/\text{Leakage}^{1}$$

---

[1]An alternative derivation of the multiplier formula emanates from the national income accounting. In a closed, private (nongovernment) economy:

(1) Y = C + I → Expenditures side of NDP
(2) Y = C + S → Income side of NDP

From equation 1, I = Y – C, so that ΔI = ΔY – ΔC. We now substitute the last equality into the denominator of the multiplier definition:

$$k = \frac{\Delta Y}{\Delta I} = \frac{\Delta Y}{\Delta Y - \Delta C}$$

Divide through by ΔY to obtain:

$$k = \frac{1}{1 - \Delta C/\Delta Y} = \frac{1}{1 - \text{MPC}} = \frac{1}{\text{MPS}}$$

These proofs of the multiplier formula rely on a comparison between the initial and final equilibria. They do not highlight the process of moving from the first to the second through successive rounds of spending. But readers familiar with the underlying mathematics may recognize in Figure 17–2 and the accompanying discussion *elements of a convergent series*. The solution to such a series also yields the same multiplier formula.

Table 17–2 Effect on Income of a $100 Rise in Investment Under Four Alternative Multipliers

	(1)	(2)	(3)	(4)	(5)	(6)
	ΔI	*MPC*	*MPS*	*k*	ΔY	ΔS
(A)	100	0.8	0.2	5 (= 1/0.2)	500	100 (500 × 0.2)
(B)	100	0.75	0.25	4 (= 1/0.25)	400	100 (400 × 0.25)
(C)	100	0.6	0.4	2.5 (= 1/0.4)	250	100 (250 × 0.4)
(D)	100	0.5	0.5	2 (= 1/0.5)	200	100 (200 × 0.5)

The size of the multiplier equals the inverse of the MPS, or the inverse of the leakage out of the spending stream at each round of spending. Since MPS + MPC = 1, we have:

$$k = \frac{1}{\text{MPS}} = \frac{1}{1 - \text{MPC}}$$

It is useful to illustrate the formula by numerical examples. Given the MPC, and therefore the MPS, the multiplier is easily obtainable. Given the multiplier (k), we can calculate the change in income for any given change in investment. In Table 17–2, this calculation is performed for four alternative MPCs, each occupying one row. Only columns 1 and 2 are given. The remaining columns are calculated according to the preceding analysis.

Again it must be recognized that the formula works in both directions. It can be applied to a decrease as well as to an increase in investment. Thus, with an MPC of 0.6 (row C) and an attendant k of 2.5, a *reduction in investment of $200 lowers income by $500.* In other words, after successive income-spending rounds worked themselves out, the economy would settle at a new equilibrium output lower by $500 than the original equilibrium. Savings decline by $200 billion (500 × MPS) to match the reduction in investment.

An upward shift in the *entire consumption function* would have an effect similar to that of an increase in investment: It would raise aggregate expenditures (vertically) by the full extent of the shift and have a multiplied effect on income (see appendix to Chapter 17). In Figure 17–3, this would be shown by the *corresponding downward shift in the savings function,* with an identical effect on income. A downward shift in the consumption function, and the associated upward shift in the savings function, would lower income by a multiple of that shift.

RECESSIONARY AND INFLATIONARY GAPS

We now return to the relation between equilibrium GDP (Y_E) and full-employment equilibrium (Y_{FE}), discussed in the preceding chapter.

If Y_{FE} exceeds Y_E, then the difference between them is the GDP gap, representing excess capacity and unemployment. Suppose Y_E = $1,900

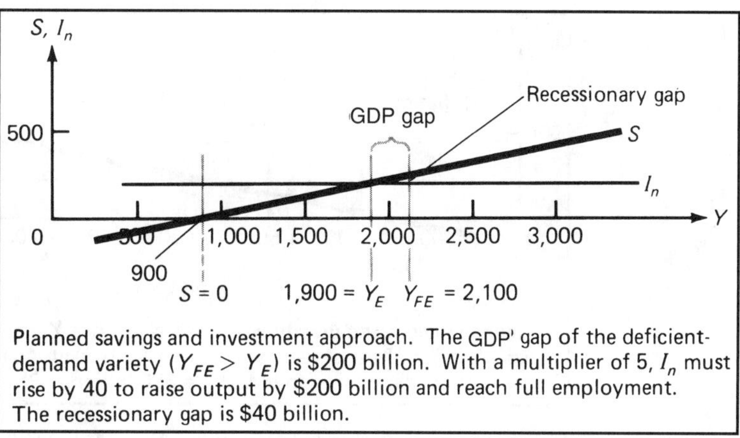

Planned savings and investment approach. The GDP' gap of the deficient-demand variety ($Y_{FE} > Y_E$) is \$200 billion. With a multiplier of 5, I_n must rise by 40 to raise output by \$200 billion and reach full employment. The recessionary gap is \$40 billion.

Figure 17–4 Recessionary Gap when Y_E = *\$1,900* Billion, Y_{FE} = \$2,100 Billion and MPS = 0.2 (k = 5)

billion, Y_{FE} = 2,100 billion, and MPS = 0.2 (k = 5). To remove the unemployment, output and income must rise by the GDP gap of \$200 billion. But the multiplier analysis demonstrated that such an expansion calls for a much smaller primary increase in investment. In fact, because k = 5, a rise in investment of \$40 billion suffices to push the economy to full-employment output: $\Delta Y = \Delta I \times k = 40 \times 5 = 200$. The **recessionary gap** measures the extent by which investment must rise to eliminate the unemployment when Y_{FE} exceeds Y_E. It equals the GDP gap divided by the multiplier:

Recessionary gap: By how much investment needs to rise to raise output to the full-employment level, when full employment output exceeds equilibrium output. It equals: GDP gap divided by multiplier, or $\frac{Y_{FE} - Y_E}{k}$.

$$\text{Recessionary gap} = \frac{\text{GDP gap}}{\text{Multiplier}} = \frac{Y_{FE} - Y_E}{k} \text{ when } Y_{FE} > Y_E$$

This is illustrated in Figure 17–4 for the figures previously given.[2]

Conversely, consider the case where Y_E exceeds Y_{FE}. The difference between them is the GDP gap. But it is of the opposite variety, representing excessive aggregate expenditures. To dampen that excess, output and income must be lowered by the size of the gap. But remember that the multiplier works in both directions. Consequently, to reduce output by a given magnitude, investment must be lowered by only a fraction of that magnitude. For example, if Y_E = \$1,900 billion, Y_{FE} = \$1,500 billion, and MPS = 0.2, then the GDP gap is \$400 billion and k = 5. In that case, a reduction of \$80 billion in investment is required to remove the GDP gap (excess aggregate expenditures) of \$400 billion, because \$80 billion × 5 = \$400 billion.

---

[2] In an alternative example, suppose that Y_E = \$1,900 billion, Y_{FE} = \$2,050 billion, and MPC = 0.6. What is the recessionary gap? The GDP gap in this case is \$150 billion. In other words, NDP or Y is \$150 billion short of full-employment output. With MPC = 0.6, the MPS is 0.4 and the multiplier is 1/0.40 = 2.5. The recessionary gap is GDP gap/k = 150/2.5 = \$60 billion. It would take a \$60 billion rise in investment to generate an expansion of output and income to the tune of \$150 billion ($\Delta Y = \Delta I \times k = 60 \times 2.5 = 150$), thereby eliminating the unemployment.

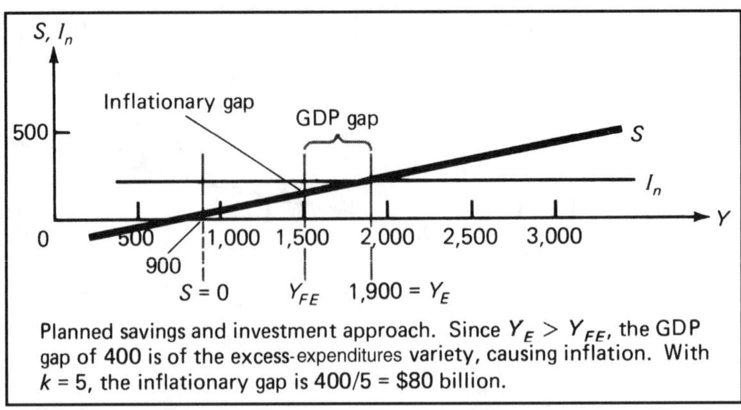
S, I_n
500
0
Inflationary gap
GDP gap
S
I_n
Y
500
1,000
1,500
2,000
2,500
3,000
900
S = 0
Y_{FE}
1,900 = Y_E
Planned savings and investment approach. Since $Y_E > Y_{FE}$, the GDP gap of 400 is of the excess-expenditures variety, causing inflation. With $k = 5$, the inflationary gap is 400/5 = $80 billion.

Figure 17–5 Inflationary Gap when Y_E = $1,900 Billion, Y_{FE} = $1,500 Billion, and MPS = 0.2 (k = 5)

Inflationary Gap: By how much investment needs to be reduced to remove inflation, when equilibrium output exceeds full-employment output. It equals: GDP gap divided by the multiplier k, or: $\frac{Y_E - Y_{FE}}{k}$.

The **inflationary gap** measures the magnitude by which investment must be reduced to eliminate the GDP gap when Y_E exceeds Y_{FE}:

$$\text{Inflationary gap} = \frac{\text{GDP gap}}{k} = \frac{Y_E - Y_{FE}}{k}, \text{ when } Y_E > Y_{FE}$$

Figure 17–5 illustrates the inflationary gap for the preceding numerical example.[3] The appendix of this chapter contains a diagrammatic presentation of the "gaps" using both approaches.

FACTORS THAT DAMPEN THE SIZE OF THE MULTIPLIER

Relaxing momentarily the assumptions underlying this analysis, we note three factors that tend to lower the size of the multiplier. They increase the leakage out of the income stream at each round of spending.

First, add the government sector, to be introduced explicitly in Chapter 18. A rise in investment gradually raises income to a new level through the multiplier process. But at each round of new spending and income, some of the added income is withdrawn into income taxes.

Second, add foreign trade—imports and exports. Imports are positively related to income: The higher the income, the more people are able and willing to import. As income rises in successive rounds of spending, another withdrawal is into imports.

Third, assume for a moment that the economy operates in region II rather than region I of aggregate supply, and observe Figure 13–5. A rise

[3]As an alternative illustration, assume that Y_E = 1,900 billion and Y_{FE} = $1,740 billion, so that the GDP gap of the excessive-expenditures variety is $160 billion. If MPC = 0.75, then MPS = 0.25 and k = 4. The inflationary gap is then 160/4 = $40 billion. It would take a $40 billion cut in investments to reduce aggregate expenditures by $160 billion, to the point of eliminating the excessive expenditures.

in investment increases aggregate expenditures in the price-output space. But not the entire increase is reflected in a rise in real output; part of it dissipates in a rise in prices.

In a more complete analysis, three factors dampen the size of the multiplier: withdrawals into taxes and into imports and a rise in the price level at each round of increased spending. It is estimated that the size of the multiplier in the United States, *with respect to GDP*, is between 1.5 and 2. That means that a permanent increase (decrease) in investment of $10 billion raises (lowers) GDP by $15–20 billion, following an appropriate time lag.

SOME PRACTICAL CONCLUSIONS

This analysis leads to certain significant conclusions, although incomplete ones, concerning the performance of the economy. Excess capacity and unemployment occur when full-employment equilibrium output (Y_{FE}) exceeds the equilibrium output (Y_E) generated by the consumption and investment schedules prevailing in the economy. Unemployment is a result of inadequate aggregate expenditures. A move toward full employment requires an upward shift in the investment or the entire consumption function (or both), either of which has a multiple effect on output (NDP) and income. Such an upward shift may come about on its own. For example, investment may rise as a result of a new discovery or invention; the consumption function may rise because people become less thrifty. However, if such changes do not occur, then there is a role for government policy in bringing them about. Government may improve the investment climate by, say, offering investors special tax breaks; or it may cause a boost in the consumption function by, say, lowering interest rates that consumers must pay when they borrow to finance purchases. Because such policies are designed to increase output and employment by changing aggregate expenditures, they are called *demand-management* policies. However, these are only examples. The entire range of government policies must await the explicit inclusion of government in the analysis.

Conversely, inflation occurs when full-employment output (Y_{FE}) *is* short of equilibrium output (Y_E) generated by the consumption and investment functions prevailing in the economy. Consumers and investors, in the aggregate, demand more goods and services than the economy is able to supply at full capacity. This causes the average price level to rise. A reduction in the investment or the consumption function is called for to eliminate the excessive aggregate expenditures. And such a decrease results in a multiple reduction in output. If the reduction does not occur on its own, then the government has a role to play in bringing it about through demand-management policies. Such measures are of the opposite variety to those undertaken in the case of a recessionary gap.

But abstracting from the role of government and confining ourselves to the private sector, the analysis makes clear that an upward shift in the aggregate-expenditures schedule—occasioned by a rise in the investment or the consumption function, or both—increases output by a multiple of that shift. A downward shift does the reverse. Herein lies the explanation of one case of self-justifying expectations. Suppose consumers expect a recession and unemployment to occur. To protect themselves against such a contingency, they become more thrifty; out of any given income, each consumer saves more for a "rainy day." This raises the savings function and correspondingly lowers the consumption and therefore the aggregate-expenditures function. In turn, the latter reduction causes a multiple decline in output and employment. The feared recession sets in. And savings decline by moving downward along the savings function.

Although a single consumer can protect herself against a "rainy day" by increasing savings, consumers in the aggregate cannot. For by increasing savings out of a given level of income, they bring about the rainy day they fear. This is sometimes referred to as a "fallacy of composition": What is true for one person is not necessarily true for all people in the economy put together.

SUMMARY

This chapter introduces the important concept of the multiplier, labeled k. A given permanent increase or decrease in investments raises or lowers output or income by a multiple of the primary change in I. The immediate effect of the primary change in investment is to change income by the same amount, and the ΔI continues during subsequent periods. But since consumption is positively related to income, the change in income generates induced changes in consumption, the extent of which depends on the MPC. The process continues in subsequent periods through successive rounds of spending, where at each round, part of the income is withdrawn from the income stream in the form of savings. The extent of the withdrawal or leakage depends on the size of the MPS. The multiplier is defined as the ratio between the total change in income and the primary change in investment, and its size is equal to the inverse of the MPS. The multiplier formula is:

$$k = \Delta Y / \Delta I = \frac{1}{\text{MPS}} = \frac{1}{1 - \text{MPC}}$$

The effect of the multiplier finds diagrammatic expression in the savings and investment approach. As we shift the investment function, the economy moves from one equilibrium point to another, with equilibrium being determined by the equality of planned savings and investment. The change in income between the two equilibrium is a multiple of the primary change in investment that brought it about.

Given the size of the multiplier and the GDP gap, we can determine by how much investment (or the consumption function) must rise in order to eliminate the excess capacity and unemployment when $Y_{FE} > Y_E$; or by how much investment must fall to eliminate the excess aggregate expenditures when $Y_E > Y_{FE}$. Two terms are defined:

$$\text{Recessionary gap} = \frac{\text{GDP gap}}{k} = \frac{Y_{FE} - Y_E}{k}, \text{ when } Y_{FE} > Y_E$$

In words, a recessionary gap occurs when full-employment output exceeds equilibrium output. The gap is the difference between the two outputs, divided by the multiplier.

$$\text{Inflationary gap} = \frac{\text{GDP gap}}{k} = \frac{Y_E - Y_{FE}}{k}, \text{ when } Y_E > Y_{FE}$$

In words, an inflationary gap occurs when equilibrium output exceeds full-employment output. The gap is the difference between the two, divided by the multiplier.

Demand-management policies are measures designed to influence the level of economic activity by bringing about changes in aggregate expenditures: increasing the investment and/or the consumption function in the case of a recessionary gap, and reducing them in the case of an inflationary gap. The objective is to change aggregate expenditures by the amount of these gaps and no more. Because of the multiplier effect, such changes would close the GDP gap. One does not want to overshoot the mark.

Individual consumers can protect themselves against unemployment by increasing savings, but consumers in the aggregate cannot; for by doing so, they bring about the very unemployment they fear.

QUESTIONS AND PROBLEMS

1. Following are values (in billions of dollars) for planned consumption and investment at alternative levels of GDP for a certain economy (in which there is no government and no foreign trade):

Possible Level of GDP	Planned Consumption	Planned Savings	Investment Schedule
240	200		20
190	160		20
140	120		20
90	80		20

a. Calculate the savings schedule.

b. What would the equilibrium level of income be? Demonstrate why the GDP would gravitate toward this equilibrium level.

c. Show graphically the equilibrium GDP in terms of the savings-investment diagram.

d. How large are the marginal propensities to save and to consume and the multiplier?

e. Suppose the full-employment level of income is 190; how big is the GDP gap? How big is the inflationary or recessionary gap, and which is it?

2. The following values (in billions of dollars) are for the U.S. economy, which is assumed to have no government or foreign trade.

Possible Level of GDP	Planned Consumption	Planned Savings	Investment Schedule
285	220		25
235	190		25
185	160		25
135	130		25

a. Calculate the savings schedule for the table.

b. Calculate the level of aggregate expenditures at each level of GDP.

c. State and explain the equilibrium level of GDP.

d. Calculate the marginal propensity to consume and the multiplier for the table. Show your work!

e. Calculate the inflationary or recessionary gap that would exist in the economy shown in the table for: (i) a full-employment level of GDP of $285 billion; and (ii) a full-employment level of GDP of $135 billion. For each, indicate whether the gap is inflationary or recessionary, the amount of the gap (not merely the amount of the GDP gap), and briefly, how your answer was obtained.

f. Suppose investment increases permanently from 25 to 45 (ΔI = 20), with $Y_{FE} = 285$.

i. What is the effect of the increase on income (output), consumption, and savings?

ii. Draw the information in the table above and the increase in investment on the savings and investment panel, and explain your results.

iii. What is the inflationary or recessionary gap (which is it?) once the new equilibrium output (Y_E) is reached?

3. What is meant by the "fallacy of composition" in the context on increased savings?

APPENDIX TO CHAPTER 17

Diagrammatic Presentation—The Two Approaches

The results obtained in the text by using the savings-investment approach to income determination can be duplicated by employing the aggregate supply and expenditures approach. A rise in investment is shown on the upper panel of Figure A17–1 by shifting upward the aggregate expenditures ($C + I_n$) function where the vertical shift equals ΔI (100 billion). On the upper panel, aggregate expenditures rises from $C + I_1$ to $C + I_2$, with a corresponding increase in investment, from I_1 to I_2. On both panels equilibrium income rises from $1.9 trillion to $2.4 trillion, or by $500 billion. The multiplier is 5.

Inspection of the upper panel reveals that a similar result would follow from an upward shift in the *entire consumption function.* That raises aggregate expenditures

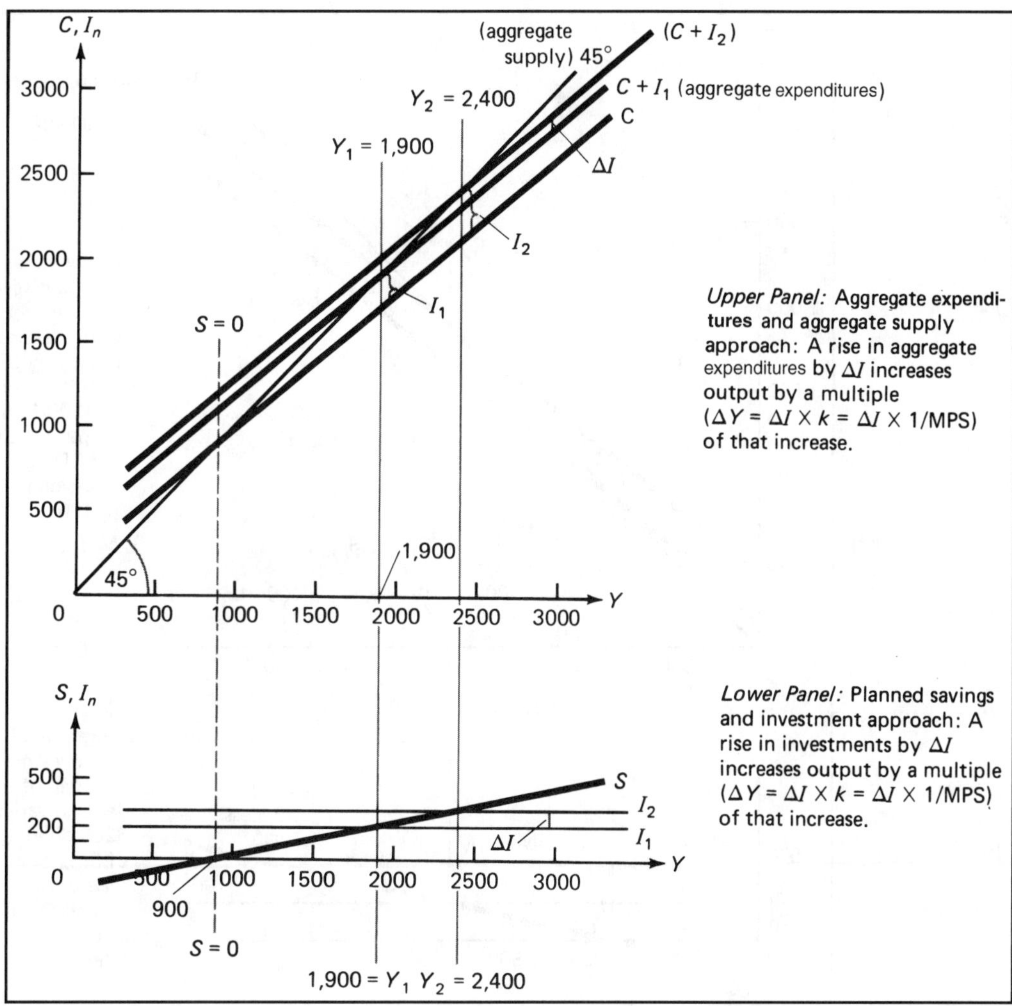

Figure A17–1 An Increase Investment, ΔI, Raises Equilibrium Income from Y_1 to Y_2: The two approaches to income determination correspond to each other.

(vertically) by the full extent of the shift, and has a multiplied effect on income. On the lower panel, it is manifested by a corresponding downward shift in the savings function, with an identical effect on income. The reader is invited to experiment by sketching such a shift and examining the effect on income.

Figures A17–2 and A17–3 describe a recessionary and an inflationary gap, respectively, using (in each case) the two complementary approaches to income determination: the aggregate expenditures and aggregate supply approach on the top panel, and the planned savings and investment approach on the bottom panel.

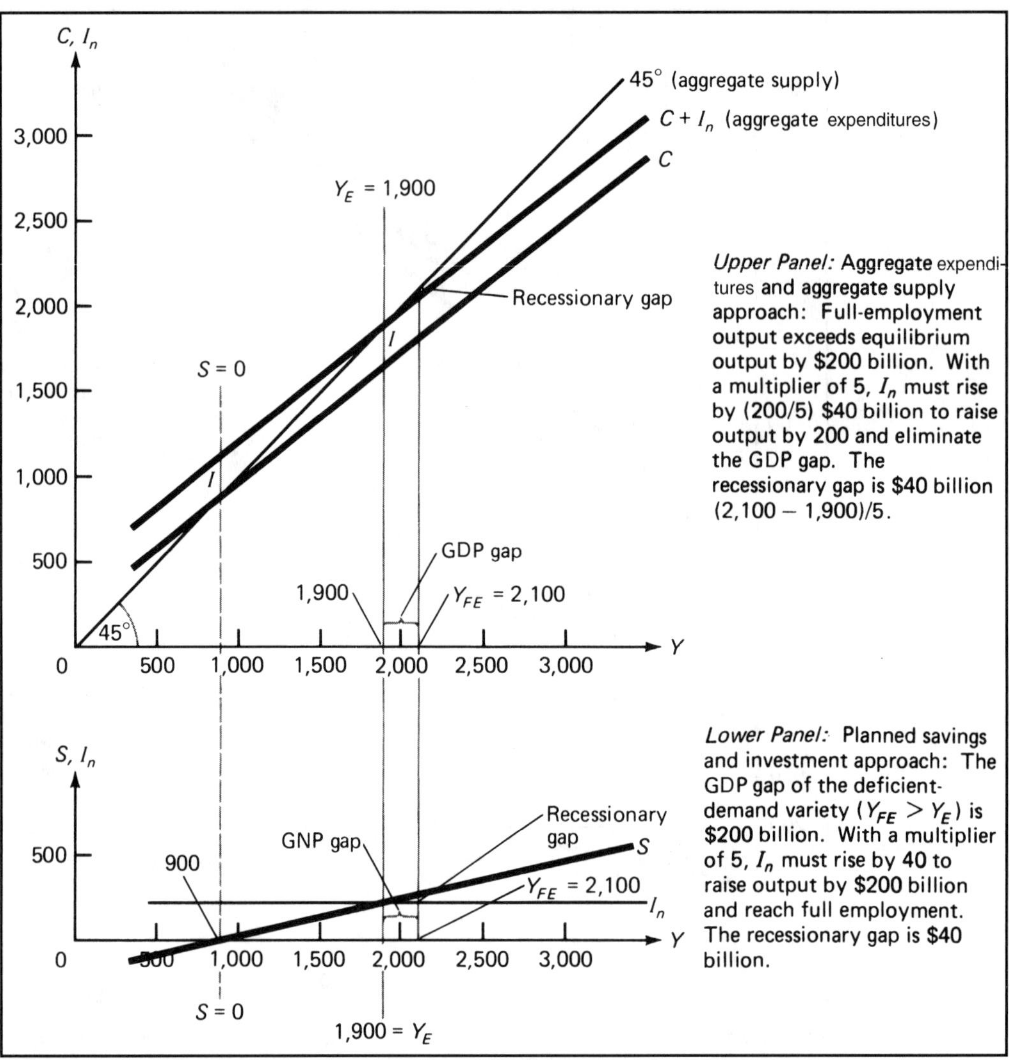

Figure A17–2 Recessionary Gap when Y_E = \$1,900 Billion, Y_{FE} = \$2,100 Billion, and MPS = 0.2 (k = 5)

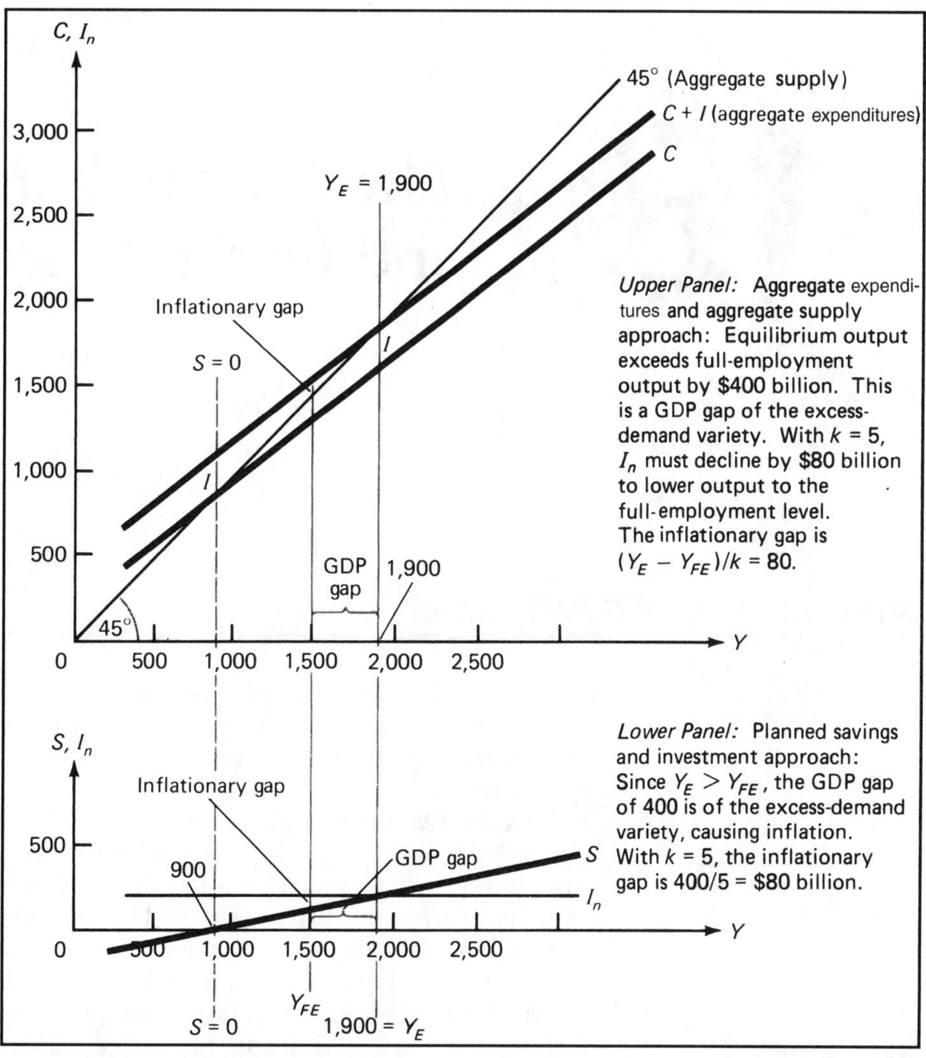

Figure A17–3 Inflationary Gap when Y_E = \$1,900 Billion Y_{FE} = \$1,500 Billion, and MPS = 0.2 (k = 5)

PROBLEMS

Refer to questions 1c and 2f at the end of Chapter 17. In each case, extend your graph to show both the aggregate expenditures and supply approach (top panel) and the corresponding savings-investment approach (bottom panel).

18 The Government Sector and Fiscal Policy

INTRODUCTION OF GOVERNMENT

We return now to the "closed-economy" case, and extend the previous analysis to incorporate the public or government sector. For the moment, we center our attention on the federal rather than state or local government.

There are two sides to government activity in the economy, and these are reflected in its budget. First, it spends money on a variety of social programs, national defense, and the like. Most of these expenditures consist of purchases from the private sector. For the purpose of analyzing their effect on the aggregate level of economic activity, we lump all government expenditures together and label them G. Second, the government collects a variety of direct and indirect taxes from individuals and business firms. All government tax revenues are lumped together and labeled T. *An excess of expenditures over tax revenues is a* **budgetary deficit**; *an excess of revenues over expenditures is a* **budgetary surplus**.

Budgetary deficit: Excess of government outlay's or expenditures (G) over tax revenues (T).

Budgetary surplus: Excess of tax revenue over government expenditures. While T is a positive function of income, G is determined politically, and (like I) is invariant with respect to income.

Introduction of taxes nullifies the equality between disposable income, personal income, national income, and GDP. Given the personal income tax, disposable income (DI) is no longer equal to personal income (PI). Rather, PI is greater than DI. But the equality between personal income, national income, and GDP remains, because of our assumption that all taxes are levied upon and collected from individuals. The assumption that business firms pay no taxes is similar to the assumption embodied in Chapter 14 that only households, and not business organizations, save. In fact, businesses do pay taxes (such as the corporate profit tax), and they do save—say, in the form of undistributed corporate profits. But the assumption simplifies the discussion while enabling us to gain important insights.

Fiscal policy: Changing government expenditures (G) and/or taxes (T) in order to achieve and maintain full-employment without inflation. A rise (reduction) in G raises (lowers) GDP. A rise (reduction) in T lowers (raises) GDP.

If equilibrium output in the economy (Y_E) does not coincide with full-employment equilibrium (Y_{FE}), the government has a role to play in pushing the economy toward full employment. One main tool for accomplishing this task is **fiscal policy.** It means **changing government expenditures and/or government taxes with a view toward attaining and maintaining full employment without inflation.** These issues are addressed in this and the next chapter.

GOVERNMENT EXPENDITURES

We begin the analysis by concentrating on the expenditures side, and assuming for the moment no taxes.

The Expenditures Schedule

A variety of factors determine the level of government expenditures. They include the social consensus (as manifested in the political process) about the desirability of social programs, the need for national defense and for foreign programs affecting the international standing of the United States, the perceived desire for a space program, and the like. Many government expenditures, such as the agricultural support program, interest on the federal debt, Social Security outlays, and veterans' benefits, are mandated by law and cannot be changed from one year to the next. Others are subject to annual modifications. In the annual budget-making process, individual expenditure items are recommended by various agencies in the administration and approved by the appropriate congressional committees, and then by Congress. An overall view of total government expenditures is in the hands of the Office of Management and Budget in the administration and the Congressional Budget Office in Congress.

Not bound by a need to balance the budget annually (see the next chapter), the federal government has considerable leeway in changing government expenditures to accommodate social and defense needs, as well as the needs of the economy. Within a wide range, the government determines the overall level of its expenditures independent of the level of GDP. As a first approximation, it is assumed that *G* is independent of GDP. The government-expenditures schedule is thus described in the *G*–GDP space as a straight horizontal line, shown in Figure 18–1 at $300 billion. Regardless of GDP, government expenditures are the same. The statement that G is invariant with respect to GDP means that **GDP does not affect *G*.** But the reverse is not the case: **Variations in government expenditures have a profound effect on GDP.** For government expenditures involve either the direct hiring of productive factors, such as personnel, or purchases of goods and services, such as military aircraft, from private firms, which in turn cause these companies to hire or buy productive factors. Either way, such expenditures inject new purchasing power into the economy. Consequently, **government expenditures constitute an injection into the income stream,** much the

Figure 18–1 The Government-Expenditures Function: Government expenditures do not depend upon the current level of GDP (but they do affect GDP). At any level of GDP, *G* is the same.

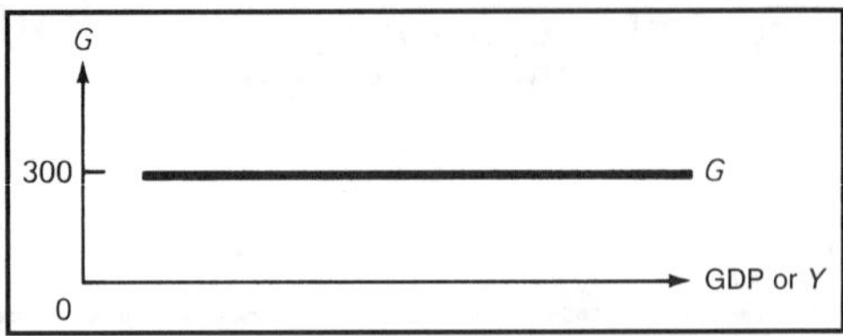

same as investment. In terms of their effect on the aggregate level of economic activity these two types of expenditure are identical.

Equilibrium Output

Ignoring for a moment taxes or, in general, how government expenditures are financed, equilibrium GDP is established by employing the two equivalent approaches used in Chapter 16. It is the level at which all output is sold, the level at which aggregate supply equals aggregate expenditures. However, aggregate expenditures is now extended to incorporate government expenditures, so that equilibrium occurs at the point where:

$$\text{GDP} = C + I_n + G$$

Equivalently, in terms of planned savings and investment, equilibrium output occurs at the point where **Planned S = Planned $(G + I_n)$.**

Only a slight extension of the analysis in Chapter 16 is required to establish this proposition. Table 18–1 presents a modified version of Table 16-1 using strictly hypothetical figures. The schedules for GDP and consumption were changed somewhat from those in Table 16-1; and a column for government expenditures (column 6) was added. The differences between the rows are: $\Delta Y = 500$, $\Delta C = 300$, and $\Delta S = 200$, so that the MPC $= \Delta C/\Delta Y = 0.6$, the MPS $= \Delta S/\Delta Y = 0.4$, and the multiplier is 2.5. At each level of GDP, G is added to I_n to obtain column 7.

Table 18–1 Hypothetical GDP (*Y*) *C*, *S*, I_n, *G* Schedules and the Determination of Equilibrium NDP ($ Billion)

	Employment (Millions of Workers)	Possible Levels of Aggregate Supply GDP (*Y*)	Planned *C*	*S*	I_n	*G*	$I_n + G$	Aggregate Expenditures $(C + I_n + G)$	Change in Inventories	Change in Output	Relation Between Planned *S* and $I_n + G$
	(1)	(2)	(3)	(4)	(5)	(6)	(7)	(8)	(9)	(10)	(11)
(A)	80	1,500	1,400	100	200	300	500	1,900	Depletion	Increase	$(I_n + G) > S$ by 400
(B)	100	2,000	1,700	300	200	300	500	2,200	Depletion	Increase	$(I_n + G) > S$ by 200
(C)	120	2,500	2,000	500	200	300	500	2,500	Constant	Equilibrium	$(I_n + G) = S$
(D)	140	3,000	2,300	700	200	300	500	2,800	Accumulation	Decrease	$(I_n + G) < S$ by 200

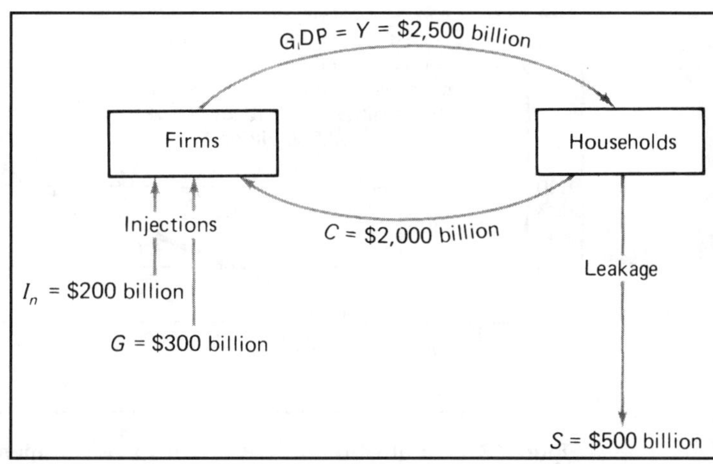

Figure 18–2 Circular-Flow Description of Equilibrium GDP (Row C): The top arrow shows income flow from firms to households (in return for productive services rendered); the bottom arrow shows a payments flow from households to firms (in return for goods and services purchased). Households withdraw savings from the income stream, and firms inject investments into the income stream. In addition, the government injects its expenditures (*G*) into the income stream.

At levels of GDP above $2,500 billion, such as row D, aggregate supply ($3,000 billion) exceeds aggregate expenditures ($2,800 billion), and equivalently planned savings exceeds planned $I_n + G$ by the same amount (column 11). The difference constitutes unintended accumulation of inventories and motivates businesses to contract output, and with it income and employment. At GDP levels below $2,500 billion, such as rows A and B, aggregate expenditures exceeds aggregate supply, and equivalently planned $I_n + G$ exceeds planned S by the same amount. The difference is reflected in unintended depletion of inventories and induces an expansion of output, income, and employment. The reader is invited to repeat the analysis by the use of circular-flow diagrams. When this is done, G should always be added to I_n on the "injection" side. Equilibrium is established at GDP = Y_E = $2,500 billion (row C).

A circular-flow diagram describing this equilibrium (an extension of Figure 16-5) is shown in Figure 18–2. Firms produce $2,500 billion of goods and services (top flow). This is aggregate supply. They sell $2,000 billion to consumers (bottom flow), $200 billion to investors, and $300 billion to the government, for total aggregate expenditures of $2,500 billion. Aggregate supply equals aggregate expenditures. Equivalently, planned savings by households of $500 billion equals planned I_n ($200 billion) plus planned G ($300 billion). There is no change in inventories and hence no incentive to change the level of output. In sum, given the C (and therefore S), I_n and G schedules, a unique equilibrium output is established that meets the preceding condition.

Diagrammatic Exposition The diagrammatic exposition of this equilibrium calls for superimposing G upon I_n. This is done in Figure 18–3, using the planned savings and investment approach. In a strictly private economy, with only S and I_n schedules, equilibrium is at Y_1. By comparing

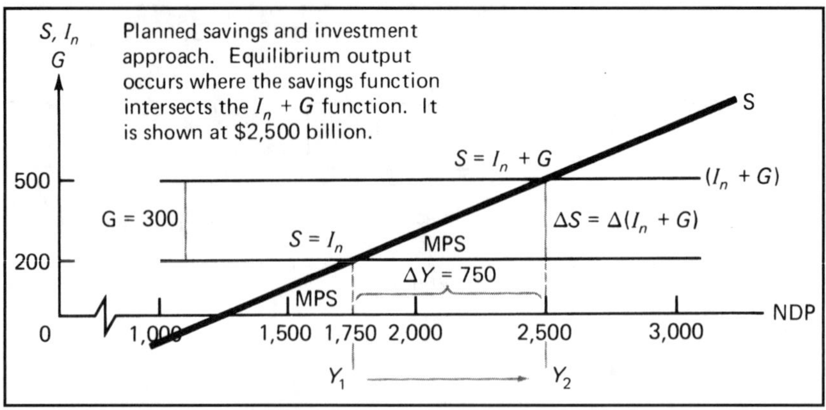

Figure 18–3 Equilibrium GDP or *Y* with Government Expenditures: Introduction of *G* raises equilibrium output or income from Y_1 to Y_2.

columns 4 and 5 of Table 18–1, it can be determined that equality between planned savings and investment occurs at the midpoint between rows A and B, where $S = I_n = \$200$ billion. Equilibrium GDP with a private economy as described here is $1,750 billion. Government expenditures, an injection into the income stream, is now superimposed vertically upon the investment function to produce the $I_n + G$ function. Equilibrium GDP rises to $Y_2 = \$2,500$ billion. At that level of income, a new, higher level of sav-

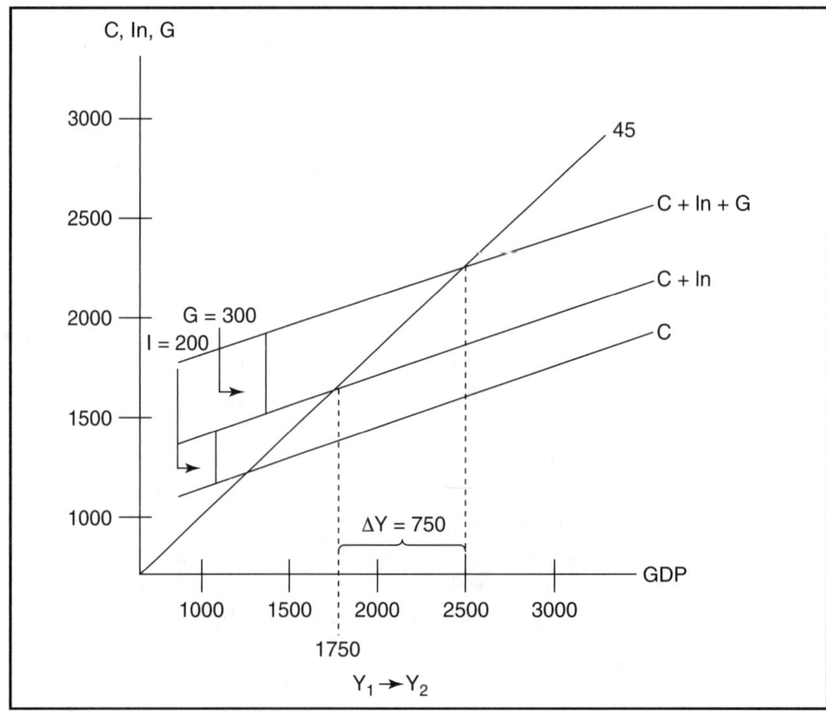

Figure 18–3A: Equilibrium with government expenditures (no taxes). Introduction of G raises output from 1750 to 2500.

ings ($500 billion; see row C) is generated to match $I_n + G$. It follows that $\Delta S = \Delta(I_n + G)$.

As an alternative geometric formulation, but with identical results, super-impose G upon (C + I) in the C, In, G – GDP space (upper panel) to obtain equilibrium GDP at 2,500. This is shown in Fig 18-3a.

Output rose from 1,750 to 2,500 as a result of adding government expenditures (no taxes) to the (C + In) function. The 750 added income reflects a multiplier of 2.5 (namely: 300 × 2.5 = 750). The appendix to Chapter 18 contains a diagrammatic exposition of the two approaches

Government expenditures multiplier: the ratio between the permanent change in output and the change in government expenditures that brought it about. k = 1/MPS

The Government-Expenditures Multiplier

A permanent introduction of, or addition to, government expenditures (all other things remaining unchanged) has a multiplied effect on the economy. The analysis is analogous to that carried out in the case of a rise in investment. Assuming that the economy starts from underemployment equilibrium, then in the period when G is introduced, income rises by the amount of G (or ΔG). In the next period, G continues on the same level. But income recipients from the first period spend on consumption a portion of that income and withdraw the remainder out of the income stream and into savings. The proportion of income so spent and "leaked" depends respectively on the MPC and MPS prevailing in the economy. In the third period, G continues. But income recipients from the second-round spenders spend part of their receipts on consumption—the proportion depending on the MPC—and save the rest. And so the process continues through the successive, and ever-decreasing, rounds of spending. And GDP converges on a new, higher level. The multiplier is again:

$$k = \frac{1}{\text{MPS}} = \frac{1}{1 - \text{MPC}}$$

In the example of Table 18–1 and Figure 18–3, the newly introduced government-expenditures amount is $300 ($G$ = 300) and the MPC = 0.6, yielding a multiplier of 1/0.4 = 2.5. As a result, GDP increases by 300 × 2.5 = $750 billion once the succession of spending rounds is completed.

Although these examples involved introduction of government spending into an otherwise private economy, the same analysis applies to *changes* in the level of government expenditures. Such changes have a multiplied effect on GDP: **A rise in government expenditures increases GDP and a reduction in such expenditures reduces GDP, both by a multiple of that change.**

Policy Implications

Since the federal government has control over its aggregate level of expenditures, variations in government expenditures can be used to *stabilize* the economy; that is, to move the economy toward a position of full employment without inflation. It is the first tool of fiscal policy. If the economy is in underemployment equilibrium (especially if it is in region I of AS), then the GDP gap can be divided by the multiplier to compute the *recessionary gap.* A rise in government expenditures by the amount of that gap would increase output to the full-employment level. For example, suppose the schedules shown in Table 18–1 prevailed in the economy, producing equilibrium GDP at $2,500 billion. If full-employment income (Y_{FE}) were $2,600 billion, then the GDP gap would be $100 billion, and of the inadequate-aggregate-expenditures variety. Given a multiplier of 2.5 [1/(1 – MPC) = 1/(1 – 0.6) = 1/0.4 = 2.5], the recessionary gap is 100/2.5 = $40 billion. A rise in government expenditures by $40 billion, from $300 billion to $340 billion, would push the economy to full employment GDP of $2,600 billion. In this case, government expenditures are used to make up for insufficient aggregate expenditures.

Conversely, if the economy suffers from "excessive" aggregate expenditures and an attendant rise in prices, then a reduction in government expenditures can be used to dampen that demand. Suppose again that the situation in Table 18–1 described the initial status of the economy, with equilibrium output set at $2,500 billion, but that full employment GDP (Y_{FE}) was at $2,425 billion. Then there would be a GDP gap to the tune of $75 billion of the excessive-aggregate-expenditures variety. With a multiplier of 2.5, this implies an inflationary gap of 75/2.5 = $30 billion, calling for a reduction of government expenditures by the same amount to eliminate the excess expenditures and curb the inflation.

It goes without saying that government expenditures have other roles to play besides stabilizing the economy. These include the provision of social goods and services such as national defense and redistribution of income from the rich to the poor. And since part of government expenditures is mandated by law and not subject to annual changes, it is not always easy to alter government spending as an economic stabilization measure. When such an alteration *is* decided upon, it is also necessary to reach a social consensus, through the political process, concerning the programs whose size ought to be changed in response to the overall economic situation. Certainly **it is easier to raise government expenditures in times of unemployment than to lower them in times of excessive aggregate expenditures,** because the beneficiaries of government programs usually object to any reduction in their size or scope. Every program has a constituency with varying degrees of political clout, These are some of the social and political constraints on the use of *G* as a tool of fiscal policy.

When President Reagan came to office in 1981, he vowed to reduce spending by amounts that would more than match the tax cut he initiated. But with his commitment to national defense, defense expenditures were increased considerably. Interest on the federal debt, amounting to $152 billion in 1988, cannot be touched; it can decline only with a reduction in market interest rates. The massive Social Security expenditures, which are indexed to the CPI, can be reduced only by politically sensitive legislation, as is the case with the agricultural support program. Payments by the government to individuals through such politically popular programs as Social Security, railroad retirement, federal employees' retirement, unemployment compensation, Medicare and Medicaid, housing assistance, food stamps, public assistance, and Supplemental Security

Income are sometimes called "entitlement programs." They are all difficult to curtail.

About three-quarters of government expenditures are considered uncontrollable; they cannot be reduced substantially without politically sensitive legislation. This explains the great difficulty encountered by Presidents Reagan and Carter in trying to reduce the size of government expenditures.

Notwithstanding these limitations, and however imperfect the tool, variations in *G* are used to stabilize the economy.

GOVERNMENT TAXES (*T*)

Taxes are levied on individual households (business taxes are assumed not to exist, for the sake of simplicity) and are received by government. The funds so withdrawn from the economy **constitute a leakage out of the income stream.** In that sense, they *play a role similar to savings* and the reverse of government expenditures.

Progressive, Proportional, and Regressive Taxes

Because the amount of taxes a person pays depends on the person's income, total tax revenue collected by the government is positively related to income. However, the extent to which taxes rise as income increases can vary widely. In particular, three gradations are distinguished that describe the change in tax *rates* (or the *proportion* of income paid in taxes) as income rises. The tax rate is *progressive, proportional,* or *regressive,* depending on whether the proportion (percentage) of *income* paid in taxes *rises, remains constant,* or *declines* as income increases. It is the *proportion* of *income* paid in taxes that distinguishes among the three cases, not the absolute dollar amount paid. These distinctions were discussed in Chapter 3; the student is advised to review them at this point.

The Tax Function

Tax function: The positive relationship between income and tax revenue where income is the independent variable (horizontal-axis) and taxes paid is the dependent variable(vertical-axis). When the tax rate (percent of income paid in taxes) rises, remains constant, or declines as income rises, the tax is called, respectively, progressive, proportional (flat-rate) or regressive.

The personal income tax is levied mainly by the federal government, but also by some of the states. The **tax function** describes a relation between income and taxes, both measured in terms of dollars. Three such possible functions are plotted on the income-tax space in Figure 18–4. The bottom panel displays a regressive tax. The tax is fixed in absolute dollar amount (at $5,000), so that its ratio to income declines as income rises. In the middle panel, the proportion of tax to income is constant at 20 percent as income rises. In the top panel, the proportion of income paid in tax rises as income rises: It is 15 percent at $20,000 income and 30 percent at $50,000 income. The function represents a progressive tax.

Figure 18–4 Diagrammatic Presentation of Three Hypothetical Income Tax Schedules ($ Thousand): Income is measured on the horizontal axis and taxes on the vertical axis.

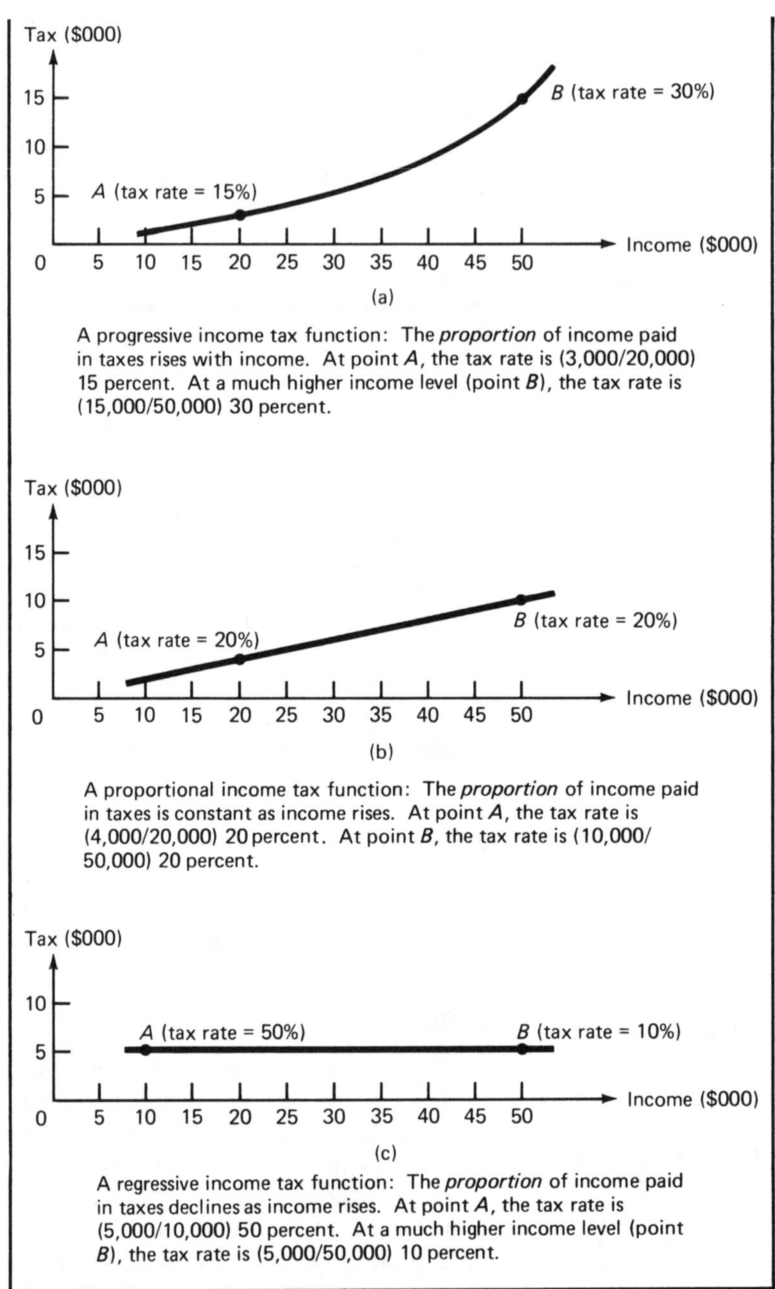

Tax ($000)
15
10
5
0
B (tax rate = 30%)
A (tax rate = 15%)
5 10 15 20 25 30 35 40 45 50
Income ($000)
(a)
A progressive income tax function: The *proportion* of income paid in taxes rises with income. At point *A*, the tax rate is (3,000/20,000) 15 percent. At a much higher income level (point *B*), the tax rate is (15,000/50,000) 30 percent.
Tax ($000)
15
10
5
0
B (tax rate = 20%)
A (tax rate = 20%)
5 10 15 20 25 30 35 40 45 50
Income ($000)
(b)
A proportional income tax function: The *proportion* of income paid in taxes is constant as income rises. At point *A*, the tax rate is (4,000/20,000) 20 percent. At point *B*, the tax rate is (10,000/50,000) 20 percent.
Tax ($000)
10
5
0
A (tax rate = 50%)
B (tax rate = 10%)
5 10 15 20 25 30 35 40 45 50
Income ($000)
(c)
A regressive income tax function: The *proportion* of income paid in taxes declines as income rises. At point *A*, the tax rate is (5,000/10,000) 50 percent. At a much higher income level (point *B*), the tax rate is (5,000/50,000) 10 percent.

Equilibrium Output with a Government Sector

Table 18–2 adds a proportional tax of 17 percent to the analysis of Table 18–1, thereby incorporating both sides of government activities: taxes and expenditures. The four possible levels of GDP or income remain as before

Table 18–2 Hypothetical GDP, T, C, S, in, G Schedules and the Determination of Equilibrium NDP ($ Billion)

	Possible Levels of GDP = Y	T(17% of Y)	Disposable Income (Y - T)	C	Y-T-C 11 S	T + S	I_n	G	$I_n + G$	Aggregate Expenditures ($C + I_n + G$)	Change in Inventories	Change in Output	Relation Between S + T and $I_n + G$
	(1)	*(2)*	*3(=1 - 2)*	*(4)*	*(5)*	*6(=2 + 5)*	*(7)*	*(8)*	*9(=7 + 8)*	*10(=4 + 7 + 8)*	*(11)*	*(12)*	*(13)*
(A)	1,500	255	1,245	1,247	−2	253	204	300	504	1,751	Depletion	Increase	$(I_n + G)>(S + T)$ by 251
(B)	2,000	340	1,660	1,496	164	504	204	300	504	2,000	Constant	Equilibrium	$(I_n + G)=(S + T)$
(C)	2,500	425	2,075	1,745	330	755	204	300	504	2,249	Accumulation	Decrease	$(I_n + G)<(S + T)$ by 251
(D)	3,000	510	2,490	1,994	496	1,006	204	300	504	2,498	Accumulation	Decrease	$(I_n + G)<(S + T)$ by 502

Notes: This table assumes a *proportional* income tax rate of 17%. Applied to Y in col. 1, it generates the taxes shown in col. 2, where ΔT between rows is constant at $85 billion, yielding a linear positive tax function. Disposable income, shown in col. 3, is obtained by subtracting government tax revenue from NDP. Between rows, $\Delta Y = 500$; $\Delta T = 85$; $\Delta DI = 415$; $\Delta C = 249$; $\Delta S = 166$. All functions are linear for simplicity.

The MPC out of disposable income is 249/415 = 0.6
The MPS out of disposable income is 166/415 = 0.4 } Total = 1

The MPC out of *Y* is 259/500 = 0.498
The MPS out of *Y* is 166/500 = 0.332
The tax rate out of Y is 0.170 } Total = 1

(The multiplier, *k*, with respect to *Y* is $= \dfrac{1}{1 - \text{MPC}} = \dfrac{1}{1 - 498} \approx 2$)

Average propensities can be calculated by the reader for each row.
The figure for I_n was modified slightly to 204 ($I_n + G = 504$) for the sake of computational accuracy.

Table 18–3 Analysis of Row A in Table 18–2

Aggregate Supply and Expenditures Approach		Planned and Realized S + T and I_n + G Approach			
Aggregate Supply (GDP)	$1,500 billion	$S + T$		$I_n + G$	
Aggregate expenditures			Planned		
C = $1,247 billion		S = $–2 billion		I_n =	$204 billion
I_n = $ 204 billion		T = $255 billion	<	G =	$300 billion
G = $ 300 billion		$S + T$ = $253 billion		$(I_n + G)$ =	$504 billion
	$1,751 billion				
			Realized		
Excess of aggregate expenditures over aggregate supply	$ 251 billion			Planned $I_n + G$ =	$504 billion
				Unplanned $I_n + G$ = (depletion of inventories) −	$251 billion
		$S + T$ = $253 billion	=	Total	$253 billion

(column 1), but the personal tax (column 2) now drives a wedge between national or personal income (Y) and disposable income (DI) At each level of GDP, DI is lower than Y by the amount of the tax, which itself grows with income.

Because taxes, like savings, constitute a leakage out of the income stream, it is possible to add taxes to savings and thus extend the analysis. But the change involved is not as straightforward as was the addition of G to I_n. Since consumption and savings are functions of disposable income, which is now smaller than Y, their functional relation to national income changes. In the case of the hypothetical figures in Table 18–2, the MPC and MPS out of disposable income remain 0.6 and 0.4, respectively. But because of the income tax of 0.17 of Y, the MPC and MPS out of Y are now 0.498 and 0.332 respectively. The average propensities with respect to Y also decline. All this yields smaller consumption and savings figures (columns 4 and 5) than in Table 18–1 and is explained in the notes at the bottom of Table 18–2. Columns 6–9 are self-explanatory.

Row A Consider row A of Table 18–2. GDP or aggregate supply of goods and services is $1,500 billion, and an equal amount of income is generated in the productive process. Out of this income, households pay $255 billion (1,500 × 17%) in taxes, leaving them with disposable income of $1,245 billion. These taxes constitute a leakage out of the income stream. Out of their DI, households spend $1,247 billion on consumption and dissave $2 billion. In turn, business firms invest $204 billion and the government spends $300 billion, both these items constituting injections into the income stream. This is summarized in the circular-flow diagram of Figure 18–5 below, where the top flow shows output or income and the bottom flow shows consumption.

Aggregate expenditures is $1,751, consisting of consumption of $1,247, investments of $204 billion, and government purchases of goods and services of $300 billion. Aggregate supply is $1,500; it is short of aggregate expenditures by $251 billion. The excess of aggregate expenditures over aggregate supply is provided out of inventories; it represents depletion of inventories. And such a depletion induces firms to increase orders from the factories, bringing about expansion of output and income.

Equivalent results are obtained from the planned savings and investment approach, now modified to incorporate $S + T$ and $I_n + G$. At the

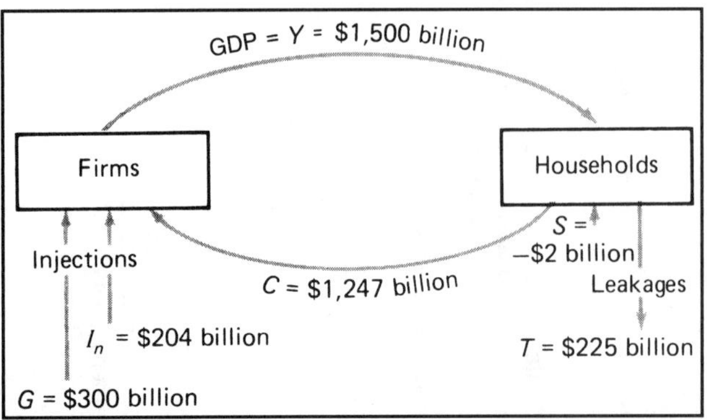

Figure 18–5 Circular-Flow Description of Row A in Table 18–3: Top and bottom arrows are, respectively, payments from firms to households for productive services rendered and payments from households to firms for goods and services purchased. Savings (in this case negative) *and taxes* are leakages from the income stream, and investments and government expenditures constitute injections into the income stream.

beginning of the period, looking ahead, households plan to pay $255 billion in taxes (on projected income of $1,500 billion) and save –$2 billion, firms plan to invest $204 billion, and the government plans to spend $300 billion, for a total injection of $504 billion. The excess of the injections over the leakages (column 13 of Table 18–2) is $251 billion, and it equals the excess of aggregate expenditures over aggregate supply, or the depletion of inventories. Since a change in inventories is counted as a part of investment, the total injections equal the total leakages in a realized sense. The two approaches are summarized in Table 18–3 on page 301.

It is the unplanned $251 billion depletion of inventories that brings the unequal $S + T$ and $I_n + G$ plans into equality in a realized sense. But such a depletion induces an expansion of output and income. Given the schedules in Table 18–2, $1,500 billion is not equilibrium GDP. It will rise, say, to $2,000 billion.

Row C As a reverse case, consider row C. Firms produce $2,500 billion of goods and services, generating an equal amount of income for households. Out of that income, households pay $425 billion in taxes, leaving them with disposable income of $2,075 billion. They spend $1,745 billion on consumption and save $330 billion. In turn, firms invest $204 billion, and the government buys goods and services to the tune of $300 billion, for a total injection of $504 billion. This information is summarized in the circular-flow diagram of Figure 18–6, where the top flow shows output or income and the bottom flow shows consumption.

Aggregate supply is $2,500 billion and aggregate expenditures are $2,249 billion, consisting of consumption of $1,745 billion, investment of $204 billion, and government expenditures of $300 billion. The excess of aggregate supply over aggregate expenditures, $251 billion, represents addition to inventories. This situation is not sustainable; firms will not go on producing output that cannot be sold. Orders from the factories diminish, and with them output, income and employment.

Equivalent results follow from the planned leakage ($S + T$) and injection ($I_n + G$) approach. At the beginning of the year, looking ahead, house-

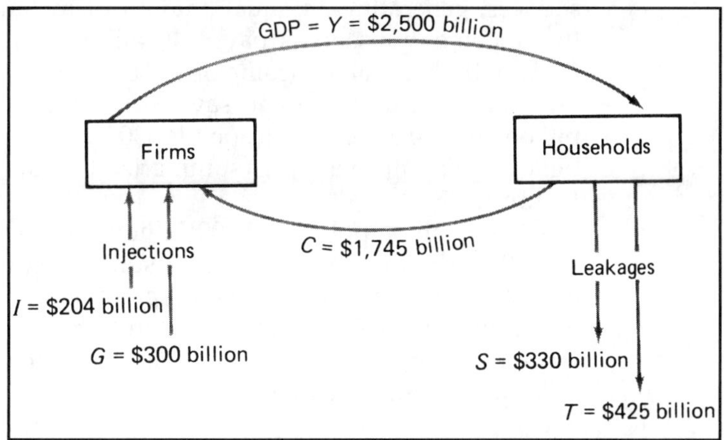

Figure 18–6 Circular-Flow Description of Row C in Table 18–2

Table 18–4 Analysis of Row C In Table 18–2

Aggregate Supply and Expenditures Approach		Planned and Realized $S + T$ and $I_n + G$ Approach			
Aggregate Supply (GDP)	$2,500 billion	$S + T$			$I_n + G$
Aggregate expenditures			Planned		
C = $1,745 billion		S = $330 billion		I_n =	$240 billion
I_n = $ 204 billion		T = $425 billion		G =	$300 billion
G = $ 300 billion		$S + T$ = $755 billion	>	$(I_n + G)$ =	$504 billion
	$2,249 billion				
			Realized		
Excess of aggregate supply over aggregate expenditures	$ 251 billion		Planned	$I_n + G$ =	$504 billion
			Unplanned (addition to inventories)	$I_n + G$ =	$251 billion
		$S + T$ = $755 billion	=	Total	$755 billion

holds plan to pay $425 billion in taxes (out of projected income of $2,500 billion) and to save $330 billion. In turn, firms plan to invest $204 billion and the government plans to purchase $300 billion in goods and services. Planned $S + T$ exceeds planned $I_n + G$ by $251 billion—precisely the excess of aggregate supply over aggregate expenditures—which is added to inventories. Since additions to inventories are counted as a part of investment, the $S + T$ equals $I_n + G$ in a realized sense. The two approaches are summarized in Table 18–4.

It is the unplanned $251 billion addition to inventories that brings the unequal leakages $(S + T)$ and injections $(I_n + G)$ plans into equality in a realized sense. The change in inventories serves as a "valve," a regulatory mechanism, of the level of economic activity. Accumulation of inventories induces firms to reduce orders from the factories; output contracts. Given the schedules of Table 18–2, GDP of $2,500 billion is not equilibrium output. It contracts, say, to $2,000 billion.

Row B: Equilibrium In row B, firms produce $2,000 billion of goods and services, generating an equal amount of income for households. Out of that income, households pay $340 billion in taxes (17 percent), leaving them with disposable income of $1,660 billion. Of that, they spend $1,496 billion on consumption and save $164 billion. In turn, firms invest $204 billion and the government spends $300 billion, for a total injection of $504 billion. This information is summarized in the circular-flow diagram of Figure 18–7.

Aggregate supply is $2,000 billion, and aggregate expenditures are also $2,000 billion, consisting of consumption of $1,496 billion, investment of $204 billion, and government spending of $300 billion. Precisely the entire output is sold to consumers, investors, and the government. There is no change in inventories, and no incentive to change the level of output; it is equilibrium GDP or Y.

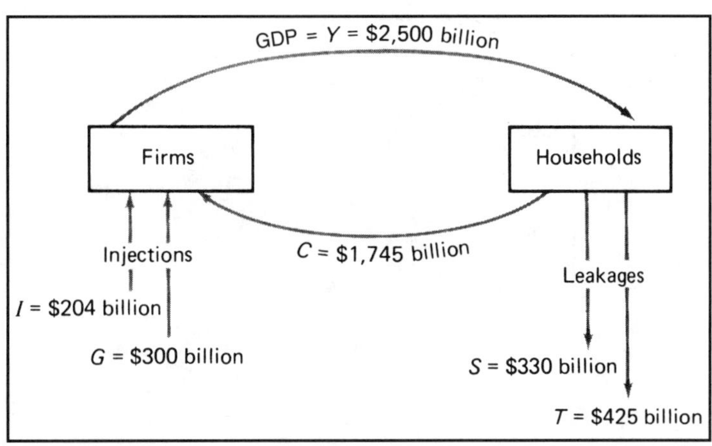

Figure 18–7 Circular-Flow Description of Row B in Table 18–3

Identical results from the leakage and injection approach. At the beginning of the year, looking ahead, households plan to save \$164 billion and to pay \$340 billion in taxes, for a planned total leakage of \$504 billion. Planned injections also add up to \$504 billion. (I_n = \$204 billion; G = \$300 billion). No change in inventories is necessary to bring the leakage and the injection into equality; they are equal in a planned sense, indicating equilibrium GDP. This information is summarized in Table 18–5.

To sum up, given the schedules of Table 18–2, there is only one unique level of GDP toward which the economy gravitates and at which it settles. Once attained, that level is sustainable. The equilibrium is at GDP = \$2 trillion. At that GDP, government tax revenue (T) is \$340 billion and government spending (G) is \$300 billion, so that the government budget has a surplus of \$40 billion.

In sum, **equilibrium GDP is the level at which aggregate supply equals aggregate expenditures**, where aggregate expenditures consists of $C + I_n + G$. **Equivalently, it is the level at which planned $S + T$ equals planned $I_n + G$.** (In a realized sense, they are always equal.) The latter result follows also from the national income accounts:

Table 18–5 Analysis of Row C In Table 18–2

Aggregate Supply and Expenditures Approach		Planned and Realized $S + T$ and $I_n + G$ Approach		
Aggregate supply	\$2,000 billion	$S + T$		$I_n + G$
Aggregate expenditures:			Planned	
C = \$1,496 billion		S = \$164 billion		I_n = \$204 billion
I_n = \$ 204 billion		T = \$340 billion		G = \$300 billion
G = \$ 300 billion		$S + T$ = \$504 billion	=	($I_n + G$) = \$504 billion
	\$2,000 billion			
			Realized	
Excess of aggregate supply over expenditures	0	$S + T$ = \$504 billion	= Planned	$I_n + G$ = \$504 billion
			No change in inventories	

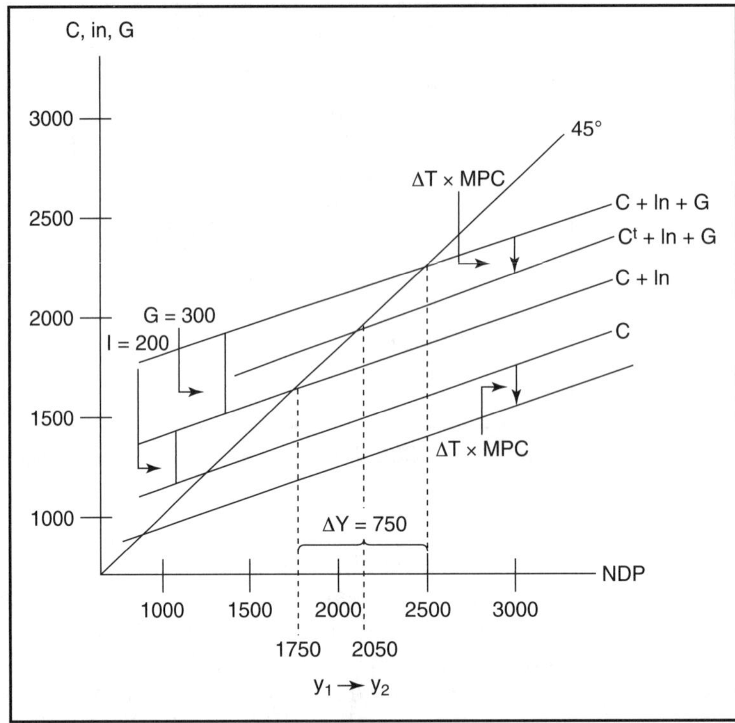

Figure 18–8 Equilibrium output with both government expenditures (G) and taxes (T). Private economy (C + I_n) equilibrium output is at 1,750. Addition of G = 300 raises it to 2500 (C + I + G). Adding taxes of 300 reduces the consumption function by (300 ¥ 0.6=) 180, so that the (C + I_n + G) function declines by the same amount, and equilibrium output drops to 2,050.

$$GDP = C + I_n + G \quad \text{Expenditures side}$$
$$GDP = C + S + T \quad \text{Income side}$$
$$\therefore I_n + G = S + T$$

Fiscal policy and taxes: Taxes are another tool of fiscal policy. An increase in tax rates reduces output, but by a smaller amount than a decrease in government expenditures. Conversely, a decrease in taxes increases output but by a smaller amount than a rise in government expenditures would. ΔGDP = ΔT(MPC) times k. A reduction in tax rates lead to government budget deficits while an increase in tax rates lead to budget surpluses.

Diagrammatic Exposition

It is most convenient to show the effect of taxes by using the upper panel of our diagram. Suppose the government introduces $300 billion in personal income taxes to match the expenditures of G = $300 billion. The effect of that would be to leave $300 billion **less** in the hands of consumers to spend. Namely, disposable income is now $300 billion **less** that the national income. Introduction of income tax reduces DI for any given level of Y. And that would induce consumers (at any level of income) to cut consumption—BUT NOT BY THE FULL AMOUNT OF THE TAX. For if the MPC is 0.6, consumption would decline by 300 × 0.6 = $180 billion while savings would diminish by 300 × 0.4 = $120 billion (MPS = 0.4). Unlike G, introduction of T has no immediate, direct impact on aggregate spending. It simply leaves less income for consumers to spend and they would cut spending by (ΔT × MPC). A tax cut leaves more money in their hand to spend and they would increase spending by (–ΔT × MPC).

Herein lie two essential differences between G and T:

a. they affect output (and income) in opposite directions. A rise in G increases output through a rise in aggregate expenditures and a reduction in G has the opposite effect. By contrast, a rise in T reduces output (and income) and a cut in T increases spending and hence output.

b. the **initial impulse** of a change in G (up or down) equals G itself, and its total effect on output is ΔG times the multiplier, k(= 1/MPS). By contrast, the **initial impulse** of a change in T (up or down) is (ΔT × MPC)—a smaller number because MPC < 1—and its total effect on output is (ΔT × MPC) times the multiplier k (= 1/MPS).

Following up on this discussion, the diagrammatic exposition of T involves lowering the entire consumption function by (T × MPC); along with it, the (C + In) function and the aggregate expenditures (C + In + G) function are lowered by the same amount. This is shown in Figure 18-8. It first reproduces Figure 18-3A which contains G and no T, with equilibrium output at 2,500. As a second step T in the amount of 300 (= G) is added, reducing the total expenditures function by 180 (T × MPC = 300 × 0.6). The new equilibrium output is 2,050; it is reduced by 450 (2,500 – 450 = 2,050). And that number is obtained by multiplying 180 (T × MPC) by the multiplier (k = 1/MPS = 1/0.4 = 2.5).

Introduction of T in equal amounts to G lowered output by NOT ALL THE WAY BACK to 1,750—the private sector equilibrium level. And that's because the initial impulse of G is greater than that of T.

To recapitulate, changes in taxes have an opposite effect on the economy to that of changes in government expenditures. An increase in taxes lowers GDP and a decrease in taxes raises GDP, in both cases by a multiple amount. Even though the multiplier formula is the same for changes in expenditures and taxes, the *multiplicand* is different. A change in *G* has a direct effect on expenditures. Hence, the primary effect on expenditures—the multiplicand in the multiplier formula—is equal to Δ*G*. By contrast, a change in taxes does not directly affect expenditures. Rather, it brings about a shift in the consumption function (in an opposite direction from the changes in taxes), which equals Δ*T* × MPC. Hence, the primary change in expenditures—the multiplicand in the multiplier formula—is lower than the change in taxes; it equals Δ*T* × MPC. It is this latter figure that must be multiplied by *k* to obtain the change in GDP.

These results may now be summarized:

1. *A rise* in government expenditures, other things being held constant, *increases* GDP by the Δ*G* times the multiplier. The rise in expenditures moves the government budget *toward a deficit.*
2. *A reduction* in government expenditures, other things being held constant, *lowers GDP* by the –Δ*G* times the multiplier. The reduction in expenditures moves the government budget *toward a surplus.*
3. A *reduction* in tax rates, other things being held constant, *increases* GDP by the Δ*T* × MPC times the multiplier. The decline in taxes, a source of government revenue, moves the government budget *toward a deficit.*

4. An *increase* in tax rates, other things being held constant, *lowers* GDP by the $\Delta T \times$ MPC times the multiplier. The rise in taxes, a source of government revenue, moves the government budget *toward a* surplus.

Items 1 and 3 suggest that **moving the government budget toward a deficit—through either a tax reduction or an increase in expenditures, or both—has a stimulative effect on the economy.** Conversely, items 2 and 4 show that **moving the government budget toward a surplus—through a tax hike or an expenditure decrease, or both—has a dampening or contractive effect on the economy.**

Policy Implications

Changes in taxes can be used by the government to stabilize the economy. They constitute the second tool of fiscal policy. An inflationary gap calls for a tax hike, to dampen private spending; a recessionary gap calls for a tax cut, to stimulate private spending. In both cases, cognizance should be taken of the multiplier process, and the change in taxes should be less than the GDP gap. One does not want to overshoot the mark. However, a dollar increase in government expenditures has a greater stimulative effect on the economy than has a dollar reduction in taxes. Consequently, **the stimulative effect of a budget deficit of a given size is stronger if the deficit is brought about by a deliberate rise in government spending than by a reduction in taxes.** Conversely, a dollar decrease in government expenditures has a greater dampening effect on the economy than a dollar increase in taxes. Consequently, **the dampening effect of a budgetary surplus of a given size is stronger if the surplus is brought about by a deliberate reduction in government spending than by a rise in taxes.** In both cases, this occurs because the primary change in spending resulting from taxes (the multiplicand) is smaller than that resulting from expenditures.

Historical examples of such government policies are not hard to find. In 1964 a tax cut under President Kennedy, followed a few years later by a rise in military expenditures under President Johnson (during the Vietnam War), produced a prolonged expansion. Similarly, the Reagan tax cut of the early 1980s helped set the stage for the economic expansion of 1983–89. By contrast, experience with a **temporary** change in taxes in the early 1970s was far from satisfactory. Evidently, only permanent changes affect people's spending behavior.

THE BALANCED-BUDGET MULTIPLIER

Suppose that, starting from an underemployment equilibrium, the government increases both expenditures and taxes by $20 billion, so that the government budget is kept in balance (assuming that it started from a balanced position, where expenditures equal taxes): $\Delta T = \Delta G =$ $20 billion. What would be the effect on GDP? The intuitive answer is that the stimulative effect of ΔG and the depressant effect of ΔT would balance each other out, so that the effect would be nil. Not so. For it was demonstrated previously that a one-dollar change in spending has a more powerful effect on the economy than a one-dollar change in taxes. A rise in government spending increases primary spending by ΔG and raises GDP by ΔG times the multiplier. A hike in taxes reduces primary spending by $\Delta T \times$ MPC and decreases GDP by $\Delta T \times$ MPC times the multiplier.

In the example at hand, assume that the MPC = 0.6, so that the multiplier is 2.5. The rise in government expenditures will *increase* GDP by:

$$\Delta \text{GDP} = \Delta G + k = 20 \times 2.5 = \$50 \text{ billion.}$$

Balanced-budget multiplier: Shows the effect on GDP of changing G and T by equal amounts (keeping the budget balanced). This multiplier always equals 1.

The hike in taxes will *decrease* GDP by:

$$-\Delta \text{GDP} = \Delta T \times \text{MPC} \times k = 20 \times 0.6 \times 2.5 = \$30 \text{ billion.}$$

The net effect on output is positive, for the rise in taxes constitutes only a partial offset to the rise in spending. GDP rises by (\$50 billion – \$30 billion) = \$20 billion—precisely the amount of ΔG or ΔT. **Although the government budget is kept in balance, GDP increases by an amount equal to ΔG. The ratio between the two changes is 1:**

$$\Delta \text{GDP}/\Delta G| \text{ when } \Delta T = \Delta G| = 20/20 = 1$$

This ratio is known as the **balanced-budget multiplier,** for it demonstrates the effect on GDP of changing G and T by equal amounts, keeping the budget in balance. *It always equals* 1.[2] The analysis, and hence the multiplier, is equally valid for a reduction in spending and an equal reduction in taxes. It would reduce GDP by the same amount.

THE OPEN-ECONOMY CASE

Chapters 17 and 18 review the case of an economy that has no foreign trade. A hypothetical country without foreign trade is referred to as a "closed" economy. But in fact no such country exists. Even in the United States, with its huge size and diversified resources, exports or imports amount to over one tenth of GDP. And imports include such critical commodities as crude petroleum and other minerals, without which the entire industrial apparatus would come to a halt. In the large European countries, exports constitute a quarter of GDP, and in the small European countries, that ratio is about one half. The latter countries are often referred to as "open" economies, to indicate the high degree to which the country is dependent on foreign trade. Many underdeveloped countries are even more open, with exports making up over 80 percent of GDP.

A short extension of the analysis to open economies is sketched below.[3]

Methodology

Introduction of foreign trade requires adding exports and imports of goods and services to the analysis in the text.

Exports (X): represent an injection into the economy and are invariant with respect to the level of domestic income. It is treated similar to I: A rise in exports increases domestic income and output by a multiple amount.

Exports of goods and services—labeled X—include sales of merchandise by Americans to residents of foreign countries as well as sales of services, such as insurance, transportation, and others, to foreign nationals. All such transactions must be paid for by foreigners, and they give rise to inflow of dollars into the United States. Since exports must come out of domestic production, they involve the sale of goods manufactured in the United States, employing American factors of production. *Exports constitute injections into the income stream,* much the same as investment. Because exports do not depend on income (they do, however, affect income), the export function (in the export-income space) is a flat horizontal line, much the same as the I_n or the G function. A **rise (or decline) in exports has a multiple effect on domestic output and income,** in the same direction.

Imports of goods and services—labeled M—include the sale of merchandise and services by foreign nationals to Americans. Such transactions must be paid for by Americans to foreigners, and they give rise to outflow of dollars from the United States. Consequently, *imports constitute a leakage out of the domestic income stream,* much the same as domestic savings. Because imports are a function of income, the import function (in the import-income space) is positively sloped and appears similar to the savings or the tax function. Any income generated in the productive process in the United States can be respent on domestic goods and services (C), or leaked out of the income stream in the form of domestic savings, taxes, or spending on *foreign* goods and services.

Ignoring government, equilibrium now obtains at the level of income where the planned injection equals the planned leakage, or where: $I_n + X = S + M$.

Exports minus imports of goods and services is called the *balance on goods and services,* labeled **net exports, X_n**. In Chapter 12 it was shown as

[2]A balanced-budget multiplier of unity is a general proposition, not a unique result of the example above. This can be demonstrated by the use of the multiplier formula. The rise in G *raises* GDP by: $\Delta GDP = \Delta G \times k = \Delta G \times \frac{1}{MPS}$

The hike in T (where $\Delta T = \Delta G$) *lowers* GDP by: $-\Delta GDP = \Delta T \times MPC \times k = \Delta T \times MPC \times \frac{1}{MPS}$

The net effect on GDP is: $\Delta GDP = \Delta G \times \frac{1}{MPS} - \Delta T \times MPC \times \frac{1}{MPS}$

Remembering that $\Delta G = \Delta T$: $\Delta GDP = \Delta G \times \frac{1}{MPS} - \Delta G \times MPC \times \frac{1}{MPS}$

Factoring out $\Delta G \times 1/MPS$: $\Delta GDP = \Delta G \times \frac{1}{MPS} \times (1 - MPC) = \Delta G \times \frac{1}{MPS} \times MPS = \Delta G$

When $\Delta G = \Delta T$, the change in GDP equals the change in G, so that the ratio between them ($\Delta GDP/\Delta G$) is 1. Hence, the balanced-budget multiplier is 1 regardless of the size of the marginal propensities.

[3]For a more complete treatment see M. E. Kreinin, *International Economics: A Policy Approach*, 10th edition (New York: Thomson Publishing, 2006).

Imports (M): represent a leakage from the domestic economy. Like savings, it is a positive function of domestic output or income. As income rises so do imports.

Net Exports *(X_n)*: Exports minus Imports of goods and services.

one of the four expenditures components of GDP. It is also an important indicator of the country's position in its transactions with the rest of the world: Is it a net exporter or a net importer of goods and services?

Some Implications

Exports constitute a channel of expenditures, much the same as investment or consumption. A rise in exports can come about for a variety of reasons: The country's prices may become more competitive; foreign taste may shift in favor of the country's products; or foreign countries may lower barriers to their imports, such as their import tariffs. If exports increase, then the nation's output rises by a multiple of that increase, and with it income and employment expand. In other words, one way to move the economy from an underemployment equilibrium toward full employment is to increase exports. This occurred in 1988–1989. Conversely, a contraction in exports—for whatever reason—produces a multiple reduction in GDP and an associated cut in employment.

Imports are a function of income: as U.S. income rises, so do imports of goods and services. A protracted and strong economic expansion, as in 1996–2000, causes imports to shoot up and brings the U.S. external balance (exports minus imports) into deficit. Conversely, when the U.S. economy plunges into a recession, imports decline on a wide front. Consequently, it should come as no surprise that the U.S. external balance improves. Incidentally, U.S. petroleum imports, along with other raw materials used in manufacturing industries, are some of the imports that decline during a recession.

However, U.S. imports are other countries' exports. A decline in U.S. imports occasioned by a recession necessarily means that the exports of raw materials and manufactured goods of say, Latin America and Canada contract. Since these countries depend heavily on the U.S. market as an outlet for their output, the reduction of their exports may be severe. And that reduction would have a multiple effect on their GDP—reducing output, income, and employment. Thus, a recession in the United States can indirectly cause a recession in countries that depend heavily on the U.S. market. Conversely, economic expansion in the United States, as in 1996–2000, raises American imports, which in turn means that exports of other countries increase, producing a multiple expansion of their output and income. There is obviously a link between the economies of different nations.

Thus far, we have assumed that the U.S. import function—the relation between imports and income—is stable. Although this is generally the case, there are exceptions. Much of the U.S. imports of finished manufactures have close domestically produced substitutes. Automobiles are a case in point. Suppose that concern over gasoline supplies causes the buying public to switch from domestic automobiles to small and energy-efficient foreign cars. Imports rise; but not because income has increased. Rather, at every level of income, more is imported and fewer domestic goods are consumed. The entire import function shifts upward, and correspondingly, the consumption function shifts downward. The result is a multiple reduction in U.S. GDP, and with it a decrease in income and employment.

Conversely, a deliberate U.S. policy to cut by half the import of crude petroleum through a vast program of producing domestic substitutes will increase GDP and with it income and employment.

Finally, the country's external transactions—both imports and exports—are intertwined with the level of domestic economic activity: Imports are affected by that level, while exports affect GDP through the multiplier process.

SUMMARY

Introduction of the government sector necessitates adding government expenditures (G) and taxes (T) to the private sector. The excess (shortfall) of tax revenue over expenditures is the surplus (deficit) in the government budget. The size of federal-government expenditures is independent of the level of GDP. They constitute an injection into the income stream, much the same as private investment. Their effect on equilibrium GDP is obtained by adding them to I_n in the planned savings and investment analysis, and to aggregate private expenditures ($C + I_n$) in the aggregate-supply and-expenditures analysis. A change in government expenditures is equivalent to a primary change in aggregate spending and has a multiple effect on GDP in the same direction.

Income taxes are a positive function of GDP. They can be progressive, proportional, or regressive, depending on whether the tax *rate* rises, stays constant, or declines with income. A proportional tax is a linear function of income and is therefore selected for analysis in this chapter. Since an income tax lowers disposable income for each given level of national income (Y), its effect is to reduce the consumption and the savings functions when expressed with respect to Y. The primary reduction in consumption expenditures is smaller than the tax. It generates the multiplier process, which lowers GDP. Equilibrium GDP with both government spending and taxes occurs at a point (1) where aggregate supply equals aggregate expeditures, which in turn is made up of $C + I_n + G$, and where C itself has been reduced as a result of the tax; or equivalently, (2) where planned $G + I_n$ equals planned $S + T$, with G being superimposed vertically upon I_n, but with T being superimposed upon a modified S, since S itself declines as a result of T. (See appendix).

A change in tax rates affects GDP by a multiple of ΔT, but in an opposite direction. The magnitude of the effect is less than that of an equal change in spending. In fact, an equal increase (decrease) in government spending and taxes raises (lowers) GDP by an amount equal to ΔG (ΔT). The balanced budget multiplier is 1.

Fiscal policy means changing government expenditures and tax rates with the purpose of stabilizing the economy. Pushing the budget toward a deficit position—by raising spending and/or lowering taxes—stimulates the economy; pushing the budget toward a surplus position—by lowering spending and/or raising taxes—depresses the economy.

In extending the analysis to the open-economy case, exports of goods and services are added to the injection side and imports of goods and services are added to the leakage side. Ignoring government, equilibrium income for the private economy obtains at the level of output where: $I_n + X = S + M$.

QUESTIONS AND PROBLEMS

1. You are given the following figures for the American economy ($ billion), which is assumed to have no foreign trade:

Possible Levels of GDP or Y	T = 20% of Y	Disposable Income DI = Y - T	C	Savings (DI - C)	I_n	G	S + T	I_n + G	Aggregate Expenditures C + I_n + G
1,400			1,100		300	400			
2,000			1,500		300	400			
2,600			1,900		300	400			
3,200			2,300		300	400			
3,800			2,700		300	400			

a. Fill in all the missing columns.

b. For each possible level of GDP, show the difference between:

i. $S + T$ and $I_n + G$

ii. Aggregate expenditures and aggregate supply

c. Compute the MPC and the MPS (with respect to DI and to Y).

d. What is equilibrium GDP? Demonstrate your result, employing the two approaches.

e. Show your results diagrammatically, using the injection-leakage approach as in Figure 18–9.

f. Assume that Y_{FE} = $3,200.

i. By how much would the government have to increase spending to reach full employment?

ii. If the government chose a tax cut, would T have to decline by more or less than ΔG to achieve the same objective? Why?

2. What are the tools of fiscal policy, and how are they employed in periods of:

a. Unemployment?

b. Excessive aggregate expenditures (inflation)?

How is the government budget affected in each case?

3. Suppose that, starting from a balanced budget, the government decreases both taxes and spending by $30 billion, so as to retain the balance. What would happen to GDP? (Show your work.)

4. What is involved in extending the analysis to the open-economy case?

APPENDIX TO CHAPTER 18

Diagrammatic Exposition of Income Determination with Both Approaches

Income determination with the aggregate expenditures as well as the S-I approach were shown separately in the text. In Figure A18–1, both approaches are combined. On the upper panel, government expenditure is superimposed *vertically* upon the $C + I_n$ function, to generate a new aggregate-expenditures function consisting of $C + I_n + G$. Its intersection with aggregate supply, the 45° line, determines equilibrium output. Introduction of G raises equilibrium GDP from Y_1 to Y_2. Note the correspondence between the two panels: Equilibrium output rises from Y_1 to Y_2 as G is added to the private sector.

Diagrammatic Exposition of Income Determination with *C*, *I_n*, *G*, and *T* Schedules

Before the introduction of taxes, there is no difference between national income (Y) and disposable income (DI). Conceptually, savings and consumption are a function of DI, but when Y = DI, they are an equal function of Y. But the addition of taxes introduces a wedge between Y and DI. At each level of Y, DI is lower. Consequently, **with respect to Y, both S and C are reduced.**

This is shown explicitly in Figure A18–2. C_1 and S_1 represent the consumption and savings function respectively, shown in columns 3 and 4 of Table 18–1. The letters A, B, C, and D represent the rows in the table. No taxes are assumed to exist at that point. By contrast, C_2 and S_2 represent the consumption and savings functions in Table 18–3 (columns 4 and 5 respectively) after taxes were introduced. They show consumption and savings *with respect to* Y; not to DI. At each level of income, consumption and savings are shown to decline by the downward pointing arrows (pinned vertically at points A, B, C, and D), with the sum of the decline in each case adding up to the tax. For example, in row B, consumption declines by $204 billion and savings decline by $136 billion, adding up to $340 billion–the amount of the tax. To recapitulate, introduction of income tax reduces DI for any given level of Y. Since consumption and savings are functions of DI, their two schedules are reduced with respect to Y. The sum total of the reduction adds up to the tax function. The results are functions C_2 and S_2 respectively (see Figures A18–2 and A18–3).

It is on the new, reduced savings schedule that the tax schedule is superimposed to obtain the total leakage function. On top of S_2 we now add vertically the dollar amount paid in taxes at each level of income. The result is the $S_2 + T$ function, which relates column 1 to column 6 in Table 18–3 (lower panel). Nothing is added explicitly in the case of the consumption function; the effect of the tax is merely to lower it from C_1 to C_2. This is shown on the upper panel of Figure A18–3: Because the consumption function (in its entirety) declines from C_1 to C_2, the aggregate expenditures function declines correspondingly from $(C_1 + I_n + G)$ to $(C_2 + 1_n + G)$.

In Figure A18–3, equilibrium GDP (Y_3 = $2,000 billion) is shown on the lower panel at the point where:

$$\text{Planned } (S_2 + T) = \text{Planned } (I_n + G)$$

and on the upper panel where:

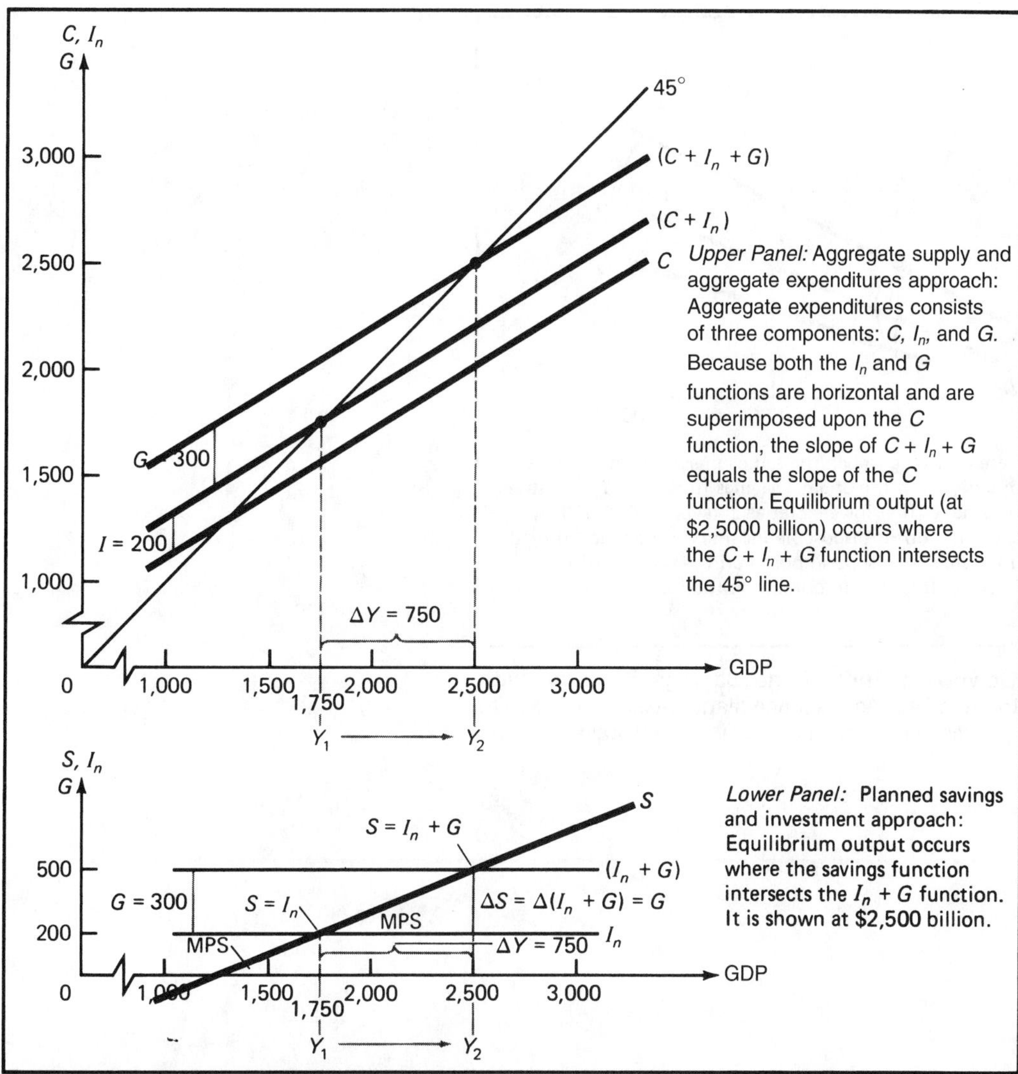

Figure A18–1 Equilibrium GDP or Y with Government Expenditures: Introduction of G raises equilibrium output or income from Y_1 to Y_2.

$$\text{Aggregate supply} = \text{Aggregate expenditures} = C_2 + I_n + G$$

Note that although on the lower panel taxes are shown explicitly, on the upper panel their effect is implicit in the downward shift of the consumption function, and therefore of the aggregate-expenditures function.

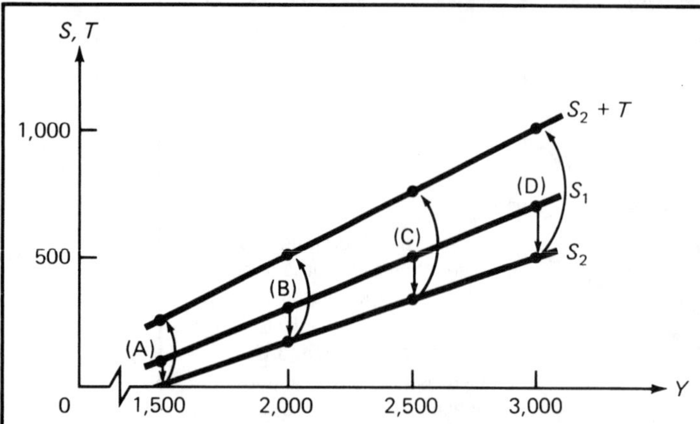

Although taxes are a leakage (much the same as savings) they are not superimposed directly upon the original savings function (S_1). Rather, the introduction of taxes first lowers S at each level of GDP (Y) by (T X MPS), because it reduces disposable income by the amount of the tax. The tax function is then superimposed on the now modified (reduced to S_2) savings function to obtain the total leakage function ($S_2 + T$).

Figure A18-2 Downward Shift of the Savings Function with Introduction of Income Tax: As a second stage, taxes are added to the revised savings function to obtain ($S_2 + T$), or total leakage.

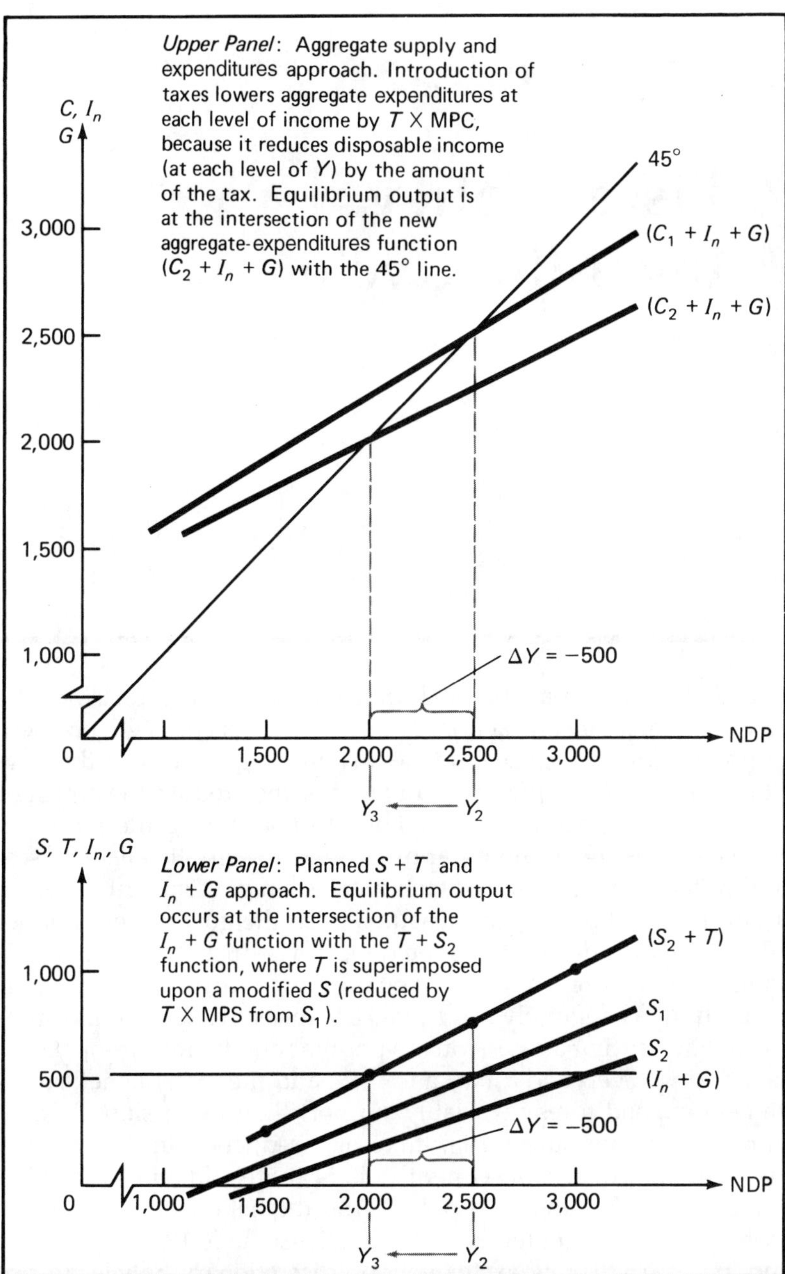
Upper Panel: Aggregate supply and expenditures approach. Introduction of taxes lowers aggregate expenditures at each level of income by T X MPC, because it reduces disposable income (at each level of Y) by the amount of the tax. Equilibrium output is at the intersection of the new aggregate-expenditures function (C2 + In + G) with the 45° line.
C, In, G
3,000
2,500
2,000
1,500
1,000
0
45°
(C1 + In + G)
(C2 + In + G)
ΔY = −500
NDP
1,500
2,000
2,500
3,000
Y3
Y2
S, T, In, G
Lower Panel: Planned S + T and In + G approach. Equilibrium output occurs at the intersection of the In + G function with the T + S2 function, where T is superimposed upon a modified S (reduced by T X MPS from S1).
1,000
500
0
(S2 + T)
S1
S2
(In + G)
ΔY = −500
NDP
1,000
1,500
2,000
2,500
3,000
Y3
Y2

Figure A18–3 Imposition of a Proportional Tax Reduces GDP from Y_2 to Y_3, namely by 500: The upper and lower panels correspond to each other.

Note: The final figures of 2,000 is a round number. In the text it is 2,050.

Fiscal Policy Over the Cycle

INTRODUCTION

Inflation tends to heat up at the peak of the expansionary phase of the business cycle. It calls for contractionary fiscal policy: a cut in government expenditures and/or an increase in taxes. These measures push the government budget *toward a surplus* position; that is, they reduce the deficit or increase the surplus. Unemployment tends to rise during the recession phase of the cycle, as the economy approaches a trough. It calls for fiscal action to stimulate economic activity: an increase in government expenditures and/or a cut in taxes. Such measures push the government budget *toward a deficit;* that is, they increase the deficit or reduce the surplus.

Although the required policies appear symmetrical in nature, their political popularity is definitely not equal. The measures required to stimulate the economy during a recession are popular and therefore enjoy congressional backing. Everybody likes a tax cut, and the many beneficiaries of government expenditures invariably support their expansion. By contrast, contractionary measures, a tax hike or a reduction in government spending, are unpopular. Consequently, it is more difficult to combat inflation than a recession by fiscal policy. And the net effect is that in the long run, the federal budget tends toward deficits (Table 19–1).

Built-in stabilizers: The government budget automatically tends toward deficit in times of recession and toward a surplus in times of expansion. This is due to the progressive nature of the income tax system and other systemic qualities of government activity. It has a stabilizing effect on the economy.

It is not necessary to rely exclusively on discretionary policies to stabilize the economy. Because of institutional innovations introduced over a period of decades, there is an **automatic tendency for the federal budget to play a stabilizing role in the economy;** that is, to move toward a deficit in times of recession and toward a surplus in times of inflation. These tendencies are known as **built-in stabilizers.**

Table 19–1 Federal Budget Receipts and Outlays 1980–2006 (Billions of Dollars, Fiscal Years)

Fiscal Year	Receipts	Outlays	Surplus or Deficit (–)
1980	517.1	590.9	-73.8
1981	599.3	678.2	-79.0
1982	617.8	745.8	-128.0
1983	600.6	808.4	-207.8
1984	666.5	851.9	-185.4
1985	734.1	946.4	-212.3
1986	769.2	990.5	-221.2
1987	854.4	1,004.1	-149.7
1988	909.3	1,064.5	-155.2
1989	991.2	1,143.7	-152.5
1990	1,032.0	1,253.2	-221.2
1991	1,055.0	1,324.4	-269.3
1992	1,091.3	1,381.7	-290.4
1993	1,154.4	1,409.5	-255.1
1994	1,258.6	1,461.9	-203.3
1995	1,351.8	1,515.8	-164.0
1996	1,453.1	1,560.6	-107.5
1997	1,579.3	1,601.3	-22.0
1998	1,721.8	1,652.6	+69.2
1999	1,827.5	1,701.9	+125.6
2000	2,025.2	1,788.8	+236.4
2001	1,991.0	1,863.9	+127.4
2002	1,853.2	2,011.0	-157.8
2003	1,782.3	2,159.9	-377.6
2004	1,880.1	2,292.2	-412.1
2005	2,153.9	2,472.2	-318.2
*2006	2,285.5	2,708.7	-423.2
*2007	2,415.9	2,770.1	-354.2

Source: Economic Report of the President, 2006, Table B.78

**Estimates*

BUILT-IN STABILIZERS

Government revenues: Without any change in fiscal policy, government tax revenues rise during expansion because more people work and hence pay taxes. The reverse happens in times of recession and unemployment.

Government Revenues

Consider first the revenue side of the budget, which consists of a variety of taxes. During the expansionary phase of the cycle, output and employment expand. Since more people are employed, there is an increase in personal income taxes paid to the government; and because incomes rise this is reinforced by the progressive nature of the personal income tax. Corporate profit taxes also increase during the cyclical expansion, because profits increase with the rise in output and sales. And so do the indirect taxes, such as sales and excise taxes.

Precisely the reverse happens during a cyclical contraction, or a recession. As output and employment decline, so do personal income taxes. Corporate profit taxes decline with the contraction of sales and profits, and so do the sales and other indirect taxes.

In sum, without any discretionary action to change tax rates, **government tax revenues rise during cyclical expansions and decline during cyclical contractions**. Assuming for a moment that federal government expenditures remain constant, there is an automatic tendency toward a

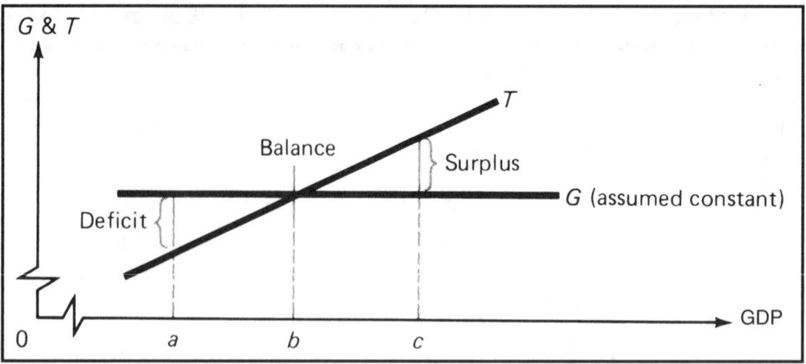

Figure 19–1 The Budget over the Cycle: During a cyclical peak when the level of output or income is high (point *c*), tax receipts are high, exceeding government expenditures; a budgetary surplus results. Conversely, during a recession when income or output is low (point *a*), tax receipts are low, falling short of government expenditures (*G*); a budgetary deficit results. At income level *b* the budget is balanced.

budgetary surplus during the expansionary phase and toward a deficit in times of recession. This is shown schematically in Figure 19–1. With *G* constant, tax revenues are less than expenditures when GDP is low (for example, at point *a*), generating a budgetary deficit. As the economy expands to point *b*, revenues rise to a point of exactly equaling expenditures, and the budget is in balance. As the economy expands further, to a point such as *c*, tax revenues rise above expenditures, yielding a budgetary surplus. All this imparts a measure of stability to the economy.

Government Expenditures

Government expenditures: Without any change in fiscal policy, government outlays increase in times of recession because more people are unemployed and receive unemployment compensation and welfare benefits. The converse happens in times of expansion.

A similar stabilizing influence occurs on the expenditures side. During a recession, unemployment expands, and that automatically increases government outlays on unemployment compensation, welfare payments to the poor, and various other subsidies. Conversely, when the economy expands, unemployment declines, and these outlays automatically shrink. Again, these factors push the federal budget toward a deficit during an economic contraction and toward a surplus during a cyclical recovery, imparting a measure of stability to the economy.

Summary

Effects on the budget: These effects on revenue and expenditures taken together, move the budget towards a surplus in an expansion and a deficit in a contraction. State and local governments budgets do NOT have this stabilizing feature. The built-in stabilizers are often insufficient and need to be supplemented by discretionary fiscal measures.

The effect of these built-in stabilizers on both sides of the budget is described in Figure 19–2. Tax revenues are shown to rise with GDP, whereas expenditures tend to decline as GDP increases. The result is **budgetary deficits during periods of low economic activity, and surpluses in periods of high economic activity.** This explains the appearance of a surplus in the Federal budget in 1998–2000 after many years of deficit, and its disappearance in 2002.

These built-in stabilizers are a feature of the federal budget. Only the federal government has abundant means of financing deficits and need not be too concerned about the debt it incurs to finance such deficits (see below). State and local governments are not in that position. Their budgets must usually be balanced. During 1983–86 and again in 1997–2002, state and local governments combined had budgetary surpluses, while in

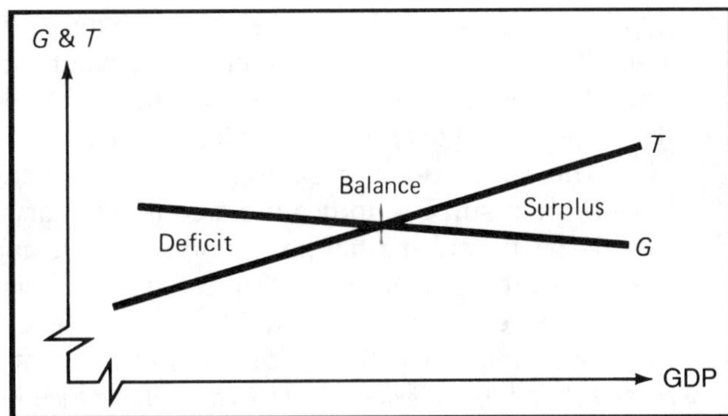

Figure 19–2 The Budget over the Cycle: Both *T* and *G* are responsive to income fluctuations. In a period of prosperity, *T* is relatively high and *G* is relatively low, producing a budgetary surplus. Conversely, in the depth of a recession, *G* is high and *T* is low, producing a budgetary deficit.

1987–88, and again in 2001–02, they showed a combined deficit. Because state and local outlays are limited to expected revenues, their budgets cannot be counter-cyclical. In boom periods, expected revenues rise, so expenditures tend to soar. Conversely, in recession periods, as revenues decline, so must expenditures, and the resulting belt-tightening measures have a dampening effect on the economy.

Not only do these fluctuations in expenditures interfere with the order and continuity of state and local programs; but they also destabilize the economy. To avoid both harmful effects, state and local governments can set up stabilization funds. Rather than increase expenditures during boom periods, they can set aside part of the expanded revenues and funnel them into such stabilization funds. And the accumulated funds can then be used in recession periods to finance ongoing programs and cushion the effect of curtailment in revenue.

Returning to the federal budget, the built-in federal stabilizers, although they move the economy in the "right" direction, are not sufficiently powerful to completely offset cyclical fluctuations. They are estimated to reduce these fluctuations by approximately one third, and must therefore be supplemented by discretionary measures (in the same direction).

DISCRETIONARY FISCAL POLICY

Discretionary fiscal measures operate in the same direction as, and thus reinforce, the built-in stabilizers. In times of recession, the federal government can raise expenditures or lower tax rates, or both, thereby pushing the budget toward a deficit and stimulating the economy. Conversely, in times of inflation, the government can lower expenditures or increase tax rates, or both, thereby pushing the budget toward a surplus and dampening the level of economic activity.

Full employment budget: what the surplus or deficit in the federal budget would have been had the economy functioned at full employment.

The Full-Employment Budget

Because of the built-in stabilizers, it is impossible to infer from the budget position in any given year whether it reflects a deliberate stimulative or depressive action. Thus, in the recession years of 1961–62, the budget showed a small deficit. But that was merely the result of a drop-off in tax revenue caused by the recession, at existing tax rates. Had there been full employment, the then-existing tax rates would have generated a substantial budgetary surplus. This is described by saying that the "full-employment budget" would have been in surplus, indicating a contractionary fiscal posture. Conversely, in 1964–65, the substantial tax cut on corporate and personal income pushed the "full-employment budget" into a deficit. This means that with the new, lower tax rates, the federal budget would have been in deficit, had there been full employment. The full-employment budget is an estimate of *what the surplus or deficit in the federal budget would have been had the economy functioned at full employment.* We use the full-employment budget, rather than the actual budget, as an indicator of the posture of fiscal policy. It is expansionary if that budget is in deficit and contractionary if that budget is in surplus. In the recession years of 1980–81 the actual deficit was over $70 billion, whereas the full-employment budget was nearly in balance, indicating a neutral posture. Only after the 1981 tax cut did the full-employment budget move into a substantial deficit, helping to produce the expansion of 1983–89.

How Big a Dose?

The first question that must be answered is how much stimulus the economy needs in a given recession, and how much dampening during a specific inflation rate. In either case, it is necessary to estimate empirically the size of the GDP gap that needs to be bridged, and the size of the multiplier (with proper allowance for the influence of price and tax changes). Only with these two figures at hand can we determine the dose of fiscal action necessary, in the form of either change in expenditures or change in tax rates.

Estimating these amounts is no mean feat. Economists have developed elaborate tools for doing so, but not with complete accuracy. The most sophisticated tool available is the **econometric model. Such a model formulates a number of relationships between economic variables and expresses them in the form of mathematical equations. These are then estimated statistically** with the help of large computers, and they provide a broad picture of the functioning of the economy. Several large models of the U.S. economy exist, each embodying hundreds of equations. And they are used, among other purposes, to answer the type of policy questions outlined above.

Models: are used to assess the effect of policy on the economy.

Models are also used to **assess the effect of alternative policy measures on the course of the economy.** At any given moment, a multitude of forces is operating on the economy, and it is necessary to isolate the effect of the policy under investigation. In order to find out the effect of a policy, we need to compare situations **with and without the policy, all other things assumed to remain unchanged.** It is the validity of this **ceteris paribus** assumption that laypeople often question when they read the writings of economists. How can it be valid if the economy is always in a state of change? The answer is that all other changes take place in the presence or in the absence of the policy under investigation. And making the assumption "other things being equal" is equivalent to comparing the situation with and without the policy. In the physical sciences, this is accomplished by controlled laboratory experiments. Since this is not possible in economics, we must use theoretical abstractions and statistical techniques to achieve the same objective.

Finally, the size of the dose is influenced by a possible tradeoff between inflation and unemployment. Recall from Chapter 13 that demand-management policies in region II of the aggregate-supply function may be subject to such a tradeoff. Stimulating the economy in times of recession runs the risk of fueling inflation. To minimize this unfavorable side effect, gentle stimulus applied over a long period is usually preferable to a strong stimulus administered in an abrupt fashion. Conversely, fighting inflation through contractionary measures may increase unemployment. A limited contractionary dose, applied over an extended period is often preferable to an abruptly administered large dose. It can gently lead the economy to a so-called soft landing, minimizing the increase in unemployment.

Timing of Policy

Lags: Recognition lag: the time elapsed between the emergence of a problem and recognition of that problem by policy makers. **Action lag:** the time elapsed between recognition and action. **Policy lag:** the time elapsed between action by the government and its effect on the economy, (6–9 months).

Past experience has shown that economic policy is not applied immediately when needed, and that, when it is applied, it does not have an instantaneous effect on the economy. We identify three types of time lags: (1) **Recognition lag** refers to the time elapsed between the rise of the needs of the economy and the recognition of these needs. It stems from delay in gathering the appropriate data about the economy. At any given point, we are fully aware only of economic conditions that prevailed a month or two earlier and not of current circumstances. This lag can be shortened by increasing the efficiency of the information-gathering apparatus. (2) **Action lag** is caused by the fact that once the need for certain measures is recognized, it takes time to mobilize the government machinery for action. Changes in tax rates require congressional approval, which may take months to pass. And changes in expenditures require planning and execution. (3) **Policy lag** is the six to nine months that past experience has shown to elapse between the time the policy button is pressed and the time its full effect on the economy is felt. Ideally, therefore, fiscal policy should be directed at conditions that will prevail half a year later. Unfortunately, the future is not known with any accuracy. This underscores the importance of economic forecasting for the conduct of policy.

Economic Forecasting There are three important methods of forecasting the economy. First is the *econometric models* mentioned in the last section. Although better suited to assessing the effect of alternative policies on the economy, they are also used to forecast the level of economic activity.

Leading-indicators: certain variables, such as orders for new machinery, that predict the course of the economy.

Second is the **leading-indicators** technique, developed originally by a nonprofit research organization, the National Bureau for Economic Research. Plotting the cyclical behavior of the economy (that is, real GDP) over many decades, the bureau has been able to identify certain indicators that consistently lead the economy. If they turn up or down, real GDP turns up or down several months later. Among these indicators are (1) building permits, which foreshadow activity in the construction sector; (2) the number of companies reporting slower deliveries, indicating a backlog of orders; (3) new orders from factories, measured in "real" terms; and (4) orders for new plant and equipment, foreshadowing changes in investment activity.[1]

[1]The other indicators are (5) stock prices; (6) money supply, adjusted for inflation; (7) average workweek; (8) unemployment claims; (9) changes in sensitive prices, such as prices of primary commodities; (10) consumer expectations.

A composite index (a weighted average) of the eleven indicators is computed and reported each month by the Commerce Department. It is used extensively to forecast the turning points in the economy. However, no significance attaches to a one or two month turn-around in the index. A trend of several months in the same direction must be established before the index can be regarded as a precursor of the economy.[2] Following is the behavior of the index in 2005–2006 reflecting economic growth:

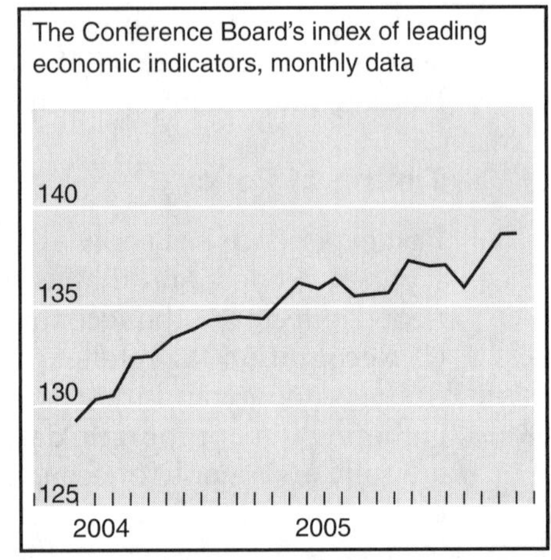

▶ WHY LEADING INDICATORS LEAD

Leading indicators are selected *because they anticipate changes* in the economy, and therefore are useful in forecasting the turning points of the business cycle. Some of them reflect decisions or commitments to economic activity in the months ahead. For example:

> *New orders for machinery and equipment, a leading indicator, reflect decisions of business firms to buy new machinery.* It takes time to convert the orders into machines. Hence, such orders tend to precede, or lead, machinery production, as well as the production of the goods the machine later helps to produce.
>
> A similar kind of decision is reflected in *obtaining a permit to build a house.* After a permit is taken out, the building can be started and is eventually completed and sold. This sequence of events takes time. Hence new building permits and housing starts lead residential construction expenditures.

Similar reasoning *applies to decisions to incorporate and to start new businesses.*

Stock prices may be a leading indicator because they are influenced by corporate profits, and profits tend to decline before the peak of a cycle. The average length of the workweek in manufacturing tends to lead the employment series: It begins to increase or decline before the number of workers employed follows suit. Similar reasoning applies to *other indicators.**

*From Goffrey Moore and Julius Shiskin, *Impact,* Washington, D C. 1979/2, pp. 56–60.

[2]In addition, the Department of Commerce compiles a composite index of *coincident indicators,* those that tend to move up or down simultaneously with the economy, and a composite index of *lagging indicators,* those that tend to trail the economy. The ratio of these two indexes tends to signal the turning points in the economy in advance of the index of leading indicators.

A third method consists of surveys of consumers' buying intentions, especially of autos and durable goods, and of corporate investment plans. These are usually combined with other information obtained from consumers and investors to indicate activity in these volatile sectors in future months.

In addition to these methods, information about prior and intended policy measures must be factored into the forecast. The "consensus forecast" embodies the outcome of all methods plus a good deal of "feel" and common sense. Forecasting contains an element of art, and a good deal of luck. It is far from being an exact science. The consensus forecast is not always accurate.

Choice Between ΔG and ΔT

Speed of policies: In a recession tax cuts stimulate spending rather quickly, while government expenditures take time to plan and carry out. Political philosophy plays a role in choosing between ΔT and ΔG.

Once the size of the policy dose and its timing are determined, it is necessary to select the desirable policy mix. The preceding chapter demonstrated that, dollar for dollar, a change in expenditures has a greater effect on the economy than does a change in taxes. That would tilt the choice in favor of expenditures. But there are other, equally important considerations bearing upon this choice.

To begin with, there is the matter of **speed**: A tax cut in a recession stimulates spending rather swiftly. By comparison, it takes time to plan and embark upon public spending programs. Also, once begun, such programs are rather difficult to terminate if the economic situation reverses itself.

A second important consideration is the matter of **political and philosophical choice** concerning the size of the public sector in the economy. A rise in government spending, in the interest of combating a recession, increases the public sector; it is generally favored by political liberals. A cut in taxes, with the same objective in mind, reduces the size of the public sector and is favored by political conservatives. All this is related to the perceived need for additional private as against public goods, and is determined through the political process.

But such questions of social choice do not stop here. If an increase in spending is chosen over a decrease in taxes, then a **choice must be made between the type of government expenditures** to be increased: defense spending, social expenditures (and if so, what type?), or whatever. Should the body politic favor the lowering of taxes, further **choices are necessary about the kind of taxes** to be cut. And that depends on (1) which group in society is to draw the benefits, and (2) which type of spending should be stimulated. A reduction in the personal income tax benefits consumers and stimulates mainly consumer spending. A reduction in the corporate profit tax benefits corporations and stockholders and stimulates investment spending (which in future years will increase the supply of goods and services). A tax reduction can zero in on stimulating investments by exempting a part of investment expenditures from profit taxes.

These considerations are reversed in times of excessive expenditures (an inflationary gap). That situation calls for either a tax hike or a reduction in government spending. Politically, a tax cut or an increase in spending is more palatable than a tax hike or a cut in spending (which always hurts some groups who are the beneficiaries of government spending). Consequently, it is easier to use fiscal policy to fight a recession than to combat inflation by dampening excessive expenditures.

FINANCING THE BUDGET

Size and Composition of the Budget

The federal administration proposes its budget to Congress in January of every year for the following fiscal year, which lasts from October 1 to the next September 30. Table 19–1 at the beginning of this chapter displays the federal budgets in recent years. On the outlay side, a large share of the budget is in the form of transfer and interest payments, which are not included in GDP, while military spending occupies a quarter of total outlays. On the revenue side, the bulk of federal receipts comes from individual and corporate taxes. About 9 percent of the budget (the deficit) is financed by borrowing. Such deficits occurred in most of the past 20 years.

Financing Deficits

Unlike state and local governments, the federal government need not worry about budgetary deficits. And indeed, it is this feature that makes the federal budget suitable for stabilization policy. But the manner in which the deficits are financed has a direct bearing on the effectiveness of fiscal policy.

There are two ways of financing the federal deficit. The first is by borrowing from the general public, business corporations, nonprofit institutions, and other organizations that have money to place in safe, interest-bearing financial instruments. This is done by **selling them various kinds of government bonds through the nation's financial markets.**[3] **The second way is by creating new money.** This is accomplished by borrowing from the central bank, and will be examined in Part 4.

Under the first method, the federal government (namely, the Treasury Department) appears on the money markets as a large borrower (debtor), or *demander of funds.* Such an increase in demand **raises the price of loanable funds, the rate of interest.** The size of the increase varies inversely with the degree of slack in the money markets—that is, the amount of idle funds in existence at the time the Treasury enters the market to sell bonds. In 1980–82, large government borrowing on tight financial markets contributed to the rise in interest rates to unprecedented levels.

Crowding-out effect: When government finances deficits by borrowing (selling bonds) interest rates rise, reducing private spending; consumers and investors are crowded-out of the market.

This *increase in the rate of interest tends to discourage some private borrowings,* which include consumer loans to finance purchases of cars, durable goods, and the like, and loans to firms to finance construction and investment activity. In other words, **some consumers and investors are crowded out of the market** (hence, this is known as the *crowding-out effect).* There

[3]A hypothesis dated back to David Ricardo in the nineteenth century suggests that government deficits financed by borrowing would have no effect on consumption. Consumers would not regard their new bond holdings as wealth because they expect in the future to pay more taxes to service and pay off the debt. And their expected tax liabilities offset the newly-found wealth. But this hypothesis has not found empirical support.

is at least some reduction in consumption and investment expenditures. Since the budget deficit is designed to stimulate the economy by, say, increasing government expenditures, the stimulus is reduced by the decline in private expenditures. That is, the rise in government spending is partly offset by a decline in private consumption and investments, thereby curtailing its stimulative effect. The large budgetary deficits during 1982–88, continuing even after the economy reached full employment, crowded out some private investments. But mainly they created problems in the foreign-trade sector of the economy.

In sum, when the federal deficit is financed by borrowing, the effect on the economy is reduced to some extent by the crowding-out effect. But the size of this reduction, and therefore the effectiveness of policy, depends on the degree of slack that exists in the money markets. If it is large, then the crowding out can be very small; for then there are ample funds to finance both ΔG and $\Delta(C + I)$.

Money creation: Financing government deficits by money creation does not lead to a crowding-out but can lead to inflation.

Under the second method, **new money is created** to finance the increase in government spending or the reduction in taxes. There is no **crowding-out effect,** and fiscal policy is fully effective. But because new money is created, **this method is inflationary.**

A reverse but symmetrical reasoning applies in times of inflation, when the government generates a budgetary surplus in order to dampen the inflation. It can use the accumulated funds to retire the outstanding debt by buying back government bonds held by the public. This method places new funds in the hands of the public, part of which may be spent to increase consumption and/or investment. This offsets, at least in part, the antiinflationary effect of the budgetary surplus. The second alternative is for the government to impound the funds accumulated through the surplus. Then there is no mitigating effect.

ALTERNATIVE BUDGET PHILOSOPHIES

Functional finance: a political philosophy which says that the main function of the federal budget is to stabilize the economy, regardless of the size of the imbalance.

Balanced-budget advocates: Conservatives advocate balancing the budget every year, regardless of the costs of doing so.

There are three fundamental approaches to the federal budget, reflecting not only economic reasoning but also the political philosophies of their proponents. At **one extreme** are adherents to **functional finance.** These tend to be political liberals, who argue that the main function of the federal budget is to stabilize the economy. That objective, they say, should be the sole focus of attention, letting the size of the imbalance fall where it may. No consideration should be given to the size of the imbalance or to its duration.

At the **other extreme** are those who **advocate balancing the federal budget every year**. These tend to be political conservatives, such as President Reagan, who believe that if left to its own devices, the government is apt to run ever-larger deficits because of the political popularity of expenditure programs and tax cuts. If the budget is left uncontrolled, its long-run effect will therefore be inflationary. Indeed, there is a movement afoot, spearheaded by Prof. Milton Friedman, to *introduce a constitutional amendment requiring the federal budget to be in balance every year*. The problem with this balanced-budget amendment approach is that it may destabilize the economy. If the government raised tax rates in a recession year in order to achieve a balanced budget, it would thereby deepen the recession and, as a result, tax revenues might decline rather than rise. Conversely, in times of inflationary boom, government revenues are expected to rise, making it possible to increase expenditures. And that in turn fuels the inflation. In short, *this proposal could make the budget destabilizing.* Additionally, it might be questioned whether the constitution is an appropriate vehicle for conducting economic policy.

Balancing the budget over the cycle: deficits in recession years should roughly equal surpluses in boom years.

Between these two extreme positions are those who advocate **balancing the budget over the cycle.** They maintain that the deficits incurred during recession years should roughly match the surpluses generated in times of prosperity, so that the budget is in balance over the entire range of the cycle. That way, the budget would not have a net inflationary or depressive effect over the long run, yet it would stabilize the economy.

As a matter of historical record, the federal budget has exhibited a succession of sizable deficits during prolonged periods of economic expansion, such as 1983–88. During these years, government revenues soared because of rapid economic expansion. Yet, there were sizable deficits, and certainly the budget was not balanced over the cycle. The budgetary deficits of the 1980s (exceeding 5 percent of GDP in some years) crowded out private investment and created problems in the foreign-trade sector (to be explored in Part 5 of this book).

THE PUBLIC DEBT

Nature and Dimension of Government Bonds

Size of debt: U.S. public debt is over half of GDP. It is financed by selling government bonds (IOUs).

To finance its budgetary deficits, the federal government markets a variety of bonds. Government bonds vary in maturity (the length of time for which they are issued) all the way from 90 days to several years. The total amount of these bonds, U.S. government IOUs, is known as the **public debt**. It is the cumulative sum of all previous annual budget deficits. Government bonds are held by individuals, manufacturing companies, banks, financial corporations such as insurance companies, and non–profit institutions. About a quarter of this debt is owed by foreigners. Whoever owns a government bond is therefore a creditor of the U.S. government.[4] The public debt has grown over the years reaching $7.6 trillion, or 63 percent of GDP, in 2005. Congressional approval is required every time the upper limit on the accumulated debt is raised.

Except for the bonds owned by foreigners, the U.S. government owes the money to Americans. In other words, we collectively owe the debt to ourselves. **When bonds mature, the government usually issues new bonds to pay off the old ones.** This function of the Treasury Department is known as **debt management**. In other words, the principal of the debt is never paid off; it is merely "refinanced" or "rolled over" by replacing maturing bonds with new bonds. What is paid out every year is the inter-

[4]However, about a third of the debt is held by agencies and funds of the U.S. government itself.

A pauper comes to a bank to apply for a $1,000 loan.

Banker: Do you have any collateral?

Loan Applicant: No!

Banker: How can you substantiate your creditworthiness?

Loan Applicant: My credit must be good; the government is trusting me for a fair share of its enormous national debt. My personal share (namely, the $5.4 trillion divided by the population) is $30,000! How can the bank deny me a loan of merely $1,000?

est on the debt; it rose from $43 billion in 1978 to $244 billion in 1997. This interest payment is called "servicing the debt."

Burden of the Debt

In many a public discourse, one can detect alarm over the size of the government debt. People see it growing every year and wonder how it will ever be paid back. Will the government eventually go bankrupt? In evaluating these concerns, both the size and the nature of the debt must be kept in mind.

Although the debt has been growing in absolute size,[5] and even in relation to the population, its ratio to GDP is half what it was in the mid-1940s (Table 19–2). And it is its relation to aggregate output or **income** that indicates the burden the debt imposes. That ratio reached a peak of 122 percent in 1946, immediately after the war. It then declined gradually over 35 years to a low of 33 percent in 1980 and 1981. In the 1980s it rose again as a result of the large federal deficits, reaching 52 percent in 1987 and 58 percent in 2000. Sizeable deficits in 2002–2005 raised the ratio to 63 percent by 2005. As of early 2006 the debt ceiling set by Congress was $8,184 billion.

Next, consider the nature of this debt. People alarmed by its sheer size usually think in terms of an individual family and ask themselves, How can a family carry such a heavy burden? But the public debt is not comparable to family debt. A family debt is owed to somebody else, an outside entity, as would be the case of a U.S. debt owed to nationals and governments of other countries. That "foreign owed" component of the debt also rose to $2.5 trillion by the end of 2005 and that number is rising. For example, in 2004–2005 over 95 percent of the deficit was financed by foreigners.

Income inequality: the income distribution of taxpayers is not the same as the income distribution of holders of government bonds. The debt contributes to income inequality.

Moreover the debt has certain effects on the economy. First, it contributes to **income inequality** in society. The income distribution of taxpayers, out of whose taxes the debt is serviced, is not the same as the income distribution of holders of government bonds, those who receive the interest payments. To the extent that public-debt ownership is concentrated in the high-income brackets, debt servicing contributes to inequality. A related

[5]Note that inflation reduces the real value of this, as of any other debt.

Table 19–2 The Public Debt as a Percent of GDP

Year	Debt Outstanding ($ Billion)	Gross Domestic Product ($ Billion)	Debt as % of GDP
1946	271	223	122
1970	381	1,013	38
1980	909	2,725	33
1998	5,478	8,626	64
1999	5,606	9,127	61
2000	5,629	9,708	58
2001	5,770	10,041	57
2002	6,198	10,373	60
2003	6,760	10,828	62
2004	7,355	11,492	64
2005	7,905	12,479	63
*2006	8,611	13,030	66
*2007	9,295	13,761	68

**Estimates*
Source: Economic Report of the President, 2006, Table B-78. B-79

Intergenerational transfers: If the crowding-out effect occurs then private investments would be curtailed and output in future years will be smaller than it would have been in the absence of public debt.

question is whether the debt creates **intergenerational transfers.** If government borrowing to finance deficits "crowds out" some private investments, then it affects the growth rate unfavorably: Output in future years will be smaller than what it would have been in the absence of the public debt.

Against these effects, one must weigh the immense value to the economy of having a sizable public debt. **Not only is there no reason to pay back the entire debt,** it would cause problems to the economy if it were liquidated. For the debt plays a crucial role in the national and international economy.

Individuals, institutions, corporations, and banks, as well as foreign institutions, often find themselves in possession of a surplus of funds. They need to **place these funds in financial instruments of varying lengths of maturity, that yield interest, and that are safe as well as liquid** (can be readily converted into cash). Government bonds are ideally suited for this purpose. Additionally, we shall see in Part 4 that government bonds play a critical role in the conduct of monetary policy. If they did not exist, something similar would have to be invented. Under present dimensions the public debt is not a drain on the economy; it serves a useful function.

On the other hand, the large annual deficits of the 1980s (which doubled the size of the debt in six years) and in 2002–2005 were a drain on the economy.

SUMMARY

Fiscal policy refers to changes in government taxes and/or expenditures to stabilize the economy, namely, reducing unemployment and minimizing inflation. Part of this stabilization role is accomplished automatically, through built-in stabilizers. During a recession, tax revenues decline and expenditures rise, without any discretionary steps being taken. The converse happens during an inflationary boom. Thus, there is an automatic tendency toward a budgetary deficit in a recession, and toward a surplus during periods of prosperity. But because the built-in stabilizers reduce cyclical fluctuations by no more than one-third, they need to be supplemented by discretionary action: Lower tax rates and/or raise expenditures during a recession; increase tax rates and/or reduce expenditure programs in times of prosperity. These are largely "demand-management" measures.

Although the direction of policy is known, we are still left with many questions requiring quantitative answers. How big a fiscal dose is needed to stabilize the economy in any given situation? That depends on the size of the "gap" and of the multiplier, both of which are susceptible to measurement by econometric models; on the tradeoff between inflation and unemployment; and on other matters. When should fiscal action be taken? That depends on the length of the various lags, and necessitates economic forecasting. What should be the composition of fiscal action? That depends on the relative effectiveness of changes in taxes and in expenditures, the speed with which each influences the economy, philosophical predilections, and other matters.

With the government budget occupying a quarter of the nation's GDP, it necessarily has a profound effect on the economy. The means of financing deficits and handling surpluses partly determine how effective fiscal policy is.

Alternative budget philosophies include functional finance, an annually balanced budget, and a balanced budget over the cycle.

There is exaggerated concern bordering on panic on the part of the general public over the size and burden of the government debt. In fact, the debt is not particularly burdensome, nor does the principal ever need to be repaid. The existence of the public debt provides some net benefits to society. But the sizable annual deficits of the 1980s did constitute a drain on the economy: they were reversed during the Clinton Administration; but returned in 2004–2005.

QUESTIONS AND PROBLEMS

1. Explain the nature and functioning of the built-in stabilizers.
2. What does the full-employment budget indicate?
3. What considerations have bearing on the (a) size, (b) composition, and (c) timing of fiscal policy?
4. How are budgetary deficits financed, and what bearing does the method of financing have on the effectiveness of fiscal policy?
5. Is the public debt a net burden to society? Discuss in full.

PART FOUR

MONEY, MONETARY POLICY, AND ECONOMIC STABILIZATION

OVERVIEW

Chapters 12 through 19 examined the need for stabilization policies and the role of fiscal policy in lowering unemployment and reducing inflation. Another way of managing aggregate expenditures with the view of promoting the same objectives is monetary policy. Relying on changes in the availability and the cost (the rate of interest) of loanable funds, monetary policy in each country is the responsibility of the central bank. In the United States, the central bank is the Federal Reserve System, dubbed the Fed.

In order to see how money is managed, and how such management affects the economy, we must first understand the nature of money, its functions, and the means by which it is created. These issues will be treated in Part 4. It will be seen that most of the nation's money supply is created by banks; and consequently, the banking system is regulated by the government more than other industries are. For that reason, bank operations will be a focus of the next chapter. Following that, we shall inquire into the nature and effectiveness of monetary policy. And Chapter 22 addresses a variety of issues concerning economic stabilization.

20 The Nature and Role of Money: How Money Is Created

FUNCTIONS OF MONEY

Medium of Exchange

Medium of exchange: Money is the means by which payments are made.

Besides "making the world go around," money is the object used in buying or selling goods and services. It is the **means of payments,** or **medium of exchange.** The alternative to such a standard object in settling transactions is the exchange of goods and services for other goods and services—a *barter system*. It was shown in Part 1 that such a system would be cumbersome in the extreme. A sophisticated and highly specialized economy cannot exist under a barter system. Although we all take the existence of money for granted, we should not lose sight of the fact that it is an incredibly useful social invention.

Unit of Account

Unit of account: money allows the values of goods and services to be measured and compared.

In addition to its principal role as a medium of exchange, money is also the **standard of value** or **unit of account.** It is the yardstick for measuring and comparing the value of goods and services. For example, in lumping all goods and services together to compute gross domestic product, we evaluate each good at its market price in terms of money. And that dollar value is the common denominator that makes possible the summation of thousands of diverse goods and services.

Store of value: Money enables people to store wealth for future use.

Other Functions

Standard of deferred payments: Debt obligations to be settled at some future date are expressed in terms of money.

A third function of money is as a **store of value.** It is a convenient vehicle for storing wealth for future use, because it can easily be used for any purpose when the need arises. A related function is as a **standard of deferred payments**. Debts and obligations to be settled at some future date are expressed in terms of money.

THE VALUE OF MONEY

Purchasing power: the amount of goods and services one dollar will buy. It varies inversely with the rate of inflation.

The effectiveness of money in performing these roles depends on the stability of its value over time. The value of money is measured by the quantity of goods and services it buys, otherwise known as its **purchasing power.** It follows that its **value over time varies inversely with the rate of inflation.** A high rate of *inflation erodes the value of money and undermines its usefulness as a stable store of value or standard of deferred payments.* Why store your wealth in the form of money if its value in terms of goods and services declines? In *cases of galloping inflation of, say, 500 percent per year, money can even lose its value as a medium of exchange and unit of account.* Price stability is required for money to perform its functions well.

FOREIGN CURRENCIES

Exchange rate: the price of one country's currency in terms of another.

In each country, a different **currency** performs the role of money. It is the dollar ($) in the United States, the yen (¥) in Japan, the pound sterling (£) in the United Kingdom, the Euro in Europe, the Canadian dollar (Can. $) in Canada, the peso in Mexico, and the ruble in Russia. The euro is the currency of 12 countries on the European continent, rather than a currency of one country backed by its government. The value of one currency in terms of another is called an **exchange rate.** And the dollar exchange rates vary everyday in response to supply and demand conditions. The means used to make payments between countries are different from those employed within a country. Our concern is with money as a medium of exchange within the United States.

FORMS OF MONEY

Commodity Money

Based on the definition and functions of money, what instruments can serve as money? Historically, certain societies used a commodity, such as cattle, as money. But *commodity money* has important disadvantages. For ideal usage, the commodity must be *divisible, uniform, storable, durable, compact, and light* (easy to carry). It is only natural that *gold and silver* evolved into the most common commodity money. But with time, it became widely recognized that there is no need to use as money a commodity that possesses intrinsic value. *Paper money,* with the denominations printed on its face, can do just as well; and it would spare society the resources required to mine gold or silver.

Paper Money

Fiat money: money which has value by government decree. **Legal tender:** Money must be accepted by all in settlement of transactions. The value of money is determined by the amount of goods and services it can buy.

As a consequence, paper money came into general use. It possesses all the desirable properties mentioned in the preceding paragraph. But it has *no intrinsic value;* the paper on which money is printed is not worth very much. Hence it is called **fiat money.** It gives its owner command over wealth *by virtue of its general acceptability* as a means of payment. Since paper money is *backed by law*—that is, decreed as money by the government—it is **legal tender.** It must be accepted by all in settlement of transactions. However, nowhere does the government offer to exchange it for anything else—gold, silver, or whatever. A dollar is convertible into twenty nickels, ten dimes, or four quarters. It is held by people because everybody is willing to accept it in exchange for goods and services. And **its value is determined strictly by the amount of goods and services it buys—by its purchasing power.**

Paper money makes up *over 40 percent* of the nation's money supply. Another 3 percent or so is in *coins:* nickels, quarters, and so on, used for handling small transactions. Since coins are made out of metal, they do have some intrinsic value, but it must be less than their face value. For if the metal of which a dime is made were worth more than a dime, people would melt dimes and sell the metal.

Checking Accounts

Checking accounts, or demand deposits: allow the depositor to write checks against the deposit in settlement of transactions.

Most payments in the economy are made not by paper notes or coins; they *are made by check.* Consequently, the sums deposited in **checking accounts**—known as **demand deposits**—in banks are an important form of money. They entitle the depositor to write checks against the deposit in settlement of transactions. About *two thirds of the nation's money consists of demand deposits.* The other third is made up of coins and paper currency in circulation outside the banking system. Together, these forms make up money supply in its narrowest sense, known as M-1.

Savings Accounts

Why are savings accounts excluded from the definition of money? Because they are not used directly as a medium of exchange. However, it often takes as little as a phone call to have funds transferred from savings to checking accounts, at which point they become means of payment. Consequently, they may be called "near money." Thus, it becomes a matter of judgment whether savings accounts in commercial banks (banks that issue checking accounts) and thrift institutions (such as savings and loan associations) should be included as well in the definition of money. A broader definition, known as M-2, adds such deposits to M-1. And even broader definitions of the money stock are available, to be discussed in a later section.

To return to the narrow definition, M-1, it is clear that commercial-bank activities play a central role in providing money to the community. Banks are in the business of accepting deposits from people with one hand and making loans and investments with the other.

Bank Deposits

Consider the deposit side first, and in particular, checking deposits. If people deposit money in a regular checking account (demand deposit), it earns them no interest. Alternatively, interest-earning checking accounts earn low interest, but require a sizable minimum balance to be kept in the account or in a savings account in the same bank. Such deposits are used mainly for safekeeping, and for the convenience of being able to write checks against the deposit. The bank must honor these checks up to the amount of the deposit (or up to the limit of an agreed-upon line of credit). It may charge customers for the check-writing service if they fail to maintain a minimum balance in an interest-bearing account. But we overlook this detail.

However, the "safekeeping" feature of the deposit does not mean that the bank keeps on hand the entire deposit. It is unlikely that all depositors would come to withdraw their money on any given day. Experience has taught banks that over any given period, some people deposit new money while others withdraw money. It is sufficient to keep on hand only a fraction—say, 20 percent—of the deposits, to meet all demands for withdrawal. The remaining 80 percent can be lent out. If all depositors came at the same time to withdraw their money, the bank would not be able to meet that demand. This is called a "run" on the bank. It happened in the 1930s and was partly responsible for the financial collapse associated with the Great Depression. But in normal periods, when confidence in commercial banks is not shaken, such "runs" do not occur. Consequently, banks operate on the principle of **fractional reserve**. They maintain in reserves only a fraction of the demand deposits they owe their depositors. The **forms that these reserves take are cash in vault and deposit with the central bank,** the bank of banks.

Fractional reserve system: a banking system in which banks keep on reserves only a fraction of the deposits they owe depositors. Reserves consist of cash and deposits with the central bank, (the Federal Reserve).

Reserve requirement: Banks are required to keep a certain percentage of deposits as reserves at all times.

Bank Loans and Investments

Banks make their profit by lending to people or by investing in securities such as government bonds, the part of their deposits that they do not keep in reserve—the 80 percent in the previous example. Of course, they receive interest on these loans and investments. Clearly, they wish to maximize the amount lent out or invested, and to minimize the fraction kept in reserve. One reason for federal control over the banking industry is to ensure that reserves are not reduced below a prudent level. Unlike any other industry, banks deal in other people's money; their **depositors need to be protected**. For that reason, *the Federal Reserve establishes minimum* *reserve requirements against deposits. A more important reason for the* **legal reserve** *requirement is the need to control the nation's money supply*; it will be explained later.

Protection to Depositors

Three other types of protection are offered depositors *against possible imprudent behavior of commercial banks:* periodic *examinations and audits of banks' books*, reviewing their business practices; laws *regulating the types and quantities of assets* in which they may place their money; and deposit insurance, *insurance of bank deposits by the Federal Deposit Insurance Corporation* **(FDIC).** Under the last provision, each checking account is insured up to $100,000, and similar insurance is available for savings accounts in savings and loan associations (S&Ls). This means that in cases of bank failure, depositors do not lose (subject to a limit of $100,000 per account); only the owners of the bank's stocks, who knowingly assumed the risk as owners of the bank, lose.

FDIC (Federal Deposit Insurance Corporation): A government agency that insures each checking account up to $100,000.

HOW CHECKS SERVE AS A MEDIUM OF EXCHANGE

A Glimpse at the Banking System

Most commercial banks in the United States do not have branches outside the state in which they operate. But that rule is breaking down as interstate banking becomes increasingly common. There are more than 14,000 commercial banks in the United States, and the system of individual banks is known as *unit banking*. It contrasts with the branch-banking system practiced in the United Kingdom, where each of eight major banks has many branches throughout the country.

Each country also has a central bank, or bank of banks. It is called the Bank of England in the United Kingdom, and the European Central Bank (ECB) on the continent of Europe. Located in Frankfurt, Germany, it is responsible for the issue of euros—the currency of 12 countries. In Japan, it is the Bank of Japan. The central bank of the United States is the **Federal Reserve System**, or the Fed. This country is divided into twelve districts, each having its Federal Reserve Bank (FRB), as shown in Figure 20-1. Some district banks have branches in other major cities within their district. Thus, the Federal Reserve Bank of Chicago (7th District) has a branch in Detroit, and the FRB of San Francisco (12th District) has branches in Los Angeles, Portland, Seattle, and Salt Lake City. At the head of the system is the Board of Governors of the Federal Reserve in Washington, D.C.

Federal Reserve System or the Fed. is the central bank of the United States.

The Fed deals only with the *government* and with *commercial banks*, not with the general public. It is sometimes called the banker's bank. *Each commercial bank keeps a balance with its district FRB. These balances are legal reserves.* The Fed is charged with the conduct of monetary policy and other matters, to be examined in the next chapter. At this point, our

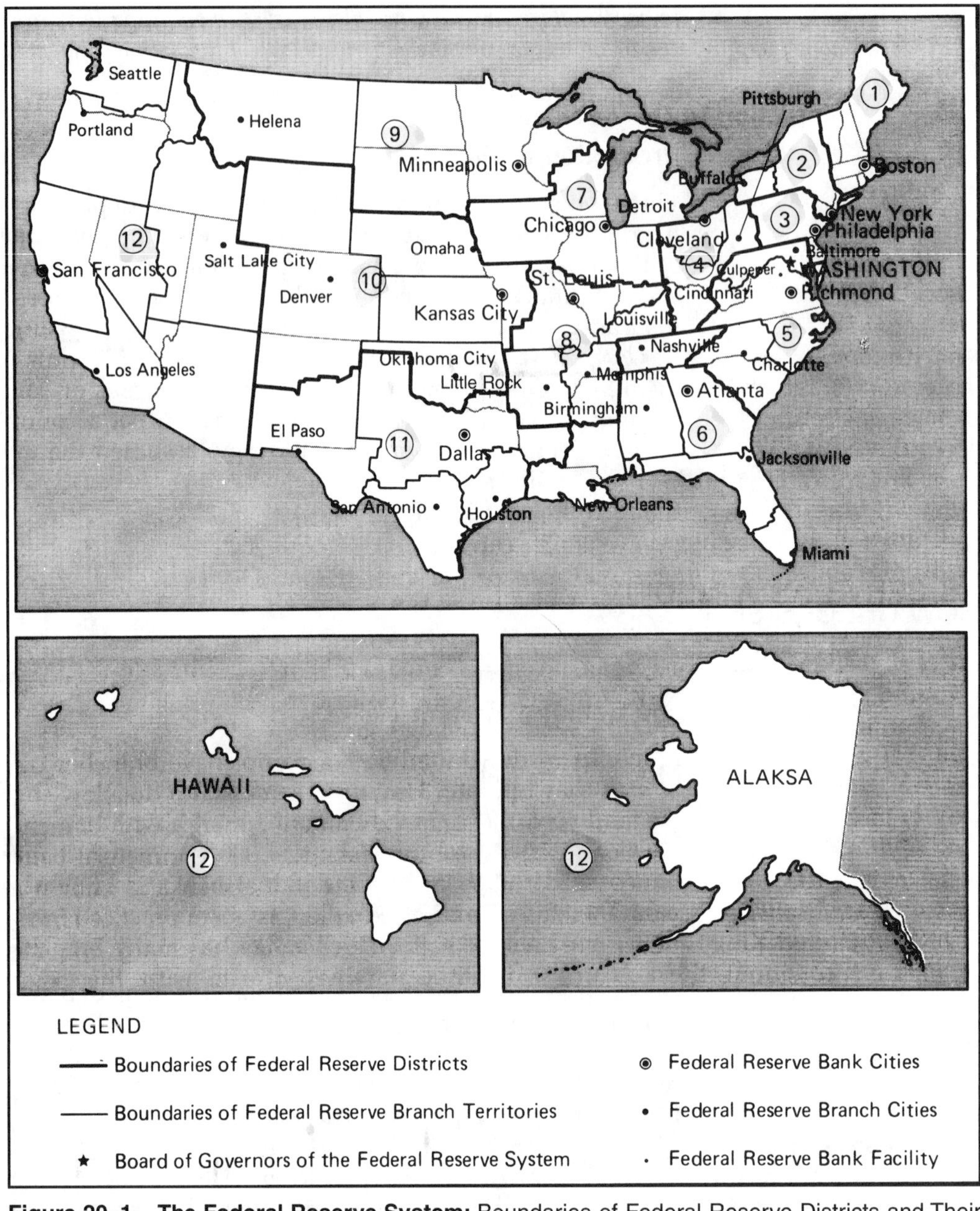

Figure 20–1 The Federal Reserve System: Boundaries of Federal Reserve Districts and Their Branch Territories. *Source: Federal Reserve Bulletin.*

interest lies in one function: the "clearing" of checks, which the Fed performs for all commercial banks, and which makes possible the use of checks as a medium of exchange.[1]

[1]Only a third of all commercial banks in the United States are members of the Federal Reserve System. They are known as "member banks"; the remaining banks are called "nonmember banks." Member banks account for three quarters of all demand deposits. But the check clearing services are provided to all banks—members and nonmembers alike.

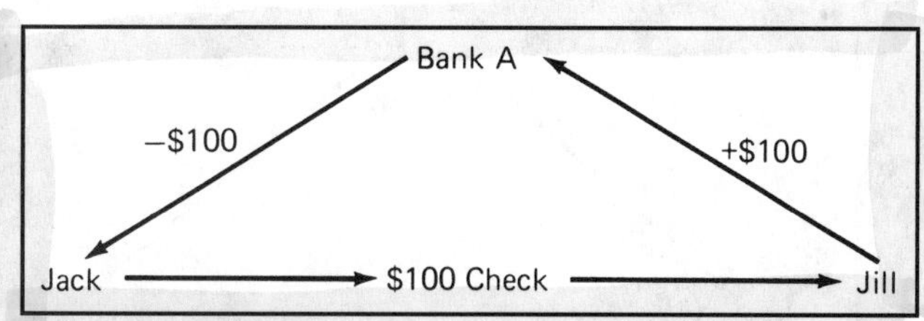

Figure 20–2 Check Clearing when Both Participants Bank at the Bank

Check clearing: Checks perform the function of money because of the check clearing system between banks, operated by the Central Bank.

The Check-Clearing Mechanism

Suppose Jack gives Jill a check for $100 drawn on his bank. She deposits the check in her bank. If they both reside in the same town and bank at the same bank, Bank A, the outcome is simple: Bank A adds $100 to Jill's account and subtracts $100 from Jack's account. This is sketched out in Figure 20–2. The bank imprints its stamp on the reverse side of the check and mails it back to Jack at the end of the month with Jack's canceled checks. When Jack receives his canceled checks, they will include his check to Jill, stamped on the back by Bank A. The check served as a medium of exchange. If Jack and Jill reside in the same city but bank at two different banks, only a slight modification of the process is needed. The banks' representatives meet at the end of each business day to exchange checks drawn upon each other's banks and subsequently adjust the accounts of their respective customers in the manner previously outlined.

Next, assume that Jack and Jill reside in two different cities, which, however, are within the same Federal Reserve district. For example, Jack banks at Bank A in Milwaukee, and Jill at Bank B in Chicago. Jack mails Jill a $100 check drawn on his account in Bank A, which Jill deposits in her account in Bank B. Bank B adds $100 to her account ("credits" her account by $100), imprints its stamp on the reverse side of the check, and sends the check to the district FRB in Chicago. The FRB of Chicago places its stamp on the reverse side of the check, adds $100 to the account that Bank B maintains there, and subtracts $100 from the account of Bank A. In other words, the district FRB credits the account of Bank B and debits the account of Bank A by $100. Since these accounts represent legal reserves of the *two banks, their reserve positions are affected accordingly.* The FRB of Chicago then mails the check to Bank B in Milwaukee, which in turn deducts $100 from Jack's account (debits Jack's account). Bank B adds its stamp to the reverse side of the check and includes it in the canceled checks that Jack will receive at the end of the month. This process is sketched out in Figure 20–3. The check has served as a means of payment. Bank B gained and Bank A lost $100 in deposits (legal reserves) with the FRB. When the canceled check returns to Jack at the end of the month, it will have the stamps of the three banks on the reverse side. As far as Jack is concerned, the canceled *check is also a legal receipt* proving that payment has been made.

Finally, consider the case in which Jack and Jill reside in two different Federal Reserve districts—say, San Francisco and Chicago, respectively.

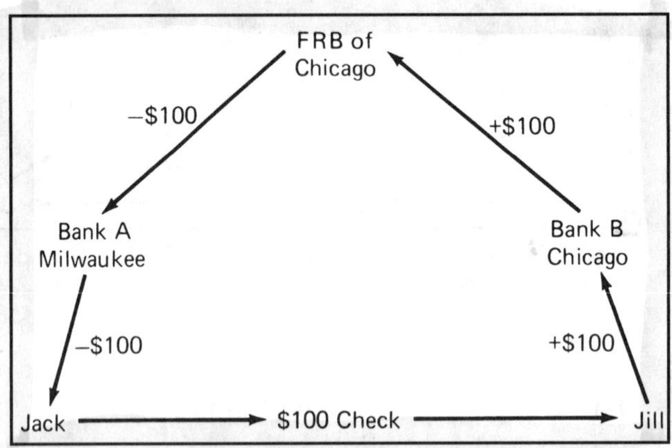

Figure 20–3 Check Clearing when Both Participants Reside in Same FR District

Then, a check from Jack to Jill requires clearing between the two FRBs, which is done through the "Inter-District Settlement Fund" at the Board of Governors in Washington, D.C. The principle remains the same, except that one layer is added to the clearing pyramid, as shown in Figure 20–4. The added layer is shown at the top: Each FRB maintains a balance with the Inter-District Settlement Fund, and the balances of the FRBs of Chicago and San Francisco are adjusted upward and downward, respectively, by $100. When Jack receives his canceled check, there will now be five stamps on the reverse side: two of the commercial banks' and three of the

Figure 20–4 Check Clearing when Participants Reside in Different Federal Reserve Districts

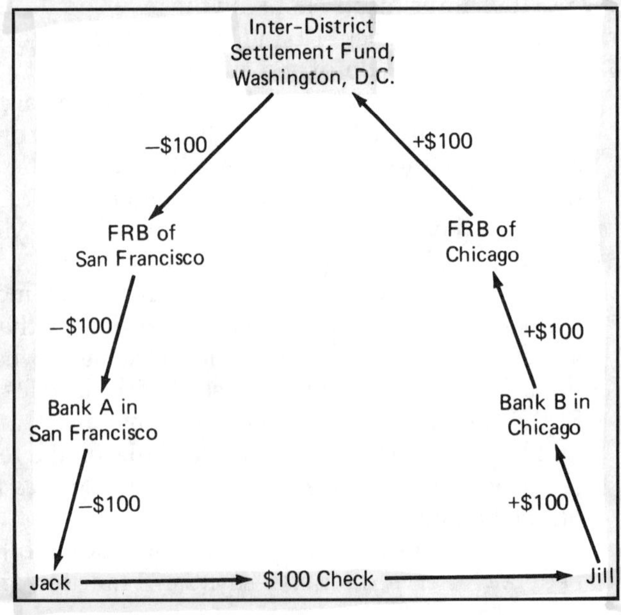

FRBs'. *The check has served as a means of payment.* Thus, since they perform the role of money, checking accounts, or demand deposits, are a component of money supply.

Because of the large distances involved, the Federal Reserve uses special plans to speed up the transfer of checks between districts. Still, a couple of days may elapse between the credit gained by Bank B in the FRB of Chicago and the debit accrued to Bank A in the FRB of San Francisco. Since commercial-bank balances with the Fed are legal reserves, there is a temporary net gain in such reserves throughout the system, known as float.

Every country has an internal clearing system for checks. And that is how checks perform the main function of money, as a medium of exchange. But there is no clearing mechanism between countries, and there is no international central bank.[2] Payments between countries are executed by different means.

ACTIVITIES OF A SINGLE BANK

Because of their importance in the economy, this section inquires more closely into the nature of commercial bank operations.

How Banks Keep Accounts

Balance sheet: A table in the form of a T, which shows what the bank owns (assets) and what the bank owes (liabilities).

Debit: Appearing on the left side of the T-account, is what the bank owes.

Credit: Appearing on the right side of the T-account, is what the bank owns.

Like any other firm, banks keep books. But our interest in their accounting practices is limited to their contribution to money supply.

A bank's **balance sheet** is an account that shows what the bank *owns*—its *assets*—and what the bank *owes*—its liabilities**.** Because it is arranged in a form similar to a capital T, it is often called a *T account.* The bank's liabilities, what it owes, are shown on the right; the bank's assets, what it owns, are tabulated on the left.

Our interest is confined to a few of these items, shown in the following T account. On the liabilities side, the main item is demand deposits of $5,000. This refers to money that customers keep in the bank in checking accounts against which they can write checks in settlement of transactions. The bank owes that money to its customers, in the sense that it must honor checks and withdrawal slips up to the limit of the balance of each account. Hence, those deposits are shown on the liabilities side.[3]

---

[2]The World Bank is sometimes thought of as an international central bank. Not so! It is a bank that raises money in the industrial countries to make loans to underdeveloped countries. If there is anything remotely resembling an international central bank, it is the International Monetary Fund (IMF). But even the IMF is nothing like a central bank, and it certainly does not perform the check-clearing function.

[3]Another liabilities item, deleted here for simplicity, is **net worth**. It's the shareholders' equity, or (in a sense) what the bank owes its shareholders. In the case of our hypothetical Bank A, it would be $500, the difference between assets and liabilities. It would balance the T account. In each bank, *assets always equal liabilities.*

Hypothetical Balance Sheet of Bank A

Assets		Liabilities	
Cash in vault	$100	Demand deposits	$5,000
Deposits with the FRB	$1,000		
Loans	$2,000		
Investments	$2,400		

The assets side includes what the bank owns and what is owed to the bank by others. The items shown are

1. Cash (paper currency and coins) in the vault.
2. Money the bank keeps on balance with the FRB of its district. This is a liability of the Fed and an asset of the commercial bank; the Fed owes it to the bank. *Vault cash and deposits with the Fed are the bank's legal reserves.*
3. Loans that the bank extends to its customers. Since the customers owe this money to the bank, such loans are an asset of the bank and a liability of the customers. The bank earns interest on its loans and investments.
4. Investments, such as U.S. government bonds owned by the bank.

Examples of Bank's Transactions

Three illustrations of how transactions affect the bank's balance sheet may be useful. First, if Jack deposits $100 cash in the bank, that sum will appear as Jack's demand deposit on the liabilities side, because the bank owes the money to Jack, and as "vault cash" on the assets side. This is seen in the following T account of the bank:

Assets		Liabilities	
Vault cash	+$100	$\text{D.D.}_{\text{Jack}}$	+$100

Should the bank transfer the money to the district FRB, the "vault cash" on the assets side will be replaced by "deposit with the FRB," as follows:

Assets		Liabilities	
Vault cash	–$100	$\text{D.D.}_{\text{Jack}}$	+$100
Dep. with FRB	+$100		

Second, suppose Mary takes out a $500 loan. The customary bank procedure is *not* to give the money out in cash. Rather, the bank opens a new checking account (demand deposit) for Mary, against which she can write checks. This is a *liability* to the bank, for it must honor these checks. In turn, the $500 appears as a loan on the *assets* side of the balance sheet, since it is money owed to the bank:

Assets		Liabilities	
$\text{Loan}_{\text{Mary}}$	+$500	$\text{D.D.}_{\text{Mary}}$	+$500

Once Mary has written the checks and the bank has honored them, Mary's D.D. disappears from the liabilities side of the T account, but the loan item remains on the assets side until it is paid up.

Finally, suppose the bank purchases a government security worth $100. If the bond is bought from an individual customer, then it would show up on the assets side of the bank's balance sheet. A likely payment arrangement is for the bank to increase the customer's demand deposit (against which he can write checks) so that that same amount appears on the liabilities side of the bank's balance sheet as a D.D.:

Assets		Liabilities	
Investments	+$100	D.D.	+$100

If the bond is bought from the FRB, it would also show up on the bank's assets side. But the payment for it is executed simply by reducing another asset item—the bank's deposits with the FRB, which are the bank's legal reserves:

Assets		Liabilities
Investments	+$100	
Deposit with FRB	–$100	

Clearly, each transaction appears twice on the bank's balance sheet. And when all items are included, *Assets = Liabilities.*

What Is the Legal-Reserve Ratio?

Reserve ratio: the ratio between legal reserves (a credit item) and demand deposit liabilities. Minimum legal reserve requirement is a level below which the reserve ratio may not fall.

In order to restrict commercial-bank lending to levels considered prudent, and also (as will be seen later) to regulate money supply, the Federal Reserve imposes minimum-reserve requirements on commercial banks. It was already suggested that banks must keep reserves against their demand-deposit liabilities. And these reserves come in two forms: vault cash, and deposits with the district FRB. Because vault cash is a relatively small item, we assume (for simplicity) that it is not part of legal reserves. Thus, the bank's **reserve ratio** is a ratio between an asset item (in the numerator) and a liability item (in the denominator):

$$\text{Reserve ratio} = \frac{\text{Deposit with the FRB}}{\text{Demand deposit liabilities}}$$

Under the now-common *fractional-reserve system* this ratio is far below 1.

In controlling the banking system, the Federal Reserve sets a minimum below which this ratio may not fall. This is known as the *minimum-legal-reserve requirement*. It ranges between 10 and 20 percent, depending mainly on the size of the city in which the bank is located.

For the sake of simplicity, assume that the required-reserve ratio is 20 percent, or 1/5, and it is wholly in the form of deposits with the FRB. If

Required reserves: the amount of reserves the bank is required to hold.

Excess reserves: reserves held over and above the amount required to satisfy the legal-minimum reserve requirement.

a bank acquires a new $5,000 demand deposit, then it is required to maintain a minimum of $1,000 in reserves. This amount is its **required reserves.** Should the bank maintain, say, $1,200 in reserves, the extra $200 is known as **excess reserves.** *Excess reserves are reserves over and above the amount required to satisfy the legal minimum-reserve requirement.*

How Much Can a Single Bank Lend?

An individual bank can lend no more than the amount of its excess reserves. To see why this is so, assume that Jack deposits $1,000 in cash in his bank, Bank A, and the bank in turn transfers the entire amount to the district FRB and places it on deposit there. Bank A's balance sheet would be affected as follows:

Bank A

Assets	Liabilities
Dep. with FRB +$1,000	D.D.$_{\text{Jack}}$ +$1,000

What is an asset to the commercial bank is a liability to the FRB; the Fed is liable to Bank A and must honor withdrawals up to $1,000. In turn, the Fed receives the cash, which appears on its assets side. The Fed's balance sheet is affected as follows:

District FRB

Assets		Liabilities	
Cash	+$1,000	Deposit of Bank A	+$1.000

Now Bank A has $200 in required legal reserves and $800 in excess reserves.

Now suppose Jill, another customer, applies for an $800 loan to purchase a washer and dryer. After ascertaining her creditworthiness, the bank makes the loan. It opens a demand deposit (checking account) in her name, against which she may write checks up to $800. A loan of $800 also appears on the bank's assets side. Combining this and the preceding step, Bank A's balance sheet will be affected as follows:

Bank A

Assets		Liabilities	
Dep. with FRB	$1,000	D.D. $_{\text{Jack}}$	$1,000
Loan$_{\text{Jill}}$	$800	D.D. $_{\text{Jill}}$	$800

Jill buys the washer and dryer from a store and pays $800 by a check drawn on her account in Bank A. Given the large number of banks in this country, the chances are that the store would have an account with another bank, Bank B, in which that check is deposited. Bank B sends the check

to the Fed for clearing and thus acquires a deposit at its district FRB. Bank B's balance sheet will be affected as follows:

Bank B

Assets		Liabilities	
Dep. with FRB	+$800	$D.D._{Store}$	+$800

In turn, the Fed credits the account of Bank B and debits the account of Bank A. Its balance sheet will be affected as follows:

Federal Reserve Bank

Assets	Liabilities	
	Dep. of Bank B	+$800
	Dep. of Bank A	–$800

After the check clears, Bank A is affected in two ways: Jill's demand deposit disappears; the bank has honored its commitment and is no longer liable. On the assets side, the bank loses $800 of its original deposit with the Fed, leaving it with only ($1,000 – $800) $200 deposit. Its balance sheet after this step will then look like this:

Bank A

Assets		Liabilities	
Dep. with FRB	+$200	$D.D._{Jack}$	$1,000
$Loan_{Jill}$	$800		

Because it lent Jill the amount of its excess reserves, the bank now has only $200 left in legal reserves, precisely enough to meet the reserve requirement against Jack's original deposit of $1,000. The other *$800 was "drained away" to other banks in the system.*

Had the bank lent Jill anything above its excess reserves—say, $850—it would have been left with *insufficient reserves* (only $150 or 15 percent) to cover Jack's deposit, once the loan was drained away to other banks. Readers can repeat the exercise, tracing the effects on the various banks, and prove to themselves that the final position of Bank A would then be:

Bank A

Assets		Liabilities	
Dep. with FRB	+$150	$D.D._{Jack}$	$1,000
$Loan_{Jill}$	$850		

In a unit banking system, a single bank can lend at most the amount of its excess reserves. Only if the bank is certain that a given proportion of the loans it makes would be redeposited in it could it lend out more. But with 14,000 unit banks in the country, this may be too much of a gamble. On the other hand, as its demand deposits increase, the bank may wish to increase its cash holdings or keep a certain amount in excess reserves, and consequently, it may lend somewhat less than its excess reserves. Despite these qualifications, which may operate in off-setting directions, a reasonable rule of thumb is that a single bank in the United States can lend exactly the amount of its excess reserves.

LENDING POTENTIAL OF THE ENTIRE BANKING SYSTEM—MONEY CREATION BY BANKS

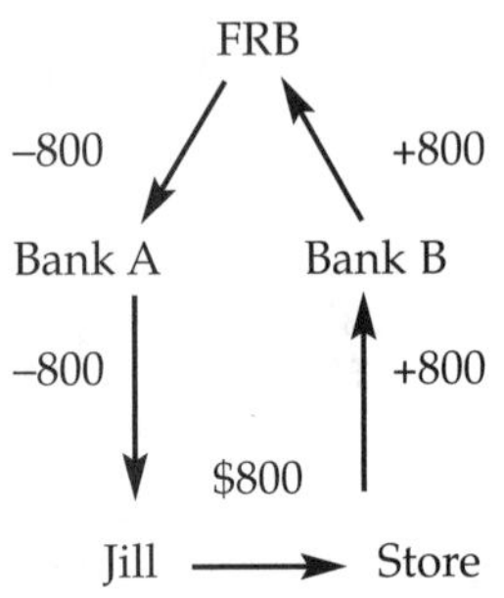

The top of the clearing pyramid shows what happens at the FRB; the right-hand side shows what happens in Bank B and the left-hand side shows what happens in Bank A.

The Mechanics of Money Creation

What is true of the individual bank is not true of the entire banking system combined. A single bank can lend only the amount of its excess reserves because these reserves are likely to be drained away to other banks. *But these other banks are part of the system.* Consequently, the banking system as a whole can lend a multiple of the excess reserves. In the process, **banks create money in the form of demand deposits.**

To demonstrate this proposition, we return to the example of Jack's depositing $1,000 cash in Bank A. No new money was created in this act. One form of money, cash, was simply converted into another form, a demand deposit. As we saw earlier, Bank A now has $800 in excess reserves, which it lends to Jill by creating a demand deposit against which Jill can write checks. After she writes her check and it is deposited in Bank B, Bank A loses the reserves, but Bank B gains them. The following T accounts recapture this transaction, which was shown in detail in previous T accounts.

Bank B

Assets		Liabilities	
Dep. with FRB	$800	D.D.$_{Store}$	$800

FRB

Assets	Liabilities	
	Dep. of Bank B	+$800
	Dep. of Bank A	–$800

Bank A

Assets		Liabilities	
Dep. with FRB	$200	D.D.$_{Jack}$	$1,000
Jill's loan	$800		

Bank A is now all "loaned out," but Bank B has excess reserves of $640—reserves of $800 minus required legal reserves of $160 ($800/5).[4]

Assume next that Nick borrows $640 from Bank B. The loan is made in the form of a demand deposit against which Nick can write checks. It affects the bank's T account as follows:

Bank B

Assets		Liabilities	
Dep. with FRB	$800	D.D.$_{Store}$	$800
Loan$_{Nick}$	$640	D.D.$_{Nick}$	$640

Next, Nick writes a $640 check to Nancy, who deposits it in her bank, Bank C. Once the check clears through the Fed, Bank B loses reserves and

[4]To figure out excess reserves, divide the D.D. *Liabilities* ($800) by 5 to obtain required reserves ($160). Then subtract the $160 from the Dep. with FRB *on the assets side* ($800) to obtain $640 in excess reserves.

Bank C gains them. On its liabilities side, Bank B honored the $640 D.D., so this item disappears. The following T accounts show the changes in Banks B and C, as well as those of the Fed's T account.

Bank B

Assets		Liabilities	
Dep. with FRB	$160	D.D.$_{Store}$	$800
Loan$_{Nick}$	$640		

FRB

Assets	Liabilities	
	Dep. of Bank B	–$640
	Dep. of Bank C	+$640

Bank C

Assets		Liabilities	
Dep. with FRB	$640	D.D.$_{Nancy}$	$640

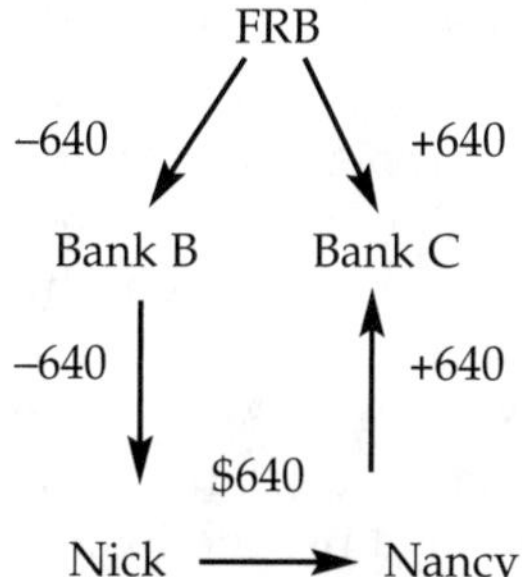

The top of the clearing pyramid shows what happens at the FRB; the right-hand side shows what happens in Bank C and the left-hand shows what happens in Bank B.

Bank B is now "loaned out." Note that it is left with an $800 demand deposit—a form of money—that was not there before. This amount is money because the store may write checks against the account.

Bank C acquires a new D.D. for $640, against which it needs legal reserves of $128 ($640/5). It has excess reserves of $512 ($640 – $128), which it can lend. Suppose Steve borrows the $512 in order to pay up a debt he owes Tina. The bank sets up the loan in the form of a D.D., and its T account is affected as follows:

Bank C

Assets		Liabilities	
Dep. with FRB	+$640	D.D.$_{Nancy}$	$640
Loan$_{Steve}$ $	$512	D.D.$_{Steve}$	$512

Next, Steve gives Tina a check for $512, which she proceeds to deposit in her bank, Bank D. That bank, in turn, sends it to the Fed for clearing, following which Bank D gains and Bank C loses $512 in reserves. This is the effect on the two banks, as well as on the FRB:

Bank C

Assets		Liabilities	
Dep. with FRB	$128	D.D.$_{Nancy}$	$640
Loan$_{Steve}$	$512		

FRB

Assets	Liabilities	
	Bank C Dep.	–$512
	Bank D Dep.	+$512

Bank D

Assets		Liabilities	
Dep. with FRB	$512	D.D.$_{Tina}$	$512

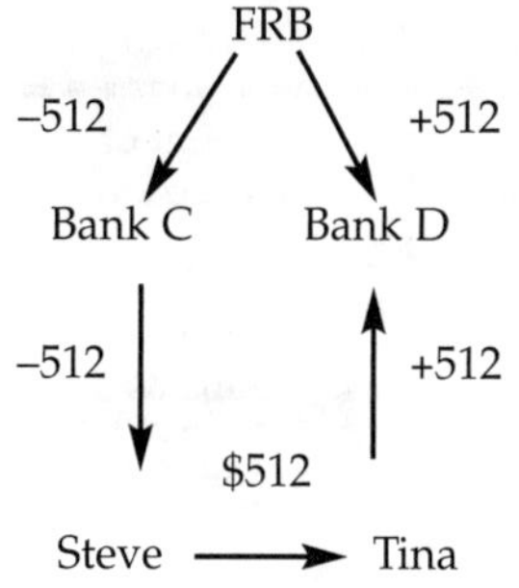

The top of the clearing pyramid shows what happens at the FRB; the right-hand side shows what happens in Bank D and the left-hand side shows what happens in Bank C.

Bank C's reserve position (deposit at the Fed) declines by $512, from $640 to $128. Steve's D.D. disappears, since the bank has honored its commitment, and Steve's loan still remains on the assets side. Nancy's D.D. remains on the books; it is newly created money, because Nancy is entitled to write checks against her deposit.

In Bank D's T account, a new $512 deposit appears, placed there by Tina. At 20 percent minimum-reserve requirements, Bank D's legal reserves are $102.40 ($512/5), and its excess reserves are $409.60 ($512 – $102.40).

Assume next that Paul borrows that amount, with the intention of paying Mary. After the loan is made, Bank D's T account is as follows:

Bank D

Assets		Liabilities	
Dep. with FRB	$512	D.D.$_{Tina}$	$512
Loan$_{Paul}$ $	$409.60	D.D.$_{Paul}$	$409.60

Paul writes a check to Mary, drawn on Bank D, which Mary deposits in her bank, Bank E. After the check clears through the Fed, the position of the banks is as follows:

Bank D

Assets		Liabilities	
Dep. with FRB	$102.40	D.D.$_{\text{Tina}}$	$512
Loan$_{\text{Paul}}$	$409.60		

FRB

Assets	Liabilities	
	Bank D Dep.	–$409.60
	Bank E Dep.	+$409.60

Bank E

Assets		Liabilities	
Dep. with FRB	$409.60	D.D.$_{\text{Mary}}$	$409.60

Bank D is now "loaned out." But Tina's D.D. of $512 is left on the books. It is newly created money, since Tina can write checks on her account. Bank E acquired a new $409.60 D.D. from Mary, against which the required reserves are $81.92 ($409.60/5), and the bank's excess reserves are $327.68 ($409.60 – $81.92). This amount it can lend to Mark by opening a D.D. in Mark's name. Mark writes a check, drawn on that account, to Linda, who in turn deposits it in her bank, Bank F. And so the process continues through a succession of banks, where each bank lends the amount of its excess reserves, and a check written against the loan is deposited in some other bank or banks in the system. The reader may wish to continue working out three additional steps.

Money Creation by the Banking System

Reviewing the entire process, we note that the initial deposit (by Jack) in Bank A created no new money. But it did *create $800 in excess reserves.* That was the basis for the subsequent series of transactions. Referring back to the T accounts, we note that each transaction left a bank with a D.D. that was not there before. Table 20–1 summarizes the new position of the banks, triggered by the $800 in excess reserves in Bank A.

The amounts listed in the third column constitute a convergent series. The numbers in the column decline, because at each step a fixed proportion, one-fifth, is "drained" into required reserves. The leftover number is therefore 80 percent of the number above it. The column sums up to

Table 20–1 Summary of the New Position of the Banks

Bank	D.D. of	Amount of D.D. Created	Amount of New Reserves	Amount of New Loans
B	Store	$800	$160	$640
C	Nancy	$640	$128	$512
D	Tina	$512	$102.40	$409.60
E	Mary	$409.60	$81.92	$327.68
.	.	$327.70	$65.54	$262.16
.	.	$262.32	.	.
.	.	$209.86	.	.
.	.	.	.	.
.	.	.	.	.
.	.	.	.	.
.	.	.	.	.
.	.	.	.	.
.	.	.	.	.
Total		$4,000	$800	$3,200

$4,000, or five *times the original excess reserves.* Since demand deposits are money, the amount of $4,000 in new money was created by the banking system. The number 5 is known as the **deposit multiplier:** *It is the number by which excess reserves are multiplied to get the total demand deposits created in the system.* It is **equal in size to the inverse of the required reserve ratio** (20 percent or 1/5, in our case), or of the proportion drained into reserves in each step:

Deposit multiplier: the number by which excess reserves are multiplied to obtain the total demand deposits that can be created by the banking system. It equals the reciprocal of the required reserve ratio. The multiplicity arises from the fact that deposits drained from one bank are deposited in other banks in the system.

$$\text{Deposit multiplier} = \frac{1}{\text{Required reserve ratio}}$$

In turn, the amount of **new money** that the banking system can create equals **the excess reserves times the deposit multiplier.** Had the legal-reserve requirement been 10 percent, the deposit multiplier would have been 10, and excess reserves of $800 would have made possible the creation of $8,000 in new deposit money. Alternatively, with a legal-reserve requirement of 25 percent, the deposit multiplier is 4, and $3,200 in new deposit money can be created if excess reserves equal $800. Likewise, the convergent series shown in the fourth column sums up to $800; it is the total amount of new reserves in the system. Finally, the convergent series in the last column adds up to $3,200; it is the total amount of new loans extended by the banking system. We can write the balance sheet of the entire banking system put together, excluding Bank A, as follows:

The Banking System

Assets		Liabilities	
Dep. with FRB	+$800	D.D.	$4,000
Loans	$3,200		

The banking system as a whole created $4,000 in new deposit money, on the basis of the original $800 in excess reserves. Given a 20 percent legal-reserve requirement, that is the maximum amount of money deposits that can be created. *Money is created when banks make loans; money is "destroyed" when loans are repaid.* Although an individual bank does not appear to create any money, the banking system as a whole creates most of our money supply. The statement, "printing money," is just a figure of speech. In fact, money is created by banks when they open demand deposits to extend loans. **Money is nothing but debt**—*either debt of the Federal Reserve* (currency notes, which appear on the liability side of the Fed's balance sheet) *or debt of commercial banks* (demand deposits). It has no intrinsic value, and *it is not redeemable in any other asset, such as gold.* It serves as a means of payment by virtue of its general acceptability, either by force of law (currency) or of custom (checks).

WHAT DETERMINES THE VALUE OF MONEY?

Scarcity of money: money needs to be scarce

The value of money lies strictly in the command it affords over goods and services. To retain and bolster this feature, money needs to be **scarce** enough so that its value in terms of goods and services is not eroded. In other words, the real value of money, its purchasing power, varies inversely with the average price of goods and services in the economy (the price index): When prices rise, the value of money declines. Herein lies the danger of inflation. When the value of money declines, it becomes less useful as a store of value, for people lose confidence in it. And in the case of hyperinflation, money may lose its usefulness even as a medium of exchange, and people may revert to barter transactions. A certain degree of price stability is required for money to perform its functions well.

Because the quantity of money relative to the quantity of goods and services available determines the value of money, it is important *to keep money relatively scarce. The regulation of money supply is an important component of monetary policy conducted by the Federal Reserve.* Left solely to commercial banks, the money stock is likely to grow all too fast. For banks make their profit by extending loans, and in that way, they create money. It is therefore important to have central control over their money-creating activity.

WHAT IS MONEY?

M_1: equals Currency + Checking accounts + Negotiated order of Withdrawal (NOW) accounts. **M_2** = M_1 + Savings deposits + Small Certificates of Deposit.

Liquidity: the ease and speed with which an asset can be converted into cash without a loss.

Earlier in this chapter, money was defined as currency in circulation (outside the banking system) and demand deposits (checking accounts). Certainly these assets perform the functions of medium of exchange and store of value. They constitute the narrowest definition of money, officially labeled by the Fed as **M_1**, where *M* stands for the money stock. Because it is possible to write checks against bank accounts that are not strictly checking accounts, M_1 also includes: (1) checking accounts in depository institutions other than commercial banks, such as credit unions and mutual savings banks; and (2) nonchecking accounts in commercial banks that can be automatically converted into checking accounts, such as the "automatic transfer from savings" and "negotiated order of withdrawal" (known as "checkable deposits")—ATS and NOW accounts.

What about savings deposits, six- and thirty-month certificates of deposit (CDs) with denominations under $100,000, and shares in money-market mutual funds? They certainly perform the store-of-value function. Although they cannot be used directly as means of payment, they can be converted into instruments (demand deposits) that can. *The ease and speed with which an asset can be converted into cash without a loss indicates its degree of* **liquidity.** A passbook savings account is totally liquid, but a six-month CD is less so: Its holder must await maturity to obtain cash for it, or must incur a loss if it is cashed prior to maturity. Still, consumer behavior in switching from one of these assets to another suggests that they are regarded as close substitutes. Also, these assets perform the "store of value" and "unit of account" functions of money. Consequently, the financial instruments listed at the beginning of this paragraph are lumped together and added to M_1 to obtain **M_2**, a broader definition of money supply. And M_3, a still broader definition, equals M_2 plus time deposits of $100,000 or more.

▶ LIQUIDITY

The term *liquidity* describes the ease with which an asset can be *converted into cash without a loss.* On the one hand, demand deposits and savings accounts are totally liquid, for they can be converted into cash upon demand. On the other end of the spectrum, real estate and industrial plants are not liquid assets. They cannot be sold instantly, and their seller may incur a loss. Corporate stocks are more liquid than real estate, since they can be sold on the spur of the moment. But because of the risk of financial loss (the selling price may be lower than the purchase price), they are still not considered completely liquid. A loss (gain) on the sale of stocks is called a **capital loss (gain)**. The same rule applies to most corporate bonds. Government bonds are generally more liquid. And next in the order of liquidity are banks' certificates of deposit and similar financial instruments. In that fashion, all assets can be ranked in the order of their liquidity.

Capital loss (gain): a loss (gain) on the sale of assets (e.g. stocks) as their prices changed since date of purchase.

Finally, the Fed has also adopted a very broad measure of liquid assets, labeled L. It equals M_3 plus other liquid assets not included elsewhere, such as commercial paper, Treasury bills and other liquid Treasury securities, and U.S. savings bonds.

Table 20–2 lists four monetary aggregates. Money supply measures, especially M_1 and M_2, grew in absolute amount in practically all years. What changes from year to year is the *rate of growth* in the money stock: In some years, that rate is high; in others it is low.

Table 20–2 Monetary Aggregates in the United States, December 2005

Aggregate	Components	$ Billions	
M_1		1,369	
	Currency outside banks		724
	Demand deposits		321
	Other checkable deposits		317
	Traveler's checks (of nonbank issuers)		7
M_2		6,601	
	M_1		1,369
	plus:		
	Savings deposits at all institutions		3,621
	Small denomination time deposits		974
	Money market funds		637
M_3			
	M_2	10,169	
	plus		6,601
	Large denomination time deposits		1,359
	Other		2,209

SUMMARY

Money is first and foremost a medium of exchange or means of payment. Its other functions are to serve as a store of value and a unit of account. Each country has its own monetary unit, and the price of one currency in terms of another is called an *exchange rate.*

Money is debt. It is not backed by any real asset, such as gold or silver. The narrowly defined money supply (M_1) consists of currency notes outside the banks, which are a liability of the Fed, and demand deposits, which are the liability of commercial banks. Demand deposits (checking accounts) can serve as a medium of exchange by virtue of the national check clearing system.

Loans are made by creating a demand deposit against which the borrower can write checks. A single bank can lend only the amount of its excess reserves, because checks drawn on it are apt to be "drained away" to other banks in the system. But the banking system as a whole can lend a multiple of its excess reserves. In doing so, it creates money. The "money multiplier" is the inverse of the legal-reserve ratio.

Banks make profits by extending loans. But in doing so, they also create money. If left unchecked, they would have an incentive to create too much money. Hence the need to control the banking industry and the size of the loans it makes. Another reason for scrutinizing banks is the need to protect people's deposits against bank failure. This scrutiny and control are a function of the central bank, the Federal Reserve System.

It is the main function of the central bank to see to it that money remains scarce relative to the goods and services produced. For money has no intrinsic value. Rather its value is derived from the willingness of people to accept it in settling transactions, which in turn requires confidence. The existence of "too much" money erodes that confidence. The Federal Reserve regulates the quantity of money in general and is responsible for the conduct of countercyclical monetary policy—varying the quantity of money and the price of loanable funds (the rate of interest) to stabilize the economy. In doing this, the Fed keeps an eye on the various definitions of money, from the narrowest (M_1) to the broadest (**M_3**, or even L).

M_3 equals M_2 plus large denomination time deposits.

QUESTIONS AND PROBLEMS

1. Assume that a person deposits in Bank A $1,000 in cash, which the bank in turn deposits at the Fed, and that the minimum required legal-reserve ratio is 10 percent.

   a. Using T accounts, show the maximum amount Bank A can lend, and why. How will its balance sheet be affected (i) immediately after the deposit? (ii) after a loan is extended? and (iii) after a check is written against the newly created D.D. and is deposited in another bank?

   b. Using a sequence of bank T accounts as in the text, estimate and show the money-creation process by the entire banking system. Show the final balance sheet of the banking system as a whole.

c. Repeat questions a and b on the assumption that the minimum reserve requirement ratio is 25 percent.

2. *a.* What are the functions of money?

   b. How do the various forms of money perform these functions?

   c. What do we mean by saying that (i) money is just debt? (ii) the only thing that backs our money is the productive capacity of the U.S. economy? What determines the "value" of money?

3. Compare and contrast (using T accounts as appropriate) the ability of one commercial bank to lend money and the ability of the entire banking system to do so.

4. Why is there a need for special supervision of the banking industry?

Monetary Policy

OBJECTIVES OF MONETARY POLICY

Long-Run Objective

Controlling the supply of money is the responsibility of the Federal Reserve System. The long-run objective is to keep money scarce enough relative to the supply of goods and services so as to maintain the stability of its value. For this purpose, the long-run growth rate in the money stock should be kept in line with the growth rate of real GDP.

Countercyclical Stabilization

At least as important as the long-run growth are variations in the growth rate of the money stock over the business cycle, designed to stabilize the economy. A large proportion of aggregate spending in the economy depends on borrowed funds, and hence on (1) the availability of money, and (2) the cost of credit, or the rate of interest. In turn, the interest rate is determined by the supply and demand for loanable funds. Therefore, by controlling and varying the rate of growth in money supply, the Fed can dampen cyclical fluctuations.

Objective of monetary policy: Stabilize the economy by changing the rate of growth in money supply. In a recession the Fed increases money supply which would lead to an increase in aggregate expenditures. Conversely, in periods of inflation the Fed reduces money supply.

In a recession, the objective is to increase aggregate expenditures so as to remove the recessionary gap. This the Fed can do by inducing an **increase in the money supply or in its growth rate.** In turn, the increase in money supply (assuming an unchanged demand for funds) lowers the rate of interest. Expenditures that depend on borrowed funds would be stimulated by the increased availability of money and the reduction in interest rates. These include investment in plant and equipment, construction, and consumer expenditures on autos, durables, and other goods. Even purchases financed by credit cards would be encouraged.

In inflationary periods, the objective is to dampen aggregate expenditures, so as to remove the inflationary gap. This the Fed can do by **tight-**

Table 21–1 Selected Items in the Fed's Balance Sheet

	Assets	Liabilities
Reserve Bank credit	Securities Loans to commercial banks	Deposits of commercial banks Federal Reserve notes outstanding

ening credit and lowering the rate of increase of the money supply, or even reducing money supply by an absolute amount. In turn, the reduction in supply raises the rate of interest. Investments and consumer expenditures that depend on borrowed funds would be discouraged and decline as a result.

Federal Reserve Balance Sheet

For the purpose of further analysis, it is useful to examine four important items on the Fed's balance sheet. These are shown in Table 21–1. On the liabilities side are listed, first, the deposits of commercial banks in the Federal Reserve. These are banks' legal reserves. Assets of the commercial banks and liabilities of the Fed, they constitute the *base* for the demand-deposit component of the **money supply**. Second are Federal Reserve notes. These are the currency notes in circulation. The part of these notes that is outside the commercial banking system is included in money supply. *Currency notes plus commercial-bank reserves are known as the* **monetary base. Money supply is a multiple of this base.**

Monetary base: equals Currency notes + commercial-bank reserves. **Money supply** is a multiple of this base. **Reserve bank credit:** Federal Reserve credit extended to the U.S. Treasury and to commercial banks.

On the assets side are shown securities, or U.S. government bonds, which are a liability of the U.S. Treasury and an asset of the Fed; and loans to commercial banks, usually a small item. Banks are generally reluctant to borrow from the Fed, but they borrow if and when they need reserves. Such borrowings show up as part of this item on the assets side, and as member-bank deposits on the liabilities side of the Fed's balance sheet. The Fed makes the loan by crediting the commercial-bank deposit. The two asset items shown in the table constitute **Reserve Bank credit;** they are the *Fed's credit extended to the U.S. Treasury and to commercial banks*, respectively. Although these assets yield revenue to the Fed in the form of interest,[1] their main purpose is the conduct of monetary policy (see below).

INTEREST RATES: SOME INSTITUTIONAL CONSIDERATIONS

The rate of interest is the price of credit, or of loanable funds. It is not the price of money.[2] There is much credit in the economy that is not money, such as loans extended by individuals to corporations and units of

[1]The profit of the Federal Reserve is turned over to the Treasury.

[2]The price or value of money is its purchasing power in goods and services.

government through the purchase of bonds. And there is some money (coins and currency notes) that is not credit.

At any given time, there is a whole structure of interest rates in the money market; various financial instruments carry different interest rates. These rates need to be sorted out.

Nominal interest rate: the interest rate prevailing in the marketplace. **Real interest rate:** Nominal rate minus the expected rate of inflation.

"Nominal" and "Real" Interest Rates

First we make a distinction between a nominal or "money" interest rate on the one hand, and a "real" interest rate on the other. Suppose Jack lends $1,000 for one year to an enterprise in need of funds. If the prevailing market interest rate appropriate for the type of risk involved in this loan is 20 percent, Jack would get back $1,200 at the end of the year, earning $200 in interest. But suppose inflation during the year was 15 percent. The real value of his $1,000, in terms of purchasing power, would then decline by $150. His earnings in "real" terms are only $50, or 5 percent.

This example suggests a general distinction between nominal and real interest rates. *The nominal or money rate is the one prevailing in the marketplace.* **The real interest rate is the nominal rate minus the expected rate of inflation;** *it indicates interest earnings in terms of purchasing power.* During several years in the mid- and late-1970s the real interest rate was negative, as the rate of inflation exceeded nominal interest rates. It pays to be a debtor under these conditions. By contrast in mid-1981 nominal rates reached 20 percent; and with inflation at 11 percent, the real rate stood at 9 percent, a twenty-year high. The real rate remained unprecedentedly high through the first half of 1982, as the sharp drop in the rate of inflation failed to be accompanied by a commensurate decline in nominal interest rates. Only in later years did the real rate drop significantly. In 1988 it stood at the 4 to 5 percent range, and in 2003–4 it was even lower.

We now turn to a discussion of the nominal interest rates prevailing in the money market.

Three Widely Cited Interest Rates

Types of interest rates: Discount rate: the interest rate charged by the federal reserve on its loans to commercial banks. **Federal-funds market:** the market for inter-bank loans. **Federal-funds rate:** the rate that commercial banks charge each other for overnight loans. **Prime rate:** the rate charged by the largest commercial banks on loans to their largest corporate customers.

There are two popularly known nominal interest rates that do not involve or relate directly to the nonbank public. The **discount rate** is the *interest rate charged by the Federal Reserve on its loans to commercial banks.* Banks borrow reluctantly from the Fed when they need to replenish their reserves, and they must pay interest, the discount rate, on these borrowings. The rate that banks charge their customers is higher than what they are charged at the Fed. Second, the **federal-funds rate** is *the rate that commercial banks charge each other.* When banks find themselves with insufficient reserves, their first act is to borrow from other banks that happen to have excess reserves. There is a very active market for such interbank loans, known as the **federal-funds market.** The interest rate on these funds, the federal-funds rate, is highly competitive and very sensitive to daily changes in financial conditions. (These are very short-term loans.)

Among the interest rates that are of direct concern to the nonbank public, the best known is the **prime rate**. *It is the interest rate charged by* *the largest banks* (such as Chase Manhattan) *on loans to their largest and most creditworthy corporate customers* (such as General Motors or General Electric). Because these loans carry minimum risk, the prime rate tends to be the lowest commercial interest rate in the market. Clearly, the corner drugstore would have to pay a higher rate on its borrowings. In fact, there is a whole *structure of interest rates* in the financial markets; they vary in size with the type of loans to which they apply. But variations in the prime rate are indicative of movements in that entire structure, which is why it is of interest to the public. This rate is widely regarded as a barometer of conditions in the money and credit markets. From 10.5 percent in mid-1985, the prime rate declined gradually to 7.5 percent in 1987 and then rebounded to reach 11 percent in early 1989, only to decline again in the late 1990's.

What Governs Market Interest Rates?

Interest rate structure: Market interest rates vary according to degree of risk, time length of loan (length to maturity), and tax exempt status of earnings.

The yield curve shows how interest rates vary with the time length of a loan.

Although many factors determine the interest rates charged on particular loans, three are paramount. First is the degree of risk involved. The higher the risk, the higher the interest rate required by lenders to part with their money. Federal government bonds are the least risky. Second is the length of time to maturity. In "normal" times, when the rate of inflation is reasonably constant and expected to remain so, long-term loans tend to carry higher interest rates than short-term ones, because they require the lender to part with money for a longer period. But this relation can be distorted in times of high inflation. If current inflation is 14 percent and long-run inflation is expected to be 7 percent, then short-term loans would carry a higher nominal interest rate (reflecting current inflation) than long-term loans (reflecting the expected long-run inflation). The third factor is the tax-exempt status of the interest earnings. Interest earned on municipal bonds (loans to states and municipalities) is exempt from the federal income tax. Consequently, other things being equal, municipalities can borrow money at lower interest rates than other borrowers. Thus, the rate of interest on municipal bonds is lower than that on corporate bonds.

The Rate of Interest and the Price of a Bond

Bond: an IOU issued by a corporation, government or other institution. Issuer of the bond is the debtor and the holder is the creditor.

Coupon: a payment of a fixed sum of money (interest) each year that the bond guarantees to the owner. As the price of a bond goes up the rate of interest goes down and vice versa.

A **bond** is an IOU[3] issued by a corporation, the government, a nonprofit institution (such as a hospital), or any other organization. The owner of the bond is a creditor, receiving interest; the issuer of the bond is a debtor, paying interest.

What a bond guarantees is a payment known as the **coupon** to the bearer, or its owner, of a *fixed sum of money (interest) each year.* In other words, we may think of a bond as *an IOU that undertakes to pay its owner a specific number of dollars each year.* Suppose that sum is $100. Given that sum, there is an **inverse relation between the price of the bond and the rate of interest** (in percent). If the rate of interest is 10 percent, then the

[3] "I owe you."

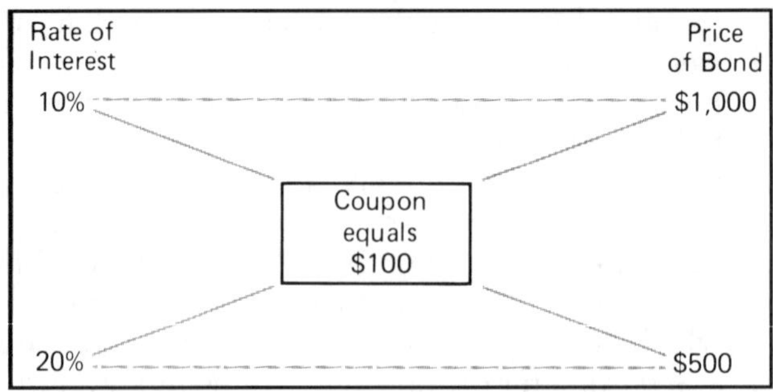

Figure 21–1 Inverse Relation between Price of Bond and Rate of Interest

market price of the bond is $1,000, because 10 percent of $1,000 equals the fixed coupon value of $100. If the rate of interest rises to 20 percent, then the price of the bond declines to $500, because 20 percent of $500 equals the fixed coupon value of $100. This is illustrated schematically in Figure 21–1. This inverse relationship between bond prices and interest rates prevails throughout the economy. It is the fixed money value of the coupon that accounts for it.[4]

TYPES OF MONETARY CONTROLS

Two sets of policy—quantitative and qualitative—are at the disposal of the Federal Reserve in attempting to change the availability of money and the cost of credit.

Quantitative Controls

Quantitative controls: Change the quantity of money or its growth rate. They include: changes in reserve requirements, changes in the discount rate; and mainly open market operations (sales and purchases of government bonds by the Federal Reserve). Only the third method is used frequently.

Quantitative or "general" **controls** change the aggregate quantity of money in the economy or its growth rate, and are not directed at any specific segment of the money market or any particular type of credit.

However, their effect is not at all evenly spread throughout the economy, because not all sectors are equally sensitive to changes in monetary conditions. When interest rates rise, the sectors affected first are those most sensitive to interest charges. Residential construction, where mortgage interest rates play an important role in financing new homes, is likely to shrink first, followed perhaps by business investments that depend on borrowed funds. The effect is apt to be most pronounced in these sectors. But ripple effects spread throughout the economy, both

[4]There exists a less direct and more tenuous relationship between interest rates and the stock market. Often, as interest rates rise, many people switch their assets from stocks to interest-bearing financial instruments (which now earn more), such as CDs. The stock market tends to decline. Conversely, when interest rates decline, people tend to get out of interest-bearing financial instruments (for they now earn less) and into stocks. The stock market tends to rise. Of course, interest rates are but one of many factors that affect the stock market.

through the multiplier mechanism and through the interrelation between sectors. The following quotation describes the latter mechanism, which operated during the collapse of the housing market (caused by high interest rates) in 1980:

> Home buying collapsed because families couldn't get mortgage money. Developers then decided that there wouldn't be much improvement for the rest of this year; consequently, the value of construction contracts they let in March dropped 25% from a year earlier. Contractors, in turn, responded by slashing purchases of new equipment.[5]

To that one may add that with fewer new homes being built, there is lessened demand for refrigerators and other durable goods.

There are three types of quantitative controls at the disposal of the Fed: changes in banks' reserve requirements, changes in the discount rate, and open-market operations, which is the policy most frequently used.

Changes in Reserve Requirements Within certain limits set by Congress, the Federal Reserve can change the minimum legal reserves that banks must maintain against their deposit liabilities. In times of **recession, the Fed lowers the required legal-reserve ratio.** This *increases excess reserves and the deposit multiplier* making it possible for commercial banks to extend loans and thereby expand money supply. That in turn encourages spending that depends on borrowed funds, with the ripple effects spreading throughout the economy. Conversely, in times of **inflation, the Fed increases legal-reserve requirements.** This *mops up excess reserves of commercial banks* and limits their ability to make new loans and thereby create new money. If there are no excess reserves at the time the action is taken, banks may be forced to call in loans, and thereby "destroy" money. Alternatively, banks can sell securities and add the proceeds to their reserves, so as to meet the new reserve requirements. In any event, money becomes "tighter" all around, and as a result, aggregate expenditures are reduced.

A change in reserve requirements is viewed as a drastic action, and *it is used only infrequently*. Its effect on money can be immediate and sizable. It also tends to discriminate between banks, since an increase in reserve requirements may find different banks in different reserve positions—some "loaned out," and others with excess reserves. The immediate effect in this case is to force the first group to borrow from the second in the federal-funds market to meet the higher required-reserve ratio. But the long-run adjustment may create different hardships on different banks.

Changes in the Discount Rate The second instrument in the hands of the Fed is changes in the discount rate–the interest rate it charges commercial banks when they borrow to replenish their reserves. That in turn forces banks to adjust in the same direction the interest rates they charge their

[5]*The Wall Street Journal*, May 8, 1980, p. 40.

customers. In times of *inflation, the Fed raises the discount rate, with the intent of raising the price of credit in the economy,* thereby discouraging spending that depends on borrowed funds. Conversely, during *a recession, the Fed lowers the discount rate,* thus lowering the price of credit and encouraging spending. As a general rule, changes in the discount rate *follow rather than lead* changes in market interest rates.

However, because commercial banks are generally reluctant to borrow from the Federal Reserve, the changes in the discount rate do not affect them directly to any significant degree. Instead, such changes are viewed as a *signal from the Fed* that it wishes to see interest rates altered throughout the economy. Banks usually heed such signals.

It is possible for interest rates to be driven so low that further reduction cannot take place. In the U.S. this has not happened since the great depression of the 1930s, but it did happen recently in Japan. Keynes dubbed this phenomenon: "the liquidity trap." It makes interest rate policy ineffective.

FOMC

The Federal Open Market Committee (FOMC) meets monthly to determine the Federal Funds rate. It's the most commonly used instrument of monetary policy.

Open-Market Operations The most flexible and most commonly used instrument of monetary policy is purchases or sales of government securities on the open market, known as **open-market operations.** A committee, consisting of members of the Federal Reserve Board and some of the district Federal Reserve Banks, sets the direction and tone of these activities. Called the **Open Market Committee,** it meets once a month to formulate policy and issue directives to the New York Fed, which is charged with executing these guidelines (because of its proximity to the all-important New York money market). It *is the existence of a large public debt that makes possible these transactions in government securities.*

First let us outline the general nature of these transactions. In times of **inflation, the Fed sells government bonds on the open market and soaks up money and/or bank reserves,** thereby reducing money supply. But inducing the public to purchase additional securities requires the Fed to **lower their price to a level that will clear the market.** Lowering bond prices is **equivalent to raising the rate of interest.** Thus, the very process of reducing money supply has the concomitant effect of raising interest rates, as is appropriate for times of inflation. The tightening of credit and the rise in interest rates discourage spending that depends on borrowed funds, with ripple effects felt throughout the economy.

In **recession** periods, the Fed does the reverse. It **buys government bonds** on the open market, thereby **pumping new money and/or reserves** into the financial system. To induce the public to sell additional bonds, the Fed must **raise their price, so that the bond market clears**. Since bond prices and interest rates are inversely related, this means a **reduction in interest rates.** And such a reduction, attendant upon open-market purchases, is precisely what the doctor ordered for a recession. The easing of credit and the reduction in interest rates encourage spending that depends on borrowed funds, with ripple effects spreading throughout the economy via the interindustry, and the multiplier mechanisms. **The most direct effect of Fed's activity is on the Federal funds rate.**

We next turn to a more detailed description of open-market operations. In times of inflation, the Fed sells government securities on the open market. If $100 worth of securities are sold to a commercial bank, they are paid for by check on the bank's account with the Federal Reserve. The balance sheets are affected as follows:

FEDERAL RESERVE

Assets		Liabilities	
Securities	–$100	Bank deposits	–$100

COMMERCIAL BANK

Assets		Liabilities
Securities	+$100	
Deposit with the Fed	–$100	

Although there is no direct effect on money supply, the bank's legal reserves decline by the full amount of the sale. Assuming that no excess reserves exist, this situation forces a contraction in money supply by $100 times the money multiplier. If some excess reserves do exist, they are "mopped up," and the result is a tightening in the money market.

As an alternative, assume that after the purchase from the Fed, the *commercial bank turns around and sells the bond to the general public.* It is paid for by a check drawn on a demand deposit at the bank. The T accounts would then appear as follows:

FEDERAL RESERVE

Assets		Liabilities	
Securities	–$100	Bank deposits	–$100

COMMERCIAL BANK

Assets		Liabilities	
Deposit with the Fed	–$100	D.D.	–$100

In this case, money supply, in the form of demand deposits, declines immediately by $100. In addition, there is a reduction of $80 in legal reserves, leading to a further multiple contraction in money supply, and a general tightening of credit conditions.

A symmetrical but opposite analysis applies to the Fed's purchase of government securities in times of recession. If a $100 security is bought from a commercial bank, paid for by a check on the banks' deposit with its district FRB, then nothing happens directly to money supply. But the commercial bank's legal reserves rise by $100. This can be seen by reversing all the signs in the first set of previous T accounts. If the bank turns around and buys the security from the public, adding $100 to the public's D.D. in return, it is as though the Fed purchased the security (indirectly) from the general public. The outcome can be seen by reversing all the signs in the second set of T accounts. Money supply, in the form of demand deposits, increases by $100, against which the bank needs to keep $20 in legal reserves (following the assumptions of the last chapter). The bank acquires $80 in new excess reserves, which may lead to a multiple expansion of money supply. In any event, credit conditions "loosen up."

Open-market operations is a flexible instrument, since it does not require the participation of all banks. Only banks that wish to buy or sell securities, and that are in position to do so in terms of their reserve position, take part. The Fed adjusts the price of the securities (or the inversely related rate of interest) to reflect financial conditions, and to make possible the desired transactions.

Note the *significance of the "Reserve Bank credit"* item on the assets side of the Fed's balance sheet. It consists of credit to banks and to the Treasury (U.S. securities). This item increases in size when the Fed buys government securities on the open market and/or extends credit to banks (thereby increasing their reserves), signaling an expansionary monetary policy. Conversely, a decline in the size of this item signals a contractionary posture by the Fed: It results from the sale of bonds on the open market and/or a reduction in loans to commercial banks.

Qualitative Controls

Besides the general policy instruments, the Fed can impose restrictions on specific types of credit extended by the banks. If it believes that inflation is fueled by consumer purchases and wishes to curtail them, the Fed can *restrict consumer credit.* It may impose limitations on the use of consumer credit cards to finance purchases. Or it may impose minimum-down-payment requirements on purchases of automobiles and durable goods, restricting the amount of credit available for such purchases. This would tend to reduce consumer expenditures.[6] Another example is the possible imposition of *margin requirements* on stock purchases, limiting the amount of credit a buyer of stocks can obtain for their purchase.

Summary of Fiscal and Monetary Policies

To Combat Recession		To Combat Inflation
	Fiscal Policies	
Raise Government Spending Lower Taxes Push Budget Towards Deficit		Lower Government Spending Raise Taxes Push Budget Towards Surplus
	Monetary Policies	
Lower Reserve Requirements Reduce Interest Rates (mainly Federal Funds Rate) Buy Government Bonds on The Open Market (increasing bank reserves)		Increase Reserve Requirements Raise Interest rate (mainly the Federal Funds Rate) Sell Government Bonds on the Open Market (reducing bank reserves)

[6]In restricting specific types of loans, the Fed exercises *control over the* assets *side of commercial bank's balance sheets.*

Moral suasion: The fed can issue "advisory statements" which banks usually follow.

In a more general way, the Fed has a profound influence on commercial banks. It can issue "advisory statements," to which banks usually adhere. This is called **moral suasion**. For example, the Fed may advise banks to limit the increase in their credit during a particular year to, say, 5 percent over the preceding year. Banks usually oblige.

INCORPORATING MONEY INTO MACROECONOMIC ANALYSIS

Money played no explicit role in the macroeconomic analysis of Chapters 15–18. It was kept in the background, and the analysis focused on the four expenditures components of aggregate output: GDP = $C + I_g + G + X_n$. But there is more than one way to view GDP. Complementing one another, each viewpoint yields additional insights. Now that we have examined monetary policy, it is time to develop an approach that recognizes explicitly the role of money. Only after incorporating money into the analysis can we assess the effectiveness of monetary policy. The monetary approach complements, rather than rivals, the expenditures approach.

The Equation of Exchange: GDP = P x Q = M x V, where: P is the price level; Q is the physical quantity of all final goods and services produced; M is money supply, defined as M_1; V is the velocity of circulation of money.

The Equation of Exchange

A useful and tradition-honored way of viewing aggregate economic activity is through the **equation of exchange**. Designed in part to highlight the role of money, it states:

$$\text{GDP} = P \cdot Q = M \cdot V$$

where:

☐ P is the price level or, conceptually, the average price of all final goods and services produced in the economy (the GDP deflator) over a year.

☐ Q is the physical quantity of all final goods and services produced during the year.

So that:

☐ $P \cdot Q$ = GDP, or the money value of all final goods and services produced in a year.

☐ M is money supply or the money stock. For the sake of simplicity, it is defined as M_1.

☐ V is the velocity of circulation of money. It is the number of times the average dollar *changes hands* to finance transactions in *final* goods and services. For example, a particular dollar may be paid by the government to an aircraft supplier in January; by the supplier to an engineer it employs in March; by the engineer to an electric company to pay an electric bill in June; and by the electric company to one of its employees in September. That dollar was used four times during the year, to finance \$4 worth of transactions. Its velocity is 4.

Thus:

☐ $M \cdot V$ is aggregate **spending** in the economy, as was shown in Chapter 13.

This equation is a truism; it is true by definition: $P \cdot Q$ is the money value of all final goods and services produced, and $M \cdot V$ is aggregate money spending on final goods and services, or the amount of money spent to purchase them. Since the money value of what is sold equals the money value of the same things purchased, the two are identical. If GDP in 2005 were \$12.5 trillion and money supply was \$1.4 trillion then the velocity of circulation (V) would be $12.5/1.4 \cong 9$. The average dollar changed hands 9 times during the year to finance transactions in final goods and services. The equation of exchange is in fact an identity.

Quantity Theory of Money: Assumes that Q is constant at the full employment level because of flexible prices and wages, and second that V is constant because of unchanging payments habit of the community. Hence changes in M cause proportional changes in P. Both assumptions were questioned by the Keynesian analysis: Q is not constant as output varies with aggregate demand; and V is not constant because of the existence of idle balances.

On a technical level, it should be noted that the size of V varies with the definition of money supply chosen. If, in the previous example, M is M-2 or \$6.7 trillion, them V is $12.5/6.7 = 1.9$, rather than 9. This problem is ignored in much of the subsequent discussion, but will be picked up again later.

The Classical Quantity Theory of Money

The classical economists adopted the equation of exchange and *added two postulates.* First, Q is constant in the short run, and is equal to full-employment output in the economy. The classical analysis had two complementary mechanisms to ensure against unemployment: savings and investment being equalized by the rate of interest, and fully flexible prices and wages clearing all markets, including the labor market. With full employment assured, the physical volume of output is fixed in the short run. It can only rise in the long run as labor and capital expand. (Keynes, concerned mainly with short-run fluctuations, retorted, "In the long run, we are all dead.")

Second, the classical economists assumed that *V is constant. For velocity is determined by the payment habits of the community, and those hardly change* from month to month. Thus, if workers are paid on a weekly basis, they gradually spend their income during the seven days following their payday. Their money balances are gradually depleted until they reach zero at the end of the week, and they get replenished by new weekly salary checks. Schematically, the movement of these money balances would appear as in Figure 21–2.

The pattern of payments and spending may be daily, weekly, biweekly, monthly, or some combination of these. The important thing is that this pattern, which determines velocity, does not change over time. Consequently, velocity of circulation is viewed as constant.

By introducing the assumptions of constant Q and V into the equation of exchange, we obtain the *quantity theory of money* in its simplest formulation:

$$M \cdot V = P \cdot Q\text{, where the bar indicates constancy.}$$

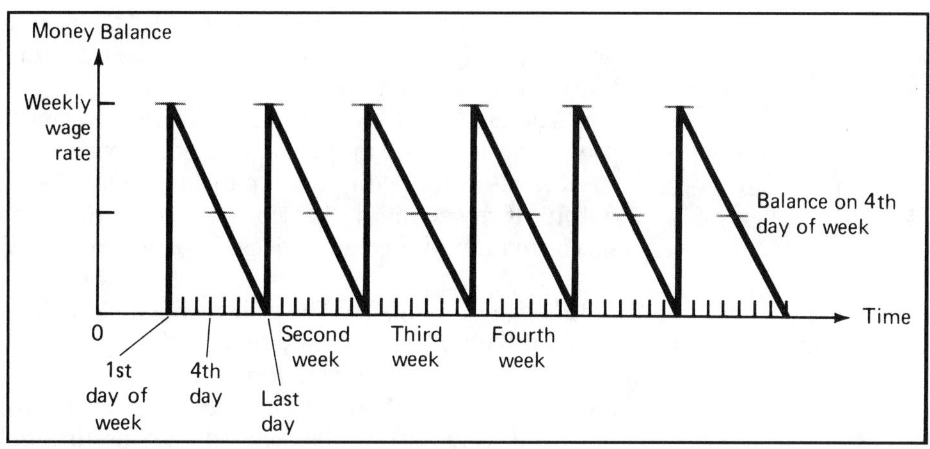

Figure 21–2 Schematic Illustration of Constant-Payment Habits: The cycle of wages and payments behaves rhythmically.

Its upshot is simple and straightforward: With a constant V, variations in money supply (M) result in proportional variations in aggregate spending (MV); and with Q also constant, *changes in* M *cause proportional changes in the price level,* P. *The central bank can influence the price level by changing the supply of money.* The main instrument available to the monetary authorities for accomplishing this (along with the infrequently used changes in reserve requirements of commercial banks) is open-market operations. Selling government bonds to the public withdraws money from circulation and reduces M; buying government bonds from the public infuses money into the economy and increases M. Monetary policy cannot affect real output, for the latter is fixed at the full-employment level. But it is extremely powerful in affecting the price level; hence it was considered the prime instrument of macroeconomic stabilization.

Questioning the Classical Assumption

The supereffectiveness of monetary policy in stabilizing prices depends on the two assumptions embodied in the quantity theory of money. Keynes challenged both assumptions.

Is Output Constant? Physical output (Q) is not constant at the full-employment level, Keynes said. Since desired investments can fall short of desired savings in the economy, aggregate demand can be inadequate to purchase the entire product at full employment. Inadequate aggregate demand is the root cause of depressions. Had prices and wages been flexible downward as well as upward, this would have presented no problem. But the rigidities in the product and factor markets prevent prices and real wages from dropping to a point that would clear the market. The supposition of the quantity theory that output is fixed in the short run at the full-employment level is wrong. In terms of the equation of exchange, MV

= PQ, a decline in aggregate spending (MV) may reduce either prices (P) or output (Q). If P is rigid, the entire brunt of a decline in spending is borne by a reduction in output.

Whether P or Q will be affected most depends on the degree of slack prevailing in the economy. This is seen in Figure 13–5. If a great deal of slack exists in the economy, expansion of spending affects mainly physical output. If the economy is at or near full employment, an increase in MV serves mainly to increase prices. In between, both P and Q may change.

Is Velocity Constant? The policy conclusion of the analysis just outlined is that full employment may require the propping up of aggregate spending, or MV. But can that be done solely by changing money supply (M), as the classicals maintained? That depends on the validity of their assumption that velocity (V) is constant, an assumption also challenged by Keynes.

Keynes maintained that monetary balances are held for two purposes: for transactions, and for precautionary and speculative reasons. People hold precautionary balances for a rainy day and speculative balances so as to be able to take advantage of unforeseen market opportunities. Precautionary and speculative balances are idle, and the following discussion lumps them together under the term *S-P.* Because they are held idle, their velocity is zero. Velocity in the transactions sphere depends on the payment habits of the community (as the classicals said) and is therefore constant. Total velocity is a weighted average of zero (for *S-P* balances) and a constant number (for transactions balances). The weights are the dollar balances in the *S-P* and transactions spheres, respectively. This is summarized thus:

Sphere	Velocity	Weight
Transactions	Constant	Transactions balances
S-P	*0*	*S-P* balances

Total velocity = A weighted average of a constant number and zero

For example, assume that transactions balances are 400 and their velocity is 5, and that *S-P* balances are 100, subject to zero velocity. In that case, velocity in the economy is:

$$V = \frac{(400 \times 5) + (100 \times 0)}{400 + 100} = 4$$

What determines the amount of *S-P* balances people hold? *The cost of maintaining idle balances is the interest earnings foregone by not placing the balances in interest-bearing assets.* Therefore, the higher the market rate of interest, the greater the cost of holding idle balances and the less *S-P* balances people would hold. Conversely, the lower the market rate of interest, the lower the cost of holding idle balances and the more *S-P* balances people would hold.

To see the credibility of this proposition, consider a corporate treasurer who has funds on hand for a period of one week because a week elapses between receipt and disbursement of these funds. Placing them for one week in interest-earning instruments is costly in terms of effort, time, and money. These are the *transactions* costs. With market interest rate at, say, 5 percent, the treasurer may simply keep the funds idle. But had interest been 15 percent, the treasurer would incur the transactions costs and invest the funds.

Thus, the rate of interest controls the allocation of total balances between the transactions and *S-P* spheres, and as a consequence, it controls the weight attached to each of the two components of velocity, and therefore the weighted average. Velocity is not a constant; it depends on the rate of interest: The higher the interest rate → the greater the cost (in terms of forgone earnings) of maintaining idle balances → the greater the share of total balances held in the transactions sphere with a positive (constant) velocity → the greater the velocity of circulation. Conversely, the lower the interest rate → the less the cost of holding idle balances → the greater the share of the total balance held in the *S-P* sphere with zero velocity → the smaller the velocity of circulation. *Velocity varies positively with the rate of interest.* All 4 arguments in the equation of exchange can vary.

This result has profound implications for the effectiveness of monetary policy. Not only is *velocity* not constant; *it has an inherent tendency to move in an opposite direction to money supply (M).* An increase in *M* lowers the rate of interest, which in turn lowers velocity. Conversely, a decrease in *M* raises the rate of interest, which in turn raises velocity. *Changes in M are offset in part by changes in V*. In terms of the equation of exchange, $MV = PQ$, this means that **changes in money supply will not necessarily change aggregate spending on the left-hand side of the equation, and certainly not in the same proportion.** If the government wishes to influence the price level (*P*) or real output (*Q*), *it may have to change aggregate spending (MV) directly. That can be done by fiscal policy:* a change in government expenditures (*G*) and/or in taxes. It cannot be accomplished by monetary policy alone. Changes in aggregate spending thus became a major tenet in the Keynesian analysis.

Today there is much controversy over the relation between money, the interest rate, and velocity. Certainly the magnitude of velocity depends on which definition of money is used—M-1, M-2, or M-3. Also, to the extent that variations in velocity can be predicted, they can be accounted for by the monetary authorities in adjusting *M*, thus improving the effectiveness of monetary policy.

EFFECTIVENESS OF MONETARY POLICY

Monetary policy has certain clear advantages over fiscal policy. It is highly flexible and can be *executed with great dispatch.* The Open Market Committee of the Federal Reserve meets monthly to determine the course of policy. It sets the target for the growth in money supply and, if required by economic conditions, can reverse course from an expansionary to a contractionary posture or vice versa without delay. There is no need for congressional approval as in the case of fiscal policy. And as a consequence, political considerations play only a secondary role in the conduct of policy. Members of the Federal Reserve Board are appointed for 14-year terms, so that electoral swings do not affect them directly. Board policies are, however, subject to congressional review, and to "moral suasion" by the White House.

Moreover, monetary policy is a powerful tool in influencing the course of economic activity. Although there is a measure of disagreement in the profession concerning the relative effectiveness of monetary and fiscal policy, there is general consensus that **"money matters,"** and that *monetary policy is a highly effective instrument.* Experience has borne that out time and again. Indeed, because of its flexibility, it is the most commonly and widely used instrument in the industrial countries.

Yet some questions about its efficacy do exist. In the first place, the Fed has direct influence only on the reserve position of commercial banks. Money supply, a multiple of the so-called monetary base, is affected only indirectly, as banks react to changes in their reserves. Experience has shown that attempts to achieve a given money-stock target on a weekly basis are often frustrated. But over a period of months, the Fed *can* be successful in achieving almost any growth target for the money supply that it sets for itself.

Second, changes in the money stock (M) do not affect spending (MV) in the same proportion. To some extent, they are offset by changes in velocity, as outlined above. Contraction in money supply is often partly offset by the use of "near money," or liquid assets, to finance transactions. Expansion in money supply may be offset by permitting money to lie idle. It is necessary for the Fed to forecast variations in V so as to offset them by changes in M.

Third, the influence of monetary changes on the economy depends on the degree of response of consumers and investors to changes in the price of credit and the availability of money. Their response to moderate changes in interest rates may not be powerful, at least in the short run. Parenthetically, it may be mentioned that changes in the rate of interest affect not only the private sector. They also change the cost to the Treasury of servicing the large public debt.

In a more general way, monetary policy is considered more effective in slowing down an inflationary boom than in stimulating a depressed economy. This asymmetry exists for the following reason. During a boom, there is a demand for goods and services; it is even excessive. Some spending can be discouraged by denying the economy the means of financing purchases and increasing the price of these means (interest rates). In a recession, the aggregate demand for goods and services is inadequate. The Fed can make available the means of financing additional purchases, but it cannot force the public to spend the money. The additional means of payment (money) may not be transformed into actual spending. "You can take a horse to water, but you can't make it drink," the popular saying goes.

Effects of Deflation: Deflation is harmful because it increases the debt burden on debtors, and makes it difficult to reduce real interest and real wages

Despite the reservations outlined here, experience has shown that monetary policy works, and works effectively. But its effect on the economy is **not instantaneous. There is a lag of six to nine months between the time the policy button is pressed and the time the effect is felt throughout the economy.** In that respect, it is similar to fiscal policy.

IS DEFLATION GOOD?

If inflation has bad consequences and needs to be controlled, one might think that deflation (declining prices) is desirable, and needs to be welcomed. NOT SO! And that for three reasons:

a) In times of deflation it becomes impossible to reduce real interest rate by lowering nominal interest rate. For example, with 2 percent deflation, a nominal rate of zero percent means a real rate of 2 percent. Since its impossible to reduce nominal rate below zero, it is not possible to bring the real rate (the one that counts) to under 2 percent. That reduces the effectiveness of monetary policy in stimulating investment and combating a recession. Japan faced this situation in the 1990s.

b) If employers are unable to reduce nominal wages, price deflation means an increase real wages, thereby discouraging employment growth.

c) Price deflation leads to redistribution of wealth from borrowers to lenders. To the extent that firms are net borrowers, their balance sheets deteriorate, and they would have trouble acquiring external financing. In the case of Japan, deflation increased the burden of corporate debt. It can only be reduced by a "burst of inflation."[7]

All this is compounded by the fact that deflation is difficult to predict. This is one reason why monetary policy should aim at low rather than zero inflation. (In addition to the fact that the cost of zero inflation is high in terms of unemployment.)

[7]See comments by Professor S. LaCroix in the Spring 2002 issue of the East-West Center *Observer*.

THE MONETARIST–FISCALIST CONTROVERSY

Monetarism: A school of thought, lead by Professor Milton Friedman, that places exclusive emphasis on monetary policy. It is distinguished from the Keynesian school in its philosophical predilaction and analytical framework.

In theory, there should be no conflict between monetary and fiscal policies. Both should be employed in concert to influence the course of economic activity. In times of recession, both monetary and fiscal policy ought to be expansionary, and in inflationary periods, both should be contractionary. The proper mix of the two policies should be determined by economic considerations, although it is also invariably influenced by political factors.

Yet there is a contemporary debate in the economics profession concerning the relative effectiveness of the two policies—between fiscalists, who adhere to post-Keynesian tenets, and the **monetarism** school, led by Prof. Milton Friedman of the University of Chicago, with views akin to those of the classical economists. The debate spills over to other, related issues, some of which will be addressed in the next chapter.

Philosophical Differences

In part, the dispute reflects great differences in philosophy and value judgments. The monetarists tend to be political conservatives, who are deeply suspicious of government intervention in the private economy. They would echo the sentiment, "The best government is the least government." The government should confine itself to the provision of public goods (such as national defense) defined as narrowly as possible; beyond that, it should merely provide a stable environment for private business. This was certainly the philosophy of the Reagan administration. In contrast, Keynesians tend to be political liberals, who have no philosophical dislike of government intervention whenever and to whatever extent it is necessary. Additionally, inasmuch as one must choose between inflation and unemployment (a question of value judgment), monetarists display greater concern than Keynesians about inflation relative to unemployment.

But the differences between the two schools of thought are not merely philosophical; they are also technical and analytical. They are embedded in the way each side views the economy and in their respective interpretations of economic phenomena. The differences in their policy recommendations are based mainly on technical considerations, although, not surprisingly, these are consistent with their philosophical predilections.

Because the debate between the two schools is at the core of the stabilization issue, this section outlines their respective positions on technical-economic (as distinguished from philosophical) matters. The explanation is confined to the two main groups at the center of the debate. Although there are divergent views within each school, they are overshadowed by the differences between the two, and this discussion treats each of them as homogeneous. The main purpose is to highlight the analytical differences between the two schools in a way that will bring into focus the differences in their policy recommendations. Before doing so, we explore two important areas where the divergent views of the two schools are easily reconcilable.

Analytical Framework

Keynesians analyze the economy by using the expenditures channels: $GDP = C + I_g + G$, an approach which lends itself readily to the study of fiscal policy. Government expenditures are shown as one channel of expenditures that influences GDP (via a multiplier mechanism), while changes in taxes affect aggregate output through their influence on C and I_g. Money does not appear explicitly in this formulation. By contrast, monetarists view the economy through a different set of glasses: The equation of exchange: $MV = PQ$. Since money supply enters here explicitly, this approach provides a direct route by which monetary policy can be examined. Indeed, the only way to influence GDP (PQ) in this formulation is by changing M or V. Fiscal policy is not recognized explicitly in this approach.

In fact it is useful to have more than one way of viewing the economy, as each can yield insights of its own. Moreover, when it comes to policy formulation, the differential approach of the two schools is more apparent than real, for it is possible to analyze monetary policy with the Keynesian tools and fiscal policy with the monetarists' tools. Consider the Keynesian expenditures approach. An increase in money supply lowers the rate of interest and that, in turn, stimulates investment and raises GDP. That way Keynesian economics provides a powerful role for monetary policy *through its effect on the rate of interest.* Conversely, fiscal policy can be analyzed, albeit indirectly, by using the equation of exchange. A rise in G, holding all else constant, pushes up the rate of interest, thereby increasing money velocity (as people hold less idle balances when the interest they can earn on alternative assets increases). Through the rise in V fiscal policy can affect GDP.

In sum, the two analytical frameworks can be viewed as complementary and reconcilable. Still, they reflect different emphasis: monetarists place the spotlight on money and monetary policy, and Keynesians on expenditures and fiscal policy.

The Aggregate-Supply Curve

Both fiscal and monetary policies are demand-management measures; they shift the aggregate demand curve along a constant aggregate supply. But the two schools of thought hold different views concerning the *shape of the aggregate-supply* curve: Keynesians believe that it is reasonably flat, while monetarists believe that it is fairly steep. This is shown in Figure 21–3, and it has profound implications to the relative effectiveness of stabilization policies (fiscal or monetary) in combating a recession or inflation.

Figure 21–3 Aggregate Supply

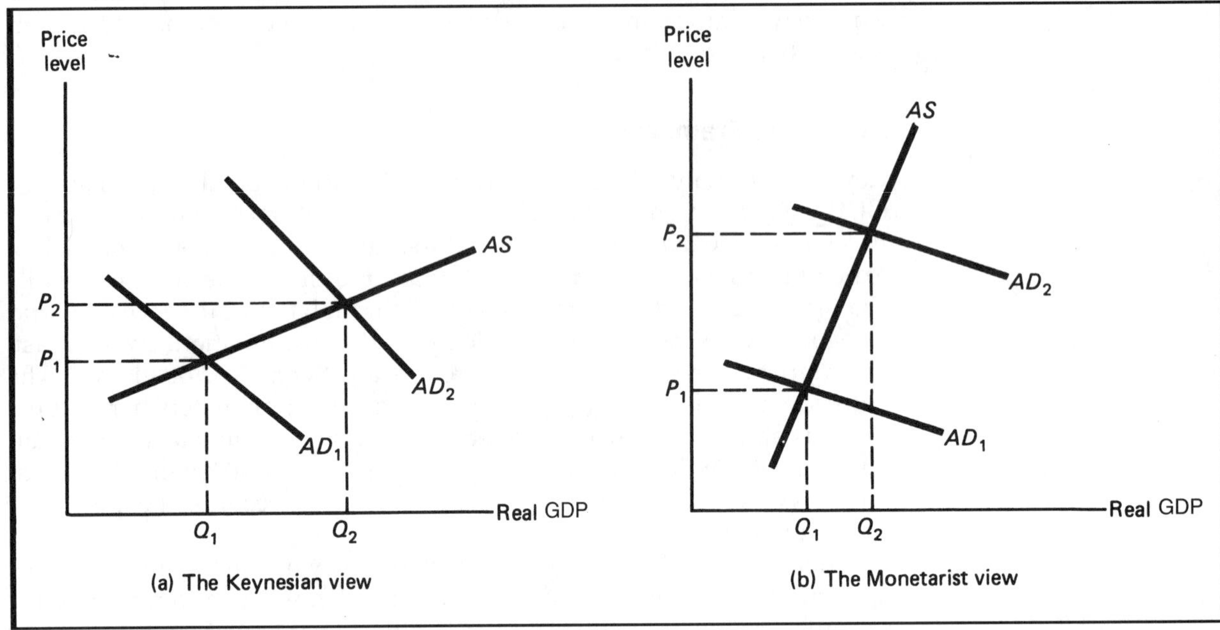

In the *Keynesian view,* the *AS* is flat (panel a). Hence, policies that increase *AD* (from AD_1 to AD_2) raise GDP considerably (from Q_1 to Q_2), at a small cost in terms of inflation (the price level rises only from P_1 to P_2). *Stabilization policies are effective in combating a recession.* On the other hand, fighting inflation requires contractionary measures that shrink *AD* (from AD_2 to AD_1). Here a small reduction in inflation is gained at a huge cost in terms of lost output (from Q_2 to Q_1). *Stabilization policies are relatively ineffective in combating inflation.*

In the *monetarist view,* the reverse is true. With a steep *AS* (Figure 21–3 panel b), combating a recession through an increase in *AD* (from AD_1 to AD_2), yields very little by way of additional output, as real GDP rises only from Q_1 to Q_2. But the cost is high in terms of inflation, as the price level rises all the way from P_1 to P_2. On the other hand, in fighting inflation the *AD* needs to be lowered from AD_2 to AD_1. A considerable reduction in inflation is attained at a small cost in terms of reduced output (from Q_2 *to* Q_1). *In the monetarist view, stabilization policies are relatively effective in fighting inflation and relatively ineffective in the fight against recession.*

Because they believe that unemployment can be cured at low cost, Keynesians are very concerned about fighting recessions. Since monetarists are convinced that the cost of combating inflation is low, they are very hawkish in the fight against inflation.

Again, the two positions are not mutually exclusive, for the flatness or steepness of the aggregate-supply curve depends on the degree of slack prevailing in the economy. *AS* is flat when the economy experiences high unemployment and large excess capacity. It is steep when the economy is at or near full employment. In its totality, the aggregate-supply curve displays the three regions shown in Chapter 12. Its policy implication is that anti-inflationary policies are effective when the economy is near full employment, while antirecessionary policies are effective when a great deal of slack exists in the economy.

We next turn to the crux of the differences between the two schools.

The Positions in Capsule Summary

First let us summarize the positions and policy conclusions of the two schools.

To the monetarists, the private economy is inherently stable and requires no government intervention. In the long run there is no tradeoff between inflation and unemployment. Money supply is the predominant factor affecting the economy: *Only money matters.* Activist fiscal policy is useless and should be abandoned. Monetary policy is so powerful that, at the present state of our knowledge, its use has a destabilizing effect on the economy. Therefore, the best policy is to let the money supply grow at a fixed percentage per year, consistent with the real growth rate of the economy (about 3 percent annually), and leave everything else to the private sector of the economy.

To the Keynesians, the private economy is not inherently stable, and government stabilization policies are required. There is a tradeoff between inflation and unemployment, at least in the short run. *Money matters, but so do fiscal policy and other influences on the economy.* Stabilization measures, both monetary and fiscal, are essential. Monetary policy should be active and countercyclical.

The Keynesian Position Restated

It will be recalled that Keynes challenged the classical analysis, first, by unlinking savings and investment, making savings a function of income rather than the rate of interest. Next, he introduced price and wage rigidities into commodities and labor markets, by denying the existence of purely competitive markets.

Prices and wages in many industries are dominated by a very few firms and large unions. Such corporations have at least partial control over the prices they charge. Known as *price makers,* they do not merely adjust to market prices; they possess varying degrees of market power. As a result of such industrial concentration, prices become rigid in a downward direction. Moreover, prices are often pushed upward even in the presence of slack and unused capacity in the economy. The same applies to real wage rates. Powerful unions, minimum-wage legislation, geographical immobility, immobility between industries (resulting in part from highly specialized skills), and other factors introduce rigidities into the labor markets. Real wages are not flexible downward and therefore cannot be relied upon to clear the labor market.[8] Involuntary unemployment (that is, excess supply of labor) can exist. And since there is no automatic mechanism that would restore full employment, a depression can be protracted.

So much for the explanation of unemployment. Since desired investment can fall short of desired savings in the economy, aggregate demand can be inadequate to purchase the entire output at full employment. Inadequate aggregate demand is the root cause of depressions. Had prices and wages been flexible downward as well as upward, this would have presented no problem. But the rigidities in the factor (and product) markets prevent real wages from dropping to a point that would clear the market. The private economy is not inherently stable, and public policy is needed to stabilize it.

Had velocity been constant, monetary policy alone could influence P or Q in the desired direction and amount. But by introducing idle balances, Keynes maintained that velocity varies positively with the rate of interest. Consequently, changes in V tend to partly offset changes in M. *All four components of the equation of exchange can vary.* Changes in money supply (M) will not necessarily change aggregate spending on the left-hand side of the equation. If the government wishes to influence the price level (P) or real output (Q), it may have to change aggregate spending (MV) directly. That can be done by fiscal policy: a change in government expenditures (G) and/or in taxes. It cannot be accomplished by monetary policy alone. Hence the introduction of fiscal policy as an important policy instrument. A change in aggregate spending (MV) may affect either P or Q, or both. Concerted *action on both the fiscal and the monetary front* is called for.

Granted that aggregate spending needs to be increased directly rather than through increasing money supply, what would such an increase affect on the right side of the equation of exchange—real output, prices, or a combination of the two? To deal with this question, Keynesian economists developed in the 1950s an analytical tool known as the **Phillips curve,** which highlights the tradeoff between inflation and unemployment. It is addressed in the next chapter, along with the controversy concerning its shape or existence.

The Monetarists' Resurgence

Phillips curve: A curve developed by a Keynesian economist to show formally the trade-off between unemployment and inflation. No longer in vogue.

The monetarist school contends that Keynesians went overboard in rejecting the classical doctrine and in downgrading the importance of monetary relative to fiscal policy. They advocate a return to at least some of the classical assumptions or variants of them. It should be stated at the outset that monetarists are concerned more with long-run developments than with short-run fluctuations.

[8]New arguments why wages are inflexible are that companies pay employees *above-market wages* to induce them to work harder, to increase discipline as well as loyalty to the company, and to keep employees from neglecting their work, or shirking. If an employee is caught shirking, he or she runs the risk of being fired. The risk is low if he or she can readily find a job at the same wage. But if the employee receives above-market wage, the loss in case of being fired is greater, and he or she would avoid neglecting his or her work. By paying above-market wages, a company might be able to reduce turnover and training costs, and improve the quality of its employees. These are reasons why wage rates do not clear the labor market.

Stability of the Private Economy Is the private economy inherently stable, or is it subject to massive and lengthy fluctuations in output and employment and therefore in need of a large dose of government stabilization measures? The answer depends greatly on the flexibility of wages and prices and the degree to which they clear the product and factor markets. And that in turn depends on the extent of competition in those markets. Although it is true that monopolistic and oligopolistic elements exist in and sometimes dominate markets, sufficient competition remains. What often is referred to as "effective competition," monetarists believe, is adequate to ensure price-wage flexibility.[9] Although short-run deviations from equilibrium are possible, in the long run prices and wages will settle at points that clear their respective markets. And that makes the private economy inherently stable in the long run. Whatever instability has been observed is in fact caused by the government's misguided attempts to stabilize the economy.

Here is an example of a self-correcting mechanism that stabilizes the economy: In times of *inflationary boom, the real value of people's liquid-assets holdings* (accumulated through past savings) *declines* as the rate of interest falls below the rate of inflation. Even the real value of current disposable income may decline if the rate of inflation is high enough. At some point, this *would induce consumers and investors to curtail their spending,* thereby cooling off the economy. Conversely, in times of *recession,* the rate of inflation is on the decline. Beyond a certain point, *the real value of people's liquid assets begins to rise,* as the rate of inflation drops below the rate of interest. Given enough time, *this process would stimulate expenditures,* thus leading the economy out of the recession.

Although Keynesians may concede the existence of such a mechanism, they emphasize that it is too weak, and that the process takes many years to complete—too long to be relevant for any political decision making.

What about the rigidities introduced into the economy by minimum-wage legislation, government control over energy prices, farm-support programs that place a floor on food prices, and monopolistic elements in both industry and labor? Would not these be the cause of unemployment? Yes, reply the monetarists. But this type, along with the frictional unemployment, is a structural phenomenon that is not susceptible to demand-management policies, either fiscal or monetary. Attempts to cure this problem by aggregate stabilization measures would only make things worse; the cure is worse than the disease. The extent of what the monetarists dub the *natural rate of unemployment* [namely, the rate of unemployment that would keep inflation from accelerating, or the Non-accelerating inflation rate of unemployment (NAIRU)] depends on workers' preferences between work and leisure (considering that leisure also carries a financial reward, in the form of unemployment compensation) and on various institutional factors that

[9]In 1981–82, for example, there were numerous instances in which unions agreed to take a cut in the money wage rates in order to preserve the level of employment. Same in 2006.

determine the rigidities introduced into the economy. *Only policies applied to specific markets to break up such rigidities and distortions and to permit the markets to function more smoothly are appropriate in this context.* In the important case of labor markets, monetarists call for the abolition of minimum-wage legislation, expansion of worker retraining and relocation programs, creation of a nationwide job bank that would impart instant information on job vacancies and available workers, and the like. When it comes to macrostabilization measures, monetarists advocate a hands-off attitude toward the economy.

Effectiveness of Monetary Policy Monetarists maintain that although velocity may not be an absolute constant, it is a *stable function of certain predictable variables.* Changes in money supply, adjusted to offset predictable changes in velocity, will have a direct, proportional (or nearly *so) effect on aggregate spending.* Hence, the quantity theory or a variant of it can be resurrected. But monetarists express it in a different form from the traditional classical way. As can be seen in Figure 21–2, the regularity of the earning-spending process that produces constant velocity implies that the money balances held by the public on a given day of any week are the same. Constant velocity implies constant money balances, since one is the inverse of the other.

Expressed in terms of the quantity-theory equation, if $MV = PQ$, then:

$$M = 1/V \cdot PQ = 1/V \cdot \text{GDP}$$

Since V is constant, so is $1/V$, and the equation may be interpreted as representing *the demand for money balances.* The public wishes to maintain money balances valued at a constant fraction of GDP. A possible equilibrium relationship may be M = \$1,000 billion; desired $1/V$ (constant) = ⅛; and GDP (= PQ) = \$8,000 billion.

Starting from such an equilibrium relationship, suppose the central bank raises money supply to, say, \$1,100 billion. People find themselves with more money balances than they wish to hold. In their attempt to get rid of these excessive balances, they increase aggregate spending until GDP (PQ) rises to \$8,800 billion. Only then will people be satisfied with the new level of monetary balances (⅛ of GDP). Conversely, if the central bank lowers the money supply from \$1,000 billion to \$900 billion, people will find themselves holding smaller balances (in relation to GDP) than they consider optimal or desirable. In attempting to build up these balances, they curtail spending until GDP declines to \$7,200 billion. Again a new equilibrium is reached. In sum, monetary policy is fully effective in producing changes in nominal GDP.[10] Variations in money supply have a

[10]Monetarists point to the close positive correlation between the growth in money and in nominal GDP over the long run (50 years) in support of their claim that money supply determines GDP. Money is the *cause* and GDP is the *effect*. Keynesians *question such a cause-and-effect* relation, maintaining that the causation can run in the opposite direction.[11]The automatic or built-in stabilizers are considered desirable and adequate.

direct effect on the economy, because demand for money balances is a stable fraction of GDP.

Keynesians deny that the public, faced (in the first case) with more money balance than it wishes to hold, would switch directly to real assets or to commodities, thereby expanding aggregate expenditures. Instead, money and financial assets are closer substitutes than money and real assets. In consequence, the excess money balances would spill first into financial assets and only indirectly into purchases of real assets. Thus, the link between money supply and spending on real assets is loose and indirect. Excess money balances would spill into real assets only to a limited degree, reducing the 1/V in the money-demand equation. An increase in money supply will raise GDP, but not by the amount suggested by the monetarists. Money matters, but it is not the only thing that matters. The money-demand equation is not stable.

Ineffectiveness of Fiscal Policy In contrast, activist fiscal policy is said to be ineffective.[11] Suppose the government decided to stimulate the economy by increasing government expenditures, leaving taxes unchanged; that is, increasing the budgetary deficit. And assume that money supply remains unchanged, so as to isolate the effect of fiscal policy. Where would the government obtain the funds to finance the increase in its deficit? By borrowing on the nation's money markets through the sale of government bonds. But in order to attract buyers, the government would have to make the bonds' yield more attractive than before, by increasing the rate of interest. In turn, that would discourage private investors from borrowing and financing expenditures that are sensitive to the rate of interest (such as construction). In short, **an increase in government spending would simply "crowd out" an equivalent amount of private spending. Aggregate expenditures would remain unchanged.** If, however, the rise in government spending were accompanied by an increase in money supply to finance such spending, there would be no crowding out and aggregate expenditures would rise. But then it is the increase in money supply that raises *MV*. Why bother to go through the government-expenditures exercise? Changes in money supply suffice. Only money matters.

In response, Keynesians maintain that (1) in times of economic slack, there is sufficient unused lending capacity in the banking system to prevent or limit the crowding-out effect; excess reserves form the basis for the needed monetary expansion; and (2) as interest rises, so does velocity, so that more spending can be financed with a given money supply. Again the argument turns in part on the constancy and predictability of velocity. The empirical evidence on the behavior of velocity is mixed. In the 1970s velocity grew smoothly at a rate of 3 percent per year. But in the 1980s it fluctuated positively with the rate of interest as the Keynesians maintain.

---

[11]The automatic or built-in stablizers are considered desirable and adequate.

Should the Fed Control Money Supply or Interest Rates? A technical matter that figures largely in the debate between Keynesians and monetarists is the question of which variable monetary policy should attempt to influence. *The Fed cannot control both the quantity of money and the price of credit (interest rate).* As in any market, either the quantity can be controlled, letting the price vary, or vice versa.

Keynesians attach great importance to the rate of interest as a regulator of investments and therefore of general economic activity. They advocate that in the conduct of monetary policy, at least one eye (sometimes both eyes) should be kept on it. Monetary policy should be geared at least in part to lowering the interest rate if the economy requires a stimulus and raising it if the economy needs to be slowed down. Indeed, until October 1979, the Fed controlled interest rates, and the money stock fluctuated outside the announced target. *To the monetarists,* the rate of interest is just a price (albeit an important one) that performs the allocative function in capital markets. Attempts to stabilize the interest rate are likely to destabilize the economy: During a boom period, the rate of interest rises in part because the demand for money rises. Attempts to stabilize it by raising money supply (leaning against the wind) only fuel the boom. Conversely, in a recession interest rates decline because the demand for money drops. Attempts to stabilize it by reducing money supply only aggravate the recession. The only proper target (or indicator) of monetary policy is money supply. *The Federal Reserve should aim strictly at affecting the growth rate of the money stock.* It cannot influence the quantity of money and the price of money at one and the same time.

In October 1979, the Federal Reserve accepted this recommendation, and for three years it adhered to money supply as the sole indicator of monetary policy, permitting interest rates to find their own level. As a result, interest rates fluctuated widely during 1980–1982. The prime rate rose from 12 percent late in 1979 to an unprecedented level of 20 percent in April 1980, then plunged back to 12 percent by June as the demand for money slackened with the onslaught of the 1980 recession, only to rise above 20 percent again by August 1981. It then declined to 12 percent with the 1982 recession. In October 1982 the Fed abandoned its exclusive reliance on the money stock as its policy guide.

To return to the monetarist view, it leaves unresolved the questions of which money-supply variable is most susceptible to Federal Reserve control and which is the most relevant for stabilization policy. The Federal Reserve has a direct influence only on the monetary base, which consists of currency in circulation and reserves of commercial banks. Money supply, even by the narrowest definition, M-1, consists of currency in circulation plus demand deposits (that is, checking accounts) in commercial banks. And in a system of fractional reserves, it is several times larger than the monetary base. Historically, M-1 was considered the most relevant money stock for stabilization purposes. However, in recent years, with changes in banking practices (such as telephonic transfers from savings to checking accounts), it is becoming apparent that a broader definition, such as M-2, is most relevant for stabilization purposes. With so many definitions of the money stock and the associated measures of velocity, the argument often revolves around which definition is chosen.

The Monetary Growth Rule

If monetary policy is considered so effective, one would expect monetarists to advocate its discretionary use to stabilize the economy. Not so. So powerful is the effect of changes in money supply on the economy, say Friedman and his followers, that the central bank must be very circumspect in the use of monetary policy. Any mistake can be exceedingly destabilizing. Moreover, monetary policy affects the economy with a considerable lag, varying between six and twelve months. As a consequence, properly executed monetary policy should be addressed to conditions that exist not at the time the policy button is pressed, but a year later. Since, at the present state of the art, economic forecasting is at best grossly inaccurate and at worst totally misleading, discretionary policy can do more harm than good. If pursued aggressively, it can cause havoc in the economy. Indeed, monetarists attribute the Great Depression to a mistaken massive contraction in money supply. The inflation of 1973, the deep recession of 1974–75, and the subsequent periods of instability were all caused—in the monetarists' view—by mismanagement of the money supply by the Federal Reserve.

To avoid such errors, the monetarists advocate the discontinuation of discretionary monetary policy as a stabilization measure. Since the private economy is inherently stable in the long run, all it needs from the government is a stable monetary framework for growth. Assuming velocity to be constant or predictable, *money supply must rise in the long run at a rate sufficient to accommodate the long-run real growth rate in the economy.* Since the increase in the labor force and in productivity generates roughly a 3 percent annual increase in real output, noninflationary growth in money supply should be about 4 percent per year. To accommodate some variations in growth as well as a certain degree of inflation, some monetarists relent and prescribe a monetary growth rate of between 4 and 5 percent per year. The government budget should be restricted to the provision of public goods and should be balanced over the business cycle (that is, no discretionary fiscal policy). Under such conditions of minimum government intervention in the economy, this monetary growth rate will ensure noninflationary stable growth in the economy.

In a *Wall Street Journal* article in early 2006 ("He has Set a Standard", *Wall Street Journal,* January 31, 2006, p. A-14) Professor Milton Friedan appears to have moderated his view and now accepts discretionary monetary policy.

The Scoreboard

We have now come full circle. Monetarists believe that the private economy is inherently stable and attribute most if not all economic fluctuations to the destabilizing effects of misguided large and rapid changes in the money stock. Fiscal policy is regarded as an ineffective stabilization measure. Based on their analytical underpinning, monetarists come up with a conclusion that corresponds to the conservative philosophical predilection: The least government is the best government. The government role should be limited to the provision of public goods through a budget that is balanced over the cycle. And the central bank should allow money supply to expand at a fixed rate that corresponds roughly to the real, long-term growth in the economy.

In contrast, Keynesians contend that the private economy requires stabilization policy; that even though money matters, other things matter as well; and that a judicious mix of discretionary fiscal and monetary policy is needed to stabilize the economy. Although they admit that variations in money supply can be destabilizing, they attribute many economic fluctuations to external shocks, such as worldwide drought or a quadrupling of oil prices. Moreover, variations in money supply are often regarded as a symptom rather than the root cause of instability, for the central bank merely accommodates the effects of other influences.

It would appear that such an important dispute should be settled by recourse to empirical tests rather than by reliance on *a priori* reasoning. But scores of empirical investigations have failed to settle the matter. One important reason for this is the inability of the statistician to infer causal relationships from mere association in timing. There is no doubt that economic fluctuations are associated with variations in money supply. All time-series charts show a rise in money supply during boom periods and a reduction (or decline in the rate of growth) in periods of recession. But can one infer from this that money-supply variations *cause* economic fluctuations (as the monetarists claim)? Why could not the line of causation be precisely the reverse (as Keynesians maintain)? Economic expansion causes business people and consumers to increase their borrowings from banks (which are assumed to have excess reserves), thereby increasing money supply, whereas economic contraction does the reverse. As long as the issue of causation is not settled, it is impossible to resolve the Keynesian-monetarist controversy.

And so the opinion columns of *The Wall Street Journal* are filled with articles advocating policies based on monetarist precepts and occasionally proclaiming the death of Keynes. Conversely, a cogent yet simple interpretation of recent events in the light of the Keynesian analysis has been presented by Nobel Laureate James Tobin of Yale University, a leading Keynesian thinker.[12] On the philosophical distance between Chicago and Yale, most professional economists would probably regard themselves closer to the East Coast. But the ranks of the monetarists have grown.

A possible compromise between the activist stance of the Keynesians and the noninterventionist posture of the monetarists may be that stabi-

[12]James Tobin, "How Dead Is Keynes?" *Economic Inquiry*, 15 (October 1977), 459–68.

lization policies should be undertaken only when there exists a sizable deflationary or inflationary gap.

SUMMARY

Monetary policy, conducted by the central bank, is an effective instrument in stabilizing and guiding the course of the economy. Like fiscal policy, it is a demand management tool. Its long-run objective is to maintain a growth rate in the money stock comparable to that of real output. Its short-run objective is to stabilize the economy so as to avoid inflation and unemployment. Both quantitative and qualitative controls are at the disposal of the Federal Reserve in attempting to meet these objectives.

In times of inflationary boom, the Fed can employ three types of quantitative measures: increase the legal-reserve ratio of banks, increase the discount rate, and sell government bonds on the open market, thereby soaking money and/or reserves out of the economy. The last tool is the one most commonly used. All three measures reduce the availability of money and increase its costs, thereby discouraging expenditures that depend on borrowed funds. Although not aimed at any particular segment of the credit market, their effect is first felt in sectors that depend most on borrowed funds, such as housing and business investments. From there they spread throughout the economy. Additionally, the Fed may employ qualitative controls, such as various restrictions on consumer credit.

In times of recession and economic slack, the Fed may reverse course, lowering reserve requirements of the banks, reducing the discount rate, and, most commonly, buying government bonds on the open market, thereby infusing money and/or reserves into the economy. These actions make money more readily available and less costly, thereby encouraging spending that depends on borrowed funds. First to be affected are expenditures most sensitive to monetary conditions; but the effect spreads gradually throughout the economy.

To assess the effectiveness of monetary policy, it is necessary to incorporate money explicitly into the analytical framework. This is done via the equation of exchange, $MV = PQ$, which is recognized as an identity, true at all times. Yet it provides fresh insights into the economy. The classical economists developed the quantity theory of money, by adding the proposition that V and Q are constant. The implication is that variations in M result in equiproportional changes in P: Monetary policy is a powerful tool in influencing the price level.

Keynes challenged the two assumptions. His claim that V is not constant weakens somewhat the ability of monetary policy to change PQ. And since Q may also vary, changes in M or MV produce variations in real output as well as in the price level. Whether P or Q is most affected depends on the degree of slack in the economy.

Questions concerning the effectiveness of monetary policy revolve around (1) the ability of the Fed to regulate the growth in money supply in the short run with any degree of precision, (2) the degree to which variations in money supply influence aggregate spending, (3) the possible existence of asymmetry, with monetary policy being more effective in controlling inflation than in abating a recession, and (4) the length of the time lag between policy and its effect on the economy. Despite these reservations, experience has shown that monetary policy is a highly effective tool. It is also a flexible instrument that can be employed with dispatch.

An important contemporary debate exists in the profession concerning the relative effectiveness of monetary and fiscal policies and related issues. On the one side are the monetarists, led by Prof. Milton Friedman. They believe that the private economy is inherently stable and attribute most if not all economic fluctuations to the destabilizing effects of misguided large and rapid changes in the money stock. Fiscal policy is regarded as an ineffective stabilization measure. Based on their analytical underpinning, monetarists come up with a conclusion that corresponds to the conservative philosophical predilection: The least government is the best government. The government role, they say, should be limited to the provision of public goods through a budget that is balanced over the cycle. And the central bank should allow money supply to expand at a fixed rate that corresponds roughly to the real, long-term growth in the economy.

On the other side are the Keynesians. They contend that the private economy requires stabilization policy; that while money matters, other things matter as well; and that a judicious mix of discretionary fiscal and monetary policy is needed to stabilize the economy. Although they admit that variations in money supply can be destabilizing, they attribute many economic fluctuations to external shocks, such as worldwide drought or a quadrupling of oil prices. Moreover, variations in money supply are often regarded as a symptom rather than the root cause of instability, for the central bank merely accommodates the effects of other influences.

QUESTIONS AND PROBLEMS

1. Suppose that, in time of a recession, the Federal Reserve buys a $100 security from (a) a commercial bank; (b) the general public. Under each alternative, show the effect of the transaction on the balance sheets of the Fed and of the commercial bank.
2. What are the objectives of monetary policy:
   a. In the long run?
   b. Over the business cycle?
3. In the first quarter of 1980, inflation in the United States reached an annual rate of 18%. Explain precisely all the quantitative and qualitative tools available to the Federal Reserve to combat this situation.

4. Explain the following:
   a. The equation of exchange
   b. The quantity theory of money

   What bearing does the controversy over the quantity theory have on the effectiveness of monetary policy?
5. Discuss the pro and con considerations relating to the effectiveness of monetary policy.
6. Explain the following concepts:
   a. The "real" rate of interest
   b. The discount rate
   c. The federal-funds rate
   d. The prime rate
7. *a.* What is the relation between the (nominal) rate of interest and the price of a bond?
   b. What factors govern interest rates charged on particular loans?
8. What are the differences between monetarists and Keynesians with respect to:
   a. The shape of the aggregate-supply function?
   b. The framework they use to analyze the economy?
   c. The stability of velocity or lack of it?
   d. Effectiveness of monetary and fiscal policy?
   e. The money supply and interest rates rules of monetary policy?
   f. The need for and effectiveness of stabilization policies?

Inflation and Unemployment Revisited

INFLATION AND MONEY SUPPLY

Part 3 of this volume reviewed the meaning, causes, and economic consequences of unemployment and inflation. Unemployment is the result of inadequate aggregate expenditures ($C + I + G + X_n$) relative to the potential (or full-employment) output of the economy. Inflation was diagnosed as an opposite case. It is caused by excessive aggregate expenditures on goods and services relative to potential output.

How are inflationary expenditures financed? This question was not addressed, because money had not yet been explicitly introduced. Yet by its very nature, inflation is a monetary phenomenon. Money must play a central role in its analysis. Inflation is defined as a process of rising price level: a continuous increase in the average price of final goods and services *expressed in terms of money.* Another way of defining inflation is as a continuous decline in the value of money in terms of goods and services. Either way, the value of money is related to a composite of goods and services available. The popular saying, "Inflation means too much money chasing too few goods," is rooted in this relationship. Although "excessive" aggregate expenditures cause inflation, these expenditures need to be financed with money.

Having incorporated money into the analysis, we now see that such expenditures may be financed to some extent by an increase in velocity of circulation. In times of inflation, nominal interest rates rise; this causes a decline in idle balances and a corresponding increase in transactions balances. Velocity rises as a result. But there is a limit to possible increases in V. Beyond that, the financing of "excessive" aggregate expenditures depends strictly on an increase in money supply. That increase occurs in the process of borrowing from the banks to finance consumer or investment expenditures. The creation of credit increases M. **Continuous inflation cannot occur without an increase in money supply.** If money supply stopped growing, inflation would cease. Indeed, central banks in Israel and Brazil were able to bring triple-digit inflation under control by curbing money supply.

Since money supply is controlled by the central bank, the Federal Reserve has the tools necessary to bring inflation under control; it can stop or slow down the creation of new money. This is what the Fed did in 1981–1982, and, indeed, the inflation rate declined from 13 percent in 1980 and 1981 to 3 percent in 1983. Conversely, by expanding the reserves of commercial banks and thereby increasing M, the Federal Reserve is responsible for inflation; as M rises, the value of money in terms of goods and services declines. Thus, the *source of inflation is too rapid an increase in the supply of money relative to the expansion of real output.* This statement underscores the role of money creation in the inflationary process. Without new money, inflation cannot continue beyond a certain point.

Paradoxically, this statement says everything and is far from the full story at one and the same time. True, it identifies the *proximate* or *immediate* cause of inflation. But it begs the obvious question: Why does the central bank go on increasing money supply beyond the growth in real output? Often this is done to accommodate other forces operating in the economy—forces such as sharp advances in energy prices or a general rise in labor costs of production. Without an accommodating increase in M, the effect of these events would be a rise in unemployment. In terms of the equation of exchange, $MV = PQ$, a rise in P, brought about by

▶ INFLATION AND MONEY

Prof. Milton Friedman, the leader of the monetarist school, wrote:

> Monetary growth is a—or the—major factor determining the rate of inflation over the longer term. The wider fluctuations in money in the 1970s than in the 1960s produced wider fluctuations in inflation as well. And the upward trend in monetary growth produced an even steeper upward trend in inflation . . .
>
> Ups and downs in monetary growth have been followed by corresponding ups and downs in inflation. The interval between changes in money and subsequent changes in inflation has been long and variable, averaging roughly two years.[a]

[a] "Monetary Instability," *Newsweek*, June 15, 1981, p. 80.

On the other hand, a Federal Reserve analysis concludes: There has been a broad consistency in the movements of money and prices, with a general acceleration since the mid-1960s. Nevertheless, short-run movements in prices often bear only a loose relation, if any, to variations in monetary expansion. In particular, price disturbances arising from supply shocks, such as those that hit the food and energy sectors in recent years, are one source of divergence between money growth and inflation. These supply disruptions also can generate pressures for monetary and fiscal accommodation; otherwise, inertia in wages and prices causes financial tensions and imposes the risk of extensive layoffs and production losses. In this way, disturbances originating in the "real" sector can spur inflationary monetary growth.[b]

[b] *Federal Reserve Bulletin*, May 1981.

external factors, would cause a contraction in real output unless M were increased to accommodate the general price rise. In such cases, it is these external factors that may be held responsible for the inflation. It is therefore necessary to probe in greater depth into the more remote causes of inflation. By employing the tools of aggregate demand and aggregate supply introduced in Chapter 13, we distinguish between demand- and supply-caused inflation.

DEMAND-PULL INFLATION WITHOUT UNEMPLOYMENT

Consider an aggregate-supply curve that is horizontally flat to the point of full-employment output, and then becomes vertical, having an upward kink at the Y_{FE} level. Displayed in Figure 22–1, it shows a situation where output can rise at a constant price level until full employment is reached. Such increases in output are induced by rightward shifts in aggregate demand, as shown by the arrows in the chart. The shifts may or may not be induced by policy measures. Beyond the Y_{FE} point, a further increase in aggregate demand, such as to AD_3, cannot raise real output; it only increases the price level. In terms of the equation of exchange, $MV = PQ$, a rise in spending increases only Q in the horizontal region of AS and only P in the vertical region. Equilibrium moves from e_1 to e_2 to e_3. Pure demand or **"demand-pull" inflation** occurs in the second region. It results from aggregate demand, financed by credit creation, in excess of full-employment output, and does not coexist with unemployment: *Either* inflation *or* unemployment conditions prevail, except at the precise point of the kink in the AS curve where neither exist. The single-minded objective of policy would then be to get the economy to that kink, at equilibrium point e_2.

Demand-pull inflation: inflation caused by rightward shifts in the aggregate demand curve. Usually caused by excessive creation of money, this type of inflation cannot coexist with unemployment.

Figure 22–1 Kinked Aggregate Supply: This is horizontal until full-employment output and vertical beyond that point.

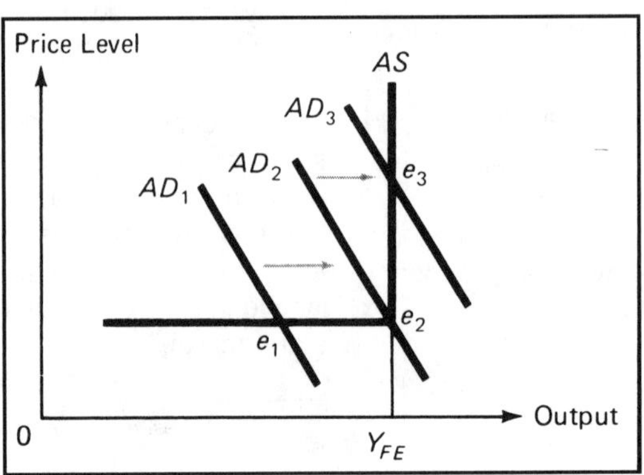

A classic case of demand-pull inflation is a war economy. When the government superimposes demand for tanks and airplanes upon a fully employed economy, there are only two ways to obtain them. First, the government can induce the private sector to abstain from consumption (that is, to save) and thereby release resources for war production. This can be accomplished either through taxation or by selling government bonds at market interest rates. But there is a limit above which taxes cannot rise without impairing work incentives, and also a limit to how much in government bonds the public will absorb. Beyond this, the government can use its power to "print money," which it does by borrowing from the central bank, and employ it to bid away goods and resources from the private sector through the market mechanism—that is, by offering to pay higher prices for them. This is what starts the inflationary process. The money spent by the government ends up in the hands of private businesspeople and workers, for it is private businesses that supply the equipment to the government. With this added purchasing power, private individuals are unlikely to stand idly by. Rather, they would try to match and outbid the government in its control over resources. And to maintain that control, the government would have to "print" more money with which to outbid the outbidders. The inflationary process is thus off and running. It occurs every time new demands for goods and services—from whatever source—appear in a fully employed economy. Note that although money creation is the proximate cause of inflation, the root cause is expansionary fiscal policy and budgetary deficits.

"PREMATURE" DEMAND INFLATION

In most industrial economies, the aggregate-supply curve is not "kinky." Rather, it begins to slope upward before full-employment output is reached, as shown in region II of Figure 13–4; see Figure 22–2. It becomes very steep in the vicinity of full employment. As aggregate demand shifts to the right, the price level begins to rise long before full employment is reached, and rises precipitously in the neighborhood of full employment.

Several factors account for the "premature" upward slope of aggregate supply. First, bottlenecks begin to appear in certain industries, even when average output for the economy as a whole is below full capacity. Some specific plants and perhaps industries already function at near full capacity, and certain labor skills are in short supply. If their prices and wage rates are bid up without corresponding declines elsewhere, the average price level rises.

A second cause is the absence of perfect competition in many sectors of the economy. Perfect competition is defined as a market condition in which so many units operate in the marketplace that no one of them has any control over the conditions of sale or purchase, including the price. It leads to price flexibility in both an upward and downward direction.

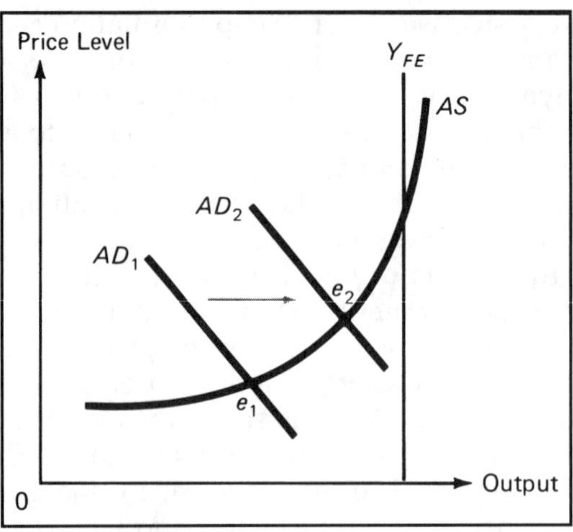

Figure 22–2 Upward-sloping Aggregate Supply: The three regions: horizontal at low-output level (Keynesian range); upward-sloping in region II (intermediate range); and very steep in region III (monetarist range) in the neighborhood of full employment.

But such conditions do not obtain in vast segments of the manufacturing sector. Many industries are dominated by very few firms and large unions, which have at least partial control over the prices and wages they charge. As a result of such industrial concentration, *not only have prices become rigid in a downward direction*, but unions and corporations use their market power (not necessarily an absolute monopoly) to push up wages and prices at times of underutilized productive capacity.

To illustrate the consequences of market power, compare the 1974 and 1975 developments in the beef and lumber industries to those in the automobile industry. All three industries suffered a drastic cut in sales. As a result, lumber and beef prices immediately plummeted, for these industries are competitive. Yet no such price reduction (beyond what the competitive dealers could offer) took place in the automobile industry. The entire brunt of reduced demand was borne by output and employment. It took a shutdown of one third of the industry to induce the auto companies to offer rebates on a few selected models and for a limited time period, without reducing list prices. Similarly, in 1981–82 it was not until nearly a third of its membership was laid off that the United Auto Workers agreed to make certain wage concessions. Additional examples can be found in steel and other industries.

A third possible cause of the upward slope of *AS* is rooted in firms' desire to keep their trained work force. They often give high wage increases even in the face of unemployment in a particular labor market.

A final reason can be found in relations between industries. Suppose the steel industry supplies products to both the automobile and the durable-goods industries. If car output expands rapidly, this is apt to raise demand for, and the price of, steel. As a consequence, the durable-goods industry—

which also uses steel as an input—is forced to raise prices even if demand for durable goods is stagnant.

Premature inflation: inflation that occurs before full employment is reached, because the aggregate supply curve gradually slopes upward.

Under these conditions, inflation appears "prematurely"; *it can and often does coexist with unemployment.* Furthermore, the closer the economy gets to full employment, the steeper the aggregate-supply curve, and the greater the price increase resulting from any upward shift in aggregate demand. A possible conflict between the twin objectives of price stability and full employment is apparent in this case. Fiscal and monetary policy can be used to stimulate aggregate spending through any of the three channels (*C*, *I*, *G*) or combinations of them, so that full employment is approached. But long before full employment is reached, prices begin to rise. And that is the reason why measures to stimulate the economy are not pushed to their ultimate conclusion—that of attaining and maintaining full employment. Conversely, contractionary fiscal and monetary policies can be employed to dampen inflation; but in the process, they create unemployment. The reason why inflation has not been wrung completely out of the economy is that this may require high unemployment. A tradeoff between inflation and unemployment occurs when demand-management policies shift the *AD* curve along region II of the *AS* curve.

SUPPLY INFLATION

Supply Shocks

Even more pervasive is the effect of supply shocks: factors that shift the aggregate-supply curve to the left. In Figure 22–3, this is shown as a shift in aggregate supply from AS_1 to AS_2. Equilibrium moves from e_1 to e_2, reflecting a decline in output (and employment) *and* a rise in prices at one

Figure 22–3 Decline in Aggregate Supply AS_1 to AS_2 along a Constant AD_1 Produces Stagflation: Output Declines and the Price Level Rises. The Fed can offset the decline in output by pumping up money supply and raising aggregate demand to AD_2. The cost is a further rise in the price level, as equilibrium moves from e_2 to e_3.

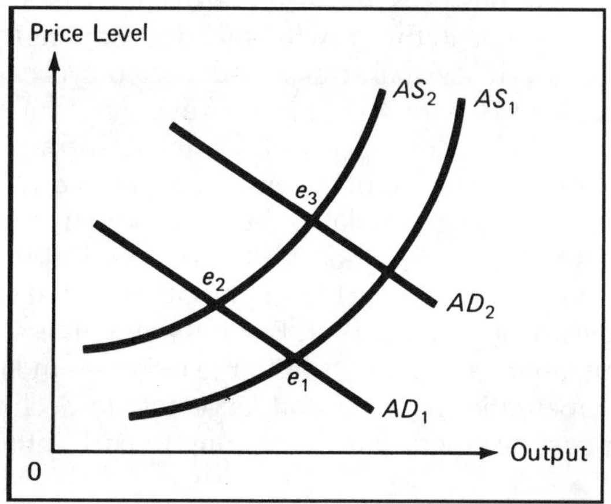

and the same time. *Stagflation* sets in. The Federal Reserve may "accommodate" the externally imposed price rise by expanding money supply, thus shifting aggregate demand from AD_1 to AD_2. Equilibrium moves from e_2 to e_3. The original level of output is restored, but at the cost of a sharply increasing price level. This was the situation in 1979.

In terms of the equation of exchange, $MV = PQ$, a sharp rise in P, triggered by an increase in energy prices, causes a reduction in Q if MV is left intact. To prevent the resulting unemployment, the monetary authorities increase MV, thereby "accommodating" the rise in P. As a result, Q is restored to its original level, but at the cost of a further increase in P. Had the Federal Reserve done the reverse, *contracting* money supply, it could have restored P to its original level, but at the cost of vastly reduced real output and a further increase in unemployment.

Causes of Supply Shocks

Supply shocks: factors causing a leftward shift in the entire aggregate supply curve. **Reverse supply shocks:** factors that shift the aggregate supply curve to the right.

Supply shocks were largely responsible for the stagflation of the mid-1970s. A constellation of circumstances converged on the economy at that time to bring about such shocks. First, the quadrupling of oil prices by the international oil cartel (OPEC) increased production costs of all firms in the economy since they all use energy as an input. Their supply schedules shifted to the left. This episode was repeated in 1979 with the doubling again of oil prices (a rise in any input price caused by resource depletion would have the same effect). Second, the imposition or tightening of environmental and safety regulations by the federal government also served to raise production costs of all firms.

A third cause was the increase in labor cost of production throughout the economy. It resulted from an increase in wage rates far beyond the increase in labor productivity (output per worker). To see the relationship between wages, productivity, and unit labor costs, assume for a moment that there is a product called "widget." If hourly pay rises 5 percent and the number of widgets produced per hour (labor productivity) also rises 5 percent, then labor production cost per widget, known as unit labor cost, remains unchanged. But if hourly pay climbs 10 percent, and the number of widgets produced per hour increases only 2 percent, the cost per widget (namely, unit labor cost) rises 8 percent. Such a rise in production costs shifts the supply curve to the left.

In the 1970s a decline in labor productivity (output per worker); a precipitous rise in energy cost; and a rise in inflationary expectations shifted aggregate supply to the left, causing stagflation. In the 1990s sharp increases in labor productivity (widespread introduction of computers etc.) constituted a reverse supply shock, bringing about non-inflationary growth.

For various reasons, such as the increases in oil prices, there was a marked decline in the growth of labor productivity in U.S. manufacturing in the 1970s. (This is apart from the expected cyclical fluctuation in productivity outlined in Chapter 13.) From an average annual rise of 3 percent between 1960 and 1973, it dropped to 1.8 percent during 1973–81. At the same time, the annual rise in hourly compensation nearly doubled. As a result, the annual increase in unit labor cost of production jumped from 1.9 to 7.7 percent (Table 22–1). Between 1981 and 1987 output per hour increased in the same proportion as hourly compensation so that unit labor cost in 1987 stood at the same level as in 1981. But 1988–89 witnessed a resumption of the rise in unit labor cost. In the 1990s large increases in labor productivity, in excess of compensation, caused unit labor cost to decline. And in 2004–2005 unit labor cost declined sharply, helping to curb inflation. Also, the rise in pro-

Table 22–1 Annual Growth Rate in Output Per Hour, Hourly Compensation, and Unit Labor Cost In U.S. Manufacturing Industries

	1960–1973	1973–1981	1981–1990	1990–2003	2004–2005
Output per hour	2.9%	1.8%	2.8%	4.0%	4.1%
Hourly compensation	1.9%	1.3%	2.2%	4.1%	3.6%
Unit labor cost	1.9%	7.7%	0.5%	-0.1%	–0.5%

Source: U.S. Department of Labor, Bureau of Labor Statistics.

ductivity, ahead of labor compensation, indicates a boost in corporate profits. Indeed, corporate profits rose significantly in 2005.

Other possible reasons for the decline in aggregate supply were a rise in inflationary expectations and competition for income shares among labor groups, as well as between labor and capital, in years of stationary real income. Both factors served to push up wage rates beyond the growth in productivity.

▶ IMPORTANCE OF PRODUCTIVITY

In the text, labor productivity was used in conjunction with labor compensation to determine unit labor cost. But productivity is important beyond its contribution to the lowering of unit labor cost and inflation. For *in the long run, productivity determines the standard of living.*

Labor productivity, in turn, depends first on the amount of machinery that each worker has to work with, or on the nation's capital stock. That is determined by the national savings rate and the ability to channel savings into productive investment, for net investment constitutes the annual addition to the capital stock. Second, productivity depends on the quality of the labor force, which is determined by the workers' technical training and education, work habits, and discipline.

A third determinant of productivity is the nation's ability to invent new products and processes and to introduce them into production. (Technological progress accounts for about half the growth in per capita output.) And that is determined by research and development (R&D) expenditures and the nation's endowment in research scientists and engineers. In 1985–87 the U.S. spent under 2 percent of GDP on civilian R&D, compared to 2.5 percent in Germany and 2.7 percent in Japan *(The Wall Street Journal,* November 16, 1988). Beyond that, productivity depends on the general political and business environment, and the availability of entrepreneurship. Because other countries are approaching and even surpassing the U.S. in all these factors, their standard of living is catching up with that of the United States.

In the late 1990s U.S. labor productivity mushroomed, partly because of technological innnovations. That helped hold inflation in check, and it increased living standards.

In all the cases, the proximate cause of high inflation was an increase in money supply. But that increase was undertaken to accommodate the supply shock that increased the price level to avoid a loss in real output. Similarly, a reduction in money supply could have averted the price rise altogether, but at the cost of reduced real output and higher unemployment. By using demand-management policies to offset a supply shock, the authorities can attain either full employment *or* price stability; they cannot attain both.

THE ROLE OF EXPECTATIONS

No discussion of the inflationary process is complete without mention of the role of expectations. In times of price stability, everybody expects stable prices to continue and behaves accordingly. But suppose prices begin to rise. Many consumers who expect the price increase to continue would advance their purchases to avoid the higher prices in the future. But by doing this, they increase present-day demand and accelerate the price rise. The expectations for price increase become self-fulfilling. The behavior of business investment can be similarly described. And labor unions that expect inflation to continue begin to factor it into their wage demands in contract negotiations. The result is ever-increasing wage rates. To the extent that they are not matched by a rise in productivity, they translate into ever-increasing prices.

Inflationary expectations are based both on past experience and on the judgment of economic agents about present and future economic conditions. Information about the course of economic policy in the near future may be incorporated into this judgment. Thus, if labor unions observe a sudden spurt in the growth rate of the money stock, they cannot help but surmise that the inflation rate will accelerate. Once inflationary expectations set in and take a firm hold, it is difficult to keep the rate of inflation constant. It tends to accelerate. A society can learn to live with a given rate of inflation as long as it is "reasonable." But that rate is *unlikely to remain at a standstill.* With inflationary expectations built in, it tends to feed upon itself and accelerate. And that can *worsen the tradeoff* between inflation and unemployment. That is why it is so important not only to keep inflation low, but to prevent its rate from accelerating. High and rising inflation can strain the social fabric.

It is *easier to bring inflation under control before it starts accelerating.* For example, in 1978, inflation was under 8 percent, and mild contractionary policies, with a small rise in unemployment, would have sufficed to contain and even reduce it. Such policies, which could have brought the economy to a "soft landing," were announced in November of that year but were not implemented. Instead, inflation was allowed to accelerate, reaching 18 percent in the first quarter of 1980. The price of failing to act in time was severe, for it required a recession and sluggish growth in 1980–81 and a deep recession in 1981–82 to bring inflation under control.

This is one reason why the Fed was concerned about the acceleration of inflation in early 1989. After several years of low or little price increases, inflation rose to 4 percent in 1988 and threatened to increase further (to the 5 to 6 percent range) in 1989, as aggregate output was bumping against capacity. To "nip that development in the bud" the Federal Reserve announced the tightening of money supply and prospective increases in interest rates, with the idea of slowing down aggregate demand, lowering the growth rate of the economy, and thereby preventing the inflation from accelerating.

THE PHILLIPS CURVE

Shifts in *AD* along the intermediate range of the *AS* curve give rise to a tradeoff between inflation and unemployment. Higher levels of unemployment tend to be associated with lower rates of price increase, and vice versa. The higher the rate of unemployment and excess industrial capacity, the more reluctant are labor unions and corporations to press for higher wages and prices. Conversely, the lower the level of unemployment and the closer the economy gets to full employment, the stronger the incentive on the part of unions and companies to press for higher wages and prices. This **inverse relationship between inflation and unemployment** is described on a chart called the Phillips curve, named after its developer, the British economist A. W. Phillips.

On its vertical axis, Figure 22–4 shows the rate of inflation (rate of *change* in the price level, rather than the price level itself, shown in Figure 22–3). The horizontal axis measures the rate of unemployment, the *inverse* of employment reflected in Figure 22–3. The Phillips curve indicates the inverse relation between the two variables.

Figure 22–4 Hypothetical Phillips Curve: Inverse Relation between Inflation and Unemployment

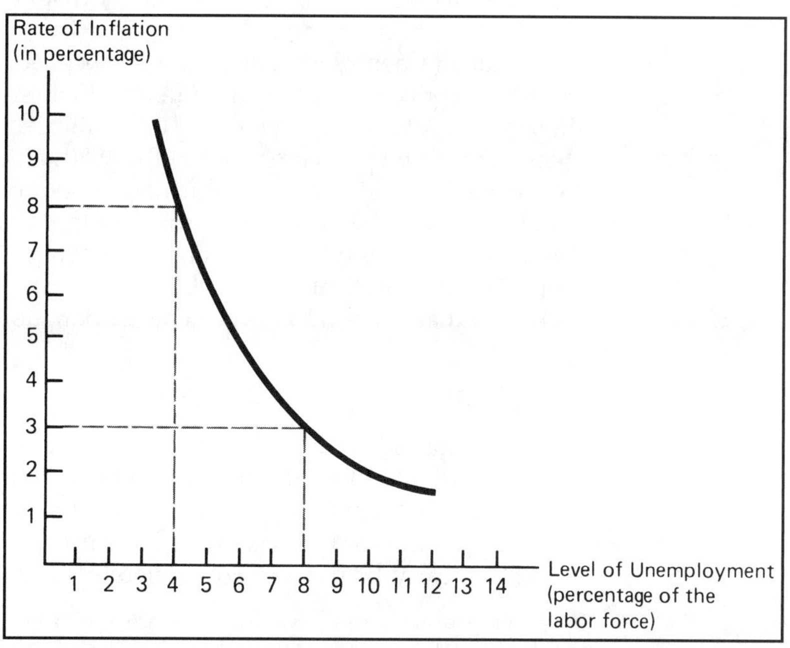

Although there is a relation between the Phillips curve and the aggregate-supply schedule, the two are not the same, since they relate to different sets of axes. In the case of *AS*, the vertical axis is the price level; in the case of the Phillips curve, it is the rate of change in the price level (inflation). In the case of *AS*, the horizontal axis is real output (GDP); in the case of the Phillips curve, it is the rate of growth in output, for that rate determines the level of employment. However, the Phillips curve shows *unemployment* rather than employment on the horizontal axis. Consequently, whereas the *AS* schedule is positively sloped, the Phillips curve has a negative slope, representing a tradeoff.

At one end of the spectrum lies the possible combination of considerable unemployment and reasonable price stability (as in the late 1950s and early 1960s); at the other end, nearly full employment along with a high rate of inflation (as in the late 1970s). Between the two extremes lie various combinations of unemployment and inflation that are "attainable." However, there have been times of both inflation and unemployment, and conversely the years 1997–2000 witnessed full employment without inflation.

Different countries have different preferences for the inflation-unemployment mix they consider tolerable. Germany, whose memories are dominated by the great post-World War I inflation, is least tolerant of inflation, and is likely to choose a mix involving a very low inflation rate even at the cost of unemployment. By contrast, the main memories in the United States and United Kingdom are of unemployment and the Great Depression. They are apt to choose a mix involving lower unemployment even at the cost of high inflation.

Figure 22–5 shows the relation between unemployment and inflation in the United States during three periods—1961–69, 1970–73, and 1976–79. In all cases, the expansion of output and corresponding decline in unemployment was attained (via expansionary policies) at the cost of rising inflation. However, the periods display distinctly different relationships. The tradeoff became much less favorable from the 1960s to the 1970s. The same rate of unemployment became associated with a higher rate of inflation, and conversely, the same rate of inflation became associated with a higher rate of unemployment. The Phillips curve shifted to the right. Moreover, if one plots the years of the 1980s and the 1990s in the diagram, what emerges are scattered points that do not reveal any particular shape. In other words, the stability of the Phillips curve in the 1950s and 1960s broke down in the 1970s. And that brought about the demise of the Phillips curve as an analytical construct, and as a way of viewing the economy.[1] Why did that happen? Two possible explanations may be suggested.

Supply Shocks

One explanation is the series of supply shocks that occurred in the 1970s. It will be recalled that the tradeoff between inflation and unemployment is a result of shifts in the *AD* curve along the intermediate range of aggregate supply. But for reasons explained earlier, economic fluctuations in the 1970s and early 1980s were dominated by factors that moved the *AS* to the

[1]Because the Phillips curve has been unstable over a long period, it has fallen into disrepute. But the existence of a trade-off between inflation and unemployment is still widely accepted. Se L. Ball and G. Mankiw, "The NAIRU in Theory, and Practice" Journal of Economic Perspective, Fall 2002, pp. 115-136.

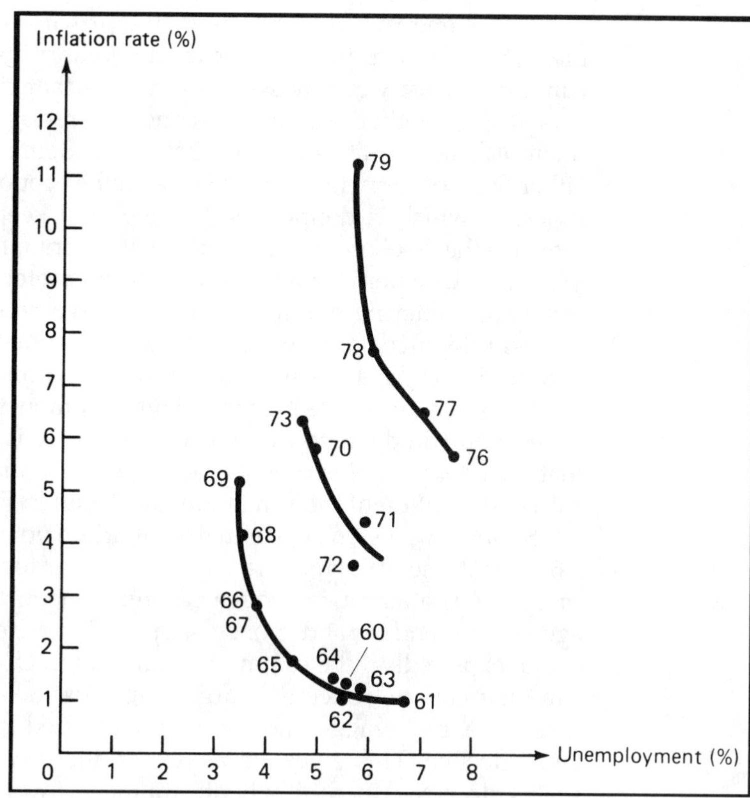

Figure 22–5 Inflation and Unemployment Rates in the United States, 1960–69, 1970–73, and 1976–79. Source: *Economic Report of the President,* January 1980 and 1982.

left. Such shifts cause *both* inflation and unemployment and they worsen the tradeoff between the two. This is one reason why the 1970s were such trying times for the economy. *Changes in AS cause* inflation and unemployment to move in the same direction, and *do not manifest a tradeoff of the Phillips curve variety.* By contrast, in the late 1990s the increased labor productivity and enhanced foreign competition constituted a *reverse* supply shock, generating full employment without inflation.

A second explanation, rooted in the monetarist view, questions the very existence of a negatively sloping Phillips curve. It is explained next.

THE PHILLIPS CURVE—AN ALTERNATIVE VIEW

In recent years, the monetarist school of thought has challenged the traditional interpretation of the Phillips curve. In particular, monetarists question the notion that unemployment can be reduced in the long run at the cost of higher inflation. And so they challenge the rationale for "activist" policy that emerges from the tradeoff concept—a policy that is contrary to their philosophy and general view of the economy.

In the long run, they maintain, the private economy is inherently stable. While short-run deviations from equilibrium are possible, in the long run, prices and wages will settle at points that clear their respective markets. Rigidities that exist in the economy produce structural and frictional unemployment that is not susceptible to demand-management policies, either fiscal or monetary. There exists in the economy a *natural rate of unemployment,* which is defined as the level that keeps inflation at a constant rate. It is the level of unemployment consistent with *nonaccelerating inflation* (NAIRU). Its extent depends on workers' preferences between work and leisure (considering that leisure also carries a financial reward, in the form of unemployment compensation) and on various institutional factors that determine the rigidities introduced into the economy.

It is the natural rate of unemployment, monetarists say, that dominates the economy in the long run. The Phillips curve is, in fact, *vertical,* pegged at that rate. And the phenomenon observed in Figures 22–4 and 22–5 above is subject to a different interpretation, displayed in Figure 22–6.

Suppose we begin at an initial equilibrium point of 2 percent inflation and a 6 percent unemployment rate (point *a*), regarded as the "natural rate." In a (misguided) attempt to reduce unemployment, the government increases aggregate spending and money supply. That raises prices. But when prices rise unexpectedly, it takes time for wages to catch up. Union contracts must run their course, collective bargaining must take place, and so on. In the meantime, real wages (money wages adjusted by the change in the price level) decline. This gives employers an incentive to hire more workers—that is, decrease unemployment. Another way of describing what happens is that the rise in prices with unchanged money wages increases profits, thereby inducing businesspersons to expand output and employment. The upshot is that we move to point *b* on the chart. Inflation rises to 4 percent, and unemployment declines.

Figure 22–6 The Monetarists' Interpretation of the Phillips Curve: In the long run the Phillips Curve is vertical, and it is set at the "natural rate of unemployment." In the short run, it is possible to lower unemployment temporarily at the cost of unanticipated rise in inflation. But to keep unemployment continuously below the natural level, the inflation rate must *accelerate.* Conversely, it is possible to reduce inflation at the cost of a temporary rise in unemployment above the natural rate.

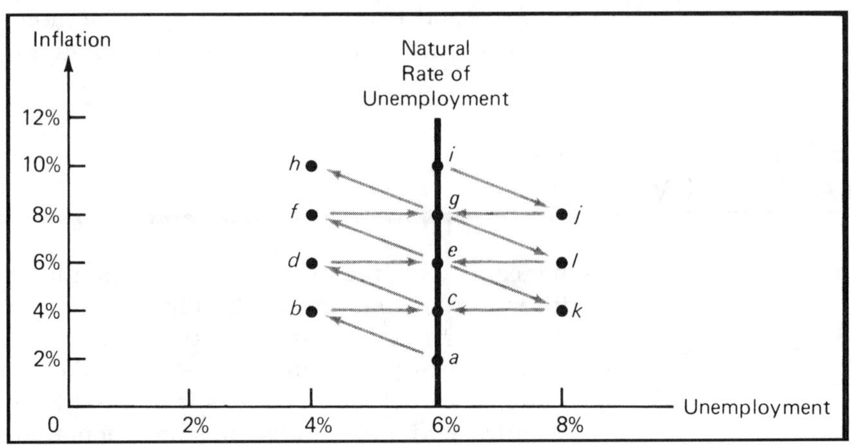

But this decline in unemployment is temporary; it does not take unions long to realize that the purchasing power of their members' paychecks has declined because of inflation. As a result, the next set of labor contracts allows for the 4 percent rate of inflation just produced. Real wages rise to their previous level, the incentive to hire more workers is removed, and unemployment returns to its previous level. In terms of Figure 22–6, we move back from point *b* to point *c*, where unemployment is back at its natural rate of 6 percent and inflation is 4 percent. The decline in unemployment was strictly temporary and was a result of unanticipated inflation.

If aggregate spending is now set at a rate that would produce 4 percent inflation, that rate of price rise becomes expected, and unions build it into their wage contracts. Unemployment is back at its natural rate. To reduce it again, the government must raise the rate of inflation further, to perhaps 6 percent, of which 2 percent is now unexpected. Again unemployment would decline temporarily, in response to the unexpected rise in inflation and the attendant reduction in labor costs. We move to point *d*. But that would last only until union wages caught up with the new rate of inflation. At that time, the economy returns to point *e*, and unemployment is back to its natural rate. This process may continue, as described on the chart. Thus, the *observed relationship is between unemployment and unanticipated inflation. In order to reduce unemployment over a protracted period, the rate of inflation must be* **accelerated.**

Monetarists view: Monetarists believe that the relationship observed by the Phillips curve is between unemployment and *unanticipated* inflation. In the long run the Phillips curve is vertical at the natural rate of unemployment.

Eventually, the rate of inflation reaches a level unacceptable to society and has to be lowered by government policy. The process must then be reversed. Suppose that starting from point *i* of 10 percent inflation, the central bank lowers the growth rate of the money stock. The rate of inflation declines unexpectedly from 10 to 8 percent. But union contracts are still based on 10 percent inflation. Real wage rates rise and employers lay off workers. Unemployment rises to 8 percent, and the economy moves to point *j* on the chart. But this is a temporary phenomenon, lasting only until unions realize that inflation has slackened and they factor the lower rate of inflation into their wage demands. Unemployment declines back to its natural rate, and the economy is back at point *g*. That process continues, as shown on the chart, until inflation is reduced to an acceptable level. Here lies the danger of boom and bust. The *monetarist's dislike for inflation is rooted partly in the belief that eventually, it must result in a recession and unemployment,* however temporary.

In the short run, the Phillips curve represents a tradeoff between unemployment and unanticipated inflation. *In the long run, unemployment cannot deviate from its natural rate.* Consequently, *the traditional Phillips curve* relationship—that between inflation and unemployment—*is vertical* and is set at the natural rate of unemployment. By implication, the aggregate-supply curve is also vertical. Attempts to lower unemployment below the natural rate will merely result in ever-accelerating inflation. There is *no scope for activist fiscal and monetary policy*—a position that is consistent with the monetarists' general predilection.

To see the relevance of this interpretation, just draw a straight vertical line at 6 percent unemployment in Figure 22–5. With some extension of the three tradeoff lines, you will obtain a diagram similar to Figure 22–6.

Rational Expectations

Rational expectations: A school of thought which denies the possibility of unanticipated inflation. Even over the short-run Phillips curve is vertical because people fully anticipate inflation.

In the monetarists' view, there exists a short-run tradeoff between unemployment and *unanticipated* inflation. But in the 1970s there emerged a new school, known as **rational expectations,** that denies the existence of unanticipated inflation.

People's expectations concerning future events have an important effect on economic variables. Consequently, economists devote considerable effort to the analysis of expectations: how they are formed, how they can best be measured, and how to incorporate them into economic analysis. For the most part, expectations' formation is assumed to be based in some way on people's past experience.

Rational expectation analysis suggests that expectations are formed in a different manner. It assumes that economic agents understand fully how the economy functions; that they possess complete information about economic events and government policies; that they know how government policies will affect the economy; and that they assimilate all that knowledge promptly in a way that guides their behavior. In other words, they *anticipate* the impact of events and policies in their own decision making, and change their behavior when new information becomes available. For example, if the authorities typically react to high inflation by reducing aggregate demand, people will soon come to anticipate such a reaction, and build it into their wage demands and other spheres of economic behavior.

How does all this apply to the case at hand? Labor unions have their own economists who read the financial press and follow government policy. When they see an increase in money supply, they rationally anticipate that inflation will follow, and they incorporate this expectation in their wage contracts without a time lag. Under these circumstances, inflation is fully anticipated.[1] The short-run Phillips curve (as well as the long-run curve) is vertical, and there is no scope whatsoever for active stabilization policies. The only thing the government should do is follow fixed and predictable (preferably preannounced) monetary and fiscal policies, thereby providing a stable framework for the private economy.

Adherents to the rational expectations hypothesis are noninterventionists in the extreme, yet they remain a vocal minority among economists. Empirical tests have failed to verify their hypothesis, and most economists believe that expectations are formed sluggishly rather than rationally.

An Emerging Consensus

Consensus: In the short run there is a trade-off between unemployment and inflation, although the formality of the Phillips curve may not hold. But in the long run unemployment is fixed at the natural rate of unemployment.

An emerging consensus among most economists appears to be as follows: In the long run, the natural rate of unemployment prevails. The Phillips curve is vertical. But in the short run, the traditional Phillips-curve relationship holds. Since the short run may last for three to four years (at least the length of most labor contracts), and because the political horizon of most democratic governments is not longer than that, there is ample room for activist fiscal and monetary policy to influence the course of the economy. These policies move the economy along a given Phillips curve—

---

[1]On a technical level, people will not err *systematically* about the direction of inflation. The difference between the actual and the expected rate of inflation will be a pure random number.

reducing unemployment at the expense of more inflation, or vice versa. Even those who deny the existence of a stable Phillips curve, accept the idea that there exists a trade-off between inflation and unemployment (see Ball and Mankiw, "The NAIRU In Theory and Practice," *Jour. of Economic Perspectives*, Fall 2002, pp. 115–136.

Behavioral Macroeconomics—Keynes Rehabilitated

Behavioral macroeconomics is a new field that rehabilitates Keynesian economics.

Just as the profession began to accept the "new classical economics," based upon price-wage flexibility, a new strand of macroeconomics appeared that offers a theoretical foundation to the Keynesian assumptions. With sticky wages and prices, explained as "almost rational," involuntary unemployment can exist; monetary policy is effective in changing real output; and the Phillips curve is rehabilitated. In addition, the new theories explain why individual savings may be insufficient for retirement and hence need to be supplemented by a government program; and why stock prices do not "rationally" reflect the expected stream of dividends—at least not in short-run fluctuations.

All this is summarized in an admirable article by George Akerlof, "Behavior Macroeconomics and Macroeconomic Behavior," *American Economic Review*, June 2002.[2]

POLICIES TO IMPROVE THE TRADEOFF

Even when inflation is caused by a leftward shift in the *AS*, the policy makers who wish to counter it by fiscal and monetary policies (demand management), must still deal with the undesirable tradeoff between inflation and unemployment. Is it possible to devise policies that would make the tradeoff more palatable by enabling us to "buy" less unemployment at any given rate of inflation, or less inflation at any given level of unemployment? The answer is *maybe*.

Greater Competition

Since one reason for the tradeoff is the market power of corporations and unions, it can be mitigated by infusing more competition into the economy. This can be accomplished by more vigorous antitrust enforcement, and by opening up the economy to unrestricted foreign competition through the complete elimination of all barriers to imports (tariffs, quotas, and the like). Potential and actual competition from foreign producers would reduce the market power of oligopolistic enterprises at home and force them to hold the lid on prices. Such actions in the field of competition and foreign trade would be beneficial on other grounds as well. Equally desirable has been the policy of the Ford, Carter, and Reagan administrations to reduce government regulation over prices and the provision of service in such

[2]For a review of stabilization policies see: *Rethinking Stabilization Policy,* a Symposium sponsored by the Federal Reserve Bank of Kansas City, August 2002.

industries as airlines, trucking, railroads, and energy. These policies constitute the "best" remedy to the tradeoff problem.

In the important case of the labor market, extensive training and retraining programs for the unemployed can be introduced, accompanied by programs to help workers relocate whenever necessary. Workers need to be equipped with skills that are needed in our increasingly mechanized and sophisticated economy. This would help alleviate the part of the unemployment problem that is considered structural in nature, and also lubricate the transition mechanism when demand shifts from one set of industries to another. Creation of a nationwide job bank that would impart instant information on job vacancies and available workers is called for. And finally, the minimum wage applying to teenagers may be lowered to motivate employers to hire the young, a group in which much of the unemployment is concentrated.

Income Policies

What if, for political or other reasons, the "best" solution is ruled out? Is there another (although inferior) remedy? We might in that case consider seriously the possible addition of **income policies** to the arsenal of policy makers. These are measures, such as price and wage controls, designed to control inflation without reducing aggregate demand. Although they are used in other countries, most Americans take a dim view of the peacetime use of direct controls, "voluntary" or otherwise. Yet when properly used, such controls can be instrumental in combating cost-push inflation. Controls should never be used in times of excessive demand, for then they only suppress and do not cure the inflation; nearly always, they lead to the appearance of black markets and cause gross misallocation of resources. But *when productive capacity is not fully utilized,* so that potential supply of goods and services is adequate, *wage-price guidelines can mitigate cost-push inflation,* and thereby partly solve the tradeoff question. Short of mandatory controls, the president can use the prestige of his office to influence price-wage decisions by persuasive arguments—that is, "jawboning." For example, an industry suffering from slumping sales and mass unemployment should be induced to *adopt a behavior like that of a competitive industry:* accept a reduction in profits, executive compensations, and wages that would permit a substantial cut in prices. The plan could be "sold" to the union on the grounds that the alternative is mass unemployment of its members, and that executives and shareowners would be required to make an even greater sacrifice. Not only would the price reduction stimulate sales directly; if similar steps were taken in all depressed industries, it would be possible to stimulate the economy without fear of inflation.

Income policies: measures, such as price and wage controls, designed to control inflation without reducing aggregate demand. President Nixon tried to impose such controls, but the attempt is generally considered a failure.

However, the issues of controls and their effectiveness in combating inflation is the subject of heated debate and disagreement among economists. Certainly, in order to work effectively, controls must be accepted and even welcomed by the general public and be administered by officials who believe in their efficacy and are dedicated to their success. At least in the United States, *the effectiveness of controls is widely doubted.*

Tax-based income policy (TIP): the government would pronounce certain guidelines for average annual percentage wage and price increases, and any company that exceeds these guidelines would be subject to a special tax. If a company falls short of the guidelines it may receive rebates on its tax liability. Never enacted by the U.S. Congress.

One form of incomes policy that was considered is known as **tax-based income policy,** or **TIP.** Under the most popular variant of the proposal, the government would enunciate each year guidelines for average percentage wage and price increases. *A corporation that grants its union a wage increase exceeding that proclaimed in the guideline would be subject to a special tax.* This would increase the cost to the company of exceeding the guideline, and would *stiffen its resistance* at the bargaining table to excessive wage increases, which later tend to be passed on to consumers in the form of price increases. Conversely, if the wage *settlement falls short of the announced guidelines, the workers and/or the company may receive special rebates on their tax liability.* This introduces an incentive to settle below the guidelines, thus lowering the rate of inflation. All this gives companies and unions a stake in combating inflation. To avoid inflation altogether, the percentage wage increments should not exceed the growth rate in labor productivity. Thus, the guidelines for wage increases should be set at a level equal to the anticipated increase in productivity plus whatever inflation the government is willing to tolerate.

Although intellectually appealing, TIP proposals ran into a maze of administrative problems and remain highly controversial. One such proposal was in fact made by President Carter in 1978, but Congress failed to enact it.

Supply-side economics: By shifting the aggregate supply curve to the right unemployment and inflation are both reduced. But the policy measures for doing so are not available in the short run.

Supply-Side Economics

In recent years, much discussion has centered around supply-management as opposed to the traditional demand-management policies. Any measures that would **shift the aggregate supply curve to the right have the advantage of lowering unemployment and inflation at one and the same time. This would shift the short-run Phillips curve to the left and improve the tradeoff.** The reduction in worldwide petroleum prices in 1981, considered a reverse supply shock, had that effect to a limited extent.

Most prominent in this context is a proposal to lower the Social Security tax paid by business. This would constitute an across-the-board reduction in business costs, and in turn would shift aggregate supply to the right, attaining the desired objective. The alternative source of financing Social Security can be either the general-fund budget of the government or perhaps revenue from a special gasoline tax imposed to induce energy conservation.

Measures to enhance incentives to invest would have the effect of increasing productivity and shifting the *AS* curve rightward. Faster depreciation on plant and equipment for tax purposes and tax credit on reinvested earnings of corporations come to mind as two possibilities. At this point, the reader is invited to review the supply-side discussion in Chapter 13.

A reduction in the personal income tax is advocated by supply-siders, not as a measure to stimulate aggregate demand but rather as a step to induce an increase in aggregate supply. That, indeed, was the underlying rationale for the 23 percent cut in the personal income tax enacted in 1981. It was claimed that a reduction in the marginal tax rates would (1) improve work incentives, and (2) promote savings and therefore stimulate investments. These arguments are considered in turn.

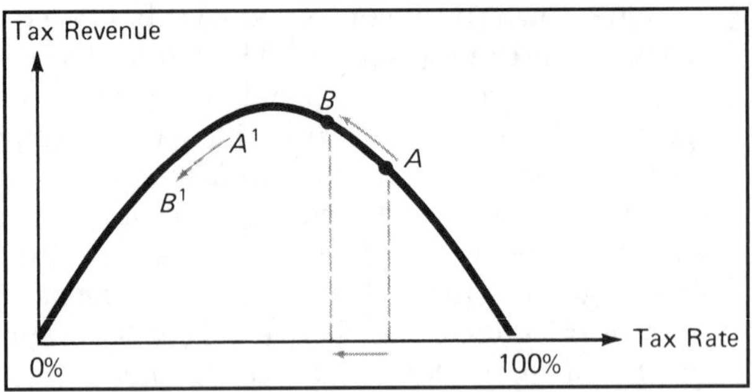

Figure 22–7 The Laffer Curve: It shows a relation between tax rates and tax revenues. Revenue is zero at 0% and 100% tax rates.

Laffer curve: shows a relation between tax rates and tax revenues. At some marginal tax rate, work disincentives are so great that tax revenue begins to decline.

Increase in Work Incentives The hypothesis that a tax cut would greatly improve work incentives is embodied in what has become known as the **Laffer curve. It postulates a relation between tax rates and tax revenues.** Tax rates and revenue are shown, respectively, on the horizontal and vertical axes of Figure 22–7. When tax rates are zero, as they are at the point of origin, the initial point on the horizontal axis, tax revenues are necessarily zero. At tax rates of 100 percent, revenue is also zero, because no one would work: Why work if all earnings must be paid in taxes to the government? And if people don't work and don't earn income, they pay no taxes. On these end points of the chart, there is no controversy; all economists agree.

What happens in between the two extreme points? As tax rates rise, displayed by a rightward movement along the horizontal axis, tax revenues begin to increase as well, as shown by an upward movement along the vertical axis. That explains the positively sloping segment of the Laffer curve. However, as tax rates increase further, they reach a level high enough to diminish work incentives. At some marginal tax rate, the disincentive to work and earn income is so strong that tax revenues begin to decline. Higher tax rates beyond that point are associated with lower tax revenues. That explains the negatively sloping portion of the curve. There is a tax rate between zero and 100 percent that yields maximum revenue—the peak of the Laffer curve.

Suppose the economy is at point *A*. Then lowering tax rates in the direction of the arrow along the horizontal axis would move the economy to point *B*: A reduction in tax rates increases work incentives so much that it results in an increase in tax revenues. In this blissful world, we can have our cake and eat it too; cut tax rates and actually increase government revenue. This is the contention of extreme supply-siders like Prof. Arthur Laffer. Indeed, they may be right with respect to a country (such as Sweden?) where marginal tax rates reach 90 percent at incomes of around $25,000. Such high rates constitute a strong disincentive to work. Reduction of such high marginal tax rates improves incentives to work, raises productivity and income, and may indeed increase tax revenue.

But in the United States, personal tax rates have not been that high, and the positively sloping segment of the line is likely to be the appropriate one.

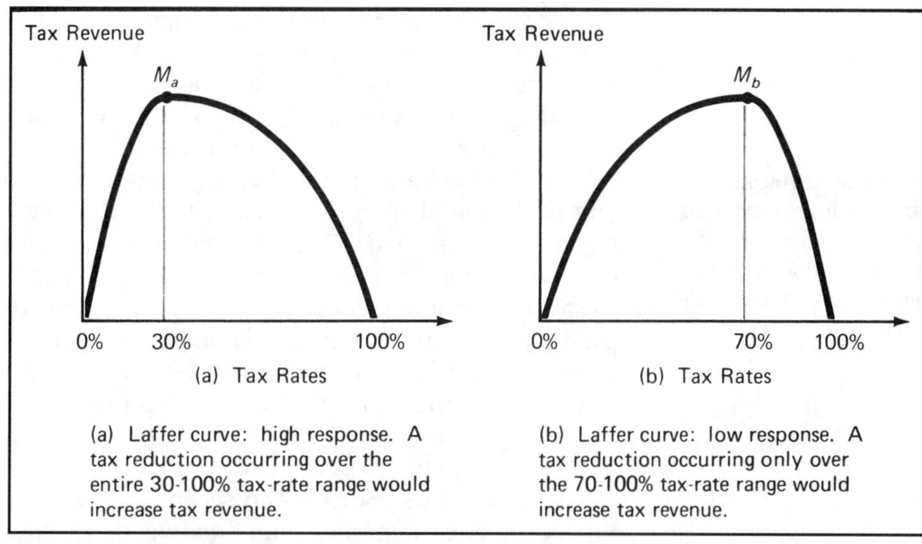

Tax Revenue
M_a
0%
30%
100%
(a) Tax Rates
Tax Revenue
M_b
0%
70%
100%
(b) Tax Rates
(a) Laffer curve: high response. A tax reduction occurring over the entire 30-100% tax-rate range would increase tax revenue.
(b) Laffer curve: low response. A tax reduction occurring only over the 70-100% tax-rate range would increase tax revenue.

Figure 22–8 How Labor Response Affects the Tax Take: Source: R.A. Krieger, "Supply Side Economics: Work and Taxes," *The Chase Economic Observer*, 1981.

In that region, a reduction in the marginal tax rate implies movement from point A^1 to B^1, thereby *reducing* tax revenue. This is the view of most economists. Although a tax cut may *stimulate additional work effort,* and hence shift the *AS* curve rightward to a limited extent, the stimulus is likely to be small—certainly not sufficient to generate an increase in tax revenue.

Not only the point on the Laffer curve at which the economy operates, but the shape of the curve itself is subject to dispute. In contrast to the symmetrical shape of the curve depicted in Figure 22–7, two alternative possibilities are shown in Figure 22–8. If the amount of labor supplied is highly responsive to changes in after-tax income, as many supply-siders claim, then even a minimal tax rate on labor income will severely discourage work effort. In this situation (panel a), the point of maximum tax revenue (M_a) may come at a relatively low tax rate. On the other hand, if the labor-supply reaction to reduced after-tax income is weak (panel b), as many critics assert, then work effort and labor income fall off very slowly as taxes rise. Only beyond point M_b, as the tax rate approaches 100 percent, will further rate hikes discourage labor enough to reduce the tax take. A study for the Treasury Department found that, as in panel b, current U.S. taxes are far below the rates necessary to elicit the Laffer effect. Total tax revenues would increase as tax rates on gross labor income rise, up to about 72 percent—far above the highest marginal tax rate on earned personal income in the United States. Indeed, the 1981 Reagan tax cut, far from increasing revenues, resulted in massive budgetary deficits of over 5 percent of GDP in 1983–86.

In sum, **a reduction in income tax rates may elicit greater work effort, but the increase is likely to be small. This is a weak supply-side measure.**

Savings and Investment A potentially more promising avenue for supply-side approaches is the stimulus the tax cuts can give to savings and investment.

Savings plays a dual role in the economy. In the Keynesian analysis, it was viewed as a *leakage or withdrawal out of the income stream.* Without any savings, there is no possibility of unemployment. When planned savings exceeds planned investments, unemployment can arise. From that point of view, a high rate of saving appears undesirable.

Effect of savings: Savings frees resources from the production of consumer goods and allows for investment to occur.

But savings also plays a critical *positive role as an engine of economic growth.* In the absence of any savings (admittedly an extreme case), all income is consumed. Since income equals output, this implies that the entire output in the economy takes the form of consumer goods, designed to satisfy consumer demand. No resources are free to be devoted to the production of investment goods (machinery and structures). And without investment, the capital stock cannot grow, and productivity does not rise. Without economic growth, living standards stagnate.

Savings plays a critical role of freeing resources in the economy from the production of consumer goods, so that they can be devoted to the production of investment goods. But for the second requirement to be fulfilled, there must exist adequate investment. *Ideally, the economy should generate sizable savings, wholly channeled into investment. That way, the economy can grow along a full-employment path. Measures to stimulate savings in the economy may thus be counted as supply-side policies.* And the view of policy makers in the Reagan administration has been tilted in this direction (see material in the following box).

Tax measures *specifically targeted to encourage savings* were included in the 1981 tax legislation. An example is the permission to employees who

▶ A NEW SAVINGS POLICY?

For three decades after World War II, attitudes and policies in the United States and the United Kingdom were shaped by the Keynesian idea that too much savings was at the root of economic depressions. Keynes downgraded the importance of savings in making room for investment and capital accumulation and thereby increasing potential output. It is claimed that these attitudes were manifested in a wide variety of antisavings policies:

> Tax rules that penalize saving; a Social Security program that makes saving virtually unnecessary for the majority of the population; credit market rules that have encouraged large mortgages and extensive consumer credit while limiting the rate of return available to the small saver; and perennial government deficits that absorb private saving and thereby shrink the resources available for investment.[a]

In contrast, the influence of Keynes was much weaker in France, Germany, and Japan, and these countries encouraged savings in both words and incentives. Partly as a result of these factors, U.S. savings have fallen in recent years, and U.S. net investment as a share of GDP has been far less than the share in other major industrial countries.

In the 1980s, there has been a radical change in the U.S. attitude toward savings. Economists on both sides of the political spectrum recommend policies that would encourage savings.

[a] Martin Feldstein, "America's New Savings Policy," *The Wall Street Journal,* August 19, 1981, editorial page.

participate in company pension plans to make additional tax-deductible contributions to Individual Retirement Accounts (IRA). Another illustration was the All-Savers certificate, which allows an exemption from income tax of up to $1,000 on the interest it earns.

But it is highly questionable whether an across-the-board income tax cut would stimulate much savings. Can it really be viewed as a supply-side measure (as its proponents contend) if most of the increase in disposable income is channeled into consumption? Is it not mainly a demand-management and only slightly a supply-side policy? Indeed the 1964 Kennedy tax cut worked because it stimulated consumption and aggregate demand when the economy was functioning at well below capacity. And in the six years following the 1981 Reagan tax cut, there has been a *decrease* in the personal savings rate: The share of personal savings in disposable income declined from 7.1 percent in 1980 to 3.2 percent in 1987. Clearly the bulk of the tax cut was channeled into increased consumption. A cut in income taxes can hardly be viewed as a supply-side measure.

In sum, supply-side policies are only those that are *specifically targeted* to increase savings and investment and, therefore, productivity. While supply-side *events* (such as the sharp decline of oil prices in the 1980s and late 1990s) can occur and shift the *AS* curve to the right, the analysis of government *policies* that can do so is still in its infancy. At best, well-targeted measures work only in the long run, after new investments come to fruition.

Indexation

Indexation: the pegging of all contracts to the cost-of-living index. In the U.S., social security payments to retirees are so pegged.

Indexation *means the pegging of all contracts in the economy to the cost-of-living index.* There are many proposals for linking wages, interest rates, and various contracts to the cost of living. But they belong in a different category from those outlined in the last three sections. Rather than attempting to reduce inflation and/or alleviating the tradeoff problem, *they accept inflation* as a fact of life, and merely *try to remove or minimize its redistributive effects.*

In a fully indexed economy, all contracts are linked to the cost of living. Wage contracts include escalator clauses that automatically raise wage rates in the same proportion as the rise in the cost of living, thereby protecting workers against unexpected inflation (expected inflation can be factored into wage contracts even without indexation).[3] Interest rates (such as variable mortgage rates) move up and down with the rate of inflation, as do dividends and other returns to productive factors. Taxes are also pegged to inflation, as the income brackets to which the tax rates apply are raised automatically in a proportion equal to the rise in the cost of living. This prevents redistribution occasioned by inflation from the private sector to the government. All contracts are similarly pegged to the rate of inflation.

---

[3]Under the monetarist interpretation of the Phillips curve, the government would be able to lower inflation without increasing unemployment. The rate of increase in wage rates could decline as inflation is reduced, thus avoiding the increase in real wages that occurs in the process and produces a temporary increase in unemployment.

In the United States, about 9 million unionized workers have escalator clauses in their wage contracts. Also, Social Security payments to the retired are indexed to the cost of living, and the federal personal income tax has been indexed since 1985. Opposition to total indexation in the United States stems from fears that a fully indexed economy would *lose much of the incentive to combat inflation.*

Postscript

The situation in 1997–99 suggests the possible existence of an "*international* Phillips curve." While the U.S. was at full employment, the rest of the world stagnated. Foreign competition forced U.S. producers to "keep a lid" on prices. If that is the case, U.S. inflation will pick up as foreign business conditions improve substantially.

SUMMARY

Inflation is a monetary phenomenon. And sustained inflation can occur only as a result of a continuous increase in the supply of money. But the statement that monetary expansion is the cause of inflation only highlights the proximate cause of inflation; it ignores the possible reasons for monetary expansion. For the Federal Reserve may increase money supply to accommodate budgetary deficits, in which case expansionary fiscal policy is the root cause of inflation. Or the Fed may increase the money stock to accommodate a great variety of supply or cost-push influences. These may include sharp increases in energy and food prices, or a rise in labor costs owing partly to lagging productivity growth. If left unaccommodated, these factors would produce unacceptably high unemployment.

Demand inflation occurs when aggregate demand is increased along the upward portion of the aggregate-supply curve. Supply or cost-push inflation occurs when, for a variety of reasons, aggregate supply moves leftward, producing stagflation. When "accommodated" by expansionary monetary policy, the inflation is exacerbated. Inflationary expectations always compound the inflation.

Both types of inflation can coexist with unemployment. Experience in the 1950s and 1960s indicated the existence of a tradeoff between inflation and unemployment, codified under the name *Phillips curve*. In the 1970s and early 1980s, economic conditions were dominated by leftward shifts in aggregate supply, and rightward shifts of the Phillips curve, where inflation and unemployment moved in the same direction. But demand-management policies designed to counter that inflation are still subject to the tradeoff. In the late 1990s the Phillips curve moved sharply to the left. An alternative (monetarist) interpretation of the Phillips curve suggests that it reflects a short-run tradeoff between unemployment and *unexpected* inflation. In the long run, the Phillips curve is vertical, pegged at the natural rate of unemployment. By implication, long-run aggregate supply is also vertical. Adherents to the rational expectations school believe that even in the short run the Phillips curve is vertical. However, the consensus among economists is that there is a short-run Phillips curve lasting for a period of up to four years. Since the length of the period coincides with the political horizon of most officeholders, activist policy is warranted.

Possible measures designed to move the Phillips curve to the left and improve the tradeoff include greater competition in both the product and labor markets; income policies, including TIP, and supply-management policies. Indexation, or the tying of all contracts to the cost of living, is a means for making inflation more tolerable, by minimizing its income-redistributive effect. But it also lowers the incentive to combat inflation.

QUESTIONS AND PROBLEMS

1. What is the proximate cause of inflation? Why is this cause inadequate in explaining the inflationary process?
2. Distinguish between demand-caused and supply-caused inflation. Analyze the two cases, and show the possible coexistence of inflation and unemployment.
3. Explain the reasons for and the nature of the tradeoff between inflation and unemployment. What happened to the Phillips curve in the 1970s? What is the monetarist interpretation of the Phillips curve? What is rational expectations?
4. Outline possible policies designed to improve the tradeoff.
5. What is indexation? What purpose does it serve?
6. What is supply-side economics? What potential policies does it include?

Recent Economic Policy in the United States

U.S. economic policies over the past forty years often reflected the trade-off between inflation and unemployment. They have shifted back and forth from the objective of dampening inflation to that of lowering unemployment.

THE 1960s

In the late 1950s and early 1960s, unemployment was fairly high by historical standards, and inflation low. During the entire 1952–62 decade, the CPI rose by less than 13 percent. President Kennedy was elected partly on the promise to "get the country moving again." And in 1964, a major tax reduction was legislated. It greatly stimulated aggregate demand, accelerated the growth rate, and pushed the economy toward full employment.

In 1966, President Johnson made a major policy decision to increase U.S. involvement in the Vietnam conflict. This translated into annual outlays approaching $30 billion, and was superimposed upon an economy approaching full employment. But for political reasons, the president decided against seeking an increase in taxes to match the rise in military expenditures. Under the circumstances, the Vietnam buildup could not help but trigger an inflationary spiral. By 1969, unemployment fell to a low of 3.5 percent of the labor force while the annual rate of inflation rose above 6 percent—very high by the then-existing historical standard.

By that time, public sentiment against the inflation became widespread, and subsequently monetary policy assumed a highly contractionary posture. For several months in 1969, the money stock was not permitted to grow at all. The purpose of this monetary contraction was to reduce the rate of inflation by generating a deliberate reduction in the rate of growth in real output and employment. As a result, a recession occurred in 1969–70—the first one in ten years.

But the rate of inflation failed to respond to the economic slowdown at the desired speed. One important reason for this lag was the cyclical behavior of labor productivity (that is, output per worker). As explained in Chapter 13, output per worker declines early in the downswing phase of the cycle. Coupled with the fact that overhead costs are spread over smaller output, the result is an increase in per-unit production costs, which is reflected in price increases. Another reason for the continued inflation was the ability of large corporations and unions to push up prices even when operating at well below capacity.

1970–1973

The inflation continued in 1970, concurrently with the spreading recession. In the winter of 1970, the Federal Reserve, recognizing the severity of the recession, began to expand money supply at about 4 percent annual rate. And following the normal six to nine months lag, unemployment leveled off at somewhat below the 6 percent mark; it remained at that level in 1971. Inflation in 1971 was around 4.3 percent. The persistent unemployment subsequently led the Federal Reserve to adopt a vigorously expansionary monetary policy. The money stock was permitted to grow at an annual rate of 7–10 percent. Coupled with an expansionary fiscal posture, these measures stimulated economic activity, and in 1971–72, the economy underwent a transformation from recession to recovery. The economy gained momentum in 1972–73, and by the fall of 1973 unemployment declined to under 5 percent.

What about the inflation? Although the induced recession of 1970 slowed down the inflation, the rate of price increase in 1970–71 was still considered unacceptably high. Consequently, as a part of the "New Economic Policy" introduced in August 1971 to deal with a wide range of domestic and international policy issues, President Nixon imposed a three-month freeze on prices and wage rates. Labeled Phase 1, it was designed to speed up price stabilization and wring out of the economy expectations of further price increases. It was followed by selective price and wage controls known as Phase II, lasting for more than a year. Early in 1973, these were replaced by the more lax surveillance procedures of Phase III. Under Phase III, decisions to change prices and wages by major corporations and unions had to be communicated to the government's Cost of Living Council, and the same applied to information about corporate profit. The administration retained the power to force a rollback of "unacceptable" price and wage increases. The rate of inflation in the United States dropped in 1972 to around 3½ percent, about one half its European counterpart. But only some of this decline could be attributed to the direct controls. In large measure, it was probably due to the increase in labor productivity during the upswing phase of the cycle; another cause was a delayed reaction on the price front to the previous recession.

However, inflationary pressure reappeared early in 1973, spearheaded by substantial increases in food prices, since rising domestic and foreign demand for food products was hitting a substantially fixed short-run supply. By mid-1973, these pressures grew so intense that the administration was forced to reverse its policy of relaxing the direct controls and impose a 60-day price freeze, to be followed again by selective controls (Phase IV). Although these controls were tighter than their Phase III counterpart, the inflation—which now appeared to be a worldwide phenomenon—continued unabated through the end of 1973, aided by dislocations produced by the energy shortage. The inflation accelerated to a double-digit rate in 1974, the highest rate since the Korean war. Yet the government decided to terminate the wage-price control program at the end of April 1974, viewing it as ineffective at controlling inflation. But this discussion is running somewhat ahead of the story.

THE 1974 STAGFLATION

By mid-1973, the economy was moving ahead at a rapid pace, and any lingering concern about a recession had completely given way to acute worry about price increases. In 1974, inflation reached double-digit proportions and became "public enemy number one." The price-wage controls were generally viewed as a failure, and major reliance in curbing the inflation was placed on monetary policy. Money supply was permitted to grow at a rate of only one-half the rate of inflation ("real" money supply declined considerably); and that, coupled with a contractionary fiscal posture, could not fail to slow down the economy.

What were the causes of the double-digit inflation in 1974? In large measure, that inflation was due to the expansionary monetary and fiscal policies undertaken in 1972 to stimulate the economy. (Incidentally, the steep rise in demand occurred simultaneously in all industrial countries.) But the normal demand-pull and cost-push influences cannot explain the great severity of the 1974 inflation. Superimposed upon them were several special factors fueling and accelerating the inflation.

First, the dollar devaluations of 1971 and 1973 increased the prices of imported commodities,[1] including those of raw materials that enter the production process. Both directly and indirectly, they contributed to inflation. Second, many investments in the United States in these years were destined for environmental cleanup—to meet the pollution standards set by the federal government. Such spendings do not contribute directly to increased supply of goods and services and are therefore inflationary.

Third, in 1973, there was a substantial escalation in the prices of many primary commodities and raw materials. In part this reflected the great surge in demand from the booming industrial countries. Most emphatically, the quadrupling of crude-oil prices by the Organization of Petroleum Exporting Countries (OPEC) cartel shifted the U.S. aggregate

[1]If the dollar declines in value from 4 deutsche marks to 3, then a 12,000 D.M. automobile rises in price from $3,000 (12,000/4) to $4,000 (12,000/3).

supply curve to the left causing stagflation. The inflationary forces caused by this factor represent a transfer of real income from the industrial to the primary-materials- and oil-producing countries.

History: The oil crisis and other factors caused stagflation in the mid-1970s. Tight money and expansionary fiscal policy raised interest rates and produced the deep 1981/82 recession which wrung inflation out of the economy. The subsequent monetary expansion produced a strong non inflationary recovery in 1983–1990. Following a short recession in 1990–91 growth resumed, and robust growth occurred during 1995–2000, to be followed by a slowdown in 2001. A recovery ensued in 2002–05.

Interestingly enough, the quadrupling of oil prices, costing American consumers some $30 billion in 1974, also constituted a "drag," on the economy by siphoning billions of dollars of consumer purchasing power into the hands of oil producers. It was akin to a tax imposed by OPEC on American consumers.

Next came the worldwide food situation, an added supply shock. The supply of food, feed, and certain other agricultural materials was seriously affected by adverse weather conditions over wide areas in 1972, particularly by the severe downturn in Soviet grain production, absence of the monsoon in Asia, the virtual disappearance of anchoveta from the coast of Peru, and the drought in Africa. Coincidentally, the output of livestock—particularly pork, poultry, and eggs—fell because profitability was adversely affected by sharp increases in the cost of feed.

Finally, a long list of U.S. government regulations served to restrict competition and therefore prevent price reductions that would benefit the consumer. The regulation of air fares is a case in point. Also, the removal of previous price-wage controls resulted immediately in widespread price increases.

Although not exhaustive, this list shows that powerful factors combined to speed up the rate of inflation and shift the *AS* curve to the left and the Phillips curve to the right, producing a less favorable tradeoff between inflation and unemployment. Nor were these forces confined to the United States. The 1974 inflation was a worldwide phenomenon; in all industrial countries except Germany, it was more serious than in the United States.

To cope with this inflation, major reliance was again placed on monetary policy. Tight growth in the money supply, coupled with energy shortages, began to slow down the economy in the first quarter of 1974, with real GDP dropping by 5.8 percent. The decline continued in the next three quarters, indicating a gradually deepening recession. As usual, the recession was not evenly spread throughout the economy. Hardest hit were the housing, automobile, and consumer-goods industries. Unemployment rose through 1974, reaching a peak in early 1975.

In the fall of 1974, the economy found itself in a state of stagflation caused by the supply shocks: a persistent double-digit inflation and a serious and deepening recession. In terms of the inflation-unemployment mix, it was the worst period in post-war history. The recession lasted five successive quarters, from the fourth quarter of 1973 through the first quarter of 1975, with the economy bottoming out in April 1975. From peak to trough, real GDP declined by 6.6 percent—double the worst previous declines of 3.3 percent that occurred in 1953–54 and 1957–58. Another indication of the severity of that recession was a postwar peak in unemployment of 9 percent of the labor force. Industrial production declined 12.5 percent from September 1974 to April 1975. The rate of inflation stood at double digits (12 percent) in 1974; it declined to under 5 percent in 1976, after the recovery got under way.

THE RECOVERY: 1975–1979

In 1975, the government moved to stimulate the economy by fiscal and monetary policies. The Tax Reduction Act of 1975 provided a $12 billion cut in personal tax withholding rates and corporate taxes for the remainder of 1975; a one-time cash payment (made in May and June), in the form of a rebate on 1974 individual income taxes, of up to $200, totaling $10 billion; and a special $50 payment to federal Social Security beneficiaries. Coupled with the increase in transfer payments (for example, unemployment insurance was lengthened to 65 weeks and its coverage was widened), it produced a budgetary deficit of $45 billion. On a "full-employment" basis, the federal budget shifted from an $18 billion surplus in 1974 to a $9 billion deficit in 1975—a highly stimulative change. With the tax cut extended to 1976, the budgetary deficit increased to $66 billion. It remained in the $45 billion range annually in 1977 and 1978. The full-employment budget was in deficit to the tune of $30 billion in 1978, extremely stimulative.

Monetary policy also assumed an expansionary posture in 1975[2] and that was accompanied by a substantial advance in the velocity of circulation, in part reflecting a permanent change in the public's payment habits.

A prolonged expansionary phase followed, fueled for the most part by an upsurge in consumer spending. By 1978–79, unemployment declined to the 5.8 percent range, but inflation also rose, from under 5 percent at the end of 1976 to 9 percent at the end of 1978. The massive budgetary deficits, occurring as they did in a period of rapid expansion, were financed largely through the creation of new money. And that combination could not help but fuel the inflation. By late 1978, concern over inflation (accompanied by concern over the depreciating dollar on the foreign-exchange markets) became paramount. And in November of that year, President Carter announced a new set of economic measures.

ANTIINFLATIONARY MEASURES, 1978–1981

Aimed at reducing the rate of inflation, the program contained four main components. The first was monetary restraint. The growth rate in the money stock was to be reduced considerably by the Federal Reserve, both through raising reserve requirements of commercial banks on large certificates of deposit and through open-market sales of government securities. The second was fiscal restraint. The deficit in the federal budget was reduced to under $27 billion in fiscal 1979.

The third component was voluntary wage-price guidelines. Under the promulgated rules, maximum wage increases would be less than 7 percent (in 1980, this was increased to a 7.5 to 9.5 percent range), and maximum price increases would be held to .05 percent less than the average increases in 1977–78.[3] Both rules applied to company averages, and various mod-

[2]In November and December 1975, the Federal Reserve enacted two successive reductions in reserve requirements, reducing required reserves by a total of $680 million, and in January 1976, the discount rate was lowered from 6 to 5 1/2 percent.

ifications were introduced as time progressed. In general, enforcement of the guidelines met with less than full success.

But the budget deficit was still too high, and the program of monetary restraint was not implemented, as attested to by the continued high rate of growth in the money stock during the subsequent months. This served to undermine the credibility of the government policy-making apparatus and to enhance inflationary expectations. By that time, inflationary expectations became deeply embedded in the economy. The annual rate of inflation continued to accelerate, surpassing 13 percent in the fall of 1979. The situation was aggravated by another supply shock, as oil prices were doubled again by the OPEC cartel. To cope with these developments, the Federal Reserve (now under the leadership of Paul Volcker) announced new steps in October 1979. These included a 1 percent increase in the discount rate, imposition of reserve requirements on certain bank deposits, and *a shift in the target of Federal Reserve policy from controlling market interest rates to controlling the money supply.* Although the growth rate in the money supply dropped as a result, no immediate effect on inflation was observed. That led to far more drastic contractionary measures, introduced by the Fed in 1980. In addition, some reductions in government expenditures were contemplated.

However, in view of the sluggish economy and the attendant decline in government revenues and increase in transfer payments, the 1980 budget was in a $60 billion deficit. This time around, the deficit—accompanied by tight money—had to be financed by government borrowing on the financial markets. Interest rates soared, and the prime rate reached 20 percent, dampening economic activity in general and the housing market in particular.

As a result of the 1980 monetary measures, real GDP declined sharply in the second quarter of that year, to be followed by sluggish growth. Because of high interest rates, that decline was spearheaded by a sharp drop in demand for housing and autos. The decline in auto sales was greatly exacerbated by the imbalance in the product mix of the domestic car industry: Producers tooled to manufacture large cars and consumer demand, responding to the rise in energy costs, shifted to small cars. From these two industries, it spread throughout the economy, resulting in the 1980 recession. It was followed by a very short recovery in the first nine months of 1981.[4] But another deep recession ensued in 1981–82 (Table 12–4). In other words, the economy plunged into the new recession before having recovered from the 1980 recession.

THE REAGAN YEARS, AND BEYOND

Mr. Reagan entered the presidential campaign of 1980 with deeply held conservative philosophical predilections. His economic program, articulated during the campaign, contained the following elements: (1) tight

[3]Congress was asked but failed to enact a wage insurance plan (a form of TIP), compensating workers through a tax rebate for a rise in the cost of living exceeding 7 percent.

[4]The shortest expansion in the postwar era.

monetary policy to control the double-digit inflation of 1979–80; (2) an across-the-board cut of about 25 percent in the marginal tax rates on personal income, and a reduction in corporate tax rates, designed to reduce the government's role in the economy; (3) a reordering of national priorities, placing greater emphasis on defense and less on social programs; (4) balance the federal budget, or at least reduce the $50 billion deficit he inherited from the Carter administration; (5) deregulate certain major industries to infuse greater competition into the economy.

While monetary policy succeeded in lowering the rate of inflation by 1982-83, the fiscal components of his program were not internally consistent. It is impossible to cut tax rates, increase defense spending and reduce the federal deficit at the same time. A way out of this dilemma was offered by what might be called a *naive* form of supply-side economics embodied in the Laffer curve. It maintained that a given percentage reduction in marginal tax rates would so stimulate work effort as to yield a proportionately greater increase in taxable income. Since government tax revenue is the product of tax rates and the income on which taxes are levied, revenue would rise, not decline, as a result. But that expectation failed to materialize as attested to by the huge federal deficits during 1982–88.

Upon his election President Reagan proceeded to implement his program. Money supply grew sluggishly (at about 5 percent annual rate) during 1981 and the first nine months of 1982 (Figure 23–1). During that period, the Fed continued to operate under the money supply rule which was adopted in October 1979 and abandoned in October 1982.[5] A 25 percent tax cut was enacted and introduced over the three year period of 1981–84. And a sizable defense build-up began. Congress refused to go along with deep cuts in social spending that would offset the rise in defense expenditures. As a result, the budgetary deficits mushroomed from $73 billion in 1980 to $128 billion in 1982 and to well over $200 billion in 1985–86, before receding to the $150 billion range in 1987–88. In 1985–86, the deficit amounted to 5.5 percent of GDP.

The combination of tight monetary policy and expansionary fiscal policy sent interest rates (both nominal and real) soaring in 1981. If the federal government appears as a huge borrower on the money markets (superimposed upon borrowing by the private sector), to finance budgetary deficits that are not financed by money creation, the demand for loanable funds rises, and their price—the rate of interest—increases. Indeed, high interest rates were the most widely discussed economic topic in 1981–82. And they threw the economy into a deep recession that lasted 16 months (July 1981–November 1982) tied with 1973–75 for the longest recession since the war. Real GDP declined by 3 percent, industrial output declined 12.3 percent, unemployment rose to 9.5 percent in 1982 (it peaked at 10.7 percent) and remained at that level in 1983, and industrial capacity utilization dropped below 70 percent. Given the high rate of inflationary expectations prevailing in the early 1980s, it required a long and deep recession to squeeze inflation out of the economy.

---

[5]During these three years M-1 grew at an annual rate of 6.1 percent, while in the following year that growth rate rose to 12.8 percent.

Recognizing the severity of the recession, the Fed abandoned its money supply rule in October 1982, and permitted the money supply to grow at a 12.8 percent rate in the subsequent year in an attempt to bring down interest rates (Figure 23–1). Indeed, rates came down substantially in 1982–83.

In the years following October 1982, the Fed adopted an *eclectic approach to monetary management, sometimes focusing on the money stock, and other times eyeing interest rates* as its main target, depending on circumstances. Money supply (M-1) grew at only 5.5 percent in 1984, but resumed a 13.8 percent annual growth rate in 1985 and 1986, only to see the growth rate decelerate to 4.0 percent in 1987–88. Monetarists criticized this behavior of the Fed as highly erratic. Interest rates (one of the Fed's targets) declined on a broad front, with the prime rate dropping from 18.9 percent in 1981 to 10.8 percent in 1983 and to 8.3 percent in 1986–87.

Responding to what has become an expansionary monetary *and* fiscal policy, the economy bottomed out in November 1982; real GDP began to grow. The economic recovery ushered in following the 1981–82 recession continued through 1989 and was one of the longest expansions since the war. Between 1983 and 1987, the average annual growth rate in real GDP was near 4 percent, far exceeding that of the European countries, and equaling that of Japan. Industrial capacity utilization rose to 84.5 percent. The unemployment rate declined from 9.5 percent in 1982–83 to under 5.4

Figure 23–1 Money Supply (M-1) in United States *Source:* Federal Reserve Bank of St. Louis, *Monetary Trends* August 1988, and January 1989.

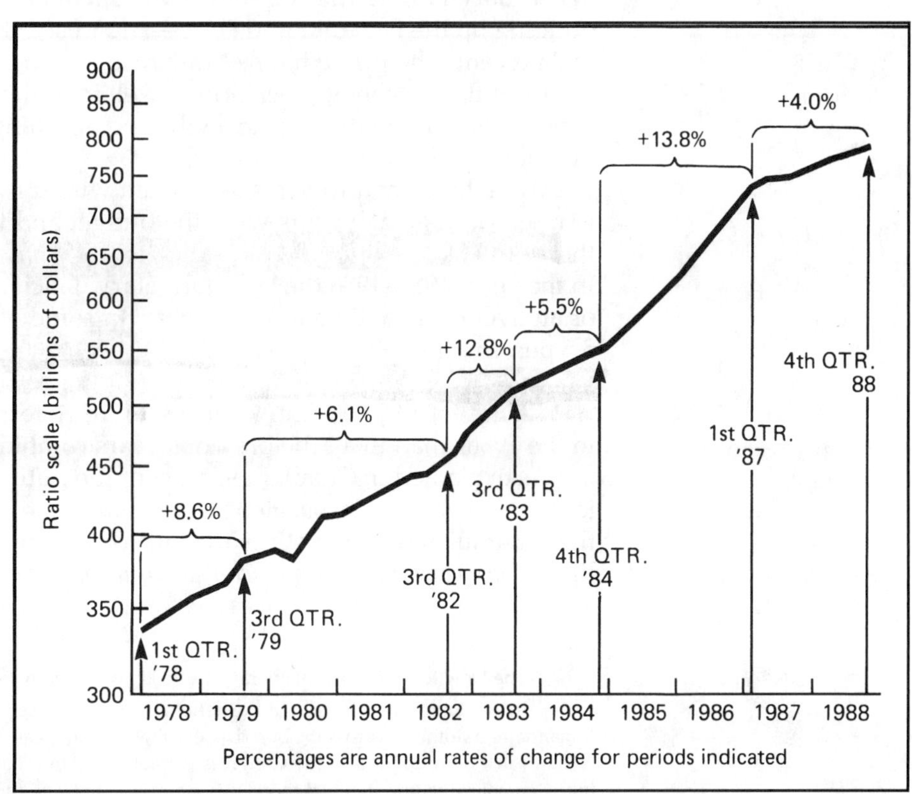

percent in early 1989, (about half that of Europe), the lowest level in 15 years. Employment in the United States rose 15 percent during this prolonged expansion, while in Europe it declined by 1 percent. Even the huge drop in stock prices on October 19, 1987 both here and abroad (often referred as the "crash"[6]) was weathered well by the economy, as it continued to grow at a respectable rate in 1988. But the policies that motivated that growth were largely demand-management rather than supply-side measures.

What about inflation? The tight monetary conditions of 1981–82 and the deep recession of these years succeeded in squeezing inflation out of the economy. The credibility of the Fed in pursuing slow monetary growth was restored, so inflationary expectations abated. This was helped along by plummeting oil prices (a reverse supply shock) as the domestic oil sector was deregulated and an oil glut developed around the world. Oil prices declined from $35 a barrel to $15. Also, the sharp rise in the exchange value of the dollar from 1981 to 1985 reduced the prices of imported goods and forced domestic producers to keep the lid on prices. As measured by the Consumer Price Index (CPI), the annual inflation rate declined from 13.5 percent in 1980 to 6.1 percent in 1982, 4.3 percent in 1984, and 1.9 percent in 1986. But fears of incipient inflation reappeared in 1987 and 1988 as the economy approached full employment, and as the exchange value of the dollar ended a three and one-half year decline from its February 1985 peak. In 1988 inflation was running at 4.5 percent, and early in 1989 there appeared signs of further acceleration, perhaps to the 5 to 6 percent range. In response, the Fed slowed the growth in the money stock to a 4.0 percent annual rate in 1987–88. Further tightening followed in February 1989, as the Fed sold government bonds on the open market—nudging up the Federal Funds rate—and raised the discount rate from 6.5 to 7 percent. The prime interest rate rose to 11.5 percent.

In sum, the economy performed well in the six year period of 1983–88, generating noninflationary growth, and reaching full employment. But inflationary signs appeared in early 1989.

Were there any problems associated with this performance? The main issues of the Reagan years were the budget and trade deficits, leading to the "Twin Towers of Debt." The first "tower" refers to the U.S. public debt. In the years 1982–1988 the U.S. budgetary deficit added up to $1.3 trillion, or an average of $180 billion per year. In some of these years it averaged 5.5 percent of GDP. As a result, the public debt—which is the cumulative total government debt incurred to finance the deficits—grew from $1.2 trillion in 1982 to $2.6 trillion in 1988. More government debt was piled up in the 1980s than in all the previous years combined.

As explained in Chapter 19, most of the public debt is owed by Americans to other Americans. Hence, the main issue is not so much the size of the accumulated debt, as it is the size of the annual deficits, which most likely *"crowded out" a significant amount of private investment.*[7] At a time

---

[6]The Dow Jones industrial average lost 500 points on that day.

[7]In an attempt to bring down the deficit, Congress passed the *Gramm-Rudman Act of 1985*. It mandates automatic, across the board, spending cuts (in areas outside Social Security and basic welfare) if the President and the Congress cannot agree upon sufficient spending cuts and tax hikes to achieve required deficit targets. The aim was to bring the budget into balance by 1991.

of full employment one would expect the budget to be in balance and even show a surplus. Although in 1987–88 the annual deficit shrunk to the $150 billion range, it was still far too high for a buoyant high-employment economy. Moreover, the 1989 plan to bail out the nation's savings and loan associations called for a further increase in federal borrowings. (Only in 1997–98 was the budget deficit eliminated.)

Not only were the deficits a problem in themselves, but their persistence reveals another dilemma in economic management during the 1980s. Congress and the President could not agree on measures to reduce the deficit: the $1/2 trillion in Social Security spending became politically sacrosanct, and the $140 billion interest on the federal debt is also a nondiscretionary expenditure. Beyond that the President rejected a tax increase or a reduction in defense spending, and the Congress refused to go along with deep cuts in social spending. This political impasse essentially immobilized fiscal policy. The only policy instrument available to stabilize the domestic economy and to influence the exchange rate of the dollar was monetary policy. Should the Fed tighten money supply and raise interest rates in 1989[8] (or beyond) to deal with an incipient inflation, it may throw the economy into a recession, and the size of the deficit would actually rise. Timing of economic measures is critical. And the most appropriate time to address the deficit was in 1987–88, when the economy was expanding, and not at some future date when growth may be slow or nonexistent. This would have restored fiscal policy as an effective instrument. To accompany deficit reduction measures (contractionary fiscal policy), the Fed could have pursued expansionary monetary policy to avoid a recession, and place the economy on an even keel.

No policy measures were taken in the late Reagan years to deal with the deficit. And the issue was largely avoided in the 1988 presidential election campaign, because raising taxes and/or lowering expenditures is a politically sensitive issue.[9] The first Bush budget (for fiscal year 1990) proposed no new taxes and left in place a sizable deficit.

Associated with the first tower is the second tower of debt. It refers to the *foreign* debt of the United States, or to what Americans owe to residents of other countries. The combination of tight monetary and expansionary fiscal policies (namely, the budget deficits) in the early 1980s pushed interest rates to levels that were high not only by U.S. historical standards, but also by prevailing international standards. American interest rates, both nominal and real, were far higher than their European and Japanese counterparts, and that relationship remained through much of the decade. The high rates attracted hundreds of

[8]In February 1989 the Fed tightened up the money supply and the interest rate rose. That action brought the monetary authorities into conflict with the fiscal authorities: A rise in interest rates increases government expenditures needed to service the $2.6 trillion public debt, and the slowdown of economic growth, attendant upon higher interest rates, lowers government revenue. Thus the Fed action in fighting inflation was seen by the administration as undermining the "rosy" assumptions on which the 1990 budget estimates were based, and leading to a higher deficit than postulated in the budget message.

[9]The resounding defeat of Mr. Mondale in the 1984 elections is often attributed to his facing up to the deficit issue and suggesting the need to raise taxes.

billions in foreign funds to our shores, seeking higher return than they could get in the other countries.[10] Many of these billions were placed in U.S. government securities, thus helping to finance the U.S. budgetary deficit. Foreigners were accumulating massive amounts of dollar assets, which were the liabilities of the United States.

In order to be placed in U.S. financial instruments, these funds had to be converted from yen, marks, or pounds into dollars. And the rise in demand for dollars, doubled the exchange value of the U.S. currency relative to other currencies between 1981 and 1985. With such a high exchange rate, American exports could not compete abroad, and American import-competing goods (such as automobiles) could not compete with foreign imports to the United States. The result was an annual trade deficit (excess of imports over exports) in the unprecedented $160 billion range, approaching, in some years, 4 percent of GDP. Although the dollar exchange rate declined between 1985 and 1998 to its 1980–81 level, the annual trade deficits remained well above the $100 billion mark. The external deficits continued throughout the 1990s. They grew sharply in 1997–98, when the U.S. prospered and the rest of the world stagnated or declined.

During the Reagan years, the United States was running massive trade deficits, and paying for them by piling up huge liabilities to foreign countries. As a result of the cumulative deficits and the associated debt, the United States became a net debtor nation for the first time since World War I. The accumulated net foreign debt exceeded ½ trillion dollars in 1988.[11] It continues to grow as long as the trade deficit persists, surpassing $3 trillion by 2006.

The 1990–91 Recession and Subsequent Recovery

By 1989/90 the expansion ran out of steam, largely because of the excessive debt accumulated in the economy. Consumers and businesses had to adjust their balance sheets, and, consequently reduced spending. That ushered in a mild and short recession, lasting from July 1990 to March 1991. The Gulf War, so brilliantly engineered by President Bush, actually exacerbated the recession by adding to the uncertainty under which consumers and companies had to function. Why, it might be asked, was the war not an economic stimulant? Several reasons suggest themselves: (a) Its costs amounted to only 1 percent of U.S. GDP. (b) Much of the war expenses were defrayed by the allied countries. And (c) the military supplies used in the war came from existing stocks, and—given the end of the Cold War—did not need to be fully replenished.

As the debt/income ratio was adjusted downward to a historical level, the recession ran its course. Spending began to increase in 1991 and the economy emerged from the recession. By and large this was an

[10]U.S. interest rates would have been even higher if it were not for the influx of foreign funds.

[11]This figure may be exaggerated, because U.S. assets abroad are evaluated at the original book value, which is well below their current market value. The United Kingdom is the largest investor in the United States, followed by Japan.

interest-rate driven recovery, as consumers and businesses responded to ever lower interest rates. For example, mortgage rates during the recession and its aftermath declined from 11 to 7 percent. Not only did that stimulate the construction sector, but homeowners were able to refinance their mortgages, sometimes twice. The resulting decline in monthly payments left them with newly-found purchasing power. Of course, interest rates on cars and durable goods declined as well, stimulating purchases that depend on borrowed funds.

But the rate of unemployment remained at the 8–9 percent range during 1991–94. And that for several reasons. First, except for the final quarter of 1992, the recovery was weak during its first 1½ years, with growth rate of one third the average of postwar recoveries. Second, unemployment always lags behind cyclical changes in output. Third, post Cold War defense cutbacks, concentrated in Southern California and the east coast, threw many workers out of their jobs. And fourth, "corporate restructuring" often involving the removal of layers of management, continued unabated. The high level of unemployment allegedly contributed to the election loss of President Bush in his bid for a second term, and to the ascent of Clinton to the presidency.

But an annual growth rate of over 3 percent was not as sustainable, and fear of inflation began to govern Federal Reserve policy. Between early 1994 and February 1995, the Fed raised the short term federal funds interest rate seven times—from 3 to 6 percent, with the intent of slowing down GDP growth. Indeed, in 1995, the growth rate slowed to 2.3 percent, and in mid-95 the Fed lowered the federal funds rate to 5.75%. In the Fall of 1998, partly due to concern for the global financial crisis, it again lowered rates three times, by ¼ percent each.

In 1996–2000, the economy gained momentum and grew at over 3.5 percent, while unemployment fell to 4.4 percent. Because of intense foreign competition and increases in productivity, the entire period of the 1990s was almost free of inflation. Yet in 1998–2000 the Federal Reserve, fearing impending inflation, raised the Federal Funds rate to 6.5 percent. Because of the high growth rate the budget deficit turned into surplus in 1998–2001. But the external trade deficit continued unabated.

THE NEW CENTURY

A recession set in in year 2001 interrupting the spectacular growth of the second half of the 1990s. First investors and then consumers retrenched, partly because of excessive accumulation of business and household debt. Unemployment rose to 5.9 percent, and continued at that level in 2002 despite a short-lived recovery in the first quarter (remember that unemployment is a lagging indicator). Corporate profitability was particularly hard hit.

In response to the recession, the Federal Reserve lowered interest rates (see Figure 23-2) until the federal funds rate reached 1 percent by mid-2003 and was kept at that level for over a year. Fiscal policy also turned expansionary with the Bush tax cuts of 2001 and 2003, and the rise in government expenditure caused partly by the Iraq war and hurricane devastation in the Gulf coast. These factors combined to stimulate the economy. The post-recession expansion gained momentum during 2003–2005, and unemployment declined to under 5 percent by early 2006. Corporate profits rose by 11.6% in 2005. Fears of inflation caused the Federal Reserve to raise the federal funds rate in monthly intervals of ¼ percent each from late 2004 to mid-2006. At the time of this writing, the outlook for 2006 is for moderate growth of around 3 percent.

Federal Funds Rate (percent)

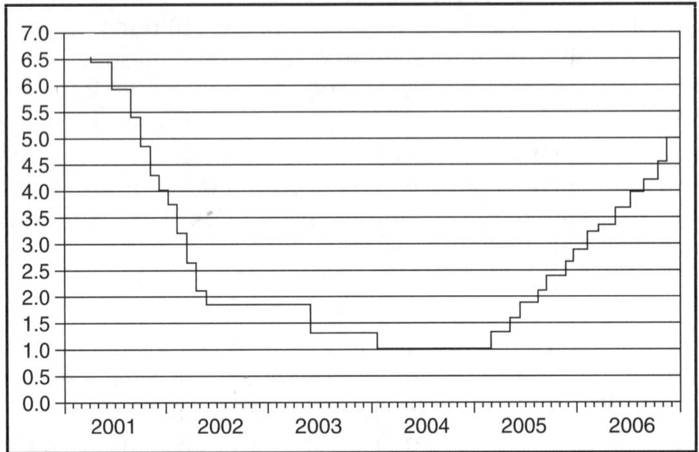

Figure 23-2 Responding to the 2001 recession, the Fed lowered interest rates in successive monthly intervals from 6.5 percent in mid-2000 to 1 percent by mid-2003 and kept it at that level through most of 2004. With the recovery, fear of inflation set in, and the rate was raised in monthly intervals of 0.25 percent through 2006 up to 5 percent in May 2006.

By the time you finish reading this chapter, the analysis contained in it will be overtaken by events. However, the tools of economic analysis acquired in this book should enable you to follow economic developments on your own. As a good budding economist, capitalize on your investment in time, tuition, and books for this course. Keep up with economic and financial news.

QUESTIONS AND PROBLEMS

1. Trace U.S. economic policies in terms of the tradeoff between inflation and unemployment, emphasizing shifts from expansionary to contractionary policies or vice versa. Can 1982 be used as an example of the tradeoff? How about 1989?
2. Explain the Reagan economic program.
3. The Reagan years witnessed noninflationary economic growth and a "twin tower of debt." Explain.
4. The Clinton years witnessed non-inflationary economic growth and "one tower of debt." Explain!

PART FIVE

BEYOND OUR SHORES

OVERVIEW

WHAT IS INTERNATIONAL ECONOMICS?

So far this book has treated the United States as a closed economy; namely, an economy without foreign trade. Although the share of foreign transactions in the U.S. economy is smaller than in that of other countries, the role played by foreign trade is significant, and it is expanding rapidly. Thus, merchandise exports constitute 8 percent of GDP in the United States (up from about 4 percent in the 1960s); 15 percent of GDP in Japan, between a quarter and a third of GDP in the large European countries; and around one half of GDP in the small European countries.

Apart from merchandise, the United States imports and exports a variety of services, such as transportation, insurance, and tourism. And finally, various forms of capital flow in and out of this country. These include: (1) direct foreign investments, such as the establishment of a branch plant abroad (a subsidiary) by an American corporation or of a stateside plant by a foreign corporation; (2) purchases and sales of foreign stocks or bonds by U.S. citizens or of American stocks and bonds by foreign nationals; and (3) transactions by Americans in foreign banks and by foreigners in American banks.

In sum, the field of **international economics is concerned with the flow of merchandise, services, capital, and labor across national boundaries.**

WHAT IS UNIQUE ABOUT INTERNATIONAL ECONOMICS?

International economics: the branch of economics that is concerned with the flow of merchandise, services, capital, and labor across national boundaries. The first subspecialty in economics.

In a very real sense, international transactions constitute an extension of domestic transactions. In both cases, trade offers the benefits of specialization. Exchange of goods and services among persons enables each individual to specialize in what he or she can do best. Domestic exchange enables each region of the country to specialize in the same manner. Thus, the exchange of Idaho potatoes, Florida oranges, Michigan-made cars, and Washington-produced aircraft, enhances the efficiency of production and raises living standards, as each region of the country specializes in what it can do best. Internationally, U.S. import of Japanese cars and Brazilian coffee and the U.S. export of grains, sophisticated computers, and jet aircraft, enable each country to specialize in what it can do best, and thereby produce more than it could without trade. And such specialization increases living standards in all countries.

Clearly the reasons for, and the benefits from, international transactions are no different from the reasons for and the benefits from internal transactions: to reap the fruits of increased output from a given amount of resources, attendant upon greater specialization. Thus, international transactions constitute an extension of domestic transactions beyond the country's national boundaries.

Why then is it necessary to distinguish between domestic and international economic relations? We study international economics as a separate field because the existence of national boundaries has profound implications for the *conduct* of trade. A few of the differences between domestic and foreign trade that emanate from this fact follow.

Exchange rate: The price of one currency in terms of another.

1. **Exchange rates.** Transactions within a country are financed by the country's own currency, usually through the writing of checks. However, a universal currency does not exist. Rather, each country issues its own currency. The price of one currency in terms of another is called an *exchange rate,* and many exchange rates fluctuate or change daily in response to supply and demand conditions in the foreign-exchange markets. International transactions often require payments or receipts in foreign currencies, and these must be converted to a domestic currency through the exchange rates, which themselves are subject to change. This introduces risks and complications that do not exist in domestic trade. Exchange-rate variations in themselves can have profound effects on the domestic economy.

   Also, because there is no international clearing system for checks, foreign payments usually require special methods, other than the writing of checks.

2. *Special Policies.* A national government can introduce a variety of restrictions on international transactions that cannot be imposed on domestic transactions. Examples are:

Tariff: a tax on an imported commodity. **Import quota:** a quantitative limitation on the amount of the commodity that may enter the country.

Voluntary export restraint: The government of an importing country negotiates with the government of an exporting country a quantitative limitation on the export of a certain commodity.

   a. A **tariff,** which is a tax on an imported commodity.

   b. An **import quota,** which places a maximum quantitative limitation on the amount of the commodity that may enter the country (for example, one million tons of steel).

   c. A **"voluntary" export restraint** (VER), where the government of an importing country (say, the United States) negotiates with the government of an exporting country (say, Japan), a quantitative limitation on the export of a certain commodity. Under such an agreement, the Japanese government limited automobile shipments to the United States during the four years of 1981–85. All VER's were abolished in 2005.

   d. Export subsidy, where the government pays exporters a sum of money for each unit they export, to make exports more competitive abroad.

   e. Exchange control, where a country (such as India) restricts the ability of its citizens to convert their money (rupees) to foreign currencies (such as the dollar).

Such measures may have profound effects on the economy. Yet they apply only to international and not to domestic transactions.

3. *Different Domestic Policies.* Each country has its own central bank and finance ministry, and hence its own monetary and fiscal policies. In turn, these determine its rate of inflation, economic growth, and unemployment. Such policies are common to all regions of the country, but they vary from one country to another. Consequently, while the rate of inflation is reasonably the same in various regions of France, it differs between France and Hungary. And that clearly affects the countries' relative competitive position in each other's market and in third markets. Indeed, many changes in international trade and financial transactions can be traced to the differences in the domestic policies pursued by different governments. Such diversity does not exist between regions of the same country.
4. *Statistical Data.* We know more about the composition, size, and direction of international trade than about the same features of domestic transactions. No one is aware of what commodities and in what quantities are traded between New York and California. There are no "border regulators" along state lines to compile such information. But when a shipment of merchandise leaves or enters the country, the exporter or importer must fill out an export or an import declaration. It includes a description of the shipment, its weight, its value, its destination (in case of exports) or source (in case of imports) and other characteristics. From those trade declarations, which are required by all countries, detailed statistics can be compiled on international trade. Such data are not available for domestic trade.
5. *Relative Immobility of Productive Factors.* Factors of production are much more mobile domestically than they are internationally. No one can prevent workers from moving from Virginia to Texas in search of better opportunities or for other reasons. But immigration restrictions, language barriers, and different social customs constitute formidable barriers to people's mobility between countries. While capital can move between countries much more easily than labor, even capital is more mobile domestically than internationally.
6. *Marketing Practices.* Differences in demand patterns, sales techniques, market requirements and the like make international transactions more cumbersome than domestic ones. Thus in April 1985 Prime Minister Nakasone of Japan urged Japanese consumers to buy foreign goods in order to reduce Japan's massive trade surpluses. He cited himself as a model, having purchased a British suit, a French tie, a foreign-made fountain pen, a German electric razor, an American tennis racket, and foreign-made golf clubs. But the initial response of the average Japanese consumer was puzzlement and bewilderment.

   "What foreign goods should we buy?" asked the usually compliant consumers!

   "How about a fondue set, a roast-beef thermometer, or a matched set of sheets and pillowcases for starters," was a reply of an official charged with making up a list of such goods.

   "What is a fondue set?" said one consumer.

"What am I going to do with an oven thermometer?" Many Japanese families don't have an oven, for they tend to steam, boil, or stew their food.

"What use do I have for American sheets?" The traditional Japanese bed—a Futon—is rolled on the floor and takes its own fitted sheets.[1]

Similarly, American exports of electrical appliances to Europe must be adjusted to the use of European electric current. Automobiles exported to the United Kingdom or Japan require the steering wheel on the right-hand side of the vehicle, as the British and Japanese drive on the left side of the road. And foreign automobiles exported to the United States must be fitted with the American-mandated pollution-control equipment.

In sum, exporters need to make special adjustments in their product design in an attempt to penetrate a foreign market.

7. *Summary.* Six areas of significant difference between domestic and foreign transaction were outlined. Although they refer to the conduct of, rather to the reasons for and benefits from trade, they highlight important and unique features. And these features call for a special field of international economics. Indeed, this is the oldest branch of economics, dating back to David Hume (1752), Adam Smith (1778), and David Ricardo (1817). It was Ricardo who first articulated the famous law of comparative advantage.

Two of the chapters in this final part of the book are devoted to international economics as previously defined. Chapter 24 reviews the fundamentals of the benefits from international trade and assesses the effects of various protective measures. Chapter 25 is devoted to exchange rates and international financial relations. In Chapter 26 we consider problems of the developing countries of Africa, Asia, and Latin America.

[1]These illustrations are drawn from *The Wall Street Journal*, April 16, 1985.

24 International Trade and Protectionism

AN EMPIRICAL GLIMPSE

International commodity trade has grown forty-fold over the last 40 years. In 1958 exports of all countries amounted to $108 billion; by 2004 it had reached $8.8 trillion. Table 24–1 presents the matrix of world exports in 2004.

Over half of world trade takes place *among* the industrial countries of North America, Western Europe, and Japan, much of it in finished manufactures. The industrial countries export mainly manufactured products to the developing countries of Latin America, Africa, and Asia and import from them primary products (raw materials and food) as well as manufacturers.

Although the share of the United States in world trade has declined in recent years, it is still the largest trading nation. The U.S. is a net exporter of food, chemicals, specialized machinery, and aircraft, and a net importer of fuels, raw materials, steel, motor vehicles, and household and consumer goods. Our single main trading partner is Canada, followed by Japan.

Next consider Japan. Devoid of natural resources, Japan imports most of the raw materials and other primary products it requires. In 2003 it imported $257 billion of such products and exported only $20 billion. On the other hand, Japan exported $439 billion of manufactured goods and imported only $218 billion. Within the manufacturing sector, Japan had sizable trade surpluses (exports greater than imports) in motor vehicles, certain types of machinery, and household appliances.

Canada, on the other hand, being well endowed with land and natural resources had a sizable surplus in primary products and a deficit in manufactured goods.

To understand the basis for international trade and the benefits that flow from it, we turn to the famous principle of comparative advantage.

Table 24-1 Network of World Trade, 2004 ($ Billion)

Origin	Destination: North America	South and Central America	Europe	Asia	Other	World
North America	742	71	216	249	45	1,324
South and Central America	93	64	59	39	15	276
Europe	367	51	2,973	308	291	4,031
Asia	533	39	417	1,201	145	2,388
Other	116	17	292	267	133	888
World	1,852	242	3,957	2,065	629	8,907

Source: World Trade Organization, *International Trade Statistics 2005*, Table A.2

THE PRINCIPLE OF COMPARATIVE ADVANTAGE

Asked why they engage in foreign trade, most businesspersons can promptly offer a superficial, yet correct answer: They purchase a commodity abroad if and when it is cheaper abroad than at home, and they sell a commodity abroad when it fetches a higher price abroad than it does domestically. In other words, relative prices at home and abroad determine which goods are exported and which are imported by any given country, namely, the commodity composition of trade.

But what makes some goods cheaper in one country and others cheaper in another? To businesspersons this is of no consequence; they simply convert one currency into another at the prevailing exchange rate and compare prices. But to economists this is the crux of the matter, for it is only by answering this question that they can determine whether such profit-maximizing behavior on the part of individual traders is beneficial to the country.

Comparative advantage: Refers to the *degree* of productivity advantage of one country over another. A country may produce two goods cheaper than another country. But if the degree to which good A is cheaper than good B is greater, it is said to have a comparative advantage in A, and a comparative disadvantage in B. It would export A and import B.

To answer this question, we refer to a principle originally enunciated early in the nineteenth century by the English economist David Ricardo: the principle of **comparative advantage.** It is most easily explained by a simplified example similar to the one Ricardo used. Assume that the world consists of two countries, say the United States and the United Kingdom, which produce two commodities, wheat and textiles. Suppose further that the only factor of production employed in producing the two goods is labor in a homogeneous form. This means that the value of each product is determined exclusively by its labor content (yielding the so-called labor theory of value). Goods move freely between the two countries but labor is mobile only domestically, not internationally. Transport

Scheme 1 Production Conditions

In	One Person-Day of Labor Produces
United States	60 bushels of wheat *or* 20 yards of textiles
United Kingdom	20 bushels of wheat *or* 10 yards of textiles

costs are also assumed not to exist. Although this is a highly simplified case, it yields considerable insight of general application.

Suppose that the production conditions prevailing in the two countries are those of Scheme 1. Clearly, labor is more productive *absolutely* in the United States than in the United Kingdom in both the textile and the wheat industries: It produces (per day) more of everything in the United States than it does in the United Kingdom.

However, it should not be inferred that because the United States is more efficient in the production of both commodities, it would produce both of them when trade opens up or that the United Kingdom would produce none. To suggest this is to deny the mutual advantage to be derived from international trade. The condition postulated here, that one country is absolutely more productive than another in most of their mutual pursuits, is common. Yet mutually beneficial trade does take place, even between countries as extremely different in productive efficiency as the United States and India.

What is important in the problem at hand is *comparative,* not absolute, advantage. A vertical comparison of the figures in Scheme 1 shows that the *degree* of American advantage over the United Kingdom is not the same in both industries. The United States has a 3 to 1 advantage in wheat, but only a 2 to 1 advantage in textiles. Comparatively speaking, therefore, the United States has a greater advantage in wheat and a lesser advantage in textiles. The United Kingdom is in the reverse position; it has an absolute disadvantage in both goods, but the extent of disadvantage is greater in wheat and lesser in textiles, because labor can produce only one third as much wheat as in the United States, but it can produce fully one half as much textiles. Since we are merely comparing the *degree* of advantage and disadvantage in producing the two goods, the analysis can be expressed by asserting that the United States has a *comparative advantage* in wheat, while the United Kingdom has a *comparative advantage* in textiles.

This situation is analogous to that of a doctor who is absolutely more efficient than a nurse in the performance of both medical and paramedical duties. But the degree of the doctor's advantage is much larger in the first type of duty than in the second. And just as it pays the doctor to concentrate on the former and hire a nurse to do the latter, so it is to America's advantage to specialize in wheat and purchase British textiles.

But this is running somewhat ahead of our story. The productivity comparison between the two countries is possible only because of the existence of an international common denominator—a given quantity of homogeneous labor. Had this been absent, the vertical comparison in Scheme 1 would have been impossible. Consequently, it is more general and meaningful to focus on an horizontal, *within-country* comparison, although the conclusion is the same in both cases.

What do we see from that vantage point? Domestically, the United States must give up 3 bushels of wheat to obtain 1 yard of textiles. Obviously, wheat is not convertible into textiles in any mechanical sense, but by foregoing 3 bushels of wheat, enough labor (and other resources if present) is released to be put into textile production to produce 1 yard of textiles. This is what the internal cost ratio of 3 to 1 (or 60 bushels of wheat for 20 yards of textiles) means: The resource cost, or the "opportunity cost," of 1 yard of textiles in the United States is 3 bushels of wheat. The United States would be *un*willing to trade 3 bushels of wheat for anything less than 1 yard of textiles, for it can do better at home. But it would be eager to purchase textiles abroad if a yard could be obtained for less than 3 bushels of wheat, because then the resource cost of textiles embodied in the wheat traded is less than that of foregoing wheat production in order to produce the textiles at home.

What is the situation from the British point of view? Domestically, the resource cost of 2 bushels of wheat is 1 yard of textiles, because by giving up 1 yard of textiles enough labor is released to produce 2 bushels of wheat. If the United Kingdom is able to obtain through trade more than 2 bushels of wheat per yard of textiles, it will trade, for the resource cost of obtaining wheat by trading away textiles is less than that of giving up textile production to produce wheat at home. But the United Kingdom would be unwilling to trade 1 yard for less than 2 bushels, for it can do better at home.

Put differently, the relative cost of producing the two commodities in the two countries can be summarized as follows: 1 unit of textiles cost 3 units of wheat in the United States and 2 units of wheat in the United Kingdom. Textiles are cheaper (in terms of wheat) in the United Kingdom. One unit of wheat costs one-third unit of textiles in the United States and one-half unit of textiles in the United Kingdom. Wheat is cheaper (in terms of textiles) in the United States.

Each country specializes in the product that it can produce more cheaply and obtains the other commodity through trade. The United States would produce and export wheat, while the United Kingdom would produce and export textiles.

In sum, the appropriate comparison for each country is between the resource cost of the commodity produced at home and the cost when it is acquired from abroad in exchange for the export good. The figures of Scheme 1 can be transformed into the limits to mutually beneficial trade, as given in Scheme 2.

Scheme 2 Limits to Mutually Beneficial Trade

1 yard of textiles {	= maximum of 3 bushels of wheat for the United States
	= minimum of 2 bushels of wheat for the United Kingdom

The United States is willing to purchase 1 yard of textiles for anything less than 3 bushels of wheat, while the United Kingdom is willing to sell 1 yard of textiles for anything more than 2 bushels of wheat. Trade can take place anywhere between these limits. Stated differently, the domestic cost ratios of the two commodities in the two countries constitute the limits to mutually beneficial trade. Within these limits, it is to the advantage of each country to concentrate on the production of the good in which it has a comparative advantage and to obtain the other product through trade.

To see that trade is indeed beneficial to both nations, select any international price ratio within the specified limits, such as 1 yard of textiles = 2½ bushels of wheat. Trading at this ratio enables each country to consume more than is possible without trade. Let us say that the United States, employing its entire labor force, produces 600 bushels of wheat, of which it consumes 400 and exchanges 200 for textiles. The United Kingdom at full production manufactures 200 yards of textiles, of which it consumes 120 and exchanges 80 for wheat. With international trade, the 200 bushels of wheat are exchanged for 80 yards of textiles (an exchange ratio of 1 yard = 2½ bushels), permitting the United States to consume 400 bushels and 80 yards and the United Kingdom to consume 200 bushels and 120 yards. Without trade, the United States can transform (in terms of resource conversion) the 200 bushels into only 66⅔ yards of textiles, making available a total of 400 bushels and 66⅔ yards. The United Kingdom, without trade, can transform the 80 yards of textiles into only 160 bushels of wheat making available 120 yards and 160 bushels. All this is summarized in Table 24–2, showing clearly that both countries benefit from the exchange.

In sum, it is comparative advantage that makes wheat cheaper in the United States and textiles cheaper in the United Kingdom. In a multicommodity world, it is necessary to *rank* products within each country by degree of comparative advantage, from the highest to the lowest productivity. The country would export goods that rank high on this scale and import goods that rank low. Under the productivity conditions of Scheme 1, the United States would produce and export wheat while the United Kingdom would produce and export textiles, to the mutual benefit of both countries.

Although comparative rather than absolute advantage governs the direction of trade, absolute advantage is also important. Because in the long run productivity determines the standard of living, the absolute U.S. pro-

Table 24–2 Production and Consumption With and Without Trade, Where the International Exchange Ratio is 1 Yard = 2½ Bushels

	United States	United Kingdom
Production at full capacity	600 bushels of wheat	200 yards of textiles
Consumption with trade (200 bushels for 80 yards)	400 bushels of wheat 80 yards of textiles	200 bushels of wheat 120 yards of textiles
Consumption without trade	400 bushels of wheat 66 ²/₃ yards of textiles	160 bushels of wheat 120 yards of textiles

ductivity advantage shown in Scheme 1 suggests that the U.S. living standard would be higher than that of the United Kingdom.

DEMAND CONSIDERATIONS

Referring back to Scheme 2, it will be observed that the internal productivity ratios provide only the limits to mutually beneficial trade. Within these limits, the actual exchange ratio is determined by the relative strength, or intensity, of each country's demand for the other country's product.

Since the demand for the imported good is expressed in terms of units of the country's own export product—the entire exchange being in barter terms—it is known as "reciprocal demand." In other words, productivity determines the limits, while reciprocal demand determines what the actual exchange ratio will be within these limits. The further apart the two domestic productivity ratios are, the more room there is for mutually advantageous trade, and the larger the benefits are that can be derived from trade by both countries, in the sense that the net increase in available goods over the no-trade position is larger. At the other extreme, when the two domestic ratios are identical, there are no advantages to trade. Each country is as well off *in isolation* (without trade) as with trade, so there is no inducement to engage in trade. In the real world before trade can commence, the difference between the two productivity ratios must be large enough to compensate for transport costs and artificial barriers to trade.

Differentiated products: Each product has various qualities, sizes, colors, etc.

In reality, demand factors often occupy a more important role than the one ascribed to them here. In the example of Scheme 1, both goods are homogeneous commodities, there is only one universal type of wheat and only one kind of textile. But much of the trade that takes place in the world is in **"differentiated products."** Each commodity has various gradations of quality, size, flavor, and so on; differences even in packaging and brand names are important. In such circumstances it is no longer true that identical productivity ratios would result in no trade. For example, it is reasonable to assume that automobile production has approximately the same rank of comparative advantage in Italy, France, West Germany, and the United Kingdom. Consequently, it would be difficult to explain the intercountry exchange of Fiats, Renaults, Volkswagens, and Austins on the grounds of productivity differentials. A large part of the explanation lies in consumer preferences for the foreign brand, even when the price equals that of its domestic counterpart. Since these cars are of roughly similar quality and size, the benefit from such trade cannot be quantified as shown in the last section. It is a gain in the mind of the consumer, derived from having an option to purchase the foreign brand.

Many industrial products are traded among nations even when productivity ratios are identical in the countries involved, because consumers may prefer the foreign brands for reasons that have nothing to do with productivity.

Since much of world trade is in differentiated products, demand considerations play an important role in determining its composition.

What Underlies Comparative Advantage?

What factors confer upon a country an advantage in certain products?

Resource-Based Advantage Nations that possess certain raw materials would acquire a comparative advantage in goods that are manufactured out of such materials. Likewise, countries that have a specific climate would acquire a comparative advantage in plants that thrive in such a climate. Thus, Saudi Arabia and Brazil have a comparative advantage in the production of petroleum and coffee, respectively, and Canada would have a comparative advantage in wheat.

Relative factor abundance: A country has a comparative advantage in a good that uses intensively its abundant factor of production.

Relative Factor Abundance Countries such as India possessing an abundance of labor relative to other productive resources would acquire a comparative advantage in products that require much labor for their manufacture (known as labor-intensive products), while countries possessing a relative abundance of capital would acquire a comparative advantage in products that require much capital for their manufacture (capital-intensive products). Thus, underdeveloped countries are highly competitive in labor-intensive products such as textiles, footwear, and lumber goods, while Japan is highly competitive in capital-intensive goods such as automobiles.

As an extension of this **relative factor abundance** principle, countries possessing an abundance of certain labor skills would acquire a comparative advantage in products that require such skills in their manufacture.

Knowledge and Technology Countries that possess an abundance of scientists and engineers and that expend much funds on research and development would acquire a comparative advantage in high-technology and knowledge-intensive products. Thus, the United States has been a world leader in computers, jet aircraft, and other high-technology items. But that leadership is being eroded as Japan and Europe advance in their level of technological sophistication.

POLICY IMPLICATIONS

To recapitulate, international trade raises the real income of the community by improving the efficiency of resource utilization. The ranking of industries in the order of their comparative advantage determines which commodities are to be exported and which are to be imported. The country's resources are most efficiently utilized if they are distributed and employed along this order. Consequently, policies that distort this ranking, such as tariffs and quotas imposed on specific commodities, result in inefficient resource allocation and loss of income to the community.

Demands of import-competing industries for protection, under one guise or another, are often unwarranted. What they are asking for is selective protection or, essentially, tariff or quota protection for themselves. That would distort the industrial ranking and lead to inefficient resource utilization. The claim that they cannot compete, either because their wage rates are "too high" or for other reasons, is essentially correct from their own self-centered point of view. But satisfaction of their demand for protection would be injurious to the economy as a whole. The reason they are not competitive is that they rank low in the order of comparative advantage. Allocative efficiency requires that they contract in size and their resources be transferred to the growing industries. Government help in this transfer process in the form of direct loans, retraining programs, and the like would contribute to efficiency all around and help alleviate human suffering.

Far from contributing to inflation, as is sometimes alleged by the popular media, international trade is anti-inflationary. Suppose that bad weather conditions cause a poor harvest in the Soviet Union, making it necessary for that country to purchase huge quantities of grain from the United States. The price of grain (as well as of meat and other products derived from grain) will rise in the United States. This always happens to the price of an exported commodity. However, this does not mean that the conduct of trade is inflationary because it overlooks what happens to the price of imports. At the most simplified level, assume that the United States barters its wheat for Russian crude oil. The United States can obtain the oil it needs either by producing it at home (say, at the Alaskan north slope) or by bartering it for wheat. Given the immensely efficient American agriculture, it is cheaper to obtain oil by bartering it for wheat. The effect on the U.S. price level would be anti-inflationary.

Thus, when imports as well as exports are considered, it is seen that the effect of foreign trade is to lower rather than to raise the average price level of all goods. Additionally, competitive pressure from foreign producers often constitutes a barrier to price increases by domestic producers. It spurs local producers to introduce the latest technological innovations and greater efficiency. In the case of the auto industry, it is often suggested that foreign competition induced the U.S. producers to introduce small cars in the late 1970s, thereby conforming to consumer preferences. And in the 1980s and 1990s, intense foreign competition forced American producers to hold the lid on prices, thereby contributing to the prevention of inflation.

It is in the interest of a country to engage in balanced, mutually beneficial, and market-directed trade. It is contrary to its interest to pursue policies that distort its comparative advantage by providing protection to inefficient industries. There is no particular advantage in being able to undersell other countries in everything. Giving up commodities in exchange for gold, IOUs, or other paper assets simply deprives the nation of the satisfactions derived from consumption.

ECONOMIC ADJUSTMENTS

It is important to recognize that comparative advantage is a dynamic rather than a static concept. It changes over time because the manifold factors that underlie comparative advantage are never at a standstill. Technological advancement, capital accumulation, acquisition of new skills, and invention of new products are commonplace in all dynamic economies. They occur practically every year and, in turn, change the ranking of industries in terms of comparative advantage. Industries that could easily meet price competition on world markets at one time may suddenly find themselves shrinking in size because of their inability to compete. Under such circumstances, it is important that resources in the economy be mobile enough to shift from sluggish to competitive sectors. The economy itself must be in a process of continual transformation to meet new circumstances.

Consider, for example, the production of desk calculators. Immediately after World War II, this was almost exclusively an American monopoly. But twenty years later, when the technology involved was no longer considered sophisticated, the Burroughs Corporation found it advantageous to move production from Detroit to Scotland where equally qualified but cheaper labor was to be found. Were the Detroit plants shut down? Not at all; they were transformed into the production of more sophisticated electronic computers. While the United States was losing its comparative advantage in calculators, it was gaining a new one in more sophisticated equipment.

But at the same time, similar changes were taking place in other countries. Consider the attempts of the developing countries to industrialize. What new industries can they establish? Apart from production based on locally available materials, it is clear that their comparative advantage lies in industries that are both technologically unsophisticated and labor intensive. Textiles, footwear, and lumber products come immediately to mind as concrete possibilities. Thus, while India and Pakistan establish textile mills, it is necessary for Great Britain and continental Europe to contract their textile industries and shift to the production of more advanced products.

Perhaps the most dramatic illustration of the dynamic nature of comparative advantage is the Japanese concern about textile imports. Toward the end of 1970, in the midst of the American industry's clamor for quota protection from Japanese textile exports, the Japanese mills themselves were becoming increasingly concerned about cheap textile imports from South Korea, Hong Kong, and Taiwan. Likewise, Korea is beginning to export steel to Japan. It can only be hoped that Japan will handle the problem by gradually shifting resources to more sophisticated industries, and not by the imposition of new restrictions on imports from other Far Eastern countries.

But here comes the hitch. What on paper is a one-paragraph description of economic transformation is in reality a severe problem of human dislocation and adjustment. Production equipment must be scrapped and new machinery installed. Workers must be retrained in new skills and sometimes relocated. At times, even entire communities are disbanded, and ghost towns appear where once there were thriving cities. In other words, the shift that benefits the entire nation occurs at the expense of considerable hardship to a minority of dislocated people. This problem is common to any type of economic change, such as the introduction of new technology, not only to change brought about by foreign trade. Public assistance in the adjustment process can help smooth over and speed up the transformation, but hardships remain nonetheless.

Consequently, it is not surprising that the industries directly affected by new import competition strive to protect their interests by demanding tariff or quota protection, with the labor unions joining in. The eventual benefit to all, after the transformation has been completed and workers moved to higher paying jobs, is lost sight of. The vested interest of the minority often prevails; certainly little attention is paid to the consuming public that stands to benefit from cheaper imports. The resulting protection of the textile industry in the United States and Europe has become a major grievance of many developing nations.

Another contemporary illustration is the insistence of the (politically powerful) Japanese farmers on import protection for farm products, which thereby perpetuates their very inefficient agricultural practices. American food exports are not allowed to penetrate that market, much to the chagrin of U.S. policy makers. Within Japan, the policy of protecting agriculture incurs the wrath of the large industrial exporters, who fear American retaliation in curbing imports of Japanese manufactured products.

To all countries, developed and developing alike, inability to transform may spell economic stagnation and continuous difficulties. Despite the hardships involved, an economy must maintain the dynamism necessary for continuous change as it adapts to shifts in comparative advantage. The government can help by maintaining a high level of aggregate production and employment so that labor and capital released from declining industries will find alternative employment. It can also provide direct assistance to alleviate the burden of interindustry transfers.

PROTECTION

In light of the gains from international trade articulated earlier, one would expect free trade to be the prevailing rule and artificial barriers to trade the exception. Yet even casual observation may convince the reader that we live in a protection-ridden world, where government interference with the free flow of goods, services, and capital is anything but an exception. In what follows we review the main instruments of protection.

Ad valorem tax: A tax levied as the fixed percentage of the value of the product. **Specific tax:** levied as a fixed dollar amount per unit of the commodity regardless of its price.

Tariff

A tariff or a duty is a tax levied on an imported commodity. It is an **ad valorem tax** if it is computed as a fixed *percentage* of the value of the product, such as 5 percent of the price of a car. It is a **specific tax** if it is computed as a fixed *dollar amount* per unit of the commodity regardless of price, such as $500 per car.

Although the main purpose of the tariff is to protect a domestic industry that produces substitutes for imported products, it also yields government revenue, for the proceeds of the tax are collected by the government. Indeed, in early American history revenue was the main purpose of levying import duties. The only tariff that yields no government revenue is one set high enough to keep out all imports, known as a **prohibitive tariff.**

Prohibitive tariff: a tariff levied at a high enough rate to keep out all imports. A tariff or a quota redistributes income away from consumers, and cause a welfare loss to the country as a whole.

A tariff raises the internal price of import, and that increase has several consequences. In the first place, it forces some consumers to curtail consumption of the imported products and switch to domestically produced substitutes. The latter are presumably less desirable; otherwise, they would have been purchased even in the absence of the tariff. Consequently, this change constitutes a welfare loss to the consumer.

Second, as the price rises, production expands in the domestic industries that produce substitutes for the tariff-ridden imports. Under conditions of full employment, this can be accomplished only by drawing resources away from other industries, which presumably rank higher in the order of comparative advantage. This is a loss in production efficiency for the economy as a whole. It is worth emphasizing that the producers of the protected commodity gain from this transformation; the loss occurs

Figure 24–1 Domestic Effects of the Tariff: A tariff in the amount P_2P_3 raises the domestic price of the imported commodity from P_2 to P_3. Imports decline from the free trade level of *ab* to the protection-ridden level of *gh*. This reduction has two components: domestic consumption declines by *bh*, and local production rises by *ag*. Government tariff revenue is represented by the shaded area. Net loss is triangles A + B.

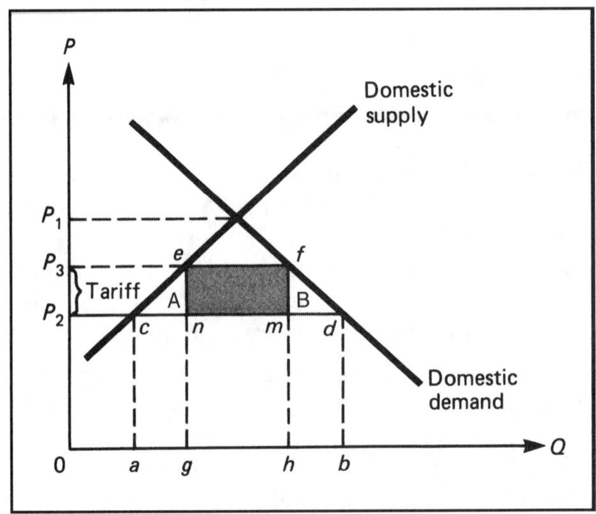

in the efficiency of the economy as a whole, as protection enables these producers to attract resources from other sectors. The consumption and production losses are partly offset by an increase in government revenue.

In sum, a tariff causes a net loss to the economy as a whole, coupled with a redistribution of income from the consuming public to the producers of the protected commodities and to the government. Because the tariff raises the price to the consumer and gives protection to the domestic producer, its domestic effects are comparable to those of a tax on the consumers combined with a subsidy to the producers.

These effects can be seen in Figure 24–1. It depicts the internal supply and demand conditions for a tariff-ridden commodity—say, shoes. In the absence of any international trade, the domestic price is set at P_1. Under free trade and in the absence of transport cost, the domestic price cannot differ from the world price, assumed here to be P_2. At P_2 domestic consumption is O*b*, production is O*a*, and imports, being the difference between the two, are *ab*.

A tariff in the amount of P_2P_3 raises the domestic price to P_3 and produces the following effects. Internal consumption of shoes declines by *hb* as consumers move along the demand curve from *d* to *f*. Thus, the tariff forces consumers to curtail consumption of the taxed commodity and switch to less desirable domestic substitutes (the consumption effect of the tariff). Domestic production of shoes rises by *ag* as producers move along the supply curve from *c* to *e* (the production effect of the tariff). In the context of the entire economy, *ag* represents the resources that the protected shoe industry is able to bid away from the other, more efficient, industries. The domestic shoe industry benefits, but production efficiency in the entire economy declines. Imports decline by *ag* + *hb*. Finally, the shaded rectangle, import volume of *ef* (= *gh*) times the tariff per unit P_2P_3, represents government revenue from the tariff.

In 2002 President Bush (II) under pressure from the steel industry and its union (the United Steel Workers), imposed a high tariff on imported steel. This raised input prices in the steel-using industries (such as autos), and created other dislocations in the economy. It resulted in a net welfare loss measured by triangles A and B. Finally, Europe and Japan threatened retaliation that could have conceivably developed into a trade war. All in all a no win situation. For all these reasons the steel tariff was removed in December 2003. The year 2002 also witnessed U.S. restrictions on the imports of Canadian lumber, and a large increase in agricultural subsidies.

Import Quotas

An import quota is a restriction on the amount of permissible import of a commodity; no more than some maximum quantity may be imported. Because it restricts the supply of imports, the import quota raises the domestic price of the imported commodity in much the same way as does the tariff. Consumption declines and consumers switch to less desirable substitutes, while domestic production of substitute products expands under the protection accorded to their producers, with resources drawn from other (presumably more efficient) industries. However, in contrast to the tariff, there is no revenue to the government. Rather, the revenue accrues to the importers, who are now able to charge a higher price for each unit of the restricted supply. Only by auctioning off the import licenses can the government recoup this revenue.

That the effects of a quota and a tariff are similar can be seen in Figure 24–1. Instead of imposing a tariff, the government restricts imports from *ab* to *gh*. The restriction raises the domestic price from P_2 to P_3. As a result, consumption of the imported commodity declines by *hb*, and production of the domestic substitute rises by *ag*. But the shaded area now accrues to the importers instead of to the government.

Despite these similarities, there are many ways in which a quota is much more harmful to the economy than a tariff. A tariff distorts relative prices, but the market mechanism is allowed to function; those who pay the tax can continue to import. A quota displaces the market altogether and substitutes for it an import-licensing mechanism, where licenses are issued by a government bureaucracy set up for that purpose. Who gets the licenses, how the imports are distributed among supplying countries, and how the annual quota is divided over the year all become subject to arbitrary decisions. In some cases the quota can even serve political ends, as when Cuba was excluded from the list of countries eligible to fill the U.S. sugar quota.

A quota leaves more scope for a domestic monopolist to inflict damage on the economy than does a tariff. Under a tariff the domestic price cannot be above the world market price plus the tariff. A domestic-competing monopolist cannot charge above that price. A quota sets no such cap on the price. Once the monopolist accommodates himself to the fixed amount of imports, he can charge any price that maximizes his profit. And usually that price would be higher than that under a tariff.

Finally, under a tariff the quantity of imports can adjust. If demand for the product rises, as it usually does in a growing economy, imports would rise to the benefit of consumers. No such adjustment is possible in case of a quota, for the quantity of imports is fixed by decree. Hence if demand rises, prices would increase.

An interesting effect of quantitative restriction is known as "quality upgrading." Suppose the Japanese are restricted in the number of cars they can ship to the United States. Why should they not switch to more luxurious and hence more lucrative models, loaded with options, and thereby increase their profit per unit? In all quantitative limitations imposed on differentiated products, the exporters attempt to compensate for the cut in quantity and reduced profits, by shipping higher-quality brands that yield higher profit per unit.

Other Protective Measures

Although tariffs and quotas are the most common restrictions on trade, they are by no means the only ones. Other restrictions are reviewed briefly.

Until 2005, all world trade in textiles and clothing was regulated by an international commodity agreement. Under it, each importing country limited the quantity of textiles it imported from each exporting nation in any given year. An annual growth factor of 2 to 6 percent was usually applied to this restricted trade. Although it was phased out in 2005, new restrictions on imports from China were imposed by the U.S. and the EU.

Dumping: A sale of a good in a foreign country at a price below that charged in the home market.

Governments often apply special duties to counteract imports said to be subsidized by foreign countries or when the foreign exporters charge a price below the price of the product in their home countries (known as **dumping**). The determination of these cases is often said to be arbitrary and capricious.

A myriad of administrative regulations are used by many countries to limit trade in many commodities. In addition governments often give preferences to local producers in the purchase of goods and services by the public sector. Exports are often promoted artificially by subsidies and other means.

Summary

What all measures of import restrictions have in common is that they raise the price to the consumer. In doing so, they harm the public welfare, while at the same time benefiting the protected industry and its workers.

The benefits to the protected industry and its workers come at a high cost to society. For example, it has been estimated that the restrictions on auto imports into the U.S. in the 1980's cost the American consumers $4 billion per year in higher prices, while saving about 20,000 jobs in the U.S. auto industry. That works out to $200,000 a year for each job saved. The steel restrictions were estimated to save U.S. jobs at the same cost. And an import quota on shoes, proposed in 1985, was estimated to save jobs at an even higher cost. It would be cheaper for society to enjoy the full benefits of free trade, and pay the displaced workers a $25,000 per year retraining and relocation subsidy, thereby realizing a net saving of $175,000 per worker.

Adjustment assistance: Aid to firms and individuals who have been hurt by imports.

Indeed, this is the public policy recommended by economists: Remove all barriers to trade, so that the society can reap the benefits of unfettered commerce. And at the same time offer direct financial help known as **adjustment assistance,** to firms and workers that are harmed by the removal of protection. Provisions for such assistance are embodied in the U.S. trade legislation.

This negative attitude towards protection was expressed in the 1985 summit communiqué of the heads of state of the seven largest industrial countries[2]: "Protection does not solve problems; it only creates problems."

---

[2]The United States, United Kingdom, Germany, France, Japan, Canada, and Italy.

THE POLITICS OF PROTECTION

Politics: Protection abounds because the losses from it are diffused, while the "benefits" are concentrated. It pays the potential gainers to lobby for protection.

Why then is protectionism so widespread? As in other areas of national concern, commercial policies do not represent a majority vote or the reasoned opinions of a single decision maker. They are a product of pressure groups vying for the attention of legislators and policy makers.

One reason why protection from foreign competition is so common is the strong incentive to lobby on the part of population groups that gain from protection, and the lack of such incentives on the part of groups that stand to lose from protection. Any specific trade restriction inflicts damage on the community at large and confers benefits on a few small groups. While the total loss to society exceeds the benefits to the gaining groups (and thus there is a net loss), the losses from protection are diffused while the gains are concentrated in very few groups.

A restriction on the entry of a foreign product, such as textiles, reduces the quantity supplied and hence raises the product's price. The main loser from such action is the consumer, who must pay the higher price. Thus, the loss is diffused over 300 million consumers, each paying a slightly higher price. Similarly the U.S. sugar quota raises sugar prices (as well as the prices of goods made with sugar) by a few cents per pound, barely noticeable to the average buyer. Furthermore, in many cases consumers are not even aware of the relation between the price hike and protection. Consequently, they have little incentive to oppose the protective measure.

However, the gains from protection are not diffused. Producers and workers in the protected industry, partly freed from the pressure of foreign competition, are able to charge a higher price for their product (such as domestic textiles). The benefits are heavily concentrated in very few groups, namely, the domestic manufacturers and labor unions in the particular industry. And the gains realized by each individual are sizable and visible. Hence, those who gain as a group have an intense interest in the outcome. They are willing to engage in intense lobbying efforts and expend large sums of money to assure a legislative outcome favorable to them.

In sum, the benefits of protectionism are concentrated and visible, while its far higher costs are diffused and invisible. Those who lose hardly know that they are being forced to bear the cost. This distribution of losses and benefits, and hence the interest of various political constituencies, explains why the pressure for protectionism is so great. There is a fundamental imbalance in the process of making trade policy; the advocates of protectionism start with a built-in advantage.

Arguments for Protection

Infant industry: A country should protect industries until they reach a size that enables them to compete on the world market. Much abused.

Against this background, we can evaluate some of the arguments heard in political and economic circles on behalf of protection.

Infant Industry From the viewpoint of the welfare of the world as a whole, the most popular claim made for tariff protection is the so-called infant-industry argument. It asserts that an industry whose existence may benefit other industries (because it creates an infrastructure or a well-trained labor pool), and which itself can benefit from economies of scale, should be allowed to grow to optimum size under a protective tariff. Once that size is attained, the tariff can be removed leaving behind a viable and competitive industry. Theoretically, this is a valid argument. Indeed, Japan's development is replete with illustrations of how an industry can be developed and fostered under protection until it reaches an optimum size.

Often there are difficulties with the practical application of this argument. First, the argument can be abused, as it has been at times by declining industries that attempt to protect their position in the market and thereby perpetuate inefficiency. Even the American steel industry advanced the argument once in an effort to convince Congress to impose import quotas on steel. Second, once it has been imposed, a tariff is rather difficult to remove, regardless of the industry's competitive standing. And finally, even in cases where the infant-industry position applies, it is more efficient to offer a direct subsidy as a means of helping the industry to expand. A tariff is equivalent to a tax on the consumer plus a (disguised) subsidy to the producer. By contrast, a direct subsidy does not contain the tax element, and the subsidy component is provided in an overt fashion. It is then open for all interested parties to inspect and evaluate. And when the time comes, it is somewhat easier to discontinue.

Domestic employment: A country should use tariffs to increase domestic employment and improve the balance of payments by reducing imports. Inefficient way to increase employment.

Domestic Employment Tariffs may at times be used to increase domestic employment or improve the balance of payments. But both objectives can be met more efficiently by fiscal and monetary policies. It was shown earlier that employment expansion through protectionism is very costly. Also, the increase in employment is accomplished at the expense of foreign countries whose exports are restricted. And foreign retaliation can create equally severe unemployment in our export industries.

In 1977–78 and again in 1981–88, there was a marked increase in the clamor for protection in the United States. In part, this was due to the massive trade deficits, which had adverse macroeconomic effects on employment and output. A similar clamor was heard in Europe where double-digit unemployment plagued the economy. Yet in both cases the most effective solution was a coordinated change in fiscal and monetary policies.

As a general rule, protection is not an effective cure to domestic economic ills be they macroeconomic in nature or problems affecting a specific industry. It merely perpetuates inefficiency and postpones the inevitable adjustment process.

Keep out cheap imports: A country should use protectionism to keep out cheap imports because they undersell local producers: A satire about an imaginary request by French candlemakers for protection from sun-light.

Keep Out Cheap Imports Demands to keep out cheap foreign imports—simply because they undersell local produce—go back many years. A famous reply to this argument is contained in a short satire by Fredric Bastiat. Titled "The Petition of the Candlemakers," it is an imaginary petition presented to the French Chamber of Deputies in the early nineteenth century:

We are subjected to the intolerable competition of a foreign rival whose superior facilities for producing light enable him to flood the French market at so low a price as to take away all our customers the moment he appears, suddenly reducing an important branch of French industry to stagnation. This rival is the sun.

We request a law to shut up all windows, dormers, skylights, openings, holes, chinks, and fissures through which sunlight penetrates. Our industry provides such valuable manufactures that our country cannot, without ingratitude, leave us now to struggle unprotected through so unequal a contest. . . . In short, granting our petition will greatly develop every branch of agriculture. Navigation will equally profit. Thousands of vessels will soon be employed in whaling, and thence will arise a navy capable of upholding the honor of France. . . .

Do you object that the consumer must pay the price of protecting us? You have yourselves already answered the objection. When told that the consumer is interested in free importation of iron, coal, corn, wheat, cloth, etc., you have answered that the producer is interested in their exclusion.

Will you say that sunlight is a free gift, and that to repulse free gifts is to repulse riches under pretense of encouraging the means of obtaining them? Take care—you deal a death-blow to your own policy. Remember: hitherto you have always repulsed foreign produce because it was an approach to a free gift; and the closer this approach, the more you have repulsed the goods.

When we buy a Portuguese orange at half the price of a French orange, we in effect get it half as a gift. If you protect national labor against the competition of a half-gift, what principle justifies allowing the importation of something just because it is entirely a gift?

The difference in price between an imported article and the corresponding French article is a free gift to us. The bigger the difference, the bigger the gift. . . .[3]

Declining industries: A country should protect industries that are lagging behind others. Inefficient: Resources should be moved to expanding industries.

Declining Industries Industries that are on the decline because demand has turned away from their products or because they lag technologically, often lobby for protection from foreign imports. But such protection only perpetuates inefficiency and prolongs the agony. It does not forestall the inevitable outcome. A far superior policy is to help labor and capital adjust by moving to other lines of production in the expanding sectors of the economy.

National Security: A country should protect industries that are essential to its national security. A subsidy is a better policy. In the U.S. the machine tool industry received VER protection on these grounds.

National Security Industries often claim that their products and the labor skills they utilize are essential to national security, and should therefore be preserved by a tariff. Whether true or not, this is not a subject on

[3]Quoted from Yeager and Tuerck, *Trade Policy and the Price System,* (Scranton, Pa: International Textbook Co. 1966).

which the economist can pass judgment, except to indicate that if it is true the industry should be directly and overtly subsidized out of the defense budget.

Revenue tariff: Levy tariffs on imports because of the revenue they generate. Used in LDCs. In the U.S. tariff revenue constitute a mere 1 percent of government revenue.

Revenue Tariff Tariffs yield only 1 percent of government revenue in the United States. Yet in 1985 a proposal surfaced in the Congress to levy a 20 percent tariff surcharge on all imports, designed to yield about $70 billion in revenue, and thus reduce the $200 billion budget deficit. Apart from probable retaliation by other countries and a possible trade war that may be triggered, it must be remembered that there are more efficient and equitable ways to raise government revenue.

Summary While protection is very common in the present-day world, rational justifications for its use are few and far between. The world as a whole, as well as most individual countries, would be better off if it were dispensed with as an instrument of national policy. The question examined next is whether there has been any progress toward this end.

APPROACHES TO FREE TRADE

Although it is in the interest of countries to abolish tariffs, it is a fact of political and economic life that they are extremely reluctant to do so. Tariff cuts appear to be as painful to the nation as tooth extraction is to the patient, for reasons discussed previously.

Any country reducing its level of protection feels that it is giving away something valuable and must obtain something in return from its trading partners. Tariff reduction has come to be regarded as a *concession* to others and is offered only *reciprocally*. **Reciprocal tariff concessions** has also become a subject of tough and prolonged international bargaining, in which each party tries to "extract" as much as possible from its partners and to "surrender" as little as possible in return.

Reciprocal tariff concessions: Countries agree to lower tariffs if their trading partner reciprocate.

The International Approach

The first approach is associated with the World Trade Organization (WTO), an international organization with a membership of 148 countries devoted to the promotion of international trade in general and the reduction of trade barriers in particular. Its members hold periodic negotiating conferences in which tariff concessions are exchanged. The reductions agreed upon by any two or more partners are then extended to all member nations. This rule is known as the Unconditional **Most Favored Nation Principle (MFN)**; it guards against discrimination in international trade. The result has been successive rounds of tariff reductions, each applying to all sources of supply on a nondiscriminatory basis.

MFN Principle: Adopted by the World Trade Organization (WTO) it prohibits discrimination by country-sources of imports.

Rounds of negotiations in the past twenty years were conducted over broad commodity categories, where the United States, Japan, and the European Community held the center stage. The last completed set of tariff reductions, known as the "Uruguay Round," was negotiated during the years 1986–93. It resulted in average tariff cuts of approximately 35 percent of the duties prevailing in the mid 1980s, with the reduction ("staged" over the nine-year period) completed by 2002. A new round (dubbed the Doha Round) began in 2001, but little progress was made by 2006.

Apart from providing a framework for negotiations on trade liberalization, the WTO also oversees countries' compliance with trade rules and adjudicates trade disputes.

As a result of many rounds of negotiations, tariff barriers around the world have come down considerably. The U.S. tariff average reached a record high of about 60 percent under the Smoot-Hawley tariff of 1930. In the postwar period, it has gradually declined to about 5 percent.

Current attention in the WTO is focused on liberalization of non-tariff barriers, trade in services, agricultural protectionism, technical regulations, and export subsidies, as well as on further tariff reductions.

The Regional Approach

Customs union: A group of countries which abolish all trade restrictions among themselves and impose a uniform tariff on imports from outside countries. The **European union** is a prime example.

A free trade area, such as NAFTA, has free trade among members but does not impose a common tariff on external imports. Each member country imposes its own restrictions.

The regional approach is exemplified by customs unions and free-trade areas. A **customs union** involves two or more countries that abolish all, or nearly all, trade restrictions among themselves and set up a *common and uniform* tariff on imports from outsiders. The **European Union (EU)**, or Common Market, is a 25 country customs union that includes the United Kingdom, Germany, France, Italy, and Spain among others. Trade among members is free of restrictions; nonmembers must pay the common external tariff. An American producer shipping to France is discriminated against in favor of a German competitor to the extent of the common duty.

In a **free-trade area**, trade among the member countries is also completely liberalized, or nearly so. But there is no common tariff against nonmember countries; each country is free to impose its own duty. The European Free Trade Association (EFTA) is a free-trade area encompassing Norway, Switzerland, and Iceland. An American exporter to Norway is discriminated against in favor of a Swiss counterpart by the level of the Norwegian duty. Australia and New Zealand also negotiated a free-trade area, as did the United States, Canada, and Mexico (the North American Free Trade Agreement or NAFTA).There exist similar regional groupings among various developing countries. Customs unions and free-trade areas are exempt from the WTO's Most Favored Nation rule.

Unlike the WTO approach, regional groupings do discriminate against outsiders. On the other hand they aim at complete removal of trade barriers within their respective regions. Certainly the EU contributed significantly to the expansion of trade among European countries.

SUMMARY

International commerce among all nations has grown rapidly in the post-war period, and it now reaches $8 trillion per year. What underlies much of this trade is the principle of comparative advantage. A country would tend to specialize in and export those commodities in which its *degree* of productivity lead over other countries is large, and import those commodities in which its degree of productivity advantage is small. Thus, mutually beneficial trade can exist even in cases where one country is absolutely more productive than another in all industries.

Relative productivity conditions set the limits to mutually beneficial trade, while demand conditions determine where within these limits the international exchange ratio would settle. Beyond that, demand considerations often generate trade in differentiated products even when not justified by relative productivity conditions.

Natural resources, relative factor abundance, relative labor skills, and relative possession of knowledge and technology are some of the factors that underlie comparative advantage. Because they tend to change over time, so does the comparative advantage configuration. Therefore, countries must continuously adjust to changing circumstance by shifting resources from declining to newly competitive industries.

Despite the distinct advantages that flow from unfettered international commerce, the world is replete with obstacles to such trade. Tariffs, quotas, VERs, and other restrictions on imports are very common. By restricting supply they raise the price to the consumer, while at the same time subsidize the domestic import-competing industry.

One reason why the pressure for protection is so rampant is that its cost is highly diffused and hidden, while its benefits are visible and heavily concentrated in a few groups. Consequently, the beneficiaries have a strong incentive to seek protection through political pressure, while the losers have little incentive to resist it.

Most arguments for protection heard in political debates do not make economic sense. Protection is a poor and inefficient way to correct domestic economic ills such as unemployment, budget deficits, difficulties of declining industries and the like. Even in the case of valid arguments, a direct subsidy is usually superior to import protection.

Significant liberalization of internal trade has taken place over the postwar period. This was accomplished internationally through the WTO and regionally through the formation of customs unions and free-trade areas. The liberalization was one of the factors responsible for the expansion of world trade.

QUESTIONS AND PROBLEMS

1. You are given the following figures on labor productivity in the United States and Germany in two industries, wheat and linen. One day of homogeneous labor can produce:

In	Wheat (Bushels)	Linen (Yards)
United States	20	20
Germany	10	15

   a. Determine and explain the comparative advantage configuration of the two countries. Which country will export what commodity and why?

   b. What are the limits to mutually beneficial trade?

   c. What determines where (within these limits) the international exchange ratio of the two goods would settle?

   d. Demonstrate with a numerical example that trade would benefit both nations.

2. What can you say about the following relationships?

   a. Absolute advantage and the standard of living.

   b. Comparative advantage and the direction of trade.

   c. Comparative advantage and the standard of living.

3. Do you agree with the following statement? "A drought in the Soviet Union which doubled the demand for Canadian wheat is inflationary to Canada." Why or why not? Explain *in full!*

4. Evaluate the following statements:

   a. "Once the United States acquires a comparative advantage in the production of jet aircraft, its position in the world markets (in that industry) is secure forever."

   b. "A tariff on textiles is equivalent to a tax on consumers and a subsidy to the textile producers and workers."

   c. "A tariff lowers the real income of the community, while at the same time it distributes income from the consumers to the governments and to the import-competing industry."

   d. "As instruments of protection go, a tariff is less harmful than a quota.

   e. "Protection is an expensive and inefficient way to create jobs."

   f. "Protection is the best way to help an industry that is lagging technologically to survive."

   g. "If consumer demand has switched from meat to fish, we should protect the meat industry from foreign competition."

   h. "The best way to reduce the budget deficit is to impose a tariff to collect revenue."

   i. "Chinese mushrooms undersell American mushrooms because Chinese labor is cheaper than American labor. We should impose a high tariff on mushrooms until China agrees to raise wage rates to the level prevailing in the United States."

5. What are the similarities and differences between a tariff and a quota?

6. State and evaluate five popular arguments for protection.
7. What are the differences between the WTO, the European Union, and NAFTA?

25 Foreign Exchanges and the International Currency System

INTRODUCTION

Chapter 24 deals with the exchange of goods and services between countries. But in reality such international exchange is not conducted as barter trade. The United States does not barter wheat for British textiles, grains for Russian oil, or aircraft and computers for Japanese cars. Rather, it sells wheat, aircraft, and computers for money and buys oil, cars, and textiles with money. Movement of goods and services among countries requires movement of money in the opposite direction. This chapter analyzes such international movements of funds. The specific topics to be covered are outlined in this section.

Exchange Rates

While the exchange of goods and services for money is also characteristic of domestic transactions, there is an important difference between internal and foreign trade. Domestic purchases and sales are financed by the country's own currency. For example, a New York buyer of Florida oranges or Idaho potatoes pays for them in dollars. In contrast, international transactions are financed in foreign currencies. A German camera maker selling his wares in New York requires payments in euros, and a Japanese auto manufacturer marketing cars in California is paid in yen.

Each country's central bank issues its own currency. Thus, Japan's currency is the yen (¥); England's currency is the pound sterling (£); Russia's is the ruble, and so on. Twelve European countries issued a common currency called the Euro (€).

International transactions require conversion of one currency into another, for while the American buyer of a German camera pays in dollars, the German seller receives payment in euros. The price of one currency in terms of another is called an exchange rate. Thus, on a recent day the U.S. dollar was worth ¥100 and 1 Euro, which by implication means that 1€ = ¥100. Each exchange rate has an inverse: If $1 = ¥100, then ¥1 = 1¢. By definition, an exchange rate involves more than one country.

Exchange rates of the major currencies are determined by supply and demand for foreign currencies on the foreign exchange markets. Physically, these markets can be described as telephone and cable lines, providing instant communication among the major banks and brokers that deal in foreign currencies. There is no "big board" on which exchange rates are posted centrally, as in a stock market.

Balance of Payments

Each country compiles an annual record of all transactions by its citizens that require dealings in foreign currencies. This record is called a **statement of international transactions**, more popularly known as the country's balance of payments.

International Currency System

Because exchange rates always involve two or more currencies, they cannot be the exclusive domain of one country. Hence, all countries band together to establish a framework within which exchange rates are determined. This is known as the *international currency system.*

It is to the aforementioned topics that the present chapter is devoted. The chapter begins with the U.S. balance of payments statement, and examines the types of transactions that give rise to foreign payments and receipts. It then considers various exchange-rate regimes, leading up to the contemporary international currency system.

STATEMENT OF INTERNATIONAL TRANSACTIONS

Statement of international transactions: an annual record, compiled by each country, of all transactions by its citizens with foreigners.

A statement of all the transactions between one country and the rest of the world, usually reported annually, is known as that country's *international transactions statement,* alternatively referred to as the country's *balance of payments.* The transactions included are merchandise trade (export and import of goods); exchange of services, such as insurance or transportation services (these are referred to as *invisible* items because, unlike commodities, they cannot be seen); and transfers of capital in both directions.

In order to facilitate the understanding of the various items appearing in the statement, it is useful to divide them into two groups: those giving rise to dollar *inpayments (plus* or *credit* items) and those resulting in dollar *outpayments (negative* or *debit* items). This dichotomy should be kept in mind throughout the exposition.

Table 25–1 offers a condensed version of the U.S. statement of international transactions for 2005. It is used in the subsequent discussion to illustrate the various items that appear in the statement.

Table 25–1 U.S. International Transactions, 2005 (Billion Dollars)

Current Account Transactions		
1. Merchandise exports	893	
2. Merchandise imports	-1,674	
3. Balance of merchandise trade		-781
4. Export of services	380	
5. Import of services	-322	
6. Balance on goods and services (lines 3+4+5)		-724
7. Income receipts on U.S. assets abroad	469	
8. Income payments on foreign assets in the U.S.	-467	
9. Government grants and private remittances	-83	
10. Balance on current account (lines 6–9)		-805
Financial Account Transactions		
11. Change in U.S. private assets abroad, net (increase/capital outflow/-)[a]	-478	
12. Change in foreign private assets in U.S., net (increase/capital inflow/+)[b]	1,072	
13. Statistical discrepancy[c]	10	
14. Capital account balance (lines 11–13)		604
15. Official reserve transactions balance (lines 10+14)		-201
16. Increase in U.S. official reserves (increase,-)	-14	
17. Rise in foreign official assets in U.S.	215	

Source: Bureau of Economic Analysis, Department of Commerce, April 2006.

[a]*An increase in U.S. assets abroad means capital outflow from the United States and has a negative sign. A decrease means capital inflow and has a positive sign.*

[b]*An increase in foreign assets in the United States means capital inflow into the United States and has a positive sign.*

[c]*What is the nature of the statistical discrepancy and how does it arise? In compiling the statistics, the United States Department of Commerce uses two sources of information for each transaction: the transaction itself and the means of payment for it. For example, information of a given U.S. export transaction can be obtained from the exporter who shipped the merchandise and from the bank through which the payment was made. All goods and services as well as capital transfers are treated in the same manner. Theoretically, the value of all transactions should add up exactly to the value of all payments. But in fact they do not. The difference is called a statistical discrepancy.*

The Current Account

Balance of trade: the difference between merchandise exports and imports. **Balance on goods and services:** The difference between export and import of goods and services. Both are part of the **current account.**

Merchandise trade constitutes the largest item in U.S. international transactions; exports of goods give rise to inpayments and are plus items, whereas imports of goods are outpayments or negative items. The two are shown on lines 1 and 2 of Table 25–1; the difference between them is the *balance of merchandise trade* or simply the **balance of trade** (line 3). In 2005 the United States has a trade deficit of $781 billion. Although it is very much a partial balance, the trade balance is reported by the Department of Commerce on a monthly and quarterly basis and is given extensive coverage by the national media. A similar balance is reported by other countries. Line 4 shows that exports of services resulted in total inpayment payments of $380 billion. These include foreign tourists visiting the United States; U.S. airlines flying foreign passengers; American ships carrying foreign freight; and U.S. banks, insurance companies, and other financial institutions selling services to foreigners. All these service transactions generate dollar inpayments, and hence are considered credit items, denoted by a plus sign.

Line 5 shows that imports of services added up to outpayments of $322 billion. These include American tourists traveling abroad, foreign airlines carrying U.S. passengers, and foreign financial institutions rendering financial services to Americans.

In all, the United States had a $58 billion (380–322) surplus on service transactions. Exports minus imports of goods and services constitute the balance on goods and services, shown on line 6 of Table 25-1. This balance amounted to a deficit of $724 billion in 2005; and it is the primary link between the international transactions statement and the national income accounts. A variant of this balance appears on the expenditures side of GDP as net exports of goods and services (X_n), where: $GDP=C+I+G+X_n$.

Line 7 of Table 25-1 shows repatriated earnings on U.S. investments abroad, an inpayment of $469 billion. Examples are the repatriated profits of American companies on their direct investments abroad (subsidiaries and branch plants); dividends realized by U.S. residents on their foreign accounts. Correspondingly line 8 shows repatriated *returns* on foreign investments in the United States, an *outpayment* of $467 billion. This item includes profits made by U.S. subsidiaries of foreign companies, dividends realized by foreigners on their holdings of shares in U.S. companies, and interest earned by foreigners on their American bonds and bank accounts. It should be emphasized that investment income refers to returns on foreign investments accumulated over previous years; the annual investments themselves are shown in the financial account.

Unilateral transfers (line 9) are an outpayments item for the United States. They include government's foreign aid program, as well as private remittances to people living abroad.

Adding lines 6–9 we obtain the balance on current account (line 10), which was in deficit of $805 billion in 2005.

Financial account: The part of the international transactions statement which records international purchases or sales of assets.

The Financial Account

We next turn to the financial account[1] of the statement which records international *purchases or sales of assets*. Line 11 in Table 25–1 shows the net change over the year in U.S. assets (other than official reserve assets) held abroad. This change is a result of U.S. financial *outpayments* (negative items) of the following varieties: (1) direct private investment abroad by American corporations, such as the establishment of foreign subsidiaries; (2) purchases of foreign securities (stocks and bonds) and deposits in foreign banks by Americans; and (3) U.S. government loans to foreign countries, less repayment of loans by foreigners. In all cases; repatriated U.S. capital is netted out. All these net outflows increase U.S. asset holdings abroad. Therefore, an *increase* (decrease) in U.S. assets abroad means capital *outflow* (inflow) and has a *negative* (positive) sign. In 2005 U.S. assets abroad increased by $478 billion.

[1]There exists a third account known as the "capital account." It includes such items as debt forgiveness. But because it is of negligible magnitude it is ignored here.

Line 12 in Table 25-1 shows the net change over the year in foreign assets (other than official reserves) in the United States. Such financial *inpayments* (positive items) include (1) direct investment in the United States by foreign corporations and (2) purchases of American securities (that is, stocks and bonds) and deposits in U.S. banks by foreigners. An *increase* (decrease) in foreign assets in the United States means a capital *inflow* (outflow) and has a positive (negative) sign. In 2005 foreign assets in the United States increased by $1,072 billion.

While all items reporting the transfer of capital are included in the financial account component of the balance of payments, the income on foreign investment—whether interest, dividends, or repatriated profits—is part of the goods and services section. These earnings are a result of investment made in previous years.

Finally, a statistical discrepancy of $10 billion in dollar inflow appeared in 2005. Its nature is explained in the third footnote to Table 25–1 and it need not detain us here.

Adding up all the financial account items (lines 11–13) we obtain the financial account balance. As shown in line 14, it was in a surplus to the tune of $604 billion in 2005. A financial account surplus means that on balance foreign funds flowed into the United States in a variety of forms. These are assets to foreigners and liabilities to the United States. They are partial offset to the U.S. current account deficit; the U.S. pays for its trade deficit by owing the money to foreigners (accumulating foreign liabilities). It is in that fashion that the trade deficits of the 1980s to date led to accumulation of large foreign debts by the United States.

Balance of Payments Deficit

Official reserve transactions balance = Current account balance + Capital account balance. Shows changes in the country's international reserve position.

Summing the current account deficit of $805 billion and the financial account surplus of $604 billion yields the overall U.S. external position. In 2005 this country had a deficit of $201 billion. Known as the **official reserve transactions balance,** it is shown in line 15.

All the inpayment and outpayment entries shown in lines 1, 2, 4, 5, 7, 8, 9, 11, and 12, constitute responses to general economic or political factors. If they do not add up to zero, the balance of payments is considered out of balance or out of equilibrium. It is in deficit when their sum is negative (private outpayments exceed inpayments). That is the item shown in line 15.

This difference between the inpayments and outpayments must somehow be settled; the means for settling it are gold, official foreign currency reserves, and official debt (the term "official" refers mainly to the central bank). These entries are brought into being by the very existence of imbalance in the private transactions. In Table 25–1 they are shown on lines 16 and 17. Their total must equal the imbalance but bear the opposite sign, thus making the entire statement add up to zero.

In 2005 foreign official reserves (held in the United States) increased by $215 billion (line 17), while U. S. official reserves increased by $14 billion (line 16), yielding a net increase of foreign reserves of $201 billion. The

U.S. paid for the deficit by owing the money to foreign central banks. The dollar reserves accumulated by foreign central banks constitute an asset to these banks and a liability (or debt) to the United States. These changes in reserves come about because U.S. and foreign central banks often intervene in the foreign-exchange market to influence the exchange rate.

MARKET-DETERMINED EXCHANGE RATES

Demand and Supply of Foreign Currencies

Floating exchange rate: A currency that fluctuates freely on the market, and its exchange rate is determined by supply and demand conditions, without government intervention. The official reserve transactions balance is zero. *Relative prices, incomes and interest rates* are the main determinants of the exchange rate.

When the exchange value of a currency fluctuates freely on the foreign-exchange markets, with its value determined daily by supply-and-demand conditions, it is known as a *freely fluctuating* or a **floating exchange rate.** In such a situation, market forces determine each exchange rate at the level that clears the market. A floating currency is said to *appreciate* when its exchange value increases and to *depreciate* when its exchange value decreases relative to other currencies.

To illustrate how the exchange rate of a floating currency is determined, Figure 25–1 shows the German foreign-exchange market, where euros are traded for dollars, which for simplicity are taken to represent all foreign currencies as far as Germany is concerned. The two intersecting curves show the demand for and supply of dollars at various euro (€) prices. They exhibit "normal" slopes: as the euro (€) price of the dollar declines, more dollars are demanded and fewer are supplied. The equilibrium exchange rate for this particular set of curves is 1€ = $1; it would vary with shifts in either demand or supply. The quantity axis indicates the number of dollars changing hands. This is similar to the price determination mechanism in the market for any commodity.

But the analysis begs the more fundamental question of what gives rise to such supply and demand, because foreign currencies are not commodities. A commodity is demanded by consumers for its own sake, to enhance consumer satisfaction, and is supplied by producers through the use of productive factors. By contrast, people do not normally require foreign currencies for their own sake, and foreign currencies are not manufactured in the same manner as are commodities. Rather, the *demand for dollars in our illustration reflects German desire to purchase foreign goods, to travel abroad and buy other foreign services, or to transfer capital abroad for investment and other purposes.* Together these items constitute the *outpayments* side of the German international transactions statement. On the other hand, the *supply of foreign currencies is derived from commodity and service exports and from the inflow of foreign capital.* These entries make up the *inpayments* side of the German international transactions statement. Thus, the demand curve in Figure 25–1 is tantamount to the German dollar outpayments curve, and the supply curve, to the German dollar inpayments curve. Since the exchange rate is determined by the intersection of the two curves, *it ensures equality between inpayments and outpayments.* A shift in one or both curves will change the exchange rate to a new level, which again clears the market. In other words, a *freely fluctuating rate will ensure equilibrium in the balance of payments.*

Shifts in the demand and supply curves occur nearly every day. For that reason, exchange rates change almost on a daily basis. In what follows we survey briefly the main factors that are responsible for such changes.

Shifts In the Demand and Supply Curves

Three main factors determine a country's inpayments and outpayments and therefore its demand for and supply of foreign currencies: (1) its rate of inflation relative to inflation abroad; (2) its real income relative to foreign incomes; and (3) its real rate of interest relative to rates abroad. In addition to income (*Y*), prices (*P*), and the rate of interest (*i*), a variety of psychological factors (originating in political disturbances and even rumors, economic expectations, and the like) affect the exchange rate. These factors are considered one at a time, in each case assuming that other factors are held constant.

Figure 25–1 Supply and Demand Curves for Dollars in Germany: Germans demand dollars to finance imports of goods and services, and to finance investment and other capital outflows to the United States. Hence, the *demand for dollars is equivalent to Germany's dollar outpayments.*

Germany's supply of dollars is derived from exports of goods and services to the United States, from American investment in Germany, and from other U.S. capital flowing into Germany. Hence, the *supply of dollars is equivalent to dollar inpayments.*

The intersection of the supply and demand curves determine the dollar–euro exchange rate and the number of dollars traded. The vertical axis shows the number of euros per dollar along with the corresponding inverse, the equivalent number of dollars per euro in each case.

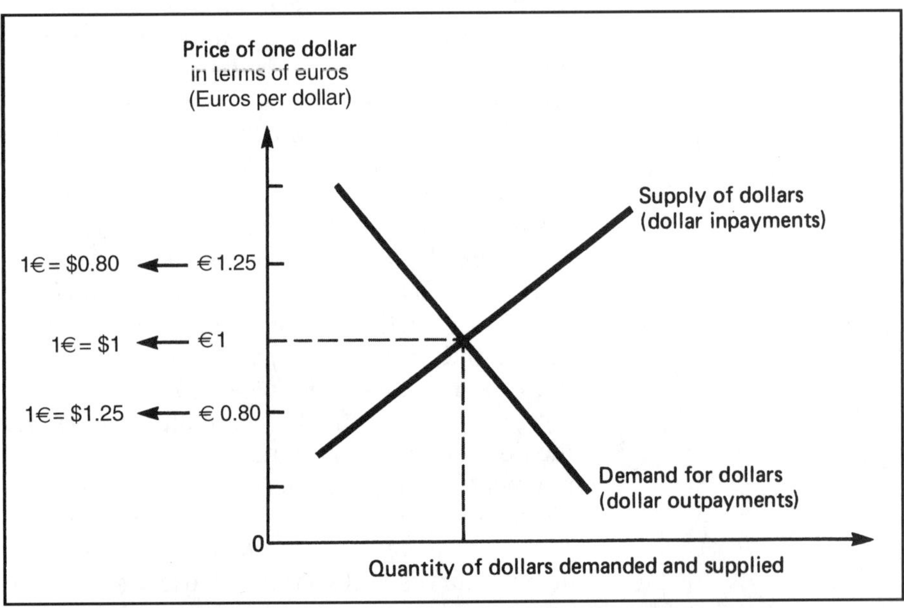

Relative Price Change Assume that the U.S. inflation rate far exceeded that of Germany and other major trading nations. This means that American goods and services would become more expensive relative to their German counterparts on both the U.S. and foreign markets. The American competitive position would deteriorate, and Germany would *sell more* on the U.S. market and *buy less* American goods and services.

In that case Germany would export more to the United States—increasing its supply of dollars; and it would import less from the United States—reducing its demand for dollars. The dollar inpayments curve in Germany would rise or shift rightward. At each and every exchange rate more dollars would be supplied. Concurrently, the dollar outpayments curve in Germany would decline, or shift leftward. At each exchange rate fewer dollars would be demanded to finance purchases in the United States. Draw the two shifts in Figure 25–1, and observe that both cause a reduction in the exchange value of the dollar. The dollar depreciates, say, from say, from 1€ to 0.80€, and correspondingly, the euro appreciates from 1€ = $1 to 1€ = $1.25. Conversely, had German inflation been in excess of U.S. inflation, the German competitive position would deteriorate and the euro would depreciate relative to the dollar. Differential inflation rates between countries have been a prime cause of currency fluctuations during the past decade.

A country with an inflation rate well above the world's average would see its currency depreciate continuously. This phenomenon is of paramount importance to the high inflation countries of South America or Russia whose currencies depreciated on a monthly basis (now stabilized).

In the very long run, the relative price behavior of any two countries is the most powerful determinant of the exchange rate between their currencies. Put differently, *the exchange rate reflects the relative rate of change in their respective domestic price levels, or the purchasing power of their currencies.* This proposition is known as the **purchasing power parity (PPP)** doctrine.

Purchasing Power Parity (PPP): In the long run the exchange rate reflects the relative price levels in the 2 countries, or the purchasing power of their currencies. In the short run PPP can be swamped by the effect of relative interest rates and other variables.

Its simplest version states that if $1 buys the same quantity of goods and services in the United States as 1€ buys in Germany, then the long-run equilibrium exchange rate would be $1 = 1€. But because the exchange rate is affected by influences other than relative price levels, the actual exchange rate can depart from purchasing power parity for an extended period. For example, in the year 2000 the dollar exchange rate was about 1.25€ while in 2005 $1 = 0.83€. Yet the purchasing power of $1 in the United States was equivalent to that of about 1€ PPP. Despite such episodes, relative price changes have a powerful influence on the exchange rate.

Relative Interest Rates Suppose that U.S. real interest rose sharply relative to interest rates prevailing abroad. Then individuals, corporations, and other economic institutions would transfer funds to the United States to be placed in high-interest-yielding securities and other financial instruments. Americans as well as foreigners would convert foreign currencies into dollars to take advantage of high stateside interest rates. The demand for dollars would rise, and with it, its value on the foreign currency markets. This can be seen in Figure 25–1 by shifting the demand for dollars curve upward (to the right) and inspecting the effect on the exchange rate.

Often the effect of changes in relative real interest rates can be powerful, especially in the short run. Indeed over the 1981–85 period it dominated the changes in the value of the dollar. High U.S. real interest rates relative to those prevailing abroad attracted foreign funds to these shores and propelled the exchange value of the dollar to a fifteen-year high. And in early 2006 the dollar apppreciated as the Federal Reserve kept raising interest rates.

Expectations Often market participants anticipate any or all of the preceding changes based on information available to them, and act before the change actually occurs. For example, a sudden spurt in the growth of the money supply leads people to expect an acceleration of the inflation rate. Anticipating that a depreciation of the currency will follow, they sell ("unload") their holdings of the currency, and as a result its value declines even before the acceleration of inflation is evident. In general, unfavorable expectations about a country's political and economic conditions and/or the strength of its currency may lead to depreciation as people sell the currency, while the reverse is true in the case of favorable expectations.

Other Factors Besides the price and income factors, the trade position of a country is affected by such imponderables as international shifts in taste and the quality and design of the country's products and accompanying services. Practically any economic change, such as the lengthening of workers' coffee breaks or an increase in the price of fuels, would affect the exchange rate through its impact on costs, prices, interest rates and incomes, which in turn influence inpayments and outpayments.

Summary All events in the economy and all government policies influence real income (Y), prices (P), or the rate of interest (i). These include changes in wage rates and productivity which affect labor production costs (and the price level), changes in energy costs, fiscal and monetary policies, and a multitude of other factors. Through their impact on Y, P, and i, they influence the exchange rate. Schematically, these relationships can be shown as follows:

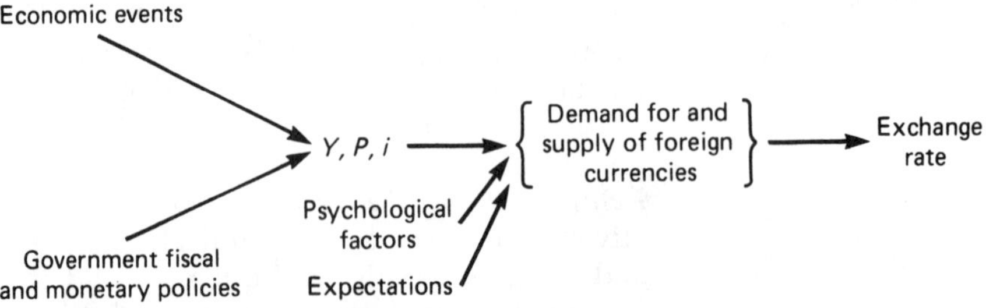

Anything that affects these factors at home and abroad influences the position of the supply and demand curves and therefore affects the exchange rate. The exchange rate is deeply rooted in the country's economic conditions; in no way can it be divorced from its own and other countries' general economic policies.

In all cases what counts are the *changes inside the country relative to changes in the rest of the world.* If prices and income rise commensurately on both sides of the border, then outpayments and inpayments may be similarly affected, with no change in the exchange rate. Also, several of the preceding *factors affecting the exchange rate may change simultaneously.* Finally, it follows from the discussion that *depreciation is not necessarily bad, nor is appreciation necessarily good.* It all depends on the factors(s) causing the exchange rate to change.

Managed float: A fluctuating currency; but the central bank intervenes in the foreign currency markets (buying or selling foreign currencies) to influence the exchange rate.

Managed Floats

Central banks often intervene in the foreign currency markets to influence the exchange rate in a direction they consider desirable. A central bank would sell its currency and buy foreign currencies in order to cause its currency to depreciate. It would purchase its own currency in exchange for foreign currencies in order to bring about appreciation of its currency, or prevent depreciation. That is how changes in a country's international reserves come about. In 1987 the major central banks spent $56 billion to support or prop up the dollar, they sold foreign currencies on private markets and bought dollars. By 2005 the number grew to hundreds of billions. Foreign reserve holdings of dollars correspondingly increased (items 16 and 17 of Table 25–1). A regime in which the central bank intervenes in the foreign-exchange market (buying or selling foreign currencies) is called a **managed float.** Most currencies of the industrial countries are under a managed rather than a free float.

Mechanism of Adjustment

By what mechanism is the balance of payments kept in equilibrium? Under a free float the exchange rate performs the function of *equating inpayments and outpayments,* both defined to include transactions in goods and services as well as capital transfers. This takes us back to the discussion of the balance of payments. Had there been absolutely no government intervention in the foreign-exchange market, that is, a **free float**, there would be no change in official reserve holdings and no deficit or surplus in the overall balance of payments. But departures from equilibrium can occur under a managed float, where changes in reserves take place because of government intervention.

Implication for the Trade Balance

But (even in a free float) overall balance of payments equilibrium *does not mean that each subcategory of the international transactions is in balance.* Countries often attach particular importance to *their balance of trade* because merchandise exports and imports have direct and important implications to domestic employment. Exports are produced at home and thus generate employment in the same way as do investments. A rise in exports has a multiplier effect on domestic output. Imports displace local production in whole or in part. So a rise in imports tends to reduce domestic output and employment.

How are exports and imports affected by the exchange rate? Consider a situation in which the dollar exchange rate depreciates from 1.2€ to 1€.

Effect on US. Exports An American jet airliner priced at $100 million cost the German buyer 120 million euros at a $1 = 1.2€ exchange rate. Its German price declines to 100 million euros when the exchange value of the dollar drops to $1 = 1€. As the dollar depreciates, the prices of all U.S. goods and services decline on foreign markets. American exports become more competitive abroad, and more of them would be produced and sold. U.S. output and employment would rise.

Effect on U.S. Imports Consider a German automobile priced at 60,000 euros. Its price to an American buyer is $50,000 at a $1 = 1.2€ exchange rate. It rises to $60,000 when the exchange value of the dollar drops to $1 = 1€. As the dollar depreciates, the prices of all imported goods and services rise on U.S. markets. Imports become less competitive with American-made substitutes. Americans would purchase fewer imports, and produce at home more domestic substitutes. U.S. output and employment would rise.

The Balance of Trade The depreciation of the dollar increases exports and reduces imports and thereby it improves the U.S. balance of trade. Indeed, the U.S. trade deficit declined as the dollar depreciated during 1985–88. Dollar appreciation has the opposite effect of increasing the trade deficit, as it did in 1981–85.

GDP and Employment Net exports (X_n) or ($X - M$) *is* one of the four expenditure channels of GDP, the others being C, I, and G. When ($X - M$) rise, real output in the economy increases through the multiplier process. Hence, depreciation of the dollar produces a rise in real GDP and in employment. However, the multiplier in an open economy is smaller than that in a closed economy because at each round of spending there is a leakage into imports as well as into savings.

As income rises, a fraction of the *increment is* channeled into savings, with its size determined by the marginal propensity to save (MPS = $\Delta S/\Delta Y$). By the same token, as income rises, a *fraction of the increment is channeled into imports*, and its size is determined by the **marginal propensity to imports**, or MPM. Analogous to the MPC and MPS, the MPM = $\Delta M/\Delta Y$, where M stands for imports. In a private open economy: MPC + MPS + MPM = 1. And a leakage into imports—its size deter-

Marginal Propensity to Import (MPM): the fraction of an additional income devoted to additional imports. ($\frac{\Delta M}{\Delta Y}$).

mined by the MPM—is added to the leakage into savings. The open-economy multiplier is:

$$k = \frac{1}{\text{leakage}} = \frac{1}{\text{MPS} + \text{MPM}}$$ [1]

Therefore, an autonomous rise in net exports ($X - M$), caused by depreciation or other reasons, would increase GDP by:

$$\Delta Y = \Delta(X - M) \quad \frac{1}{\text{MPS} + \text{MPM}}$$

The multiplier works in reverse for an autonomous decline in ($X - M$).

Dollar Appreciation All the effects on exports, imports, the trade balance, and U.S. output and employment operate in reverse when the exchange value of the dollar rises. The student is invited to follow the same reasoning for an appreciation of the dollar from 1€ to 1.25€.

Finally, there is a time lag between exchange-rate changes and their effects on the economy.

THE U.S. TRADE DEFICITS, 1983–1988

It will be recalled from Chapter 23 that the first two Reagan years were characterized by large budgetary deficits and tight monetary policy. This policy mix led to very high U.S. (real and nominal) interest rates relative to foreign rates, attracting massive amounts of foreign funds to these shores. The resulting demand for dollars propelled the dollar exchange rate to a level well above that justified by economic fundamentals such as the relative purchasing power of currencies. As the dollar doubled in value relative to major European currencies, American producers found it increasingly difficult to compete at home and abroad. As a result, the U.S. balance of trade reached unprecedented annual deficits of $125 to $160 billion in 1984–88.

While the high dollar was responsible for about two-thirds of the deficits, other causes were: (1) the rapid growth rate of the U.S. economy relative to that of its main trading partners, leading it to absorb more imports (income effect) than foreign countries were buying from the United States; (2) the "belt tightening" measures undertaken by the major debtor countries of Latin America, leading them to curtail imports from the United States, their traditional supplier; and (3) the expansion

[1]For a more complete analysis see M. E. Kreinin, *International Economics*, 10th ed. (New York: Harcourt Brace Jovanovich, 2006.

▶ DETERMINANTS OF A COUNTRY'S IMPORTS AND EXPORTS

Although many factors determine a country's imports and exports, two are paramount: (1) the country's real income, or the growth in income, relative to that in the rest of the world; and (2) the country's competitive position, which in turn may change if its inflation rate is different from that in other countries, or if its exchange rate changes.

Imports: (1) Imports are positively related to a country's real income or output. As domestic income and output rise, the country needs more imported materials, and its citizens can afford to spend more on imported goods and services. During a period of strong recovery, the economy absorbs more imports from the rest of the world. Conversely, imports shrink during a cyclical contraction.

(2) A rise in the country's rate of inflation relative to that prevailing elsewhere or an increase in the exchange value of its currency make it less competitive and increase its imports.

Imports rise with the rise in real output or income, in the inflation rate, and in the exchange value of the country's currency.

Exports: (1) "Our" exports are the rest of the world's imports. Therefore, exports are positively related to the growth rate in real output or income of the country's trading partners.

(2) The higher the country's inflation rate or the exchange value of its currency, the less competitive it is, and the smaller its exports.

Exports rise (decline) with the rise (decline) in other countries' real income and output, with the decline (rise) in the country's inflation rate and in the exchange value of its currency.

of agricultural production in many countries, reducing their farm imports from the United States.

U.S. output and employment were adversely affected. The economic recovery during that period would have been stronger, and unemployment lower, had the dollar not been overvalued. (On the other hand, foreign countries exporting to the United States were able to increase their exports, output, and employment). But mainly the overvalued dollar accounted for the lopsided nature of the recovery in the 1980s. Sectors that do not participate in international trade, such as construction and services, grew rapidly, while the traded-goods sectors, mainly manufacturing and agriculture, were adversely affected. The growth in their output was slow, and at times they completely stagnated.

Figure 25–2 shows variations in the exchange value of the dollar relative to the other major currencies (in index form) after an adjustment is made for differential inflation rates between the United States and

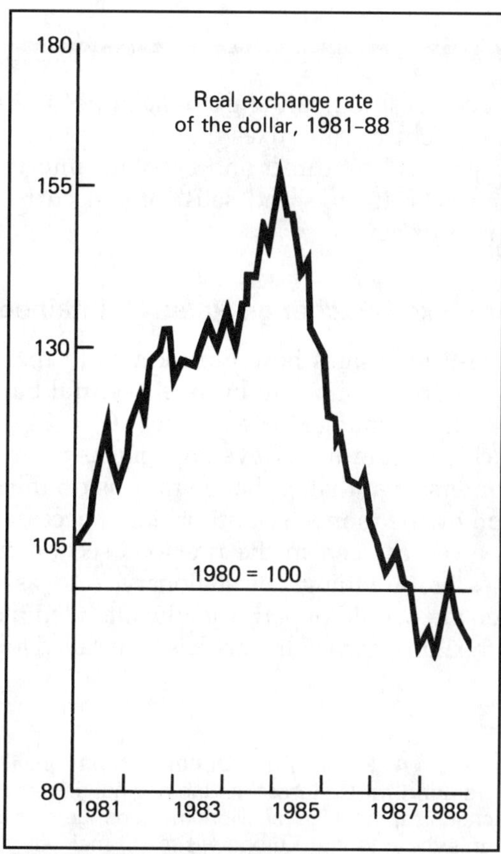

Figure 25–2 Real Exchange Rate of the Dollar, 1981–1988: Source: IMF Survey November 14, 1988.

other countries. It is seen that the dollar peaked in February 1985 after a four-year rise. Since then the dollar declined, mainly as a result of the narrowing of interest-rate differentials between the United States and abroad. By the end of 1987, the dollar's exchange value was back to its level in 1980. And in 1988 the effect of the depreciation (after a two and one-half-year lag) was felt across many America industries. Exports rose, the trade deficit diminished substantially, and employment in the traded-good sectors expanded. But the annual trade deficit remained very high, rising to over $400 billions in years 2000–2002, and to $780 billion in 2005.

Fixed exchange rate: The central bank sets exchange value of its currency at a pre-announced level and maintains it by buying and selling foreign currencies in exchange for the domestic currency.

In direct contrast to floating-exchange rates is a system of **fixed-exchange rates.** Each central bank fixes the exchange value of its currency at a pre-announced level by direct and constant intervention in the foreign currency markets: It buys and sells foreign currencies in exchange for the domestic currency.

How Are Fixed-Exchange Rates Maintained?

Figure 25–3 illustrates how Europe would fix or peg the euro exchange rate to the dollar. Suppose Europe's central bank estimates the long-run equilibrium exchange rate to be 1€ = $1, and decides to fix the euro-exchange rate at this level. As long as the market supply and demand curves intersect at that exchange rate, as do the solid lines in Figure 25–3, no action by the monetary authorities is necessary.

However, as seen in the previous section these supply and demand schedules are anything but stationary. And as they change, the market-exchange rate would depart from the intended fixed level. Market intervention by the European central bank is then called for to maintain the fixed rate.

Figure 25–3 A Fixed Euro-Dollar Exchange Rate; Excess Demand for Dollars: With the original demand and supply schedules, the initial equilibrium exchange rate is $1 = 1€. That is the rate that Europe wishes to maintain fixed. When demand for dollars rises to *D´*, an excess demand for dollars in the amount *bc* is created at the fixed exchange rate. To maintain that rate, the European central bank sells *bc* dollars in exchange for euros on the Europe's money market. Europe's foreign currency reserves are depleted by *bc*, and its domestic money supply (euros outside the central bank) declines.

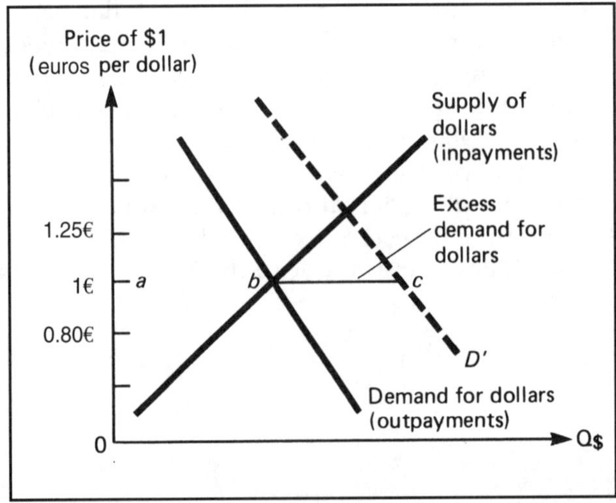

Excess Demand for Dollars Suppose the demand for dollars rises to the dashed D′ in Figure 25–3, perhaps because of a rise in European inflation. Then at the $1 = 1€ exchange rate, the demand for dollars is *ac* while their supply is *ab*, generating an excess demand for dollars in the amount of *bc*. The European central bank would sell *bc* dollars from its foreign currency reserves on the European market in exchange for euros to maintain the fixed-exchange rate.

Two things happen when Europe's central bank sells dollars and buys euros: (1) its foreign currency reserves are depleted, and (2) the European money supply (denominated in euros—the currency of issue) declines.

▶ FOREIGN CURRENCY INTERVENTION

In order to maintain a fixed-exchange rate, a country needs foreign currency reserves, otherwise known as international reserves. Such reserves are held by the central bank, in the form of strong and widely used *foreign* currencies, gold, or other assets acceptable to all countries. For example, dollars and yen are reserves for Europe but euros are not. Dollars are reserve for Japan but yen are not. Euros and yen are reserves for the United States, but dollars are not.

Because of the importance of the U.S. dollar as a global currency, countries hold most of their foreign currency reserves in dollars. Dollars are used in private transactions in all countries, enabling central banks to buy and sell dollars in exchange for their respective domestic currency. Therefore, most countries use U.S. dollars to intervene on their foreign currency market. Dollars are reserves for all countries *except* the United States.

Each country's money supply is denominated in its own currency: euros in Europe, yen in Japan, and dollars in the United States. It consists of currency in circulation and demand deposits in commercial banks, and does *not* include currency and deposits in the hands of the central bank.

Central bank intervention in the foreign currency markets means buying or selling foreign currencies (into and out of the country's reserve holdings) for the domestic currency. Hence, intervention changes the country's foreign currency reserves and its domestic money supply.

When the central bank sells foreign currencies for the domestic currency, its foreign currency reserves are depleted. Since it absorbs local currency, the domestic money supply (outside the central bank) declines.

Conversely, when the central bank buys foreign currencies for the domestic currency, its foreign currency reserves increase. Because it pays in domestic currency, the domestic money supply (held outside the central bank) expands.

The U.S. dollar plays three roles in most countries: It is a *transaction* currency for the private sector, the *intervention* currency for the central bank, and it is the major *reserve* currency of the central bank.

As explained in the display box above, Europe needs foreign currency (or other international) reserves to maintain a fixed-exchange rate. Those are held primarily in dollars. Because of the importance of the U.S. dollar as a worldwide transactions currency for the private sector, dollars can be bought and sold on private markets in all countries. Europe's domestic money supply is made up of euros held outside the central bank. Consequently, when the European central bank sells dollars in exchange for euros, it loses *bc* dollars in reserves, and absorbs an equivalent amount of euros from the private sector. Hence, Europe's domestic money supply shrinks. (This example is hypothetical. The euro is NOT on fixed rate).

A similar situation would arise when the *supply of dollars* schedule *declines,* or shifts to the left. An excess demand for dollars emerges, requiring the central bank to sell dollars in exchange for euros. The student is invited to redraw the initial supply and demand equilibrium, then shift the supply curve to the left, and trace the effects of currency intervention on Europe's reserves and domestic money supply.

Excess Supply of Dollars A converse situation occurs when the demand schedule for dollars declines or the supply increases, (perhaps because of a reduction in European inflation), generating excess supply of dollars at the fixed-exchange rate. This calls for foreign currency intervention by the European central bank of the opposite variety: It would purchase dollars in exchange for euros.

Figure 25–4 displays the situation just described. The fixed-exchange rate is set at \$1 = 1€. As demand declines (moves leftward) to the dashed D′, an excess supply of dollars in the amount *bc* appears: the difference between dollars supplied (*ac*) and dollars demanded (*ab*). The central bank buys *bc* dollars in exchange for euros to maintain the \$1 = 1€ exchange rate. In so doing it increases the country's foreign currency reserves, and at the same time expands its money supply (currency and deposits outside the central bank).

A similar situation would arise if the *supply of dollars schedule* rose (shifted to the right). Again an excess supply of dollars appears, requiring the European central bank to purchase dollars in exchange for euros on the money market.

In all cases the actual intervention by the central bank in the money market is done in a simple manner. The bank stands ready to buy or sell dollars (in exchange for the local currency) in unlimited amounts at the predetermined fixed-exchange rate. That is sufficient to maintain that rate.

A Measure of the Balance of Payments Deficit

In a system of fixed-exchange rates, the change of the country's foreign currency reserves is the measure of its overall external deficit or surplus (line 15 of Table 25–1).

An excess demand for dollars, as portrayed in Figure 25–3, means that private *outpayments exceed inpayments* at the fixed-exchange rate. The country is in an external *deficit.* The excess of outpayments over inpay-

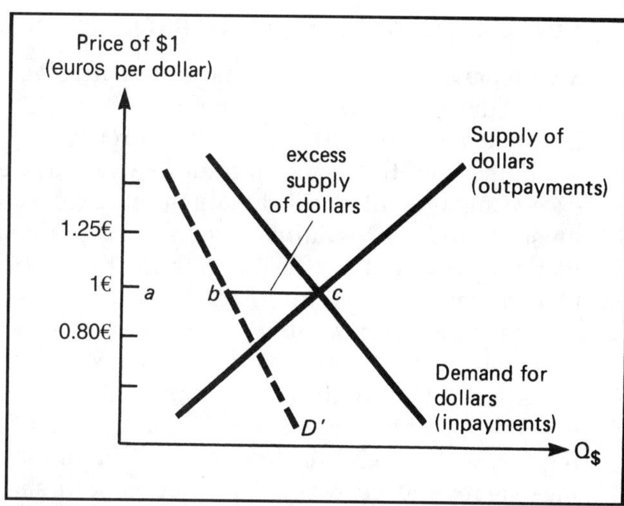

Figure 25–4 A Fixed Euro-Dollar Exchange Rate; Excess Supply of Dollars: With the original supply and demand schedules, the initial equilibrium exchange rate is $1 = 1€. This is the rate which Europe wishes to maintain fixed. When demand for dollars declines to D′, an excess supply of dollars in the amount *bc* is created at the fixed exchange rate. To maintain that rate the European central bank buys *bc* dollars in exchange for euros on the European money market. Europe's foreign currency reserves increase by *bc*, and its domestic money supply (euros outside the central bank) expands.

ments is made up by dollar sales out of the country's (Europe's) central reserves. Hence, the depletion in foreign currency reserves measures the size of the deficit.

An excess supply of dollars, as portrayed in Figure 25–4, means that private *inpayments exceed outpayments* at the fixed-exchange rate. The country is in an external *surplus*. The excess of inpayments over outpayments is made up by dollar purchases into the country's (Europe's) central reserves. Hence, the increase in foreign currency reserves measures the size of the surplus.

In a *fixed-exchange rate* regime, the change in the country's international reserves constitutes the measure of its external imbalance. In a regime of a *freely floating* exchange rate, no change in reserves occurs. The external imbalance is fully reflected in exchange-rate variations. Under a *managed-float* regime, the external imbalance is manifested in a combination of changes in the exchange rate and in the country's international reserves.

How Long Can the Fixed-Exchange Rate Be Maintained?

Maintenance of the fixed-exchange rate involves central bank intervention in the currency markets, buying or selling foreign currencies (mainly dollars) in exchange for the domestic currency.

If the country is in continuous external deficits, then outpayments exceed inpayments, and dollars are in excess demand. The central bank must sell dollars to maintain the exchange rate. This it can do as long as its dollar reserves last, or as long as it can obtain dollar loans from the United States or from international institutions.

Devaluation: Occurs under a fixed exchange rate regime when a country declares a (discrete) reduction in the exchange value of its currency.

Once the country runs out of reserves, or even when it is threatened by exhaustion of reserves, maintenance of the exchange rate becomes impossible. The country would have to let the exchange value of its currency drop, for example from 1€ = $1.25 to 1€ = $1. In a fixed-exchange rate regime, such a step is called **devaluation** of the currency. While in a floating-rate regime, currency depreciation occurs in small daily amounts controlled by market forces, devaluation of a fixed currency is done by sizable amounts at infrequent intervals, and is executed by a government decree. But it is market forces that force the government to devalue the currency.

If the country experiences continuous external surpluses, then its inpayments exceed outpayments, creating an excess supply of dollars. The central bank buys dollars into central reserves in exchange for the local currency. Theoretically, such accumulation of foreign currency reserves can go on forever, for the European central bank can "print" the euros it needs to sell in exchange for dollars. The ECB issues euros but not dollars.

Revaluation: Occurs when a country increases the exchange value of its currency.

However, the increase in dollar reserves is not without cost to Europe. The expansion of domestic money supply attendant upon the dollar purchases is inflationary. And besides, the central bank may not wish to accumulate reserves beyond a certain amount considered prudent and reasonable. Consequently, at some point Europe may decide to increase the exchange value of the euro, for example, from 1€ = $1 to 1€ = $1.25. In a fixed-exchange rate regime, such an action is called currency **revaluation.** Unlike appreciation of a floating-exchange rate, revaluation of a fixed currency is done by sizable amounts at infrequent intervals, and is executed by government decree. But it is market forces that force the government to revalue its currency.

Fixed-exchange rates were practiced by most countries during two extended periods: The Gold Standard (1870–1914) and the Bretton Woods period (1944–1973), when the U.S. dollar served as the core of the system. After functioning for 30 years, the Bretton Woods system collapsed in 1973 under the onslaught of market forces. It is the consensus of most economists that no system of fixed-exchange rates could have survived the financial turmoil of the 1970s: poor harvests, global inflationary pressures, the soaring oil prices in 1973–79, deep recessions in 1973–75 and 1980–82, and large intercountry differentials in inflation rates and productivity growth. Bretton Woods was replaced by the contemporary mix of floating and fixed rates.

Terminology of Exchange Rate Changes

Exchange Rate Regime	Rise in the Exchange Value of the Currency	Decline in the Exchange Value of the Currency
Floating (small daily changes)	Appreciation	Depreciation
Fixed (large changes at infrequent intervals)	Revaluation	Devaluation

THE CURRENT INTERNATIONAL CURRENCY SYSTEM

Since March 19, 1973, the international currency system has been a mixture of fixed- and floating-exchange rates.

Fluctuating Currencies

Of the major currencies, the U.S. dollar, the British pound sterling, the Japanese yen, and the Canadian dollar are allowed to float on the market, with their exchange rates determined by demand-and-supply conditions. Often the monetary authorities of each country intervene in the foreign-exchange market in order to smooth out fluctuations, to maintain orderly conditions, or to prevent their currency's exchange rate from moving upward or downward to a degree that they consider excessive or undesirable. Although such intervention can at times be massive, there is no official commitment to contain exchange fluctuations within fixed limits.

Such floats are known as *managed* or "dirty" floats, as distinguished from *free* or "clean" floats, which occur when no official intervention takes place.

The European Monetary Union; the Euro

In an unprecedented move, 12 European countries (Germany, France, Italy, Spain, Portugal, Holland, Belgium, Luxemburg, Ireland, Austria, Finland, and Greece) replaced their national currencies with a common currency, the EURO. A common Central Bank (called the European Central Bank, or ECB) was established, located in Frankfurt, to control the supply of Euros, establish common interest rates for the participating countries, and otherwise run monetary policy for them. Each country gave up its independent monetary and exchange rate policies. The Euro *fluctuates* against the dollar, yen, and pound sterling.

Fixed-Exchange Rates

Many currencies, of developing countries, are pegged by government action to one of the major currencies—mainly the dollar. However, dealing in some of these currencies (such as the Indian Rupee and the Chinese Yuan) is not free but subject to government restrictions. Some currencies are pegged to a weighted basket of major currencies.

Summary

International Monetary Fund: the organization which coordinates foreign exchange policies and provides credit to countries in need. **The Euro:** a currency of 12 European countries, that also have a common central bank (ECB).

The contemporary international currency system is a "hybrid" of four exchange-rate regimes: **single floats, a common currency (the EURO), currencies pegged to a major currency, and currencies pegged to a basket of major currencies.** Individual countries sometimes switch from one regime to another mainly from a fixed to flexible exchange rate. At the core of the system is an international organization, the **International Monetary Fund (IMF)**, which coordinates foreign exchange policies and provides credit to countries in difficulties.

CONTEMPORARY PROBLEMS IN THE INTERNATIONAL ECONOMY

What are the main issues in the international arena at the beginning of the 21st century? Most informed observers would list the following:

1. Sizeable bilateral trade imbalances between the United States (deficits) and far eastern countries, such as China and Korea (surpluses).
2. Persistent European unemployment, with its rate averaging 10 percent, after having endured for years at the double-digit level. (Even Germany has unemployment well above historical levels.) It is partly Keynesian in nature, caused by inadequate aggregate demand, where European governments refuse to stimulate their economies for fear of inflation. In part it is a classical phenomenon, caused by a variety of factors in the labor market that militate against full employment, such as labor market rigidities; above-market-equilibrium, real wage rates; and incentives on the part of the public and private sectors for people to remain unemployed. These incentives often come in the form of excessively high unemployment compensations and welfare payments.[2]

---

[2]Not only is European unemployment much higher than in the United States, but the length of time that a worker remains unemployed is significantly longer: an average of 3–4 months in the United States and a year in Europe. Recently, a new explanation of European unemployment surfaced, called the insider-outsider theory. It centers on market power of incumbent workers and firms. Incumbent employees ("insiders") have market power, because firms want to avoid labor turnover costs (screening, training, and so on). They use it to negotiate above-market wages, without regard to the interest of the unemployed ("outsiders"). Outsiders are disenfranchised from the process of wage formation. Because of turnover costs, insiders can drive their wages above competitive level without risk of dismissal. Incumbent firms exercise monopoly power because of barriers to entry, so that new firms cannot enter and hire the outsiders. Such barriers are higher in Europe than in the United States.

3. Tight protection of agriculture in the major developed countries, resulting in huge farm surpluses and trade disruptions, and costing tens of billions of dollars per year.
4. Large debt of some the developing countries.[3] It was brought on partly by internal economic mismanagement and partly by circumstances beyond the control of LDCs.

SUMMARY

Exchange Rates International transactions require buyers and sellers to deal in foreign currencies. The price of one currency in terms of another is called an exchange rate. Exchange rates may be floating, with their values determined daily by demand for and supply of currencies in the marketplace. A decline in the value of a floating currency is called *depreciation,* and a rise in its value is called *appreciation.*

There exist two variants of floating-exchange rates. In a *free* float, the exchange rate is determined strictly by market forces without any government intervention. In a *managed* float, the government intervenes in the market, selling and buying foreign currencies in exchange for the domestic currency, to influence the exchange rate in one direction or another.

Alternatively, the exchange rate can be *fixed* by the government at a predetermined level. This is done by the central bank selling foreign currencies when they are in excess demand and buying foreign currencies when they are in excess supply, at the fixed-exchange rate. Each central bank sells and buys foreign currencies (mainly dollars) in exchange for the domestic currency. To accomplish this, a country needs international reserves. Most countries hold such reserves in the form of foreign currencies (mainly dollars), gold, and the ability to borrow from the International Monetary Fund (IMF).

Changes in the value of a fixed-exchange rate occur in discrete and infrequent intervals, and are of sizable amounts. A reduction in the exchange value is called *devaluation,* and an increase in the exchange value is called *revaluation.* Both are executed by government decree.

Historical examples of fixed-exchange rates are the gold standard (1870–1914) and the Bretton Woods period (1944–1973). The contemporary international currency system consists of floating currencies, a common currency in Europe, currencies pegged to a major currency (mainly the U.S. dollar), and currencies pegged to a basket of major currencies.

[3]The U.S. external debt is not similar in all respects to that of LDCs such as Mexico and Brazil. True, in both cases it is a result of a country living beyond its means. But there the analogy ends, and two differences emerge. The U.S. debt occurs because foreigners wish to hold dollar assets, while Mexico's debt—whatever its causes—did not come about because of high world demand for pesos. Second, the American debt is denominated in dollars, of which the United States is the country of issue. LDC debt is also denominated in dollars, which these countries do not issue (but their debt burden declines when the dollar depreciates).

Balance of Payments Each country maintains a record of its international transactions known as the balance of payments. The statement consists of inpayments and outpayments items. Inpayments include exports of goods and services, and inflow of capital in various forms. Outpayments include imports of goods and services, unilateral transfers, and outflow of capital in various forms.

Partial balances can be computed from the statement as follows: the balance of trade is the exports minus imports of merchandise; the balance on goods and services is the exports minus imports of merchandise and services; the balance on current account equals exports of goods and services minus imports of goods and services and unilateral transfers.

Finally, the overall balance of payments position, known as the official reserve transactions balance, is all private inpayments minus all private outpayments It is in a surplus if inpayments exceed outpayments and in a deficit when outpayments exceed inpayments.

In a fixed-exchange rate regime the overall deficit or surplus reflects the country's external position, and it is settled by changes in official international reserves. In a free-float regime, there can be no deficit or surplus, since exchange-rate variations equalize inpayments and outpayments. The country's external position is fully reflected in the movements of its exchange rate. Under a managed float, the country's external position is manifested in a combination of exchange fluctuations and its overall payments imbalance.

Freely Floating Rates In this regime the exchange rate is determined by the intersection of demand for (outpayments) and supply of (inpayments) foreign currencies. But these demand and supply schedules are shifted daily by all developments in the economy as well as by government economic policies. In particular, changes in real income, inflation rate, and interest rates affect the location of the demand and supply curves and therefore the exchange rates. So do various expectations and psychological factors.

A rise in the rate of inflation, a decline in interest rates, and adverse expectations would cause the currency to depreciate. A decline in the rate of inflation, a rise in interest rates, and favorable expectations would cause the currency to appreciate. In all cases, what counts is domestic circumstances relative to conditions prevailing abroad.

For these reasons exchange rates fluctuate on a daily basis. A country on a free-float regime needs no international reserves, because exchange fluctuations always equate inpayments and outpayments, thereby maintaining equilibrium in the balance of payments. But a country on a managed-float regime requires reserves with which to influence the float.

Although the overall balance of payments is in equilibrium under a free float, partial balances may not be. In particular, the United States in 1983–2006 had sizable trade and current account deficits, offset by large inflows of capital. That condition originated from an overvalued dollar (relative to purchasing power parity), triggered by high U.S. real interest rates in the early 1980s.

Fixed-Exchange Rates A government may choose to keep the exchange value of its currency fixed relative to other currencies. It must then stand ready to buy and sell foreign currencies (mainly dollars) in exchange for the domestic currency at the fixed price (exchange rate). To do so it needs to keep sizable international reserves.

In case of excess demand for foreign currencies, the central bank sells dollars in exchange for the domestic currency. Its foreign currency reserves are depleted and the domestic money supply shrinks. This can go on as long as foreign currency reserves last. When they are exhausted, the country may have to devalue its currency.

In case of excess supply of foreign currencies, the central bank buys dollars in exchange for the domestic currency. Its foreign currency reserves and the domestic money supply both rise. This can go on as long as the government is willing to accumulate reserves, or until fears of domestic inflation, triggered by the rise in money supply, become paramount. At that point the government may choose to revalue its currency.

When an external deficit occurs under a fixed-exchange rate, equilibrium can be restored by contractionary domestic policies or by devaluation. An external surplus can be eliminated by expansionary domestic policies or by currency revaluation.

The Contemporary Scene The contemporary international currency system consists of managed floats, a common currency in Europe, and fixed-exchange rates. The dollar is the main transactions, intervention, and reserve currency. The IMF is active in overseeing currency intervention by central banks, extending credit to countries in deficit, and it also helps countries in financial difficulties.

Major problems on the contemporary scene include bilateral trade imbalances, European unemployment, and Japan's banking problems.

QUESTIONS AND PROBLEMS

1. You are given the following figures for Japan's international transactions (in trillions of yen):
   a. Calculate:
      The balance of trade
      The balance of goods and services
      The balance on current account
      The official reserve transactions (overall) balance
   b. Would you conclude from the figures that the Japanese yen is a freely floating currency? Why or why not?

c. What is the link between the following figures and Japan's National Income Accounts?

Merchandise exports	+100
Merchandise imports	–150
Service transactions (net)	+100
Unilateral transfers	– 10
Private capital outflow	– 20
Private capital inflow	+100

d. What are the inpayments and outpayments items in the preceding statement?

2. Using a supply and demand diagram, as in Figure 25–1, show the equilibrium exchange rate for a freely floating yen at: ¥100 = $1 or ¥1 = 1¢. Now illustrate successively the effect of the following events on the exchange rate (assume that all other things are held constant):
   a. A precipitous rise in Japan's inflation.
   b. A sharp drop in Japan's real interest rates.
3. Redraw your original diagram for the foreign-exchange market in question 2. But now assume that the yen is on a fixed-exchange rate. Next, introduce successively:
   a. A reduction in the supply of dollars to Japan (perhaps caused by a decline in the U.S. inflation).
   b. A rise in the supply of dollars to Japan (perhaps caused by an increase in the U.S. inflation).

   In each case show and explain what Japan's central bank would do to maintain the fixed-exchange rate. How would each of the bank's actions affect Japan's international reserves and its domestic money supply?
4. How would an overall external surplus of a country be manifested if its currency is on:
   a. A fixed-exchange rate regime?
   b. A free-float regime?
   c. A managed-float regime?

   Explain fully!
5. Why might a country need international reserves? What forms do such reserves take?
6. Explain the following terms:

exchange rate	managed float
freely floating exchange rate	depreciation
fixed-exchange rate	appreciation
devaluation	balance of trade
revaluation	balance on goods or services
inpayments	balance of payments
outpayments	purchasing power parity
	international reserves

7. What might account for the combination of a robust growth in the U.S. service sector and the stagnating U.S. manufacturing sector in 1985?
8. How long can a fixed-exchange rate be maintained? At what points may a country have to devalue or revalue its currency?
9. Describe the contemporary international currency system.
10. List four major problems on the contemporary international scene.

26 Problems of the Developing Countries

LIVING CONDITIONS IN LDCS

Less Developed Countries (LDCs): Countries in Africa, Asia and Latin America, that are relatively underdeveloped. The poorest countries are concentrated in Africa, while some Asian and Latin American countries made considerable development strides.

For those of us living in North America, and perhaps familiar with living conditions in Western Europe and Japan, it is difficult to imagine the abject poverty that exists in the **less developed countries (LDCs)** of Asia, Africa, and Latin America.[1] Nearly two thirds of the world population, residing in these three continents, live in circumstances of persistent hunger and disease that defy statistical exposition or verbal description. It is true that pockets of poverty exist even in the United States. But the widespread conditions of hopelessness and starvation in many LDCs are not within the range of our normal experience. They have to be seen to be believed.

A short visit to Calcutta, India would make the statement somewhat tangible. Visitors would be struck by streets full of little children begging for alms. Or they may note a large railroad station that is home to hundreds of families who merely spread a blanket on the floor and call it home (and these are the lucky ones, for they have a roof over their heads). Children, with their stomachs bulging from disease, go untreated. And people debilitated by hunger are everywhere in sight. A visit to Lagos, Nigeria would produce the same impressions.

In many LDCs large families reside in one-room shanties without water supply or a source of energy, let alone any of the modern amenities. Open sewer systems and lack of sanitation are everywhere in evidence. Sparse harvests permit only a starvation diet, and many die of famine in drought years. Since the years of the 1970s, half a million people are reported to have died in Bangladesh, a quarter of a million in Ethiopia, a similar number in the Sahal region of Africa, and over half a million in India. Graphic pictures of such episodes sometimes appear on Western

[1] The terms: *less developed countries, underdeveloped countries,* and *developing countries* are used interchangeably to describe the relatively low-income countries of Africa, Latin America, and Asia.

television, as they did in the case of Ethiopia in the mid-1980s, or in conjunction with "Live Aid"—a July 1985 rock concert (televised worldwide) that raised $50 million for famine relief. Disease is widespread, but medical attention is scant or nonexistent.

In rural areas, where most people live, women and young children work in the fields. Water and other supplies must be brought from places several miles away from home, carried on a person's head or back. Children have no schools to attend; nor is there a medical facility available to help the sick. Hence, illiteracy is high and infant mortality widespread.

SELECTED STATISTICAL INDICATORS

Per capita income: GDP divided by population in a country. This is a statistical indicator used to measure the country's level of development.

It is difficult to reduce such shocking descriptions to a set of numbers. Yet the statistics reveal a gapping disparity between the industrial and the underdeveloped countries. One statistic commonly used to measure the level of development is **per capita income,** or *per capita GDP* (GDP divided by the number of people in the country). In the United States and

Table 26–1 Per Capita GDP in Developed and Less Developed Countries, 2004 (Dollars)

Low-Income Economies ($765 or less)	$440
Kenya	400
Bangladesh	400
Cameroon	630
Lower-Middle Income Economies ($766–$3,035)	$1,490
Indonesia	810
Sri LAnka	930
Ukraine	970
Philippines	1,080
Egypt, Arab Republic	1,390
Colombia	1,810
Thailand	2,190
Brazil	2,720
Turkey	2,800
Upper-Middle Income Economies ($3,036–$9,385)	$5,440
Argentina	3,810
Malaysia	3,880
High- and Upper-Middle Income Oil Exporters	
Saudi Arabia	9,240
Kuwait	17,960
High-Income Economies ($9,386 or more)	
Korea, Rep.	12,030
Singapore	21,230
France	24,730
Germany	25,270
United Kingdom	28,320
Japan	34,180
United States	37,870

Source: World Bank, World Development Indicators Database, 2005

Averaging out growth rates or incomes among groups of countries is useful if the *dispersion* among them is not great. When the dispersion is large, averages can conceal as much as they reveal, and should be supplemented by additional measures.

Cartoons often view averages skeptically. One suggests that "with one foot in the oven and the other in the freezer your average temperature is OK." In another cartoon *(The Wall Street Journal*, February 28, 1984) a doctor is shown reporting laboratory tests to a patient, and stating: "Blood pressure's high, metabolism low, cholesterol high, blood sugar low—it all averages out pretty good." These of course overstate the point just to be humorous.

certain European countries this figure is well above $30,000 per year. In low-income LDCs it is below $500 per year (see Table 26–1). Infant mortality is about 10 deaths per 1,000 live births in the United States, and 150 deaths per 1,000 live births in Bangladesh. Life expectancy at birth is 75 years in the United States and 50 years in India. And the adult literacy rate is 99 percent in the United States, and 26 percent in Bangladesh.

Another pervasive problem in many LDCs is an extremely unequal domestic income distribution. While the masses live in abject poverty, there exists a very small class of extremely wealthy people.

Of the several indicators of underdevelopment mentioned earlier, per capita income or per capita output is the one most commonly used. Over 70 percent of the world population lives in the LDCs (21 percent in China alone), and they account for only one fifth of global output. In sharp contrast, the 18 percent of the world's population living in the industrial market-economy countries of North America, Western Europe, and Japan account for 62 percent of global output. That is what generates the large disparity in worldwide income, with U.S. per capita income being twentyfold that of the average LDC.

Has this gap between the "have" and "have not" countries narrowed in recent years? Between 1965 and 1986 the real GDP of the LDCs grew faster than their rate of population growth, so that per capita GDP rose at over 2.5 percent per year. In the industrial countries population growth was insignificant, and per capita GDP grew at about 2.5 percent. Yet *the gap* between the two groups, measured in dollars, *grew wider*. For a 2.5 percent growth rate translates to $250 when applied to a $10,000 base, and only to $12.50 when applied to a $500 base.

Growth among the LDCs has not been uniform, and the average rate of 2.5 percent conceals substantial differences between countries. Rapid growth occurred in a dozen LDCs, most notably China, India, South Korea, Singapore, Taiwan, and Hong Kong. On the other hand several LDCs, especially in Africa, stagnated.

For this and other reasons, it is useful to divide the LDCs into four subgroups. (1) The oil-rich countries of the Persian Gulf. With sparse population and large oil revenues, their per capita income is among the highest in the world. Yet they remain underdeveloped in terms of their economic structure and level of industrialization. (2) A dozen or so LDCs that grew rapidly in the postwar period and attained a semi-industrial status. Known as the new industrial countries (NICs), they include Mexico, Brazil, Colombia, Korea, Taiwan, Hong Kong, and Thailand. (3) The bulk of the LDCs, with per capita income of roughly \$1,600–\$4,000. China and India, with one third of the world population between them, are growing rapidly (although still poor). (4) The 36 countries classified as the least developed among the LDCs. With a combined population of 300 million, these countries are at the bottom of the development hierarchy. Their average per capita income is under \$400, their literacy rate is one quarter of the adult population, and their growth rate barely exceeds their population growth.

IMPEDIMENTS TO LDCS' GROWTH

Impediments to growth include Rapid Population growth; Scarcity of capital; Inadequate Infrastructure; Scarcity of Human Capital; and Lack of Technological know-how.

Why do most LDCs (outside the NICs) find it difficult to break out of the cycle of poverty and embark upon a process of self-sustained growth? Most commonly, LDC growth is hampered by a rapid expansion of population and by a slow rise in real GDP. In turn, the slow growth rate of GDP can be traced to several critical factors: (1) scarcity of capital; (2) absence of infrastructure, otherwise known as "social overhead capital," such as roads, railways, electricity, and other related items that are prerequisites to sustained growth; (3) inadequate human capital; (4) unemployment and underemployment; and (5) inhibitive social environment.

These factors are considered in succession. But it should be mentioned at the outset that the countries which are now fully developed required several generations to overcome these impediments and reach their present status. Sustained economic growth and high living standards are fairly recent historical phenomena. The industrial revolution in Britain is only two centuries old. And in the prior era living standards in Europe had stagnated for centuries.

Rapid Population Growth

In the decades since the war, population in the various developing countries grew at an annual rate of between 2 to 4.5 percent, a rate that would double the population every 30 years. By contrast, population in the developed countries expanded at under 1 percent annual rate. According to projections prepared by the World Bank, world population would grow from 4.8 billion people in the 1980s to 9.8 billion in year 2050. But the increase is expected to be very uneven. Population in the developed countries would rise from 1.2 to 1.4 billion, while that of the LDCs would mushroom from 3.6 to 8.4 billion. Such a rapid population expansion keeps per capita income low even when real GDP is increasing rapidly. It can frustrate or even abort the development effort.

Why is population in countries like India growing so rapidly? Two demographic factors determine the rate of population growth: the birth rate, or the number of births per 1,000 population; and the death rate, or the number of deaths per 1,000 population. The difference between the two (birth rate minus death rate) is the rate of population growth.

A high birth rate is characteristic of many poor societies for several reasons. It is a century-old tradition in LDC societies to have large families. In rural cultures children are the only guarantee of economic support at old age. Children are needed to help in the fields from a young age. The opportunity cost of rearing children, in terms of work that needs to be foregone by the mother, is low. And because of limited education, birth control measures are not readily available and family planning is not widely practiced.

On the other hand, the death rate in LDCs has declined due primarily to public health improvements, introduced first by the colonial powers and subsequently by United Nations' agencies. It is the combination of high birth rate and declining death rate that produces the high rate of population growth.[2]

Governments of several LDCs have attempted to escape this Malthusian spectre by reducing birth rates. But the achievements to date, although tangible, fall short of the spectacular. They also vary greatly from one country to another. Educational programs of family planning and distribution of contraceptive information have met with some success in countries where the educational level is reasonably high. A compulsory sterilization program in India aroused such public indignation that it led to the downfall of the government. But educational programs met with considerable success in three Indian states.

China embarked upon a program of financial incentives to limit family size. Under the plan, government support is provided for the first child. But for the second child and beyond, support is withdrawn and financial penalties are imposed. A combination of public education, social pressures, and economic measures has slowed population growth in China to a 1 to 2 percent annual rate. An active family planning program in Indonesia also met with a measure of success. But in many other LDCs population problems remain very serious and widespread.

Scarcity of Capital

A rise in real output requires an increase in labor productivity, which in turn depends on the increased availability of machines and structures. And capital formation can come about only through a process of saving and investment. People must abstain from consumption and the resources so released need to be channeled into the construction of plants and equipment. But very poor people, who require all their income to finance subsistence-level existence, cannot save. And the very wealthy in the LDCs tend to channel their savings into foreign bank accounts or to the acquisition of luxury consumer goods. The saving rate in LDCs is exceedingly low.

---

[2]*The World Development Report, 1984*, published by the World Bank in Washington, D.C., is devoted largely to the problem of population and development.

Such meager savings as are generated are not usually directed toward investment. Many LDCs do not have a tradition of using resources for productive investments and they lack economic incentives to do so; they are also devoid of entrepreneurs, able and willing to assume the risk involved in investment activity. Their governments often fail to provide a stable political and social environment conducive to investment activity. With small domestic markets, prices that are distorted beyond recognition by government policy, lack of the needed infrastructure, and a near absence of an entrepreneurial class, it is difficult to expect much investment to occur. Finally, social and economic prestige in many LDCs goes to government bureaucrats and other functionaries, rather than to the successful businessperson, further reducing the attraction for competent people to enter the business world.

LDCs are caught in a *vicious circle* in the area of capital formation. *Because poor countries cannot save, they cannot invest and accumulate capital. Hence, productivity remains low and real GDP does not grow. And because they fail to develop, the rate of saving remains very low.*

A variety of domestic measures have been employed to deal with this problem, including "forced saving" by taxation or through inflation. But they produced meager results in nonauthoritarian countries.

One possible solution is an inflow of direct foreign investment from abroad. By investing in LDCs, foreign companies do both the saving and the investing on behalf of their host countries. They also bring with them technological and managerial know-how. Although this is an attractive solution to the scarcity of capital, it is fraught with obstacles.

Multinational corporations do not always find investment in LDCs attractive. Political instability, fear of expropriation, small market size, inadequate infrastructure, limited availability of skilled labor, and a (frequently) inhospitable economic environment tend to limit such investment activity. For their part, potential host LDCs have mixed feelings about foreign investment and their policies toward the multinationals are often self-contradictory. They welcome the capital and the know-how that comes with foreign investment, but they fear possible abuses and alleged "exploitation" by the multinational corporations. They are also reluctant to have important segments of their economy owned and controlled by foreign companies, who may not serve the best interest of the host country. (But of late MNCs invested heavily in China).

For these and other reasons, many LDCs have special laws that apply to foreign investors. Examples are the limitation on foreign ownership to 49 percent of a local subsidiary; mandatory employment of a minimum number of local personnel; or a requirement that a minimum proportion of the subsidiary's output be exported. These laws constitute a deterrent to foreign investment in LDCs.

Inadequate Infrastructure

A fundamental prerequisite for economic development is the existence of "social overhead capital" or infrastructure. That includes roads, railroads, port facilities, an electrical network, schools, hospitals, and other prerequisites of modern economic life. They must be in place before development can proceed.

As often as not, such facilities are lacking. The LDC government has a critical role to play in creating an adequate infrastructure, as it does in establishing a stable political, legal, and social system within which business can flourish. Grants and loans from the industrialized nations or from international institutions (such as the World Bank) are a useful means for addressing this problem and setting the stage for sustained growth.

Scarcity of Human Capital

Many LDCs are short of human capital—engineers, electricians, machinists, construction workers, draftsmen, and other skilled workers. Educational facilities to train such technicians are grossly inadequate. Also scarce are people trained in advanced farming methods, who are able to impart such knowledge to farmers. Finally, the scarcity of entrepreneurs, able and willing to assume the risks involved in investment and other business transactions, was mentioned earlier.

Overcoming these shortages in human capital involves more than just training a cadre of able individuals. It calls for changes in the social value system. In many countries the skills that are critical for development carry low social esteem, and therefore they appear unattractive to young people. High status and prestige attaches to liberal arts education and government service, rather than to technical training and business activity. These social beliefs need to be modified.

Technology

Technological backwardness characterizes most of the LDCs. On the surface this appears to be one area in which decades of painstaking work can be shortcut by borrowing and adapting technologies that already exist in advanced countries (and which had taken decades to develop). But apart from possible reluctance of the industrial countries to transfer technology freely to the LDCs, such a transfer faces two fundamental problems.

First, Western technology is not usually appropriate for LDCs. Inventions and innovations in the advanced countries tend to be of the labor-saving variety. This is because labor is a scarce resource in these countries, while capital is abundantly available. But in the LDCs unskilled labor is the abundant factor while capital is scarce. Sophisticated technologies that emphasize the saving of labor are unsuited for them. Second, putting advanced technology into widespread use requires a cadre of engineers and technicians, and these are not adequately available in most LDCs.

For these reasons, technological advance would have to proceed slowly. Only appropriate technologies can be borrowed (usually from the less advanced industrial countries), while others may have to be developed anew.

Unemployment

An important and highly disconcerting feature of many LDCs is the existence of large-scale unemployment or underemployment. Many people in the rural areas are underemployed in a sense that their marginal contribution to output is minimal. And as young people are attracted to cities with few or even nonexistent employment opportunities, unemployment rates in urban centers can reach one third of the labor force. In some countries, above-equilibrium wage rates add to the unemployment problem.

Government Intervention in the Economy

Many LDCs' governments intervene in various sectors of their economies in an attempt to influence the growth process and steer the economy in a direction the government considers desirable. Administrative controls over prices, wages, and interest rates, subsidies, credit rationing, protection from foreign competition, unstable currencies, occasional expropriation of private property, and public ownership and management of enterprises are all tools that have been used in one form or another. In the process governments often interfere with the functioning of markets, distort prices, and destroy the incentive system. Market decisions are transferred from individual businesspersons to the hands of incompetent bureaucrats. Economic development is often the casualty of these practices.

SELECTED ISSUES IN DEVELOPMENT STRATEGY

Economic development is an internal matter that must be accomplished by the LDCs themselves. The industrial countries can help (see next section) but cannot do the job for them. In pursuing their development strategy, LDCs often encounter controversial issues, a few of which are reviewed briefly.

Balanced versus Unbalanced Growth

Balanced growth: Occurs when all sectors of the economy grow in concert with each other.

Unbalanced growth: A few key industries are targeted for growth. They are expected to spill over to other industries.

Once it commences, how should economic growth proceed? One view holds that all sectors of the economy need to grow in tandem for the process to be sustained—**balanced growth.** Economic sectors are interdependent. Each industry depends on others for inputs and/or for a market for its products. A balanced growth strategy would enable each industry to grow in tandem with industries that support it or that are supported by it. A contrary school of thought supports an **unbalanced growth** strategy. A few key industries should be targeted for rapid development. Because they require inputs from other industries, and in turn supply inputs to a third set of industries, their growth would foster spontaneous development elsewhere in the economy.

Economic Planning versus Reliance on Market Forces

Many LDCs have opted for a comprehensive or partial government control over the development process, where the government develops and attempts to implement a succession of "five-year plans."

One school of thought maintains that given the absence of the preconditions for development, planning is the only effective way to proceed. The contrary view is that governments often do more harm than good by destroying the system of market incentives, and that only the market mechanism can produce an effective and sustained growth process. Certainly the few traditional LDCs that reached the semi-industrial stage had done so by injecting a large dose of market incentives into the economy. Even China has moved to liberalize its economy in recent years, by allowing markets to function in agriculture and industry, as a partial substitute to comprehensive government planning and controls. It also opened its economy to foreign trade. It grows at 8–10 percent annually.

Import Substitution versus Export Promotion

Imports and exports occupy a large, if not a dominant, share of the economy in many LDCs. Consequently, their foreign trade policy is important. Two alternative trade approaches to economic development can be distinguished: import substitution and export-oriented strategies.

Import substitution: A country imposes high tariffs and other import restrictions to keep out imports and produce at home the good that would have been imported.

Under the policy of **import substitution,** a country erects high tariffs and quantitative barriers to imports, and behind this shelter it expands domestic production to replace imports. Usually the country starts by producing nondurable consumer goods, which require labor-intensive and unsophisticated techniques. Once this easy stage is completed, further import substitution becomes increasingly difficult. The next step is to turn to the final processing of assembly-type commodities, generating a shift in the composition of imports away from these final products and toward intermediate and capital goods.

This strategy was common among many LDCs, in particular the countries of Latin America. But it has insulated the LDC economy from the world economy and created a variety of market distortions. For example, by subsidizing capital-goods import it created an incentive to use capital-intensive techniques regardless of the country's factor endowments. This is one reason why the growth in industrial production in many LDCs has not been accompanied by a rapid growth in industrial employment. The policy also penalizes the export sectors, since it tends to be accompanied by overvalued currencies.

Export promotion: Provide incentives for firms to increase exports. Country develops by integrating itself into the global economy, emphasizing industries in which it has a comparative advantage.

Because of such problems, many developing countries such as Taiwan, South Korea, Singapore, and Brazil have opted for an **export-promotion** strategy. This involves a change in the system of incentives in favor of exports. Countries may even introduce a variety of fiscal incentives to increase exporters' earnings (such as export subsidies) or to reduce exporters' costs (such as reducing or removing duties on imported inputs or reducing the exporters' income taxes). Some countries (such as Mexico and Taiwan) established duty-free processing zones into which inputs are imported duty free and from which final goods are exported after processing. In other cases, tariff rates have been reduced and harmonized, or the currency has been devalued to a realistic level. The major effect has been to expand the export of labor-intensive manufactured products and to avoid the establishment of insulated, highly inefficient domestic industries. Indeed, over the past decade there has been a sharp increase in the volume of manufactures exported from LDCs; however, most of it is accounted for by only ten countries.

Although import substitution up to a certain point can be beneficial, the development experience of countries following export-oriented strategy has tended to be more favorable. They have done better in terms of growth rate and expansion of employment than countries developing strictly via import substitution. Reliance on exports made it possible for LDCs to break through the limitation of small market size, set up firms that can realize economies of scale, foster market incentives, dismantle or simplify government controls, and integrate the country more fully into world markets.

THE ROLE OF THE INDUSTRIAL COUNTRIES

Although economic development is an internal process, where success or failure depends largely on the policies of the LDC governments, the industrial countries can play a helpful role. Indeed the LDCs have promulgated the need for a "New International Economic Order" (NIEO) that calls on the developed countries to increase their contribution to development. This suggested contribution is to be in several forms.

Increased Foreign Aid

The current level of official global foreign assistance is over $50 billion per year. Such government aid, prompted by a combination of humanitarian and political reasons, amounts to 0.5 percent of the GDP of the advanced countries. For the United States the proportion is even lower. LDCs regard this level as inadequate, and request the industrial countries to provide assistance to the tune of 1 percent of their GDP.

Also, much of today's aid is "tied" to purchases in the respective donor country. Recipient LDCs are not free to shop around for the cheapest sources of supply; they must spend the money in the country from which the aid was obtained. Because this provision reduces the real value of foreign assistance, LDCs call for "untying" the aid.

Along with increased aid, LDCs request expanded technical assistance programs, and better means for transferring advanced technology to their countries.

Export Markets

Because the industrial countries provide a market for most of LDCs' exports, export-oriented growth requires adequate access to the markets of the developed countries. LDCs demand duty-free access for their manufactured exports into the industrial countries, as well as the removal of many nontariff barriers. Some of these demands have already been met.

But in cases of several labor-intensive products (such as textiles or footwear), where the LDCs have a clear comparative advantage, international trade is heavily regulated by quantitative restrictions. Manufacturers and labor unions in the industrial countries, who fear a flood of cheap imports, pressure their governments to maintain and even tighten these restrictions. A case in point is restrictions on Chinese textile export.

Although both the LDCs and the consumers in the industrial countries have much to gain from the elimination of these trade barriers, the political clout of the protected industries prevents their removal.

Primary Products

About 75 percent of LDC exports consist of raw materials and food products, lumped together under the title "primary products." LDCs complain that because of inelastic global supply and demand schedules, the prices of these products fluctuate excessively on world markets. This, they maintain, causes sharp annual fluctuations in their foreign-exchange earnings and inhibits their development. To remedy this alleged problem, LDCs call for global schemes to stabilize commodity prices. They demand a series of international commodity agreements, which buy and sell the commodity into and out of central stocks, as a means of stabilizing prices.

PROSPECTS FOR THE LDCS

Can the LDCs break away from the cycle of poverty and reach a "takeoff stage" of self-sustained growth? The prospects today appear far brighter than they did 25 years ago, as the development process has taken hold in quite a few countries. Some countries achieved an economic transformation in a few short decades. The most outstanding example is Japan, a country totally devoid of natural resources. From one of the world's impoverished nations, it has risen to become one of the world's richest and most advanced. China and India, with one third of the world population between them, opened their economies to foreign trade and investment, and have been growing at an annual rate of 7–10 percent. China has become the fourth largest economy after the U.S., Japan, and Germany, although its *per capita* income is still low. A dozen countries in Asia and Latin America (the NICs) have been transformed to a semi-industrial stage, and a second tier of NICs (such as Thailand) has also appeared.

However, they all sustained a setback during the crisis of 1997–2000 (from which they fully recovered by 2002), and Argentina faced a financial crisis in 2002. Additionally, in recent years many LDCs have become self-sufficient in grains, thereby conserving foreign currency that used to be expended on food imports. While most of the people in LDCs live in countries that are growing, there are numerous LCDs, especially in Africa, which continue to stagnate.

Future success depends in large measure on the country's ability to limit population growth, to generate savings and investment, and to integrate itself into the world economy. Most LDCs are small countries, whose internal markets are too small to realize economies of scale in production and distribution. Bangladesh, for example, has a nonagricultural income approximately 3 percent that of Sweden and less than 2 percent that of Canada, neither of which is regarded as an economy large enough to forego the benefits of specialization and international trade. Consequently, full integration of the LDCs into the world economy is their most promising path. This means a market-oriented strategy at home, and an export-promotion approach in foreign trade. Indeed, the LDCs that have grown rapidly have pursued that strategy.

Although the prospects for most LDCs depend largely on policies pursued at home by their own governments, the process can be helped by foreign economic assistance, and by the industrial countries maintaining flourishing and open markets for LDCs' exports.

SUMMARY

Over two thirds of the human race inhabits the underdeveloped continents of Africa, Asia, and Latin America. People in LDCs live under conditions of poverty and disease. Their average per capita income is a fraction of what it is in the advanced industrial countries, and the gap between the two groups has widened in absolute dollar terms. The only exception to that has been a handful of NICs that succeeded in breaking out of the poverty cycle.

Several factors account for the persistent poverty of the LDCs. Rapid population growth means that even if aggregate real output grew significantly, per capita output or income would grow slowly, if at all. In turn the rapid population growth is due to a high birth rate that is typical of low-income societies. Growth in real output is hampered by meager savings and low capital formation. Low-income people cannot save, and the lack of proper skills and of a stable environment inhibit investment. Although foreign investment can help break this cycle, there are problems in fostering such investment. To the low capital formation, one must add the following factors that inhibit growth: inadequate social overhead capital, scarcity of human capital, technological backwardness, and an economic and social environment not hospitable to business enterprises.

Although the main impetus to growth must come from the LDCs themselves, the advanced countries can help by increasing foreign aid and by keeping their markets open to LDC exports. Since both industrial and developing countries are a part of the same universe, all have a stake in the success of the development enterprise.

QUESTIONS AND PROBLEMS

1. *a.* Compare and contrast the LDCs and the industrial countries in terms of per capita income and other development indicators.
   b. Has the gap between the "haves" and "have nots" been narrowed?
2. What are the two vicious circles in which LDCs are trapped? Explain fully!
3. What are the main impediments to development and what can be done about them?
4. Explain the following terms:

   export promotion policy
   import substitution policy
   unbalanced growth
   balanced growth
   per capita income
   "tied" foreign aid
   NICs
   social overhead capital
   foreign investment

INDEX

Index

A

B

C

D

E

F

G

H

I

J

K

L

M

N

O

P

Q

R

S

T

U

V

W